The Law of Large-Scale Claims

The Law of Large-Scale Claims

Product Liability, Mass Torts, and Complex Litigation in Canada

JAMIE CASSELS AND CRAIG JONES

The Law of Large-Scale Claims
© Irwin Law Inc., 2005

All rights reserved. No part of this publication may be reproduced, stored in a retrieval system, or transmitted, in any form or by any means, without the prior written permission of the publisher or, in the case of photocopying or other reprographic copying, a licence from Access Copyright (Canadian Copyright Licensing Agency), 1 Yonge Street, Suite 1900, Toronto, Ontario, M5E 1E5.

Published in 2005 by

Irwin Law
347 Bay Street
Suite 501
Toronto, Ontario
M5H 2R7

www.irwinlaw.com

ISBN: 1-55221-085-3

Library and Archives Canada Cataloguing in Publication

Cassels, Jamie
    The law of large-scale claims : product liabilty, mass torts, and complex litigation in Canada / Jamie Cassels and Craig E. Jones.

Includes bibliographical references and index.

ISBN 1-55221-092-8

    1. Complex litigation—Canada. 2. Torts—Canada. 3. Class actions (Civil procedure)—Canada. 4. Products liability—Canada.

I. Jones, Craig E. (Craig Elton), 1965- II. Title.

KE8349.C38 2004   347.71'053   C2004-904384-6
KF8840.ZA2C38 2004

The publisher acknowledges the financial support of the Government of Canada through the Book Publishing Industry Development Program (BPIDP) for its publishing activities.

Printed and bound in Canada.

1 2 3 4 5   08 07 06 05 04

Summary Table of Contents

PREFACE *xvii*

INTRODUCTION *1*

PART ONE: **Sources of Liability** *9*

CHAPTER 1. Causes of Action in Product Liability *11*

CHAPTER 2. Causes of Action in Mass Tort *102*

CHAPTER 3. Remedies in Large-Scale Claims *167*

PART TWO: **Problems of Proof and Causation** *201*

CHAPTER 4. The Problem of Indeterminate Causation *203*

CHAPTER 5. Problems of Proof *249*

CHAPTER 6. The Problem of Corporate Groups *273*

PART THREE: **The Law of Aggregate Claims** *307*

CHAPTER 7. Class Proceedings *309*

CHAPTER 8. Some Emerging Issues Regarding Class Actions *360*

PART FOUR: **Interjurisdictional Dimensions** *389*

CHAPTER 9. Conflict of Laws in Large-Scale Claims *395*

CHAPTER 10. Interjurisdictional Class Actions *433*

CONCLUSION. The Future of Large-Scale Claims in Canada *468*

TABLE OF CASES *471*

INDEX *501*

Detailed Table of Contents

PREFACE *xvii*

Introduction 1

A. Special Problems of Large-Scale Claims 1

B. The Role and Limits of Law 3

    1) The Problematic "Substantive/Procedural" Distinction 3
    2) The Inadequacy of Reliance on Precedent 5

C. Product Liability and Mass Tort 6

PART ONE: SOURCES OF LIABILITY 9

CHAPTER 1.

Causes of Action in Product Liability 11

A. Historical Foundations 11

    1) Evolution of Contract-Based Product Liability 11
    2) The Evolution of Tort-Based Product Liability 13

B. Basic Principles of Negligence Law Applicable to Products 16

    1) Introduction 16
    2) Large-Scale Duties of Care 16
    3) Standard of Care 20
    4) Causation 26
    5) Damage and the "Pure Economic Loss" Bar 28

C. Types of Product Liability Claims in Negligence 32

    1) Manufacturing Defects 32
    2) Design Defects 36
        a) Generally 36
        b) Tests for Design Defect 37
            i) Risk-Utility Test 38
            ii) The Consumer-Expectations Test 41
            iii) Blended Theories 42
        c) Case Study: Risk-Utility and Tobacco 43
            i) Are Cigarettes an "Unreasonably Dangerous" Design? 43
            ii) Efforts to Expand Risk-Utility in Tobacco Litigation 45

D. Failure to Warn 48

    1) Overview of the Duty to Warn 48
    2) The Knowledge of the Defendant 52
        a) The "Duty to Research" 52
        b) Imputation of Industry-Wide Knowledge of Dangers 53
    3) The Content of the Warning 55
        a) Clear and Adequate Communication 55
        b) Obviousness 56
        c) The Knowledgeable User 57
        d) The Relevance of "Dependency" 57
        e) Compliance with Standard Warning 58
    4) The Duty to Warn Is a Continuing One 58
    5) The Learned Intermediary Rule 59
    6) Causation in Duty-to-Warn Cases 60
    7) Reliance on Other Sources for Warning 63

E. Consumer Protection Legislation in Canada 64

    1) Overview 64
        a) Division of Powers 64
        b) Federal Legislation 65
        c) Provincial Legislation 66
    2) Unfair Trade Practices and Misleading Advertising 66
    3) Liability from Warranties and Implied Terms 68
    4) The Sale of Goods Acts 70
        a) Overview of the Legislation 70
        b) The Implied Warranty of Fitness for Particular Purpose 70
        c) The Implied Condition of Merchantability 77
        d) Privity of Contract 82

5) Special Rules for the Production and Dissemination of Defective Medical Products 84
   a) Breach of Implied Warranty and Privity of Contract in the Medical Context 84
   b) Statutory Warranties and Privity Problems 86

F. Strict Liability 91
   1) Strict Liability in the United States 91
   2) Strict Liability in Canada 95

CHAPTER 2.
Causes of Action in Mass Tort 102

A. Introduction 102

B. Intentional Torts 103

C. Statutory Causes of Action 104

D. Negligence 105
   1) Breach of Common Law Standards 105
   2) Breach of Statutory Standards 105
      a) Breach of Statute as Evidence of Negligence 105
      b) Breach of Statute as a Mass Tort 107
   3) Affirmative Defences in Negligence 107
      a) Intervening Act of Another 107
      b) Contributory Negligence 109
      c) Voluntary Assumption of Risk and Waiver of Liability 110

E. Nuisance-Based Claims 113
   1) Private Nuisance 113
   2) Nuisance and Negligence 115
   3) Problems with Private Nuisance as a "Mass Tort" 116
   4) Public Nuisance 117
   5) *Rylands v. Fletcher* Actions 120

F. Liability from Statements and Silence 124
   1) Deceit 124
   2) Negligent Misrepresentation 127
   3) Misrepresentation in Securities Cases 130

G. Unjust Enrichment 132

H. Conspiracy   135

   1) Civil Conspiracy Generally   135
      a) The "Injurious Purpose" Test   136
      b) The "Unlawful Means" Test   137
   2) Conspiracy in Non-Commercial Cases   140
      a) The Requirement of Agreement   141
      b) The Requirement of Intent   141
   3) New Applications of the Tort: Hunt v. Carey Canada Inc.   142

I. Vicarious Liability   144

J. Breach of a Special Duty   146

   1) Fiduciary Duties   146
   2) Voluntarily Assumed Duty   149

K. Misfeasance in a Public Office   150

L. Defamation and Hate Speech   154

   1) Group Defamation at Common Law   154
   2) Statutory Actions for Defamatory or Hateful Statements   155

M. Constitutional Claims   158

   1) Claims Based on the Invalidity of Laws   158
   2) Recovery for Breaches of *Charter* Rights   161
      a) Overview of Civil *Charter* Claims   161
      b) Does a *Charter* Damages Claim Require Bad Faith or Malice?   164

CHAPTER 3.
Remedies in Large-Scale Claims   167

A. Introduction   167

B. Statutory Remedies   167

C. Compensatory Damages   169

   1) Generally   169
   2) Future Care   170
   3) Lost Earning Capacity   173
   4) Pain and Suffering   174

D. Special Issues and Approaches in Mass Tort and Product Liability Cases   175

1) Individualization versus Aggregation 175
2) Medical Monitoring 178
   a) In the United States 178
   b) In Canada 180
3) Fear of Disease (Emotional Distress) 181
4) Enhanced Risk 183

E. Punitive Damages 184

1) Generally 184
2) Punitive Damages in Product Liability Cases: United States and Canada 185
3) The Law in Canada: Principles and Quantum 189
4) Punitive Damages in Class Actions 192

F. Restitution and Disgorgement of Profits 193

1) Generally 193
2) Restitution Explained and Illustrated 194
3) Restitution as an Alternative Measure of Damages for Civil Wrongs 195
4) Restitution in Contractual Settings and Other Emerging Issues 196
5) Restitution in Mass Tort Cases 197

G. Injunctions 198

PART TWO: PROBLEMS OF PROOF AND CAUSATION 201

CHAPTER 4.
The Problem of Indeterminate Causation 203

A. Causation Problems in Large-Scale Wrongs 203

B. The Inadequacy of the "But For" Test 205

C. Liability "In the Air" 210

D. Some Approaches to Indeterminate Causation 212

1) Statutory Reform of Causation Rules 212
2) Probabilistic Discounting 214
3) Alternate Liability 215
4) Liability Based on Concert in Action, Enterprise Theory, or Market Participation 218

5) Liability for Medical Monitoring 222
6) From Burden-Shifting and "Loss of Chance" to Probabilistic Causation 223
   a) Onus-Shifting 223
   b) Probabilistic Discounting 226

E. Risk-Based Liability: The Fairchild Decision 232
   1) Is Proof of Causation Really Necessary? 233
   2) Inferences of Law and Fact versus Risk-Based Liability 234
   3) Where Would Risk-Based Liability Apply? 235

F. Proposed Application in Mass Tort Cases 237

G. The Reception of Fairchild in Canada 245

CHAPTER 5.
Problems of Proof 249

A. The Use of Statistical Evidence in Mass Tort 249

B. Deemed Knowledge 256
   1) Deeming Knowledge at Common Law 256
   2) Deeming Knowledge Via Statute 257

C. Destruction of Documentary Evidence 259
   1) Introduction 259
   2) Particular Relevance in Product Liability Context 260
   3) History of the Spoliation Doctrine 262
   4) Remedies for Spoliation 264
      a) As an Independent Tort 264
      b) As a Basis for Drawing Adverse Inferences and Presumptions 268
      c) As an Evidentiary Tool 269
      d) To Restrict Available Defences 270
   5) Is There a Remedy if the Destruction Is Negligent? 271

CHAPTER 6.
The Problem of Corporate Groups 273

A. The Implications of the Corporate Group 273

B. Limited Liability and Tort Creditors 274

C. Modern Corporations and "Judgment-Proofing" Strategies 278

D. "Piercing the Corporate Veil" 281

D. Successor Liability 286

- 1) Introduction 286
- 2) The Asset Purchase Liability Bar 288
- 3) The Emergence of Successor Liability in U.S. Product Liability Cases 288
- 4) "Product Line Liability" 291
- 5) Application of Successor Liability Rules in Canada 292
- 6) Does U.S.-Style "Successor Liability" Have a Place in Canadian Tort Law? 297
    - a) Successor Liability in a Fault-Based System 297
    - b) Pleading Successor Liability in Canadian Courts 299

F. Enterprise Liability 300

- 1) Introduction 300
- 2) Jurisprudence 303
- 3) Statutes 305

PART THREE: THE LAW OF AGGREGATE CLAIMS 307

CHAPTER 7.
Class Proceedings 309

A. Introduction 309

B. The Purposes of Claims Aggregation 312

C. Foundations of Canadian Class Action Policy 318

- 1) Origins of Aggregative Proceedings 318
    - a) Common Law, Equity, and the Rules of Court 318
    - b) U.S. Federal Rule 23 324
    - c) Development of "Mass Tort" Class Action Claims in the U.S. under Rule 23 325
- 2) Canadian Reform 331
- 3) Scope of Reform 334
- 4) Objectives of Reform 335

D. Features of Canadian Class Actions 338

- 1) Certifying the Class 338

2) Common Issues 342
3) Preferability 345
4) Notice Requirements and Opt-Out Rights 347
5) Aggregate Assessment of Damages and Non-Restitutionary Distribution 348
6) The "Common Law Class Action" 349

E. Representative Actions after *Western Canadian Shopping Centres v. Dutton* 350

1) "Representative Proceedings" and "Class Actions" 351
   a) Representative Action 352
   b) Class Proceeding Distinguished 353
   c) The Plaintiffs' Option? 354
      i) Do Statutory Class Action Regimes Supplant "Representative Proceedings" Rules? 355
      ii) Subsequent Treatment of *Dutton* in Representative Proceedings Brought Pursuant to Rules of Court 357

CHAPTER 8.
Some Emerging Issues Regarding Class Actions 360

A. Is Deterrence the Most Important Benefit of Class Litigation? 360

B. Do Class Actions Really Conserve Judicial Resources? 363

C. Need the Representative Plaintiff Have a Claim Against Each Defendant? 366

D. The "Public Law" Vision of Class Counsel as Private Prosecutor 368

E. Financing the Class Action 369
   1) Litigation as Investment 369
   2) Cost Awards and Indemnification Agreements 370

F. Carriage Motions and Competing Claims 374

G. Collusion in Settlement 379
   1) To the Prejudice of Claimants 379
   2) To the Prejudice of Non-Settling Defendants 382

H. "Strike Suits" and "Blackmail" Settlements 384

I. Problems of the "National Class" and Extraprovincial Notice 389

Part Four: Interjurisdictional Dimensions 395

CHAPTER 9.
Conflict of Laws in Large-Scale Claims 397

A. Introduction 397
B. An Overview of Conflict of Laws Analysis 397
C. The "Constitutionalization" of Private International Law 399
   1) *Morguard* 399
   2) *Hunt* 401
   3) The Future Direction 402
D. The Constitutional Context 403
   1) The Legislative Authority 404
   2) Comity, Order, and Fairness 405
E. Jurisdiction Over the Defendant 407
   1) *Jurisdiction Simpliciter* and the "Real and Substantial Connection" Test 407
   2) *Jurisdiction Simpliciter* and Multiple Defendants 409
   3) Comity Internationally after *Spar Aerospace* and *Beals v. Saldanha* 410
   4) Jurisdiction *Forum Conveniens* 413
   5) "Fairness and Justice" 414
F. Choice of Law and Applicability 416
   1) Choice of Law 416
      a) In Tort-Based Claims 416
      b) Choice of Forum and Law in Contract-based Cases 417
   2) Applicability of Provincial Statutes 420
G. "Blocking Provisions" 423
H. Enforcement of Judgments 426
   1) Enforcement of Canadian Judgments Within Canada 426
   2) Enforcement of Canadian Judgments Internationally 427
   3) Enforcement of Foreign Judgments in Canada 429
   4) Enforceability as an Element of Jurisdictional Analysis 430

CHAPTER 10.
Interjurisdictional Class Actions   433

A. Introduction   433

B. National Classes vs. Province-by-Province Certification   434
   1) Why the National Class is Preferable   434
   2) Objections to the National Class   438
      a) Provincial Sovereignty   439
      b) Jurisdiction and Notice   440
      c) Choice of Law   442
      d) Opt-In vs. Opt-Out   443

C. Jurisprudence   444
   1) *Morguard* and *Hunt* Revisited   444
   2) The *Dutton* Decision   447
   3) Interpreting the Legislation: Opt-In vs. Opt-Out   449
      a) National Classes in British Columbia   450
      b) National Classes in Ontario   452
      c) National Classes in Quebec   459
   4) The Unanswered Question: Sufficiency of Notice   460

D. The Future of the National Class   465

CONCLUSION
The Future of Large-Scale Claims in Canada   468

TABLE OF CASES   471

INDEX   501

Preface

In this book we discuss a number of areas of law that are usually studied and taught separately. In doing so, we are conscious that each field we touch upon — product liability, torts, corporation law, evidence, conflict of laws, class actions, and the law of remedies, to name only the most significant — is itself the topic of excellent full-length treatises, in some cases running to several volumes. We do not pretend that this book should replace any of these comprehensive works.

Instead, our idea builds on a recognition that there is a field of practice — and, increasingly, of legal study — that demands a working comprehension of all the topics covered here and, more important, the way they interact in the modern courtroom. In the United States, virtually every law school offers courses in this field, which is usually termed "complex litigation." Canadian schools appear only now to be catching up, as our litigation itself, in the dawning class action era, begins to resemble more closely the American model in some important respects.

Some parts of this book are based on material we have, together or individually, previously published. Certain elements of our discussion on class actions have been adapted from Craig Jones' book *Theory of Class Actions*; portions of the "Remedies" section have been adapted from Jamie Cassels' text on that subject (both books are published by Irwin Law); parts of our section on problems of proof and causation are shared with an article we co-authored for the *Canadian Bar Review*; and the section on national class actions is largely reproduced in an article by Craig Jones in the inaugural edition of the *Canadian Class Action Review*. Some of the theoretical analysis underscoring the uniqueness of the legal problems in mass tort situations derives from Cassels' book *The Uncertain Promise of Law: Lessons from Bhopal* (Toronto: University of Toronto Press, 1993). In each case, we have tried to ensure that the work included here has been updated to reflect recent changes to the law.

We are grateful to Jeffrey Miller at Irwin Law, who embraced this notion from the beginning and supported our endeavour through the inevitable delays wrought by our professional obligations. Our colleagues at the University of British Columbia, the University of Victoria, and in the profession have been generous with their time and thoughts. Elliott Myers, QC, and Elizabeth Araujo, who have developed considerable expertise in the application of private international law rules to mass tort and product liability cases, provided inspiration and insight as the project developed. Kimberley Kuntz contributed her thoughts and research in several areas, most notably the emerging jurisprudence surrounding the destruction of documentary evidence in mass tort claims. Daniel Webster, QC, and Tom Berger, OC, QC, were constant (if unknowing) sources of ideas. We are grateful also to Peter Burns, QC, and Vaughan Black, who reviewed drafts of our work on probabilistic causation, and John Kleefeld, who provided helpful suggestions on topics related to class actions.

Throughout this project, we have had the assistance of colleagues and students at the University of British Columbia and the University of Victoria, including Claire Hatcher, Ben Berger, and Zoran Bozic. Vida Mehin, at that time an articled student at Bull, Housser and Tupper, provided invaluable assistance with editing and arrangement.

Needless to say, responsibility for any errors or oversights in this book is ours alone.

Introduction

A. SPECIAL PROBLEMS OF LARGE-SCALE CLAIMS

On its simplest level, the ambition of this book is to explain the legal rules applicable to cases of large-scale claims, typically in "product liability" and "mass torts." But what does that mean, exactly?

"Product liability" generally refers to a series of overlapping regimes of public and private law governing the extent to which those involved in the production or distribution of goods can be liable to persons who suffer loss or injury as a result of flaws in design, manufacture, or condition of those goods. Because, as we note below, the realities of mass production mean that most such flaws will be reproduced numerous times in the production or distribution process, modern product liability law can be viewed as a subspecies of a broader topic, which we here refer to by its most common appellation, "mass tort," though the term is regrettably inexact.

The term "mass tort" is used in a wide variety of contexts, from single-incident disasters with a host of victims both immediately apparent (as in, for instance, an airplane crash) to those apparent only with the passage of time (in the case of delayed-onset diseases allegedly resulting from tortious exposure to substances such as Agent Orange or, for example, the catastrophic gas leak from a Union Carbide plant in Bhopal, India). More common examples can be drawn from product liability cases, where the failure of a product can occur more or less immediately or some time in the future.

Beyond the problems such incidents create from a practical point of view owing to the sheer numbers of victims, unique difficulties arise for the substantive law of civil obligations. For instance, because of the inexactness of scientific understanding of disease and injury processes, in many cases it will not be possible to match a harm with a cause. We may know, for instance, that a particular type of cancer can be caused by a certain substance, but it might also be caused by a host of other factors, both wrongful and innocent. How can the law link the harm with the wrongful cause, or with any particular wrongdoer, as traditional tort law requires?

In our view, any comprehensive analysis of the subject must begin with the recognition that mass torts are a particular — and to some extent inevitable — consequence of the nature of a modern industrial society. Contemporary economies of scale dictate that it is better, cheaper, and more efficient to provide products or services that are generic to large numbers of consumers. Any wrongful or negligent decision made in the course of the provision of such goods and services, therefore, is likely to have ramifications for larger numbers of consumers than in the paradigmatic — that is, bipolar — "duty" relationships for which the law of tort was initially developed. This is so whether the product mass-produced is a poorly operated mode of transportation, a faulty product, or a misleading prospectus.

The modern economy has a second aspect that is relevant to our undertaking: the sheer scale of industrial production necessary to satisfy widespread demand for consumer goods and services is such that catastrophic disasters in the production or distribution of various products can be of such a magnitude so as to cause widespread harm to victims who have no consumer relationship — direct or indirect — with the wrongdoer at all. Industrial pollution — as exemplified by the Bhopal disaster — is perhaps the most obvious example, but less spectacular cases of such non-contractual harm are common, such as when a tire failure causes accidents that injure passengers or other motorists with no contractual relationship, however indirect, with the manufacturer. In such circumstances, libertarian notions based on privity of contract and the voluntary assumption of risks in a competitive marketplace offer no comprehensive solution.

The change wrought by industrialization was recognized as early as 1897 by the great American jurist Oliver Wendell Holmes, Jr, who remarked in a lecture that

> [o]ur law of torts comes from the old days of isolated, ungeneralized wrongs, assaults, slanders, and the like, where the damages might be taken to lie where they fell by legal judgment. But the torts with which our courts are kept busy today are mainly the incidents of certain well known

businesses. They are injuries to person or property by railroads, factories, and the like. The liability for them is estimated, and sooner or later goes into the price paid by the public.[1]

This particular type of "generalized" wrong — which we might describe as widespread and diffuse damage arising from centralized causes (usually wrongful or negligent business decisions) — is difficult to encapsulate within the traditional tort or contract relationships, which focus on reciprocal relationship between two individuals and are in many ways vestiges of pre-industrial legal principles.

The size and complexity of the modern economy — and the increasing globalization of trade — raise other issues that must be considered in any book of this type: the legal world is divided into geographic jurisdictions; the marketplace, increasingly, is not. The impact of large-scale wrongs is less likely to be confined to any particular nation, province, or state. How the rules of domicile and conflict of laws play out in the context of large-scale claims is therefore important to any comprehensive understanding of the topic.

In the United States, practitioners, courts, and academics, recognizing the unique challenges involved, have defined a field known as "complex litigation" to facilitate the study and resolution of the types of claims described here. The Judicial Council of California says: "Complex litigation refers to cases that require exceptional management to avoid placing unnecessary burdens on the court or the litigants and involve such areas as antitrust, securities claims, mass torts, and class actions."[2] Large-scale claims have generated significant changes to both substantive and procedural rules as courts struggle to reconcile modern models of production and consumption with the requirements of justice in the enforcement of private and public obligations. It is this struggle to which this book is addressed.

B. THE ROLE AND LIMITS OF LAW

1) The Problematic "Substantive/Procedural" Distinction

This book adopts the perspective that the division of legal rules into "substantive" and "procedural" categories for separate study is often unhelpful.

---

[1] O.W. Holmes, "The Path of the Law" (1897) 10 Harv. L. Rev. 457 at 467. Holmes originally delivered the paper as a lecture on 8 January 1897, at the dedication of a new hall at the Boston University School of Law.
[2] Judicial Council of California, Fact Sheet: Complex Civil Litigation, June 2003.

We take the view that, particularly in a study of mass tort litigation, substantive and procedural rules must be considered together.

While substance/procedure distinctions may make perfect sense for many purposes, rigorous examination of one at the expense of the other ignores the way that substance and procedure interact to produce particular outcomes — and it is outcomes that are most important to the parties, as well as to litigators and students of policy. Rights and remedies, it is often remarked, are functionally indistinguishable.

The question of who bears the onus of proof on a particular question — say the causation of a particular disease — is theoretically irrelevant to the legal rights of the parties. But in a situation of causal uncertainty, the "information deficit" will enure to the detriment of the party who bears the burden — at common law usually the plaintiff. If the information deficit is systemic to a particular type of claim, then each such claim will fail, and often there is a sense that an injustice is occurring — victims are going uncompensated, and wrongdoers are escaping liability. Courts and legislatures can react by adjusting the substantive law (for instance, by designing a cause of action that is not based on traditional causation) or the procedural law (by, for instance, changing laws of evidence that make the burden easier to meet). Other changes, such as relaxing or reversing the burden on the issue of causation under particular circumstances, are difficult to classify as strictly procedural or substantive.

Class actions, upon which significant portions of this work necessarily focus, are another example of the profound substantive impact of procedural rules. It is trite to say that, without aggregation of claims, many wrongs that result in small individual losses would go unaddressed; class action procedures make such claims viable to pursue; in the result, many areas of the law that had lain largely dormant have blossomed into a hotly contested jurisprudence. Competition law, securities law, and, of course, product liability law owe their current vitality in large part to procedures permitting collective action against the wrongdoer.

In the United States, as we noted earlier, substance and procedure in mass tort and product liability cases are increasingly studied together under the rubric of the term "complex litigation." While this term is perhaps no more accurate than any other in describing the scope of its topic, it adequately represents the trend towards an outcome-focused, pragmatic approach to the analysis of substantive and procedural rules applicable to large-scale claims. It is an approach we find largely lacking in Canadian commentary, and it is hoped that this book may in some measure serve to correct this deficit.

Although in this book we break our discussion of certain procedural devices — and in particular the class action lawsuit — into discrete sections for separate discussion, wherever possible, we also examine and describe the ways that substance and procedure work together either to advance or to frustrate plaintiffs, defendants, or broad social goals. We examine ways in which technically procedural devices — such as evidentiary rules or the availability of aggregate claims — may have as profound an effect on outcomes as any substantive right established by common law or statute.

Our overall approach might be described as "functionalist." Whenever it is possible to understand and elucidate the goals behind legal rules, we believe that is the function of the law to advance those goals, and we explore the ways that this does or does not occur.

2) The Inadequacy of Reliance on Precedent

Another challenge in setting out the law applicable to large-scale wrongs is its deep and continuing uncertainty. Stakes in large-scale litigation are notoriously high. Most mass tort claims are today pursued as class actions, and if certified as such, they usually settle. The amount for which they settle is a result of the parties' assessments of the chances of the suits' success, which in turn are based on an assessment that the court will accept theories of liability and calculation of quantum that may have no established precedent. Unfortunately, this process compounds the uncertainty, since it produces few decisions to guide future decision makers.

A good example of this is the question of market-share liability. Established in the 1970 California litigation involving DES — a drug designed to prevent miscarriage — this theory holds manufacturers of generic products liable to victims in proportion to their market share in circumstances where the degree of their actual contribution to the harm in the population cannot be otherwise measured. This is a form of probabilistic or "risk-based" liability, because market share is essentially serving as a proxy for the probability that any particular manufacturer caused the harm complained of.

In the thirty years since the California Supreme Court applied market-share liability in *Sindell*,[3] no Canadian court has confirmed that the doctrine is available to plaintiffs in Canada. Yet, at the same time, no court has permitted a claim based on market-share liability to be struck as disclosing no reasonable cause of action. Plaintiffs and defendants involved in a suit

---

3   *Sindell v. Abbott Laboratories*, 26 Cal.3d 588 (1980).

where market-share theory is advanced therefore conduct their litigation largely in the dark, and settlements are concluded based on each party's assessment of the probability that market-share liability might be imposed, viewed through the filter of their respective degrees of risk-tolerance.

It is more than simply ineffective to look only to established Canadian jurisprudence to determine the rules of liability and damages in mass tort cases; to do so would be irresponsible. The student, like the practitioner and the judge, must be prepared to anticipate a host of legal principles, some of which might at first appear quite unnatural but which might be applied should the case proceed to trial.

C. PRODUCT LIABILITY AND MASS TORT

We believe that it is useful to break down our consideration of the substantive law applicable to mass wrongs into two broad categories or bases of liability: product liability and mass tort liability more generally.

Product liability has evolved relatively recently along with the tumultuous evolution of economic life into one of mass production and marketing. Product cases have often been the basis from which mass tort law generally has developed, yet product liability itself is not derived entirely from the law of tort. Product liability often involves plaintiffs and defendants who are, at least nominally, "known" to each other in the sense that they occupy positions along a line from production to consumption (though this is, of course, not always so); as a result, product liability cases are rooted as much in ideas of contract and consensual relationships as in the broader, more public-law duties found in the law of tort.

Beyond product liability *per se* is another type of mass wrong, in this case founded upon more "ordinary" tort liability, particularly on breaches of the duty that defendants owe regardless of any economic relationship between defendant and plaintiff. A polluter, for instance, may owe duties to those likely to be affected by its toxic emissions, not simply to the purchasers of its product or its employees; an airline might owe a duty to take precautions against disaster quite apart from those owed to its customers; an automobile manufacturer owes duties to all reasonably foreseeable victims of an unsafe car, not only to the car's owners or occupants.

The main distinction is that the first basis of liability, product liability, has evolved in part from contract theory — in the relationship formed between customer and producer; there are persistent questions of consent, contract, and voluntary assumptions of risks that do not arise (or at least do not arise in the same way) when the duty is owed to a stranger. This, of course, is not a hard-and-fast distinction; some product liability cases involve strangers and some non-product mass tort cases involve persons in contractual relationships with one another.

We believe it is important that mass torts beyond product liability receive treatment in this book, because they present so many of the same fundamental problems of resolution as do claims arising from mass marketing of products. This overlap necessarily requires some repetitiveness of discussion; we have minimized this by treating the substantive law of product liability, arguably the more complex and better developed area of complex litigation, first, followed by a discussion of other causes of action that may be increasingly encountered by practitioners and students of the field.

Part One:
Sources of Liability

1. Causes of Action in Product Liability

A. HISTORICAL FOUNDATIONS

In modern society the phenomena of mass production and distribution of products has made "product liability" a fertile field of mass litigation, involving the modern law of contract and tort. However, the production and distribution of products, and the injuries caused by them when they are somehow defective, is a very old social problem and we begin this chapter with a brief historical account of the law of contract and tort in relation to products in order to provide a context to understand the shape of the present law, its current constraints, and its possible future directions.

1) Evolution of Contract-Based Product Liability

The law of implied warranties dates back to the fifteenth century, its evolution parallelling that of contract law. The doctrine first arose as a tort for uttering a false statement inducing a sale, under the assumption that the seller had actually deceived the buyer into making a bad purchase by uttering an untrue statement as to the good's quality. The action was conceived in the nature of misrepresentation, with the buyer detrimentally relying upon the seller's skill and judgment. While the buyer's damages were limited to the difference between the price paid and the value of the goods received, the buyer could succeed without being required to prove that the seller knew about the defect or that his or her statement was actually untrue.

In the eighteenth century, the development of the law of the sale of goods was extended further, allowing for the bringing of warranty actions in *assumpsit*. The courts continued to search for a breach of contract, on the basis of a stated promise, permitting the seller to claim expectation damages in the amount of the difference between the value of the goods sold and the value that they would have been worth had they been fit for their intended use.

By the nineteenth century, implied warranties were assessed from the perspective of an implied promise. In the early 1800s an English court held that, in a sale of goods by a person dealing in those goods, there was an implied promise that the goods would be of "merchantable" quality, provided that the buyer had not had an opportunity to inspect the goods before sale. In *Gardiner v. Gray*,[1] for example, Lord Ellenborough stated the following:

> I am of the opinion ... that the purchaser has the right to expect a saleable article answering the description in the contract. Without any particular warranty, *this is an implied term in every such contract*. Where there is no opportunity to inspect the commodity, the maxim of caveat emptor does not apply. He cannot without a warranty insist that it shall be of any particular quality or fitness, but the intention of both parties must be taken to be, that it shall be saleable in the market under the denomination mentioned in the contract between them.

The action remained a contractual one but no longer required an express promise: it was accepted that a seller warranted that his or her goods would be reasonably fit for ordinary use regardless of the intent of the parties. The courts further determined that the doctrine of implied warranties should not be limited to financial losses incurred by the actual sale by measuring the difference between the value of the goods paid for and the value of the goods received. Rather, it was recognized that damages could be measured according to the injury suffered through the use of the chattel. The courts therefore began to allow for consequential damages on the basis that the seller should be liable for all damage that ought reasonably to have been contemplated as liable to result from a breach of promise.

The notion that a seller of goods provides a warranty as to their fitness without making an express representation has been codified in Canada

---

1 (1815), 171 E.R. 46 [emphasis added].

through English and later Canadian (provincial) legislation such as the *Sale of Goods Acts*.[2] These Acts will be the subject of further discussion later in Part One of this book.

An action for liability under the *Sale of Goods Act* may succeed if a product defect is established; however, the requirement of privity of contract prevails and plaintiffs must also meet a number of specific requirements set out in the legislation. Therefore, unless there is provincial consumer protection legislation in place, an injured party will have a difficult time succeeding against a *manufacturer* pursuant to the notion of implied warranties.

In summary, while implied warranties are not solely creatures of statute, the courts have tended to limit their application to cases involving sales, recognizing that warranties are little more than implied promises between individuals. This has meant that manufacturers, distributors, retailers, and suppliers of defective products have been named, often without success, as defendants in product liability actions. How can the law justify its limitation of liability to a finding of an agreement between sellers and buyers? In many cases, after all, it is not the actual sale that occasions the loss, for individuals can be easily injured by products and objects that they themselves have not purchased. The continuing individual focus of the law of contract means that it cannot yet play a robust role in large-scale claims.

2) The Evolution of Tort-Based Product Liability

Until early in the twentieth century, claims relating to product liability were almost exclusively limited to the law of contract. The concept of privity of contract — the notion that only the parties to a contract can claim damages for a breach — was applied to manufactured goods, with a predictably constraining effect. What made things more difficult for jurists, however, was that during the nineteenth century they were confronted by a wide range of cases involving strangers. The advent of railroads and motor vehicles created a series of largely unforeseen injury situations involving persons who were in no way directly connected with one another, least of all through contract. The initial reluctance of the English common law courts to address this new reality is well illustrated by the 1842 decision of *Winterbottom v. Wright*,[3] in which a passenger brought a suit for personal injuries against the supplier of a mail coach that had broken down. The court limited the liability of the manufacturer and supplier on grounds of a lack of privity of contract. In so holding, Lord Abinger declared that "the

---

2 For instance *Sale of Goods Act*, R.S.O. 1990 c. S-1; *Sale of Goods Act*, R.S.B.C. 1979, c. 370.
3 (1842), 152 E.R. 402 [hereinafter *Winterbottom*].

most absurd and outrageous consequences, to which I can see no limit,"[4] would result if it were held that a defendant who contracted with Party A should be held liable to Party B for failure to perform that contract.

When possible, courts struggled to expand notions of contract to accommodate the new reality of the mass marketing of goods, but with limited success. The seminal case of *Carlill v. Carbolic Smoke Ball Co.*[5] appeared to accept the notion that manufacturers could be liable for statements made to the world at large regarding the efficacy of their products. In truth, though, that decision was much narrower, dealing with a fairly unique set of facts (wherein the manufacturer had offered a reward if the purchaser of the "smoke ball" found it ineffective at preventing influenza). The issue was not, in that case, whether the product — a rubber ball that puffed out a mist of powdered carbolic acid — was ineffective, or even dangerous; rather, it was whether the manufacturer's promise to pay one hundred pounds was enforceable.

However, efforts to expand contractual remedies could not keep pace with the social context of industrialization. Mass production, consumerism, rapid transportation, machinery, and fewer personal relations between individuals in the chain of commerce created strong pressure for a more generalized civil remedy for personal injury.

In the twentieth century, the law of product liability was at last freed from the shackles of privity of contract, finding a home in the duties that were being recognized in the law of negligence. In the United States, the case of *McPherson v. Buick Motor Co.*,[6] penned by Justice Benjamin Cardozo, declared that any object negligently manufactured was inherently dangerous and, as such, could be the basis for a claim in tort. The seed of this new liability took root in the British Commonwealth, and earlier than is sometimes supposed. Linden notes that "it is commonly, although wrongly, believed that this development worked its way into the law of the Commonwealth ... through the decision of *Donoghue v. Stevenson*."[7] In fact, two Canadian cases preceded this famous House of Lords decision.

In 1919 Mr. Justice Drysdale of the Nova Scotia Supreme Court decided a case surprisingly analogous to the later decision in *Donoghue v. Stevenson*.[8] In *Buckley v. Mott*,[9] the plaintiff was injured when he ingested a

---

4   *Ibid.* at 405.
5   [1893] 1 Q.B. 256 (C.A.).
6   217 N.Y. Supp. 382 (1916).
7   A.M. Linden, *Canadian Tort Law*, 7th ed. (Toronto: Butterworths, 2001) at 568.
8   [1932] A.C. 562.
9   (1919), 50 D.L.R. 408 [hereinafter *Buckley*].

quantity of powdered glass contained in a chocolate cream bar manufactured by the defendant. Despite the fact that Buckley had purchased the candy from a retailer and, as such, there was no contractual relationship between the parties, Drysdale J. found that "there was a duty to the public not to put on sale such a dangerous article as the chocolate bar in question."[10] Accordingly, he found that the defendants were liable in negligence and awarded the substantial sum of $700 plus costs.

Ross v. Dunstall[11] involved a claim against the manufacturer of a particular sportsman's rifle. The rifle in question was capable of firing even when the bolt was unlocked, thereby putting the user at risk, and a number of individuals had been injured as a result of this design defect. The Court found that there was evidence that the defect could have been readily remedied by a simple change in design and that, in addition, the manufacturer had failed in its duty to warn potential consumers of the danger. Although the decision was based on the Quebec *Civil Code*, Anglin J. stated that "[w]hile English law is not applicable to these cases I am inclined to think that under it the defendant would likewise be liable." He went on to make the following, and strikingly modern, statement about product liability:

> The duty of a manufacturer of articles (such as rifles), which are highly dangerous unless designed and made with great skill and care, to possess and exercise skill and to take care exists towards all persons to whom an original vendee from him, reasonably relying on such skill having been exercised and due care having been taken, may innocently deliver the thing as fit and proper to be dealt with in the way in which the manufacturer intended it should be dealt with. The manufacturer of such articles is a person rightly assumed to possess and to have exercised superior knowledge and skill in regard to them on which purchasers from retail dealers in the ordinary course of trade may be expected to rely. From his position he ought to know of any hidden sources of danger connected with their use. The law cannot be so impotent as to allow such a manufacturer to escape liability for injuries — possibly fatal — to a person of a class who he contemplated would use his product in the way in which it was used caused by a latent source of danger which reasonable care on his part should have discovered and to give warning of which no steps have been taken.[12]

So the principles enunciated in *Donogue v. Stevenson* were circulating in Canadian law well prior to that famous case. *Buckley* and *Ross* are both

---

10 *Ibid.* at 409.
11 (1921), 62 S.C.R. 393 [hereinafter *Ross*].
12 *Ibid.* at 403.

departures from liability constrained by contract and demonstrate incipient conceptions of a duty to warn, liability for both design and manufacturing defects, and proximate cause based upon reasonable foresight. The next century would see Canadian law build upon these ideas, entrenched by the House of Lords in *Donoghue v. Stevenson*, thereby establishing a mature law of negligence-based product liability.

B. BASIC PRINCIPLES OF NEGLIGENCE LAW APPLICABLE TO PRODUCTS

1) Introduction

As is true for all claims of negligence, a plaintiff must establish the following elements to be successful in a negligence claim arising from product liability:

- that the defendant owed a legal duty of care to the plaintiff;
- that the defendant's impugned actions failed to meet a reasonable standard of care;
- that the defendant's actions were both the factual and proximate cause of the plaintiff's injuries; and
- that the plaintiff suffered damage as a result of the defendant's actions.

Accordingly, it is appropriate to review briefly the general applicability of these elements to the area of product liability.

2) Large-Scale Duties of Care

The "neighbour principle," enunciated in *Donoghue v. Stevenson*, established a general duty of care premised on the notion of foreseeability. Lord Atkin articulated the duty as arising with respect to "persons who are so closely and directly affected by my act that I ought reasonably to have them in contemplation as being so affected when I am directing my mind to the acts or omissions which are called in question."[13] This approach revolutionized the law of civil liability from one built upon an incremental analysis of discrete relationships to one based upon a general duty owed by all. Yet the concept of duty of care is not merely one of foreseeability. In *Anns v. Merton London Borough Council*,[14] the House of Lords refined the idea of duty of care, by creating a two-stage analysis:

---

13 *Donoghue v. Stevenson*, supra note 8 at 580.
14 [1978] A.C. 728 (H.L.) [hereinafter *Anns*].

> First one has to ask whether, as between the alleged wrongdoer and the person who has suffered damage there is a sufficient relationship of proximity or neighbourhood such that, in the reasonable contemplation of the former, carelessness on his part may be likely to cause damage to the latter — in which case, a prima facie duty of care arises. Secondly, if the first question is answered affirmatively, it is necessary to consider whether there are any considerations which ought to negative, or to reduce or limit the scope of the duty or the class of person to whom it is owed or the damages to which a breach may give rise.[15]

Thus, policy considerations, which may include factors such as the needs and realities of modern society, play an important part in the duty-of-care analysis. This second branch of the duty-of-care analysis permits an open assessment of the costs and benefits that recognizing a particular duty would have for society. It also permits the court to modify or reduce the scope of the duty in order to fit these needs. So, while there is a presumptive duty of care owed to all persons foreseeably affected by an individual's actions, the defendant is afforded an opportunity to negate or limit this duty by advancing policy reasons as to why the general duty is too broad. The Supreme Court of Canada accepted this two-stage analysis in *Kamloops (City) v. Nielson*.[16]

This two-stage approach to duty of care raises significant questions in the context of product liability: Who owes a duty of care with respect to a given product? To whom is this duty owed? What is the nature and extent of this duty? Do all products give rise to this duty? The second branch raises the important question of the social utility of negligence-based product liability — are there any social or economic reasons why the duty of care should be limited?

Donoghue v. Stevenson remains the leading statement regarding the duty of care owed in the context of product liability. Specifically, it recognizes that a duty of care exists between a manufacturer and an ultimate consumer:

> [A] manufacturer of products, which he sells in such a form as to show that he intends them to reach the ultimate consumer in the form in which they left him with no reasonable possibility of intermediate examination,

---

15 *Ibid.* at 751–52.
16 [1984] 2 S.C.R. 2. Note that, in *Murphy v. Brentwood District Council*, [1990] 2 All E.R. 908 (H.L.) [hereinafter *Murphy*], the House of Lords rejected the two-stage test of *Anns, supra* note 14, as being too expansive. The Supreme Court of Canada considered and rejected *Murphy, supra,* in *Canadian National Railway Co. v. Norsk Pacific Steamship Co.,* [1992] 1 S.C.R. 1021 at 1155.

and with the knowledge that the absence of reasonable care in the preparation or putting up of the products will result in an injury to the consumer's life or property, owes a duty to the consumer to take that reasonable care.[17]

The duty to take care in the design and manufacture of a given product is firmly established in Canadian law. Yet, as demonstrated by *Lambert v. Lastoplex Chemicals Co.*,[18] this duty is not limited to care in production but includes a responsibility on the part of a manufacturer to warn of dangers inherent in the product's use. In this case, the plaintiff had purchased two cans of lacquer sealer manufactured by the defendant. The sealer was highly volatile and, although there was a warning on the product not to expose it to open flame, there was no indication of the dangers of fumes spreading and, themselves, igniting. The plaintiff was sealing a floor in his basement when the pilot light from a gas furnace one room away caused an explosion, in which the plaintiff was badly burnt and his house badly damaged. Laskin J. (as he then was) wrote the following for the Court:

> Manufacturers owe a duty to consumers of their products to see that there are no defects in manufacture which are likely to give rise to injury in the ordinary course of use. Their duty does not, however, end if the product, although suitable for the purpose for which it is manufactured and marketed, is at the same time dangerous to use; and if they are aware of its dangerous character they cannot, without more, pass the risk of injury to the consumer.[19]

The manufacturer's duty extended to ensuring that sufficient warning was given with respect to dangers inherent in the use of the product. Consequently, there is a firmly established duty owed by a manufacturer to the ultimate consumer, one that requires care in the design, production, and distribution of the product.

It is also now clear that it is not only the "manufacturer of products" who owes such a duty. Any person in the chain of distribution to the ultimate consumer (importers, wholesalers,[20] distributors, retailers[21]) may be liable for a failure to use reasonable care in performing his or her function.

---

17   *Donoghue v. Stevenson, supra,* note 8 at 599.
18   (1972), 25 D.L.R. (3d) 121 (S.C.C.) [hereinafter *Lambert*].
19   *Ibid.* at 124–25.
20   *O'Fallon v. Inecto Rapid Canada Ltd.*, [1940] 4 D.L.R. 276 (B.C.C.A.).
21   See *Nernberg v. Shop-Easy Stores Ltd.* (1966), 57 D.L.R. (2d) 741 (Sask. C.A.). In this case, the defendant retailer was held liable for injuries caused by a crack in a glass jar purchased from its store.

In *Pack v. Warner (County) No. 5*,[22] the court was faced with a situation in which the plaintiff claimed damages for injury to his cattle that resulted from spraying them with a chemical that was not recommended by the manufacturer for that purpose. The county, which performed the spraying, added the distributor as a third party to the proceedings, claiming that they had a duty to warn subsequent users of the unsuitability of the chemical. The court agreed, finding that the distributor owed a duty of care to the plaintiff, and allowed the defendant county to indemnify against the distributor in the amount of 50 percent. In reaching this decision, the court relied upon the statement by Stable J. that "I do not think that it matters whether the man is a manufacturer or whether he is a distributor."[23]

Even those outside the chain of distribution but involved in installing or maintaining the product can be held liable. In *Lemesurier v. Union Gas Co. of Canada*,[24] the plaintiff sued the defendant installer of a fireplace for damages resulting from a gas explosion. Although the accident was traced to the faulty design of the fireplace, the court held that the installer should have recognized this deficiency and, accordingly, found the defendant liable. Similarly, in *Marschler v. G. Masser's Garage*,[25] the repairer of automobile brakes was held liable to an injured third party for his negligence. This duty of care even extends to inspectors and certifiers, whereby an inspector can be held liable for failing to detect a defect in a given product.[26] It is apparent that the group of individuals who may owe a duty of care with respect to a product is broad, indeed — virtually any person who becomes involved in the production, distribution, or use of a product is potentially liable for injuries resulting from his or her negligence.

Nor is protection limited to the "ultimate consumer," as suggested in *Donoghue v. Stevenson*. Any person who can reasonably be expected to use or consume the product is also protected by this duty. Indeed, in *Bow Valley Huskey (Bermuda) Ltd. v. Saint John Shipbuilding Ltd.*,[27] the court concluded broadly that "... liability for defective products extends beyond the

---

22 (1964), 46 W.W.R. 422 (Alta C.A.).
23 *Watson v. Buckley*, [1940] 1 All E.R. 174 at 183 (K.B.). In this case, the plaintiff was permitted to recover from the defendant distributor for injuries suffered from using a hair dye.
24 (1975), 8 O.R. (2d) 152 (H.C.J.). See also *Hansen v. Twin City Construction Co.* (1982), 19 Alta. L.R. (2d) 335 (Q.B.).
25 (1956), 2 D.L.R. (2d) 484 (Ont. H.C.).
26 See *Ostash v. Sonnenberg* (1968), 63 W.W.R. 257 (Alta. C.A.), a tragic case in which three children died and a man became dangerously ill as a result of the failure of a government gas inspector to detect a flaw in the home's furnace.
27 (1995), 126 D.L.R. (4th) 1 (Nfld. C.A.), var'd [1997] 3 S.C.R. 1210 [hereinafter *Bow Valley*].

owner or consumer to anyone who is reasonably foreseeable as being affected by the negligent conduct of the manufacturer."[28]

Finally, a product liability analysis requires a consideration of the kinds of products that are captured by the general duty of care. Although *Donoghue v. Stevenson* seemed to suggest a more limited approach that would encompass only food and drink or common household items, the intervening years have made clear that virtually all products give rise to such a duty.[29] The only useful distinction to be drawn is for those products that can be described as "inherently dangerous," for which there is an elevated duty to warn, as will be discussed below.

Clearly, the vast expansion of relationships of responsibility described here is an appropriate legal adaptation to the impersonal systems of mass production and distribution in the modern world. However, as we will see, establishing the requisite elements of the cause of action continues to be relatively individualized and the law is often only awkwardly applicable in cases of mass claims.

3) Standard of Care

Once a duty of care is established, the next question is: What is the content of that duty? The answer is found in the standard of care. Because liability under negligence law is not "strict" or "absolute," it is not enough to show that the actions of a defendant were harmful. Having established the existence of a duty of care, the plaintiff must prove that the defendant's actions fell below an acceptable level and thus breached the *standard* of care. The product, process, or distribution must be shown to be *defective*, and the defect must be traceable to the failure by the manufacturer to use *reasonable care*. It must be shown that there was some fault in designing, testing, producing, or distributing the product.

To what level of care ought we to hold a defendant? The English case of *Vaughan v. Menlove*[30] established the general rule that a defendant must "adhere to the rule which requires in all cases a regard to caution such as a man of ordinary prudence would observe."[31] The test of what a "reasonable person" would do has been modified to fit particular contexts in which claims of negligence arise. For example, in cases of alleged medical negli-

---

28 Ibid. at 28.
29 See A.M. Linden, *Canadian Tort Law*, 5th ed. (Toronto: Butterworths, 1993) at 550–52 for a list of the kinds of products that have attracted a duty of care.
30 (1837), 132 E.R. 490 (C.P.).
31 Ibid. at 493.

gence, the proper standard of care is that "which could reasonably be expected of a normal, prudent practitioner of the same experience and standing ...."[32] Similar modifications of the test have occurred in the area of product liability. As such, the law expects a manufacturer of products to exercise the degree of care that could reasonably be expected of a prudent manufacturer. Simply put, the manufacturer has "a duty to take reasonable care in the manufacture of its product."[33]

This assessment of reasonableness will be influenced by a number of factors, including the foreseeability of injury from a product or activity (probability), the severity of the potential consequences should the risk materialize (gravity), the social utility of the activity or product, and the cost of precautions (including, in the case of products, the feasibility of tests and processes). There is also a set of specific guidelines that the courts will use to assess reasonableness. The first is industry standards. A useful guide to determining the requisite standard of care is the general practice in the defendant's industry. As stated in *Edmonton (City) v. Lovat Tunnel Equipment Inc.*:[34]

> Generally, a manufacturer will not be held liable for employing materials and manufacturing methods commonly used and accepted at the time of manufacture (*London v. Lancashire Guarantee & Accident Co.*, [1944] 1 D.L.R. 561 at 564 (S.C.C.)), although the weight to be given to common practice or industry standards in determining whether reasonable care was taken varies.[35]

Some courts have gone so far as to suggest that "trade custom is *prima facie* proof of a standard of reasonable care."[36] However, it is also clear that compliance with an industry standard is not dispositive of the question of negligence. In a number of cases, courts have found that the defendant complied with industry standard but that the standard was itself insufficient, and, therefore, assigned liability.[37]

One example is *Mayburry v. Ontario (Liquor Control Board)*.[38] In that case, the plaintiff sued Bacardi Canada and the Ontario Liquor Board for injuries suffered when a carbonated alcoholic beverage slipped to the ground

---

32 *Crits v. Sylvester* (1956), 1 D.L.R. (2d) 502 at 508 (Ont. C.A.).
33 *Mississauga (City) v. Keifer Racaro Seating Inc.*, [2001] O.J. No. 1893 at para. 3 (C.A.).
34 (2000), 88 Alta. L.R. (3d) 283 (Q.B.).
35 *Ibid.* at para. 251.
36 *Moss v. Ferguson and Latham* (1979), 35 N.S.R. (2d) 181 para. 28 (T.D.).
37 See *Murphy v. Atlantic Speedy Propane Ltd.* (1979), 103 D.L.R. (3d) 545 (N.S.T.D.); *Williams v. St. John (City)* (1983), 53 N.B.R. (2d) 202 (Q.B.).
38 [2001] O.J. No. 1494 (S.C.J.).

and exploded, sending a shard of glass into Ms. Mayburry's eye. The bottle was not coated with a "retentive polymer coating," which would have reduced the distance that the glass fragments travelled. The court found that the alcohol industry had never used such a coating but nevertheless found that Bacardi was liable for 40 percent of the damages, noting that the absence of an industry standard "does not mean that a manufacturer does not have a responsibility to employ an available safer design where it would be reasonable to do so."[39] As Edgell notes, "courts cannot accept a standard of care that gives undue weight to cost saving or outdated standards, or which arises from compromise or from the lowest common denominator."[40]

Similar considerations apply to legislative standards. Where a legislative standard exists, failure to comply with that requirement is strong evidence of a breach of the standard of care.[41] However, compliance with a legislative standard is not conclusive on the issue of liability. The Supreme Court of Canada effectively summarized the law relating to legislative standards in the case of *Ryan v. Victoria (City)*:[42]

> Legislative standards are relevant to the common law standard of care, but the two are not necessarily co-extensive. The fact that a statute prescribes or prohibits certain activities may constitute evidence of reasonable conduct in a given situation, but it does not extinguish the underlying obligation of reasonableness. ... Thus, a statutory breach does not automatically give rise to civil liability; it is merely some evidence of negligence. ... By the same token, mere compliance with a statute does not, in and of itself, preclude a finding of civil liability. ... Statutory standards can, however, be highly relevant to the assessment of reasonable conduct in a particular case, and in fact may render reasonable an act or omission which would otherwise appear to be negligent. This allows courts to consider the legislative framework in which people and companies must operate, while at the same time recognizing that one cannot avoid the underlying obligation of reasonable care simply by discharging statutory duties.[43]

One can see this approach applied in *Willis v. FMC Machinery & Chemicals Ltd.*[44] In that case, the plaintiffs sued the defendant chemical company for damage caused to their crops from the application of a particular

---

39 Ibid. at para. 159.
40 D.F. Edgell, *Product Liability Law in Canada* (Toronto: Butterworths, 2000) at 30.
41 See *R. v. Saskatchewan Wheat Pool*, [1983] 1 S.C.R. 205.
42 [1999] 1 S.C.R. 201.
43 Ibid. at para. 29.
44 (1976), 68 D.L.R. (3d) 127 (P.E.I.T.D.).

herbicide. The government had approved the herbicide for use, but the court nevertheless held that the defendants were liable, stating only that "the federal authorities may also have been negligent in granting registration to a product before sufficient trial experiment has been conducted."[45]

Another factor that can affect the standard of care expected from the manufacturer has to do with the nature of the product being produced. The law is clear that manufacturers of inherently dangerous products or products designed for human consumption will be held to a high standard of care. The leading decision on products that pose some heightened risk is that of the Supreme Court of Canada in *Hollis v. Dow Corning Corp.*[46] This case, which involved a claim of negligence against the defendant manufacturers of breast implants, established the following principle:

> In the case of medical products such as the breast implants at issue in this appeal, the standard of care to be met by manufacturers in ensuring that consumers are properly warned is necessarily high. Medical products are often designed for bodily ingestion or implantation, and the risks created by their improper use are obviously substantial. The courts in this country have long recognized that manufacturers of products that are ingested, consumed or otherwise placed in the body, and thereby have a great capacity to cause injury to consumers, are subject to a correspondingly high standard of care under the law of negligence ....[47]

Although the Court is specifically dealing with medical products, the general principle applies to manufacturers of all products that pose a particular risk to consumers. In *Heimler v. Calvert Caterers Ltd.*,[48] the plaintiff contracted typhoid fever from food consumed at a wedding. One of the defendant catering company's employees was a typhoid carrier and failed to take proper hygienic precautions. The court found that "the standard of care demanded for those engaged in the food-handling business, is an extrememly high standard ...."[49] Similarly high standards are imposed upon manufacturers of inherently dangerous items such as weapons, chemicals, and some appliances. In *Buchan v. Ortho Pharmaceutical (Cana-*

---

45   *Ibid.* at 157.
46   [1995] 4 S.C.R. 634 [hereinafter *Hollis*]. Appeal dismissed. Leave to appeal to S.C.C. granted from a judgment of the B.C.C.A. (1993), 81 B.C.L.R. (2d) 1, ordering a new trial (with respect to Birch) and dismissing an appeal (with respect to Dow Corning Corp.) from a judgment of Bouck J., [1990] B.C.J. No. 1059, allowing Hollis's action against Dow Corning Corp. and dismissing her action against Birch.
47   *Ibid.* at para. 23.
48   (1975), 8 O.R. (2d) 1 (C.A.).
49   *Ibid.* at 1.

da) Ltd.,[50] the court held that the standard of care for manufacturers of such hazardous materials is higher and, indeed, "may be so high that it approximates to or almost becomes strict liability."[51]

This latter comment raises a subtle issue regarding standard of care in product liability cases. At the outset of this section, it was stated that liability in this area is neither strict nor absolute. Strict liability would exist where, once the plaintiff showed that he or she suffered damage from the defendant's product, the onus shifts to the defendant manufacturer to prove that due diligence was exercised. Absolute liability exists where liability will be imposed without regard to the care exercised by the defendant. Except in certain narrow fields,[52] Canadian common law requires the plaintiff to demonstrate, on a balance of probabilities, that the defendant was negligent and caused the injuries in question. Therefore, liability is not legally strict nor is it absolute. However, Canadian courts have applied the evidentiary doctrine of *res ipsa loquitur* in some cases of product liability and the effect of this doctrine is to allow inferences that effectively transform the case into one of strict liability.

Res ipsa loquitur means "the thing speaks for itself." When applied to product liability in the context of standard of care, this doctrine states that, once the plaintiff has succeeded in establishing a *prima facie* case that the standard of care was not met, it will be incumbent upon the defendant to dispel this inference. The onus never shifts, but the doctrine allows the court to infer negligence where sufficient circumstantial evidence exists. *Farro v. Nutone Electrical Ltd.*[53] is a good example of this doctrine being applied. In this case, the plaintiff homeowner was suing the defendant for damages resulting from a fire in the plaintiff's home. The plaintiff was able to demonstrate that the fire was likely started by an overheated motor in a ceiling exhaust fan manufactured by the defendant. The plaintiff was not, however, able to establish precisely what defect caused the fire and, as a result, could not demonstrate the exact nature of the defendant's careless behaviour. The trial judge dismissed the action because, absent evidence of the conduct alleged to be below the applicable standard of care, liability

---

50 (1984), 8 D.L.R. (4th) 373 at 386 (Ont. H.C.), aff'd (1986), 25 D.L.R. (4th) 658 (Ont. C.A.) [hereinafter *Buchan*].
51 *Ibid.* at 386.
52 Strict liability is applied in cases of vicarious liability of employers, for instance, and in the *Rylands v. Fletcher* tort, each of which is discussed in more detail in Part Two. Strict liability can also be imposed by statute, and several such regimes are described throughout this book.
53 (1990), 68 D.L.R. (4th) 268 (Ont. C.A) [hereinafter *Farro*].

could not be assigned. The Court of Appeal reversed this decision, stating the following:

> Having found that the fan motor caused the fire, the learned trial judge, with great respect, placed too heavy a burden on the appellants to show how the particular defect occurred. There was evidence of sufficient weight and cogency to support an inference that the fan motor was defective when it left the manufacturer's plant.[54]

The defendant had been unable to rebut this inference and, therefore, was found liable in the amount of $60,000.

The Supreme Court of Canada has since said that the doctrine of *res ipsa loquitur* does not shift the onus of proof and, therefore, liability is not technically strict.[55] It is merely an evidentiary guideline to be employed by trial judges when weighing the evidence. Owing to confusion on this issue, the Court suggested that the discrete doctrine of *res ipsa loquitur* should be discarded. However, Major J., on behalf of a unanimous Court, was careful to state that the evidentiary principle for which it stood should be retained:

> It would appear that the law would be better served if the maxim was treated as expired and no longer used as a separate component in negligence actions. After all, it was nothing more than an attempt to deal with circumstantial evidence. That evidence is more sensibly dealt with by the trier of fact, who should weigh the circumstantial evidence with the direct evidence, if any, to determine whether the plaintiff has established on a balance of probabilities a *prima facie* case of negligence against the defendant. Once the plaintiff has done so, the defendant must present evidence negating that of the plaintiff or necessarily the plaintiff will succeed.[56]

Accordingly, standard of proof analyses always depend on the plaintiff establishing, on a balance of probabilities, that the defendant's impugned actions were unreasonable.

Is is sometimes said that products liability law in the United States is based on a theory of strict liability. As we have said several times, this is not the case in Canada. But U.S. law and the principle of strict liability do influence Canadian law and we will therefore return to this issue in some detail in the concluding section of this chapter.

---

54 *Ibid.* at 273.
55 *Fontaine v. British Columbia (Official Administrator)*, [1998] 1 S.C.R. 424 [hereinafter *Fontaine*].
56 *Ibid.* at para. 27.

4) Causation

Not all careless acts respecting products will attract liability. As is the case for any action founded in negligence, the plaintiff must demonstrate that the impugned actions were the cause of the damage suffered. As stated in *Stewart v. Pettie*, "[t]he plaintiff in a tort action has the burden of proving each of the elements of the claim on the balance of probabilities. This includes proving that the defendant's impugned conduct actually caused the loss complained of."[57] To satisfy this requirement, a plaintiff must establish both that the defendant's carelessness was the cause-in-fact of the injury and that this causative link is sufficiently close, or *proximate*, to satisfy a second requirement, that of legal causation.

In the context of product liability, factual causation is made out where the plaintiff is able to establish that the defendant's actions or omissions led, in some way, to the injury suffered. That is, there must be some causative link between the alleged carelessness and the damage incurred by the plaintiff. The substance of this link is irrelevant at the cause-in-fact stage of the analysis; that is, any factual cause whatsoever ought to satisfy this portion of the causation analysis.

Yet a number of hurdles to establishing cause-in-fact are present in cases of product liability. First, the complexity and technical nature of product liability cases can make it particularly difficult for a plaintiff to establish with certainty the source of a particular injury. If, for example, an injury resulted from a fault in a complex mechanical system, it may be apparent that the machine caused the harm but difficult to pinpoint what precisely went wrong. However, the Supreme Court of Canada, in *Snell v. Farrell*,[58] made clear that the inability to show causation with this degree of precision should not be a bar to liability. Rather, "an inference of causation may be drawn although positive or scientific proof of causation has not been adduced."[59] The Court held that this inference was especially appropriate where the facts lay in the knowledge of the defendant — a common state of affairs in product liability cases.

Second, where a product is mass-produced by a number of manufacturers, it can be extremely difficult for an individual to establish which manufacturer's product caused the harm complained of. The classic example is that of tobacco litigation, where plaintiffs may have smoked a number of brands of cigarettes. In this context, it would be virtually impossible to determine which

---

57 *Stewart v. Pettie*, [1995] 1 S.C.R. 131 at para. 60.
58 [1990] 2 S.C.R. 311.
59 *Ibid.* at para. 33.

product was the cause-in-fact of the injury. In the United States, two concepts have arisen to cope with this difficulty: industry-wide liability[60] and market-share liability.[61] In England, the recent decision of *Fairchild v. Glenhaven Funeral Services Ltd.*[62] adopted an approach imposing liability for risk-creation, without causation in fact being shown. Although these concepts have been referred to in Canada and may be found in some statutes, they have not been adopted in common law. These matters are discussed later in this work.

There are a host of other causation-related barriers that a plaintiff might have to overcome in the context of product liability litigation. Owing to their importance and complexity, issues regarding factual causation will be discussed in greater detail in a subsequent section of this book. For present purposes, it is sufficient to note these general issues and to acknowledge that, despite the relaxed *Snell v. Farrell* standard, an absence of factual causation has been and remains grounds for denying recovery in product liability cases.

But, even if this factual cause is demonstrated, negligence is limited by the notion of proximate cause, or remoteness, which in the end is a question of policy. In *R. v. Goldhart*,[63] the Supreme Court of Canada articulated the function and rationale for the concept of remoteness:

> The happening of an event can be traced to a whole range of causes along a spectrum of diminishing connections to the event. The common law of torts has grappled with the problem of causation. In order to inject some degree of restraint on the potential reach of causation, the concepts of proximate cause and remoteness were deployed. These concepts place limits on the extent of liability in order to implement the sound policy of the law that there exists a substantial connection between the tortious conduct and the injury for which compensation is claimed.[64]

Questions of foreseeability can arise at any of the duty stage (who is my neighbour?), the standard-of-care stage (one need only take care to prevent reasonably foreseeable risks) or when causation is being assessed. In each context, the concept of proximity functions to limit the defendant's liability. However, in the causation analysis, it is with this notion of remoteness that the *adequacy* of the causative link between a particular product and the injury comes into question. In essence, the courts must ask whether or not the factual cause is sufficiently *proximate* or *foreseeable* to attract liability:

---

60   *Hall v. Dupont de Nemours & Co.*, 345 F. Supp. 353 (E.D.N.Y. 1972).
61   *Sindell v. Abbott Lab.*, 607 P.2d 924 (Cal. 1980).
62   2002 UKHL 22.
63   [1996] 2 S.C.R. 463.
64   *Ibid.* at para. 36.

> You must use reasonable care to avoid acts or omissions which you can reasonably foresee would be likely to injure your neighbour ... persons *who are so closely and directly affected by my act that I ought to have them in contemplation as being so affected when I am directing my mind to the acts or omissions which are called in question.*[65]

The basis of liability is that "one who brings himself into a relation with others through an activity which *foreseeably* exposes them to danger if proper care is not observed must exercise reasonable care to safeguard them from that danger."[66] Unlike intentional torts such as battery, for which a defendant is liable for all harm caused by his or her actions, this element of remoteness limits a careless defendant's liability. Thus, a manufacturer that carelessly designs, produces, or distributes a product will be liable only for those injuries that are reasonably foreseeable. Yet it should be noted that the manufacturer need not specifically foresee the severity of the injury or the precise way in which it occurred: "It is enough to fix liability if one could foresee in a general way the sort of thing that happened. The extent of the damage and its manner of incidence need not be foreseeable if physical damage of the kind which in fact ensues is foreseeable."[67]

5) Damage and the "Pure Economic Loss" Bar

It is implicit in the need for a causation analysis that, unlike the intentional torts, which are sometimes actionable without proof of damage, a claim in negligence will be successful only if the plaintiff can establish that the defendant's impugned acts caused damage or injury. Indeed, Conrad J.A., in dissent (though not contradicted on this point), stated in a recent Alberta case that "it is well established that damage is the gist of an action in negligence."[68] The requirement for damage is a natural extension of the principle that the essence of negligence law is compensatory, not punitive. This general rule applies equally to product liability cases. Accordingly, a plaintiff seeking recovery on the basis of a claim of product liability grounded in negligence must convince the court not only that the product was defective in some way but also that this defect resulted in some kind of loss to the plaintiff.

Several movements are afoot in law that might undermine this central proposition. The idea of pure economic loss, developed in *Rivtow Marine Ltd.*

---

65 *Donoghue v. Stevenson*, supra note 8 [emphasis added].
66 *Buchan*, supra note 50 at 666, cited to (1986), 25 D.L.R. (4th) 658 (Ont. C.A.) [emphasis added].
67 *Assiniboine South School Division 3 v. Hoffer* (1971), 21 D.L.R. (3d) 608 at 614 (Man. C.A.), aff'd 40 D.L.R. (3d) 480 (S.C.C.).
68 *Wavel Ventures Corp. v. Constantini*, [1997] 4 W.W.R. 194 at para. 83 (Alta C.A.).

v. Washington Iron Works,[69] might provide an opening to pursue claims where damage has not occurred, but the possibility of harm leads the plaintiff to make expenditures to avoid it.[70] In *Rivtow*, the Court allowed compensation for "down time" incurred when cranes were taken out of commission for preventative maintenance when one of them had failed on account of cracks.

Recovery for "pure economic loss" has potential application in product liability litigation. Recently, class actions have been launched against Shell Canada, which has admitted that an additive to its "Bronze" grade gasoline left a residue in fuel systems that could lead to engine failure. While Shell has offered to compensate any Bronze gasoline user who experienced problems with their fuel-injection systems, the class action seeks to have Shell pay for inspection and cleaning of affected cars even before problems are experienced. The claim has passed the initial stage of judicial authorization (certification) and will be closely watched.[71]

Similar claims are also becoming more common where the risk of harm requires that potential victims undergo medical monitoring or other preventative or diagnostic procedures. Such a claim is advanced in the Phen-Fen diet pill litigation, where the products are alleged to cause occasional heart-valve failures. The hearing judge refused to dismiss the medical-monitoring claim, and on appeal it was noted that such claims have been advanced previously in Canada[72] and that the "issue is arguable and should not be excluded at this stage of the proceeding."[73] Medical-monitoring pleadings had been allowed to proceed in at least two other cases,[74] neither of which offered a final resolution of the legal question.

Nevertheless, it is important to distinguish the type of complaint requiring medical monitoring (i.e., where the product is potentially dangerous) from ones, perhaps like the *Shell* case, where the harm is pecuniary only and where the plaintiffs must rely on either contractual or statutory duties owed by the defendant, rather than negligence. Edgell writes:

---

69 [1974] S.C.R. 1189 [hereinafter *Rivtow*].
70 The leading works on pure economic loss in Canada are Bruce Feldthusen, "Economic Loss in the Supreme Court of Canada: Yesterday and Tomorrow" (1990–91) 17 Can. Bus. L.J. 356; Bruce Feldthusen, *Economic Negligence: The Recovery of Pure Economic Loss*, 4th ed. (Toronto: Carswell, 2000); and Bruce Feldthusen, "Liability for Pure Economic Loss: Yes, But Why?" (1999) 28 U. W. Austl. L. Rev. 84.
71 *Scarola v. Shell Canada Ltée.*, [2003] J.Q. no 8973 (S.C.).
72 *Wilson v. Servier Canada Inc.* (2000), 50 O.R. (3d) 219 (S.C.).
73 *Ibid.* at para. 12.
74 *Nantais v. Telectronics Proprietary (Canada) Ltd.* (1995), 127 D.L.R. (4th) 552 (Ont. Gen. Div.), leave to appeal denied (1995), 129 D.L.R. (4th) 110 (Ont. Gen. Div.), leave to appeal denied (1996), 28 O.R. (3d) 523 (C.A.); and *Anderson v. Wilson* (1999), 44 O.R. (3d) 673 at 675–76 (C.A.).

> [I]t seems that there is a duty, independent of any contractual obligation, to take reasonable care to manufacture and design products which are not "unsafe" or "dangerous." Breach of such a duty can be pursued in negligence by persons who are not parties to the contract and even by contracting parties (subject to contractual limitations or waivers of that right).
>
> However, if the product were not unsafe or dangerous, but merely shoddy or substandard or failed to live up to expectations, then it seems that there would likely be no duty of care owed independent of the contractual obligations. In such a case, a party who is a stranger to the contract would have no cause of action. The distinction then between shoddy and dangerous products would be very important.[75]

At present, the principal bar to recovery for pure economic loss in tort remains intact. An excellent illustration of this in the product liability context is *Zidaric v. Toshiba of Canada Ltd.*[76] In that case, Toshiba had installed allegedly faulty components in certain of its computers. The plaintiff attempted to sue on the basis of negligence.

Cumming J. noted that there was no contractual relationship between the manufacturer and the plaintiff. Contractual remedies, such as recission, were therefore not at issue. He also found that there was nothing dangerous about the computers in issue; rather, the allegation was that they were shoddily made. Consequently, no duty to warn of a risk arose. He said at paragraphs 8–10:

> ¶ 8 The loss claimed is properly characterized by the law as a pure "economic loss." This can be defined as a loss that is "a diminution of worth incurred without any physical injury to any asset of the plaintiff." *A.G. (Ont.) v. Fatehi*, [1984] 2 S.C.R. 536, at p. 542 per Estey J. In *Winnipeg Condominium Corporation No. 36 v. Bird Construction Co.*, [1995] 1 S.C.R. 85 La Forest J. at p. 96 set forth the approach for analysis as to the very limited occasions when there can be recovery for a pure economic loss under tort law.
>
> ¶ 9 In my view, the defective computer at issue in the case at hand comes within the category of the "negligent supply of shoddy goods." *Winnipeg Condominium* involved a defective building which created a serious risk of personal injury if the building was not repaired. The claim alleges that the faulty floppy disk microde for the Toshiba laptop could conceivably cause a serious loss of data in certain circumstances (for example, medical

---

75 Dean F. Edgell, *Product Liability Law in Canada*, supra note 40 at 160.
76 [2000] O.J. No. 4590 (S.C.J.).

records supposedly saved on a floppy disk and not retained on the hard drive). However, the pleading does not, of course, suggest any risk of personal injury or property damage from the defective computer itself.

¶ 10 Moreover, there is no claim for a cost of repair, being the only damages compensable under the *Winnipeg Condominium* regime for recovery. In my view, the claim cannot be conceived as falling within any one of the categories whereby pure economic loss can be recovered under tort liability. As well, it is admitted that there has been a relatively simple corrective software application available free of charge from TCL after 1999 which can correct the defect. The recovery in *Winnipeg Condominium* was limited to "the reasonable cost of repairing the defect and mitigating the danger." (at pp. 121, 125). It is admitted there is no cost to repairing the defect of the product in the instant situation.

Cumming J. concluded that the plaintiff's proper recourse would be in an action in contract against the vendor of the goods. He struck the plaintiff's negligence claim as disclosing no reasonable cause of action.

The opposite conclusion was reached in another class action, *Reid v. Ford Motor Co.*[77] In that case, the plaintiffs argued that a defect in the ignition systems of certain Ford vehicles was in fact dangerous:

¶ 26 The plaintiff's claim in negligence is that the TFI modules in the proposed class vehicles are defective and that the TFI defect poses a danger to the public. The plaintiff argues that the general rule that a plaintiff cannot sue in tort for pure economic loss does not apply in the case of a dangerous defect and that this case falls squarely into the category of cases for which the Supreme Court of Canada has confirmed a cause of action exists. *Winnipeg Condominium Corporation No. 36 v. Bird Construction Co.*, [1995] 1 S.C.R. 85.

The failure of the TFI module would cause the engine to stall. This would, as Gerow J. noted, cause power brakes and power steering to stop functioning. There was therefore (at least on the pleadings) a risk of both personal injury and property damage, and mitigation of that risk would require expenditures on repairs. Taking the pleadings on their face, the hearing judge found they described an action in negligence and granted certification of the class proceeding.

---

77   2003 BCSC 1632.

C. TYPES OF PRODUCT LIABILITY CLAIMS IN NEGLIGENCE

Tort lawyers typically divide negligence-based product liability into three basic categories: injuries caused by a manufacturing defect, those caused by a design defect, and those caused by a failure to warn of a risk. A manufacturing defect involves goods that cause harm when, because of some error in production, the goods fail to conform to their intended, and presumably adequate, specifications (e.g., if critical bolts in a car are insufficiently tightened). A design defect occurs when the goods are manufactured properly but are unduly dangerous because of the way in which they were designed in the first place (e.g., a gas tank that is liable to explode in rear-end collisions). A failure to warn occurs when the goods are carefully designed and manufactured but nevertheless carry an inherent danger (e.g., flammable spirits). In these cases a manufacturer has a duty to provide proper instructions and warnings, and a failure to do so that results in injury may also result in liability.

1) Manufacturing Defects

In Canada, in order to be liable for manufacturing defects, one must be found negligent. Negligence may be established by showing that the product was carelessly manufactured, packaged, or installed and that the resulting flaw in the product injured the plaintiff. This form of product liability is the simplest and probably the first form of product liability recognized in the courts. Indeed, *Donoghue v. Stevenson*[78] was itself a manufacturing-defect case. In the case of manufacturing defects, negligence is established where it is shown that the defendant's method for producing the goods was deficient (e.g., that the particular goods fell below the usual quality owing to contamination or an error in the manufacturing process) and that this deficiency caused harm to another. The core allegation in *Donoghue v. Stevenson*[79] was that the manufacturers of the ginger beer were careless in production by allowing a snail to be put into the bottle, resulting in injury to the plaintiff.

Shandloff v. City Dairy Ltd.[80] is a good example of a manufacturing defect case. The plaintiff was injured when, sucking chocolate milk through a straw, she consumed a number of shards of glass. The bottle was opaque, so she was unable to detect the glass before she drank its contents. The Court of Appeal affirmed the trial judge's finding of liability, stating that "a

---

78 *Donoghue v. Stevenson*, supra note 8.
79 *Ibid.*
80 [1936] 4 D.L.R. 712 (Ont. C.A).

manufacturer who prepares and puts upon the market food in a container which prevents examination by the ultimate consumer is liable to the ultimate consumer for any defects which exist in the goods so marketed which arise from negligence or lack of care."[81] A more recent example of a manufacturing defect case is *LeBlanc v. Marson Canada Inc.*[82] In this case, the defendant was injured when a tub containing chemical hardener used in a fibreglass repair kit burst, spraying the chemical onto his face and eyes. Based upon the trial judge's finding that the container failed during "normal use by Mr. LeBlanc," the Court of Appeal found the manufacturers liable, stating that "the tube having failed during normal use, the trial judge was entitled to infer that it was defective. The presence of such a defect spoke of negligence on the part of the appellant [manufacturer]."[83]

As these cases demonstrate, establishing liability on the basis of manufacturing defects is generally a straightforward proposition. The plaintiff is alleging that there is a deviation between what the manufacturer intended to produce and what was actually sold to the consumer and that this deviation resulted in the injury. This is opposed to design defects, discussed below, in which the product was manufactured according to specifications but the plaintiff is alleging that the specifications themselves were flawed. In a manufacturing defect case, the plaintiff has the luxury of being able to show that the manufacturer failed to live up to its own design. Once such a flaw is demonstrated, liability tends to flow naturally. A good example is the case of *Arendale v. Canada Bread Co. Ltd.*[84] Here, an eleven-year-old girl was injured when she ingested a piece of packaged bread that had a small piece of glass imbedded in it. As it turned out, there were pieces of glass in most of the slices in the loaf, to the point that "these [pieces of glass] could be seen gleaming when the loaf was held up to the light."[85] The court held that "if glass was in the bread on delivery, a *prima facie* case is established" because "[t]he defendant was under a duty to take reasonable care that its products were free from defects likely to cause harm or damage to the ultimate user."[86]

The ease with which liability is made out in such cases may suggest that there is an onus shift in cases of manufacturing defect. Yet, as has already been discussed, and as the Supreme Court made clear in *Fontaine*,[87]

---

81   Ibid. at 719.
82   (1995), 146 N.S.R. (2d) 392 (C.A.) [hereinafter *LeBlanc*].
83   Ibid. at paras. 3–4.
84   [1941] 2 D.L.R. 41 (Ont. C.A.) [hereinafter *Arendale*].
85   Ibid. at 42.
86   Ibid. at 44.
87   *Fontaine, supra* note 55.

the onus of proof in product liability cases never actually shifts. Rather, these are cases in which an inference adverse to the defendant is drawn without the plaintiff having to adduce "scientific" proof of liability. In this respect, the court in *Arendale*[88] made reference to a *prima facie* case and, later, the doctrine of *res ipsa loquitur*. Similarly, in *LeBlanc*,[89] the court referred to an "inference of negligence." The manufacturing defect cases are merely examples of cases in which the circumstantial evidence is such that the plaintiff is able to make a *prima facie* case so strong that liability will flow unless the defendant dispels this inference. Such an inference is often reasonable both because of the nature of the defect and the fact that the defendant has exclusive control over and knowledge of the manufacturing process. As the court stated in *Smith v. Inglis Ltd.*, "[r]arely could a plaintiff prove by direct evidence that a defect existed when the product containing it left the factory. Often that fact may be readily inferred and indeed be overwhelmingly obvious ...."[90] *Grant v. Australian Knitting Mills*,[91] a case that involved injuries suffered from exposure to an irritable substance that had contaminated the defendant's product in the manufacturing process, stands as the best articulation of how this inference operates: "Negligence is found as a matter of inference from the existence of the defects taken in connection with all the known circumstances: even if the manufacturers could by apt evidence have rebutted that inference they have not done so."[92] Therefore, a manufacturer faced with proof that a person was injured as a result of a defect in one of its products will have to displace a strong evidentiary inference. In the practical result, while there is no legal shift of onus, the defendant in a manufacturing defect case may well be placed in a position similar to bearing the legal burden.

The standard of care of a manufacturer for defects in a product is heightened in cases where the product is intended to reach the consumer in the same condition in which it leaves the manufacturer and where there is no opportunity for intermediate inspection, which would allow detection of a defect. This proposition is best exemplified by two very similar cases from the Ontario Court of Appeal. The first, *Mathews v. Coca-Cola Company of Canada*,[93] involved a patron of a restaurant who was served a bottle of Coca-Cola. The beverage tasted strange and, on further examination, it was

---

88 *Arendale, supra* note 84.
89 *LeBlanc, supra* note 82.
90 *Smith v. Inglis Ltd.* (1978), 83 D.L.R. (3d) 215 at 219 (N.S.C.A.).
91 [1936] A.C. 85 at 101 (P.C.).
92 *Ibid.*
93 [1944] O.R. 207 (C.A.).

discovered that there was a dead mouse in the bottle. The plaintiff became ill and sued Coca-Cola. The court found the manufacturer liable, arguing that it was not reasonable for the consumer or vendor to have made an intermediate inspection and so the manufacturer was responsible for taking a heightened degree of care in detecting flaws in its products. Similarly, in *Zeppa v. Coca-Cola Limited*,[94] the plaintiff, while drinking a bottle of Coca-Cola, was injured when she consumed a quantity of glass particles that were in the drink. The jury in this case found that Coca-Cola had manufactured and sold the bottle of pop and that the contents of the bottle, when consumed by Mary Zeppa, were the same as the contents of the bottle when it left the plant. However, the jury also found that there had been no negligence on the part of Coca-Cola. Faced with these seemingly irreconcilable findings, the court held that the jury's finding of an absence of negligence was in error and arose because of faulty instructions it had received. The court imposed liability and stated the following:

> The jury having found that the particles of glass which caused the injury in the instant case were in the bottle of Coca-Cola when it left the manufacturer, a presumption of negligence against the respondent arose, in my opinion, in the facts of this case. It was not a case where one would expect any examination of the product after it left the manufacturer and before consumption in order to ascertain if it contained some injurious substance and it is not, in my opinion, a case where the consumer would be expected to observe the injurious substance.[95]

This heightened standard where there is no means of making an intermediate inspection does not apply solely to products intended for human consumption. In *Castle v. Davenport-Campbell Company Ltd.*,[96] the plaintiff had purchased a pump for his furnace, manufactured by one of the defendants. The other defendant installed and serviced the pump. The pump turned out to be defective and the furnace emitted smoke, which damaged the house. At issue was whether or not the appellant and/or defendant service company were also negligent in some way for not detecting the fault. The court held that only the manufacturer was liable, noting that the product was sold to the defendant service company as a sealed and finished unit and, consequently, there was no reasonable prospect of intermediate inspection.

---

94 [1955] 5 D.L.R. 187 (Ont. C.A.).
95 *Ibid.* at 194.
96 [1952] O.R. 565 (C.A.).

2) Design Defects

a) Generally

Another way to establish liability for injuries caused by products is to prove that the product was defectively designed. Design defect cases are still rare in Canada, but it is established that a manufacturer owes a duty not to manufacture a dangerous product if the same product can be manufactured with a substantially reduced risk of injury.[97] The legal requirements for establishing liability in a design defect claim were succinctly laid out in the recent case *Kreutner v. Waterloo Oxford Co-operative Inc.*[98] This case involved an allegation that the defendant manufacturers had negligently designed the valve on a propane tank, and that this negligence led to a serious explosion and fire. The court unanimously dismissed the plaintiffs' claim for lack of evidence but, in the process, Borins J.A. stated the following: "... to succeed in this case the plaintiffs are required to identify the design defect in Sherwood's valve, establish that the defect created a substantial likelihood of harm and that there exists an alternative design that is safer and economically feasible to manufacture."[99] Thus, to succeed in a claim of negligent design, a plaintiff must (a) point to a specific design defect; (b) demonstrate that this defect created a risk of harm; and (c) establish that there is an alternative design that is both safer and economically realistic to produce.

In *John Deere*,[100] the defendant was the manufacturer of a riding lawnmower on which the gas tank had been placed too near the battery, thereby creating the risk of fire by a spark igniting gasoline vapours. This design eventually did cause a fire, and the plaintiffs claimed damages for the losses that incurred as a result. The court found that there were alternative safer designs available; whether the lawnmowers might have been more costly to produce was immaterial. It reasoned that "[a] manufacturer does not have the right to manufacture an inherently dangerous article when a method exists of manufacturing the same article without risk of harm. No amount of or degree of specificity of warning will exonerate him from liability if he does."[101] On this basis, the manufacturer was held to be negligently responsible for the defective design of the mower.

Of course, many products have dangerous features that cannot be said to be design defects. This certainly does not automatically lead to liability. In

---

97 *Nicholson v. John Deere Ltd.* (1986), 34 D.L.R. (4th) 542 (Ont. H.C.) [hereinafter *John Deere*].
98 (2000), 50 O.R. (3d) 140 (C.A.).
99 *Ibid.* at para. 8.
100 *John Deere, supra* note 97.
101 *Ibid.* at 549.

the case of alleged *design* defects, it must be shown that the plaintiff's design of the product was negligently deficient — that is, not only that the design of the product was dangerous, but that it was unnecessarily or carelessly dangerous. To establish this, it must generally be shown that there was an alternative design, available to the defendant or discoverable through the use of reasonable care, that would have reduced the danger. This is a negligence test. The issue is not simply whether the product is dangerous but whether there is a reasonable and safer alternative design. In *John Deere*, it is important to note that the court found not only that the placement of the gas tank was dangerous but that there was a safer and technically feasible alternative.

It is also important to note that the law does not necessarily require a manufacturer to adopt the *safest possible* design. In *Dallaire v. Paul-Émile Martel Inc.*,[102] the plaintiff alleged that, among other things, the defendant had been negligent in its design of a conveyor on which the plaintiff was injured. The Supreme Court of Canada held that the injury suffered by the child plaintiff was wholly the result of his own negligence and that of his father and, therefore, the manufacturer was not liable. However, Gonthier J., for the Court, stated the following in *obiter*:

> It is perhaps true that the conveyor could have been designed to be safer, and it is true that without protection the worm screw [which caused the accident] did represent a danger. However, the respondent had provided adequate covers capable of ensuring safety and which could be used without great difficulty.[103]

Since the manufacturer had acted reasonably in its design, the mere existence of a *safer* design did not lead to a finding of liability.

b) Tests for Design Defect

The key issue in design defect cases is how to determine the standard of care expected in the design of products. It is not reasonable to expect that all products must be designed so as to be perfectly safe. We tolerate certain risks inherent in products because we value their use. A knife may cause a cut, but it is neither defective nor carelessly designed. Nor do we even expect all similar products to have the same level of safety (consider the vastly different range of safety in different automobiles). The question for courts is not whether a product is dangerous but whether it is *unreasonably* dangerous. How is this determined?

---

102 [1989] 2 S.C.R. 419. Although this was a Quebec case interpreting the *Civil Code*, the reasoning does not seem necessarily limited to the civil law.
103 *Ibid.* at para. 12.

i) Risk-Utility Test

Perhaps the most prominent standard is the risk-utility test. This approach weighs the risks associated with the design of a product against the utility of the product in that particular design configuration. Among the factors that may be considered by a court in this analysis are the following:

> (1) utility of the product to the public as a whole and to the individual user; (2) the nature of the product — that is, the likelihood that it will cause injury; (3) the availability of a safer design; (4) the potential for designing and manufacturing the product so that it is safer but remains functional and reasonably priced; (5) the ability of the plaintiff to have avoided injury by careful use of the product; (6) the degree of awareness of the potential danger of the product which reasonably can be attributed to the plaintiff; and (7) the manufacturer's ability to spread any costs related to improving the safety of the design.[104]

In both Canada and the United States, the existence of an alternative design is only one factor to be considered in weighing the risks of a product against its utilities.[105]

The American-style risk-utility test has been applied in product liability cases in Canada and it is instructive to compare the weight that various courts have attributed to the different factors to be considered in the risk-utility analysis.

In *Rentway Canada Ltd. v. Laidlaw Transport Ltd.*,[106] the plaintiff alleged that the defendant was negligent in its design of a steering tire and the lighting on a tractor trailer. In considering the issues, Granger J., for the court, gives an instructive review of the American risk-utility approach to design defect actions. He adopts the following passage from *Boatland of Houston, Inc. v. Bailey*[107] to emphasize that the availability of a safer alternative is clearly relevant (though not determinative) in the risk-utility analysis: "Since defectiveness of the product in question is determined in relation to safer alternatives, the fact that risks could be diminished easily or cheaply may influence the outcome of the case." Another consideration in balancing a product's utility against the likelihood and gravity of injury from its use is the technological context existing at the time of its manufacture:

---

104 *Voss v. Black & Decker Manufacturing Co.*, 450 N.E.2d 204 at 208–9 (N.Y.C.A. 1983).
105 *O'Brien v. Muskin Corp.*, 463 A.2d 298 (N.J. 1983) [hereinafter *O'Brien*]; and *John Deere*, supra note 97.
106 (1989), 49 C.C.L.T. 150 (Ont. H.C.J.) [hereinafter *Rentway*].
107 609 S.W.2d 743 (Tex. 1980) [hereinafter *Boatland*].

... the more scientifically and economically feasible the alternative was, the more likely that a jury may find that the product was defectively designed. A plaintiff may advance the argument that a safer alternative was feasible with evidence that it was in actual use or was available at the time of manufacture. Feasibility may also be shown with evidence of the scientific and economic capacity to develop the safer alternative.[108]

In applying the risk-utility analysis to the facts in *Rentway*,[109] Granger J. found that the risks to the public far outweighed the utility of the trailer's particular design. Even so, the court ultimately held that the plaintiff had failed to demonstrate that the negligent design was the cause-in-fact of the accident and the resulting injuries.

The case of *Baker v. Suzuki Motor Co.*[110] was also decided on the basis of a risk-utility analysis. On the facts of *Baker*, the plaintiff's motorcycle burst into flames following a highway collision. The fire was caused by the ignition of gasoline, which had leaked from the fuel tank as a result of the accident. The plaintiff was seriously burned and sued the manufacturers of the motorcycle for negligence in the design of the gas cap.

The case turned on the plaintiff's failure to adduce evidence of a reasonable alternative design. The court held that the design was part of an *industry-wide practice*, and that no negligence could be found to exist without *evidence that the manufacturer had the means to take steps to prevent the inherent risks without creating others*:

> [T]he [p]laintiff [is required] to prove on a balance of probabilities that the manufacturer has not used reasonable efforts to reduce any risk to life and limb by showing that other reasonable choices were available to the manufacturer that would have avoided damage. The plaintiff has not done so here.[111]
>
> ...
>
> Ultimately I conclude that the social utility of supplying motorcycles outweighs the known risk of harm. Many individuals will undoubtedly conclude that risk is not worth taking, particularly where the vehicle is used solely for recreational purposes. However, that decision and those risks must be made and assumed on an individual basis. Where the chance is taken and harm ensues from inherent risk, the manufacturer is not liable.[112]

---

108   *Ford Motor Co. v. Nowak*, 638 S.W.2d 582 at 585–86 (Tex. C.A. 1982) quoting from *Boatland*.
109   *Rentway, supra* note 106.
110   (1993), 12 Alta. L.R. (3d) 193 (Q.B.) [hereinafter *Baker*].
111   *Ibid.* at para. 116.
112   *Ibid.* at para. 131.

It is important to note that, in *Baker*, the criticisms waged by the plaintiff against the fuel system of the Suzuki 850 were criticisms common to all conventional motorcycles designed at the time. The court found that

> [t]o accept these as negligent design, even though this type of fuel system admittedly leaks gas in certain types of collisions, would require me to ignore industry-wide practice at the time of design and would lead to the imposition of strict liability on manufacturers for motorcycle fires. Absent evidence that safer motorcycles could have been built, i.e., ones which not only removed the risk of fire but also the other risks the fuel system addressed in priority to that one, to find Suzuki liable would amount to a finding of strict liability.[113]

In the more recent case of *Tabrizi v. Whallon Machine Inc.*,[114] the Supreme Court of British Columbia also applied the risk-utility analysis. Again, the viability of an alternative design was key in its decision. In this case, the plaintiff was employed at a fish-canning plant. In the course of her duties, she was crushed and seriously injured when the machine she operated closed in on her.

Based on an application of the risk-utility analysis, the court in *Tabrizi*[115] concluded that it was reasonable to expect that the manufacturer would have designed the product in a safer manner. The functions of the machine were not dependent on the existence of the particular hazard that brought about the plaintiff's injuries, and there would have been no utility trade-off and only minimal cost implications to lessen significantly the likelihood of such harm. Thus, the defendant had failed in its duty to manufacture a reasonably safe product. It should be emphasized, however, that in this case there was an *easily achievable alternate design*, and because the *hazard was fairly obvious*, the plaintiff was held 70 percent responsible for her own injuries.

On the evidence in *Tabrizi*,[116] there was a substantial likelihood of harm from the machine, and it was entirely feasible to have designed the machine in a safer manner. Romilly J. also found that it is informative, though not determinative, to consider industry standards in the relevant manufacturing sector when attempting to determine whether a product is reasonably safe. Romilly J. cited *Meisel*:[117]

---

113   *Ibid.* at para. 129.
114   (1996), 29 C.C.L.T. (2d) 176 (B.C.S.C.) [hereinafter *Tabrizi*].
115   *Ibid.*
116   *Ibid.*
117   *Meisel v. Tolko Industries*, [1991] B.C.J. No. 105 (S.C.) [hereinafter *Meisel*], which cited Professor Fleming, *The Law of Torts*, 7th ed. (Sydney: The Law Book Co., 1987).

Since the standard of care is determined by reference to community valuations, considerable evidentiary weight attaches to whether or not the defendant's conduct conformed to standard practices accepted as normal and general by other members of the community in similar circumstances.

...

> Conformity with general practice ... usually dispels a charge of negligence. It tends to show what others in the same "business" considered sufficient, that the defendant could not have learnt how to avoid the accident by the example of others ....

While accepting that industry standards and practices should be weighed when applying the risk-utility analysis, Romilly J. stressed that he would not place as much weight on the relevance of industry practice as did the court in *Meisel*.[118] Indeed, Romilly J. cites *Murphy v. Atlantic Speedy Propane Ltd*.[119] in support of the proposition that even widespread industry customs can be found to be negligent in certain circumstances.

It should be noted that the *Murphy*[120] case was one in which the court found that the practice of the industry in not carrying out periodic inspections was negligent. Those facts are distinguishable from a case in which an entire product line — such as cigarettes — could be wiped out as a result of a finding of negligence based on design defect. In *Tabrizi*,[121] as well, it was only the design of a single machine that was at issue.

ii) The Consumer-Expectations Test

Another test used to determine standard of care that has risen to some favour in the United States is the consumer-expectations test.[122] Rather than stepping back and attempting to balance abstractly the risk of a product with its utility, this test asks whether the design of the product in question met the safety expectations of the "ordinary consumer."[123] In these terms, a manufacturer may be held to be liable where the expectations of the ordinary consumer are not met. As to the question of who constitutes the ordinary consumer, one American court held that the ordinary consumer is one who would be foreseeably expected to purchase the specific product involved.[124] It would seem, therefore, that the ordinary consumer

---

118 Ibid.
119 (1979), 103 D.L.R. (3d) 545 (N.S.T.D.) [hereinafter *Murphy*].
120 Ibid.
121 *Tabrizi*, *supra* note 114.
122 In Canada, this test was mentioned, but not applied, in *Ragoonanan*, *infra* note 137.
123 See *Campbell v. General Motors Corp.*, 642 P.2d. 224 (Cal. Sup. Ct. 1982); *Robinson v. Reed-Prentice Div. of Package Machinery Co.*, 403 N.E.2d. 440 (N.Y. 1980).
124 *Woods v. Fruehauf Trailer Corp.*, 765 P.2d. 770 (Okla. Sup. Ct. 1988).

might be understood to include those who are knowledgeable about the product in question.

There is some debate in American courts as to whether the risk-utility test and the consumer-expectations test are really distinguishable. Some U.S. courts have held that the two tests are really two aspects of the same standard,[125] arguing that, in the assessment of risk-utility, balancing is being performed from the perspective of the ordinary consumer. That is, *in the eyes of the consumer*, does the risk associated with the product outweigh its utility? Other courts have disagreed. While they have argued that the consumer-expectations test may overlap with risk-utility where the potential dangers are relatively apparent, the complex or scientific nature of some defects, and therefore the obscure nature of the risks associated with use of the product, would simply not be within the ken of the consumer (pharmaceuticals would be a good example). Consequently, while the consumer-expectation test may be useful in a manufacturing defect case, it would seem inappropriate in complex design defect situations. While the *Restatement (Third) of Torts: Product Liability*, acknowledges that both tests — risk utility and consumer expectations — are used in the U.S., depending on the jurisdiction, it notes that the second is merely a variant of the first in most cases, and involves defining consumer expectations in terms of risk-utility. In those few U.S. jurisdictions where the consumer-expectations test has been the prevailing one, the tide is turning, and the writers of the *Restatement* predict that the numbers may continue to diminish.[126]

iii) Blended Theories

Barker v. Lull Engineering Co.[127] is an American case that stands for a kind of intermediate or blended theory of design defect liability. The test reflected in this case is a "two-pronged" approach, whereby the plaintiff can make out a claim in design defect negligence by showing *either*[128] (1) that the product failed to meet the consumer-expectations test; or, (2) that the design of the product caused the injury and the utility of the product does not outweigh the risks associated with its use.[129] It is important to note that, on this second branch, the defendant bears the onus of demonstrating that the utility outweighs the risk.

---

125 *Phillips v. Kimwood Machine Co.*, 269 Or. 485 (1974) [hereinafter *Phillips v. Kimwood*].
126 *Restatement (Third) of Torts: Products Liability* §2 (1998) [hereinafter *Restatement Third of Torts: Products Liability*].
127 20 Cal. 3d. 413 (Sup. Ct. 1978).
128 Only one of the two prongs need be established: *Curtis v. State of California*, 128 Cal. App. 3d. 668 (5th Dist. 1982).
129 This test is also evident in *Donaghue v. Stevenson*, *supra* note 8.

c) Case Study: Risk-Utility and Tobacco

i) Are Cigarettes an "Unreasonably Dangerous" Design?

One obvious and intriguing application of risk-utility analysis is in the context of cigarettes. There is some experience with the risk-utility test in the context of tobacco litigation, although the test has not yet been applied unequivocally to hold that cigarettes are defective. Many commentators speak of the "risks" associated with smoking that could be weighed in a risk-utility analysis: risk of addiction, risk of contracting smoking-related diseases such as heart disease and lung cancer, risks of economic harm owing to reduced productivity, risk of fires caused by cigarettes and the resultant damage to property, and the risk of causing discomfort and illness to passive smokers. On the "utilities" side of the equation, it has been held that the collateral economic benefits of a product, such as employment for those who manufacture it and tax revenue for the government, are not to be considered as part of a product's utility. In *Cipollone v. Liggett Group, Inc.*,[130] the defendants argued at 289-90 that, in determining liability according to the risk-utility analysis, a jury should take into consideration "profits made, employees hired, benefits to suppliers of goods and services, taxes generated and even charitable activities or contributions made by the defendant manufacturer." The court held, however, that

> [t]he analysis was never meant to balance the risk to the consumer against the general benefit to society. Rather, the sole question presented is whether the risk to the consumers exceeds the utility to those consumers. The manufacturer of a highly dangerous or defective product with no or limited utility to a consumer should not escape liability by demonstrating that the manufacturer of the product makes money for the stockholders, for workers, for contractors, for suppliers, for municipalities, for the IRS, etc. It is the benefit and utility to the cigarette smoker which is here in issue, and not the benefit to the cigarette industry or those in turn, who benefit from its existence.[131]

The court in *Cipollone*[132] reasoned that "to permit the defendants to introduce the evidence that they here propose would undercut the very goals of strict liability law insofar as it suggests that the defendants' interest in mak-

---

130 644 F. Supp. 283 (D.N.J. 1986) [hereinafter *Cipollone*].
131 *Ibid.* at 290.
132 683 F. Supp. 1487, 1493-95 (D. N.J. 1988), aff'd in part, rev'd in part, 893 F.2d 541 (3d. Cir. 1990), cert. granted, 111 S. Ct. 1386 (1991).

ing a profit could transform an otherwise insufficient evaluation of their product's safety into a reasonable one."[133]

In the *Cipollone* case[134] the court did consider allegations of a "safer" (palladium) cigarette and held that the evidence was at least sufficient to put to a jury — that tobacco companies have long been aware of the dangers of smoking, and that a safer alternative design has existed for decades. However, the court held that there was no proof that, had the defendants marketed a safer cigarette, the plaintiff would have switched to it or, if she had, that it would have prevented her cancer (the evidence showed only that it would have reduced the risk by a mere 8 percent to 17 percent). Thus, the plaintiff failed to show that the design defect was a factual cause of the injury sustained.

There was additional evidence discovered in *Cipollone*[135] (though not discussed by the court) that at least three of the major cigarette manufacturers, namely Lorillard, Philip Morris, and R.J. Reynolds, had indeed developed cigarettes that reduce the risk of cancer. The evidence indicated that R.J. Reynolds had taken its research further and actually developed a smokeless cigarette, patented in 1964 and marketed under the brand name *Premier* in 1988 and 1989. The design of the *Premier* was such as to allow for the delivery of the nicotine and flavour that smokers apparently desired, while eliminating many of the dangerous by-products. The market testing of the *Premier* smokeless cigarette was terminated in February 1989. Some allege that it was terminated because of a conspiracy among the tobacco companies but Reynolds took the position that the product was unacceptable to consumers because of its high price and bad taste.[136] If this latter position was true, then the product was not a "viable alternative."

Cipollone is not a strong authority for liability. It is hardly a "design defect" case in the traditional sense because it does not hold that, in light of the available alternatives, the defendants should have ceased marketing conventional (unsafe) cigarettes. Had this been the court's intent, it would

---

133   *Supra* note 130 at 288. Note that, since the same goals of economic efficiency and product safety underlie product liability negligence theory as well as the theory of strict liability, it may be argued that collateral benefits should likewise not be a factor in a risk-utility analysis in Canada.

134   *Cipollone, supra* note 132.

135   *Ibid.*

136   See L. Gordon & C.A. Granoff, "A Plaintiff's Guide to Reaching Tobacco Manufacturers: How to Get the Cigarette Industry off its Butt" (1992) 22 Seton Hall L. Rev., 851 at 884 [hereinafter "Tobacco Manufacturers"]; J.W. Henges, "Cigarettes: Defectively Designed or Just Extremely Dangerous?" (Fall 1993) Okla. City University L. Rev. 18, 3., 559 at 593; and D. DeMott, "The Biggest Deal Ever" (1989) Duke Law Journal 1 at 16.

have been unnecessary to require the plaintiff to prove that she would have switched brands (the wrong would have been in marketing the defective product). Nor does the case represent a clear finding that there is an available alternative cigarette that is significantly safer or that it was negligent of the manufacturer to continue to market conventional cigarettes.

Most recently, in the ongoing *Ragoonan* litigation,[137] Cumming J. accepted the risk-utility test in the context of a claim by a plaintiff alleging that the defendant manufacturer (ITC) was negligent in designing cigarettes capable of starting fires, when ITC knew how to manufacture "fire-safe" cigarettes. The plaintiff's house was destroyed and her daughter and brother died in a fire caused by an unextinguished cigarette. The judge was faced with a motion by the defendants to strike out the pleading on the basis that no reasonable cause of action was disclosed. Cumming J. refused to do so. He explicitly adopted the risk-utility test formulated in the American and Canadian jurisprudence and said that "the risk-utility theory of liability for the defective design of a product is a plausible legal theory in support of the asserted cause of action in the plaintiff's pleading."[138]

The consumer expectations test has not led to liability in the case of tobacco. In *Roysdon v. R.J. Reynolds Tobacco Co.*,[139] the court considered the consumer expectation argument. It rules that the defendant's cigarettes posed no greater risks than those "known to be associated with smoking." The court concluded that, because tobacco has been used for some four hundred years, and knowledge of its dangers is "widespread," the cigarettes that caused the plaintiff's injury were not defective as a matter of law.

ii) *Efforts to Expand Risk-Utility in Tobacco Litigation*

There have been suggestions that the risk-utility test can in some cases be used to argue that an entire product category is defectively designed. The idea would be that certain products are so inherently dangerous, and so devoid of social or personal utility, that their mere design, manufacture, and sale is negligence *per se*. In other words, even when there is no safer alternative design (for a gun, a cigarette, a type of knife), the product is defectively designed merely by virtue of having been designed. This is an argument that has surfaced in tobacco litigation.

In both Canada and the United States, the existence of an alternative design is sometimes said to be only one factor to be considered in weigh-

---

137 *Ragoonanan Estate v. Imperial Tobacco Canada Ltd.* (2000), 51 O.R. (3d) 603 (S.C.J.) [hereinafter *Ragoonanan*].
138 *Ibid.* at para. 138.
139 849 F.2d 230 (6th Cir. 1988).

ing the risks of a product against its utilities.[140] However, the majority view now is that proof of an available alternative design is a necessary condition for success of a design defect claim. In other words, most courts have rejected a theory of strict liability under which a product can be said to be defective even though there is no safer alternative.

For example, the *Restatement on Product Liability* states:[141] "To establish a *prima facie* case of defect, the plaintiff must prove the availability of a technologically feasible and practical alternative design that would have reduced or prevented the plaintiff's harm." Thus, in those states in which the *Restatement* has been accepted, no matter how dangerous the product, and how devoid of utility, it will not be called defective if the danger is related to an inherent characteristic of the generic product, especially when that danger is recognized by the consumer. Another way of stating this is that, when there is no safer alternative, a product will not be called "defective" even if it is devoid of utility. The product may be ultra-hazardous and anti-social, but it is not *defective* (e.g., an exploding cigar).

Some states are asserting that, even in the absence of proof that there is a safer alternate design for cigarettes, the product should be considered *per se* defective. Unlike any other product, cigarettes cause injury when used exactly as intended. The argument is that the risks and costs of tobacco use vastly outweigh its social utility and the product should be considered presumptively defective.

In the absence of proof that there is a safer cigarette, liability under the theory that cigarettes are unreasonably dangerous *per se* would require a court to accept the conclusion that cigarettes are simply unsafe as a "product category" and cannot be saved even by adequate warnings about their dangers. This would mean that some products are so manifestly unreasonable and devoid of utility that liability would attach even in the absence of proof that there is a reasonable alternate design. This theory raises interesting questions about the institutional capacity of courts to act essentially as a regulatory authority. The theory is controversial in the U.S. and probably not a viable one in Canada.[142] There is no case in Canada in which a product has been declared defective in the absence of an alternative. Several American cases have considered the theory in respect to cigarettes.

---

140 See *O'Brien, supra* note 105 and *John Deere, supra* note 97.
141 *Restatement of Torts: Product Liability, supra* note 126.
142 See J.A. Henderson, Jr & A.D. Twerski, "Closing the American Product Liability Frontier: The Rejection of Liability Without Defect" (1991) 66 N.Y.U.L. Rev. 1263 at 617–18.

On the extreme end of strict liability for a product *per se* is *Wilks v. American Tobacco*.[143] The court held that, unlike alcohol cigarettes are dangerous because even when used as intended they cause disease and death. The product is, therefore, "defective and unreasonably dangerous." The court based its finding of absolute liability on the public policy objective of placing the cost and risk on the manufacturer. The court also held that (a) the plaintiff was not obliged to prove that the product was unreasonably dangerous; (b) he was not required to prove that he was unaware of the danger; (c) liability is not precluded solely because the danger is obvious; (d) assumption of risk did not apply except where the plaintiff's conduct can be shown to be "venturous" and the sole proximate cause of his injury; and (e) contributory negligence applies only when it can be shown that the plaintiff has misused or abnormally handled the product. However, the plaintiff, who had a history of other ailments that may have contributed to his death, was unable to establish smoking as the cause of death.

In *Kotler v. American Tobacco Co.*,[144] a federal district court in Massachusetts considered and flatly rejected the analysis, reasoning that, unless the purely hedonistic consumer's preference for a product is considered "utility," then a large percentage of manufactured products would fail a risk-utility analysis. However, as one commentator points out, the court did not take notice that other products such as alcohol, refined sugars, and saturated fats — harmful in large quantities or over a long period of time — are safe and can even be useful in small quantities. The same cannot be said about tobacco, which is deadly even when used exactly as intended.[145]

A similar result was reached in *Gianitsis v. American Brands, Inc.*[146] In that case, the plaintiff smoker asked for a simple determination of whether he could bring a design defect cause of action under a risk-utility theory. The court emphatically declined to adopt such an "expansive doctrine of strict product liability" with respect to cigarettes. Noting that the plaintiff was proposing a theory of liability that could effectively destroy an industry, the court would not allow a design defect claim without proof of an alternative design.

In *Gilboy v. American Tobacco Co.*[147] the Louisiana Court of Appeal undertook a type of risk-utility analysis to find that cigarettes were not

---

143 61 USLW 2708 (Miss. Cir. 1993).
144 731 F. Supp. 50 (D. Mass. 1990), aff'd 926 F.2d 1217; cert. granted and judgment vacated 505 U.S. 1215, 112 S.Ct. 3019.
145 "Tobacco Manufacturers," *supra* note 136 at 882.
146 685 F. Supp. 853 (D.N.H. 1988).
147 572 So.2d 289 (La. App. 1990).

unreasonably dangerous *per se*, and so declined to hold the tobacco companies strictly liable. Following *Halphen v. Johns-Manville*,[148] the court held at page 114 that the test for whether a product is unreasonably dangerous *per se* is "if a reasonable person would conclude that the danger-in-fact of the product, whether foreseeable or not, outweighs the utility of the product ... A warning or other feature actually incorporated in the product when it leaves the manufacturer's control, however, may reduce the danger-in-fact." Here, the court held that the warning reduces the danger and also that the policy rationale of strict liability does not apply to cigarettes, where "someone who voluntarily smokes cigarettes for a lifetime, and then tries to hold the manufacturer and others liable for the harm he was aware of all along."[149] The court held that knowledge of the health hazards of smoking is widespread, the labels warn consumers of the risks, and that smoking is a voluntary act. If, in these circumstances, strict liability were to be applied, it would open the floodgates of claims in respect to other "dangerous" products such as alcohol. This seems not quite accurate since, as pointed out in *Wilks*, cigarettes are uniquely dangerous because they cause disease and death when used exactly as intended.

D. FAILURE TO WARN

There is a third "class" of negligence-based product liability cases that involves a failure on the part of a defendant to explain adequately to consumers the risks inherent in the product or use of the product. In these cases, there has been neither a defect in the manufacture nor a flaw in the design. Rather, the product is just as the manufacturer or distributor[150] had intended, but this product carries with it certain risks of which the consumer must be made aware.

1) Overview of the Duty to Warn

The essence of the duty to warn is the concept of an individual's responsibility for his or her own conduct. Inseparable from the idea of fault-based liability is the idea that one should not be able to recover for a risk knowingly taken. Sir Francis Bacon said: "*Nam et ipsa scietia potestas est,*" or

---

148 *Halphen v. Johns-Manville Sales Corp.*, 484 So.2d 110 (La. 1986).
149 *Supra*, note 147 at 291
150 It is uncontroversial that the duty to warn is not limited to the manufacturer: *Fleming on Torts*, 3d ed., at 486: "... a distributor is required to warn of dangers of which he actually knows or had reason to know."

"knowledge itself is power."[151] However, defining what level of "knowledge" is necessary before a risk can be said to have been "voluntarily" assumed is not easy.

The problem is compounded by the way the human brain assesses risks; detailed, probabilistic analyses presented statistically, while perhaps the most accurate way of communicating the risks associated with a product, are invariably inexact in any individual case; on the other hand, in some cases, general warnings that do not communicate the details of risks lead people to believe that risks are actually greater than they are.[152]

The principle of the duty to warn in Canada was enunciated by Laskin J. (as he then was) in *Lambert*[153] where he stated:

> Manufacturers owe a duty to consumers of their products to see that there are no defects in manufacture which are likely to give rise to injury in the ordinary course of use. Their duty does not, however, end if the product, although suitable for the purpose for which it is manufactured and marketed, is at the same time dangerous to use; and if they are aware of its dangerous character they cannot, without more, pass the risk of injury to the consumer.

The leading case in this area of law is *Hollis v. Dow Corning Corp.*[154] *Hollis* involved a woman who had undergone breast-implant surgery to correct a congenital deformity. One of the implants ruptured and Ms. Hollis suffered severe medical consequences. The trial judge found Dow liable for negligent manufacture, but this finding was overturned by the Court of Appeal. The Court of Appeal held that there was no manufacturing defect but, concluding that Dow had failed to issue adequate warnings about the risk of rupture occurring, imposed liability on that basis. The Supreme Court of

---

151 Bacon, *De Haeresibus Meditationes Sacrae* (1597).
152 See several works by W. Kip Viscusi present the rational choice theory of risk assessment: *Risk By Choice: Regulating Health and Safety in the Workplace* (Cambridge, Mass.: Harvard University Press, 1983); (with Wesley A. Magat) *Learning about Risk: Consumer and Worker Responses to Hazard Information* (Cambridge, Mass.: Harvard University Press, 1987); and *Fatal Tradeoffs: Public and Private Responsibilities for Risk* (New York: Oxford University Press, 1992). Viscusi controversially argues with respect to smoking that, "if people understood the lung cancer risk accurately as opposed to overestimating it, the societal smoking rate would increase by 6.5–7.5%" W. Kip Viscusi, *Smoke Filled Rooms* (Chicago: U. Chicago Press, 2002) at 163. Viscusi's views are countered by other law and economics scholars; see, for instance, Jon D. Hanson, "Taking Behavioralism Seriously: The Problem of Market Manipulation" (1999) 74 N.Y.U. L. Rev. 630.
153 *Lambert*, supra note 18 at 124–25.
154 *Hollis*, supra note 46.

Canada affirmed the Court of Appeal decision and, in the process, stated the following general principle with respect to manufacturers' duty to warn: "It is well established in Canadian law that a manufacturer of a product has a duty in tort to warn consumers of dangers inherent in the use of its product of which it has knowledge or ought to have knowledge."[155] Thus, a manufacturer will be held liable where it is aware, or ought to be aware, of dangers associated with the use or consumption of its product. The Supreme Court made clear that the duty upon a manufacturer to warn consumers of risk associated with its products is merely an extension of the general duty to take care imposed by tort law and that the rationale for the rule lay in the disparity of knowledge between manufacturer and consumer:

> The rationale for the manufacturer's duty to warn can be traced to the "neighbour principle," which lies at the heart of the law of negligence, and was set down in its classic form by Lord Atkin in *Donoghue v. Stevenson* …. When manufacturers place products into the flow of commerce, they create a relationship of reliance with consumers, who have far less knowledge than the manufacturers concerning the dangers inherent in the use of the products, and are therefore put at risk if the product is not safe. The duty to warn serves to correct the knowledge imbalance between manufacturers and consumers by alerting consumers to any dangers and allowing them to make informed decisions concerning the safe use of the product.[156]

Based as it is upon the "neighbour principle," the duty to warn is a potentially broad one. The duty extends to all those who may reasonably be affected by the potentially dangerous product, including those persons who are not party to the sale.[157] Furthermore, the manufacturer must warn not only of dangers inherent in the proper use of the product but also of dangers that could arise from foreseeable misuse. Yet a manufacturer need not warn of risks that are known to the consumer or otherwise obvious.[158] As Galligan J.A. stated in *Deshane v. Deere & Co.*: "[t]he law does not impose a duty to warn of a danger which is so obvious and apparent that anyone would be aware of it. Thus, the manufacturer of a butcher knife is not under a legal duty to warn consumers that the butcher knife may cut flesh."[159] However, where a supplier is *aware* that a consumer intends to put

---

155   *Ibid.* at para. 20.
156   *Ibid.* at para. 21.
157   *Bow Valley*, supra note 27.
158   *Shulz v. Leeside Developments Ltd.* (1978), 90 D.L.R. (3d) 98 (B.C.C.A.).
159   *Deshane v. Deere & Co.*, (1993), 50 C.P.R. (3d) 449 at 465 (Ont. C.A.).

a product to a dangerous use for which it was not intended, that supplier is under a duty to possible third persons not to sell the product.[160]

Lem v. Barotto Sports Ltd.[161] is demonstrative of this latter point. In this case, the plaintiff had purchased a machine that reloaded expended shotgun shells. The manufacturer and retailer provided instructions on the proper use of the machine. But Mr. Lem, an experienced hunter, did not follow all of the instructions strictly. As a result, he reloaded some shells that, though they appeared normal, were defective and when he fired these shells he was injured. The plaintiff claimed that the defendants had a duty to provide warnings about the possible risks involved in misusing the machine. Although the Court of Appeal in *Lem*[162] found that Mr. Lem had ignored key indications that he was misusing the machine in a manner that was not foreseeable by the defendants, it did state that "the duty of the manufacturer is to give adequate warning ... not only as to such that would arise out of the contemplated proper use of the product, but also as to such that might arise out of *reasonably foreseeable fault* on the part of the purchaser in its contemplated use."[163]

Having identified the existence of a duty, *Buchan*[164] raises more fully the issue of what will satisfy the duty — what is the content of the duty to warn? The plaintiff in that case suffered a serious stroke shortly after beginning to take oral contraceptives. The court was satisfied that there had been no defect in design or manufacture but, rather, that the risk of stroke was one inherent in the use of the product. The manufacturer's product information and marketing approach failed to alert either the patient or the doctor of the risks associated with the drug. As such, the court imposed liability, stating as follows:

> [The warning] should be communicated clearly and understandably in a manner calculated to inform the user of the nature of the risk and the extent of the danger; it should be in terms commensurate with the gravity of the potential hazard, and it should not be neutralized or negated by collateral efforts on the part of the manufacturer. The nature and extent of any given warning will depend on what is reasonable having regard to all the facts and circumstances relevant to the product in question.
>
> ...
>
> The duty is a continuous one requiring that the manufacturer warn, not only of dangers known at the time of sale, but also of dangers discovered after the product has been sold and delivered ....

---

160 *Good-Wear Treaders Ltd. v. D & B Holdings Ltd.* (1979), 98 D.L.R. (3d) 59 (N.S.C.A.).
161 (1976), 1 C.C.L.T. 180 (Alta. C.A.) [hereinafter *Lem*].
162 *Ibid.*
163 *Ibid.* at para. 22 [emphasis added].
164 *Buchan, supra* note 50.

> Ordinarily, the warning must be addressed directly to the person likely to be injured. It is not, however, necessary that that be done in every case. Where, for example, the product is a highly technical one that is intended or expected to be used only under the supervision of experts, a warning to the experts will suffice....[165]

This passage raises a number of issues touching upon the duty to warn, which will be dealt with in turn.

2) The Knowledge of the Defendant

a) The "Duty to Research"

As described, manufacturers and distributors have a duty to warn only of dangers of which they knew or ought to have known at the relevant times.

The obvious question, then, is what dangers ought a manufacturer to know? To put it another way, what is the extent of manufacturers' duty to find out about possible dangers that inhere to the use of their product?

Many products, of course, have vigorous safety-testing requirements imposed by statute or regulation. Manufacturers of machinery, electrical products, pharmaceuticals, automobiles, and so on each have rigorous standards imposed by law. But does compliance with regulations, if any, absolve a manufacturer from seeking out knowledge of the harm of its products?

Recent cases speak for the proposition that a manufacturer has a duty to become an expert on any harmful effects of its product. The general rule is that defendants will be held liable for failing to warn of dangers that were reasonably foreseeable or scientifically discoverable at the time of the victim's exposure. Such was the basis of the decision in the famous asbestos case of *Borel v. Fibreboard Paper Products Corp.*,[166] a case involving asbestos.

This view is consistent with recent Canadian decisions such as *Buchan* and *Hollis*, both *supra*, which have held that "[a] manufacturer of prescription drugs occupies the position of an expert in the field; this requires that it be under a continuing duty to keep abreast of scientific developments pertaining to its product through research, adverse reaction reports, scientific literature and other available methods."[167]

---

165 *Ibid.*, cited to (1986), 25 D.L.R. (4th) 658 (C.A.) at 667–68.
166 493 F.2d 1076, 1088 (5th Cir. 1973), cert. denied, 419 U.S. 869, 95 S. Ct. 127 (1974).
167 *Buchan, supra* note 50 at para. 40, cited by MacEachern C.J.B.C. concurring in *Hollis*, *supra* note 46.

b) Imputation of Industry-Wide Knowledge of Dangers

In another asbestos case, *Dartez v. Fibreboard Corp.*, the Fifth Circuit Court of Appeals went beyond even the "state of the art" rules of industry knowledge and held that constructive knowledge imputed from one manufacturer to another could impose a duty to warn:

> Defendants contend that Smith's testimony is irrelevant because it relates only to Johns-Manville. Their contention reflects a misunderstanding of a critical issue in any product liability action: the state of the art pertaining to any possible risks associated with the product. Dartez was required to establish that the dangers of asbestos were reasonably foreseeable or scientifically discoverable at the time of his exposure before these defendants could be found liable. *Borel v. Fibreboard Paper Products Corp.*, 493 F.2d 1076, 1088 (5th Cir.1973), cert. denied, 419 U.S. 869, 95 S. Ct. 127, 42 L. Ed. 2d 107 (1974).
>
> *Borel* holds all manufacturers to the knowledge and skill of an expert. They are obliged to keep abreast of any scientific discoveries and are presumed to know the results of all such advances. Moreover, they each bear the duty to fully test their products to uncover all scientifically discoverable dangers before the products are sold. *Id.* at 1089–90. The actual knowledge of an individual manufacturer is not the issue. If the dangers of asbestos were known to Johns-Manville at the time of Dartez's exposure, then the same risks were scientifically discoverable by other asbestos corporations. Therefore, the testimony of the medical director of the industry's largest member is relevant to plaintiff's attempt to meet the evidentiary burden defined by *Borel*.
>
> ...
>
> ... Defendants assert that this testimony was prejudicial because it allowed the jury to find these defendants liable for the knowledge and conduct of Johns-Manville. But this argument misses the point of *Borel* — *the knowledge of one manufacturer can be a proper basis for concluding that another manufacturer should have warned of a specific danger*.[168]

This "imputing" of knowledge from one manufacturer to another was also a feature of the Florida Supreme Court's decision in *Carter v. Brown & Williamson*.[169] The *Carter* court had to decide whether, in introducing evidence of Brown & Williamson's knowledge (as opposed to that of American Tobacco Co., which had manufactured the cigarettes smoked by the

---

168 *Dartez v. Fibreboard Corp.*, 765 F.2d 456 at 461 (5th Cir. 1985) [emphasis added].
169 778 So.2d 932 (Sup. Ct. Fla. 2000) [hereinafter *Carter*].

Carters prior to that company's merger with B&W), the Carters had advanced an unpleaded cause of action. Because Brown & Williamson had merged with ATC, it was suggested that the introduction of evidence of, essentially, B&W's historical wrongdoing had a prejudicial effect, since B&W was now the defendant as successor to ATC. The court explains:

> During the trial, the Carters presented the testimony of ATC officials, including a former CEO and a former research director, who testified that ATC never conducted any tests to determine whether smoking was harmful or whether nicotine was addictive. The Carters argue that the Brown & Williamson documents were relevant to establish the state of the art pertaining to possible risks associated with smoking, i.e., that had ATC conducted testing, it would have learned of the harmful nature of smoking. However, the district court below concluded that "the focus placed on the objectionable documents was less on what Brown & Williamson, and therefore other manufacturers, knew, and more on Brown & Williamson's alleged failure to disclose all that it knew, an allegation not attributable to ATC by virtue of its position in the industry."[170]

The *Carter*[171] court, relying on *Borel* and *Dartez*, *supra*, confirmed that "Florida courts have also recognized that '[a] manufacturer has the duty to possess expert knowledge in the field of its product.'"

The American decisions appear to establish:

- the duty of a manufacturer to research and to possess expert knowledge in the field;
- the presumption that each manufacturer knows of all advances in knowledge, with "actual knowledge" not an issue; and, most important
- the principle that the knowledge of one manufacturer can be imputed to another for the purposes of proof of "failure to warn."

The sum of these rules is that, at least in Florida and in the U.S. 5th Circuit, a duty-to-warn case can be made entirely through evidence of the knowledge of another manufacturer in the same industry.

Buchan[172] was extensively relied upon when the Supreme Court of Canada affirmed the Court of Appeal's decision in *Hollis*[173] and was even cited by the two dissenting members of the Court. Although the Supreme Court has not spoken authoritatively on whether the evidence of one man-

---

170   Ibid. at 942.
171   Ibid. at 943.
172   Buchan, *supra* note 50.
173   Hollis, *supra* note 46.

ufacturer's knowledge may be imputed to another, the affirmation of *Hollis*[174] and the endorsement of *Buchan*[175] seem to suggest that these cases accurately express the law in Canada on the issue.

3) The Content of the Warning

a) Clear and Adequate Communication

In *Hollis*, the Supreme Court of Canada explicitly noted that "[a]ll warnings must be reasonably communicated and must clearly describe any specific dangers that arise from the ordinary use of the product."[176] This requirement, which gives content to the duty to warn, is consistent with the Court's stated rationale for the rule, which is to address the imbalance in knowledge between manufacturer and consumer. If the warning is not clear and understandable, as well as sufficiently thorough, this policy goal would not be achieved. But the more difficult issue is to determine what level of specificity and clarity is necessary in order to satisfy this requirement. In *Hollis*, the Court concluded as follows:

> The nature and scope of the manufacturer's duty to warn varies with the level of danger entailed by the ordinary use of the product. Where significant dangers are entailed by the ordinary use of the product, it will rarely be sufficient for manufacturers to give general warnings concerning those dangers; the warnings must be sufficiently detailed to give the consumer a full indication of each of the specific dangers arising from the use of the product.[177]

The warning, therefore, must be commensurate with both the gravity and the likelihood of the danger. This requirement is consistent with the general approach to standard of care, which requires a heightened level of caution where there is a likelihood of some harm or a risk of serious harm. In *Hollis*, the Court concluded that, since medical products like breast implants are designed for bodily ingestion or implantation, the risks are high and, accordingly, the warnings must meet a high standard.

This notion of the proportionality between risk and warning has been articulated and applied in a number of other decisions. In *Lambert*,[178] a man had been applying a lacquer sealer in his basement, in which there was also

---

174 *Ibid.*
175 *Buchan, supra* note 50.
176 *Hollis, supra* note 46 at para. 20.
177 *Ibid.* at para. 22.
178 *Lambert, supra* note 18.

a natural gas furnace and water heater. The sealer container had general warnings about inflammability on the label and these warnings were read by the plaintiff. However, when he was almost finished sealing the floor, he noticed a line of fire spreading across the floor and, though he tried to escape the basement, was caught in the ensuing explosion and injured. Laskin J. (as he then was) stated the following:

> Where manufactured products are put on the market for ultimate purchase and use by the general public and carry danger ... although put to the use for which they are intended, the manufacturer, knowing of their hazardous nature, has a duty to specify the attendant dangers, which it must be taken to appreciate in a detail not known to the ordinary customer or user. A general warning, as for example, that the product is inflammable, will not suffice where the likelihood of fire may be increased according to the surroundings in which it may reasonably be expected that the product will be used. The required explicitness of the warning will, of course, vary with the danger likely to be encountered in the ordinary use of the product.[179]

The Court held that the warnings on this product "lacked the explicitness which the degree of danger in its use in a gas-serviced residence demanded."[180]

Of course, a manufacturer need not warn of every possible permutation of the danger; a general warning sufficient to instil the appropriate caution will generally be appropriate. As Isley C.J. stated in *Tanner v. Atlantic Bridge Co.*: "In my opinion, the duty of the appellant was not to warn the respondent against the danger of 'the precise concatenation of circumstances which led up to the accident' ... but only against the danger of circumstances which were of a *'type or kind'* which it might reasonably have foreseen."[181]

b) Obviousness

It is accepted that there is no duty to warn where the danger is obvious. A concise statement of this principle can be found in *Andrulonis v. United States*: "[T]he focus of the 'obviousness' inquiry is upon the objective reasonableness of the supplier's judgment about whether users will perceive the danger .... The danger must be so apparent or so clearly within com-

---

179 *Ibid.* at 125.
180 *Ibid.* See also *O'Fallon v. Inecto Rapid (Canada) Ltd.*, [1940] 4 D.L.R. 276 (B.C.C.A.).
181 (1996), 51 M.P.R. 293 at 296 (N.S.S.C.) [emphasis in original].

mon knowledge that a user would appreciate the danger to the same extent that a warning would provide."[182]

The obviousness rule is narrow: only failures to provide warnings that would be completely redundant to a reasonable consumer are excused under the obviousness rule.

c) The Knowledgeable User

Even in cases where there is a general duty to warn because the danger is not "obvious," the duty does not extend to those persons who can be said to be "knowledgeable users."

In *Allard v. Manahan*,[183] the suit was brought by the estate of a worker killed attaching a two-by-four to a cement wall with a nail gun, when a nail ricocheted off the wood and struck him in the head. The operator's manual failed to warn users that it was unsafe to use the tool on any two-by-fours without a particular type of guard. The court found that the particular occurrence was something of a freak accident, not reasonably foreseeable. It dismissed the action, holding that a manufacturer's duty to warn was restricted to instances where an operator cannot be expected to be aware of the danger; the court's focus in this case on the victim's considerable experience in using the nailer reflects the subjective nature of the inquiry in many failure-to-warn cases, particularly where they involve machinery or equipment employed by experienced professionals, as opposed to novice or dilettante consumers.

d) The Relevance of "Dependency"

There appears little doubt that the idea of "dependency" plays an important role in the standard of care in duty-to-warn cases. In *Hollis* as elsewhere, the differential between the relative knowledge of risks of plaintiff and defendant, coupled with the particular vulnerability of persons with respect to items ingested or implanted, led to this conclusion that the defendant failed in its duty.

This "dependency" aspect also arose in the decision of Macdonald J. in *Robb v. Canadian Red Cross Society*,[184] a case dealing with transfusions of infected blood by the Canadian Red Cross Society (CRCS). In that case, His Lordship said at paragraph 72:

> The CRCS faces, in the context of the analysis, an exacting and high standard. The first factor which puts the standard at a high level is the nature

---

182 *Andrulonis v. United States*, 924 F.2d 1210 at 1222 (2d. Cir. 1991).
183 [1974] 3 W.W.R. 588 (B.C.S.C.).
184 [2000] O.J. No. 2396 (S.C.), rev'd (but not on this point) [2001] O.J. No. 4605 (C.A.).

of the relationship between the CRCS and Canadian hemophiliacs, who comprise a sick and vulnerable population. They depended on the CRCS for the supply of factor concentrates that were essential to their survival. Since the CRCS was in the unique position of being the only supplier of blood products in Canada, hemophiliacs had no other options. Their relationship with the CRCS was one of total dependency. Although not pleaded, it is very close to a fiduciary relationship.

But "dependency" is not confined to medical cases; in fact, the information deficit faced by consumers compared to manufacturers informs the entire jurisprudence surrounding the duty to warn. Where the deficit is widest, duties will be more likely to be found, and the standards for the appropriate warning will be highest; in cases where the victim is well positioned compared to the manufacturer, either a duty will not be found or its standard will be a low one.

e) Compliance with Standard Warning

With regard to the failure to warn, compliance with labelling standards, worked out in conjunction with health authorities, may *prima facie* satisfy a company's duty to warn. However, in *Buchan*,[185] the Ontario Court of Appeal held a drug manufacturer liable for failure to warn notwithstanding its compliance with statutory warnings. Compliance is relevant but not conclusive. Particularly if it could be proved that the defendant had earlier and better knowledge of the risks, strenuously resisted efforts to place warnings, or, through parallel activities such as advertising or marketing campaigns, minimized the content of those warnings, a defence of compliance would likely fail.

4) The Duty to Warn Is a Continuing One

The duty to warn of dangers associated with the use of a product do not attach only to initial warnings by way of labelling or instructions. Rather, the courts have been explicit that the duty to warn is a continuing one. A manufacturer who newly becomes aware of risks or discovers some new danger must take steps to warn the consumer. In *Hollis*,[186] the Supreme Court stated that "[t]he duty to warn is a continuing duty, requiring manufacturers to warn not only of dangers known at the time of sale, but also of dangers discovered after the product has been sold and delivered."[187]

---

185 *Buchan, supra* note 50.
186 *Hollis, supra* note 46.
187 *Ibid.* at para 20.

In *Rivtow Marine Ltd. v. Washington Iron Works*,[188] the plaintiffs had purchased two cranes for use on its log barge. After a similar crane collapsed on another company's barge, killing its operator, the plaintiffs recalled its barge from operation and inspected it. The inspection revealed cracks in the mountings of the plaintiffs' cranes that were similar to those that had caused the collapse on the other barge. The defendant companies had become aware of this risk some time after selling the cranes to the plaintiffs but had not issued a warning. The plaintiffs sought compensation for the cost of repair and for the lost productive time. Ritchie J., for the majority of the Supreme Court, held that "the knowledge of the danger involved in the continued use of these cranes for the purpose for which they were designed, carried with it a duty to warn those to whom the cranes had been supplied and this duty arose at the moment when the respondents or either of them became seized with the knowledge."[189]

5) The Learned Intermediary Rule

While the general rule is that a manufacturer must issue a warning to the ultimate consumer, this is not always the case. Where the product is one that is necessarily subject to inspection by, or its use is under the supervision of, an expert, the manufacturer can discharge its duty to warn by informing this "learned intermediary" of the risks associated with the product. Similarly, if the product is such that it is unrealistic to expect the manufacturer to inform the consumer directly (food supplied to a restaurant, for example), a warning to an informed intermediary may suffice.

In *Hollis*,[190] the defendant company claimed that it could rely upon this rule because the breast implant was a technical product that never reached the consumer before being used. The Supreme Court described the operation of the learned intermediary principle as follows:

> ... the "learned intermediary" rule is less a "rule" than a specific application of the long-established common law principles of intermediate examination and intervening cause developed in *Donoghue v. Stevenson* .... Generally, the rule is applicable either where a product is highly technical in nature and is intended to be used only under the supervision of experts, or where the nature of the product is such that the consumer will not realistically receive a direct warning from the manufacturer before

---

188   *Supra* note 69.
189   *Ibid.* at 200.
190   *Hollis, supra* note 46.

using the product. In such cases, where an intermediate inspection of the product is anticipated or where a consumer is placing primary reliance on the judgment of a "learned intermediary" and not the manufacturer, a warning to the ultimate consumer may not be necessary and the manufacturer may satisfy its duty to warn the ultimate consumer by warning the learned intermediary of the risks inherent in the use of the product.[191]

Dow argued that it had discharged its duty to warn by passing on product information to the doctor who had inserted the implants, but the Court refused to apply this rule. The Court pointed out that "the 'learned intermediary' rule presumes that the intermediary is fully appraised of the risks, and can only provide shelter to the manufacturer where it has taken adequate steps to ensure that the intermediary's knowledge of the risks in fact approximates that of the manufacturer."[192] The information supplied was not adequate, particularly because no mention had been made of the risk of rupture during the course of ordinary activity. Consequently, the manufacturer had not discharged its duty.

In *Bow Valley*,[193] the defendant manufacturer argued that it should be entitled to rely upon the learned intermediary rule because it had informed the rig builder of the risk of fire. The court rejected this argument, however, noting that the rule applied only where the product was highly technical or warning the consumer was an unreasonable expectation. It concluded as follows:

> Thermaclad was not a highly technical product, nor did its use and application require expert supervision. Nor was it unrealistic to expect Raychem to have warned BVHB, the ultimate consumer, directly. There was direct contact between BVHB and Raychem, independent of SJSL. Raychem actively sought the business of BVHB, and the trial judge found that the Thermaclad was owner-directed supply. In these circumstances Raychem had both the opportunity and the duty to warn BVHB directly.[194]

6) Causation in Duty-to-Warn Cases

As in all areas of negligence, it is not sufficient to establish merely that the manufacturer failed in its duty to warn the consumer. The plaintiff must also prove that the injuries suffered were a product of this failure — a

---

191   *Ibid.* at para. 28.
192   *Ibid.* at para. 32.
193   *Bow Valley, supra* note 27.
194   *Ibid.* at para. 37.

causative link must be established. In duty-to-warn cases, the causation analysis has some unique contours. Since the essence of a breach of the duty to warn is a failure to pass on adequate information to the consumer, causation will be made out only where it is established that, had the information been properly communicated, the consumer's choice or use of the product would have been different. But what is the appropriate test to be applied?

In *Hollis*, the Supreme Court was asked to consider precisely this question. The trial judge had applied the modified objective test, usual in medical informed-consent cases, which was posed as follows: "[W]ould a reasonable person in Ms. Hollis' particular circumstances have consented to the surgery if she had known all the material risks?" La Forest J. rejected the application of the modified objective test and held that, owing to the nature of the relationship between manufacturer and consumer, the proper test in manufacturers' liability cases was purely subjective. Thus, the proper inquiry was simply, "[W]ould Ms. Hollis have consented to the surgery if she had known all the material risks?" La Forest J. approved of the reasoning of Robins J.A. in the court below:

> The considerations applicable to and the responsibilities involved in a doctor-patient relationship differ markedly from those of a manufacturer-consumer relationship. As between doctor and patient, there is a direct and intimate relationship in which the relative advantages and disadvantages of a proposed medical treatment, including the taking of a drug, can be considered, discussed and evaluated. As between drug manufacturer and consumer, the manufacturer is a distant commercial entity that, like manufacturers of other products, promotes its products directly or indirectly to gain consumer sales, sometimes, as in this case, accentuating value while under-emphasizing risks. Manufacturers hold an enormous informational advantage over consumers and, indeed, over most physicians. The information they provide often establishes the boundaries within which a physician determines the risks of possible harm and the benefits to be gained by a patient's use of a drug. Manufacturers, unlike doctors, are not called upon to tailor their warnings to the needs and abilities of the individual patient; and, unlike doctors, they are not required to make the type of judgment call that becomes subject to scrutiny in informed consent actions.[195]

The Court was satisfied, on the evidence, that Ms. Hollis would not have had the surgery if properly informed and, therefore, it found there to be the nec-

---

195 *Supra*. note 46 at para. 45.

essary causative link. Accordingly, if a manufacturer fails in its duty to warn a consumer of risks associated with the use of its product, causation will be established where it is proven that the consumer in question would not have used the product had he or she been provided with the proper information.

Hollis also raised the issue of how to analyse causation in cases that involve a learned intermediary. Dow argued that, even if it had provided the necessary information to the doctor, he would not have informed Ms. Hollis and, therefore, there was no causative link. Dow took the position that it was incumbent upon Ms. Hollis to prove that the doctor would have passed the warning on to her. The Court rejected this argument, noting that Dow's position would require her to disprove the hypothetical that the doctor would have failed in his legal duty to obtain informed consent. The situation was analogous, the Court held, to the *Cook v. Lewis*[196] situation in which one of two possible defendants is liable. In such a situation, once all of the elements of the negligence claim are made out, it is up to the defendants to sort out liability between them because the plaintiff does not have access to the requisite information:

> We know that Dow's failure to warn was a cause of her injury; whether Dr. Birch's actions in the hypothetical situation posited by Dow might also have been a cause is not a matter for Ms. Hollis to prove. Ms. Hollis, who was in a position of great informational inequality with respect to both the manufacturer and the doctor, played no part in creating the set of causal conditions leading to her injury. Justice dictates that she should not be penalized for the fact that had the manufacturer actually met its duty to warn, the doctor still might have been at fault.[197]

In the result, the principle is as follows:

> The ultimate duty of the manufacturer is to warn the plaintiff adequately. For practical reasons, the law permits it to acquit itself of that duty by warning an informed intermediary. Having failed to warn the intermediary, the manufacturer has failed in its duty to warn the plaintiff who ultimately suffered injury by using the product. The fact that the manufacturer would have been absolved had it followed the route of informing the plaintiff through the learned intermediary should not absolve it of its duty to the plaintiff because of the possibility, even the probability, that the learned intermediary would not have advised her had the manufacturer issued it. The learned intermediary rule provides a

---

196 [1951] S.C.R. 830.
197 *Hollis, supra* note 46 at para. 57.

means by which the manufacturer can discharge its duty to give adequate information of the risks to the plaintiff by informing the intermediary, but if it fails to do so it cannot raise as a defence that the intermediary could have ignored this information.[198]

Where a manufacturer fails to perform its duty to warn, it cannot defend itself by arguing that, even if it had informed a learned intermediary, that intermediary may not have fulfilled his or her own legal duties.

7) Reliance on Other Sources for Warning

A manufacturer cannot necessarily rely on warnings from other sources to discharge its duties to warn consumers (or intermediaries). In a passage in turn cited at length and with approval by Prowse J.A. in *Hollis*,[199] the Ontario court said in *Buchan*:

> In determining whether a drug manufacturer's warnings satisfy the duty to make adequate and timely warning to the medical profession of any dangerous side-effects produced by its drugs of which it knows, or has reason to know, certain factors must be borne in mind. A manufacturer of prescription drugs occupies the position of an expert in the field; this requires that it be under a continuing duty to keep abreast of scientific developments pertaining to its product through research, adverse reaction reports, scientific literature and other available methods. When additional dangerous or potentially dangerous side-effects from the drug's use are discovered, the manufacturer must make all reasonable efforts to communicate the information to prescribing physicians. Unless doctors have current, accurate and complete information about a drug's risks, their ability to exercise the fully-informed medical judgment necessary for the proper performance of their vital role in prescribing drugs for patients may be reduced or impaired.

The Ontario court continued:

> [A]s a general proposition, a manufacturer cannot justify a failure to warn by claiming that physicians were in a position to learn of the risks inherent in its products through other sources. *The manufacturer's duty to warn continues notwithstanding that the information may be otherwise available.* In this regard, I respectfully agree with the apt observations of Linden J. in

---

198 *Ibid.* at para. 61.
199 (MacEachern C.J.B.C. concurring), *Hollis, supra* note 46.

Davidson v. Connaught Laboratories et al. (1980), 14 C.C.L.T. 251 (Ont. H.C.J.) at p. 276:

> A drug company cannot rely upon doctors to read all the scientific literature outlining the specific dangers involved in the many drugs they have to administer each day. They are busy people, administering to the needs of the injured and the sick. They have little time for deep research into the medical literature.[200]

Again, the *Buchan*[201] case dealt with the duty of a manufacturer to warn the learned intermediary, not the consumer. However, it is difficult to see any distinction, and the fact that there is no learned intermediary between a manufacturer of consumer products and his or her customer, in our view, only makes the case stronger that a manufacturer cannot rely on other sources of warning unless these warning were in fact effective — that is, unless they make the harm so "obvious" that the manufacturer's warning would be entirely redundant.

E. CONSUMER PROTECTION LEGISLATION IN CANADA

1) Overview

a) Division of Powers

Section 91 of the *Constitution Act, 1867* grants jurisdiction to the federal government over, *inter alia*, trade and commerce, criminal law, banking, and weights and measures, as well as vesting it with a general authority to make laws for "peace, order and good government" of the country. These heads of power have supported federal consumer protection laws, most notably those dealing with safety of goods, labelling, banking, telecommunications, misleading advertising, and marketplace-competition rules.

Section 92 of the *Constitution Act* permits provincial legislation with respect to property and civil rights within the province (including laws respecting torts and contracts), the administration of justice within the province, and matters of a local or private nature. This has permitted the provinces to legislate consumer protection with respect to tort and negligence law generally, sale of goods and services, trade practices, warranties, licensing and regulation of businesses, some safety standards, and securities law.

---

200 *Buchan*, *supra* note 50, ctied to (1986), 25 D.L.R. (4th) 658 at 678 and 680 (C.A.).
201 *Ibid.*

b) Federal Legislation

There are several federal statutes that provide some elements of consumer protection in specific industry sectors or with respect to certain products, including foods and drugs,[202] textiles,[203] electricity and gas,[204] precious metals,[205] and radiation-emitting devices.[206] In addition, there are a host of federal statutes of a more general application, providing broader protections to consumers. The most significant of these is the *Competition Act*, which is administered by the Competition Bureau, Industry Canada. The *Competition Act* sets out a series of offences based on anti-competitive behaviour, in an effort "to provide consumers with competitive prices and product choices."[207] The Act also establishes laws regarding misleading advertising, false testimonials/representations, double ticketing, "pyramid" selling and multi-level marketing schemes, referrals,[208] "bait-and-switch" selling, and promotional contests.

The *Consumer Packaging and Labelling Act*,[209] administered by the Consumer Products Branch, sets out requirements for the packaging, labelling, sale, importation, and advertising of prepackaged and certain other products. The Act prohibits the sale, import, or advertising of such products that lack proper labels or packaging (as determined by regulation) or that display false or misleading representations. Related legislation, the *Weights and Measures Act*,[210] establishes requirements for numerical counts or metric unit of measurement of net quantity in packaged products to be contained in a declaration on a product label.

The *Hazardous Products Act*[211] governs the sale and importation of certain hazardous substances.[212] Dealing in such products under this Act is

---

202 *Food and Drug Act*, R.S.C. 1985, c. F-27; *Meat Inspection Act*, R.S.C. 1985, c. T-10; *Fish Inspection Act*, R.S.C. 1985, c. F-12.
203 *Textile Labelling Act*, R.S.C. 1985, c. T-10.
204 *Electricity and Gas Inspection Act*, R.S.C. 1985, c. E-4.
205 *Precious Metals Marking Act*, R.S.C. 1985, c. P-19.
206 *Radiation Emitting Devices Act*, R.S.C. 1985, c. R-1.
207 *Competition Act*, R.S.C. 1985, c. C-34, s. 1.1.
208 The Act's s. 56 (referral sales) permits such schemes where "licensed or otherwise permitted by or pursuant to an Act of the legislature of a province." The sections were found not to violate *Charter* equality rights based on province of residence: *R. v. CLP Canmarket Lifestyle Products Corp.*, [1988] 2 W.W.R. 170 (Man C.A.).
209 R.S.C. 1985, c. C-38.
210 R.S.C. 1985, c. W-6.
211 R.S.C. 1985, c. H-3.
212 In particular, those that are not otherwise regulated under the *Food and Drugs Act*, *Explosives Act*, R.S.C. 1985, c. E-17; *Pest Control Products Act*, R.S.C. 1985, c. P-9; or the *Nuclear Energy Act*, R.S.C. 1985, c. A-16.

either prohibited outright (Schedule I) or regulated (Schedule II). In the case of regulated substances, the Act sets out requirements for labelling.

c) Provincial Legislation

The provincial legislative schemes show varying degrees of uniformity. Statutes governing unfair trade practices are roughly uniform, laws of general application applying across the broad range of transactions. Other schemes of consumer protection vary widely. For instance, the various Consumer Protection Acts, such as that in Ontario,[213] while providing some broad consumer remedies regarding conditions and warranties, is in large part focused on cost-of-credit disclosure and direct sellers.

2) Unfair Trade Practices and Misleading Advertising

As noted, the federal *Competition Act*, in addition to addressing anti-competive practices, also contains prohibitions on misleading marketing activity. For instance, section 74.01 states:

> 74.01 (1) A person engages in reviewable conduct who, for the purpose of promoting, directly or indirectly, the supply or use of a product or for the purpose of promoting, directly or indirectly, any business interest, by any means whatever,
> (a) makes a representation to the public that is false or misleading in a material respect;
> (b) makes a representation to the public in the form of a statement, warranty or guarantee of the performance, efficacy or length of life of a product that is not based on an adequate and proper test thereof, the proof of which lies on the person making the representation; or
> (c) makes a representation to the public in a form that purports to be
>   (i) a warranty or guarantee of a product, or
>   (ii) a promise to replace, maintain or repair an article or any part thereof or to repeat or continue a service until it has achieved a specified result,
> if the form of purported warranty or guarantee or promise is materially misleading or if there is no reasonable prospect that it will be carried out.

However, the *Competition Act* provides a statutory civil remedy only with respect to offences relating to anti-competitive practices, not with respect to matters considered "reviewable" under part VII.1, like those above (unless the activity has been reviewed, found unlawful, and has contin-

---

213 *Consumer Protection Act*, R.S.O. 1990, c. C-31.

ued).[214] Consumers who have suffered loss as a result of such activities must seek their remedies at common law or under other legislation, although, of course, the statutory provisions in the *Competition Act* may assist in establishing a breach of duty in any particular case.

At present, eight provinces have enacted legislation prohibiting "unfair" business practices and misleading advertising, and these two areas have become the principal sources of product liability claims.

In Alberta, the *Unfair Trade Practices Act*[215] addresses misrepresentations regarding the attributes of a product or service offered. In addition, it explicitly prohibits a vendor from exerting undue pressure, taking advantage of the consumer's inability to understand, knowingly concealing a substantial defect, charging grossly unfair prices, and selling on credit while knowing that the consumer is unlikely to be able to pay in full.

In British Columbia and Newfoundland, the *Trade Practice Act*[216] and the *Trade Practices Act*[217] set out a list of deceptive or unfair trade practices and unconscionable acts or practices that are substantially the same as Alberta's, with the addition of two prohibitions: entering into a transaction knowing the consumer will not receive a substantial benefit; and entering into a transaction with such harsh and adverse terms so as to be inequitable to the consumer.

The *Business Practices Acts* in Ontario[218] and Prince Edward Island[219] similarly provide a list of acts and practices that are deemed to be unfair or unconscionable consumer representations. In Quebec's *Consumer Protection Act*,[220] the list of unfair business practices mirrors the kind of misrepresentations covered in the common law provinces but does not include the more general provisions aimed at unconscionable or inequitable bargains, aspects that may be more specifically addressed in the *Civil Code*.

Like Quebec's legislation, Manitoba's *Business Practices Act*[221] focuses on misrepresentations rather than unconscionability or inequity in bargains. Aside from its list of prohibited deceptive practices, the Act defines "unfair business practice" differently from other provinces, prohibiting a vendor from taking advantage of the fact that the consumer is "not in a position to protect the consumer's own interests."

---

214 *Competition Act, supra* note 207, s. 36.
215 R.S.A. 1980, c. U-3.
216 R.S.B.C. 1979, c. 406.
217 R.S.N. 1990, c. T-7.
218 R.S.O. 1990, c. B.18.
219 R.S.P.E.I. 1988, c. B-7.
220 R.S.Q., c P.-40.1, ss.215–53.
221 S.M. 1990–91, c.6.

In Saskatchewan, the *Consumer Protection Act*[222] is a comprehensive statute covering such matters as implied warranties, privity of contract, and consumer remedies, in addition to dealing with unfair practices. Unlike Manitoba's models but like that of most other provinces, the Act prohibits taking advantage of a consumer by way of one-sided agreements, setting prices excessively above market rates, or exerting undue pressure and influence.

Each of these statutes, either explicitly (through statutory rights of action) or implicitly (by establishing standards that provide evidence of standards of care at common law), can provide platforms for consumer actions, whether individually or in the aggregate.

3) Liability from Warranties and Implied Terms

As we described at the beginning of Part One, prior to the twentieth century, an action for breach of contract was the primary remedy for harms caused by defective products. Since there was no generalized tort of negligence, a consumer injured by a product or service would have to sue for breach of warranty to recover damages. The contract remedy was severely restricted by the need to establish a warranty, as well as by the requirement of "privity" — the need to demonstrate that there was a contractual relationship between the plaintiff and defendant. This requirement often barred remote third-party users from bringing an action for injuries suffered from products that they had not directly purchased, and also insulated manufacturers from suits by consumers (since the consumer had a contract with the vendor rather than the manufacturer). When the House of Lords replaced this narrow contractual basis of duty by the more expansive notion of "neighbourhood" or foreseeability in *Donoghue v. Stevenson*,[223] the law of negligence appeared essentially to swallow the law of contract whole for purposes of product liability actions.

Currently in Canada, the federal government has legislative control over interprovincial trade and commerce, which permits it to regulate various products. The federal government therefore sets safety standards for motor-vehicle manufacturers and regulates in the areas of food and drugs and hazardous products. Each of the Canadian provinces has legislative authority over local matters including the *Sale of Goods Act*, and warranty and consumer protection concerns. All of the provinces except Quebec have, to varying degrees, modelled their product liability legislation upon English law.

---

222 S.S. 1997, c. 30.1.
223 *Donoghue v. Stevenson, supra* note 8.

Section 14(2) of the English *Sale of Goods Act, 1893*,[224] which itself is a reflection of the English common law, reads as follows:

> 14(2): Where goods are bought by description from a seller who deals in goods of that description (whether he be the manufacturer or not), *there is an implied condition* that the goods shall be of merchantable quality; provided that if the buyer has examined the goods, there shall be no implied condition as regards defects which such examination ought to have revealed.

This provision has been adopted in many parts of the common law world, including the various provinces of Canada. Article 2 of the American *Uniform Commercial Code* also contains a similar term. This means that, in nearly all common law jurisdictions, there are long-established minimum requirements of quality in things sold that every buyer is entitled to expect, unless there is an express agreement to the contrary. Such standard may be read into almost every sale of goods made by a dealer in the common law world.

However, the association of warranty with reliance upon an implied promise has also led to the assumption that implied warranty cannot exist without a sale. Courts will often search for the existence of a contract, or limit the finding of breach of implied warranty to circumstances arising directly between buyer and seller. In our modern industrialized world, the association of implied warranty with the occurrence of a sale has resulted in the denial of justice for many injured parties. Where a defective product causes injury to a third party (not the actual purchaser), he or she may be denied the right to sue for breach of implied warranty and may be forced to meet the high burden of proving negligence. For example, in *Lyons v. Consumer Glass Co.*,[225] the infant plaintiff was injured by a bottle purchased by his mother, yet the court refused to extend the warranty to him because he was not a party to the contract. The court affirmed that privity of contract was required to found an action and that a remote consumer is not a "buyer" for the purposes of the *Sale of Goods Act*.

---

224 *Sale of Goods Act, 1893*, 56 and 57 Vic., c. 71 [emphasis added].
225 (1981), 28 B.C.L.R. 319 (S.C.).

4) The Sale of Goods Acts

a) Overview of the Legislation

Each common law province has enacted stand-alone legislation known as the "Sale of Goods Act,"[226] patterned on the English model discussed earlier, and some have further legislation setting out particular warranties.[227] While the details vary, the purpose of these statutes is to introduce (or in some cases to confirm) the warranties that accompany consumer transactions. The British Columbia *Sale of Goods Act* provides that there are no implied warranties or conditions as to the quality or fitness of goods, except in certain circumstances. Section 18 does offer some protection to the buyer who relies on the seller. It provides:

> ... where the buyer or lessee expressly or by implication makes it known to the seller or lessor of the particular purpose for which the goods are required, so as to show that the buyer or lessee relies on the seller's or lessor's skill or judgment, and the goods are of a description which it is in the course of the seller's or lessor's business to supply, whether he is the manufacturer or not, there is an implied condition that the goods are reasonably fit for such purpose; except that in the case of a contract for the sale or lease of a specified article under its patent or other trade name, there is no implied condition as to its fitness for any particular purpose.
>
> Where goods are bought by description ... there is an implied condition that the goods shall be of merchantable quality; but if the buyer or lessee has examined the goods there is no implied condition as regards defects which such examination ought to have revealed.

b) The Implied Warranty of Fitness for Particular Purpose

The "particular purpose" referred to in most Sale of Goods Acts does not mean "special purpose"; rather, it has been interpreted to apply to the ordinary purpose for which goods are normally used. A purchaser is not entitled to expect that the goods will be fit for any purpose, yet he or she may take comfort in knowing that the implied condition of fitness will extend to virtually all cases where goods are put to their "normal" everyday use, especially where there is only one use for the goods.

---

226 *Sale of Goods Act*, R.S.B.C. 1979, c. 370; *Sale of Goods Act*, R.S.A. 1980, c. S-2; *Sale of Goods Act*, S.S. 1978, c. S-1; *Sale of Goods Act*, R.S.M. 1987, c. S10; *Sale of Goods Act*, R.S.O. 1990, c. S.1; *Sale of Goods Act*, R.S.N.S. 1989, c. 408; *Sale of Goods Act*, R.S.N.B. 1973, c. S-1; *Sale of Goods Act*, R.S.P.E.I. 1988, c. S-1; *Sale of Goods Act*, R.S.N. 1990, c. S-6.

227 See, for instance, *Consumer Products Warranties Act*, S.S. 1978, c. C-30; *Consumer Product Warranty and Liability Act*, S.N.B. 1978, c. C-18.1.

In *Venus Electric Ltd. v. Brevel Products Ltd.*,[228] Dubin J.A. referred to what is stated in 77 Corp. Jur. Sec., 325, at 1178:

> A warranty of fitness has to do with the intrinsic qualities and characteristics of the property sold ... An implied warranty that goods are reasonably fit for the purpose must be reasonably construed in the light of common knowledge with respect to the nature of the article sold. While such warranty requires that goods be reasonably suited or fitted to the purpose for which sold, nothing further is required, and *it is not necessary, for example, that the article purchased be perfect or the best of its kind*, nor is there any implied warranty that the article is as suitable for the purpose as other articles of the same kind. *The warranty does not constitute an agreement that the goods can be used with absolute safety or that they are perfectly adapted to the intended use* ...

In *Lalese Enterprises v. Arete Tchnologies Inc.*,[229] it was found that, where the purchaser of a custom-designed computer system makes it known to the developer/vendor of the use to which it is intended to be put, even where the purchaser knows that the developer/vendor has never designed a retail computer software system before, the vendor is under an obligation to supply goods reasonably fit for the purpose intended. While the plaintiff in such circumstances is not entitled to receive a perfect computer system, entirely free from defects, if the system provided does not prove to be even reasonably operational, the purchaser is entitled to rescind the contract and to claim consequential damages.

The limitations of the "fitness" requirement were made particularly clear in the case of *Baker v. Suzuki Motor Co.*[230] In that case, discussed above, the plaintiff ("Baker") was seriously injured when the motorcycle manufactured by the defendant collided head-on with a truck and burst into flames. The resulting injuries left Baker painfully incapacitated, with the use of only one of his four limbs. Evidence revealed that the fire was caused by fuel leaking from the motorcycle and that the gasoline cap on the motorcycle had come off during impact. The court dismissed the plaintiff's claim against both the seller and the manufacturer on the basis that the motorcycle was reasonably fit for the purpose intended.

In writing for the majority, Bielby J. noted that "in Canada, the law does not impose strict liability on manufacturers of goods, so that they are liable

---

228 (1978), 19 O.R. (2d) 417 at 424 (C.A.) [emphasis added].
229 [1994] B.C.J. No. 1867 (S.C.).
230 *Baker, supra* note 110.

for all injuries caused by those goods, no matter what the circumstances." The law does not require manufacturers to create products that are foolproof or incapable of causing injury. The court found that, since Suzuki admitted to knowing that its motorcycles would leak fuel when subjected to certain forces, it clearly did not purport to manufacture motorcycles that would withstand the force of a high-impact, head-on collision. The motorcycle was therefore reasonably fit for the purpose intended, and accordingly, the court ruled out the plaintiff's claim for breach of implied warranty under contract.

With regard to the co-defendant seller, the court found that Baker had not relied upon the seller's skill and judgment. Baker had ridden motorcycles for most of his life and knew of the risks associated with them. He clearly knew what he wanted when he purchased the motorcycle and relied upon his own skill and judgment so as to not give rise to an implied warranty of fitness *vis-à-vis* the seller. This left Baker with the assertion that Suzuki had been negligent, notwithstanding that there had been no breach of contract. The court found that the plaintiff had no claim in negligence since there were no other reasonable choices available to the manufacturer at the time that the motorbike was designed to reduce the its risk to life and limb.

Given that the court in *Baker*[231] found that Suzuki did know about the danger that the gas cap might come off the gas tank during a high-impact collision, and given that motorcycles may reasonably be expected to be driven at the speed at which they become susceptible to high-impact collisions, one might argue that Baker had a strong argument to make that Suzuki had failed to warn him sufficiently of the risk(s) associated with the motorcycle.

However, in the *Lambert*[232] case, which we have discussed earlier, Laskin J. further pointed out that the manufacturer's duty may be "discharged" in circumstances where the injured plaintiff has "special knowledge" of the risk of injury. Such *"volenti"* negligence defence can be used if it can be established that the plaintiff knew of the risk of injury involved in using a less-than-perfect product and willingly assumed it. Similar reasoning was effectively used in the *Baker* case to dispense with the plaintiff's claim. There, the court concluded that

> ... [no] evidence was led to show that Baker would have declined to ride the motorcycle if he knew of the risk of this type of fire. He had ridden motorcycles for most of his adult life .... He also clearly knew that more risks were associated with riding motorcycles than with driving automo-

---

231 *Baker, ibid.*
232 *Lambert, supra* note 18 at 575.

biles. ... I find that he knew riding motorcycles was risky. If he had been told in advance that fires resulted from a small proportion of motorcycle collisions, I doubt that he would have been surprised. I accept that he would not have declined to ride this motorcycle because of that risk.[233]

The court's reasoning, and the absence of widely enforceable strict liability laws in Canada, might suggest that manufacturers of dangerous products need do little more than argue that they either did not intend to design a crash-worthy product or that the users of such products accepted the risk of danger in their use. These conclusions may be contrasted with negligence claims that have succeeded on the basis of "crashworthiness," which are discussed in the context of the defence of "intervening acts" in the next chapter.

In *Fording Coal Ltd. v. Harnischfeger Corp. of Canada Ltd.*,[234] the court examined an express warranty as to the fitness of a mining shovel sold by the respondent to the appellant. The parties had agreed that the express warranty would not override the warranties and conditions implied by the *Sale of Goods Act*. The respondent operated an open-pit coal mine at Elkford, British Columbia, and had previously purchased mining shovels from the appellant. Each shovel contained a large roller that was critical to its functioning. The respondent alleged that the roller supplied to it by the appellant contained a defect that had arisen during the manufacturing process. The result was that the roller lasted for only 25 percent of its anticipated lifespan, culminating in repair costs to the respondent of close to $400,000, in addition to other financial losses suffered during the thirty-two–day repair process.

At the time of purchase, the parties had negotiated a one-year express warranty agreement which, by the time the shovel was rendered inoperable five years later, had long expired. While the parties had expressly agreed that their contract would not override the *Sale of Goods Act*, the appellant submitted that, for the court to infer that the goods were still subject to a warranty of reasonable fitness, would be to impose upon the seller a commercially unreasonable obligation to guarantee that the goods be free from defect throughout their normal life expectancy.

At trial, Mr. Justice Macdonald concluded that the implied warranties and conditions in the *Sale of Goods Act* allocate the risk of an inherent defect to the seller. By having agreed to incorporate into their contract the

---

233 *Baker, supra* note 110 at para. 135.
234 (1990), 1 B.L.R. (2d) 313 (S.C.), aff'd (1991), 8 B.C.A.C. 250.

implied warranties contained in the *Sale of Goods Act*, the defendant was not permitted to limit the purchaser's protection to the terms of a long-expired express warranty. Notwithstanding that four years had passed since the expiration of the express warranty, the trial judge concluded that the goods were not durable for a reasonable period considering the nature of the article sold. The defendant was held liable for the cost of repairs to the shovel and for losses directly resulting from the shovel being inoperable during the repair period.

On appeal, Madam Justice Rowles upheld the trial judge's findings yet concluded that, while goods are expected to be reasonably suitable for the purpose for which they are sold, they are not required to be perfect:

> The defect rendered the roller susceptible to failure in a manner that could not be anticipated or ascertained by normal inspection. That failure was likely to occur within the roller's normal life span and hence while the shovel was in operation. The result of the failure was likely, therefore, to be catastrophic. That is enough to show that the roller, and hence the shovel which contained it, was not of merchantable quality. *The obligation that the shovel not contain an undetectable defect that will probably cause it to suffer catastrophic failure falls short of an obligation that it be "perfect" or "the best of its kind."* [Emphasis added.][235]

The purchaser also does not have to make "known to the seller" the exact manner in which he or she intends to use the goods. Where the buyer's purpose for using the goods is the manner in which the goods are normally used, there is no need for the purchaser to convey that intention to the seller. Courts will frequently find that the buyer relied on the fitness of the goods from the very fact of having purchased them. Furthermore, there is very little evidence required to establish that the buyer relied on the "skill or judgment" of the seller, particularly where the purchaser is unfamiliar with the product. The protection thus provided is meant to safeguard consumers from far more knowledgeable and savvy sellers against whom they have little bargaining power.

In *I.J. Manufacturing Ltd. v. Wolkowski*,[236] the plaintiff, I.J. Manufacturing, sold the defendant, Wolkowski, windows for a new house, payments for which were to be made in instalments. When the windows proved faulty, Wolkowski refused to pay the remaining $8,235 owing to the plaintiff. I.J. Manufacturing filed a builder's lien and then sued Wolkowski for

---

235 *Ibid.* at para. 28.
236 [1996] B.C.J. No. 2449 (S.C.).

the balance owing. Wolkowski brought a counter-claim in the amount of $56,436 for breach of contract. He alleged that the windows were not reasonably fit for use and that they did not meet industry standards because as ice and condensation had built up on their insides, they leaked, and they bore obvious scratches that could be attributed to faulty manufacturing.

The defendant asserted that the plaintiff had breached the implied conditions and warranties regarding quality, fitness, or durability set out in section 18 of the *Sale of Goods Act*. The plaintiff countered that, in order for these implied conditions to extend beyond what might reasonably be expected under contract, the purchaser must have made known to the seller any unusual expectations that he had of the product, and further, that the buyer must have specifically relied upon the seller's skill and knowledge.

The court rejected the plaintiff's argument and concluded that the defendant was entitled to the protection of the implied warranty notwithstanding that he had sought nothing exceptional. Wolkowski simply wanted windows that would perform for the purposes of residential home construction. He had shown the plans of his proposed residence to the plaintiff for the purpose of obtaining a price estimate for the work negotiated. Such was found to be sufficient evidence that he had communicated to the plaintiff his intended use for the goods sold.

The court further found that the plaintiff understood that people who purchased its windows were relying on its skill and judgment to ensure that they worked properly. That, taken together with the fact that plaintiff had failed to meet "The Canadian National Standard for Windows," adopted under the *British Columbia Building Code*,[237] was sufficient to establish that the plaintiff had breached the implied warranty and condition of reasonable fitness for purpose under section 18 of the *Sale of Goods Act*.

Damages were assessed on the basis of full replacement, pursuant to section 52 of the *Sale of Goods Act*, which included the cost of preparation, removal, and reinstallation, as well as a landscaping and clean-up allowance. Note, however, that where the buyer has more information about the product available to him or her than the seller, the court may decline to hold the seller liable on the basis that the purchaser did not in fact "rely" on the seller's skill or judgment. Such is also the case where the buyer puts the goods to extraordinary or exceptional use.

The Sale of Goods Acts further generally require that the goods be of a description that is in the course of the seller's business to supply. While the

---

237 *British Columbia Building Code* contained within the *Local Government Act*, R.S.B.C. 1996, c. 323.

buyer should not lose protection simply as a result of the seller entering into a new field of business or making a singular effort to supply goods outside his or her everyday field, such criteria have been used to deny a purchaser recovery notwithstanding that the buyer relied on the seller's skill and judgment.

In *Kordyban v. Windmill Orchards Ltd.*,[238] the plaintiff, Kordyban, was a medical doctor who decided that he would become a part-time orchardist although he had no experience in the orcharding business. He was introduced by a friend to the defendant, Boerboom, whom the friend considered to be an expert on apple orchards. Kordyban purchased a 5.5-acre parcel of an existing apple orchard across the street from Boerboom's orchards.

An arrangement was made between Kordyban and Boerboom whereby Boerboom would remove the existing apple trees and replant the orchard with new ones. When the project failed, Kordyban sued the defendant for breach of contract, negligence, and breach of section 18 of the *Sale of Goods Act*. One of Kordyban's complaints was that the posts required to support the apple trees and orchard-irrigation system were not pounded far enough into the ground, and therefore were not reasonably fit for their intended purpose.

The defendant admitted that he had made a mistake with regard to approximately 185 posts that supported the overhead irrigation system as well as the apple trees. He acknowledged that he should have used longer posts and pounded them another foot into the ground. Yet the plaintiff's claim of an implied condition of fitness with respect to the posts failed because there was no evidence that the defendant was ever in the business of selling posts. Such finding appears illogical when one considers that the defendant was clearly an expert in the business of apple orchards, that he had contracted with the plaintiff to establish an apple orchard on his behalf, and that the posts were essential to the formation and maintenance of a sound orchard.

The court allowed the plaintiff's claim of an implied condition of fitness with respect to defective apple trees on the basis that the defendant was in the business of selling apple trees. Yet, while the court accepted the defendant's testimony of his mistake with respect to the posts supporting the overhead irrigation system, Tysoe J. concluded that such constitutes only an admission that he did not exercise the requisite standard of care in installing the posts. The court's adoption of such a plain reading of the section is problematic. If the defendant is found to have ventured into a novel

---

238 [2000] B.C.J. No. 407 (S.C.).

or only partially related field, a plaintiff may risk not being able to recover even where the defendant has clearly committed a wrong. Moreover, it suggests that such defendants may be found liable only according to a much higher standard of care rather than that prevailing under a direct breach of contract with the plaintiff.

c) The Implied Condition of Merchantability

The phrase "goods bought by description" found in the *Sale of Goods Act* has been interpreted to mean all sales in the ordinary course of business from which there stems an express or implied description of the goods sold. The implied condition of merchantability applies to virtually every sale in the ordinary course of commerce. The corollary, of course, is the requirement of a sale and not some other type of contract, such as an agreement for the provision of services. The meaning of "merchantable quality" has proven difficult to define. Two frequently cited judicial interpretations include the following, from the Saskatchewan Court of Appeal: "'The phrase ... is, in my opinion, used as meaning that the article is of such quality and in such condition that a reasonable man acting reasonably would after a full examination accept it under the circumstances of the case in performance of his offer to buy that article, whether he buys for his own use or in order to sell again.'"[239] The court stated in *Grant v. Australian Knitting Mills Ltd.*: "Whatever else merchantable may mean, it does mean that the article sold, if only meant for one particular use in the ordinary course, is fit for that use."[240]

These two definitions suggest that the goods must have the appearance of resale value as well as be fit for their ordinary general use. A product that looks acceptable but harms its user is obviously not of merchantable quality. However, a second-hand or superficially damaged product that is scratched or torn may still be put to its ordinary use and therefore may not necessarily be viewed as unmerchantable.

The determination as to whether a good is of "merchantable quality" is therefore ultimately a question of fact. It will be up to the court to determine, within the context of each case, whether the plaintiff's claim is justifiable on one or several grounds. In *Gee v. White Spot Ltd.*,[241] the British Columbia Supreme Court found that a restaurant was liable under the *Sale*

---

239 *International Business Machines Co. Ltd. v. Scherban*, [1925] 1 W.W.R. 405 at 409 (Sask. C.A.) citing *Bristol Tramways & Carriage Co. v. Fiat Motors Ltd.*, [1910] 2 K.B. 831 at 841. Note that this definition must be read in consideration with Lord Wright's finding in *Grant v. Australian Knitting Mills Ltd.*, [1936] A.C. 85 (P.C.) that goods are not merchantable simply because they look acceptable.
240 *Ibid.* at 99.
241 (1986), 7 B.C.L.R. (2d) 235 (S.C.).

of Goods Act to a customer who contracted botulism poisoning following consumption of a meal purchased at the defendant restaurant. In so finding, the court acknowledged that the purchase of a meal in a restaurant was a contract for the sale of goods under section 18 of the *Sale of Goods Act* rather than a contract for the provision of services. The court noted that "an item on a menu offered for a fixed price is an offering of a finished product and is primarily an offering of the sale of a good or goods and not primarily an offering of a sale of services."[242] From such finding, the court concluded that there is an implied warranty, in cases involving food purchased in restaurants, that the food supplied is reasonably fit for human consumption and therefore of merchantable quality.

In contrast, in *Wharton v. Tom Harris Chevrolet Oldsmobile Cadillac Ltd.*,[243] the court concluded that a whine in the stereo system of a new car will not render it of "non-merchantable quality" under the *Sale of Goods Act*, although the purchaser may be entitled to general damages for the inconvenience of trying to have the problem fixed. In that case, the plaintiff's husband had purchased a new Cadillac car for her. Shortly after delivery, the plaintiff detected a buzzing noise coming from the stereo speakers that appeared to increase with acceleration of the car. In an effort to have the problem rectified, the plaintiff made twenty-six trips over a two-and-a-half-year period, on a 400-km round-trip journey from the remote town where she lived to the Tom Harris Chevrolet Oldsmobile Cadillac car dealership in Nanaimo, British Columbia. While the problem was ultimately corrected and the car sold, the plaintiff sued both the dealership (which was not the same dealer from whom the vehicle had been purchased) as well as the manufacturer, General Motors of Canada Ltd. (the "defendants"), for the difference between the purchase price of the Cadillac of $62,714.40, minus the sale price of $31,000.00, plus special damages for travel to and from Nanaimo and hotel accommodation.

The court found that the vehicle was not rendered "unmerchantable" because of the sound problem since it provided reasonable and reliable transportation throughout the period that the plaintiff owned it. However, the defendants were found to have been negligent with respect to the long delays to effect a repair. While the failure of the sound system dealt with only one aspect of the operation of the vehicle, the court further found that the plaintiff could be compensated under an implied warranty that the sound system within the vehicle would operate properly. Such result is sur-

---

242 *Ibid.* at para. 15.
243 [2002] B.C.J. No. 233 (C.A.).

prising considering that it was the plaintiff's husband, and not the plaintiff, who purchased the vehicle from a dealer in California. While the court does not address this point, one wonders how the court could have concluded that there was an implied warranty of merchantability concerning the sound system with regard to the two defendants in question when the plaintiff had not directly contracted with either one at the point of purchase and sale in relation to the stereo's fitness.

Under the circumstances, relaxing the doctrine of privity of contract seems appropriate; yet if intended this would be a sufficiently important development to merit express judicial analysis.

In *Farmer v. Interbake Foods Ltd.*,[244] it was found that a manufacturer could be held liable to a consumer for both breach of implied warranty of fitness under the *Sale of Goods Act* and for negligence. In that case, the plaintiff was rendered physically and mentally ill after consuming several cookies, manufactured by the defendant, which were later discovered to have been infested with maggots. The plaintiff consumed the biscuits in a dimly lit room and was unable to detect the presence of maggots until his daughter later discovered them (after the plaintiff had been rendered ill by their consumption). The court found that the manufacturer was liable to the plaintiff in contract under the *Sale of Goods Act* in addition to its liability for failure to discharge the tort law duty that it owed to the plaintiff at common law.

When products are unmerchantable pursuant to the statutory warranties, plaintiffs frequently seek simultaneous relief against the manufacturer in negligence. The way manufacturers deal with problems communicated to them through the supply chain can affect their liability in such cases. In *Strandquist v. Coneco Equipment*,[245] four unrelated companies ("the plaintiffs") purchased a piece of logging equipment known as a feller-buncher from a merchant, Coneco Equipment ("Coneco"). The machines all required a great deal more cleaning than had been recommended by the manufacturer in order to offset the high risk of fire outbreak owing to the unusually excessive amount of debris build-up and oil leakage during operation. Notwithstanding that the plaintiffs all followed meticulous cleaning schedules, each of the machines caught fire during operation and were all eventually destroyed.

The plaintiffs sued both the manufacturer, Timberjack Inc., and the vendor, Coneco. The vendor was found liable to the plaintiffs for breach of

---

244 (1982), 49 N.S.R. (2d) 111 (S.C.T.D.).
245 (1996), 45 Alta. L.R. (3d) 272 (Q.B.), aff'd [1999] A.J. No. 1438 (C.A.).

implied warranty of merchantability under the *Sale of Goods Act*, on the basis that it had become aware that the machines required far more maintenance work than any other machine it sold. Both Timberjack Inc. and Coneco were in constant communication regarding warranty problems. Notwithstanding that Coneco was entitled to rely upon the manufacturer to test the machines and to ensure that they did not pose a fire hazard, the court found that Coneco continued to sell the machines knowing of the problems that they presented. The manufacturer was found liable to the plaintiffs for negligently manufacturing a machine that it knew or ought to have known presented a dangerous fire hazard.

Similarly, in *McMorran v. Dominion Stores Ltd.*,[246] the plaintiff bought a carbonated soft drink that had been manufactured by the defendant manufacturer and that had been sold to him by the defendant retailer. When the plaintiff opened the bottle, the crown was launched upwards and injured the plaintiff in the eye. The plaintiff succeeded against the vendor for breach of implied warranty of fitness under the *Sale of Goods Act*.

Because the defect in the product was present when the plaintiff purchased the bottle from the vendor, the plaintiff also succeeded in establishing that the injury was caused by the negligence of the manufacturer. The vendor was entitled to indemnity from the manufacturer based on breach of contract, which the court found to be "implied where one defendant is exposed to liability without any fault of his own by the negligent act of the co-defendant, unless the act is clearly illegal in itself."

The common law courts have further determined that price is not a conclusive factor in determining merchantability. If goods are sold at a price that is so low that it does not even remotely compare to their ordinary retail value, one might assume that the goods are not merchantable. However, small differences in price are not necessarily to be taken as any indication of the merchantable quality of the product. Where goods are sold at a reduced price, that is not necessarily an indication that they are unmerchantable, nor is it a viable excuse for the seller to claim that the provision of an unmerchantable product at a low price somehow justifies or even necessarily communicates to the consumer that they are unfit for their ordinary use and essential prupose.

Section 18 of the British Columbia *Sale of Goods Act* further provides that there is no implied warranty concerning defects that an examination by the buyer ought to have revealed. The effect of this provision has been

---

246 (1977), 14 O.R. (2d) 559 (H.C.J.).

to provide protection to buyers who make either no examination of the product at all or merely a superficial examination, but not to those who carefully assess the goods before purchase. In many cases, an examination can reveal little to the average consumer who inspects the product and is simply not able to assess its merchantability. A consumer who purchases a used vehicle, for example, may not be able to determine simply by looking under to hood whether the engine is in good order.

Many factors, such as a lack of knowledge, skill, experience, or simple oversight, may contribute to the consumer's inability to detect an "apparent" defect in a product. Would the consumer be better off purchasing the product without making such cursory inspection and take the risk that he or she may ultimately be injured by it? Or is it better that the buyer examine the product and risk that his or her own unskilled assessment may result in the loss of the benefit of the warranty? In either case, it would appear that the section operates unfairly against purchasers.

A related point concerning prejudice against the purchaser is that recent case law has indicated that the law of implied warranty will not apply if the purchase is made in the course of a private sale. In *Witherell v. Buchanan Estate*,[247] the defendant placed a car for sale on a used car lot. The plaintiff was told that the car he purchased was not a used car and that it was being sold on an "as is" basis. The plaintiff had test-driven the car on two separate occasions and had been advised by the defendant to have it inspected by his own mechanic. Since the plaintiff's mechanic was unavailable, the plaintiff went ahead and bought the car without having it inspected. When the car broke down within the following ten days, the plaintiff brought an action for damages against the seller. The New Brunswick Court of Appeal found that, under the *Consumer Product Warranty and Liability Act*[248] in that province, the defendant was not a "distributor" within the meaning of the *Consumer Product Act* (which is similar to the *Sale of Goods Act* requirement that the defendant be "in the business" of supplying or manufacturing the product at issue). The sale was merely a private sale for which there was no express or implied warranty. The plaintiff was found to have assumed all risk for the vehicle's reliability at the point of purchase.

A final relevant point to a discussion of implied warranty of fitness and merchantability is that clear and direct language is required in order for parties to contract out of the statutory protection of the *Sale of Goods Act*. In

---

247 (1995), 169 N.B.R. (2d) 14 (C.A.).
248 S.N.B. 1978, c. 18.1, ss. 1(1), 12 [hereinafter *Consumer Product Act*].

Queen Charlotte Lodge Ltd. v. Hiway Refrigeration Ltd.,[249] the plaintiff purchased a used refrigeration unit from the defendant Hiway Refrigeration Ltd. to transport frozen goods to the plaintiff's fishing lodge in the Queen Charlotte Islands. While in transit from Vancouver to the Queen Charlotte Islands, the refrigeration unit ceased functioning and most of the frozen goods were spoiled and had to be discarded by the plaintiff. The plaintiff claimed, and the court agreed, that section 18 of the British Columbia *Sale of Goods Act* imposed an implied condition upon the sale that the refrigeration unit would be reasonably fit for the particular purpose made known to the seller by the buyer. It was further found that the plaintiff relied on the defendant's skill or judgment in the selling of such units.

However, a central issue was that the words "NO WARRANTY" in quotation marks were written on the invoice that the defendant provided to the plaintiff. The defendant argued that such words were sufficient to permit it to contract out of the implied warranty provisions contained in the Act. The court concluded that, although section 20(2) of the *Sale of Goods Act* permits the contracting out of section 18 in the case of used goods, such intention must be made very clear. The court rejected the defendant's argument that small businesses would be prejudiced by having to include more expansive language within their sale documents and concluded that "it is possible to find clear and simple language that makes the seller's position clear but does not leave the buyer at a distinct disadvantage."

d) Privity of Contract

The remedy for breach of implied warranty is limited to buyers. Canadian and English law requires that a contract exist between the seller and buyer in order for liability to be found. When damages for breach of warranty are claimed for consequential losses, which are often sought by persons other than the buyer, difficulties can arise. Defective goods typically cause injury not only to the buyer but to the buyer's family, acquaintances, neighbours, or anyone else within enough proximity to the defective product to be affected by it. Limiting recovery to the buyer suggests that a vast number of individuals harmed by defective products will be denied compensation for their injuries.

In the classic case of *Buckley v. Lever Bros.*,[250] the plaintiff mailed in two soap box lids to the defendant to obtain a "special offer" consisting of an apron and twelve clothespins. One of the clothespins broke and blinded the

---

249 [1998] B.C.J. No 13 (S.C.) [in Chambers].
250 [1953] 4 D.L.R. 16 (Ont. H.C.J.).

plaintiff in one eye. Since the terms of the offer had required her to send in fifty cents along with the soap box tops, the plaintiff was able to establish that a contract existed and hence that a breach of implied warranty had occurred under the *Sale of Goods Act*.

Yet a careful reading of the court's decision suggests that the result would have been different had the plaintiff not been required to remit some monetary value for the defective product. If the clothespins had been offered as part of an entirely gratuitous promotional gimmick, the plaintiff may not have been able to bring the case within the context of a sale and thereby may not have succeeded on the grounds of breach of implied warranty. However, regardless of whether the fifty cents were remitted or not, the result is the same: a detective product was put into the stream of commerce by the defendant, causing injury to the plaintiff. Moreover, had one of the plaintiff's family members, or an innocent bystander, been similarly injured by the defective product, they would not have been able to claim against the defendant for breach of implied warranty since the law of product liability limits recovery to those plaintiffs who have directly contracted with the defendant.

In *Sigurdson v. Hillcrest Services Ltd.*,[251] for example, the driver of a car succeeded against the seller of a defective brake hose, but the driver's wife and children, who were also passengers of the car at the time of the accident, were prevented from recovering. While such injured persons might have had a remedy against the manufacturer of the defective products in negligence, that remedy would have been valueless if the manufacturer were insolvent, absent from the jurisdiction, or otherwise unknown. In *Trueman v. Maritime Auto and Trailer Sales Ltd.*,[252] the plaintiff purchased a mobile home from a dealer. The plaintiff received a warranty card from the manufacturer that was required to be signed and returned to the manufacturer by the plaintiff to become effective. The plaintiff failed to return the card. The trailer subsequently suffered from moisture and condensation problems; however, the manufacturer offered a solution to the plaintiff. The plaintiff rejected the manufacturer's suggestions and brought a claim against the manufacturer for recission.

The New Brunswick Court of Appeal rejected the plaintiff's claim on the grounds that there was no privity of contract between the buyer and manufacturer, except for the manufacturer's express warranty. Given that the plaintiff had failed to comply with the terms of the warranty card, in

---

251 [1977] 1 W.W.R. 740.
252 (1977), 19 N.B.R. (2d) 8 (C.A.).

failing to return it to the manufacturer, the plaintiff was not able to establish that a contract between herself and the manufacturer had come into existence. Such reasoning suggests that it will be especially difficult for injured plaintiffs to establish privity of contract between themselves and manufacturers (where there is an intermediary dealer involved) in cases where an express warranty has not been accepted or complied with. This case further begs the question of whether a third party who was not the actual purchaser of the product would have had any chance of success at all *vis-à-vis* the manufacturer. While the issue of implied warranty was not addressed on these facts, the fact that both the trial division and appeal courts were quick to find the absence of a contract suggests that a wide number of plaintiffs will have a difficult time pleading breach of contract or breach of warranty against manufacturers in cases such as these.

5) Special Rules for the Production and Dissemination of Defective Medical Products

An interesting and often litigated area where problems concerning privity frequently arise is that of implied warranties and defective health-care products. When defective medical products are distributed by medical practitioners, the question becomes one of establishing liability (as between doctor and/or manufacturer) and affording adequate compensation. Two related issues are frequently raised in such cases: the duty to warn and the implied warranty of fitness for purpose.

As we have explained previously in this chapter, a manufacturer has a duty to warn consumers (by disseminating product information to those in the best position to digest and distribute knowledge that can prevent harm, such as doctors and other medical professionals) of the risks and dangers inherent in the use of a product. The doctor also has a duty to warn patients of the risks inherent in a given medical procedure. Failure to observe such requirements may expose both the doctor and manufacturer of defective medical products to liability in negligence. Another possible outcome is that the injured party seeks to hold either the doctor or manufacturer liable for breach of implied warranty at common law or under the *Sale of Goods Act*.

a) Breach of Implied Warranty and Privity of Contract in the Medical Context

Problems with an attempt to establish breach of implied warranty at common law are evident when the victim-patient tries to demonstrate privity of contract between him- or herself and the manufacturer and finds that the chain of distribution was fatally disturbed when the doctor provided or administered the defective product. Such is highly problematic given that frequently the patient is able to acquire the product only through his or her physician. The recent case of *Hollis v. Birch*[253] provides a good example of how this chain of distribution works to thwart what might otherwise be a successful product liability lawsuit.

In that case, the plaintiff, Ms. Hollis ("Hollis"), received defective breast implants from her physician, Dr. Birch. The plaintiff made a claim against Dr. Birch under the British Columbia *Sale of Goods Act* on the grounds that she and Dr. Birch had entered into contract and that he had failed to provide her with implants that were reasonably fit for their intended purpose. The trial judge found that no contract existed between Hollis and her physician with respect to the implants on the grounds that there was no intent to enter into contract and no consideration provided. In the alternative, the trial judge found that no contract of the sort involved in this case was contemplated in the *Sale of Goods Act*. Hollis succeeded against Dow Corning Corporation ("Dow") for negligent manufacture of a breast implant that ruptured within seventeen months of being implanted. The plaintiff's claim against Dr. Birch was dismissed.

With regard to the trial court's finding that there was no contract between Hollis and her physician, the agreement to undergo complex and often painful medical treatment, for which there are inherent risks involved, should constitute ample consideration at common law. In *Goldthorpe v. Logan*,[254] the Ontario Court of Appeal found that submission to treatment may constitute valid consideration for the formation of a contract at common law. In that case, the court awarded damages in contract (yet did not find liability in negligence) to a plaintiff who had undergone electrolysis treatments that had been advertised by the defendant. The court found that "[t]hese parties had a common intention, and there was good consideration present. It was constituted by the detriment or inconvenience sustained by the female plaintiff. Her submission to the treatments, in accordance with the advertisements, was a benefit sought by the advertiser."

The plaintiff in Hollis did ultimately prevail in the Court of Appeal and Supreme Court of Canada on the basis that the defendant manufacturer had failed properly to warn her of the risks. However, absent this, she would not have succeeded against either the manufacturer or doctor in contract.

---

253 *Hollis, supra* note 46.
254 [1943] 2 D.L.R. 519 (Ont. C.A.).

With regard to the issue of implied warranty of fitness under section 18 of the *Sale of Goods Act*, the court agreed with the finding of the trial judge that the provisions of the *Medical Service Act*[255] and the nature of the agreement between Hollis and Dr. Birch suggest that the parties did not enter into a contractual relationship, in part because the procedure was covered by the provincially funded Medical Services Plan.

If Hollis had been able to purchase the implants directly from the manufacturer, and use them for their intended purpose, she may have had a greater claim to breach of implied warranty. Yet, because she was able to purchase them only through her physician, and since she was required to have them implanted by her physician, the chain of distribution was not sufficient to establish a direct link between the manufacturer and the defective product.

b) Statutory Warranties and Privity Problems

Contracts that are primarily for the provision of medical services will generally not fall within the requirements of implied warranty under the *Sale of Goods Act*. The *Sale of Goods Act* applies only to sale transactions that primarily concern the provision of goods under contract. However, where defective goods are supplied by some means other than a sale, the injured party should not be faced with a broad application of *caveat emptor* and barred from recovery merely because he or she was supplied with the harmful product after the point of sale. Surely, in such a case, the plaintiff's injuries are causally connected to the sale of the defective product and the party who ultimately distributes them should be liable.

However, the courts have developed a body of case law that distinguishes between contracts for sale and contracts for services, primarily limiting the application of the *Sale of Goods Act* to loss caused by defective products supplied under a contract of sale. Liability for the provision of defective services has long been found to require proof of negligence. In *Greaves & Co. Contractors v. Baynham, Mickle & Partners*,[256] Lord Denning concluded that "[t]he law does not usually imply a warranty that [a supplier of services] will achieve the desired result, but only a term that he will use reasonable care and skill. The surgeon does not warrant that he will cure the patient. Nor does the solicitor warrant that he will win the case."

Where defective goods are supplied in the process of performing a contract for the provision of medical services, the courts have consistently held that no liability under the *Sale of Goods Act* may arise. This is based essen-

---

255 R.S.B.C. 1979, c. 255.
256 [1975] 3 All E.R. 99 at 103–4 (C.A.).

tially on policy. Liability in contract law (for breach of warranty) is strict in the sense that no matter how much care has ben exercised, if goods covered by a warranty are not "fit" or merchantable, the supplier is liable. Courts are reluctant to extent the reach of strict liability to medical practitioners who may supply those "goods" in the course of providing complex medical service. One argument supporting such an approach is that the medical practitioner is merely an intermediary figure who cannot be expected to be responsible for each and every possible product defect occasioned by the manufacturer. Should it be the responsibility of the doctor to examine thoroughly each product before he or she supplies it to the patient? What about products containing defects that cannot be detected by ordinary means? Why should medical practitioners be held liable for defective products that they themselves did not create and that they genuinely believed, relying upon the representations of the manufacturer, to be free from harm?

A leading American case on this subject is *Perlmutter v. Beth David Hospital*,[257] where the plaintiff brought an action to recover damages for injuries sustained as a result of undergoing a blood transfusion in the defendant hospital. The plaintiff did not advance a claim under negligence but sought to recover only for breach of warranty of reasonable fitness and quality under New York's *Sales Act*. The plaintiff's claim therefore turned on whether the supply of blood constituted a "sale" within the meaning of the Act.

The court held that the contract between the plaintiff and the hospital was clearly one for services, the essence of which was that the patient had bargained for, and the hospital had agreed to make available, "the human skill and physical materiel [sic] of medical science to the end that the patient's health be restored." The supply of blood was merely incidental to the provision of service by the hospital. The court noted that, while "certain items of medical material" may pass from the hospital to the patient during the course of medical services, such is not sufficient to make such transaction a sale; moreover, not every transfer of personal property amounts to a sale. Fauld J., writing for the majority, stated:

> ... It has long been recognized that, when service predominates, and transfer of personal property is but an incidental feature of the transaction, the transaction is not deemed a sale within the *Sales Act*.
>
> ...
>
> If, however, the court were to stamp as a sale the supplying of blood — or the furnishing of other medical aid — *it would mean that the hospi-*

---

[257] 308 N.Y. 100 (C.A. 1954) [hereinafter *Perlmutter*].

tal, no matter how careful, no matter that the disease-producing potential in the blood could not possibly be discovered, would be held responsible, virtually as an insurer, if anything were to happen to the patient as a result of "bad" blood .... [T]he fact is that, *if the transaction were to be deemed a sale, liability would attach irrespective of negligence or other fault.* The art of healing frequently calls for a balancing of risks and dangers to a patient. Consequently, *if injury results from the course adopted, where no negligence or fault is present, liability should not be imposed upon the institution or agency actually seeking to save or otherwise assist the patient.* [Emphasis added.][258]

Given that the primary nature of the agreement between the hospital and the plaintiff was for the provision of medical treatment and other related services, from which the receipt of blood through transfusion was only a minor part, the plaintiff was unable to establish a cause of action for breach of implied warranty under the *Sales Act*.

Perhaps the medical practitioner's function is merely to advise his or her patients of the inherent risks of accepting medical products and treatment and to perform medical service(s) with utmost responsibility and care. To hold all medical practitioners liable in contract for the products that they supply to patients in the course of their business invites numerous policy considerations of remoteness, foreseeability, acceptance of risk, and to what extent the "parties" to contract consented to be bound.

However, to limit a plaintiff's recovery for injuries caused by a clearly defective product on the basis that the medical practitioner was not negligent or reckless in its provision, and that the patient did not directly "contract" with the manufacturer at the point of sale (assuming that, if he or she had in fact purchased the product him- or herself directly from the manufacturer, such issues of liability would not arise), does deprive highly deserving injured persons of a remedy. If the medical practitioner is able to deny liability on the basis of a finding that he or she was not negligent or reckless in the provision of the product and the manufacturer is able to deny liability on the basis that the injured party did not contract with it, who will compensate the plaintiff for the harm suffered? In *ter Neuzen v. Korn*,[259] for example, the plaintiff was infected with HIV after participating in an artificial-insemination program. The Supreme Court of Canada ultimately held that the agreement between the doctor and patient for the supply of the defective semen did not fall within the scope of the *Sale of Goods Act*, or breach of implied warranty at common law, since the "contract" con-

---

258 *Ibid.* at 104, 106.
259 (1995), 127 D.L.R. (4th) 577 (S.C.C.) [hereinafter *ter Neuzen*].

cerned the provision of medical services and was not primarily concerned with the sale of goods (i.e., semen).

We would ask whether the non-contractual approach to medical issues should be as absolute as it seems.

An agreement for the supply of semen is far more akin to a contract of sale than a vast number of other "contracts" in medical-related product liability cases. Consider the *Perlmutter*[260] case above, where a plaintiff became ill and was sent to hospital seeking treatment. At that point, one could safely assume that the patient had at best only a vague idea what medical procedures would be performed in an effort to affect a treatment or cure. In such a case, the patient is clearly seeking the provision of medical services and has little or no idea of the manner in which they will be performed. Should certain medical goods be supplied to the plaintiff in the course of such treatment, including the provision of blood through transfusion, they would clearly be incidental to the patient's main undertaking with the hospital, which is the performance of medical services.

In *ter Neuzen v. Korn*,[261] however, Ms. ter Neuzen contracted with a specific doctor to have his nurses obtain semen from an anonymous donor and transport it quickly back to his offices where it was implanted within her. She went to Dr. Korn for the purchase of a particular product, human semen, of which the provision of services through implant was an important, but not exclusive, part. This is reinforced by the fact that, while Ms. ter Neuzen could have obtained semen directly from any other willing donor, she specifically sought to purchase it from Dr. Korn who also had the means to implant it within her in order to achieve the desired effect.

Therefore, she privately sought out and personally paid Dr. Korn for the semen obtained through his office in manner of the sale of a good. This aspect of the "contract" was akin to a commercial transaction where a particular product was obtained and sold to a willing purchaser for a particular price. A secondary aspect of the arrangement was the insemination, the cost of which was paid for by Ms. ter Neuzen's publically funded medical services plan. Nonetheless, both the trial court jury, and subsequently the Court of Appeal and Supreme Court of Canada found that the contract between the parties was primarily for the provision of services, and not for the sale of goods. This suggests that plaintiffs who are supplied defective products in the context of medical cases will have an extremely difficult time recovering against the medical professionals who ultimately provide the products to them.

---

260 *Perlmutter, supra* note 257.
261 *ter Neuzen, supra* note 259.

With regard to whether a common law warranty existed, the trial judge instructed the jury that there are common law conditions and warranties that exist outside the *Sale of Goods Act*. But these amount to the same thing as a claim in negligence. The Court of Appeal concluded that, under the common law warranty, a contract for the sale of medical services merely requires that a physician meet the standards of a reasonably competent person practising in his field and does not imply that he warrants that the services will be effective. The Court of Appeal drew upon Bouck J.'s reasoning in *Hollis*,[262] where he concluded that "[a]bsent any negligence on the part of the medial practitioner, it would be unreasonable for the law to hold the doctor to the strict warranty that the blood or prosthesis are of good quality and reasonably fit for the purpose for which they were intended."

The Supreme Court of Canada held in the *ter Neuzen*[263] case that the common law doctrine of implied warranty is inapplicable to biological products used in medical procedures because they carry intrinsic risks that cannot necessarily be detected through the use of reasonable care. Sopinka J. found that the same policy considerations that apply to the *Sale of Goods Act* are found under the common law doctrine of implied warranty. More specifically, the doctrine of implied warranty under either the common law or *Sale of Goods* legislation cannot be applied in the provision of medical services since that would mean that "a medical practitioner would be held strictly liable for the biological products employed in the medical procedures, notwithstanding that it would be impossible for the doctor to detect any risks." Such would overlook the essential point, expressed by Sopinka J., that "different considerations"[264] apply in the context of the medical profession than apply in the everyday commercial context.

Yet the inability of a seller or supplier to detect hidden flaws or dangers in a product does not normally exclude the assertion of implied warranty for fitness of purpose. A party is entitled to hold a vendor liable for the sale of a defective product produced by a negligent manufacturer. Why should it be only in cases concerning the medical profession that injured parties are denied recourse against those who provide defective products to them? From the plaintiff's perspective, the question of knowledge should largely be considered irrelevant. In the context of Canada's publicly funded health care system, there is a further barrier to such contractual claims.

The *Sale of Goods Act* applies only to sale transactions — if a defendant makes a gift of goods to the plaintiff, the law may provide no remedy for the

---

262 *Hollis, supra* note 46 at para. 87.
263 *ter Neuzen, supra* note 259.
264 *Ibid.* at 607.

receipt of goods that turn out to be of a lesser standard than the donor described. However, as long as our courts continue to require a contract between the plaintiff and the defendant in order to establish liability for breach of implied warranty, plaintiffs in receipt of defective medical products will continue to face an inordinately high burden in proving their cases.

With our publicly funded medicare system, one might wonder whether patients could ever be construed as entering into a contract of sale with suppliers of medical products. Should such suppliers be immune from the consequences of implied warranties of fitness simply because a doctor is interposed between them and the end user?

F. STRICT LIABILITY

1) Strict Liability in the United States

As the legal approaches in the United States and Canada are somewhat analogous, Canadian courts often turn to U.S. jurisprudence for guidance and as a comparative reference point in order to analyze the current state of Canadian law. As such, developments in U.S. case law and legal theories, while not always adopted in Canada, are nonetheless persuasive and influential. The realm of products liability is laden with clear parallels in the way the Canadian and American courts have implemented their laws and policies; however, notable distinctions still exist between the two. In light of this, it is important that one not hold an insular view of products liability and embrace an analysis of U.S. law. With the volume of products liability cases in the U.S. far exceeding that in Canada and the U.S. being a basis for pioneering litigation in the field, this section of the book encourages the reader to keep abreast of the comparative differences that will increasingly have an impact on Canadian courts.

In the United States, liability for *manufacturing defects* (as opposed to design defects) is said to be "strict." An injured consumer needs to prove only that the injury was caused by a defective product (i.e. a product that deviated from the manufacturer's usual specifications due to an error in the manufacturing process) in order to recover. The consumer need not establish that the defect in the manufacturing process was caused by carelessness or negligence. This is strict liability. There have been occasional suggestions that strict liability be extended to design defects as well as manufacturing defects. The theory is that the design of some products should be considered defective *per se*. As we have discussed earlier, this theory has made some headway but is certainly not "mainstream" law in the U.S.

Strict liability in the U.S. derives from both tort and contract. In contract law (in Canada and the U.S.), liability for breach of condition and warranty is "strict" in the sense that if the goods are unfit or unmerchantable, it is no defence that the vendor used reasonable care. But because of the rules of privity of contract, that liability only exists as between parties to a contract (e.g. between a seller and a buyer) and does not protect third party users of products, or create a liability by a manufacturer (as opposed to a vendor) to the ultimate consumer. However, in the U.S. privity rules have been substantially relaxed in many states. Therefore, unlike the situation in Canada, U.S. consumers can frequently rely on contractual strict liability in actions against manufacturers and others with whom they do not obviously have a contract. A landmark 1960 decision of the Supreme Court of New Jersey illustrates how the law rapidly evolved from a general preference for warranty law into a widespread acceptance of strict liability. In *Henningsen v. Bloomfield Motors, Inc.*,[265] Mr. Henningsen purchased a Chrysler car from a dealer in Bloomfield. One day, while Mrs. Henningsen was driving it, the car suddenly turned sharply to the right and hit a wall. An action was brought by Mrs. Henningsen against both the manufacturer and dealer. The court found both the defendants liable, without any requirement for negligence or privity of contract. In so concluding, the court noted that:

> [T]he burden of losses consequent upon the use of defective articles is borne by those who are in a position to either control the danger or make an equitable distribution of the losses when they do occur.
>
> ...
>
> Accordingly, we hold that under modern marketing conditions, when a manufacturer puts a new automobile into the stream of trade and promotes its purchase by the public, an implied warranty that it is reasonably suitable for use as such accompanies it into the hands of the ultimate purchaser. Absence of agency between the manufacturer and the dealer who makes the ultimate sale is immaterial.

While the idea that manufacturers could be held liable to those other than their immediate vendors had been viewed as dangerous and radical, it quickly spread throughout the United States, such that by the early 1960s it had become widely accepted in virtually every American jurisdiction.

At the same time, the law of torts had been moving substantially towards a strict liability approach in product defect cases. In an early Cali-

---

265 161 A.2d. 69 at 81 and 84 (N.J. 1960).

fornia case, *Escola v. Coca Cola*,[266] where the plaintiff had been injured by an exploding bottle, the Supreme Court of California held that she could recover on the basis of a strong inference that the defect was caused by negligence (relying on the doctrine of *res ipsa loquitor*). Justice Traynor went even further and stated that

> In my opinion it should now be recognized that a manufacturer incurs an absolute liability when an article that he has placed on the market, knowing that it is to be used without inspection, proves to have a defect that causes injury to human beings .... Even if there is no negligence, however, public policy demands that the responsibility be fixed wherever it will most effectively reduce the hazards to life and health inherent in defective products that reach the market.[267]

In the later case of *Greenman v. Yuba Power Products Inc.*,[268] in which a plaintiff was injured from the use of a power tool, Justice Traynor, writing for a unanimous majority of the California Supreme Court, held that California would from then on decide products liability cases under a system of strict liability in tort.

These developments served as the basis for s. 402A of the *Restatement (Second) of Torts*, which the American Law Institute formally adopted one year later. The *Restatement* approach provides that a seller will be held liable for the sale of "any product in a defective condition unreasonably dangerous to the consumer." The standard used to define "defect" is that established by the producer's own industry; strict liability can therefore be established against a manufacturer simply by showing a failure to conform to industry standard in relation to a particular product.

The following are a number of policy reasons:

a) the manufacturer should be provided with an incentive to invest in safety research and design innovation, and will tend to produce safer and more resilient products;
b) the manufacturer, in an advanced consumer society, where certain product injuries are inevitable, is best able to spread the risk of injury through the price of the product;
c) the consumer expects a certain level of safety in relation to consumer products, regardless of negligence — simply placing goods into the

---

266 24 Cal.2d 453 (Sup. Ct. 1994).
267 *Ibid.* at 461–62.
268 59 Cal.2d 57 (1963).

stream of commerce is akin to making a representation that they meet a certain standard;
d) the financial burden of inevitable injuries should be internalized by the industry in order to set a socially accurate price for their products and activities in order to achieve efficient level of production;
e) as a matter of justice, the beneficiaries of an industry should pay the full costs created by their enterprise and products;
f) due to informational and resource inequalities, the consumer frequently lacks the resources to demonstrate negligence.

In order to recover under strict liability, the buyer must prove that there was a defect in the goods, that they were "unfit or unmerchantable" and that the defect resulted in his or her injuries. However, the goods do not have to be perfect, or even absolutely "harmless" to a buyer. A product cannot be considered "defective" merely because it is dangerous. There must be some test or standard against which it can be judged. A knife is dangerous but not necessarily defective. Nor does strict liability cover all accidents caused by products. In order for a plaintiff to recover under s. 402A, his or her injury must have been caused not just by a product created by the manufacturer, but by a *defective* product. For example, in *Griffiths v. Peter Conway Ltd.*,[269] the plaintiff alleged that he had been afflicted with skin dermatitis from wearing clothing sold by the defendant. The court refused to hold the defendant liable, finding that the plaintiff was uniquely sensitive and that no ordinary user would have contracted the skin disease in the same way. Such an approach reveals that for the doctrine of strict liability to apply, the product must actually be defective, and not cause injury merely as a result of the plaintiff's own susceptibility to harm.

There are still some interesting differences in the application of the law depending upon whether the case is framed in tort or contract. *Denny v. Ford Motor Co.*[270] provides a good illustration of those differences. In that case, the plaintiff was injured when the Ford Bronco II that she was driving rolled over. The plaintiff provided evidence showing that sport utility vehicles, and in particular the Ford Bronco, are more likely to be involved in rollover accidents than other vehicles. Ford countered that the features that increased the risk of rollover were specifically designed to enhance the vehicle's unique off-road capabilities. The jury found that the Bronco was not "defective" as required under s.402A to hold Bronco liable on a strict products liability basis (in tort), but did conclude that Ford was liable to

---

269 [1939] 1 All E.R. 685 (C.A.).
270 87 N.Y. 2d. 248 (C.A.) 1995).

Denny on a breach of implied warranty basis. While the features that made the vehicle prone to rollover were necessary to its function as an off-road vehicle (and therefore the risk of rollover did not outweigh its off-road capabilities), it was not fit for the ordinary intended use to which it was put (city driving on paved roads). The New York Court of Appeals upheld the jury's finding that the vehicle was "not defective but was unmerchantable" and concluded that products liability and warranty actions are not identical: the warranty claim could succeed even though the products liability claim had failed. The court reasoned that warranty actions are based on contract law (on the basis of whether the goods are fit for their ordinary use) while strict liability relies on risk allocation in negligence/tort (balancing the risks/benefits of a product against its social utility).

2) Strict Liability in Canada

There is no doctrine of strict liability in Canada for product liability. Canadian courts have not yet established that manufacturers should be held strictly liable for defects inherent in the design and manufacture of their products, and continue to insist on some proof of carelessness (or breach of contract). Such was articulated by the Ontario Court of Appeal in *Phillips v. Ford Motor of Canada*[271] where Schroeder J.A. stated that:

> While the scope of *M'Alister (or Donoghue) v. Stevenson*, [1932] A.C. 562 has been greatly extended, and is no longer limited to articles of food and drink ... our Courts do not, in product liability cases, impose upon manufacturers, distributors or repairers, as is done in some of the States of the American union, what is virtually strict liability. *The standard of care exacted of them under our law is the duty to use reasonable care in the circumstances and nothing more.* [Emphasis added]

This traditional position was reiterated by the Supreme Court of British Columbia in relation to asbestos-related property damage in *Privest Properties Ltd. v. Foundation Co. of Canada*.[272] Here, the plaintiff building owners and managers, in the course of renovations, discovered asbestos in the fireproofing. The plaintiffs sued the defendant manufacturer, alleging that the asbestos was installed without their knowledge or consent and that it caused a danger to the health and safety of the building's employees and its occupants. The plaintiff's argument that the strict liability approach accept-

---

271 (1971), 18 D.L.R. (3d) 641 at 653 (Ont. C.A.), rev'g [1970] 2 O.R. 714 at 739 (H.C.J.) [hereinafter *Phillips*].
272 (1995), 11 B.C.L.R. (3d) 1 (S.C.), aff'd (1997), 31 B.C.L.R. (3d) 114 (C.A.) [hereinafter *Privest*].

ed in the United States should be adopted in this case was rejected. The court noted that while the strict liability approach currently dominates the products liability sphere in the United States, it must be left to the appellate courts to decide whether such "stricter versions of liability" should be accepted in Canada. In the alternative, the court noted that the strict liability approach requires proof that injury was caused by a defective product. Here, there was no evidence that the fireproofing, nor the asbestos levels contained within, were inherently dangerous. Drost J. stated

> In product liability cases, Canadian courts have always insisted upon some degree of fault. Unlike the courts in many of the American states, they have, thus far at least, rejected the doctrine of strict liability.[273]

This position is frequently reiterated by trial courts.[274]

The apparent gulf between U.S. law and Canadian law on the issue of strict liability may not be so wide as it seems. Through the robust use of inferences, and the setting of fairly stringent standards of care, Canadian courts hold manufacturers to very high levels of accountability that arguably come close to strict liability. And on occasion, some Canadian judges do appear to have come close to suggesting a theory of strict liability. Such statements are sometimes made when the product in question is particularly dangerous. For example, in *Phillips*, Haines J. stated that in most cases of product liability the manufacturer owes a duty only to ensure that goods are "free from defects which arise from negligence or lack of care ...." But "where the product is a dangerous or potentially dangerous thing, the duty of care so owed approximates an absolute liability."[275] This decision was overruled by the Ontario Court of Appeal. Two of the judges on appeal specifically disagreed with the views of Haines J. Schroeder J.A. stated at 657: "... our Courts do not, in product liability cases, impose upon manufacturers, distributors or repairers, as is done in some of the States of the American Union, what is virtually strict liability. The standard of care exacted of them under our law is the duty to use reasonable care in the circumstances and nothing more."

Yet the distinction may approach the illusory in cases of things that are inherently dangerous or ultrahazardous (firearms, explosives, etc.) or designed for intimate human use or ingestion, where courts have held that there is a very high standard of care. In *Buchan*, it was said that "this stan-

---

273 *Ibid.* at para. 281.
274 *Baker, supra* note 110; *Meisel, supra* note 117; *Holt v. PPG Industries Canada Ltd.* (1983) 25 C.C.L.T. 253 (Alta. Q.B.) [hereinafter *Holt*].
275 *Supra* note 271 at 739.

dard of care may be so high that it approximates to or almost becomes strict liability."[276] Once again, liability on appeal was upheld (on the basis of a failure to warn), but the court expressly refused to consider the argument of strict liability.

Though they come close, such cases do not establish strict liability. They are instead an application of the principle of ordinary negligence law that, as the danger becomes more readily foreseeable, and the consequences more severe, the standard of care becomes higher.[277] This point is explained in *Rae and Rae v. T. Eaton Co. (Maritimes) Ltd.*[278] in which it was held that there is no liability even for dangerous things in the absence of negligence:

> ... [the] test of liability is not whether the product sold was or was not a "dangerous thing," but considering its nature and all relevant circumstances whether there has been a breach of duty by the manufacturer which he owed to the injured person. The duty is to use that due care that a reasonable person would use under all the circumstances. And one of the most important circumstances — and often the controlling circumstance — is the character of the article sold and its capacity to do harm.

It is also sometimes said that proof that a product was dangerous or defective and that it caused injury is sufficient to trigger an inference of negligence, and that this approaches strict liability. In *Holt v. PPG Industries Canada Ltd.*, Stratton J. stated that "it seems increasingly clear that the trend in Canadian/English Courts is to allow an inference of negligence to be more readily drawn particularly as against a manufacturer. This inference, however, comes into prominence only in the event that the product in question is found to be defective ...."[279]

While courts will sometimes infer negligence from proof of defect and resulting injury, they will do so only where there is no reasonable alternate explanation of the defect that does not involve negligence. Allegation and proof of negligence is still formally necessary.[280] Proof that a product is defective and that it caused injury is not alone sufficient to establish liability. In *Meisel v. Tolko Industries Ltd.*,[281] the Supreme Court of British Columbia reaffirmed that manufacturer liability requires proof that the product

---

276 *Buchan*, supra note 50, cited to (1984), 8 D.L.R. (4th) 373 at 386 (S.C.).
277 Linden, 5th ed., *supra* note 29 at 573.
278 (1961), 28 D.L.R. (2d) 522 at 535 (N.S.S.C.).
279 *Holt*, supra note 274 at para. 30.
280 *MacLachlan & Mitchell Homes Ltd. v. Frank's Rentals and Sales Ltd.* (1979), 10 C.C.L.T 306 (Alta. C.A.).
281 *Meisel*, supra note 117.

was defective; that the injury was caused by the defect; and that the manufacturer was negligent in allowing the defect to occur.

In the recent case of *Hollis*,[282] the British Columbia Court of Appeal held that the mere fact that a breast implant had ruptured did not establish that the product was defective, or that the manufacturer was liable. Nor was the maxim *res ipsa loquitur* applicable because the evidence did not exclude other possible (non-negligent) causes of rupture (the manufacturer was held liable for a failure to warn of the risk of rupture, which it was held to be aware of at the relevant time). The court stated that "in making these comments about strict liability, [it] is not suggesting that strict liability is the standard to apply in a product liability case such as this. That is an intriguing question, but one which does not have to be resolved on these facts."

As Waddams points out, "the formal requirement of proof of negligence extends the litigation process, involving the plaintiff in delay and expense, two things the plaintiff can often ill afford."[283] It is therefore to be expected that courts will, where appropriate, seek to ease this burden. But, while inferences of negligence and the doctrine of *res ipsa loquitur* do frequently lessen the burden on the plaintiff, *res ipsa loquitur* or similar inferential devices do not reverse the onus of proof. Nor do they "cast upon the defendant the burden of disproof of negligence, for this would come dangerously close to a fictional use of the maxim as a foundation for the doctrine of strict liability."[284]

Linden succinctly summarizes the current state of affairs with respect to the application of strict liability in product liability cases in Canada:

> Strangely, this doctrine has not so much as tiptoed across the Canadian border, despite the fact that most of the manufactured goods sold in Canada are produced in the United States or by Canadian corporations owned by American interests. Although the processing methods are the same, and the advertising is the same, the protection afforded a Canadian consumer by Canadian courts is less than that accorded to an American consumer by United States civil courts. More startling is the fact that American corporations are more prone to civil liability in their homeland than they are in Canada. Whether strict liability in tort will be kept out of

---

282 *Hollis, supra* note 46.
283 S.M. Waddams, *Product Liability*, 3d ed. (Toronto, Carswell, 1993) at 61.
284 *Phillips, supra* note 271 at 658, *per* Schroeder J.A.

Canada forever, or whether it will eventually be adopted, is a tantalizing but unanswered question at this time.[285]

Professor Fleming described in 1990 the "transformation" from fault-based to strict liability that occurred in the American law of product liability in the 1960s and came to "dominate" the field of product liability in the United States. After reviewing similar changes occurring at the same time in European countries, Professor Fleming asked: "How much longer can Canada afford to stand aside?"[286] The question may be ripe for reconsideration.

The possible policy reasons for the adoption of the strict liability standard are set out at length in the *Restatement (Third) of Torts* but principally include the creation of safety incentives and issues of economic fairness.[287] There has never been, it would appear, a conscious and principled rejection of these arguments by a Canadian appellate court.

In fact, these same principles have been found to govern in another "strict liability" context. In the recent case of *Bazley v. Curry*,[288] the Supreme Court of Canada imposed strict (that is to say, without fault) vicarious liability on an employer of a sexual predator who had molested several children under the employer's care. The rationale offered by the Court is so perfectly applicable to the product liability setting that it is a surprise that it has not been more widely referenced. McLachlin J. said that strict employer liability was justified on the following "policy" grounds:

> 30 First and foremost is the concern to provide a just and practical remedy to people who suffer as a consequence of wrongs perpetrated by an employee. Fleming expresses this succinctly (at p. 410): "a person who employs others to advance his own economic interest should in fairness be placed under a corresponding liability for losses incurred in the course of the enterprise." *The idea that the person who introduces a risk incurs a duty to those who may be injured lies at the heart of tort law.* As Cardozo C.J. stated in *Palsgraf v. Long Island R. Co.*, 162 N.E. 99 (N.Y. 1928), at p. 100, "[t]he risk reasonably to be perceived defines the duty to be obeyed, and risk imports relation; it is risk to another or to others within the range of apprehension."

---

285 A.M. Linden, *Canadian Tort Law*, 6th ed. (Toronto, Butterworths, 1997) at 573.
286 John G. Fleming, "Product Liability" in *Donoghue v. Stevenson and the Modern Law of Negligence: The Paisley Papers* (Vancouver: Continuing Legal Education Society of British Columbia, 1991).
287 American Law Institute, *Restatement (Third) of the Law of Torts: Product Liability* (Washington, D.C.: American Law Institute, 1998) at 5–15.
288 [1999] 2 S.C.R. 534 [hereinafter *Bazley*].

31 However, effective compensation must also be fair, in the sense that it must seem just to place liability for the wrong on the employer. Vicarious liability is arguably fair in this sense. *The employer puts in the community an enterprise which carries with it certain risks. When those risks materialize and cause injury to a member of the public despite the employer's reasonable efforts, it is fair that the person or organization that creates the enterprise and hence the risk should bear the loss.* This accords with the notion that it is right and just that the person who creates a risk bear the loss when the risk ripens into harm. *While the fairness of this proposition is capable of standing alone, it is buttressed by the fact that the employer is often in the best position to spread the losses through mechanisms like insurance and higher prices, thus minimizing the dislocative effect of the tort within society.* "Vicarious liability has the broader function of transferring to the enterprise itself the risks created by the activity performed by its agents" (*London Drugs*, per La Forest J., at p. 339).

32 The second major policy consideration underlying vicarious liability is deterrence of future harm. Fixing the employer with responsibility for the employee's wrongful act, even where the employer is not negligent, may have a deterrent effect. *Employers are often in a position to reduce accidents and intentional wrongs by efficient organization and supervision. Failure to take such measures may not suffice to establish a case of tortious negligence directly against the employer. Perhaps the harm cannot be shown to have been foreseeable under negligence law. Perhaps the employer can avail itself of the defence of compliance with the industry standard. Or perhaps the employer, while complying with the standard of reasonable care, was not as scrupulously diligent as it might feasibly have been.* [Emphasis added.]

If one were to replace the term "employer" in the above passages with the term "manufacturer," the reasoning employed by the Supreme Court in *Bazley* provides a textbook justification for the adoption of strict liability for manufacturing defects in Canada. In fact, to these (mostly economic) "policy considerations" we would add another: If the strict liability regime in the United States makes recovery for plaintiffs easier (as it certainly appears to do), the continued resistance to its employment in Canada, given almost unrestricted trade between the two countries, makes less and less economic sense because of a simple observation: there seems no reason to believe that Canada's more conservative regime has led manufacturers to reward Canadians' stoicism with lower prices on goods sold in both countries.

If Canadian consumers pay the same price for commonly sold goods as their American counterparts (subject to distribution and other incidental costs), and this price includes a virtual "insurance premium" to protect manufacturers from tort liability (as it must), then more restrictive rules in Canada will mean that Canadian consumers are effectively subsidizing the superior insurance enjoyed by Americans.

2. Causes of Action in Mass Tort

A. INTRODUCTION

While the U.S. courts have, as we shall see in Part Three, vacillated over the appropriateness of aggregate resolution of mass tort claims, virtually all of the proposals for legislative reform in Canada have indicated that aggregation could assist the broadest possible variety of tort claims. When considering the causes of action available to a mass tort plaintiff, reference might be made, for instance, to the Manitoba Law Reform Commission's *Report on Class Actions*, which gives an indication of the broad types of litigation that might be furthered by class proceedings statutes:

> Class actions are useful in tort cases for mass disaster claims (claims arising from single incident mass accidents, such as train derailments and environmental disasters) and for creeping disaster claims (claims for bodily injury arising from consumer products, such as tobacco and asbestos, or medical products, such as intra-uterine devices, breast implants, contaminated blood, jaw implants, silver mercury fillings and heart pacemakers). Other uses include "claims of group defamation, nuisance, the principle in *Rylands v. Fletcher*, various statutory torts, damages claims for breach of *Charter* rights, claims arising from illegal strikes, negligent house construction, and negligent misstatement."[1]

---

[1] Manitoba Law Reform Commission, *Class Proceedings* (Report #100) (Winnipeg: Manitoba Publications Branch, January 1999) at 17–18.

The purpose of this chapter is to consider the various causes of action for which mass tort claims might conceivably be brought.

B. INTENTIONAL TORTS

Most discussion in this book of sources of tort liability deals with tortious conduct that falls, one way or the other, within the category of "negligence." However, this is not to say that mass tort liability cannot be founded on intentional torts; it certainly can. Some torts, like deceit, are by their nature often "directed" at large numbers of people. More commonly, there is increasing acceptance that vicarious liability of corporations or institutions can be founded upon the intentional torts of employees or volunteers.[2]

Relatedly, the action filed by victims of British Columbia's eugenic sterilization program framed their complaint (*inter alia*) in battery, as is customary in cases of allegations that medical procedures were performed without consent.[3] While the claim failed, the court appeared to recognize that battery could, in certain cases, be appropriate in mass claims given sufficient central direction.[4]

One intentional tort with a natural, but so far unexplored, application in mass claims is that of "interference with economic relations," or more commonly "inducing breach of contract." In the recent decision of *Verchere v. Greenpeace Canada*,[5] the defendant environmental group, and some of its members, were successfully sued for unlawfully preventing licensed logging by chaining themselves to equipment. The court awarded damages to the plaintiffs, who were loggers prevented from working during the period of the protest. While there were in *Verchere* only three plaintiffs, it is not difficult to see how similar disruptions (either in the envronmental or labour context[6]) could give rise to claims by hundreds or even thousands of affected workers.[7]

---

2   *Rumley v. H.M.T.Q.*, [2001] 3 S.C.R. 184.
3   *Malette v. Shulman* (1990), 67 D.L.R. (4th) 321 (Ont. C.A.); *Norberg v. Wynrib*, [1992] 2 S.C.R. 226.
4   *D.E. (Guardian at litem of) v. British Columbia.*, 2003 BCSC 1013 at paras. 183–88. However, such direction may actually require the establishment of agency or some other form of vicarious liability, or perhaps concert in action, since the court found at para. 185 that "[w]hatever force is required to constitute a battery must be applied directly by the defendant to the plaintiff's person. Battery is not committed where the act of the defendant only indirectly affects the plaintiff (*Non-Marine Underwriters, Lloyd's of London v. Scalera*, [2000] 1 S.C.R. 551)."
5   2004 BCCA 242 [hereinafter *Verchere*].
6   See, for instance, *Torquay Hotel Co., Ltd. v. Cousins*, [1969] 2 Ch. 106 (C.A.).
7   The Court in *Verchere*, *supra* note 5, described at paras. 33–36 the elements of the tort of interference in these terms:

Other intentional torts, such as misfeasance in public office, appear to provide a fertile ground for mass claims, and, where appropriate, such causes of action receive separate treatment in this chapter.

C. STATUTORY CAUSES OF ACTION

Many statutes, whether or not they have regulatory components such as the *Competition Act* (discussed in more detail elsewhere in this book), establish civil causes of action. Some are unlikely ever to become the subject of mass tort litigation: for instance, the British Columbia *Livestock Act*,[8] provides for strict liability for harm done by animals unlawfully at large on neighbouring property. Others, however, appear tailor-made to address more widespread harm, such as the liability that can result from nuclear accidents in the federal *Nuclear Liability Act*.[9] In British Columbia alone, a cursory review of the statutes reveals civil causes of action relating to the operation of mines,[10] pipelines,[11] securities,[12] and the practice of architecture,[13] to name but a sample. It is certainly possible to envisage the breach of any of these statutorily created standards giving rise to numerous claims.

It is not our intention here to canvass each statutory cause of action and its possible application in mass tort contexts. However, the student and practitioner are well advised to review all regulatory statutes concerning the activity in dispute to see whether a civil cause of action has been provided (or restricted) by statute.

---

1) that the plaintiffs had a valid and enforceable contract at the time of the alleged interference;
2) that the Defendants knew of the existence of that contract;
3) that the defendants, by unlawful (wrongful) means, caused the breach of the plaintiffs' contract;
4) that the Defendants intended the breach of the plaintiffs' contracts;
5) that the Plaintiffs suffered damages as a result of that interference.

8   R.S.B.C. 1996, c. 270, s. 11.
9   R.S.C. 1985, c. N-28.
10 *Mines Act*, R.S.B.C. 1996, c. 293, s. 17.
11 *Pipeline Act*, R.S.B.C. 1996, c. 364.
12 *Securities Act*, R.S.B.C. 1996, c. 418, s. 131.
13 *Architects Act*, R.S.B.C. 1996, c. 17, s. 66.

D. NEGLIGENCE

1) Breach of Common Law Standards

There is nothing extraordinary in the application of common law principles of negligence in the mass tort context. If one considers the basic elements of a negligence action — duty, breach of duty (by failure to observe the lawful standard of care), and damage caused by the breach — it is readily apparent that in many, if not most, circumstances, the first and second elements are "generic." That is to say, the duty is to a neighbourhood; if a defendant falls below the standard of care expected, then it can be said to have breached its duty to all members of that neighbourhood. On the face of it, it is mainly the third element, damage causally related to the breach, that makes a mass negligence claim so different from an individual action.

2) Breach of Statutory Standards

a) Breach of Statute as Evidence of Negligence

It is established in Canada that there is no right, at common law, to sue a defendant for "breach of statute" *per se*.[14] This has not always been the case. Prior to *R. v. Saskatchewan Wheat Pool*,[15] there existed in Canada, as in England, a nominate tort of breach of statute, though its actionability was subject to arcane and obfuscative rules that few could articulate, let alone deal with on the basis of principle.[16]

In *Saskatchewan Wheat Pool*, Mr. Justice Dickson reviewed the history of the cause of action for statutory breach and the various approaches taken in different countries. Recognizing that simplification of the law in the area was badly needed, he said: "Breach of statute, where it has an effect upon civil liability, should be considered in the context of the general law of negligence. Negligence and its common law duty of care have become pervasive enough to serve the purpose invoked for the existence of the action for statutory breach."

Following *Saskatchewan Wheat Pool*, the approach adopted by Canadian courts is to consider statutory standards as evidence of standard of care,

---

14 Of course, some penal or regulatory statutes, including many discussed in this book, do set out civil remedies for offences they describe. Here we discuss regulatory or penal regimes that do not explicitly provide for civil remedies.
15 [1983] 1 S.C.R. 205 at 225 [hereinafter *Saskatchewan Wheat Pool*].
16 A.M. Linden, *Canadian Tort Law*, 6th ed. (Toronto: Butterworths, 1997) at 204, rightly complained: "Little guidance was available as to which effect should be accorded a statutory violation and why. There was no rhyme or reason to it."

the departure from which alone is strong and often sufficient evidence of negligence. Statutory standards may also be relevant in certain intentional tort cases,[17] although, because of the availability of the negligence analysis, and the fact that most crimes are already recognized torts, this is one area seldom explored.

In the modern analysis, the "liability is not to be regarded as created by the statute, where there is no express provision for it";[18] it is, in other words, judicially created liability, designed with reference to the statutory regime but not dependent upon it. It does not follow, however, that because statutory standards can be used as a sword, they can also be employed as a shield. Compliance with regulations, while frequently invoked by defendants, particularly in heavily regulated industries, is not necessarily sufficient to discharge a defendant's duty in negligence.[19]

Nor will the law restrict its reference in negligence cases to standards gleaned from traditional statutory sources. In the wake of *Saskatchewan Wheat Pool*, Canadian courts have been able to look at municipal as well as provincial or federal laws as evidence of duty and standard of care.[20] Indeed, in one instance of an injury arising in the course of a rugby game, the official rules were said to establish the appropriate standard.[21] These developments make sense if the provisions in question are viewed as indicative of social expectations, a degree of consensus as to reasonable risk.

Increasingly, courts are confronted with claims based on a breach of the constitution. On occasion, these claims are premised on negligence, with the *Charter* used as evidence of the appropriate standard of care. We discuss mass litigation of constitutional claims later in this chapter.

---

17   *Whistler Cable Television Ltd. v. I.P.E.C. Canada Inc.* (1992), 17 C.C.L.T. (2d) 16 at 23 (B.C.S.C.) (describing a "tort of statutory breach distinct from negligence liability" for breaches of the *Broadcast Act*); also *Wild Rose Mills Ltd. v. Ellison Milling Co.* (1985), 32 B.L.R. 125 at 134 (S.C.) (breach of statutory warranties of fitness and merchantability); and *Patenaude v. Roy* (1988), 46 C.C.L.T. 173 (Que. S.C.) (private right of action for breach of *Charter* rights).
18   *Baird v. Canada (A.G.)* (1983), 148 D.L.R. (3d) 1 at 9 (F.C.A.).
19   This was the case even before the liberalization arising from *Saskatchewan Wheat Pool*, supra note 15: see, for instance, *Bux v. Slough Metals Ltd.*, [1974] 1 All E.R. 262 at 272 (C.A.). ("There is ... no presumption that a statutory obligation abrogates or supersedes the employer's common law duty or that it defines or measures his common law duty either by clarifying it or cutting down — or indeed by extending it ... The statutory obligation may exceed the duty at common law or it may fall short of it or it may equal it.")
20   Courts had been previously reluctant to do so: e.g., *Porter v. Joe* (1979), 106 D.L.R. (3d) 206.
21   *Hamstra v. B.C. Rugby Union* (1989), 1 C.C.L.T. (2d) 78 at 85 (B.C.S.C.).

b) Breach of Statute as a Mass Tort

Because of the increasingly detailed regulation of daily life, and particularly of industry and commercial activity, it is not surprising that many, if not most, mass claims involve some allegation that a statute has been breached. Many of these cases, of course, rely upon civil causes of action established by securities and consumer protection legislation and so on. Increasingly, though, reliance is being had on other statutes, such as the *Criminal Code of Canada*,[22] that create what might be termed "widespread duties."

Class actions have been launched premised entirely upon breaches of statute in fields such as securities litigation (for misrepresentations in a prospectus, for instance),[23] banking law (increasingly with respect to allegations of criminal interest rates), and, even more frequently, with environmental torts.

3) Affirmative Defences in Negligence

We have so far discussed certain affirmative defences as they arise in the context of particular causes of action; we raised the question of the learned intermediary and compliance with statutory warnings defences, for instance, in the specific context of a failure to warn. Nevertheless, there are certain defences that apply more broadly to all negligence-based actions, and so we discuss several of them here as distinct topics.

a) Intervening Act of Another

Product liability cases in particular may raise issues of whether the manufacturer's error was — in law — the true cause of the harm, or whether in fact a third party who breached an independent duty to the victim is legally responsible for the harm. As Professor Edgell writes, the "success of [the intervening act] argument hinges on the foreseeability of the intervening act."[24] He cites the Ontario Court of Appeal: "[A] break in the line of causation, is subject to the qualification that if the intervening act is such that it might reasonably have been foreseen or anticipated as the natural and probable result of the original negligence, then the original negligence will be regarded as the proximate cause of the injury, notwithstanding the intervening act ...."[25]

It is, of course, tempting to introduce the plaintiff's knowledge of the "intervening act" to snap the chain of causation and relieve the defendant

---

22 R.S.C. 1985, c. C-46.
23 For instance, *Pearson v. Boliden*, [2002] B.C.J. No. 2593 (C.A.).
24 Dean F. Edgell, *Product Liability Law in Canada* (Toronto: Butterworths, 2000) at 83.
25 *Cotic v. Gray* (1981), 33 O.R. (2d) 356 at 378–79.

of all liability. In *Smith v. Inglis Ltd.*,[26] the plaintiff had received an electric shock caused by a manufacturing defect in the refrigerator's electrical system. The shock would not have occurred except that the plaintiff, though knowing that the grounding prong had been removed from the refrigerator's electrical cord, had used the unit regardless. The court held that it was foreseeable that the grounding prong would be removed to fit a two-prong outlet, such that any defect in the refrigerator could cause such an injury. The court ordered a reduction of damages due to contributory negligence.

Initially, U.S. courts were reluctant to find that an auto manufacturer had a duty to foresee negligent driving and resulting crashes; manufacturers were liable only for accidents caused or contributed to by any malfunctioning of the vehicle itself.[27] The logic was that automobile accidents were outside the "intended use" of the vehicle.

Today, however, U.S. courts have almost unanimously held that an auto maker is under a duty to design a "reasonably crashworthy" automobile.[28] The decisions in these cases are premised on the reality that collisions occur in the course of the ordinary use of the automobile and, consequently, it is foreseeable that injuries will occur if the car fails to withstand collision as well as may be reasonably expected. This notion has taken root in Canadian law as well. In *Gallant v. Beitz*,[29] Linden J. held that the liability of a negligent driver and a claim against the vehicle manufacturer for additional injuries allegedly caused by the vehicle's lack of crashworthiness were both issues to go to trial.

U.S. courts have, however, refused to extend this principle to impose a duty on cigarette manufacturers to make "fire safe" cigarettes,[30] or on firearm manufacturers to design a gun that, when mishandled, will not go

---

26 (1978), 6 C.C.L.T. 41 (N.S.C.A.). See also, *Good-Wear Treaders v. D. & B. Holdings Ltd.* (1979), 8 C.C.L.T. 87 (N.S.C.A.), aff'g (1978), 28 N.S.R. (2d) 316 (T.D.).
27 See *Evans v. General Motors Corp.*, 359 F.2d 822 (7th Cir. 1966).
28 *Camacho v. Honda Motor Co.*, 741 P.2d 1240 (Col. 1987). See also *Huff v. White Motor Corp.*, 565 F.2d 104 (7th Cir. 1977); *Daly v. General Motors Corp.*, 575 P.2d 1162 (Cal. 1978); *Knippen v. Ford Motor Co.*, 546 F.2d 993 (D.C. Cir. 1976); *Ward v. Honda Motor Co.*, 33 Va. Cir. 400 (1994); *Passwaters v. General Motors Corp.*, 454 F.2d 1270 (8th Cir. 1972).
29 (1983), 42 O.R. (2d) 86, 148 D.L.R. (3d) 522 (H.C.J.).
30 *Sacks v. Phillip Morris Inc.*, 1996 U.S. Dist. LEXIS 15184 (D. Md.), aff'd 139 F.3d 892 (4th Cir. (Md.) 1998); *Kearney v. Phillip Morris Inc.*, 916 F. Supp. 61 (D. Mass. 1996) at 7–11; *Frulla v. Phillip Morris Inc.*, (W.D. Tenn. 10 January 1990) [unreported]; *Lamke v. Futorian Corp.*, 709 P.2d 684 (Sup. Ct. Okla. 1985); *Griesenbeck v. American Tobacco Co.*, 897 F. Supp. 815 (D.N.J. 1995).

off and injure an innocent third party.[31] Canadian courts have proven more flexible, choosing to employ analyses of whether there were reasonably available alternative designs and the risk vs. utility of the product's use in assessing the question.[32]

b) Contributory Negligence

The role of fault-based liability is mainly to provide compensation to victims and deterrence against wrongdoing. Negligence law is not meant simply to be an insurer; it should exact compensation from wrongdoers to the benefit of victims in order to compensate and regulate behaviour, but it follows that if society is to avoid unnecessary accident costs, victims too should be encouraged by the law to avoid acting recklessly in a way that might exacerbate risks.

Contributory negligence is the principal doctrine that has developed to regulate the behaviour of potential victims. In its initial formulation, contributory negligence was a complete defence; that is, a victim could not recover from a wrongdoer if his or her own negligence contributed to the loss complained of. The rule did not require even that the plaintiff was the *principal* author of his or her misfortune: Lord Blackburn in an early case stated the rule bluntly: "[I]f there is blame causing the accident on both sides, however small that blame may be on one side, the loss lies where it falls."[33]

The reform of contributory negligence laws dates in Canada to the enactment of apportionment legislation, beginning in Ontario in 1924.[34] It soon caught on in all the provinces and later spread to England and most of the United States.

British Columbia's *Negligence Act*[35] is typical of apportionment schemes:

> 1 (1) If by the fault of 2 or more persons damage or loss is caused to one or more of them, the liability to make good the damage or loss is in proportion to the degree to which each person was at fault.
>
> (2) Despite subsection (1), if, having regard to all the circumstances of the case, it is not possible to establish different degrees of fault, the liability must be apportioned equally.

---

31 *Mavilia v. Stoeger Industries*, 574 F. Supp. 107 (D. Mass. 1983). But see *White v. Smith & Wesson*, 97 F. Supp.2d 816 (N.Dist. Ohio 2000).
32 See, for instance, *Baker v. Suzuki Motor Co.* (1993), 12 Alta. L.R. (3d) 193 (Q.B.); *Ragoonanan v. Imperial Tobacco Canada Ltd.* (2000), 4 C.C.L.T. (3d) 132 (Ont. S.C.J.).
33 *Cayzer, Irvine & Co. v. Carron Co.* (1884), 9 App. Cas. 873 at 881 (H.L.).
34 *Negligence Act*, S.O. 1924, c. 32.
35 R.S.B.C. 1996, c. 333.

(3) Nothing in this section operates to make a person liable for damage or loss to which the person's fault has not contributed.

Ontario's *Negligence Act*[36] addresses plaintiff negligence separately:

3. In any action for damages that is founded upon the fault or negligence of the defendant if fault or negligence is found on the part of the plaintiff that contributed to the damages, the court shall apportion the damages in proportion to the degree of fault or negligence found against the parties respectively.

The apportionment regime established under the provincial statutes is not limited to negligence actions; where the defendant can show that the plaintiff's loss was due to his or her own "fault," the defendant can plead and rely on the negligence actions even where the plaintiff's claim is for an intentional tort such as battery or fraud[37] or where the action is framed in breach of contract.[38]

In mass claims, apportionment legislation has benefits for both plaintiffs and defendants. For defendants, it can reduce liability for virtually any type of claim where the behaviour of the victims is at issue; for plaintiffs, aggregate litigation is facilitated because, absent the "absolute bar" to recovery in contributory negligence, membership in the class will be much easier to establish.

The standard of care by which plaintiffs will be judged is the same as that governing defendants, and all the rules determining that standard, such as regulatory laws, may also be raised with respect to the plaintiff's behaviour. But, in an apportionment regime, this is not as conclusive as it once was. Where a manufacturer could at one time not have been held liable if its product caused harm only when used illegally (for instance, a tire that fails only at speeds over the legal limit), this is no longer necessarily the case.

c) Voluntary Assumption of Risk and Waiver of Liability

Another affirmative defence often raised in large-scale claims is that the plaintiffs voluntarily assumed the risk of a certain activity. The idea that one who consents to running a risk should not recover, or *volenti non fit injuria*, has been characterized in two ways: first, as negating the duty of care owed by the defendant (the tort model); and second, as a waiver of an

---

36 R.S.O. 1990, c. N-1.
37 See, for instance, *Brushett v. Cowan* (1987), 42 C.C.L.T. 64, rev'd in part (1990), 69 D.L.R. (4th) 743 (Nfld C.A.); *Andersen v. Stevens* (1981), 125 D.L.R. (3d) 736 (B.C.S.C.).
38 *Tompkins Hardware v. Northwestern Flying Services* (1982), 22 C.C.L.T. 1 (Ont. H.C.).

existing cause of action (a contract model). McLachlin J. (as she then was) put it this way: "The negation or limitation of duty of care approach looks at all the circumstances, including the contract, to determine what was the common law duty between the parties. The waiver approach assumes a standard duty of care, but says that the plaintiff's right to sue for breach of that duty has been removed."[39]

Volenti is crucial in product liability cases where a duty to warn is alleged; that is to say, there is no duty to warn a person with full knowledge of the risks. In *Bow Valley Husky (Bermuda) Ltd. v. Saint John Shipbuilding Ltd.*,[40] Madam Justice McLachlin speaking for the Court on this point, said:

> 22 [K]nowledge that there may be a risk in some circumstances does not negate a duty to warn. Liability for failure to warn is based not merely on a knowledge imbalance. If that were so every person with knowledge would be under a duty to warn. It is based primarily on the manufacture or supply of products intended for the use of others and the reliance that consumers reasonably place on the manufacturer and supplier. Unless the consumer's knowledge negates reasonable reliance, the manufacturer or supplier remains liable. This occurs where the consumer has so much knowledge that a reasonable person would conclude that the consumer fully appreciated and willingly assumed the risk posed by use of the product, making the maxim *volenti non fit injuria* applicable[.]

This aspect of *volenti* has been discussed at some length in our discussion of the duty to warn. We therefore turn our attention to the question of waiver. In what circumstances will a party be found to have waived his or her right to sue, even if the defendant has breached his or her duty?

In order to apply the contract or "waiver" model of the *volenti* defence, it is not enough that the defendant show that the plaintiff was aware of the possibility of harm. Since the *volenti* defence is a complete bar to recovery (rather than an apportionment device such as contributory negligence), the courts tend to view it restrictively. While it is standard for defendants in negligence cases to plead both *volenti* and contributory negligence, the former will assist only where the plaintiff has assumed both the physical *and the legal risk* involved in the activity.[41]

---

39 *London Drugs Ltd. v. Kuehne & Nagel International Ltd.*, [1992] 3 S.C.R. 299 at para. 276.
40 [1997] 3 S.C.R. 1210 [hereinafter *Bow Valley*].
41 See, for instance, *Car and General Insurance Corp. v. Seymour*, [1956] S.C.R. 322; *Dubé v. Labar*, [1986] 1 S.C.R. 649.

A good illustration of this principle is the case of *Crocker v. Sundance Northwest Resorts Ltd.*[42] There, the plaintiff had become inebriated and participated in a downhill inner-tubing event under the defendant's supervision. His tube upended and Crocker was paralysed. The Court held:

> 33 In the present appeal an attempt could be made to found a *volenti* defence either on (a) Crocker's voluntary participation in a sport that was obviously dangerous or (b) the fact that Crocker signed a waiver form two days before the competition. I will examine each of these bases in turn.
>
> 34 The first basis can be disposed of in short order. Crocker's participation in the tubing competition could be viewed as an assumption of the physical risks involved. Even this, however, is dubious because of the fact that his mind was clouded by alcohol at the time. It is well-nigh impossible to conclude, however, that he assumed the legal risk involved. Sliding down a hill in an oversized inner tube cannot be viewed as constituting *per se* a waiver of Crocker's legal rights against Sundance.
>
> 35 The argument that Crocker voluntarily assumed the legal risk of his conduct by signing a combined entry and waiver form is not particularly convincing either. The trial judge, having heard all the evidence, drew the following conclusion on the issue of the waiver at pp. 158–59:
>
>> I find that no attempt was made to draw the release provision to Mr. Crocker's attention, that he did not read it, nor in fact, did he know of its existence. Therefore, Sundance had no reasonable grounds for believing that the release truly expressed Mr. Crocker's intention. In fact, in so far as he was signing anything other than an application form, his signing was not his act.
>
> Given this finding of fact, it is difficult to conclude that Crocker voluntarily absolved the resort of legal liability for negligent conduct in permitting him, while intoxicated, to participate in its tubing competition. I would conclude, therefore, that Crocker did not, either by word or conduct, voluntarily assume the legal risk involved in competing. The *volenti* defence is inapplicable in the present case.

The basic requirements of an effective waiver are that its terms must be known to the plaintiff, which usually requires that the defendant take reasonable steps to bring it to the plaintiff's attention; that the defendant must put the waiver before the plaintiff at the time the bargain is made (or, if it is

---

42 [1988] 1 S.C.R. 1186.

subsequent, it must be the subject of a new agreement with consideration etc.); and that its language must be clear and unambiguous and should infuse in a reasonable person a sense of the scope of the legal rights being waived.[43] As in the case of many "form"-type agreements, a standard-form waiver will ordinarily be construed strictly against the party that drafted it.[44]

In the setting of mass-marketed goods, it is difficult for defendants to rely on waivers. Any waiver that is inside the packaging at the time of the purchase, for instance, is almost certainly not enforceable; similarly, waivers printed on receipts or tickets given to the plaintiffs after purchase do not meet the generally accepted criteria.

An interesting issue arises with respect to software-use agreements that, after purchase, seek to limit the liability of the manufacturer through a requirement that the purchasor not break the seal of the software if the terms are not acceptable. On its face, such an agreement is almost certainly ineffective to limit product liability in tort, and possibly also with respect to claims based on contract or implied warranties of fitness. However, contract claims might fail where they rely on the same document that is claimed not to be effective in limiting liability.[45]

E. NUISANCE-BASED CLAIMS

Environmental litigation is increasing in Canada as elsewhere. Mass claims concerning the harmful use of land will likely be pled in accordance with principles established under basic negligence law, as well as under the tort of nuisance and the *Rylands v. Fletcher* tort of strict liability. These causes of action, and ways in which they overlap and converge, is the subject of this section.

1) Private Nuisance

Nuisance is described as follows in J.G. Fleming, *The Law of Torts*: "The gist of private nuisance is interference with an occupier's interest in the beneficial use of his land."[46] Nuisance is an action based upon strict liability, except perhaps in cases of personal injury, where there is some debate as

---

43 *Bow Valley, supra* note 40; *Ochoa v. Canadian Mountain Holidays Inc.*, [1996] B.C.J. No. 2026 (S.C.); *Tilden Rent-a-Car v. Clendenning* (1978), 18 O.R. (2d) 601 (C.A.).
44 See, for instance, *Murray v. Sperry Rand Corp.* (1979), 96 D.L.R. (3d) 113 (Ont. H.C.J.).
45 See, for instance, *Rudder v. Microsoft Corp.* (1999), 47 C.C.L.T. (2d) 168 (Ont. S.C.J.), where a forum selection clause on a "click" software agreement was held valid, in part because the putative class members were relying on a breach of the same agreement as the foundation of their claim.
46 J.G. Fleming, *The Law of Torts*, 8th ed. (Sydney: Law Book Company, 1992) at 416.

to whether proof of negligence is required.[47] Otherwise, the plaintiff need show only causation and damages; it is no defence that the defendant has taken all reasonable precautions. However, the requirement that, to establish a nuisance, one must show an "unreasonable" interference with the use and enjoyment of property infuses some flexibility in the application of the law. Street, in *The Law of Torts*, puts it this way: "A person then, may be said to have committed the tort of private nuisance when he is held to be responsible for an act indirectly causing physical injury to land or substantially interfering with the use or enjoyment of land or an interest in land, where, in the light of all the surrounding circumstances, this injury or interference is held to be unreasonable."[48]

In *St. Pierre v. Ontario (Minister of Transportation & Communications)*,[49] McIntyre J. adopted the following passage from Fleming, *The Law of Torts*:

> The paramount problem in the law of nuisance is, therefore, to strike a tolerable balance between conflicting claims of landowners, each invoking the privilege to exploit the resources and enjoy the amenities of his property without undue subordination to the reciprocal interests of the other. Reconciliation has to be achieved by compromise, and the basis for adjustment is the reasonable user. Legal intervention is warranted only when an excessive use of property causes inconvenience beyond what other occupiers in the vicinity can be expected to bear, having regard to the prevailing standard of comfort of the time and place. Reasonableness in this context is a two-sided affair. It is viewed not only from the standpoint of the defendant's convenience, but must also take into account the interest of the surrounding occupiers. It is not enough to ask: is the defendant using his property in what would be a reasonable manner if he had no neighbour? The question is, is he using it reasonably, having regard to the fact that he has a neighbour?[50]

The test of reasonableness is an objective one: that is, whether there is an interference that would be substantial, not just with reference to the plaintiff, but with reference to any reasonable person in the plaintiff's position.[51] In

---

47 See, for example, *Ross v. Wall* (1980), 114 D.L.R. (3d) 758 (B.C.C.A.) (negligence must be shown to establish liability for a collapsing awning; liability in nuisance is not more strict than in negligence).
48 H. Street, *The Law of Torts*, 6th ed. (Toronto: Butterworths, 1976) at 219.
49 [1987] 1 S.C.R. 906.
50 *Ibid.* at para. 7, citing J.G. Fleming, *The Law of Torts*, 4th ed. (Sydney: Law Book Company, 1971) at 346.
51 *Ibid.* at 421; *Clerk & Lindsell on Torts*, 17th ed. (London: Sweet & Maxwell, 1995) at 895; *Walker v. Pioneer Construction Co. (1967) Ltd.* (1975), 8 O.R. (2d) 35 at 48–49 (H.C.J.).

Tock v. St. John's Metropolitan Area Board,[52] La Forest J. noted the balancing that courts had undertaken in assessing alleged nuisances. Citing *Walter v. Selfe*[53] and *Bamford v. Turnley*,[54] he said:

> There it was observed that the very existence of organised society depended on a generous application of the principle of "give and take, live and let live." It was therefore appropriate to interpret as actionable nuisances only those inconveniences that materially interfere with ordinary comfort as defined according to the standards held by those of plain and sober tastes. In effect, the law would only intervene to shield persons from interferences to their enjoyment of property that were unreasonable in the light of all the circumstances.

If an activity is carried out pursuant to legislative authority, no action for nuisance will succeed. However, Canadian courts have interpreted this defence restrictively; it is not enough to show that legislation *permitted* an activity that is otherwise a nuisance; to escape liability, a defendant must show that it was *mandated* to do the given activity, or at least that the activity complained of was an inevitable consequence of the mandated activity. If it is within the defendant's discretion to carry out its activities in a way that does not create a nuisance, the defendant's duty is to exercise that discretion in a way that avoids infringing on the rights of others. Fleming writes:

> The basic rule, as generally formulated, is that if the nuisance is an unavoidable consequence of the authorised undertaking, and was not negligently carried out, it is implicitly legalized and not actionable. Thus villagers near a new oil refiner, authorised by statute, could not complain of irreducible air pollution, nor residents adjoining a railway of vibrations from passing trains or the noise of cattle traffic in the station yard.[55]

2) Nuisance and Negligence

Klar describes the current state of the law in Canada with respect to the overlap between nuisance and negligence as follows:

> If the case is one in which the defendant has created the nuisance, he will be liable in nuisance despite the lack of his negligence. Certain cases, such as *Royal Anne Hotel v. Ashcroft* and *Smith v. Richardson* have treated the

---

52 [1989] 2 S.C.R. 1181 at 1191.
53 (1851), 64 E.R. 849.
54 (1862), 122 E.R. 27.
55 J.G. Fleming, *The Law of Torts*, 7th ed. (Sydney: Law Book Company, 1987) at 408.

defendant as having created a nuisance when he created the condition on his land which resulted in the nuisance. These cases have held the defendants strictly liable. Other cases ... have held that unless the defendant has actually created the nuisance itself he will not be liable for it unless he permitted it to continue after he knew or ought to have known of its existence. The distinction in this approach seems to rest in the fact that certain courts have held that creating the condition which results in a nuisance is tantamount to having created the nuisance, whereas other courts have held that there will be no liability unless the defendant in creating the condition knew of the likelihood of danger and failed to do anything about it.[56]

This passage suggests that, when a defendant creates a nuisance or the potential of a nuisance, the exercise by the defendant of reasonable care may be one factor to consider but it is not conclusive.

3) Problems with Private Nuisance as a "Mass Tort"

Nuisances are often "mass torts," in that what is a nuisance to a single neighbour is also often a nuisance to many, whether caused by noise or pollution in the air, water, or ground. Despite this, aggregate claims for nuisance are relatively rare. This is in part because the principal remedy for nuisance is an injunction, not damages; there are therefore fewer advantages to pursuing an action as a class.[57] However, another important issue barring certification can be that liability to any plaintiff is dependent on the degree of interference, and the reasonableness of interference, with that plaintiff's rights to enjoy property. As such, defendants can sometimes defeat certification on the basis of a lack of "commonality" among claims.[58]

---

56 Lewis Klar, *Tort Law*, 3d ed. (Toronto: Carswell, 2003) at 230.
57 This is not always the case. Nuisance may give rise to damages where the injury to the plaintiff's legal rights is small, it is one which is capable of being estimated in money, it can be adequately compensated by a small money payment, and it would be oppressive to the defendant to grant an injunction: *Shelfer v. London Electric Lighting Co.* (1895), 1 Ch. 287.
58 This was the case, for instance, where a class action was launched against the operators of an airport for unacceptable levels of noise in the neighbouring homes: *Sutherland v. Vancouver Int'l Airport Authority* (1997), 15 C.P.C. (4th) 329 (B.C.S.C.) [hereinafter *Sutherland*]. Nevertheless, courts in Quebec have certified actions based on civil causes of action similar to nuisance for noise and related harm caused by an illegal gravel removal operation and the operation of hydroplanes: See W. Branch, *Class Actions in Canada* (Toronto: Canada Law Book, 1997) at 538 [hereinafter *Class Actions*] (citing *Robitaille v. Constructions Desourdy Inc.* (1998), 78 A.C.W.S. (3d) 877 (Que. C.A.)); and *Filteau v. Aviation Roger Forgues* (unreported, 30 January 30, Quebec 200-06-000001-951, Que. S.C.)).

under the common law, the government would have to show the harmful effects of pollution from a particular site and identify according to common law rules the party responsible. However, under the *Waste Management Act*, the government determines by regulation the class of harmful substances and the levels of concentration that will indicate a "contaminated site." The *Waste Management Act* then makes present and past operators liable for the remediation of the site:

> 27 (1) A person who is responsible for remediation at a contaminated site is absolutely, retroactively and jointly and severally liable to any person or government body for reasonably incurred costs of remediation of the contaminated site, whether incurred on or off the contaminated site.

Two common law defences, "compliance with regulation" and "Crown licence," are removed from the defendants by the operation of subsection 3:

> (3) Liability under this Part applies
> (a) even though the introduction of a substance into the environment is or was not prohibited by any legislation if the introduction contributed in whole or in part to the site becoming a contaminated site, and
> (b) despite the terms of any cancelled, expired, abandoned or current permit or approval or waste management plan and its associated operational certificate that authorizes the discharge of waste into the environment.

The *Waste Management Act* and its Canadian counterparts[65] are hardly unique and in fact closely parallel the recovery scheme in the U.S. "superfund" environmental legislation, the *Comprehensive Environmental Response, Compensation and Liability Act*.[66]

Recently, the Supreme Court of Canada has issued what appears to be an invitation for governments to be more proactive in pursuing public environmental claims on a *parens patriae* basis. In *British Columbia v. Canadian Forest Products Ltd.*,[67] the Court confirmed that the Crown's right to sue in the public interest went well beyond those areas in which it had been traditionally exercised, and extended to compensatory claims, even where the government had not suffered traditionally-quantifiable losses.

Binnie J., for the Court, canvassing the history of the Attorney General's *parens patriae* jurisdiction and the American doctrine of the public trust, rejected the idea that the Attorney General's right to sue on behalf of

---

65 *Ibid.*
66 1980, 42 U.S.C., s. 9607(a).
67 [2004] 2 S.C.R. 74 [hereinafter *Canfor*].

the public was limited to seeking abatement or other injunctive relief. He wrote at paragraph 81:

> It seems to me there is no legal barrier to the Crown suing for compensation as well as injunctive relief in a proper case on account of public nuisance, or negligence causing environmental damage to public lands, and perhaps other torts such as trespass.

In *Canfor*, the issue was environmental losses causes by the defendant forest company's negligence. But the Court in no way limited its analysis of the right to recover to forestry cases *per se*. Binnie J. noted that, in addition to negligence, *Canfor*'s misfeasance also constituted a public nuisance, which the Court defined very broadly as "any activity which unreasonably interferes with the public's interest in questions of health, safety, morality, comfort or convenience."[68]

The Attorney General's free standing right to recover pecuniary and consequential damages arising from the defendants' wrongs is "an important jurisdiction that should not be attenuated by a narrow judicial construction."[69]

5) *Rylands v. Fletcher* Actions

We have discussed at some length the American jurisprudence regarding strict product liability, and its continued rejection by Canadian courts. This is not to say, however, that strict liability can have no application in mass tort claims. One area in which strict liability is established in Anglo-Canadian common law deals with the unnatural use of land and the escape of dangerous things therefrom. Here, the principle to be followed is that set out in *Rylands v. Fletcher*.[70]

The basis of the rule in *Rylands* is the statement by Blackburn J. that: "... the person who for his own purposes brings on his lands and collects and keeps there anything likely to do mischief if it escapes, must keep it in at his

---

68 *Ibid.* at para. 66, adopting the definition from *Ryan v. Victoria (City)*, [1999] 1 S.C.R. 201 at para. 52.
69 *Ibid.* at para. 76 *per* Binnie J. In *Canfor*, the majority's discussion of the full extent of the Crown's power to sue in the public interest was *obiter*, as Binnie J. found that the Attorney General had not framed its claim on that basis and so could not recover beyond the damages to which it was entitled as an ordinary commercial litigant. Lebel J., writing for himself, Fish and Bastarache JJ. in dissent, adopted, at para. 158, Binnie J.'s analysis of "of the Crown's ability to sue in the public interest," but would have gone further and applied it in that case.
70 (1866), L.R. 1 Ex. 265, aff'd (1868), L.R. 3 (H.L.) [hereinafter *Rylands*].

peril, and, if he does not do so, is *prima facie* answerable for all the damage which is the natural consequence of its escape."[71] This principle has been applied to the use of explosives and herbicides[72] but has not evolved into a generalized principle of liability.

In affirming the *Rylands* decision in the House of Lords, Lord Cairns introduced the requirement that, for the tort to be made out, the storage of the dangerous thing must be a "non-natural" use of the land. He stated that, if the harmful escaping substance (in *Rylands*, stored water) had been kept in the course of natural use, there would be no liability. This indicates a narrowing of Lord Blackburn's statement of the rule[73] and, of course, introduces a perilously subjective element into the analysis: what is the "natural" use of land?

In *Carmel Holdings Ltd. v. Atkins*,[74] Craig J. struggled with the overlap between nuisance and *Rylands v. Fletcher* actions. In that case, an oil storage tank had leaked, causing damage on neighbouring property. Craig J. recognized that strict liability on the basis of *Rylands v. Fletcher* depended on an "unnatural" use of the land. He said:

> ¶ 34 Whether there has been a non-natural, unreasonable, extraordinary, abnormal or special use of property is, in many cases, a perplexing issue. A decision on any particular case may tend to be arbitrary. Often, the distinction between what is classified as a natural use and what is classified as a non-natural use is simply a matter of degree. The defendant Atkins operates an apartment building. He must supply heat and hot water for his tenants. Obviously, he must store fuel oil on his property in order to have a supply always available. Is the storage of 1,200 gallons of fuel oil a natural use of the land? Would the storage of a much larger amount — say 6,000 gallons — be a non-natural use of the land, having regard to the size of the building and the number of tenants? On the other hand, the defendant knew or ought to have known that if 1,200 gallons of fuel oil "escaped" from the tank it could cause damage to the owners of adjoining properties and inconvenience in the form of nauseous smell. Moreover, the defendant Atkins was aware of the fact that his tanks were embedded in sand on rock, that the rock sloped downward through the

---

71   Ibid. at 279.
72   *Mihalchuk v. Ratke* (1966), 55 W.W.R. 555 (Sask. Q.B.).
73   In *J.P. Porter Co. Ltd. v. Bell*, [1955] 1 D.L.R. 62 (N.S.S.C.), MacDonald J. suggested that there are really two rules in *Rylands v. Fletcher* — Blackburn J.'s in the Exchequer Court decision and that of Lord Cairns on the appeal.
74   [1977] 4 W.W.R. 655.

plaintiff's property and that, therefore, if anything should happen to either tank the natural flow would be to the plaintiff's property. In these circumstances, there should be a strong onus on the defendant to ensure that the oil does not escape to the plaintiff's property.

¶ 35 In all the circumstances, I think that the defendant Atkins should be liable on the basis of the rule in *Rylands v. Fletcher*. Even if the rule in *Rylands v. Fletcher* were not applicable, because the storage of 1,200 gallons of fuel oil was considered to be a natural use of the property, I think that the defendant Atkins is liable in nuisance. The storage of 1,200 gallons of fuel oil on the property was a potential nuisance because of the damage it could do if it escaped. Mr. Atkins was aware on Friday or Saturday, at the latest, that there very likely was a leak, and he did nothing about it. ... If he had acted promptly, much of the damage to the plaintiff's property may well have been prevented ....

Even in its narrow *Rylands v. Fletcher* context, Anglo-Canadian courts appear to be deeply suspicious of strict liability. The House of Lords has recently narrowed the scope of this principle in England by reintroducing a negligence principle — requiring that the event must be reasonably foreseeable. In *Cambridge Water Co. v. Eastern Counties Leather plc.*,[75] the Lords rejected the American approach to strict liability in respect to ultrahazardous operations by requiring that the plaintiff prove that damage of the relevant type was a reasonably foreseeable consequence of the operation.

The *Cambridge*[76] decision has been applied in the Canadian case of *Smith Bros. Excavating Windsor Ltd. v. Camion Equipment & Leasing Inc. (Trustee of)*,[77] in which the court held that in order to apply strict liability it must be shown that the damages resulting from the escape were reasonably foreseeable. However, if those damages are reasonably foreseeable, a defendant may be subject to a higher standard of care than he would be in negligence. For instance, in *Jones v. Mobil Oil Canada Ltd.*,[78] the court seemed to blend theories of strict liability, negligence, and nuisance together. In that case, the defendant had operated flare pits that, when put out of commission and buried, contaminated ground water supplies, affecting grazing cattle. The plaintiff, a cattle rancher, brought an action pleading negligence, nuisance, and *Rylands v. Fletcher*. The court held Mobil to be strictly liable in nuisance; however, it found that, even if some degree of

---

75 [1994] 1 All E.R. 53 (H.L.) [hereinafter *Cambridge*].
76 *Ibid.*
77 (1994), 21 C.C.L.T. (2d) 114 (Ont. Gen. Div.).
78 (1999), 72 Alta. L.R. (3d) 369 (Q.B.).

negligence was required (and notwithstanding the fact that the court had already found that the defendant could not be held liable under the ordinary rules of negligence), Mobil nonetheless had failed to meet a heightened standard of care. The court held:

> ¶ 149 In this case, Mobil, through its predecessor Canadian Superior, created the condition on the land that led to the nuisance ... Mobil bears strict liability for this nuisance, even though it quite properly proceeded to correct the situation when the nuisance became apparent. If it had not, its liability may have been compounded by negligence.
>
> ¶ 150 ... There is persuasive authority to the effect that the standard of care to be applied to such conduct under the tort of nuisance should be a higher standard of care than is applied in negligence actions ....
>
> ¶ 151 [I]n nuisance, a court must be satisfied that the defendant has done all it reasonably could and all that was practicable to avoid the nuisance, even where, as in this case, the special use the defendant makes of the property benefits the community as a whole. The natural resource industry is a steward of lands in Alberta together with the ranching and farming community, and for policy reasons should bear the burden of the highest standard of care where there is the possibility of injury arising from nuisance. In this case, I am not satisfied Canadian Superior met this standard of care in its disposal of the flare pit, even if its method of disposal was consistent with past industry practice.

Because nuisance is also an issue in many cases where *Rylands v. Fletcher* is pleaded, commentators and courts alike have had difficulty distinguishing the two and can even treat them as synonymous. Some commentators have emphasized the difference in temporal terms: that *Rylands v. Fletcher* is applicable to a "single disastrous escape," whereas nuisance relates to an ongoing state of affairs.[79] Thus, the diligence with which a defendant responds to the problem is relevant in nuisance but not in strict liability. This explanation is only partly satisfactory, though, and until the Supreme Courts revisits the problem in a principled way, plaintiffs will likely continue to plead both causes and courts will continue to adopt whichever analysis most closely fits the facts before them.

There arises a possibility that the days of *Rylands* in Canadian law are numbered, especially since the decision of the High Court of Australia in

---

79   J.G. Fleming, *The Law of Torts*, 2d ed. (Sydney: Law Book Company, 1961) at 285, *Salmond on Torts*, 16th ed. (London: Sweet & Maxwell, 1973) at 322.

Burnie Port Authority v. General Jones Pty. Limited.[80] There, a 5–2 majority of the High Court held that the Rylands v. Fletcher strict liability should no longer be part of the law of Australia, but ought rather be subsumed within negligence, nuisance and trespass.

The Burnie decision was viewed with equal measure of alarm and relief in academia,[81] but Canadian courts have so far declined to follow the Australian example, and have, where appropriate, continued to apply Rylands, apparently feeling themselves bound by the Supreme Court's relatively recent affirmation of Rylands in Tock v. St. John's Metropolitan Area Board.[82] The House of Lords, too, has recently reaffirmed the availability of the tort in England and Wales, and arguably even refined it somewhat, in Transco plc v. Stockport Metropolitan Borough Council.[83]

F. LIABILITY FROM STATEMENTS AND SILENCE

1) Deceit

Deceit is the deliberate misleading of one person by another into a course of action taken to the former's detriment. The terms "fraud" and "deceit" and "wilful misrepresentation" are unfortunately inexact and, as Fleming has pointed out, are often more accurately considered as elements of other torts rather than a tort in themselves:

> We have repeatedly had occasion to notice that misrepresentation may be a mode of committing various torts, without there being any call to treat it as a separate or independent basis of liability. Thus, a battery may be committed by gaining consent to physical contact through misrepresenting its true character, intentional infliction of nervous shock may be procured by telling a lie, or a conversion committed by obtaining possession of goods through fraud. Besides, many forms of negligent misconduct involve misrepresentation, even if this aspect is frequently obscured and submerged amidst other attendant factors. For example, the liability of

---

80 (1994), 179 C.L.R. 520 (H.C. Aust.).
81 See, for instance, Jane Swanton, "Another Conquest in the Imperial Expansion of the Law of Negligence" (1994) 2 Torts L.J. 101; John Fleming, "The Fall of a Crippled Giant" (1995) 3 Tort L. Rev. 56.
82 [1989] 2 S.C.R. 1181. See, for instance, John Campbell Law Corp. v. Strata Plan 1350, [2001] B.C.J. No. 2037 (S.C.); Spika v. City of Port Alberni, 2002 BCSC 700.
83 [2003] UKHL 61. Vaughan Black has an excellent summary of the recent travails of Rylands v. Fletcher in "Rylands v. Fletcher Update," in Continuing Legal Education Society of British Columbia, Torts Update (2004).

manufacturers and occupiers is, in essence, based on a false assurance as to the safety of their products or premises, even though the duties in question are rarely defined by reference to the fact of implied misrepresentation as such.[84]

Nevertheless, deceit remains an independent cause of action. Lord Henshell established in *Derry v. Peek*[85] that deceit requires proof "... that a false representation has been made (1) knowingly, or (2) without belief in its truth, or (3) recklessly, careless whether it be true or false." At first, this might appear to be the language of negligence, but, in practice, the standard of *scienter* — the degree of deliberacy — involved in deceit is a high one. It is not enough that the party making the representation is negligent — even grossly negligent — of the truth; he or she must, at the very least, be found to have consciously decided to ignore the question of truth. Lord Henshell in *Derry* continued:

> Although I have treated the second and third as distinct cases, I think the third is but an instance of the second, for one who makes a statement under such circumstances can have no real belief in the truth of what he states. To prevent a false statement being fraudulent, there must, I think, always be an honest belief in its truth. And this probably covers the whole ground, for one who knowingly alleges that which is false, has obviously no such honest belief. Thirdly, if fraud be proved, the motive of the person guilty of it is immaterial. It matters not that there was no intention to cheat or injure the person to whom the statement was made.

Klar lists the elements of the tort of deceit as follows:

(a) the defendant made a false representation of fact to the plaintiff
(b) the defendant
    (i) knew the representation was false;
    (ii) had no belief in the truth of the representation; or
    (iii) was reckless as to the truth of the representation
(c) the defendant intended that the plaintiff should act in reliance on the representation,
(d) the plaintiff did act on the representation
(e) the plaintiff suffered a loss by doing so.[86]

---

84 *Fleming on Torts*, 7th ed. at 597.
85 (1889), 14 App. Cas. 337 at 374 (H.L.) [hereinafter *Derry*].
86 Lewis N. Klar *et al.*, *Remedies in Tort*, vol. I (Scarborough, ON: Carswell, 1987) c. 5 at 5-11 and 5-14.

The misrepresentation of the fact can occur orally, in writing, or by conduct intended to induce the representee to a misapprehension of fact. Klar states:

> § 20 A representation of fact may be inherent in a statement of opinion, and the existence of the opinion in the person stating it is a question of fact. Thus if the facts are not equally known to both sides, a statement of opinion by the one who knows the facts best involves very often a statement of a material fact, for he impliedly states that he knows facts which justify his opinion. Accordingly, statements of opinion which do not represent the real opinion of the representator are misrepresentations; and an opinion may be so grossly erroneous that the court will conclude it could not have been honestly held.[87]

Half-truths are also actionable. Lord Cairns stated in *Peek v. Gurney*: "[T]here must ... be some active misstatement of fact, or, in all events, such a partial and fragmentary statement of fact, as that the withholding of that which is not stated makes that which is stated absolutely false."[88] Lord Steyn said in *Smith New Court Securities Ltd. v. Scrimgeour Vickers (Asset Management) Ltd.* that "... a cocktail of truth, falsity and evasion is a more powerful instrument of deception than undiluted falsehood."[89]

Silence, too, can in limited circumstances constitute deceit. In *Sidhu Estate v. Bains*,[90] the British Columbia Court of Appeal said:

> ¶ 31 The circumstances required for silence to be actionable misrepresentation are articulated in Spencer Bower & Turner, *The Law of Actionable Misrepresentation*, 3d ed. (London: Butterworths, 1974) at 101:
>
>> A misrepresentation may be made by silence, when either the representee, or a third person in his presence, or to his knowledge, states something false, which indicates to the representor that the representee either is being, or will be, misled, unless the necessary correction be made. Silence, under such circumstances, is either a tacit adoption by the party of another's misrepresentation as his own, or a tacit confirmation of another's error as truth.

If a plaintiff believes that he or she can prove the higher standard of fraud, as opposed to negligence, in the misrepresentation, he or she enjoys the

---

87 *Ibid* at 5-21.
88 [1861–73] All E.R. Rep. 116 at 129 (H.L.).
89 [1997] A.C. 254 at para. 50 (H.L.).
90 [1996] B.C.J. No. 1246 at para. 31 (C.A.).

advantage of not having to demonstrate that the consequent losses were foreseeable, since "it does not lie in the mouth of the fraudulent person to say that they [the losses] could not reasonably have been foreseen."[91]

It is not difficult to see why deceit is rarely pleaded in cases of misrepresentation. Most types of consumer transactions, real estate and other professional advisory situations, and securities offerings, which were all once fertile ground for the tort, are now governed by statutory regimes, many of which establish civil rights of recovery without necessity of proving all the elements of deceit. Where such regulatory legislation does not assist, the development of the law of negligence to cover many types of misrepresentation fills the gap in most cases more than adequately.

2) Negligent Misrepresentation

In the seminal case of *Hedley Byrne & Co. v. Heller & Partners Ltd.*,[92] the House of Lords held that misrepresentations could constitute actionable breaches of duty in certain circumstances. The basic elements of the tort of negligent misrepresentation are as follows:

1) the duty of care must be founded upon a "special relationship" between the person making the representation and the person receiving it;
2) the representation must be untrue, inaccurate, or misleading;
3) the representation must be made in breach of the standard of care applicable in the circumstances;
4) the person receiving the representation must have acted reasonably in relying on the negligent misrepresentation; and
5) the reliance must have resulted in damages being suffered.

In *Hercules Management Ltd. v. Ernst & Young*,[93] the Supreme Court of Canada adopted five general indicia of reasonable reliance, which had been proposed by Professor Feldthusen:

(1) The defendant had a direct or indirect financial interest in the transaction in respect of which the representation was made.
(2) The defendant was a professional or someone who possessed special skill, judgment, or knowledge.
(3) The advice or information was provided in the course of the defendant's business.

---

91 *Doyle v. Olby (Ironmongers) Ltd.*, [1969] 2 Q.B. 158 at 167 (C.A.).
92 [1964] A.C. 465 [hereinafter *Hedley Byrne*].
93 [1997] 2 S.C.R. 165 at para. 43 [hereinafter *Hercules Management*].

(4) The information or advice was given deliberately, and not on a social occasion.

(5) The information or advice was given in response to a specific enquiry or request.

The most difficult area in applying the tort has been determining what constitutes a "special relationship" so as to give rise to the duty owed in the circumstances. In *Hercules Management*, above, the Supreme Court adopted the test developed in *Anns v. Merton London Borough Council*,[94] to assist in determining the existence of such a "special relationship." Lord Wilberforce held, in *Anns* at 751–52:

> First one has to ask whether, as between the alleged wrongdoer and the person who has suffered damage there is a sufficient relationship of proximity or neighbourhood such that, in the reasonable contemplation of the former, carelessness on his part may be likely to cause damage to the latter — in which case a prima facie duty of care arises. Secondly, if the first question is answered affirmatively, it is necessary to consider whether there are any considerations which ought to negative, or to reduce or limit the scope of the duty or the class of person to whom it is owed or the damages to which a breach of it may give rise.

The *Anns* test, in the context of negligent misrepresentation, consists of two basic elements. First, the court will ask whether, given the nature of the relationship between the party making the representation and the party receiving it, the prospect of harm to the latter should have been in the reasonable contemplation of the former. Second, the court will consider whether there are any policy considerations that should limit the scope of the duty, the persons to whom it is owed, or the damages to which its breach might give rise.

Early cases of negligent misrepresentation, particularly in England, set out a requirement that (a) the defendant must know the identity of either the plaintiff or the class of plaintiffs who will rely on the statement, and (b) that the reliance losses claimed by the plaintiff stem from the particular transaction in respect of which the statement at issue was made.[95]

---

94 [1978] A.C. 728 (H.L.) [hereinafter *Anns*].
95 See, for example: *Candler v. Crane, Christmas & Co.*, [1951] 2 K.B. 164 at 181–82 and 184 (C.A.) *per* Denning L.J. (dissenting); *Hedley Byrne*, *supra* note 92; *Caparo Industries plc. v. Dickman*, [1990] 1 All E.R. 568 *per* Lord Bridge at 576 and *per* Lord Oliver at 589. The more narrow application of the tort was also evident in the Supreme Court of Canada's decision in *Haig v. Bamford*, [1977] 1 S.C.R. 466.

This restrictive reading was formally rejected by the Supreme Court in *Hercules Management*. There, La Forest J. held at paragraph 28:

> 28 While I would not question the conclusions reached in any of these judgments, I am of the view that inquiring into such matters as whether the defendant had knowledge of the plaintiff (or class of plaintiffs) and whether the plaintiff used the statements at issue for the particular transaction for which they were provided is, in reality, nothing more than a means by which to circumscribe — for reasons of policy — the scope of a representor's [sic] potentially infinite liability. As I have already tried to explain, determining whether "proximity" exists on a given set of facts consists in an attempt to discern whether, as a matter of simple justice, the defendant may be said to have had an obligation to be mindful of the plaintiff's interests in going about his or her business. Requiring, in addition to proximity, that the defendant know the identity of the plaintiff (or class of plaintiffs) and that the plaintiff use the statements in question for the specific purpose for which they were prepared amounts, in my opinion, to a tacit recognition that considerations of basic fairness may sometimes give way to other pressing concerns. Plainly stated, adding further requirements to the duty of care test provides a means by which policy concerns that are extrinsic to simple justice — but that are, nevertheless, fundamentally important — may be taken into account in assessing whether the defendant should be compelled to compensate the plaintiff for losses suffered. In other words, these further requirements serve a policy-based limiting function with respect to the ambit of the duty of care in negligent misrepresentation actions.

Hercules Management concerned alleged misrepresentations made in an auditor's report, which had allegedly been relied upon by shareholders to their detriment. One of the Court's concerns when deciding whether policy considerations should negate liability was whether to do otherwise would lead to "indeterminate liability." The Court settled this question through the application of a rational litmus test: where the reliance by the shareholders was precisely the sort of action the representation was meant to encourage, concerns over the indeterminacy of liability would be, at the least, muted. In that case, though, the Court found that the auditor's statements had been prepared for a more general purpose: assisting the shareholders in the oversight of the company's activities. To the extent that the auditor's negligence interfered with that right, the shareholder's proper

---

96 *Hercules Management, supra* note 93 at para. 28.

recourse was through derivative, rather than direct, actions following the rule in *Foss v. Harbottle*.[97]

Subsequent decisions have made it clear that, even following the acceptance of the applicability of the general *Anns* test to negligent misrepresentation, the extension of liability into new areas will be approached conservatively in the class action era. The decision in *Cooper v. Hobart*,[98] while not strictly speaking a case of negligent misrepresentation, nevertheless illustrates the point nicely. In that case, the regulator of insurance brokers was sued for failing to oversee the activities of Eron Mortgage Corporation, to the detriment of its investors. The Supreme Court of Canada found that the claim disclosed no cause of action, since there was no duty owed by the registrar in placing his office's *imprimateur* on Eron.

3) Misrepresentation in Securities Cases

Securities regulation is currently the domain of the several provinces, and each has enacted essentially similar legislation.[99] The function of the Acts was described in *Pearson v. Boliden* at paragraph 2:[100]

> Most of the Acts create a "closed system" of securities trading and thereby regulate initial distributions of shares to the public, takeover bids, insider trading and the disclosure of information relating to publicly-traded shares. (See generally D. Johnston and K.D. Rockwell, *Canadian Securities Regulation* (2d ed., 1998) Ch. 5, and M. Gillen, *Securities Regulation*

---

97 (1843), 2 Hare 461. The rule was explained by the Court of Appeal in *Prudential Assurance Co. v. Newman Industries Ltd. (No. 2)*, [1982] 1 All E.R. 354 at 367 (C.A.) as follows:

> The rule in [*Foss v. Harbottle*] is the consequence of the fact that a corporation is a separate legal entity. ... The company acquires causes of action for breaches of contract and for torts which damage the company. No cause of action vests in the shareholder. When the shareholder acquires a share he accepts the fact that the value of his investment follows the fortunes of the company and that he can only exercise his influence over the fortunes of the company by the exercise of his voting rights in general meeting. ... If it is right that the law ... should in certain restricted circumstances confer further rights on a shareholder the scope and consequences of such further rights require careful consideration.

98 [2001] 3 S.C.R. 537.
99 Securities Acts. See *Securities Act*, R.S.B.C. 1996, c. 418; *Securities Act*, S.A. 1981, c. S-6.1; *Securities Act*, 1988, S.S. 1988, c. S-42.2; *Securities Act*, R.S.M. 1988, c. S.50; *Securities Act*, R.S.O. 1990, c. S.5; *Securities Act*, R.S.Q., c. V-1.1; *Securities Act*, R.S.N.S. 1989, c. 418; *Security Frauds Prevention Act*, R.S.N.B. 1973, c. S-6; *Securities Act*, R.S.P.E.I. 1988, c. S-3; and *Securities Act*, R.S.N. 1990, c. S-13, all as amended.
100 2002 BCCA 624.

in Canada (2d ed., 1998) at 74–79.) Most require the registration or licensing of brokers, dealers and other market intermediaries, and establish securities commissions or similar bodies which have rule-making, investigative and adjudicative functions.

Prior to share distribution, a prospectus must generally be filed and a copy provided to each investor. In most provinces, there is a statutory requirement that the prospectus contain full, true, and plain disclosure of all material facts relating to the distribution; in Quebec, there is a parallel requirement that the prospectus must not contain any misrepresentation likely to affect the value or market price of the shares.

Ontario was the first province to enact legislation providing a civil cause of action for misrepresentations made in securities prospectuses.[101] Subsequently, each province enacted similar legislation modelled on Ontario's Act. However, the first fifty years of such legislation passed without a single reported decision in a lawsuit by shareholders for misrepresentation; this has changed in recent years with the advent of the class action lawsuit. Since the enactment of such regimes in the 1990s, a number of cases under the Securities Acts have been filed.[102]

Most of the Securities Acts provide for a civil cause of action[103] in any person who has purchased the offered securities "during the period of distribution" or "in a distribution," against the issuer or vendors of the securities, the underwriters, and other persons specified, for any damages arising from a misrepresentation contained in the prospectus.

The principal innovations of the statutory causes of action for misrepresentations in a prospectus are twofold. First, there is no requirement to establish the "special relationship" between plaintiff and defendant: the parties responsible are set out in the Acts themselves. Second, each statute provides for "deemed reliance" — the plaintiff purchaser is deemed to have relied on the misrepresentation. Thus, the securities legislation vaults the plaintiff past the two principal obstacles of the common law actions of misrepresentation or deceit.[104] This is particularly crucial in class actions, cer-

---

101 *Securities Act*, S.O. 1947, c. 98.
102 See *Pearson v. Boliden Ltd.*, supra note 100; *Kerr v. Danier Leather Inc.* (2001), 7 C.P.C. (5th) 74 (Ont. S.C.J.); and *CC&L Dedicated Enterprise Fund (Trustee of) v. Fisherman* (2001), 18 B.L.R. (3d) 240 (Ont. S.C.J.). Other securities class actions alleging a variety of causes of action include *Carom v. Bre-X Minerals Ltd.* (2000), 51 O.R. (3d) 236 (C.A.) and *Stern v. Imasco Ltd.* (1999), 38 C.P.C. (4th) 365 (Ont. S.C.).
103 The exception is New Brunswick, which provides for no civil cause of action and leaves purchasers subject to the laws of that province with only their common law remedies.
104 See, for example, *Hercules Management*, supra note 93.

tification of which depends on commonality of issues, which is threatened to the extent that defendants can emphasize individualistic issues such as "special relationship" and "detrimental reliance."[105]

The causes of action in the Securities Acts generally protect only purchasers of securities who make their purchases during the period of distribution outlined in the Act.[106] This has been interpreted to exclude purchasers on the secondary market, whenever they made their purchases, from the statutory cause of action.[107]

G. UNJUST ENRICHMENT

Particularly in cases dealing with generic contractual relationships, consumers are increasingly relying upon the cause of unjust enrichment to seek a remedy against a defendant who has, by whatever means, collected money to which he or she is not entitled. The three-part test for unjust enrichment and restitution is set out in *Pettkus v. Becker*.[108] The three elements are

a) an enrichment of the defendant;
b) a corresponding deprivation of the plaintiff; and
c) an absence of a juristic reason for the defendant's enrichment.

In cases where the plaintiff has paid money to the defendant under an illegal contract, the application of parts (a) and (b) are straightforward. The British Columbia Supreme Court considered restitution in the context of criminal interest in *Vandekerhove v. Litchfield*.[109] Skipp J. described the enrichment of the lender in these terms at page 755:

---

[105] John J. Chapman, "Class Proceedings for Prospectus Misrepresentations" (1994) 73 Can. Bar Rev. 492.

[106] The exception to this general rule is in s. 141 of the Manitoba Act, which does not limit its application to the primary market in a "closed system":

> 141. Where a receipt for a prospectus has been issued by the director, notwithstanding that the receipt is thereafter revoked, every purchaser of the securities to which the prospectus relates shall be deemed to have relied upon the statements made in the prospectus whether the purchaser has received the prospectus or not, and, if a material false statement is contained in the prospectus, every person who, at the time of the issue of a receipt for the prospectus, is a director of a company issuing the securities or a person or company that signed the certificate required by section 52 is liable to pay compensation to all persons or companies who have purchased the securities for any loss or damage the persons or companies have sustained as a result of the purchase ....

[107] *Pearson v. Boliden, supra* note 100.
[108] [1980] 2 S.C.R. 834 [hereinafter *Pettkus*].
[109] (1993), 103 D.L.R. (4th) 739 (B.C.S.C.) [hereinafter *Vandekerhove*].

The benefit derived by the lender is the amount of the "overpayment" of interest by the borrower. According to the cases dealing with s. 347 of the *Criminal Code*, it would seem to be clear that the lender would not have been able to enforce payment of interest under the 1982 Loan Agreement in civil proceedings. The lender is in receipt of interest that he was not entitled to; hence he has been enriched at the expense of the borrower.

The difficulty arises in evaluating the third branch of the *Pettkus*[110] test: whether it would be unjust to allow the defendant to retain the benefit. Prior to *Garland v. Consumers' Gas Co.*[111] it was unclear whether the plaintiff must prove the absence of a juristic reason, thereby placing him or her in the unfortunate position of proving a negative, or whether the defendant must prove the presence of a juristic reason.[112] Moral and policy questions are properly considered under the juristic reason branch of the inquiry. The question to be asked is whether the enrichment and detriment, morally neutral in themselves, are unjust.

The concept of injustice in the restitutionary context was described by McLachlin J. in *Peel v. Canada*:[113]

> First, the injustice lies in one person's retaining something which he or she ought not to retain, requiring that the scales be righted. Second, the required injustice must take into account not only what is fair to the plaintiff; it must also consider what is fair to the defendant. It is not enough that the plaintiff has made a payment or rendered services which it was not obliged to make or render; it must also be shown that the defendant as a consequence is in possession of a benefit, and it is fair and just for the defendant to disgorge that benefit.[114]

In *Garland*,[115] the Supreme Court of Canada held that the proper approach to the juristic reason analysis is in two parts. First, the plaintiff must make out a *prima facie* case, showing that no juristic reason from an "established category" exists to deny recovery. The "established categories" identified by the Court included a contract, a disposition of law, a donative intent, and other valid common law, equitable or statutory obligations. The burden then shifts to the defendant to show that there is another reason to

---

110 *Pettkus*, supra note 108.
111 [2004] 1 S.C.R. 629 [hereinafter *Garland*].
112 J. Ziegel, "Cases and Coments: Criminal Usury, Class Actions and Unjust Enrichment in Canada" (2002) J.C.L Lexis 6 at 7.
113 [1992] 3 S.C.R. 762 at 804 [hereinafter *Peel*].
114 *Ibid.*
115 *Supra* note 111.

deny recovery. In this second analysis, courts should consider two factors: the reasonable expectations of the parties and public policy considerations.

Today, it appears that "unjust enrichment" is most likely to be litigated, as in *Garland*, in the context of illegal rates of interest contrary to section 347 of the *Criminal Code* of Canada (which establishes a maximum legal interest rate of 60 percent per year). Such cases are of particular importance to students of mass wrongs because of the frequently generic nature of loan arrangements at financial institutions and other credit-based businesses.[116]

As described by Huddard J. in *Mira Design Co. v. Seascape Holdings Ltd.*,[117] the purpose of section 347 is "to punish everyone who enters into an agreement or arrangement to receive interest at a criminal rate. The penalty is severe, and designed to deter persons from making such agreements ... It is designed to protect borrowers. There is no penalty imposed on a person who makes an agreement to pay, or pays, interest at a criminal rate."

Establishing a collection of an illegal interest rate does not necessarily lead to the conclusion that such interest should be disgorged. Courts in some cases have found restitution appropriate,[118] and others have found it to be not.[119] Reviewing the Canadian law, one commentator has suggested that disgorgement of criminal interest should be presumptively appropriate.[120] This is essentially the approach taken by the Supreme Court of Canada in *Garland*, discussed above.

The remedy of restitution is further discussed in chapter 3 of this book.

---

116 See, for instance, the claims described in the B.C. :payday loan" litigation: *MacKinnon v. Vancouver City Savings Credit Union*, 2004 BCSC 125; *MacKinnon v. National Money Mart Co.*, 2004 BCSC 140; *MacKinnon v. National Money Mart Co.*, 2004 BCCA 137.
117 (1982), 36 B.C.L.R. 355 at 362 (S.C.).
118 *Vandekerhov*, *supra* note 109 (overturned on other grounds) at 756, emphasizing the deterrent effect of disgorgement.
119 *Garland v. Consumers' Gas Company Ltd.*, [2001] O.J. No. 4651 (C.A.) (rev'd *supra* note 111). The court held that the existence of a regulated fee structure was a juristic reason because allowing restitution of fees that were approved as part of a regulated fee structure would be unfair to the defendant. The argument presented by the defendant was that the regulator sets fees for all services and that by setting the late payment penalties at the illegal amount, the regulator must have lowered fees for other services in an effort to control the revenues of the company. Therefore, overall, the defendant could not be said to have been enriched by the illegality.
120 J.S. Ziegel, "Cases and Comments: Criminal Usury, Class Actions and Unjust Enrichment in Canada" (2002) 18 Journal of Contract Law (Australia) at 11.

H. CONSPIRACY

1) Civil Conspiracy Generally

Civil conspiracy has been called "a somewhat awkward and obscure tort."[121] The common law tort of conspiracy is an offshoot of the crime of the same name. The tort essentially consists of an agreement plus concerted action taken pursuant to the agreement, resulting in damage to the plaintiff. Unlike the crime, proof of damage is essential and the agreement must have been executed in order for the tort of conspiracy to be actionable.[122] The cause of action requires an agreement between two or more people either to (a) act lawfully, but with the predominant goal of harming the plaintiff (the "injurious purpose" test); or to (b) act unlawfully, where they know the plaintiff is likely to be harmed by their unlawful action (the "unlawful means" test).

In the leading case of *Canada Cement*, the Supreme Court of Canada defined the tort as follows:

> Although the law concerning the scope of the tort of conspiracy is far from clear, I am of the opinion that whereas the law of torts does not permit an action against an individual defendant who has caused injury to the plaintiff, the law of torts does recognize a claim against them in combination as the tort of conspiracy if:
>
> (1) whether the means used by the defendants are lawful or unlawful, the predominant purpose of the defendants' conduct is to cause injury to the plaintiff; or
>
> (2) where the conduct of the defendants is unlawful, the conduct is directed towards the plaintiff (alone or together with others), and the defendants should know in the circumstances that injury to the plaintiff is likely to and does result.
>
> In situation (2), it is not necessary that the predominant purpose of the defendants' conduct be to cause injury to the plaintiff but, in the prevailing circumstances, it must be a constructive intent derived from the fact that the defendants should have known that injury to the plaintiff would ensue.[123]

---

121 *671122 Ontario Ltd. v. Sagaz Industries Canada Inc.* (1998), 40 O.R. (3d) 229 (Gen. Div.) per Cumming J.
122 *Lonrho v. Shell Co. Ltd.*, [1982] A.C. 173 at 188 (H.L.) [hereinafter *Lonrho*], Diplock L.J., cited with approval in *Canada Cement LaFarge Ltd. v. British Columbia Lightweight Aggregate Ltd.*, [1983] 1 S.C.R. 452 [hereinafter *Canada Cement*].
123 *Ibid.* at 471–72.

To a large extent, if another tort can be proved, conspiracy is redundant, for the allegation adds little to the causes of action already itemized (though the conspiracy allegation may permit the application of joint and several liability). Yet in one respect the cause of action adds something new because *an injurious action which, if done by one person would not be a tort, may constitute the tort of conspiracy if done by two.*

a) The "Injurious Purpose" Test

The "injurious purpose" test for the tort of conspiracy was considered by the Supreme Court of Canada in *Canada Cement*.[124] In that case, Estey J., for the Court, quotes the statement in *Salmond on Torts*[125] that "the common law is clear" that the tort is made out where there is a "combination wilfully to do an act causing damage to a man in his trade or other interests ... if damage in fact is caused." The intent to injure or cause damage to the plaintiff was required.

If the "sole or predominant" motive of those acting in concert is to advance a personal interest rather than to cause injury to the plaintiff, then such an agreement is not actionable as conspiracy. Any self-serving advancement or benefit (economic, personal, or otherwise) will also apparently suffice to avoid liability. In other words, "[a]n ordinary commercial transaction, the predominant purpose of which is to advance economic interests, does not constitute a conspiracy even though the complaining party may suffer an economic loss as a result."[126] This is true even if injury to the plaintiff is inevitable.[127]

Malice, or the lack of it, is also not determinative, but the purpose of the combination must be "wholly destructive by prevailing community standards." Because motives will so often be mixed, the test before *Hunt*[128] had always been to find the "real" or "predominant" purpose in the combination. Both or all members of the combination must have the same desire to damage or harm the plaintiff.[129]

---

124 *Canada Cement, supra* note 122.
125 R.F.V. Heusten, *Salmond and Heuston on the Law of Torts*, 18th ed. (London: Sweet & Maxwell, 1981) [hereinafter *Salmond on Torts*].
126 *Belsat Video Marketing Inc. v. Astral Communications Inc.* (1998), 54 O.T.C. 84 at para. 53 (Gen. Div.) per Rosenberg J., aff'd (1999), 118 O.A.C. 105 (C.A.).
127 See *Positive Seal Dampers Inc. v. M & I Heat Transfer Products Ltd.* (1991), 2 O.R. (3d) 225 at 237–38 (Gen. Div.); *Lonrho, supra* note 122 at 463–64; L. Rainaldi, ed., *Remedies in Tort*, vol. 1 (Toronto: Carswell, 1987) at 3–19.
128 *Hunt v. T&N plc* (1989), 117 N.R. 361 (B.C.C.A.) per Esson J.A. [hereinafter *Hunt v. T&N*].
129 See Fleming (7th ed.) at 706–8; *Canada Cement, supra*, note 122 at 471–72 (S.C.R.) per Estey J.; *Crofter Hand Woven Harris Tweed Co. v. Veitch*, [1942] A.C. 435 (H.L.) (cited

After *Hunt*, there is a serious question of whether the "predominant purpose" test has application to product liability cases involving failure to warn. This will be discussed below.

b) The "Unlawful Means" Test

In *Canada Cement*, the Supreme Court broadened the scope of the common law tort when it extended the tort to include "cases in which this intention to injure is absent but the conduct of the defendants is by itself unlawful, and in fact causes damage to the plaintiff."[130] Estey J. identified the additional elements of such a claim as three: the conduct of the defendants is unlawful, the conduct is directed towards the plaintiff (alone or together with others), and the defendants should know in the circumstances that injury to the plaintiff is likely to and does result.

The "unlawful means" might be the commission of a crime or a tort or the infringement of a guaranteed constitutional right.[131] The "constructive intent" of this second type of conspiracy may be explained like this: once the unlawfulness of the acts is established, the inquiry into the object of the conspiracy becomes superfluous since an injurious purpose can be inferred.

This type of conspiracy was alluded to in a number of English cases decided prior to the House of Lords decision in *Lonrho*;[132] these English cases led the learned author of *Salmond on Torts*[133] to conclude:

> A second form of actionable conspiracy exists when two or more combine to injure a third person by unlawful means — e.g. the commission of a crime or tort, or the infringement of a guaranteed constitutional right .... In such a case it is irrelevant that the object of the conspirators in using those means may be legitimate. Combinations of this kind must be contrasted with what might be called "*Quinn v. Leathem* conspiracies," where the means are legitimate but the object is not .... Hence a conspiracy may be actionable if either the end or the means, or both, are unlawful.

Lord Diplock in *Lonrho*[134] declined to accept this analysis, however, observing in his judgment that

---

with approval in *Canada Cement, supra* note 122). "Unless both are liable, neither is": *McKernan v. Fraser* (1931), 46 C.L.R. 343 at 401–9 *per* Evatt J.
130 *Canada Cement, supra*, note 122 at 468.
131 See also *Starkman v. Canada (Attorney General)*, [2000] O.J. No. 3764 (S.C.J.); *Duca Community Credit Union Ltd. v. Giovannoli*, [2000] O.J. No. 1199 (S.C.J.).
132 *Lonhro, supra* note 122.
133 *Salmond on Torts, supra* note 125.
134 *Lonhro, supra* note 122 at 189 and 464.

... in none of the judgments in decided cases in civil actions for damages for conspiracy does it appear that the mind of the author of the judgment was directed to a case where the damage-causing acts although neither done for the purpose of injuring the plaintiff nor actionable at his suit if they had been done by one person alone, were nevertheless a contravention of some penal law.

As a result, Lord Diplock concluded that the House of Lords had an "unfettered choice" in defining the scope of the tort of conspiracy, and elected to limit the civil action to acts done in combination for the predominant purpose of injuring the interests of the plaintiff.

The history of this tort in the United States has been quite different. While there are cases to the contrary, the courts generally have for many years concluded that the tort of conspiracy to injure forms no part of the law.[135] In order to establish a civil conspiracy in the United States, a plaintiff must prove:

1. two or more persons;
2. an object to be accomplished;
3. a meeting of the minds on the object or course of action to be taken;
4. *the commission of one or more unlawful overt acts*; and
5. damages as the proximate result of the conspiracy. [Emphasis added][136]

It appears, that in the United States, civil conspiracy is not a cause of action in itself but rather a set of preconditions which, if fulfilled, can lead to the sharing of liability among defendants.[137] This seems to be the case in all

---

135 See Prosser, *Law of Torts*, 4th ed. at 291; *Civil Conspiracy*, L.S.U.C. Special Lectures 1973, 495 at 502.
136 *Re TMJ Implants Prods. Liab. Litigation*, 113 F.3d 1484 at 1498 (8th Cir. 1997).
137 Conspiracy is "sustainable only after the underlying tort claim has been established." *Hanten v. School District of Riverview Gardens*, 183 F.3d 799 (8th Cir. 1999) at 809 (quoting *K&S Partnership v. Continental Bank*, 952 F.2d 971 (8th Cir. 1991) at 980). "Actionable civil conspiracy must be based on an existing independent wrong or tort that would constitute a valid cause of action if committed by one actor." *Posner v. Essex Ins. Co.*, 178 F.3d 1209 (11th Cir. 1999) at 1218 (quoting *Williams Elec. Co. v. Honeywell, Inc.*, 772 F. Supp. 1225, 1239 (N.D. Fla. 1991)) (applying Florida law); *Applied Equip. Corp. v. Litton Saudi Arabia Ltd.*, 869 P.2d 454 (Cal. 1994) at 457 ("Standing alone, a conspiracy does no harm and engenders no tort liability. It must be activated by the commission of an actual tort."); *Stoldt v. Toronto*, 678 P.2d. 153 (Kan. 1984) at 161 ("Conspiracy is not actionable without commission of some wrong giving rise to a cause of action independent of the conspiracy."); *Alleco, Inc. v. Harry & Jeanette Weinberg Found., Inc.*, 665 A.2d 1038 (Md. 1995) at 1045 ("No action in tort lies for conspiracy to do something unless the acts actually done, if done by one person, would constitute a tort.") (citation omitted); *Alexander & Alexander of N.Y. Inc. v. Fritzen*, 503

U.S. states; at the very least, we have been able to find no exception.[138] The law as expressed in *Canada Cement* and *Hunt v. T&N*, therefore, represents a rather abrupt departure from both *Lonrho* and from the U.S. jurisprudence on conspiracy.

N.E.2d 102 (Ct. App. N.Y. 1986) at 102–3 ("[A] mere conspiracy to commit a tort is never of itself a cause of action. ... Allegations of conspiracy are permitted only to connect the actions of separate defendants with an otherwise actionable tort.").

138 See *Hanten v. School Dist. of Riverview Gardens*, 183 F.3d 799 (8th Cir. 1999) at 809; *Gaming Corp. of America v. Dorsey & Whitney*, 88 F.3d 536 (8th Cir. 1996) at 551 ("[C]onspiracy is based on the commission of an underlying tort.") (applying Minnesota law); *Halberstam v. Welch*, 705 F.2d 472 (App. Ct. D.C. Cir. 1983) at 479 ("Since liability for civil conspiracy depends on performance of some underlying tortious act, the conspiracy is not independently actionable; rather, it is a means for establishing vicarious liability for the underlying tort.") (applying District of Columbia law); *Cunningham v. PFL Life Ins. Co.*, 42 F. Supp.2d 872 (N.D. Iowa 1999) at 884 ("[C]onspiracy does not state an independent cause of action, but rather requires the commission of an underlying wrong for which liability may be extended to an additional defendant by virtue of a conspiracy.") (applying Iowa law); *University System of New Hampshire v. United States Gypsum Co.*, 756 F. Supp. 640 (D.N.H. 1991) at 652 ("For a civil conspiracy to exist, there must be an underlying tort which the alleged conspirators agreed to commit. Conspiracy, then, serves as a device through which vicarious liability for the underlying tort may be imposed on all who commonly plan, take part in, further by cooperation, lend aid to, or encourage the wrongdoers' acts.") (applying New Hampshire law); *Re North Dakota Personal Injury Asbestos Litig. No. 1*, 737 F. Supp. 1087 (D.N.D. 1990) at 1095 ("One of the parties must commit some act in pursuance of the agreement that is itself a tort for civil conspiracy to exist.") (applying North Dakota law); *McGlasson v. Barger*, 431 P.2d 778 (Colo. 1967) at 780 ("[U]nless a civil action in damages would lie against one of the conspirators, if the act was done by him alone, it will not lie against many acting in concert.") (quoting *Pullen v. Headberg*, 127 P. 954 (Colo. 1912) at 955); *O'Neal v. Home Town Bank*, 514 S.E.2d 669 (Ga. Ct. App. 1999) at 675 ("Absent the underlying tort, there can be no liability for civil conspiracy."); *Cohen v. Bowdoin*, 288 A.2d 106 at 110 (Me. 1972) ("[C]onspiracy' fails as the basis for the imposition of civil liability absent the actual commission of some independently recognized tort; and when such separate tort has been committed, it is that tort, and not the fact of combination, which is the foundation of the civil liability."); *Admiral Ins. Co. v. Columbia Casualty Ins. Co.*, 486 N.W.2d 351 (Mich. Ct. App. 1992) at 359 ("Because [plaintiff] has failed to state any tortious action, its conspiracy action must also fail."); *Middlesex Concrete Prods. & Excavating Corp. v. Carteret Industrial Ass'n*, 181 A.2d 774 (N.J. 1962) at 779 ("[A] conspiracy cannot be made the subject of a civil action unless something has been done which, absent the conspiracy, would give a right of action."); *Nix v. Temple University of Commonwealth System of Higher Educ.*, 596 A.2d 1132 (Pa. Super. Ct. 1991) at 1137 ("'Absent a civil cause of action for a particular act, there can be no cause of action for civil conspiracy.'") (quoting *Pelagatti v. Cohen*, 536 A.2d 1337 (Pa. Super. Ct. 1987) at 1342).

The Canadian tort of conspiracy is generally referred to as existing as two independent types, "conspiracy to injure" and "conspiracy by unlawful means." It is also possible, however, to view the elements of the latter as a presumption that establishes the former without a showing of predominant intent to injure. Professor Burns has said, in a passage endorsed by Estey J. in *Canada Cement*, that "[t]he main effect of a finding that a conspiracy by unlawful means has been made out is to exclude the negative defence of predominant legitimate motive, that is, the advancement of the defendants' own legitimate interests."[139]

2) Conspiracy in Non-Commercial Cases

The tort of conspiracy is thought to be confined largely to the commercial realm (dealing with matters of unfair competition and economic harms). It has not yet been a source of liability in personal injury and product liability cases. In the leading case on conspiracy (*Canada Cement*[140]), the Supreme Court of Canada stated:

> The tort of conspiracy to injure, even without the extension to include a conspiracy to perform unlawful acts where there is a constructive intent to injure, has been the target of much criticism throughout the common law world. It is indeed a commercial anachronism as so aptly described by Lord Diplock in *Lonrho* ... In fact, the action may have lost much of its usefulness in our commercial world, and survived in our law as an anomaly.[141]

However, the use of conspiracy in product liability and personal injury cases is an open question. In *Hunt v. Carey Can. Inc.*,[142] the Supreme Court of Canada refused to strike out conspiracy pleadings against asbestos manufacturers who allegedly withheld information regarding the dangers of asbestos. Commenting on the defendant's argument, Wilson J. stated:

> While there has clearly been judicial reluctance to extend the scope of the tort beyond the commercial context, I do not think this Court has ever suggested that the tort could not have application in other contexts. ...
> While courts should pause before extending the tort beyond its existing confines, careful consideration might conceivably lead to the conclusion that the tort has a useful role to play in new contexts.[143]

---

139 P. Burns, "Civil Conspiracy: An Unwieldy Vessel Rides a Judicial Tempest" (1982) 16 U.B.C. L. Rev. 229 at 254.
140 *Canada Cement, supra* note 122.
141 *Ibid.* at 473.
142 *Hunt v. Carey Canada Inc.*, [1990] 2 S.C.R. 959 [hereinafter *Hunt v. Carey*].
143 *Ibid.* at para. 48.

The issue faced by courts in determining whether to extend the tort of conspiracy is whether "the fact of combination creates an evil which does not exist in the absence of combination." Wilson J. decided that it may well be that an agreement between corporations to withhold information about a toxic product might give rise to harm of a magnitude that could not have arisen from the decision of just one company to withhold such information. This was for a trial judge to consider.

a) The Requirement of Agreement

To establish conspiracy, a number of elements must be established. First, there must be an agreement or common design; mere parallel activities or imitative conduct is insufficient. In *Burnside v. Abbott Industries*,[144] the plaintiffs argued that each defendant, individually and in concert with each other, manufactured and marketed the drug DES as a preventative for miscarriage although the defendants knew or should have known of its potential carcinogenic effects and its experimental status. The court found that the plaintiff failed to allege the manner in which a conspiratorial scheme was devised and carried out. There was no evidence of meetings, telephone calls, joint filings, cooperation, consolidation, or joint licensing. The plaintiff, the court found, alleged no more than a contemporaneous and negligent failure to act.

b) The Requirement of Intent

In addition to "common design," it must also be established that the defendants *intended to injure* the plaintiff. Mere negligence is insufficient; the predominant purpose must be to cause injury to the plaintiff, rather than simply promote the defendants' interests. This requirement presents a challenge in product liability or other cases alleging a trade-off of safety for profits.

In the leading case of *Canada Cement*,[145] the plaintiff, a supplier of lightweight aggregate, went out of business after a client began using another supplier. Prior to these events, the respondent and appellant had an arrangement whereby the appellant purchased most of its lightweight aggregate for a concrete compound from the respondent.

The defendant had, in another action, pleaded guilty to the charge of conspiring to prevent or unduly lessen competition contrary to the *Combines Investigation Act* (now the *Competition Act*). While the result of this conspiracy was to render the plaintiff unable to compete effectively, Estey J., for the Supreme Court, noted that there was no finding of any intention by the appellants to injure the respondent in its business. The market-shar-

---

144 505 A.2d 973 (Super. Ct. Pa. 1985).
145 *Canada Cement, supra* note 122.

ing agreements were not alleged or found to have been entered into with the plaintiff in mind, nor to have had as their object injury to the respondent. They were simply self-serving.

But perhaps it is too harsh to say that conspiracy always requires that the *predominant* purpose was to harm the plaintiff. This invites a characterization game — a corporate defendant will always be able to argue that it acted from its own self-interest first and foremost, even if that self-interest was promoted through harming another. A more objective application of *Canada Cement* would accept that a defendant may be acting in its own interest primarily, but if it decides that its interests are best furthered through harm to another, and combines with another to affect the harm, an actionable conspiracy might be found.

3) New Applications of the Tort: *Hunt v. Carey Canada Inc.*

There is only one reason for the existence of the tort of conspiracy: to give redress for common action that caused damages over and above what would have occurred absent the combination. In most product liability cases, conspiracy may arise as a result of the withholding of information — and the agreement to withhold information — about the dangers of a product.

There is much support for this proposition, found in the *obiter* of asbestos decisions in the *Hunt v. Carey* litigation. In that case, the plaintiff alleged both types of conspiracy when he said:

> 18. After about 1934, some or all of the defendants conspired with each other with the predominant purpose of injuring the plantiff [sic] and others who would be exposed to the asbestos fibres in the Products, by preventing this knowledge becoming public knowledge and, in particular, by preventing it reaching the plaintiff and others who would be exposed to the asbestos fibres in the Products.

> 19. Alternatively, after about 1934, some or all of the defendants conspired with each other to prevent by unlawful means this knowledge becoming public knowledge and, in particular, to prevent it reaching the plaintiff and others who would be exposed to the asbestos fibres in the Products, in circumstances where the defendants knew or ought to have known that injury to the plaintiff and others who would be exposed to the asbestos fibres in the Products would result from the defendants' acts.[146]

---

146 *Hunt v. Carey*, *supra* note 142 at para. 4.

The application to strike Hunt's pleadings appears to have focused on paragraph 18 above, alleging a "conspiracy to injure." At the least, it is in this area where the judgments were focused. In the British Columbia Court of Appeal, Esson J.A. recognized that an industry-wide agreement to suppress health information, which would cause damage where individual suppression of information might not, may well provide a valid basis for the extension of the tort of conspiracy. He said:

> The language of predominant purpose and direct damage, which is relied on here as demonstrating that the action must fail, has arisen in that very special context. In this case, there is one element of the context which is similar to that in the *Canada Cement* line of cases. That is that the defendants are alleged to have conspired in protection of their own economic interests. But in all other major respects the context is different. The plaintiff has suffered personal injury. He alleges that the defendants conspired to suppress information and, by so doing, created a foreseeable risk of causing him the harm which he has suffered. *Put another way, he alleges that he would not have suffered that injury but for the conspiracy to suppress the true facts as to the dangerous propensities of asbestos.* [Emphasis added.][147]

Wilson J., in *Hunt v. Carey Canada Inc.*, endorsed this reasoning:

> I note that in *Frame v. Smith, supra*, at p. 126, I was not prepared to extend the tort of conspiracy to the custody and access context both because such an extension was not in the best interests of children and because such an extension would not have been consistent with *the rationale that underlies the tort of conspiracy:* "namely that the tort be available where the fact of combination creates an evil which does not exist in the absence of combination." But in the appeal now before us it seems to me much less obvious that a similar conclusion would necessarily be reached. If the facts as alleged by the plaintiff are true, and for the purposes of this appeal we must assume that they are, then it may well be that *an agreement between corporations to withhold information about a toxic product might give rise to harm of a magnitude that could not have arisen from the decision of just one company to withhold such information.* There may, accordingly, be good reason to extend the tort to this context. [Emphasis added.][148]

So, while the *Hunt* litigation did not go further than to hold that the pleadings ought not be struck out, the surrounding discussion provides support

---

147   *Hunt v. T&N plc*, [1989] B.C.J. No. 876 (C.A.).
148   *Hunt v. Carey, supra* note 142 at para. 49.

for the extension of the tort of conspiracy to the product liability sphere, where "the fact of combination creates an evil which does not exist in the absence of combination."

Pleadings fashioned after those in *Hunt v. Carey* have survived challenge in a lawsuit against a tobacco manufacturer in Canada: *Spasic v. Imperial Tobacco Ltd.*[149] It appears that there have been no subsequent product liability cases that have further pushed open the door left ajar by *Hunt v. Carey*.

I. VICARIOUS LIABILITY

Vicarious liability is a type of "strict" liability — liability without fault — that may in certain circumstances be imposed on employers for the torts of their employees. In Canada, vicarious liability is governed by the common law test known as the *Salmond* test,[150] the purpose of which is to determine whether an employer will be found strictly liable for its employee's conduct. Under this test, employers are vicariously liable for an employee's tort if it falls within the "scope of employment":

> An employee's wrongful conduct is said to fall within the course and scope of his or her employment where it consists of either (1) acts authorized by the employer or (2) unauthorized acts that are so connected with acts that the employer has authorized that they may rightly be regarded as modes —although improper modes — of doing what has been authorized: *Canadian Pacific Railway Co. v. Lockhart*, [1942] A.C. 591 at 599 (P.C.).[151]

In *Bazley v. Curry*,[152] the Supreme Court of Canada expanded upon the unauthorized mode test. In that case, the defendant society, which provided "total intervention" care for troubled children, hired someone who turned out to be a pedophile who molested numerous students in his charge. There was, of course, no suggestion that the molestation had been "authorized" by the society.

First, the Court held that the judge must examine precedent, and, if factually similar cases clearly determine that an employee's act is either independent of the employer (where vicarious liability will not apply) or an unauthorized mode of carrying out an authorized act (where it will), then

---

149 [1998] O.J. No. 125 (Gen. Div.).
150 R.F.V. Heuston and R.A. Buckley, *Salmond and Heuston on the Law of Torts*, 19th ed. (London: Sweet & Maxwell, 1987) at 521–22.
151 *Ibid.* at 220.
152 [1999] 2 S.C.R. 534 [hereinafter *Bazley*].

the judge must apply the precedent. If there is no such clear precedent, then the question in each case is whether there is a connection between the employment enterprise and the wrong that justifies the imposition of liability for policy reasons. These policy reasons are set out in terms (as we noted earlier) similar to the economic justifications for strict product liability in the United States: the employer introduced the risk and thus should bear the costs where the risk materialized; the employer benefited from the activity in which the risk was created; the employer was in a better position to "insure" against the risk and charge more for services in compensation (i.e., the cost of harm is "internalized" within the activity in question); and the employer will be in a better position to put in place safeguards to ensure that the risk is controlled.

While it couched its justification for imposing strict liability in economic terms more applicable to for-profit businesses, the *Bazley* Court rejected the position that non-profit organizations should be exempt from vicarious liability. Non-profit societies play a valuable role in society and many individuals benefit from their work, but this should not exempt them from liability — in a scenario where one party creates the risk and another party is harmed, the one who created the risk should bear the loss. From a policy perspective, the same considerations apply to non-profit organizations as do for-profit organizations.

Bazley was applied in *Matusiak v. British Columbia and Yukon Territory Building and Construction Trades Council*.[153] In that case, employees of MacMillan Bloedel, who were members of Building and Trade Unions (BTU), protested the presence of workers represented by the Canadian Iron and Steelworkers Union. The campaign culminated in illegal picketing and a riot by BTU members.

With respect to the first part of the *Salmond* test, the court found that the plaintiffs were threatened, intimidated, and harassed by BTU members while their supervisors, who had knowledge of their members' activities, either participated or took no active steps to prevent their actions. Given this, the court found it unreasonable to say that the defendants did not authorize or condone the actions of its members. Having found the wrongful acts authorized under the first part of the *Salmond* test, the court nevertheless went on to the second part of the test, in the event that the actions were not authorized.

First, the court found there were no precedents that governed the case and it therefore looked at the unauthorized mode test. In addressing the

---

153 [1999] B.C.J. No. 2416 (S.C.).

issue from a policy perspective, the court considered countervailing policy reasons why vicarious liability should not be imposed on unions. It concluded that, while unions should be able to engage in a philosophical protest involving the strong expression of opinions, in this case, the presence of physical assaults, property damage, intimidation, threats, and harassment made it appropriate to make a finding of vicarious liability. In sum, the court found at that

> ... the evidence overwhelmingly establishes the defendants' vicarious liability to the plaintiffs. There is no question but that the illegal picketing engaged in by the BTUs' members, and encouraged by the BTUs' leaders, not only provided the opportunity for the BTUs' members to commit the wrongs against the plaintiffs, but also materially enhanced the risk of harm, in the sense of significantly contributing to it. In my opinion, there is a significant connection between the creation and enhancement of the risk and the wrongs complained of by the plaintiffs.[154]

J. BREACH OF A SPECIAL DUTY

1) Fiduciary Duties

A fiduciary duty is a duty of the utmost good faith, requiring the party with the fiduciary duty to place the interests of the fiduciary above its own. In her dissent in *Frame v. Smith*, Madam Justice Wilson summarized the jurisprudence and principles with respect to fiduciary relationships and listed a number of categories of relationships that qualify as fiduciary: "the relationships between directors and corporations, solicitors and clients, trustees and beneficiaries, agents and principals, life tenants and remaindermen, and partners." She agreed that "the categories of fiduciary relationships are never closed" and that "[a]n extension of fiduciary obligations to new 'categories' of relationship presupposes the existence of an underlying principle which governs the imposition of the fiduciary obligation."[155]

Wilson J. described the three general characteristics of relationships in which a fiduciary obligation had been imposed:

1) the fiduciary has scope for the exercise of some discretion or power;
2) the fiduciary can unilaterally exercise that power or discretion so as to affect the beneficiary's legal or practical interests; and

---

154 *Ibid.* at para. 95.
155 *Frame v. Smith*, [1987] 2 S.C.R. 99 at para. 57.

3) the beneficiary is peculiarly vulnerable to or at the mercy of the fiduciary holding the discretion or power.[156]

She specified that the vulnerability referred to in the third element "... arises from the inability of the beneficiary (despite his or her best efforts) to prevent the injurious exercise of the power or discretion combined with the grave inadequacy or presence of other legal or practical remedies to redress the wrongful exercise of the discretion or power."[157]

The Wilson list of indicia of fiduciary relationships was adopted by the Supreme Court of Canada in Mr. Justice Sopinka's majority judgment in *Lac Minerals Ltd. v. International Corona Resources Ltd.*,[158] though not as a test. Similarly, La Forest J. found it a "useful guide" for analysing relationships in *Hodgkinson v. Simms*,[159] and added that, to establish a fiduciary duty in specific circumstances out of a particular relationship where fiduciary obligations are not innate, a party must show that the other has relinquished its own self-interest and agreed to act solely on behalf of the other party.

The Supreme Court of Canada's approach to fiduciary duty has allowed the categories of relationships to extend to the relationships between condominium developers and purchasers and to the relationships between condominium boards of directors and unit holders.[160] It is often remarked that the breadth of fiduciary law in Canada has expanded far beyond that in other jurisdictions.[161]

Fiduciary obligations can also be created between the Crown, or representatives of the Crown, and subjects. In *Guerin v. Canada*,[162] Dickson J. (as he then was) wrote: "[W]here by statute, agreement, or perhaps by unilateral undertaking, one party has the obligation to act for the benefit of another and that obligation carries with it a discretionary power, the party empowered thus becomes a fiduciary. Equity will then supervise the relationship by holding him to the fiduciary's strict standard of conduct."

Of course, once a fiduciary relationship is established, there is still the question of whether it has been broken. Canadian decisions have been

---

156 *Ibid.* at para. 60.
157 *Ibid.* at para. 63.
158 [1989] 2 S.C.R. 574.
159 [1994] 3 S.C.R. 377.
160 *2475813 Nova Scotia Ltd. v. Rodgers*, 2001 NSCA 12; *Strata Plan 1229 v. Trivantor Investments International Ltd.*, [1995] B.C.J. No. 557.
161 For a discussion of the expansion of the scope of the fiduciary concept in Canadian law, see D.W.M. Waters, "The Reception of Equity in the Supreme Court of Canada (1875–2000)" (2001) 80 Can. Bar Rev. 620.
162 [1984] 2 S.C.R. 335 at 384.

inconclusive as to whether breach can be accomplished through simple negligence or whether the fiduciary must prefer his or her own interest to that of his or her beneficiary.[163] The Supreme Court of Canada had an opportunity to settle the question in *Authorson v. Canada (Attorney General)*[164] but did not, preferring to restrict its finding to whether Parliament could legitimize such a breach, if a breach it was. The Court found in the affirmative.

The question of negligence remains important. If a fiduciary's negligence can give rise to equitable relief, affirmative defences otherwise available in negligence will not apply. As Clements and Park explain:

> Arguably, if the negligent performance of a service by a fiduciary amounts to a fiduciary breach, the threshold for liability may be lower than currently thought necessary for such a finding. A lower threshold is particularly important to plaintiffs because of the remedies a fiduciary breach affords. A reason that a litigant seeks to maintain concurrent causes of action is the expectation of preferable remedies in equity.
>
> In *Canson Enterprises Ltd. v. Boughton & Co.*, the Supreme Court was evenly divided as to whether the causation, foreseeability, mitigation, and contributory negligence doctrines of the common law should now be built into the equitable compensation remedy. Equitable remedies are more favourable to the plaintiff. A defendant in breach of fiduciary duty may not be able to argue that the plaintiff's recovery should be limited by the principle of contributory negligence. Further, the plaintiff's recovery may not be limited by traditional common law principles of remoteness and foreseeability. Therefore, the plaintiff wants a finding of breach of fiduciary duty in order to enhance its recovery.[165]

One of the most fertile grounds for mass claims for breach of fiduciary duties is with respect to the management of pension funds. In a recent article, Ward Branch and Craig Ferris describes several actions arising from pension issues. While not confined to claims based on special duties (and indeed the claims often overlap with those based on contract), the fiduciary nature of pension stewardship is an important factor in most cases:

> As the availability of class actions has expanded so to has the number of pension cases which are being launched as class actions. Numerous

---

163 Simon A. Clements and Juliane T. Park, "*Authorson v. Canada*: Opportunity Lost?" (2003) 82 Can. Bar. Rev. 535.
164 *Authorson v. Canada*, 2003 SCC 39, [2003] 2 S.C.R. 40 [hereinafter *Authorson*].
165 Clements and Park, *supra* note 163 at 538.

examples can be made as the types of pension claims which are being filed as class actions:

(a) Whether the Department of Veteran Affairs was a trustee of a pension plan and, if so, whether it breached its fiduciary duty?
(b) Whether there was a shortfall in benefits paid to members and whether the plan's sponsor failed to make required contributions to the plan?
(c) Whether contribution holidays were illegal, whether assets and liability transfers adversely affected certain plan members and whether plan amendments constituted a breach of fiduciary duty?
(d) Whether a plan actuary was fiduciary to members of the plan?
(e) Whether surplus was used improperly?
(f) Whether a partial termination of a plan occurred?
(g) Whether plan members are entitled to surplus, whether plan sponsor failed to properly insulate assets prior to plan termination, whether administrator expenses were properly paid, whether contribution holidays were illegal, and whether surplus payments from the fund were unlawful?[166]

2) Voluntarily Assumed Duty

The notion of negligence in the performance of a voluntarily assumed duty is part of the law of Canada. It is quasi-contractual; that is, there may be no contractual obligation for a person to do a thing, but the assumption of responsibility is sufficient. Three elements must be established: (a) an undertaking, (b) reasonable reliance on the undertaking, and (c) a resulting loss to the "beneficiary."[167] To hold a defendant liable for negligent performance of a voluntarily assumed duty, a plaintiff must demonstrate that he or she reasonably relied, to his or her detriment, on the gratuitous undertaking of the defendant. Reliance on a casual undertaking is not reasonable, nor is reliance on an undertaking made by an individual who is not skilled in the field.

To give but one recent example of the application of the law, in *Maxey v. Canada Permanent Trust*,[168] the plaintiff was informed by his bank (which held his mortgage) that he had neglected to insure his house and that if he

---

166 W.K. Branch and C.A.B. Ferris, "Pension Class Actions" (paper presented at the Canadian Pension Benefits Institute 2003 Western Regional Conference), online at <www.branmac.com>.
167 See Linden, 5th ed., *supra* note 62.
168 (1984), 27 C.C.L.T. 238 (Man. C.A.).

did not do so the bank would insure it and charge the cost to the mortgage. The bank insured its own interest and the house burned down. The plaintiff argued that he had assumed that if he did nothing the bank would insure the entire house. The court held that the bank was not liable, stating that "there must be something more. The relationship between the parties must be such as to create a trust or other duty ..." Missing in this case were a sufficiently clear undertaking, a sufficient relationship to give rise to a duty, and sufficiently reasonable reliance.

K. MISFEASANCE IN A PUBLIC OFFICE

The tort of misfeasance in a public office originated in *Ashby v. White*.[169] There, the defendant had maliciously and fraudulently deprived the plaintiff of the right to vote through the exercise of his statutory power as an elections officer. Although the defendant possessed, via statute, the power to deprive certain persons from participating in the election, the court found that he could not do so for an improper purpose. For some time after the tort was established, however, it was considered that "misfeasance in a public office" was actionable only where a public officer misused a power actually possessed.

The seminal case of *Roncarelli v. Duplessis*[170] incorporated the tort into Canadian law and refined it considerably.[171] There, the premier of Quebec had abused his liquor licensing authority to target Mr. Roncarelli, whose advocacy for persecuted Jehovah's Witnesses under the Duplessis regime had angered the Duplessis government. After *Roncarelli*, it appeared that the essential elements of the tort were that the defendant has taken an action to the detriment of the plaintiff, pursuant to a discretion granted by statute but with clear departure from the lines or objects of the statute and with malice (in the sense that the person was acting for an improper purpose alien to the purpose of the statute).

Rand J. said in *Roncarelli* at 140:

> In public regulation of this sort there is no such thing as absolute and untrammelled "discretion," that is that action can be taken on any ground

---

[169] (1703), 2 Ld. Raym. 938.
[170] [1959] S.C.R. 121 [hereinafter *Roncarelli*].
[171] While the *ratio* in *Roncarelli* was based on the Quebec civil law, subsequent cases have referred to it as establishing the tort of misfeasance in a public office in Canada. See, for example, *Powder Mountain Resorts Ltd. v. British Columbia* (2001), 94 B.C.L.R. (3d) 14 (C.A.) [hereinafter *Powder Mountain*]; and *Alberta (Minister of Public Works, Supply and Services) v. Nilsson* (2002), 220 D.L.R. (4th) 474 (Alta. C.A.).

or for any reason that can be suggested to the mind of the administrator; no legislative Act can, without express language, be taken to contemplate an unlimited arbitrary power exercisable for any purpose, however capricious or irrelevant, regardless of the nature or purpose of the statute. Fraud and corruption in the Commission may not be mentioned in such statutes but they are always implied as exceptions. "Discretion" necessarily implies good faith in discharging public duty; there is always a perspective within which a statute is intended to operate; and any clear departure from its lines or objects is just as objectionable as fraud or corruption. Could an applicant be refused a permit because he had been born in another province, or because of the colour of his hair? The ordinary language of the legislature cannot be so distorted.

In *Home Office v. Dorset Yacht*,[172] Lord Reid proposed at 1031 that a cause of action exists even without the deliberate malice exhibited by the defendant in *Roncarelli v. Duplessis*: "[T]here must come a stage when the discretion is exercised so carelessly or unreasonably that there has been no real exercise of the discretion .... The person purporting to exercise his discretion has acted in abuse or in excess of his power. Parliament cannot be supposed to have granted immunity to persons who do that."

The two types of abuse of statutory power were acknowledged by Newbury J.A. for the majority of the British Columbia Court of Appeal in *Powder Mountain Resorts Ltd. v. B.C.*:

[T]he tort of abuse of public office will be made out in Canada where a public official is shown either to have exercised power for the specific purpose of injuring the plaintiff (i.e., to have acted in "bad faith in the sense of the exercise of public power for an improper or ulterior motive") or to have acted "unlawfully with a mind of reckless indifference to the illegality of his act and to the probability of injury to the plaintiff."[173]

In 2003, the Supreme Court of Canada adopted *Powder Mountain*'s broad view of the tort in the case of *Odhavji Estate v. Woodhouse*.[174] The case involved a civil suit arising from a fatal police shooting of a robbery suspect; the officers involved had allegedly not complied with statutory rules to facilitate the independent investigation of the incident.

In *Odhavji*, the Court noted that there were two types of actions that could attract liability under the tort of misfeasance in a public office: "Cat-

---

172 [1970] A.C. 1004 (H.L.).
173 *Powder Mountain, supra* note 171 at para. 7.
174 [2003] 3 S.C.R. 263 [hereinafter *Odhavji*].

egory A," where a statutory authority was exercised with the intent to injure a member of the public; and "Category B," where a public officer acts without authority but with knowledge both that he or she has no power to do the act complained of and that the act is likely to injure the plaintiff. Iacobucci J., for the Court, said:

> 23. ... What distinguishes one form of misfeasance in a public office from the other is the manner in which the plaintiff proves each ingredient of the tort. In Category B, the plaintiff must prove the two ingredients of the tort independently of one another. In Category A, the fact that the public officer has acted for the express purpose of harming the plaintiff is sufficient to satisfy each ingredient of the tort, owing to the fact that a public officer does not have the authority to exercise his or her powers for an improper purpose, such as deliberately harming a member of the public. In each instance, the tort involves deliberate disregard of official duty coupled with knowledge that the misconduct is likely to injure the plaintiff.

Iacobucci J. continued to define the parameters of the tort of public misfeasance:

> 26 ... [M]isfeasance in a public office is not directed at a public officer who inadvertently or negligently fails adequately to discharge the obligations of his or her office: see *Three Rivers*, at p. 1273, *per* Lord Millett. Nor is the tort directed at a public officer who fails adequately to discharge the obligations of the office as a consequence of budgetary constraints or other factors beyond his or her control. A public officer who cannot adequately discharge his or her duties because of budgetary constraints has not deliberately disregarded his or her official duties. The tort is not directed at a public officer who is *unable* to discharge his or her obligations because of factors beyond his or her control but, rather, at a public officer who *could* have discharged his or her public obligations, yet wilfully chose to do otherwise.
>
> ...
>
> 28 ... The requirement that the defendant must have been aware that his or her conduct was unlawful reflects the well-established principle that misfeasance in a public office requires an element of "bad faith" or "dishonesty." In a democracy, public officers must retain the authority to make decisions that, where appropriate, are adverse to the interests of certain citizens. Knowledge of harm is thus an insufficient basis on which to conclude that the defendant has acted in bad faith or dishonestly. A public officer may in good faith make a decision that she or he knows to be adverse to interests of certain members of the public. In order for the con-

duct to fall within the scope of the tort, the officer must deliberately engage in conduct that he or she knows to be inconsistent with the obligations of the office.

29 ... Liability does not attach to each officer who blatantly disregards his or her official duty, but only to a public officer who, in addition, demonstrates a conscious disregard for the interests of those who will be affected by the misconduct in question. This requirement establishes the required nexus between the parties. Unlawful conduct in the exercise of public functions is a public wrong, but absent some awareness of harm there is no basis on which to conclude that the defendant has breached an obligation that she or he owes to the plaintiff, *as an individual*. And absent the breach of an obligation that the defendant owes to the plaintiff, there can be no liability in tort. [Emphasis in original.]

Of particular interest in this passage is the reference to "the interests of those who will be affected by the misconduct in question." While the balance of the discussion is framed in individualistic terms, it appears clear that the Court is willing to embrace a view of the tort as encompassing duties owed to entire classes of persons, rather than the traditional application, which in most cases actually appeared to require malice directed at a particular person. Thus, the "neighbourhood" to whom a public officer owes a duty in misfeasance appears to parallel that to which he or she would owe a duty in negligence, with the proviso that there must be a "conscious disregard" for the interests of potential victims.

In *Odhavji* itself, one allegation was that the chief of police had failed to ensure that the officers involved in a fatal shooting comply with statutory requirements to cooperate with an independent investigation, and that the chief "knew or ought to have known" that this would harm the plaintiffs. The Court said:

38 The statement of claim also alleges that the defendant officers and the Chief "knew or ought to have known" that the alleged misconduct would cause the plaintiffs to suffer physically, psychologically and emotionally. Although the allegation that the defendants *knew* that a failure to cooperate with the investigation would injure the plaintiffs satisfies the requirement that the alleged misconduct was likely to injure the plaintiffs, misfeasance in a public office is an intentional tort that requires subjective awareness that harm to the plaintiff is a likely consequence of the alleged misconduct. At the very least, according to a number of cases, the defendant must have been subjectively reckless or wilfully blind as to the possibility that harm was a likely consequence of the alleged misconduct

.... It is clear ... that the phrase "or ought to have known" must be struck from the statement of claim. [Emphasis in original.]

The clarification and (arguably) expansion of the tort of misfeasance in public office in *Odhavji* could have important implications for the law of mass tort. Governments, perhaps to their regret, have become a principal target of the class proceedings legislation they initiated; now, where a government official can be shown to have acted outside authority, knowing that this action would cause harm to a particular group, liability may attach for the resulting harm.

L. DEFAMATION AND HATE SPEECH

1) Group Defamation at Common Law

At common law, a successful plaintiff in a defamation action must show that the words complained of referred to the plaintiff individually.[175] Quite often, though, defamatory words are directed at entire groups. Can members of such groups complain that they are individually tarred, as when somebody declares "all lawyers are thieves"? Can defamation be a "mass tort"? Certainly the Manitoba Law Reform Commission, in the passage cited in the introduction to this chapter, seemed to think so. However, statements directed generally at large groups have historically been characterized as mere abuse, without sufficient individuality for the right of recovery of any member of the group to be triggered.[176]

Where, however, the plaintiff can satisfy the court that the defamation concerns a group that is sufficiently narrowly defined, and therefore its members sufficiently identifiable, a cause of action might lie in individual members.[177] Because in such a rare case the cause of action will necessarily belong to every member of the group (because of the requirement that they are necessarily disparaged through reference to the group), a mass claim might be commenced.

In *Kenora Police Services Board v. Savino*, the defendant had suggested that racism was a problem within the Kenora police force. The court refused to certify the case as a class action, holding that the statements did

---

175 *Aiken v. Ontario (Premier)* (1999), 45 O.R. (3d) 266 (S.C.J.).
176 *Knupffer v. London Express Newspaper Ltd.*, [1944] A.C. 116 at 122, per Lord Atkin (H.L.).
177 See *Aiken v. Harris*, supra note 175; *Knupffer v. London Express Newspaper Ltd.*, ibid. See also *Elliott v. Canadian Broadcasting Corp.* (1995), 25 O.R. (3d) 302 (C.A.) [hereinafter *Elliott*]; and *Campbell v. Toronto Star Newspapers Ltd.* (1990), 73 D.L.R. (4th) 190 (Ont. Div. Ct.).

not mean that every member of the force was necessarily a racist.[178] The decision followed other cases where rights of collective action were denied to members of disparaged groups.[179] However, in *Elliott v. Canadian Broadcasting Corporation*, Abella J.A., concurring, left open the possibility that a cause of action in libel could assist members of a large group.[180]

The general rules applicable to determining whether each member of a disparaged group has been defamed are set out by Peter A. Downard: "Each case must be considered on its own facts. The larger the group and the more general the reference, the less likely it is that the words will be found to have referred to a particular plaintiff. In recent years, for example, it has been held that a reference to 'the teachers' unions' and 'the union bosses' is insufficiently specific."[181]

2) Statutory Actions for Defamatory or Hateful Statements

Two provinces appear uniquely suited to permit civil actions[182] on behalf of entire groups maligned through certain speech. In British Columbia, there exists a seldom-noticed statute called the *Civil Rights Protection Act*.[183] That Act provides for a civil cause of action, actionable *per se*, for hate speech directed at racial, religious, national, or ethic groups. It provides:

> 1 In this Act, "prohibited act" means any conduct or communication by a person that has as its purpose interference with the civil rights of a person or class of persons by promoting
> (a) hatred or contempt of a person or class of persons, or
> (b) the superiority or inferiority of a person or class of persons in comparison with another or others,
> on the basis of colour, race, religion, ethnic origin or place of origin.
>
> 2 (1) A prohibited act is a tort actionable without proof of damage,
> (a) by any person against whom the prohibited act was directed, or

---

178 *Kenora Police Services Board v. Savino* (1996), 3 C.P.C. (4th) 159 (Ont. Gen. Div.).
179 *McCann v. The Ottawa Sun* (1993), 16 O.R. (3d) 672 (Gen. Div.) *per* Chilcott J.; *Seafarers International Union of Canada v. Lawrence* (1979), 24 O.R. (2d) 257 (C.A.).
180 *Elliott*, *supra* note 177 at 305 (C.A.).
181 Peter A. Downard *et al.*, "Class Action and Defamation: Haitian and Arab Taxi Drivers Authorized to Institute Class Action Against Radio Host André Arthur," <www.fasken.com> (accessed 31 December 2003).
182 We do not here address actions brought before administrative tribunals under human rights legislation, which frequently contain protections against some forms of discriminatory or hateful speech.
183 R.S.B.C. 1996, c. 49.

(b) if the prohibited act was directed against a class of persons, by any member of that class.

It appears that the cause of action has been asserted only in individual cases, and so far not successfully. It has not yet formed the basis for a class action.

In Quebec, the *Civil Code* contains no specific defamation provisions but does protect reputation, and claims for defamation may proceed under its general provisions.[184] The Supreme Court has held that the relevant statutory provisions are, *inter alia*, found in the Quebec *Charter of Human Rights and Freedoms*:

> 4. Every person has a right to the safeguard of his dignity, honour and reputation.
>
> ...
>
> 49. Any unlawful interference with any right or freedom recognized by this Charter entitles the victim to obtain the cessation of such interference and compensation for the moral or material prejudice resulting therefrom.
>
> In case of unlawful and intentional interference, the tribunal may, in addition, condemn the person guilty of it to exemplary damages.[185]

In addition, Quebec's *Civil Code*, which the Supreme Court called "the foundation of all other laws,"[186] provides:

> 3. Every person is the holder of personality rights, such as the right to life, the right to the inviolability and integrity of his person, and the right to the respect of his name, reputation and privacy.
>
> ...
>
> 35. Every person has a right to the respect of his reputation and privacy.[187]

---

184 In *Prud'homme v. Prud'homme*, [2002] 4 S.C.R. 663 [hereinafter *Prud'homme*], L'Heureux-Dubé and LeBel JJ., on behalf of the Court, found that Quebec civil law does not provide for a specific claim for defamation. Instead, defamation claims are based on Article 1457 of the Quebec *Civil Code*, which establishes the general tort scheme applicable to civil liability. The Court held at para. 32: "[I]n an action in defamation, the plaintiff must establish, on a balance of probabilities, the existence of injury, of a wrongful act, and of a causal connection, as in the case of any other action in civil, delictual or quasi-delictual liability. (See N. Vallières, *La presse et la diffamation* (1985), at p. 43; *Houde v. Benoit*, [1943] Que. K.B. 713, at p. 720; *Société Radio-Canada v. Radio Sept-Îles Inc.*, [1994] R.J.Q. 1811 (C.A.), at p. 1818.)"
185 *Charter of Human Rights and Freedoms*, R.S.Q., c. C-12.
186 *Prud'homme*, supra note 184 at para. 9.
187 *Civil Code of Québec*, S.Q. 1991, c. 64.

Group defamation actions have succeeded in Quebec in the past. In 1915 a speaker engaged in a vitriolic attack against Jews in Quebec City. Carroll J. of the Quebec Court of Appeal summarized the defendant's comments as follows:

> The accusation, in my view, may be summarized as follows: Jews are required to listen to the teachings of the Talmud. The Talmud teaches that these crimes are not crimes when committed against Christians. The Jew is the same everywhere — and after having listed all the abominations committed by the Jewish race, the conference speaker stated: Are you beginning to understand that the Jew is a man belonging to a separate species and that his presence amongst us is not desirable — what the Jew has done elsewhere, he will also do here if allowed.
>
> After having stated that his conference was not a personal aggression, the respondent stated what he said applies in Quebec and that he excluded no Jew of Quebec from the accusations he had brought against the Jewish race.[188]

The trial judge had found that no action in defamation existed given the generality of the language. The Court of Appeal disagreed, finding that the fact that there were only a small number of Jewish families in the city at that time supported an action by one of them in defamation:

> Undoubtedly, attacks against a race, even where such attacks are violent, cannot give rise to a claim in damages. Anyone who writes, may write anything they like against a group, subject to the restriction that, where any person of the group is specifically targeted by the libel and incurs damages, that person is entitled to a claim in the courts. Where the group is numerous, there is no right of claim, because the injury in such a case is not deemed to specifically target an individual. Whether or not a group is or is not sufficiently numerous to give rise to an action, is a question of fact left to the discretion and wisdom of the courts.[189]

In 1998 André Arthur, a Montreal radio show host, accused that city's Haitian and Arab taxi drivers of being incompetent and ignorant on his call-in program. He suggested that they could not speak French, that their taxis smelled, and that there must be corruption in the granting of licences. He referred to Arabs as "fakirs" and said that Haitians speak "ti-nègre," an insulting term denoting Black slang.

---

188 *Ortenberg v. Plamondon* (1914), 24 Que. K.B. 69 at 73. The English translation cited here was provided in the subsequent Quebec Court of Appeal decision of *Malhab v. Métromédia CMR Montréal Inc.*, infra note 190.

189 *Ibid.* at 73.

A class action was brought by a Lebanese taxi driver on behalf of 1,000 Haitian or Arab taxi drivers in the city. Again, the Superior Court found that the comments could not support individual rights of action sufficient to make a class claim, and again, the Court of Appeal quashed the trial court's decision. The court certified ("authorized") a class consisting of taxi drivers whose first language was either Arabic or Creole.[190]

M. CONSTITUTIONAL CLAIMS

Unconstitutional actions by government actors are not "torts" in any recognized sense of the word. They are, however, wrongs that can give rise to remedies, and because of the government's pervasive influence in society, they are frequently wrongs having a diffuse and massive impact, just like more traditional mass torts. It is therefore not surprising that lawyers and academics have begun to explore in earnest methods of employing techniques familiar from other areas of practice — principally the use of the class action suit — to assist in the resolution of constitutional questions.

There are two main areas of redress available for unconstitutional actions by government. Section 52 of the *Constitution Act, 1982* provides that laws inconsistent with the constitution are of no force or effect; and section 24(1) of the *Charter* permits any competent court to award damages for constitutional breaches.

1) Claims Based on the Invalidity of Laws

Most constitutional mass claims have been brought on the basis of section 52; that is, the argument is that a law (usually a law imposing taxes or other fees) is unconstitutional, and thus the government, either as a general proposition or in accord with the equitable principle of unjust enrichment, must return the illegally collected fees to those who have paid them.

The idea is fairly novel; until quite recently the common law generally accepted that there are "sound public policy reasons" to deny a general right of recovery of moneys "voluntarily" paid to the state as taxes under an invalid statute.[191] However, it has been pointed out since that Madam Justice Wilson delivered a powerful dissent in *Air Canada* and that in England the House of Lords has reversed the common law rule against recovery.[192]

---

190 *Malhab v. Métromédia CMR Montréal Inc.* (2003), 226 D.L.R. (4th) 722 (Que. C.A.).
191 *Air Canada v. British Columbia*, [1989] 1 S.C.R. 1161.
192 *Woolwich Building Society v. Inland Revenue Commissioners (No. 2)*, [1992] 3 All E.R. 737 (H.L.).

Moreover, Lamer C.J.C. and McLachlin J. (as she then was) expressly refrained from speaking to the issue.[193] When the issue arose again in *Nanaimo Immigrant Settlement Society v. British Columbia*,[194] the court found that the question was open.

The difficulty with pursuing constitutional actions against the government, even if the common law would permit recovery, is that the government enjoys the ability to change the law pertaining to the claims. While creative counsel have attempted to argue in several cases that the constitutional concept of the "rule of law" bars such retroactive denial of litigative rights, all such arguments have so far been unsuccessful, and as it stands the government enjoys a wide latitude in erasing its own debts. Laws to this effect were passed, and approved in *Air Canada*, above, and by Hutchinson J. in his fourth decision in the British Columbia charities litigation.[195] In the recent Supreme Court decision of *Authorson v. Canada*,[196] where Parliament had passed a law depriving disabled war veterans of the right to sue for certain interest they were owed dating as far back as the First World War, the Court was blunt:

> 62 The respondent and the class of disabled veterans it represents are owed decades of interest on their pension and benefit funds. The Crown does not dispute these findings. But Parliament has chosen for undisclosed reasons to lawfully deny the veterans, to whom the Crown owed a fiduciary duty, these benefits whether legal, equitable or fiduciary.

Beyond the substantive problems in pursuing a mass constitutional claim, there is also a lively debate as to whether class action lawsuits are appropriate in constitutional cases. Obviously, if only a declaration of invalidity is sought, that could be as easily achieved in an individual action (indeed, more easily, since a declaratory action would not require notice to the class, etc.). An early blow was dealt in the decision of the Supreme Court of Canada in *Guimond v. Quebec (Attorney General)*.[197] In that case, the plaintiff had been sentenced for failing to pay fines under a law that he challenged on the basis of the *Charter* and the *Quebec Charter of Human Rights and Freedoms*. He sought both a declaration of constitutional invalidity and "compensatory and moral damages" under the Quebec *Civil Code*. The case was initially dismissed for disclosing no "serious colour of right"

---

193 *Peel (Regional Municipality) v. Canada*, [1992] 3 S.C.R. 762 at 805.
194 [2001] B.C.J. No. 209 (C.A.).
195 *Nanaimo Immigrant Settlement Society v. British Columbia*, [2003] B.C.J. No. 2874 (S.C.).
196 *Authorson*, supra note 164.
197 [1996] 3 S.C.R. 347 (hereinafter *Guimond*].

for judicial determination. The Court of Appeal of Quebec had reversed that judgment, but the Supreme Court of Canada restored the earlier decision. In doing so, the Court took a restrictive view of the available procedure when damages are sought under section 24(1) of the *Charter*. Gonthier J. observed at paragraph 19:

> Although it cannot be said that damages can never be obtained following a declaration of constitutional invalidity, it is true, as a general rule, that an action for damages under s. 24(1) of the *Charter* cannot be coupled with a declaratory action for invalidity under s. 52 of the *Constitution Act, 1982*. The respondent based his claim for damages under s. 24(1) on a bare allegation of unconstitutionality. The facts did not warrant a departure from the general rule.

Then, at paragraph 20, Gonthier J. added that "it is not necessary to pursue a class action to obtain a declaration of constitutional invalidity and therefore, that it is generally undesirable to do so ...."

Subsequent to *Guimond*, however, lower courts have shown an increasing willingness to permit constitutional class actions to proceed. Reed J., in *Pawar v. Canada*,[198] distinguished *Guimond* on the basis of legislative differences between the "authorization" requirements of Quebec class action law and the Federal Court Rules, and said at paragraph 8:

> The comments at p. 361 of the *Guimond* decision relate to a provision of the Quebec *Civil Code of Procedure*. It differs in content from the Rule 1711. More importantly, however, those comments are obiter and leave open the question of when a class action is an appropriate vehicle for pursuing a challenge to the constitutionality of a legislative provision. For the reasons given by the prothonotary, the circumstances in this case are of such a type to make it appropriate to allow the litigation to be pursued by way of a class action.

Constitutional class actions have been allowed to proceed in *Howard Estate v. British Columbia*,[199] where the court certified a claim brought to recover probate fees paid pursuant to an allegedly invalid regulation, and in *Nanaimo Immigrant Settlement Society v. British Columbia*.[200]

---

198 [1997] F.C.J. No. 1288 (T.D.).
199 (1999), 66 B.C.L.R. (3d) 199 (S.C.).
200 *Supra* note 195.

2) Recovery for Breaches of *Charter* Rights

a) Overview of Civil *Charter* Claims

Section 24(1) of the *Canadian Charter of Rights and Freedoms*[201] provides the basis for an award of damages arising from a breach of the rights guaranteed in that document:

> 24. (1) Anyone whose rights or freedoms, as guaranteed by this Charter, have been infringed or denied may apply to a court of competent jurisdiction to obtain such remedy as the court considers appropriate and just in the circumstances.

Nevertheless, as Kent Roach describes, Canadian courts remain reluctant to award damages in *Charter* cases and prefer to view such cases through the lenses of traditional tort; this is particularly so where the breach "is not accompanied by traditional pecuniary loss."[202] Roach devotes considerable attention to the case of Jane Doe,[203] whose claim that the Toronto Metropolitan Police had failed to protect her from a serial rapist the police knew to be active in the area was upheld. Roach writes approvingly of the plaintiff's creative approach to pursuing her claim but notes that the substantial damages eventually awarded were made on the basis of common law principles of negligence, not on a breach of the constitution *per se*. However, duties based on the *Charter* can, as in *Jane Doe*, influence the outcome of the negligence analysis.[204]

M.L. Pilkington argues that recovery should be possible under section 24(1) independently of a tort claim, to facilitate recovery even in a case where tort law would not allow it, where the injury resulted directly from the breach of a *Charter* right.[205] She notes that "some *Charter* rights have no analogue in the law of torts," and even "where there is an analogue in the law of torts, it will not necessarily protect the victim's constitutional interests." Finally, she notes:

> [E]ven where the common law of tort would provide compensation for the actual injury suffered, the victim should not be confined to a common law

---

201 *Canadian Charter of Rights and Freedoms*, Part I of the *Constitution Act, 1982*, being Schedule B to the *Canada Act 1982* (U.K.), 1982 c. 11 [hereinafter *Charter*].
202 Kent Roach, *Constitutional Remedies in Canada*, looseleaf (Aurora, ON: Canada Law Book Inc., 2003) at 11-3 [hereinafter Roach].
203 *Doe v. Toronto (Metropolitan) Commissioners of Police* (1998), 58 D.L.R. (4th) 396 (Ont. H.C.J.).
204 Roach, *supra* note 202 at 11-6.
205 M.L. Pilkington, " Monetary Redress for *Charter* Infringement" in Robert J. Sharpe, ed., *Charter Litigation* (Toronto: Butterworths, 1987) at 307.

remedy ... Where a wrongful act gives rise both to an action at common law and an application for monetary redress under section 24(1) of the *Charter* it is not appropriate, in my view, to apply the principle that a court should seek to decide a case on other than constitutional grounds.[206]

Even if there is no injury as that term is understood at common law, Pilkington argues that a victim of a *Charter* breach should nonetheless be able to recover. She says: "The primary purpose of a remedy under section 24(1) of the *Charter* should be to redress the infringement of the constitutional right, regardless of whether it has resulted in actual injury."[207]

However persuasive Pilkington's arguments may be in certain individual cases of, for instance, police abuse, it is difficult to consider *per se* actionability in "mass" constitutional claims, lest liability become simply indeterminate. If a court finds that, for instance, certain restrictions on advertising are breaches of the *Charter*'s rights of free expression, who would be entitled to a pecuniary award? Each person who had, in accord with the law, decided not to advertise? If a policy of denying prisoners the right to vote is declared unconstitutional, is every prisoner so deprived permitted to recover, whether or not he or she would actually have exercised the franchise? While such a policy would exert a powerful deterrence incentive on the government, it could also paralyse the lawmaking process.

Auton (Guardian at litem of) v. British Columbia (Minister of Health) is perhaps the best example of the reluctance exhibited by courts when faced with constitutional "mass tort" claims. In that case, the petitioners sought declarations that the denial of funding for effective autism treatment was a violation of section 7 and of section 15 of the *Charter*, an order that the provincial government must fund both past and future treatment, and damages for failure to pay the cost of the treatment in the past or, alternatively, an order under section 24(1) of the *Charter* for indemnification for the cost of past and future treatment. The claim was initially launched as a class action, but Allan J. denied certification, allowing instead an application by the named petitioners to proceed by way of judicial review.[208]

In a subsequent decision,[209] Allan J. found that the provincial Crown had violated the section 15 equality rights of the infant petitioners, and, in later reasons on remedy,[210] she ordered certain treatment to be funded and

---

206 *Ibid.* at 311.
207 *Ibid.* at 313.
208 (1999), 12 Admin. L.R. (3d) 261 (B.C.S.C.).
209 (2000), 78 B.C.L.R. (3d) 55 (S.C.).
210 (2001), 84 B.C.L.R. (3d) 259 (S.C.).

a sum paid to the adult petitioners for what she termed "symbolic damages" for breach of *Charter* rights.

In reviewing the decisions of Allan J., the British Columbia Court of Appeal held that it should not interfere with the remedies ordered. Saunders J.A., writing for the majority, said:

> Unlike an action in tort or contract in which a party is entitled to damages proved to have been occasioned by the wrongdoing, damages are not automatic for a breach of *Charter* rights. In my view the last ten words of s. 24(1), "as the court considers appropriate and just in the circumstances" entitle a trial judge to considerable deference as to the remedy fashioned.[211]

While noting that the "discretionary" remedy under section 24 "is subject to differing views," the court mentioned at paragraph 95 some useful criteria that might be considered. The court suggested that it was relevant that the duty of the government had not been "obvious on the authorities" at the time of the alleged breach and that it was an issue "raised, for the first time within the jurisdiction." Also relevant was that "Madam Justice Allan did not find bad faith of government administrators or misfeasance in their performance of public responsibilities."[212] These factors, in the view of the court, supported the award of damages in an amount less than full compensation.

As for who should be awarded damages, the spectre of an opening floodgate was also raised, since the trial judge had "noted that many other children and families were in the same situation as the petitioners before her."[213]

The Court of Appeal concluded:

> [98] Madam Justice Allan chose to describe the damages awarded as "symbolic." A similar lack of specificity is found in the term "moral damages" awarded in *Du-Lude v. Canada*, [2001] 1 F.C. 545 (C.A.). While the term "symbolic damages" indicates a lack of definitive criteria for assessment of the quantum of damages, I do not consider that the generality of the term establishes an error in law entitling the petitioners to additional damages. A modest sum is, perhaps, an adequate way to recognize the breach of *Charter* rights, treating the petitioners alike, partially offsetting the out of pocket costs of the adult petitioners, and recognizing the policy reasons that often negate any award of damages for a *Charter* breach and

---

211 *Auton v. British Columbia*, [2002] B.C.J. No. 2258 at para. 96 (C.A.).
212 *Ibid.* at para 97.
213 *Ibid.*

which may have supported an order dismissing the entire claim for damages, an issue which is not before us.

[99] In all the circumstances, I would not interfere with the quantum of damages awarded.

The *Auton* decision was overturned by the Supreme Court of Canada,[214] which found that no constitutional violation had occurred. Having reached this decision, the Court offered no guidance with respect to the appropriateness of the remedies set out in the decisions of the courts below.

b) Does a *Charter* Damages Claim Require Bad Faith or Malice?

Bad faith and malice, touched upon by the *Auton* decisions, were also pivotal in a challenge to the Manitoba government's Winnipeg Centre Courthouse Perimeter Security Program, by which most persons entering the courthouse complex in Winnipeg were subject to a search of their person and belongings. The legality of the program had been successfully challenged, with the Court of Appeal deciding that the searches were arbitrary and breached section 8 of the *Charter*.

The search program nevertheless continued pursuant to an order signed by the chief justice of the Court of Queen's Bench shortly after the decision of the Court of Appeal. That process was also set aside by the Court of Appeal on the basis of a breach of section 8.[215] A few days later the Legislature enacted the *Court Security Act*,[216] pursuant to which the searches then continued.

The plaintiff brought a *Dutton* class action (i.e., a class claim in a province without class proceedings legislation), on behalf of all persons "unlawfully searched" between the inception of the program and the coming into force of the Act. The plaintiff asserted that, in this relevant period, about 546,000 searches were conducted, and claimed for $500 in respect of each search, for a total of $273,000,000.

The Court of Queen's Bench upheld a decision of a Master dismissing the action,[217] relying heavily on the court's finding that damages would not be appropriate, *inter alia* because of a lack of bad faith or malice. That decision was overturned, the Court of Appeal agreeing with the plaintiff that such a finding could not be made absent evidence and indeed before a state-

---

214 *Auton (Guardian at litem of) v. British Columbia (Attorney General)*, 2004 SCC 78.
215 *R. v. Gillespie* (2000), 145 Man.R. (2d) 229 (C.A.).
216 C.C.S.M., c. C.295.
217 *Neufeld v. Manitoba* (2001), 161 Man.R. (2d) 18 (Q.B.).

ment of defence had even been filed.[218] The court restored the plaintiff's claim, but there has, as yet, been no resolution of the substantive issues.

In *Shewfelt v. Canada*,[219] a prisoner in British Columbia claimed damages under section 24(1) because he had been prevented by statute from voting in the 1988 federal election. Although the Supreme Court had since ruled in another case that the statutory denial of the right to vote was unconstitutional,[220] Holmes J. held that, absent bad faith or malice, damages were not available against a government for legislative wrongs. In so doing, Holmes J. noted that there is "no evidence [the plaintiff] suffered any loss or damage different from any other inmate."[221] He applied the principles articulated by Lamer C.J.C. in *Schachter v. Canada*,[222] including that "an individual remedy under s. 24(1) of the *Charter* will rarely be available" in combination with an action to declare a provision unconstitutional and that "no retroactive s. 24 remedy will be available."

Other decisions have held that a finding of malice, while possibly sufficient, is not a necessary precondition to an award of damages pursuant to section 24(1) of the *Charter*. In *Krznaric v. Chevrette*,[223] Pardu J. nevertheless noted that it is the exception rather than the rule that damages would be awarded without such a finding.

Too restrictive interpretations of section 24(1) seem to make the section largely redundant. If a plaintiff is required to show either malice or bad faith, along with actual damage caused, in order for damages to be awarded, and if remedies are unlikely in cases where the unconstitutional behaviour was mandated or permitted by statute, then the *Charter* remedy appears to offer nothing above that for "misfeasance in a public office," and indeed the latter tort seems more useful. On the other hand, as noted earlier, too broad an application of the *Charter* remedy will lead to claims that, in the aggregate, appear absurd, such as the almost $300 million sought by the plaintiffs for the inconvenience of weapons searches upon entering the Winnipeg courthouse. While the *Charter* is an important tool for advancing the public interest in being free of such searches that fall short of justification, it is in turn difficult for persons so inconvenienced to insist that the indignity they allege requires that their fellow citizens pay them money; in

---

218 *Neufeld v. Manitoba*, [2002] 11 W.W.R. 395 (C.A.).
219 [1997] 4 W.W.R. 292 (B.C.S.C.).
220 *Sauvé v. Canada (Attorney General)*, [1993] 2 S.C.R. 438.
221 *Supra* note 219 at para. 23 (B.C.S.C.).
222 (1992), 93 D.L.R. (4th) 1 (S.C.C.).
223 [1997] O.J. No. 4712 (Gen. Div.).

such cases, the public interest seems to be twice abused, and the deterrent effect on future government actions questionable.

Other illegal search cases, however, do seem to call out for more substantial remedies. In June 2003 a lawsuit was filed in Vancouver regarding a blanket policy of strip-searching prisoners at a local detention centre,[224] allegedly in violation of established rules setting out that such searches were constitutional only where justified on a case-by-case basis. In the United States, several such actions have been permitted to proceed as constitutional class actions.[225] If an institution carries on a grossly humiliating and invasive procedure as a matter of policy, particularly when it knows that such a policy has no legal basis, then the situation demands a remedy more than the simply declaratory. However, whether the *Charter* would, in such a case, provide a better basis for pursuing the case than traditional torts like assault, battery, and misfeasance in public office remains to be seen.

---

224 See <www.cbc.ca/stories/2003/10/30/stripsearch031030> (accessed 31 December 2003).

225 See, for instance, *Bledsoe v. Combs*, 2000 U.S. Dist. LEXIS 7434 (S.D. Ind.) and *Noon v. Sailor*, 2000 U.S. Dist. LEXIS 7419 (S.D. Ind.); *Tardiff v. Knox County*, 2003 U.S. Dist. LEXIS 19924 (D. Me.); *Spinner v. City of New York*, 2003 U.S. Dist. LEXIS 19298 (E.D.N.Y.).

3. Remedies in Large-Scale Claims

A. INTRODUCTION

The remedy of choice for victims in large-scale claims will almost certainly be a damages award. The main purpose of a damages award is to compensate the plaintiff for any harm that has been suffered — whether that harm is physical, financial, or (though with limits) emotional and psychological. Secondarily, the law of damages may sometimes be deployed as a type of fine or punishment to deter defendants from particularly reprehensible conduct. This chapter will provide an overview of the law of damages — both compensatory and punitive. Beyond damages, the law also offers other remedies that have limited, though important, scope in product liability and other mass tort cases. Orders may be made that defendants disgorge profits made as a result of the unlawful activity; courts may make non-monetary orders (injunctions) where appropriate in order to require defendants to refrain from a course of conduct that is causing harm (or likely to cause harm); and, in some rare circumstances, courts may order defendants to take steps to undo harms that have already occurred.

B. STATUTORY REMEDIES

Most of the actions triggered by violations of statutory provisions do not require that a civil cause of action be granted in the statute. We have discussed at some length the action in negligence that may be available when statutory standards are not met. Similarly, statutes imposing statutory terms of contract[1] will give rise to actions at common law rather than under the statute *per se*.

Yet, there are examples of statutes that do grant or confirm civil remedies where they might not otherwise exist. We have discussed earlier the civil right of action created in provincial securities legislation;[2] we have also described how provincial "polluter pays" legislation can create civil causes of action in governments or individuals who have paid to clean up environmental damage.[3] We have also discussed the remedies that might be available in the mass tort setting under the *Charter of Rights and Freedoms*.

Space does not permit a comprehensive review of statutes that create civil liabilities in ways that may be relevant to mass tort actions. However, in any discussion of remedies in a book on large-scale claims, some consideration of this subject is warranted.

As a general rule, sanctions under *federal* law are strictly penal in nature. The important exception is the *Competition Act*, which provides both penal and civil sanctions. Under the Act, a person in contravention of its provisions may be liable for a fine or to imprisonment for a term ranging from a maximum of one year to a maximum of five years (depending on the offence), or to both a fine and imprisonment. In addition, the Act provides a civil remedy to any person who has suffered losses due to a breach of the Act, without any regard to a conviction. This civil remedy has

---

1   Such as the implied warranties codified in the Sale of Goods Acts. *Sale of Goods Act*, R.S.B.C. 1979, c. 370; *Sale of Goods Act*, R.S.A. 1980, c. S-2; *Sale of Goods Act*, S.S. 1978, c. S-1; *Sale of Goods Act*, R.S.M. 1987, c. S.10; *Sale of Goods Act*, R.S.O. 1990, c. S.1; *Sale of Goods Act*, R.S.N.S. 1989, c. 408; *Sale of Goods Act*, R.S.N.B. 1973, c. S-1; *Sale of Goods Act*, R.S.P.E.I. 1988, c. S-1; *Sale of Goods Act* R.S.N. 1990, c. S-6.

2   Securities Acts. See *Securities Act*, R.S.B.C. 1996, c. 418; *Securities Act*, S.A. 1981, c. S-6.1; *Securities Act*, 1988, S.S. 1988, c. S-42.2; *Securities Act*, R.S.M. 1988, c. S.50; *Securities Act*, R.S.O. 1990, c. S.5; *Securities Act*, R.S.Q., c. V-1.1; *Securities Act*, R.S.N.S. 1989, c. 418; *Security Frauds Prevention Act*, R.S.N.B. 1973, c. S-6; *Securities Act*, R.S.P.E.I. 1988, c. S-3; and *Securities Act*, R.S.N. 1990, c. S-13, all as amended.

3   Provincial legislation includes the *Environment Management Act*, R.S.B.C. 1996, c. 118; *Environmental Protection and Enhancement Act*, R.S.A. 2000, c. E-12, ss. 2(i), 112, 113(1), 114(1), 116; *Environmental Management and Protection Act, 2002*, S.S. 2002, c. E-10.21; *Contaminated Sites Remediation Act*, S.M. 1996, c. C.205; *Environmental Protection Act*, R.S.O. 1990, c. E.19; *Pesticides Act*, R.S.O. 1990, c. P.11; *Ontario Water Resources Act*, R.S.O. 1990, c. O.40; *Crown Forest Sustainability Act*, 1994, S.O. 1994, c. 25; *Environment Act*, S.N.S. 1994-95, c. 1; *Environmental Protection Act*, S.N.L. 2002, c. E-14.2; *Environmental Protection Act*, R.S.P.E.I. 1988, c. E-9; *Environmental Protection Act*, R.S.N.W.T. 1988, c. E-7.

been upheld as valid legislation under the federal government's trade and commerce power in *General Motors v. City National Leasing*.[4]

All eight provinces with trade practices legislation[5] provide for both general and punitive or exemplary damages; however, in Ontario and Prince Edward Island only an "unconscionable representation" will trigger punitive damages. Rescission, or the nullification of a contract, is available in all eight provinces with trade practices legislation, although it is not specifically mentioned in the Saskatchewan legislation.

Equitable remedies may also be available to the consumer under the trade practices statutes. Specific performance may be awarded in Alberta, British Columbia, Newfoundland, Manitoba, Saskatchewan, and Quebec. Quebec also allows courts to order the execution of the obligation at the vendor's expense, or provide for the reduction of consumer obligations under the unfair contract. In Alberta, British Columbia, Newfoundland, Saskatchewan, and Manitoba, the court may grant injunctions or make declarations regarding unfair practices.

Nor are the civil remedies available only at the instigation of consumers. In Alberta, British Columbia, Newfoundland, Saskatchewan, and Manitoba, the director of trade practices (or the equivalent) may become a party to the consumer's action, and may even commence and maintain actions against a supplier on behalf of consumers.

C. COMPENSATORY DAMAGES

1) Generally

The primary purpose of a damages award is *restitution in integrum*. Damages are a sum of money that is designed (so far as possible) to put the plaintiffs in the position as though they had not been injured. Thus, when persons are physically injured, a damages award will be fashioned to compensate them for any financial losses they suffer (in terms both of actual

---

4   [1989] 1 S.C.R. 641. Only if the "pith and substance" of the federal law is not to create a civil remedy but rather concerns a matter within federal power will a civil remedy based on the law be valid. In *MacDonald v. Vapor Canada*, [1977] 2 S.C.R. 134, a provision granting a civil remedy under the *Trade-Marks Act* was struck down on the basis that it was "simply a formulation of the tort of conversion" and therefore in substance a provincial matter.

5   *Unfair Trade Practices Act*, R.S.A. 1980, c.U-3; *Trade Practice Act*, R.S.B.C. 1979, c. 406; *Trade Practices Act*, R.S.N. 1990, c. T-7; *Business Practices Act*, R.S.O. 1990, c. B.18; *Business Practices Act*, R.S.P.E.I. 1988, c. B-7; *Consumer Protection Act*, R.S.Q., c. P-40.1; *Business Practices Act*, S.M. 1990–91, c.6; *Consumer Protection Act*, S.S. 1997, c. 30.1.

expenses associated with care and rehabilitation and of financial losses as a result of lost work and other opportunities); for their expected future losses (in terms both of the costs of care and diminished income); and also for their pain and suffering.

The common law lays out a clear schema for the calculation of such damages.[6] First, the court will assess past or "special" losses; they are actual proven expenses and losses incurred until the time of trial. They will typically include medical expenses, the costs of care incurred to date, and lost income from employment. Proving and recovering these costs is relatively straightforward (though, in an adversarial system not without controversy over whether an expense incurred was truly the result of the injury and whether it was a reasonable expense). More complex is the question of future damages — the estimated losses that the plaintiff will continue to incur into the future as a result of the injury.

Future losses are divided into three heads: the cost of care; lost earning capacity; and pain and suffering. The cost of care is an amount of money (assessed in a present-day lump sum) that will fully cover the plaintiff's reasonably anticipated personal, medical, and therapeutic expenses arising out of the injury. Lost earning capacity is the difference between the plaintiff's economic prospects before and after the injury. In both cases, establishing the appropriate amount is a complex task, one that requires lawyers, experts, and ultimately the court to look far into the future and make a determination about the course of the plaintiff's physical condition and resulting needs and likely personal and economic prospects over the remainder of his or her lifetime. Awkwardly, the entire future loss must then be calibrated in terms of a single present-value lump sum, thus increasing the complexity of the court's task.

2) Future Care

In a nutshell, the following summarizes the assessment of damages for future care:

Future Prospects and Level of Care: Expert evidence must be adduced to permit the court to predict (as best as possible) what the plaintiff's future will hold — whether the injury is permanent, whether it will worsen over time, or whether the plaintiff might recover from it. Then, other experts will help

---

6   *Andrews v. Grand & Toy Alberta Ltd.* (1978), 83 D.L.R. (3d) 452 (S.C.C.); *Arnold v. Teno* (1978), 83 D.L.R. (3d) 609 (S.C.C.); and *Thornton v. Prince George School District No. 57* (1978), 83 D.L.R. (3d) 480 (S.C.C.) [hereinafter *The Trilogy*]; Jamie Cassels, *Remedies: The Law of Damages* (Toronto: Irwin Law, 2000).

to predict the likely costs resulting from these injuries. So, for example, where there is a serious physical injury, the plaintiff may require long-term physiotherapy, drugs, medicines, and future medical procedures that may not be fully covered by any public insurance plan. The plaintiff may require a nurse or attendant for some or all of the day; additional costs for transportation; and special needs in relation to shelter (e.g., wheelchair accessibility). In many instances, a judgment call will have to be made as to the appropriate level of care. For example, where the injury is catastrophic and results in serious impairment of function, the question will be whether the plaintiff should be cared for in an institutional setting, a group home, or the plaintiff's own house. Of course, the choice made will have a dramatic influence on the cost. The overriding principle is that, while the expenditure must be one that a reasonable person should make, the plaintiff is entitled to any costs that are reasonably justifiable in the circumstances, and simply "keeping the cost down" is not a reason to deny the plaintiff a legitimate expense. So, for example, in many cases the plaintiff is awarded the cost of living in his or her own home, with an attendant.

Contingency Deductions: Possible future changes in circumstances (e.g., chance of early recovery or of a worsening condition) must be taken into account. For example, as a result of the primary injury, the plaintiff may face a risk of secondary future injuries or complications that require further expenditures. If there is some evidence of such a possibility, it can be taken into account as a "contingency" and assigned a value based on the probability that it might occur. Other contingencies may reduce the award — for example, the possibility of early recovery. Even in the absence of specific evidence of contingencies, the courts often apply a factor (usually to reduce the award) to take into account the "vicissitudes of life." The theory here is that, even if the plaintiff had not been injured, he or she might have encountered other forms of adversity in life (natural illness and misfortune) as a contingency.

Collateral Benefits: In many cases, monetary compensation from the defendant will not be the only source of support for an injured plaintiff. In Canada, the provincial health insurance schemes will cover most of the direct medical expenses. The plaintiff may have additional private insurance. Family and friends may provide in-kind support. Where such assistance is likely to be forthcoming, defendants often make the argument that its value should be taken into account in setting the damages award. For example, if the plaintiff's spouse is likely to provide voluntary care for the plaintiff, there is no need for a damages award to cover the cost of nursing or attendance. Not surprisingly, courts take a hard look at such arguments.

While the value of public health insurance is, in fact, taken into account in determining the cost of care, most other "collateral benefits" received by the plaintiff (such as private insurance and family assistance) are not. While this may have the ultimate effect that the plaintiff is, in fact, "overcompensated" (in that the damages award may cover expenditures that are not going to be made), this is thought to be preferable to giving the defendant the benefit of the plaintiff's own foresight and expense in purchasing insurance, or to "conscripting" family members to provide services to the plaintiff that ultimately accrue to the financial benefit of the defendant.

Duration of Care: The costs of care must, of course, be estimated over the plaintiff's entire remaining lifespan. Where the injury has in fact shortened the plaintiff's likely lifespan, it is the actual remaining lifespan and not the pre-injury lifespan that governs the amount of the award. This may seem harsh, but it is not the purpose of compensatory damages to punish the defendant or overcompensate the plaintiff. If damages were awarded for costs of care beyond the actual life of the plaintiff, the funds would serve no useful purpose except to increase the value of the plaintiff's estate (note that courts take a different approach to this issue in relation to lost income).

Discounting to Present Value: The award of damages is a present-value lump-sum award, arrived at by estimating all the future losses. Because the losses are in the future, the amount required to compensate them in present-value terms is a different sum of money. The primary variables, of course, are the rate of inflation and the rate of interest. Because of inflation, future losses or costs are likely to be higher than present-day costs. However, the sum of money awarded today will not be expended until the future and will, therefore, be earning interest if properly invested (and will therefore be a larger amount in the future). The "discount rate" is a factor that takes into account the impact of both inflation and interest on damages awards. Essentially, the discount rate is the difference between long-term inflation and long-term interest rates and, in most provinces, is set at about 3 percent. In other words, it assumes that the purchasing power of a dollar today, if properly invested, will exceed the rate of inflation by about 3 percent. In the end, therefore, the present-day lump-sum award will in fact be smaller than the anticipated future loss.

Taxation: The courts will also attempt to compensate for the effect of taxation, at least in some respects. For instance, an award for the cost of future care will be "grossed up" (i.e., increased) to compensate for the effects on the award of income tax. Paradoxically, however, awards for past loss of income and future loss of earning capacity will not be similarly "grossed down."

3) Lost Earning Capacity

The award for lost earning capacity is an amount that is designed to measure the difference in the plaintiff's pre- and post-injury economic prospects. The following summarizes the courts' approach:

Pre-accident Prospects: First, the court must determine how the plaintiff might have fared economically had the injury not occurred. At the time of the injury, the plaintiff may have had a certain level of income that provides a starting point for the analysis, but the court must take into account the fact that the plaintiff might have improved his or her prospects. In the case of children and young people, the exercise is even more hypothetical since the plaintiff will have no economic track record. In such cases, experts will be brought in to testify as to the likely economic profile of the plaintiff given his or her level of education and other personal characteristics. The amount assessed by the court is based on the pre-tax income of the plaintiff.

Post-accident Prospects: Further evidence will be necessary to determine the plaintiff's post-accident prospects. Will the plaintiff be able to work at all, and at what level? Is there a chance that his or her condition will deteriorate further or in fact improve? What level of income might the plaintiff expect to achieve over his or her lifetime? An estimation of the plaintiff's residual earning power is necessary in order to determine the net loss.

Positive Contingencies and Lost Chances: A person's actual earnings at the time of an injury are rarely a full indication of his or her actual lifetime earning capacity. Individuals advance in their work and careers, receive promotions, change jobs, and sometimes radically improve their prospects. Such positive contingencies are sometimes simply factored in generally to the court's estimate of pre-accident earning capacity. But, especially in situations where there are significant positive contingencies that are unique to the individual plaintiff, those "lost chances" will be separately valued. For example, in cases where, at the time of the accident, the plaintiff is employed in an occupation but there is evidence that he or she is planning a significant change, the "value" of that change can be factored into the award. In *Conklin v Smith*[7] a young man lost his leg in an accident. He had been taking steps towards his goal of becoming a commercial airline pilot and could no longer do that. The court agreed that there was a reasonable possibility that he might have achieved his goal and awarded the amount

---

7   [1978] 2 S.C.R. 1107.

of $5,000 per year to compensate for this lost chance. The sum awarded is roughly the value of the lost opportunity, discounted by the probability that it would or would not have occurred.

Negative Contingencies: Just as there are positive chances that affect a person's economic prospects, so are there negative chances — such as sickness, unemployment, economic downturns, and so on. Typically, courts will make a general assessment of these "negative contingencies" and make a general deduction from the award (often in the range of 10–20 percent).

Collateral Benefits: An accident victim will frequently receive income assistance from private insurance, social assistance, family members, or charitable organizations. This income does, in fact, make up for some of the income loss suffered as a result of the accident. However, it is practically never deducted from the award for lost income. The courts are more comfortable tolerating some element of "overcompensation" of the plaintiff as opposed to "subsidizing" the defendant by giving him or her credit for amounts intended to benefit the plaintiff.

Duration and Discounting: The award for earning capacity is calculated by determining the stream of lost income over the plaintiff's entire pre-accident working life (i.e., to age sixty-five unless there is evidence that the plaintiff would have retired earlier or would have died earlier). Even in cases where the injury has significantly shortened the plaintiff's actual lifespan, the award is still based on the pre-injury lifespan, since this represents the actual loss suffered by the plaintiff. The future loss is then discounted to a present-day lump sum as described above.

4) Pain and Suffering

The third major head of damages for personal injury is "non-pecuniary damages." These damages include compensation for pain and suffering and lost enjoyment of life. Canadian courts take a distinctive and rather restrictive approach to these damages for the reason that they are so difficult to measure and so potentially unlimited in amount. In an effort to achieve some consistency among awards, and also to control the ultimate amounts, the Supreme Court of Canada developed two tools in a trilogy of 1978 cases.[8] The first is a cap on the total amount of damages in even the

---

8   *The Trilogy, supra* note 6. In this "trilogy," the Supreme Court made clear that it was influenced by the policy concern to avoid the escalation of damages.

most serious cases. Originally set at a rough figure of $100,000 in 1978, the cap has been increased for inflation since that time.[9]

The second tool articulated in the damages trilogy is a "functional approach" to the assessment of non-pecuniary damages. Courts do not try to value pain and suffering in the abstract but rather take a pragmatic approach, asking what uses can money be put to in order to alleviate the plaintiff's suffering and lost enjoyment of life. While in most cases courts do award "conventional" sums, the functional approach at least provides a basis for a rational and evidence-based approach to quantifying damages.

D. SPECIAL ISSUES AND APPROACHES IN MASS TORT AND PRODUCT LIABILITY CASES

Product liability cases — especially those involving hazardous substances and toxic exposures — raise particularly challenging issues for the law of damages. Unlike a single-incident, traumatic physical injury, toxic torts may have less obvious causal chains, long disease-latency periods, and uncertain future outcomes and effects. Courts, particularly in the United States, have developed unique damages orders to deal with some of these features.

1) Individualization versus Aggregation

It will be obvious from the above description that personal injury damages are highly individualized. Each question — the degree of physical injury and impairment, the economic consequences of the injury, the future prognosis — is unique to each individual who suffers harm. Thus, while personal injuries will usually be the central problem in a mass tort case, there is no easy way to deal with such injuries except on a case-by-case basis. Later in this book we discuss the advantages — indeed the necessity — of aggregating actions in mass tort claims, yet when it comes to providing a remedy such aggregation is very difficult, if not impossible, to achieve.

Thus, while it is conceptually and procedurally easy to understand how a class or representative action provides the appropriate vehicle in large-scale products liability and other tort cases, when the matter comes to damages the case is virtually always "disaggregated." The most dramatic illustration of this occurred in the Bhopal litigation. In that case, a 1984 chemical spill from a Union Carbide plant in India injured hundreds of

---

9   *Lindal v. Lindal*, [1981] 2 S.C.R. 629, held that inflation was a factor that could be considered to warrant an increase in the cap. At the time of this writing, the amount adjusted for inflation would be approximately $300,000.

thousands of nearby residents. The Indian government brought a single action (*parens patriae*) on behalf of all the victims and eventually settled the case for $470 million dollars. While the aggregate settlement was achieved in 1992, the government then had to establish a tribunal system to assess individual compensation for the victims, and indeed, as late as 2004, this system had still failed to complete the task of distributing all of the funds to injured individuals.[10]

In Canada, class action legislation frequently provides for aggregate assessment of damages, but such aggregation only can occur when the damages for individuals is identical or measurable in a simple arithmetical way that does not really require individualization. An example would be in a securities case where the harm caused by a misrepresentation is exactly proportionate to the number of shares owned by each class member. Another example might be a contractual claim for a defective product where the damages are measured simply by the cost of replacing a part, where that cost is identical for each plaintiff. However, when it comes to personal injuries, the semblance of similarity is gone. Indeed, one of the historical reasons for the absence of class action jurisprudence in products liability law is due to the fact that the individual nature of damages undermines the claim to commonality amongst the class members. Indeed, attempts to certify class actions have failed because of the individual nature of the damages problems so substantially outweighs the other common issues.[11]

An example of the problem is *Bywater v. Toronto Transit Commission*[12] in which a class proceeding was certified for about 100 people who had been injured in a subway fire. The Court would not, however, consider an aggregate assessment of damages, saying

> In my view, the case at bar is not appropriate for an aggregate assessment of damages. The action advances claims for personal injury, property damage and claims under the Family Law Act. These claims cannot, "reasonably be determined without proof by individual class members" as required by s. 24(1)(c). Furthermore, each individual claim will require proof of the essential element of causation, which, in the words of 24(1)(b), is "a question of fact or law other than those relating to an assessment of damages."

---

10 See Jamie Cassels, *The Uncertain Promise of Law: Lessons from Bhopal* (Toronto: University of Toronto Press, 1993).
11 *Caputo v. Imperial Tobacco Ltd.*, [2004] O.J. No. 299 (S.C.J.).
12 [1998] O.J. No. 4913 at paras. 18–19 (S.C.J.).

In addition, the assessment of damages in each case will be idiosyncratic. All of the usual factors must be considered in assessing individual damage claims for personal injury, such as: the individual plaintiffs [sic] time of exposure to smoke; the extent of any resultant injury; general personal health and medical history; age; any unrelated illness; and other individual considerations. Indeed here, the representative plaintiff was suffering from and experiencing symptoms of food poisoning at the time of the incident. The property damage claims of class members must be assessed individually as the underlying facts will vary from one class member to the next.

Despite the difficulty of awarding damages in the aggregate, most class proceedings legislation does permit courts to provide special rules and procedures for a more expeditious and less costly approach to the determination of individual issues such as damages. For example, under the B.C. *Class Proceedings Act*,[13] once the common issues have been decided, a court may put in place special procedures for the determination of the remaining individual issues. The court may appoint experts to prepare reports or to conduct inquiries into the individual matters (and report back to the court), and may make special rules for expedited and streamlined procedures to deal with those issues. In doing so, "the court must choose the least expensive and most expeditious method of determining the individual issues that is consistent with justice to members of the class or subclass and the parties ..."[14]

As mentioned, class action legislation also provides for aggregate assessment of damages[15] — though these provisions are generally only easily invoked when the damages to each class member are the same, or can be determined without individual proof. Some courts have indicated a willingness to go somewhat farther and to apply aggregate techniques in "simple" personal injury cases. Even where there are many individuals, their losses may be sufficiently similar, and of a modest amount, so as not to warrant individualized assessment. In *Anderson v. Wilson*,[16] the Ontario Court of Appeal considered an application for class certification for patients who had had possible exposure to Hepatitis B from electroencephalogram tests (EEGs). While the lower court had certified as a class those who had contracted Hepatitis B, those who had subsequently tested negative had *not* been certified as a class. The Court of Appeal held that not only should they

---

13   R.S.B.C. 1996, c. 50.
14   *Ibid.*, s.27
15   See, for example, s. 28 of the B.C. *Class Proceedings Act, ibid.*
16   (1999), 44 O.R. (3d) 673 (C.A.), leave to appeal to S.C.C. refused [1999] S.C.C.A. No. 476 [hereinafter *Anderson*].

be a class, but in obiter suggested that the damages for nervous shock in this case might be assessed in the aggregate: "... the nature of the overall claim lends itself to aggregate treatment because individual reactions to the notices would likely be similar in each case — fear of a serious infection and anxiety during the waiting period for a test result."[17]

So while the court seems reluctant to consider anything other than individual awards for economic loss or personal physical injury sustained in class proceedings matters, *Anderson* suggests they are more willing to consider aggregate damages for types of injury (e.g. mental suffering) where the individual damages are not generally computed with mathematical precision in any event. No other cases have yet gone so far in suggesting a willingness to depart from individual justice in relation to personal injury damages. Class Action legislation and procedures are discussed fully in subsequent chapters.

2) Medical Monitoring

In some cases, plaintiffs may be able to prove that they have been exposed to a harmful substance, but that the real anticipated harm is not yet manifest. The traditional law of damages deals with such cases rather bluntly. If no harm or injury has yet occurred, the case may simply be dismissed. If there is some indication of harm, albeit minor, the cause of action is made out; the court will award damages for the harm that has already occurred, and then, in a speculative exercise, will award damages for the further consequences that might yet occur in the future. This all-or-nothing approach is unsatisfactory. If no harm has yet occurred (though is likely to occur in the future), the plaintiff receives no compensation whatsoever. If some minor harm has occurred, the cause of action is established and the court will speculate about the future. This exposes both the plaintiff and the defendant to very real risks of both under- and over-compensation.

a) In the United States

Medical monitoring/surveillance damages are awarded in order to assist plaintiffs in tracking their health and detecting latent diseases early in their development. *Ayers v. Jackson Township*[18] was the first case in the United States to recognize future medical-surveillance costs. The plaintiffs were residents who sued for damages when their water was contaminated by toxic pollutants. The Supreme Court of New Jersey agreed with the trial

---

17 *Ibid.* at 679.
18 106 N.J. 557, 525 A.2d 287 (Sup. Ct. 1987).

award and overturned the appellate reversal. The judgment stated that "it is inequitable for an individual, wrongfully exposed to dangerous toxic chemicals ... to have to pay his own expenses when medical intervention is clearly reasonable and necessary."[19]

American courts have been inconsistent in their requirement for actual physical injury. Some courts have disallowed these "speculative" damage awards altogether because there is no manifested physical injury.[20] In *Herber v. Johns-Manville Corporation*,[21] the court required that there be a manifest injury, or at least a reasonably probable or greater than average risk of developing a future disease. However, courts seem to be leaning towards a more plaintiff-favoured approach. In *Merry v. Westinghouse Elec. Corp.*,[22] the court held that a plaintiff asking for medical-monitoring compensation need demonstrate only the potential for physical injury, not the physical injury itself. Since this case, other courts have adopted the same modified stance and awarded future medical-monitoring damages on the basis of potential, rather than manifest, physical injury.[23]

Medical-monitoring claims may also be bolstered by statutory authority. In the United States, the *Comprehensive Environmental Response, Compensation and Liability Act*, or *CERCLA*,[24] has been thought to provide some support for such claims, depending upon the court's interpretation of "necessary cost of response" under the statute. Medical monitoring has often been deemed to fall under this provision. In *Williams v. Allied Automotive, Autolite Division*,[25] the court found that medical-testing expenses incurred to assess the effect of the exposure on the public, rather than on individuals' health, are recoverable response costs under *CERCLA*.[26] Another case also distinguished between individual versus public interest. The court determined that the individual claim for medical-surveillance damages did not fall under "necessary costs of response" but public interest would warrant these damages.[26]

---

19 *Ibid* at 312.
20 *Ball v. Joy Mfg. Co.*, 755 F. Supp. 1344 (S.D. W. Va. 1990).
21 785 F.2d 79 (3d Cir. 1986).
22 684 F. Supp. 847, 849 (M.D. Pa. 1988).
23 See also: *Paoli R.R. Litig.*, 916 F.2d 829 (3d Cir. 1990); *Burns v. Jaquays Mining Corp.*, 156 Ariz. 375, 752 P.2d 28 (Ct. App. 1987).
24 42 U.S.C. §§ 9601–6987 (1988).
25 704 F. Supp. 782 (N.D. Ohio 1988).
26 *Brewer v. Ravan*, 680 F. Supp. 1176, 1179 (M.D. Tenn. 1988). Contrary to the *Brewer* line of cases are those in which the courts do not interpret the language of *CERCLA* so generously, such as *Ambrogi v. Gould, Inc.*, 750 F. Supp. 1233 (M.D. Pa. 1990).

There are numerous benefits in requiring defendants to pay for ongoing medical monitoring — at least in the United States. First, many plaintiffs could not afford to pay for this required monitoring themselves as individuals; yet many diseases are more difficult (and expensive) to treat as they progress. The overall costs of *not* establishing payment for such a regime are therefore much higher if the plaintiff is left to his or her own devices. Second, through such screening procedures, the medical community learns more about toxic exposure and effective ways to treat it. Finally, the potentially expensive ongoing monitoring serves a deterrent function to potential tortfeasors, since it more accurately internalizes the costs of the harm done.

b) In Canada

These advantages of medical-monitoring claims are not quite so obvious in Canada. In light of a scheme of universal health insurance, the cost argument is not as persuasive. Potential victims of toxic exposure will have access to basic medical services for the purpose of monitoring their health. However, provincial health insurance schemes may not cover all the required (or desired) forms of monitoring, and increasing restrictions on forms of testing and treatment may result in an increase in the frequency of lawsuits claiming these costs in Canada.

There is only one mass tort case in Canada discussing medical-monitoring claims in any detail: *Wilson v. Servier Canada Inc.*[27] This was a class action proceeding in which the plaintiffs had ingested potentially dangerous diet pills, Ponderal or Redux. Neither representative plaintiff had present physical injury but wished to determine through medical screening if they had suffered any adverse health effects. The claim sought special damages for medical costs for two groups. First, there were class members who did contract diseases, allegedly due to the ingestion of Ponderal or Redux, who claimed their medical costs. Second, there were those persons who needed to determine whether they had the diseases allegedly resulting from the ingestion of Ponderal or Redux. The defendants objected to this proposed inclusion of a claim for the latter group, presumably on the basis that, without manifest symptoms, they had no cause of action. The court considered American case law on medical screening and monitoring. It held in this case that, if exposure to a toxic substance is proven to increase significantly the risk of contracting a serious disease, then plaintiffs should be compensated for the cost of medical screening made necessary by their exposure. The court also paid keen deference to the fact that a Health Canada advisory recommended that persons who had taken either drug should consult with their physician immediately.

---

27 (2000), 50 O.R. (3d) 219 (S.C.J.) [hereinafter *Wilson*].

Given that medical monitoring expenses are borne largely by the public health care system, there is some potential in Canada for such claims to be brought by health authorities. However, despite the universal health care system and statutes permitting subrogation, in Canada, such claims brought by government medical plans on behalf of mass tort victims have been rare,[28] although it appears that this may be changing. There are several reasons for the rarity. Aside from the uncertainty of medical-monitoring claims,[29] not all Canadian provinces even have statutes permitting subrogation for the recovery of such expenses,[30] in part because such clauses have proven cumbersome and inefficient in individual actions. Also, it is not certain whether such statutes are sufficient to grant full control of the proceedings to the government insurer (a problem that sometimes plagues private insurers as well).[31] Multijurisdictional class proceedings complicate this matter further; since many consequential health care costs arising as a result of exposure in one province are actually felt in another.

3) Fear of Disease (Emotional Distress)

Especially in cases involving toxic agents, where the effects are ultimately unknown, a person may live not only with a manifest injury but with psy-

---

28 The claim has been advanced in the Phen-Fen diet pill litigation, where provincial health plans are claiming as subrogees for the cost of medical monitoring. The hearing judge refused to dismiss the claim, and on appeal it was noted that medical-monitoring claims have been advanced previously in Canada: see *Wilson, ibid.* Cumming J. found that the question of whether a subrogated claim can be maintained for the cost of medical monitoring was a common issue. *Wilson* at para. 133, leave to appeal dismissed: (2000), 52 O.R. (3d) 20 (S.C.J.). The court of appeal found (at para. 18) that the "issue is arguable and should not be excluded at this stage of the proceeding." Medical-monitoring pleadings had been allowed to proceed in *Nantais v. Telectronics Proprietary (Canada) Ltd.* (1995), 127 D.L.R. (4th) 552 (Gen. Div.), leave to appeal refused (1995), 129 D.L.R. (4th) 110 (Gen. Div.), leave to appeal denied (1996), 28 O.R. (3d) 523 (Gen. Div.); and *Anderson v. Wilson* (1999), 44 O.R. (3d) 673 at 675–76, 175 D.L.R. (4th) 409 (C.A.). Neither case offered resolution of the legal question.

29 See *ibid.* American courts have disagreed about whether a plaintiff can recover medical-monitoring costs where the monitoring confirms that the disease is not present. Some cases regard the test as being whether the exposure to a toxic substance is the "proximate cause" of a "significantly increased risk" of contracting a serious latent disease: see *Barnes v. American Tobacco Co.*, 161 F.3d 127 at 138–39 Pa. (3d Cir. C.A. 1998); *Ayres v. Jackson*, 525 A.2d 287 (N.J. 1987) at 298 and 311. Some aspects of the issue are discussed by the United States Supreme Court in *Metro-North Commuter Railroad Co. v. Buckley*, 521 U.S. 424 (1997) at 441–44.

30 Ontario has such a plan (*Health Insurance Act*, R.S.O. 1990, c. H.6, ss. 30–36), but B.C. as yet does not.

31 Craig Brown, *Insurance Law in Canada* (Toronto: Carswell, 2001) at 13–21 *et seq.*

chological trauma associated with his or her uncertain condition. Damages are sometimes claimed for "fear of cancer" or "fear of future harm." This head of damage is designed to compensate victims of toxic exposure for the fear they sustain in knowing that they have been exposed to cancer-causing agents. Again, the manifest physical injury requirement presents an obstacle to plaintiffs making this claim. The traditional common law rule is that, in negligence cases, emotional distress must go hand-in-hand with physical injury. However, the toxic tort context has demanded a modification of this rule for plaintiffs who do not have, as of yet, a physical injury.

In *Potter v. Firestone Tire and Rubber Co.*[32] the plaintiffs resided next to a landfill in which the defendant's hazardous wastes were dumped. The plaintiffs did not have any manifest physical injuries at the time of trial. However, the court found the negligence of this company to be so malicious and offensive that a new interpretation of the "physical injury rule" was required. The court held that "in the absence of a present physical injury ... recovery of damages for fear of cancer in a negligence action should be allowed only if the plaintiff ... proves that the fear stems from a knowledge, corroborated by reliable medical and scientific opinion, that it is more likely than not that cancer will develop in the future due to the toxic exposure."[33] While an important decision, this case sets a high threshold. It is a rare type of exposure that will make it "more likely than not" that cancer will result; far more often, the probability of disease manifestation is only incremental, but not necessarily less worrying. While some limit must be set to prevent purely speculative or spurious claims, the 50-percent "more likely than not" rule is a virtually insurmountable threshold.

Another creative way around the physical injury rule was seen in the case of *Laxton v. Orkin Exterminating Co.*[34] The court held that, "if the plaintiffs ingested any amount of the toxic substance, it is the judgment of the court that there is at least a technical physical inquiry."[35] An obvious concern under this head of damage is the potential for spurious claims. Absent a physical injury requirement, the floodgates could certainly be opened for fraudulent or exaggerated claims. Utah Supreme Court Justice Durham noted in *obiter* in *Hansen v. Mountain Fuel Supply Co.*[36] that, through "advances in the field of psychiatry and psychology, it is now possible to establish emotional illness

---

32   863 P.2d 795 (Cal. Sup. Ct. 1993) [hereinafter *Potter*].
33   *Ibid* at 800.
34   639 S.W.2d 431 (Tenn. 1982).
35   *Ibid.* at 434.
36   858 R.2d 970 (Utah 1993).

with some degree of certainty."[37] Fear of disease damages fill a void in compensation for those plaintiffs who do not qualify for traditional tort remedies because of their lack of manifest injury. However, medical monitoring and other expenses relating to future care are not included under this head of damage. This is purely a compensation of toxic tort victims for the anguish and shock they have suffered as a result of the exposure.

A probabilistic approach to the fear of future disease is possible in aggregate claims where it would not be particularly helpful in individual actions. For instance, if it is known that a person's exposure to disease has been increased from 1 percent to 4 percent as a result of exposure, the true "cost" of the concern can be, at least on one level, measured: it will be the cost of insuring against the increased risk (even though the risk falls far short of the "more likely than not" requirement of *Potter*). This calculation is complicated by the fact that most of the insurance is already in place through universal health care, but the principal is sound: the "fear of disease," at least to the extent that it is rational, is measurable in terms of insurance costs, and this can be a basis on which it can be measured in the aggregate with some accuracy.

4) Enhanced Risk

When a plaintiff clearly suffers a physical injury, he or she is entitled to damages compensating him or her for that injury and those damages will also take into account the risk of future complications and aggravations (the risk of future injury in these cases can be treated as a "contingency" and accorded a value based on the probability that it will occur). However, there are two other types of cases where a plaintiff might want to claim specific damages for enhanced risks. The first is where there is as yet no injury but the defendant's wrongdoing has exposed the plaintiff to a serious risk of future disease. It might be that the plaintiff fears that the defendant will be impossible to locate or sue in the future so it would be better to bring a lawsuit when the wrongdoing is discovered and claim damages for the possible future injury. Such claims for increased risk or prospective injury have occasionally been brought in the United States.

In *Potter*[38] the disposal of hazardous materials in a landfill exposed the neighbouring plaintiffs to carcinogens in their drinking water. The court acknowledged that the plaintiffs had no physical injury as of yet; rather,

---

37 *Ibid* at 975, citing T.M. Dworkin, "Fear of Disease and Delayed Manifestation Injuries: A Solution or Pandora's Box" (1984) 53 Fordham L. Rev. 527, 532–33.
38 *Supra* note 32.

there was "an enhanced but unquantified risk of developing cancer in the future due to the exposure."[39] The risk of cancer or other disease remains until physical symptoms start to emerge. This is out of the control of the toxic tort victim and adds to the anxiety that individuals feel about that risk.[40]

Claims for prospective injury are difficult to establish and are not currently available in Canada. The courts here would demand a "wait and see" approach. Technically, this is because the plaintiff does not even have a cause of action in negligence unless there is some injury. From a policy point of view, it is because, while there may be some small risk that by the time the injury is manifest the defendant may be judgment-proof for some reason, there is an even greater risk that claims in advance of any actual injury would be too speculative and costly to manage.

There is a third category of "increased risk" cases. These are situations in which the plaintiff has suffered from some wrongdoing and some type of injury or disease, but it is impossible to say with certainty that the wrongdoing "caused" the injury or disease. The most that can be said is that it increased the risk of the disease. For example, in *Wilson v. Johns-Manville Sales Corp.*,[41] an employee was exposed to asbestos, developed asbestiosis, and later died from a heart attack. The estate of the plaintiff sought damages for the enhanced risk because the asbestiosis had increased the risk of cardiopulmonary problems. The court hesitated under this head of damage because of the "all-or-nothing" nature of awarding damages to similarly situated plaintiffs. Like other aspects of this section, this case raises the question of the appropriateness of "probabilistic" assessment of liability and damages, which will be addressed at some length in chapter 4.

E. PUNITIVE DAMAGES

1) Generally

In cases where the conduct of the defendant has been particularly egregious, the courts will go beyond compensatory damages and award an additional amount designed to punish the defendant and to deter such behaviour in the future. Punitive damages are frequently available where the cause of action involves an intentional tort, for such cases are instances where the defendant's conduct is likely to meet the threshold requirements

---

39 *Ibid.* at 801.
40 K.W. Miller, "Toxic Torts and Emotional Distress: The Case for an Independent Cause of Action for Fear of Future Harm" (1998) 40 Ariz. L. Rev. 681 at 689.
41 684 F.2d 111 (D.C. Cir. 1982).

for punitive damages — conduct that is "high handed," "reprehensible," "callous," or "malicious." This sort of damages is less likely to be available in product liability and negligence cases because the conduct of the defendant is usually inadvertent. However, there are cases where the inadvertence is so callous that it warrants punitive damages. For example, in *Robitaille v. Vancouver Hockey Club Ltd.*,[42] a hockey player's injuries were ignored by his team's manager and doctor, who told him that his problems were "all in his head." These injuries were subsequently aggravated when he continued playing and became permanently disabled. The court held that the negligence of the defendants went beyond carelessness, was "arrogant and high-handed," and thus deserving of punitive damages.

Similarly, where a medical doctor went ahead with an operation in complete disregard of current medical knowledge and performed what amounted to experimental surgery on the plaintiff, punitive damages were awarded for the negligence.[43] There, the British Columbia Court of Appeal stated that, in cases of negligence, "if the defendant has acted in good faith, then generally exemplary damages are not awarded against him. On the other hand, where the defendant deliberately exposes the plaintiff to a risk without justification an award of exemplary damages may be appropriate."[44]

2) Punitive Damages in Product Liability Cases: United States and Canada

In the United States, punitive damages play a major role in product liability and other tort cases. The U.S. jury has a much more robust role in civil trials than in Canada and is embedded in legal thinking (and the constitution) as the appropriate body to reflect community values and to hold corporate wrongdoers accountable. Readers will have encountered press reports of astounding jury verdicts in the millions and sometimes billions of dollars — usually awarded against large corporate defendants in relation to injuries caused by defectively designed automobiles, faulty medical products, tobacco, and sometimes even spilled coffee that was too hot. These decisions (while usually reduced on appeal or in post-trial negotiations) are celebrated by many as the most effective means of ensuring corporate social responsibility. However, the celebration is not universal. Indeed, there is probably no more fiercely debated legal topic. Consider the different reactions to the reports of a $145-billion punitive damages award

---

42   (1981), 30 B.C.L.R. 286 (C.A.).
43   *Coughlin v. Kuntz* (1989), 42 B.C.L.R. (2d) 108 (C.A.).
44   *Ibid.* at 119.

in a lawsuit against a tobacco manufacturer (the *Engle* case[45]): "The American Medical Association called the verdict 'a victory for public health,' and the American Cancer Society commended the jurors for 'their courage and wisdom.' But the U.S. Chamber of Commerce called the decision 'an obscene symptom of a court system that is out of control.'"[46]

Critics of punitive damages argue that jury awards are frequently "irrational" in that they are neither based on nor measured by predictable rules and principles. It is a matter of some debate whether they are awarded *against* the right defendants or awarded *to* the right plaintiffs. While corporations are legal entities, they are not moral agents. An award of punitive damages against a corporation penalizes shareholders but may leave the actual decision makers relatively untouched. Punitive damages are a cause for increased insurance and other costs, and thus increase the prices of products. It is also the case that the selection of the beneficiaries of punitive damages can sometimes be irrational. Punitive damages awards are often made in relation to systemic wrongdoing that has affected many people, and the size of some awards is frequently a reflection of the fact that the jury has taken into account a historical pattern of misconduct. Yet a single plaintiff who receives the first punitive damage award may receive a massive windfall solely by virtue of being first in line. Of course, it may be argued that subsequent plaintiffs may also claim punitive damages, but this then raises the spectre that the defendant will pay many times over for the same wrongdoing.

Large U.S. jury awards are frequently reduced on appeal or through negotiations after trial. In response to increased concern over the size of these awards, the U.S. Supreme Court in *BMW of North America Inc. v. Gore*[47] has now laid down some principles regarding excessiveness. According to the pre-*Gore* standard of review, a court should set aside damages as excessive only if there was "'no rational connection between the evidence on damages and the verdict.'"[48] Further, trial judges were empowered to reduce only those jury verdicts that were "'monstrously excessive.'"[49] In determining whether the damages were excessive, courts were instructed first to look at the "totality of the evidence" and then to make a comparison to sim-

---

45 *R.J. Reynolds Tobacco Co. v. Engle* [the final decision was not published]. See generally, *R.J. Reynolds Tobacco Co. v. Engle*, 672 So.2d 39 (Fla. Ct. App. 1996).
46 Marc Kaufman, "Tobacco Suit Award: $145 Billion; Florida Jury Hands Industry Major Setback" *The Washington Post* (15 July 2000) A Section.
47 517 U.S. 559 (1996) [hereinafter *Gore*].
48 *Terrell v. Village of University Park*, 1994 WL 30960 (N.D. Ill. 1994), quoting *Abernathy v. Superior Hardwoods, Inc.*, 704 F.2d 963 (7th Cir. 1983).
49 Ibid., quoting *Joan W. v. City of Chicago*, 771 F.2d 1020, 1023 (7th Cir. 1985).

ilar cases.[50] Thus, the standards for reviewing punitive awards were extremely subjective and vague. Lower courts had little guidance in determining what limits to place on punitive damages.

In *Gore* an Alabama jury awarded an automobile purchaser $4 million in punitive damages as a result of the distributor's failure to disclose that the automobile had been repainted after being damaged prior to delivery. On appeal, the Alabama Supreme Court reduced the amount of the award to $2 million.[51] The U.S. Supreme Court held that the award of $2 million in punitive damages was grossly excessive in relation to legitimate punitive-damages objectives and thus an arbitrary deprivation of property in violation of the constitution's due process clause.[52]

Writing for the Court, Justice Stevens established three guideposts to determine when punitive damages verdicts are so excessive as to be unconstitutional. First, a court should look to the degree of reprehensibility of the conduct that gave rise to the punitive award.[53] For example, trickery and deceit are more reprehensible than negligence.[54] Second, courts should compare the ratio of punitive to compensatory damages.[55] Justice Stevens noted, however, as the Court had in *Haslip*,[56] that no mathematical formula can determine when a ratio of punitive to compensatory damages is excessive; instead, case-by-case analysis is necessary.[57] Finally, the majority instructed that punitive damages awards should be compared with existing civil or criminal sanctions for comparable misconduct.[58]

This structured, but still relatively open, test has conferred greater discretion and authority upon judges to control jury verdicts. It has been technically applied in numerous instances to hold that a specific punitive damage award was so excessive as to violate the constitutional right to due process.[59] And its general tenor has been picked up by many judges gener-

---

50 Ibid.
51 See: *BMW of North America, Inc. v. Gore*, 646 So.2d 619 (Ala. 1994) judgment re'd by 517 U.S. 559, 116 S.Ct. 1589.
52 *Gore, supra* note 48 at 568.
53 Ibid. at 575.
54 Ibid. at 576.
55 Ibid. at 580.
56 *Pacific Mutual Life Insurance Co. v. Haslip*, 499 U.S. 1 (1991).
57 *Supra* note 48 at 582–83.
58 Ibid. at 583.
59 See, for example: *Watkins v. Lundell*, 169 F.3d 540, 547 (8th Cir. 1999) (finding a $3.5-million punitive damages verdict for fraudulent business practices to be unconstitutional); *FDIC v. Hamilton*, 122 F.3d 854 (10th Cir. 1997) (holding that a $1.2-million punitive damages verdict for fraud is unconstitutional); *Continental Trend Resources v. OXY USA*, 101 F.3d 634, 642 (10th Cir. 1996) (striking down a $30-million punitive damages ver-

ally to require juries to exercise greater restraint. The widely reported award of $2.7 million against McDonald's Restaurant in relation to scalding hot coffee was reduced to $480,000.[60] A $290-million punitive damages award against Ford Motor for deaths caused when a Ford Bronco rolled over was set aside on the basis that the jury process had been "infested with passion and prejudice."[61] Similarly, a $4.9-billion award against General Motors for a defectively designed gas tank was reduced to $1.09 billion because the jury had been "animated by passion and prejudice."[62] (It should be pointed out that, as much as U.S. courts have been open to the arguments of violations of the due process rights, they have also been merciless towards legislative attempts at "capping" punitive damages awards.)[63]

Unlike the situation in the United States, punitive damages have not usually been awarded in product liability cases in Canada. There are several

---

dict for tortious interference with contract as unconstitutional); *Life Ins. Co. of Ga. v. Parker*, 726 So.2d 619 (Ala. Sup. Ct. 1998) (finding that a $200,000-punitive damages award for insurance fraud and misrepresentation violates due process); *Ford Motor Co. v. Sperau*, 708 So.2d 111, 125 (Ala. Sup. Ct. 1997) (finding that a $6-million punitive damages verdict for fraud and misrepresentation violates due process); *American Pioneer Life Ins. Co. v. Williamson*, 704 So.2d 1361, 1367 (Ala. 1997) (holding that a $2-million punitive damages verdict for insurance fraud and breach of contract violates due process); *Cates Construction v. Talbot Partners*, 62 Cal. Rptr. 2d 548 (Ct. App. 1997) (striking down a $28-million punitive damages verdict for breach of good faith and fair business dealing as unconstitutional); *Langmead v. Admiral Cruises*, 696 So.2d 1189 (Fla. Ct. App. 1997) (finding that a $3.5-million punitive damages verdict for failure to pay plaintiff's salary while she was injured violates substantive due process); *Parrott v. Carr Chevrolet*, 965 P.2d 440 (Or. Ct. App. 1998) (holding that a $1-million punitive damages verdict for fraudulently selling a vehicle without disclosing extensive defects is unconstitutional); *Apache Corp. v. Moore*, 960 S.W.2d 746, 750 (Tex. Ct. App. 1997) (striking down as unconstitutional a punitive damages verdict of $562,500 for negligently causing a gas well to explode). Note: virtually all of the cases finding punitive damages verdicts to be unconstitutional on grounds of excessiveness involved economic harm.

60 *Liebeck v. McDonald's Restaurants, Inc.*, 1995 WL 360309 at 1 (D.N.M. 1994).
61 Joseph B. White, "Judge Sets Aside $290 Million Award Against Ford Motor, Orders New Trial" *The Wall Street Journal* (17 September 1999).
62 Carolyn Whetzel, "Motor Vehicles: California Court Cuts Punitives in GM Case from Record $4.9 Billion to $1.2 Billion," *BNA Prod. Liab. Daily* (BNA, Los Angeles) (30 August 1999) at D2, or: Eric Malnic, "GM Files Appeal of $1.2-Billion Verdict, Calling Trial Unfair Accident: Lawyers Say Judge Excluded Key Evidence, Including the Car's Safety Record and the Fact That Driver Who Rear-Ended Vehicle Was Drunk. Six People Were Severely Burned in Fiery Crash" *Los Angeles Times* (7 December 2000).
63 See, for example: William Glaberson, "Ohio's Top Court Strikes Down Tort Reform Law. Ruling Is a Setback to Lawmakers Seeking Caps on Damage Suits" *Chicago Tribune* (17 August 1999); David Shepardson, "Judge Tosses Out Jury Award Cap: State's Limit on Product Liability Damages Is Unconstitutional, Circuit Court Rules" *The Detroit News* (23 December 1999).

reasons for this. First, juries are rarely used in civil cases in Canada. Damages awards, therefore, are more a product of formal law rather than community justice. Second, product liability generally involves inadvertent negligent conduct that does not meet the threshold test for punitive damages. Third, in contrast to U.S. law, Canadian courts have traditionally confined the inquiry in punitive damages cases to conduct that is aimed specifically at the plaintiff rather than conduct aimed at a class of people.[64] Thus, where the gist of the defendant's wrongdoing is disregard for the welfare of its consumers generally, this may not be as relevant in a claim by an individual plaintiff.

This requirement has been criticized by the Ontario Law Reform Commission since it renders punitive damages ineffective as a tool to "control systematic wrongdoing."[65] The rule may be fading. In *Vlchek v. Koshel*[66] the Supreme Court of British Columbia refused to strike out a claim for punitive damages though it could not be proved that the defendant intended to injure the specific plaintiff. The court held that the defendant might nevertheless be liable for punitive damages when its actions were simply directed against a class of persons, so long as those actions were "malicious or reckless to such a degree as to indicate complete indifference to the consequences that might flow therefrom, including the welfare and safety of others."[67] In *Van Oirschot v. Dow Chemical*,[68] the Alberta Court of Appeal confirmed an award of $10,000 in punitive damages against the defendant who callously failed to warn the plaintiff of the risks of using a herbicide. There was an element of individual wrongdoing in this case, however, because of the defendant's high-handed conduct after the plaintiff's crop failed and its attempt to stonewall the plaintiff's action by waiting for the evidence to decompose. In summary, while Canadian law is evolving most cautiously, punitive damages are in principle available in product liability and mass tort cases where the wrongful conduct is sufficiently extreme.

3) The Law in Canada: Principles and Quantum

The fundamental principles and rules surrounding punitive damages have been restated with clarity by the Supreme Court of Canada in *Whiten v. Pilot*

---

64 See S.M. Waddams, *Product liability*, 3d ed. (Scarborough, ON: Carswell, 1993) at 62; *Vorvis v. Insurance Corp. of British Columbia*, [1989] 1 S.C.R 1085.
65 Ontario Law Reform Commission, *Report on Exemplary Damages* (Toronto: OLRC, 1991) at 14–15.
66 (1988), 30 B.C.L.R. (2d) 97 (S.C.).
67 *Ibid.* at 102.
68 (1995), 31 Alta. L.R. (3d) 212 (C.A.).

Insurance Company.[69] This case involved a claim of "bad faith" against an insurer that had wrongfully, and without justification, withheld insurance payments from plaintiffs whose house had been destroyed in a fire. The defendant alleged, with no real basis, that the fire was the result of arson by the plaintiffs. The case made its way to the Supreme Court for two reasons. First, the basis of the claim for punitive damages (bad faith breach of contract) was relatively novel and required clarification. Second, the amount of the award was controversial. A jury had awarded $1 million, which had been reduced on appeal to $100,000.

The Supreme Court of Canada confirmed that "bad faith" breach of contract can be considered an independent actionable wrong sufficient to found a claim for punitive damages. It then reinstated the jury award of $1 million. The majority affirmed the test set out in *Hill v. Church of Scientology of Toronto*[70] by Cory J.: "Punitive damages are awarded against a defendant in exceptional cases for 'malicious, oppressive and high-handed misconduct that offends the court's sense of decency.'"[71] In considering the amount of the award, the Court held that there should not be artificial categories or formulae but that the amount of the award must be rationally related to the underlying objective of the law — deterrence of malicious wrongdoing. The amount of damages should be sufficient to remove any profit from wrongdoing and include a strong financial disincentive, but also must be proportionate to the wrongdoing. The test to employ is whether "a reasonable jury, properly instructed, could have concluded that an award in that amount, and no less, was rationally required to punish the defendant's misconduct, as discussed below."[72]

In assessing the jury verdict, a court must be satisfied that the award of punitive damages is a rational response to the defendant's wrongdoing, and that the amount is proportionate to that wrongdoing. And, in determining whether the amount bears an appropriate relation to the wrong, the court will assess whether the award is

i) proportionate to the blameworthiness of the defendant's conduct;
ii) proportionate to the degree of vulnerability of the plaintiff;
iii) proportionate to the harm or potential harm directed specifically at the plaintiff;
iv) proportionate to the need for deterrence;

---

69 (2002), 209 D.L.R. (4th) 257 (S.C.C.) [hereinafter *Whiten*].
70 [1995] 2 S.C.R. 1130 [hereinafter *Hill*].
71 *Supra* note 70 at para. 36.
72 *Ibid.* at para. 97.

v) proportionate, even after taking into account the other penalties, both civil and criminal, which have been or are likely to be inflicted on the defendant for the same misconduct; and
vi) proportionate to the advantage wrongfully gained by a defendant from the misconduct.

Obviously, after *Whiten*, "blameworthiness" will be central to any punitive damages claim. The Court considered at paragraph 113 the factors to be weighed in assessing this element:

> ¶ 113 The level of blameworthiness may be influenced by many factors, but some of the factors noted in a selection of Canadian cases include:
>
> (1) whether the misconduct was planned and deliberate: *Patenaude v. Roy* (1994), 123 D.L.R. (4th) 78 (Que. C.A.), at p. 91;
> (2) the intent and motive of the defendant: *Recovery Production Equipment Ltd. v. McKinney Machine Co.* (1998), 223 A.R. 24 (C.A.), at para. 77;
> (3) whether the defendant persisted in the outrageous conduct over a lengthy period of time: *Mustaji v. Tjin* (1996), 30 C.C.L.T. (2d) 53 (B.C.C.A.), *Québec (Curateur public) v. Syndicat national des employés de l'Hôpital St-Ferdinand* (1994), 66 Q.A.C. 1, *Matusiak v. British Columbia and Yukon Territory Building and Construction Trades Council*, [1999] B.C.J. No. 2416 (QL) (S.C.);
> (4) whether the defendant concealed or attempted to cover up its misconduct: *Gerula v. Flores* (1995), 126 D.L.R. (4th) 506 (Ont. C.A.), at p. 525, *Walker v. D'Arcy Moving & Storage Ltd.* (1999), 117 O.A.C. 367 (C.A.), *United Services Funds (Trustees) v. Hennessey*, [1994] O.J. No. 1391 (QL) (Gen. Div.), at para. 58;
> (5) the defendant's awareness that what he or she was doing was wrong: *Williams v. Motorola Ltd.* (1998), 38 C.C.E.L. (2d) 76 (Ont. C.A.), and *Procor Ltd. v. U.S.W.A.* (1990), 71 O.R. (2d) 410, at p. 433 ... (H.C.);
> (6) whether the defendant profited from its misconduct: *Claiborne Industries Ltd. v. National Bank of Canada* (1989), 69 O.R. (2d) 65 ... (C.A.);
> (7) whether the interest violated by the misconduct was known to be deeply personal to the plaintiff (e.g., professional reputation (*Hill*, supra) or a thing that was irreplaceable (e.g., the mature trees cut down by the real estate developer in *Horseshoe Bay Retirement Society v. S.I.F. Development Corp.* (1990), 66 D.L.R. (4th) 42 (B.C.S.C.)); see also *Kates v. Hall* (1991), 53 B.C.L.R. (2d) 322 (C.A.). Special interests have included the reproductive capacity of the plaintiff deliberately sterilized by an irreversible surgical procedure while the plaintiff was confined in a provincial mental institution, although no award of punitive damages

was made on the facts (*Muir v. Alberta*, [1996] 4 W.W.R. 177, 132 D.L.R. (4th) 695 (Alta. Q.B.)); the deliberate publication of an informant's identity (*R. (L.) v. Nyp* (1995), 25 C.C.L.T. (2d) 309 (Ont. Ct. (Gen. Div.)). In *Weinstein v. Bucar*, [1990] 6 W.W.R. 615 (Man. Q.B.), the defendant shot and killed plaintiffs' three companions and breeding German Shepherds who had merely wandered onto the defendant's property from a neighbouring yard. Here the "property" was sentimental, not replaceable, and, unlike the trees, themselves sentient beings.

The Court concluded that an examination of all of these factors in the present case could, in fact, reasonably lead a jury to suppose that $1 million would be necessary to reflect properly the community's disapproval and to deter this type of conduct in the future.

4) Punitive Damages in Class Actions

One difficult issue concerns the relation between punitive damages and class actions. Some have argued that punitive damages should not be available in class actions because punitive damages are based on personal wrongdoing towards a plaintiff. In a class action there is typically no "personal wrongdoing" done by the defendant against individual plaintiffs, or, if there is personal wrongdoing, it is individualized and therefore not suitable for resolution in the context of class actions. The degree of turpitude (and the degree of injury) among the various members of the class may be very different. This has led some to argue that punitive damages cannot properly be assessed in class actions.

Courts of Canada seem to have figured their way out of the dilemma. In the case of *Chace v. Crane Canada Inc.*,[73] a number of people brought actions or made insurance claims with respect to damages caused by the failures of the toilet tank manufactured by the defendants. The trial court gave judgment for the plaintiffs because Crane had been aware that toilet tanks produced at a certain plant during a specified period had had a higher in-service failure rate as compared to its other plants. On the appeal, Crane submitted that it was not possible for a court to treat punitive damages as common to all persons within a class because an assessment of punitive damages required an examination of the conduct of a defendant with respect to a particular plaintiff. However, the court, citing *Huff v. Price*,[74] held:

---

73   (1997), 14 C.P.C. (4th) 197 (B.C.C.A.) [hereinafter *Crane*].
74   *Huff v. Price* (1990), 76 D.L.R. (4th) 138 (B.C.C.A.).

Punishment of a morally culpable defendant is the purpose of punitive damages. Deterrence of such conduct is the reason for the punishment. The amount of the award is to be measured by the degree of moral culpability, the amount of compensatory damages, and the profits earned from the wrongful acts. ... This being so, a class proceeding seems particularly well-suited for the hearing of a claim for punitive damages.[75]

This holding was applied, for example, in Ontario. On 23 April 1999, Via Rail train 74 was derailed near Thamesville, Ontario. The plaintiffs moved for certification of a class action in which the proposed classes consisted of passengers on the train and their family members. The claim included one for punitive damages. The court in *Brimner v. Via Rail Canada Inc.*,[76] held at paragraph 23 that "... a train wreck is the classic example used repeatedly in decided cases as the type of mass tort in which the issue of responsibility is best resolved in a class action. Here we have, in addition, a claim for punitive damages." The Court in *Brimner v. Via Rail Canada Inc.* cited *Crane* for the proposition that the suit, including the claim for punitive damages, was an archetypical mass tort appropriately pursued as a class action.

F. RESTITUTION AND DISGORGEMENT OF PROFITS

1) Generally

An important, but less frequently acknowledged, purpose of damages is to prevent unjust enrichment. In these instances the aim of a damages award is to strip a wrongdoer of ill-gotten gains. While such an approach does incidentally provide compensation to the injured party, the focus is more on the unjust benefit to the wrongdoer than on the loss to the plaintiff.

The idea is concisely put by the American Law Institute in its *Restatement of the Law of Restitution, 1937*, section 1: "A person who has been unjustly enriched at the expense of another is required to make restitution to the other."

Unjust enrichment need not be "positive," in the sense that the defendant has actually made money as a result of the wrong; it can also be "negative," as explained by McLachlin J. (as she then was) in *Peel (Regional Municipality) v. Canada*:

> To date, the cases have recognized two types of benefit. The most common case involves the positive conferral of a benefit upon the defendant,

---

75 *Crane*, supra note 73 at para. 24.
76 (2000), 50 O.R. (3d) 114 (S.C.).

for example the payment of money. But a benefit may also be "negative" in a sense that the benefit conferred upon the defendant is that he or she was spared an expense which he or she would have been required to undertake, i.e., the discharge of a legal liability.[77]

2) Restitution Explained and Illustrated

Restitutionary remedies are particularly attractive when the defendant's conduct has been morally wrongful and has enriched the defendant but the harm to the plaintiff is difficult to establish or the amount of compensatory damages would be small. Restitution was, of course, made explicitly available in the old quasi-contract cases, and it has been awarded in more recent constructive trust cases as well. However, restitutionary motives are also implicit in many damages awards in ordinary contract and tort cases where the point of the award seems less compensatory than instructive (i.e., to teach the defendant that "wrongdoing does not pay").

The purpose and utility of restitutionary damages is nicely illustrated by the decision of the Supreme Court of Canada in *Lac Minerals Ltd. v. Int'l Corona Resources Ltd.*[78] LAC approached Corona for the purpose of discussing a joint venture. In the course of their discussions, Corona disclosed confidential information to LAC, which demonstrated the strong potential of significant mineral deposits on property that adjoined property being developed by Corona. LAC purchased the adjoining property and developed a successful mine. The Supreme Court held that this was a breach of confidence.

The remedy granted by the Court was a constructive trust. The deal anticipated between the parties had been that, while Corona might acquire the property, the parties would probably negotiate a joint venture based on 50/50 ownership. Thus, LAC argued that the measure of compensatory damages should be 50 percent of the value of the mine. This is what Corona would have received had there been no wrong. Sopinka J., dissenting on this point, accepted this measure. The majority, however, awarded to Corona the entire property in the mine, less LAC's development costs. As La Forest J. explained:

> The essence of the imposition of fiduciary obligations is in its utility in the promotion and preservation of desired social behaviour .... The approach taken by my colleague Sopinka J., would, in my view, have the effect not of encouraging bargaining in good faith, but of encouraging the contrary. If by breaching an obligation of confidence one party is able to acquire an

---

77 [1992] 3 S.C.R. 762 at 790.
78 [1989] 2 S.C.R. 574.

asset entirely for itself, at a risk of only having to compensate the other for what the other would have received if a formal relationship between them were concluded, the former would be given a strong incentive to breach the obligation and acquire the asset. In the present case, it is true that had negotiations been concluded, LAC could also have acquired an interest in the Corona land, but that is only an expectation and not a certainty. Had Corona acquired the Williams property, as they would have but for LAC's breach, it seems probable that negotiations with LAC would have resulted in a concluded agreement. However, if LAC, during the negotiations, breached a duty of confidence owed to Corona, it seems certain that Corona would have broken off negotiations and LAC would be left with nothing. In such circumstances, many business people, weighing the risks, would breach the obligation and acquire the asset. This does nothing for the preservation of the institution of good faith bargaining or relationships of trust and confidence. The imposition of a remedy which restores an asset to the party who would have acquired it but for a breach of fiduciary duties or duties of confidence acts as a deterrent to the breach of duty and strengthens the social fabric those duties are imposed to protect.[79]

There may be some objection to using a case involving a constructive trust to illustrate a point about damages. But, in our view, there is no substantial difference. Restitutionary remedies may take the form of a cash award or a property award. The underlying motive is the same (the primary difference being in the effect of the remedy on third parties).

3) Restitution as an Alternative Measure of Damages for Civil Wrongs

Restitution is the standard remedy in cases involving breach of trust or fiduciary duty. It also underlies many damages awards in tort. Restitution is explicitly employed in cases of "waiver of tort," detention of goods,[80] and certain trespass cases (where a person unlawfully uses another's land for their own gain but cause no damage to the land).[81] Restitution is also frequently implicit in punitive damage awards. For example, in defamation cases, damages are often measured by an amount sufficient to strip the wrongdoer of gains earned by publishing a libel — regardless of the actual damage done to the plaintiff's reputation.[82] In tort cases involving the wrongful use of

---

79   Ibid. at 672–73.
80   *Strand Electric and Engineering Co. Ltd. v. Brisford Entertainments Ltd.*, [1952] 2 Q.B. 246.
81   *Whitwam v. Westminster Brymbo Coal Co.*, [1896] 2 Ch. 538.
82   *Broome v. Cassell & Co.*, [1972] A.C. 1027 (H.L.).

another's property, damages are awarded in a measure equal to the wrongful gain to the defendant, despite the fact that there may have been no harm done to the plaintiff's property. For example, in *Austin v. Rescon Const. (1984) Ltd.*[83] and *Townsview Properties Ltd. v. Sun Construction and Equipment Co. Ltd.*,[84] the defendants trespassed by installing anchor rods below the surface of the plaintiff's property as part of the shoring for the foundation of a large building. While there was only nominal damage to the plaintiff's property, the defendant saved anywhere from $21,000 to over $30,000 by using the rods. The Court of Appeal increased the award of exemplary damages from $7,500 to $30,000 in order to eliminate the defendant's profit entirely.

Under the doctrine of waiver of tort, a victim is permitted to elect to pursue the restitutionary claim to recover the benefits secured by the wrongful activity of the tortfeasor as an alternative to suing for the victim's claim for damages. Use of the term "waiver" is somewhat misleading — the plaintiff may pursue the remedies in the alternative in a single action; if successful, he or she is entitled to an award on the basis of the measure yielding the higher quantum. In *United Australia Ltd. v. Barclays Bank Ltd.*,[85] Viscount Simon, L.C. put it this way: "Where 'waiving the tort' was possible, it was nothing more than a choice between possible remedies, derived from a time when it was not permitted to combine them or to pursue them in the alternative, and when there were procedural advantages in selecting the form of *assumpsit*." In *The Law of Restitution*, Lord Goff and G. Jones state: "... a tortfeasor should be personally liable to make restitution for any benefit gained at the plaintiff's expense ... This makes good legal as well as economic sense."[86] In *Amertek Inc. v. Canadian Commercial Corporation*,[87] the availability of restitution in a deceit case was made clear: "In my view, if the Plaintiffs succeed in proving the tort of deceit, they are entitled to waive the tort and recover in a restitutionary claim the value of the benefits obtained by the Government Defendants through their wrongful acts."

4) Restitution in Contractual Settings and Other Emerging Issues

It is generally said that restitution has no place where there is a contract between the parties. So long as the plaintiff can be fully compensated, there

---

83 (1989), 36 B.C.L.R. (3d) 21 (C.A.).
84 (1973), 2 O.R. (2d) 213 (H.C.J.), var'd (1974), 7 O.R. (2d) 666 (C.A.).
85 [1940] 4 All E.R. 20 (H.L.).
86 Lord Goff and G. Jones, *The Law of Restitution*, 5th ed. (London: Sweet & Maxwell, 1998) at 778.
87 [2003] O.J. No. 3177 at para. 372 (S.C.J.).

is no harm done in permitting a defendant to retain the savings or benefits of breaching a contract. A recent decision of the English House of Lords has raised the issue to the surface. *Attorney General v. Blake*[88] was a claim for breach of contract against a former secret service employee for disclosing confidential information in his autobiography in breach of his contract (the only cause of action). The plaintiff, who suffered no pecuniary loss by reason of the breach, sued the defendant for his earnings on the book. The House of Lords held at paragraphs 32 and 33 that, in rare circumstances, restitution, or account, could be a remedy for breach of contract:

> When, exceptionally, a just response to a breach of contract so requires, the court should be able to grant the discretionary remedy of requiring a defendant to account to the plaintiff for the benefits he has received from his breach of contract. ... the plaintiff's interest in performance may make it just and equitable that the defendant should retain no benefit from his breach ....
>
> A useful general guide, although not exhaustive, is whether the plaintiff has a legitimate interest in preventing the defendant's profit-making activity, and hence, in depriving him of his profit.

The House of Lords held that the Crown had a legitimate interest in preventing former employees from profiting from the disclosure of official information and that there should be no financial incentive to breach their obligation.

5) Restitution in Mass Tort Cases

Restitution is not a common remedy in product liability or mass tort cases. However, restitutionary motives are definitely to be found underlying many punitive damages awards when the award is based on a desire to strip manufacturers of the profits that had been anticipated from a particular design or product. In numerous cases the award is justified on the basis that the manufacturer should not have "weighed lives against profits" and the award is designed to remove any incentive to do so.

Perhaps the most notorious example of this is the case of the Ford Pinto. In *Grimshaw v. Ford Motor Company*,[89] the auto manufacturer was sued when one of its cars exploded in a rear-end collision, killing the driver and severely disfiguring a thirteen-year-old boy. A California jury subsequently returned a $126-million civil judgment.

The Pinto's unguarded fuel tank was subject to rupture by exposed differential bolts even at speeds of as little as twenty-one miles per hour. As

---

88   [2000] H.L.J. No. 47.
89   119 Cal. App. 3d 757 (1981).

became clear in the course of the trial, Ford had rejected safety designs costing between only $1.80 and $15.30 per Pinto. Instead, Ford had calculated the damages it would likely pay in wrongful death and injury cases in a "costs/benefits" analysis. Ford estimated that the flaws in the Pinto's design would probably cause 2,100 burned vehicles each year, resulting in 180 burn deaths and an equal number of serious burn injuries. Ford calculated the cost of resulting civil suits at $200,000 per death, $67,000 per injury, and $700 per vehicle, for a grand total of $49.5 million. Safety designs costing between only $1.80 and $15.30 per Pinto, on the other hand, could have cost approximately $137 million per year.

In lawsuits against tobacco manufacturers in the United States, restitution frequently underlay both the theory of liability and the claim for damages. In many of the claims (which were ultimately settled), it was argued that the tobacco manufacturers committed fraud and misrepresentation in order to earn wrongful profits. In addition, in the claims by the states, it was argued that the companies had been further wrongfully enriched in that the state had been required to incur medicare expenses that should rightfully have been borne by the companies.[90]

G. INJUNCTIONS

Another potentially powerful set of remedies in mass tort cases are injunctions. An injunction is a specific order by a court to a person to refrain from a wrongful or potentially harmful activity, or to take positive steps to prevent harm from occurring. Obviously, injunctions are useful only when the harm from wrongdoing has just begun, or is merely threatened, or is a continuing form of harm. Injunctions are widely used in cases involving nuisance — where there is a use of land by the defendant that wrongfully interferes with the use and enjoyment of neighbouring land (or air or water). Such cases may involve pollution (of land, water, or air) and are particularly compelling when there is a demonstrable threat to the health of others.

An injunction is available only when the plaintiffs are able to establish a right that is being violated (or about to be violated) and that the result will be "irreparable harm." Irreparable harm is harm that is substantial and not easily remedied by an award of damages. Serious interference with the enjoyment of one's property, or serious risk to one's health or safety, qual-

---

[90] For a critical view of the state tobacco litigation, see Robert A. Levy, "Tobacco Medicaid Litigation: Snuffing Out the Rule of Law" (1997) 22 So. Ill. U.L.J. 601.

ify as irreparable harm. For example, in *Canada Paper Co. v. Brown*[91] an injunction was granted to prohibit the operation of a mill that was emitting undue quantities of sulphate fumes.

Injunctions come in many forms, depending upon the circumstances of the case. When there is only a threatened harm, the plaintiff may seek a *quia timet* injunction to prohibit the risky activity. Such injunctions are difficult to obtain because the law must balance the risk of the defendant's activity (which has not yet caused any actual harm) against the cost of prohibiting what might turn out to be an entirely legitimate and harmless activity (at considerable cost to the defendant). Thus, the courts have established the test of "imminent harm" as the threshold for granting such injunctions. The plaintiff must demonstrate that the harm is likely to occur and that if it does occur it will cause harm that is substantial and cannot easily be stopped or repaired.[92] *Quia timet* injunctions have been used in cases involving pollution and contamination that pose a threat to health, but they have not been used in product liability cases. The reason for this is, of course, that generally the risk factor is unknown prior to the actual harm. However, it is conceivable that, if a company was about to launch a product that was somehow discovered to be dangerous, and no regulatory mechanisms were in place to prevent the distribution of the product, a *quia timet* injunction might be available. Indeed, various pieces of consumer protection legislation (such as the Trade Practices Acts) explicitly provide for all forms of injunctions as a remedy against suppliers who are engaged in deceptive practices.[93] These are potentially powerful remedies in cases involving products that are sold with representations concerning their quality or safety that are untrue.

It will be apparent that the primary limit on the usefulness of injunctions is that the harm must not yet have occurred. In most mass tort cases resulting in serious injury, there will simply not be the necessary foreknowledge of harm to make this a useful remedy. However, in the limited class of cases where the harm can be anticipated — or where it involves a slow and incremental process (such as pollution) rather than a single-incident catastrophe — the injunction can be a powerful remedy. Injunctions are particularly attractive remedies when there are large numbers of persons involved. In such cases an award of damages is likely to be inadequate, or at least administratively cumbersome given that there would need to be a multiplicity of actions.

---

91   (1922), 63 S.C.R. 243.
92   *Fletcher v. Bealey* (1885), 28 Ch. D. 688.
93   *Trade Practices Act*, R.S.B.C. 1996, c. 457.

Part Two:
Problems of Proof and Causation

4. The Problem of Indeterminate Causation

A. CAUSATION PROBLEMS IN LARGE-SCALE WRONGS

In mass tort cases, especially those involving large numbers of persons who have been exposed through negligence to toxic substances that cause adverse health effects through non-observable modes of causation (often called "toxic torts"), the traditional rules of law and procedure often appear both inefficient and unfair. Modes of procedure and evidence that require proof and assessment on a particularistic, individual-by-individual basis do not easily accommodate claims based on non-traumatic, gradual, or cumulative harms.

Much has been written recently on the problem of causation, since the conceptual framework of nineteenth-century tort law has had to evolve to meet claims for injury compensation for harms that are more widespread and causally complex. The variety of products, processes, and activities that can cause injury have vastly expanded during that time. Modes of mass production and distribution ensure that the potential consequences of error are more widely felt and scientific understandings of causal relationships have vastly expanded (and complicated) our understanding of the links between products, activities and environments, and harms to human health.

Tort scholars and courts have debated doctrinal innovations such as onus-shifting and presumptions and procedural innovations such as science panels[1] and the aggregation of claims through the aggressive use of class action suits.[2] Certainly, these methods have potential to ease some of the problems of particularistic proof. But dealing with large-scale claims on a probabilistic basis may require more than procedural innovation and advanced methods of proof of causation. In fact, it may require that we re-examine the necessity of establishing precise causal connections between plaintiff and defendant *at all*.

In the 1970s and early 1980s, Posner,[3] Calabresi,[4] and others[5] considered the question of causation in law in terms of economic efficiency, laying the groundwork for many of the "instrumentalist," "functionalist," or "utilitarian" proposals that followed. The late 1980s led to further analyses by Fleming,[6] Moore,[7] Brennan,[8] Wright,[9] and Ginsberg and Weiss,[10] all of whom canvassed possible solutions to what Fleming called "the problem of the indeterminate defendant."[11] Proposals for reform that included the imposition of liability on the basis of risk — rather than harm — were

---

1   T.A. Brennan, "Causal Chains and Statistical Links: The Role of Scientific Uncertainty in Hazardous-Substance Litigation" (1987–88) 73 Cornell L. Rev. 469.
2   Harvard's David Rosenberg has been perhaps the most outspoken champion of the latter approach, and we have discussed procedural options elsewhere: See D. Rosenberg, "Class Actions for Mass Torts: Doing Individual Justice by Collective Means" (1987) 62 Ind. L.J. 561; D. Rosenberg, "Of End Games and Openings in Mass Tort Cases: Lessons from a Special Master" (1989) 69 B.U. L. Rev. 695; D. Rosenberg, "Individual Justice and Collectivizing Risk-Based Claims in Mass-Exposure Cases (1996) 71 N.Y.U. L. Rev. 210; D. Rosenberg, "Mandatory-Litigation Class Action: The Only Option for Mass Tort Cases" (2001) 115 Harvard L. Rev. 831. See also C. Jones, *Theory of Class Actions* (Toronto: Irwin Law, 2002); J. Cassels, *The Uncertain Promise of Law: Lessons from Bhopal* (Toronto: University of Toronto Press, 1993) at 75–95.
3   R.A. Posner, "A Theory of Negligence" (1972) 1 J. Legal. Stud. 29; R.A. Posner, "The Concept of Corrective Justice in Recent Theories of Tort Law" (1981) 10 J. Legal Stud. 187.
4   G. Calabresi, "Concerning Cause and the Law of Torts" (1975–76) 43 U. Chi. L. Rev. 69.
5   See the discussion of "actuarial causation" in J.D. Fraser & D.R. Horwarth, "More Concern for Cause" (1984) 4 Leg. St. 131. The initial role of the legal economists in the causation debate is well summarized in H.L.A. Hart & T. Honoré, *Causation in the Law*, 2d ed. (London: Oxford, 1985) at 67–81.
6   J.G. Fleming, "Probabilistic Causation in Tort Law" (1989) 68 Can. Bar. Rev. 661.
7   M.S. Moore, "Thomson's Preliminaries About Causation and Rights" (1987) 63 Chi.-Kent L. Rev. 497.
8   Brennan, *supra* note 1.
9   R.M. Wright, "Causation in Tort Law" (1985) 73 Calif. L. Rev. 1735.
10 Ginsberg & Weiss, "Common Law Liability for Toxic Torts: A Phantom Remedy" (1981) 9 Hofstra L. Rev. 859.
11 Fleming, *supra* note 6; McLachlin, J., "Negligence Law — Proving the Connection" in Mullany & Linden, eds., *Torts Tomorrow, A Tribute to John Fleming* (Sydney: L.B.C Information Services, 1998) at 18.

greeted with deep suspicion by those who saw tort law not from a functional but from a "corrective justice" point of view, such as Epstein[12] and Weinrib,[13] and the question became a significant focus of the debate between the economic analysts of law and those purporting an independent, normative, or moral role for tort.[14] Despite the differences in approach, most who confronted the issue seemed to agree that causal uncertainty presents central questions for philosophers and lawyers alike.[15]

Mass claims present both unique problems of causation and also unique opportunities for dealing with causal indeterminacy in a principled and effective way. Ideas of "probabilistic causation," inherently difficult in individual cases, begin to make sense when harm is viewed in aggregate populations. Indeed, it is in mass tort claims where the most interesting innovations in causation analysis can be expected.

B. THE INADEQUACY OF THE "BUT FOR" TEST

There are both factual and legal elements to the traditional analysis of causation in tort and in negligence in particular. Generally, one must demonstrate causation in fact according to the "but for" test, asking whether the plaintiff would have escaped loss but for the defendant's conduct. Then the question of proximate cause arises — whether the link in question is close enough to merit the imposition of legal responsibility.[16] This might be char-

---

12 Epstein's views were set out in detail in R. Epstein, "A Theory of Strict Liability" (1973) 2 J. Legal. Stud. 151; R. Epstein, "Causation — In Context: An Afterword" (1987) 63 Chi.-Kent L. Rev. 653.
13 E.J. Weinrib, "Causation and Wrongdoing" (1987) 63 Chi.-Kent L. Rev. 407.
14 The original debate is captured in R.A. Posner, "Epstein's Tort Theory: A Critique" (1979) 8 J. Legal Stud. 457.
15 M. Kelman, "The Necessary Myth of Objective Causation Judgments in Liberal Political Theory" (1987) U. Chi.-Kent L. Rev. 579 at 580 "[T]he two liberal theories of the state dominating mainstream legal thought, libertarianism and efficiency-orientation, both rely to an alarming extent on the false premise that causal uncertainty is a peripheral issue."
16 *Horsley v. MacLaren*, [1972] S.C.R. 441. The question of "remoteness" and the related idea of "foreseeably" is most famously discussed in the case of *Palsgraf v. Long Island Railroad Company*, 248 N.Y. 339 (N.Y.A.D. 1928), rearg. den. 249 N.Y. 511 (N.Y. 1928) [hereinafter *Palsgraf*], where an extraordinary unlikely igniting of fireworks at a train station led to a bystander's injury from falling scales. The *Palsgraf* rules were modified in *Derdiarian v. Felix Contracting Corp.*, 51 N.Y.2d 308 at 315 (Ct. App. 1980) to break the "causal nexus" where "the intervening act is extraordinary under the circumstances, not foreseeable in the normal course of events, or independent of or far removed from the defendant's conduct."

acterized as a scientific question, followed by a question that is heavily infused with notions about rights and responsibilities and is viewed as a question of policy.

Both aspects of this process have been highly individualistic. The model of responsibility for harm upon which the law of tort has been built focuses on the identification of a single wrongdoer who, through observable chains of either mechanical or organic causation, can be said to be uniquely responsible for the injury caused. This model has, of course, been substantially embellished to deal with multiple defendants and multiple plaintiffs, and has also developed a "robust" approach to the inference of causation in certain cases, yet at bottom it is still built on the individualistic premises of nineteenth-century tort law.

There is a maturing awareness in various common law communities of the limitations of the traditional tort law approach to causation, particularly in the case of delayed-onset diseases. In 1998 Madam Justice McLachlin (as she then was), writing extrajudicially, put it this way:

> Why are courts now asking questions that for decades, indeed centuries, did not pose themselves, or if they did, were of no great urgency? I would suggest that it is because too often the traditional "but-for," all-or-nothing, test denies recovery where our instinctive sense of justice — of what is the right result for the situation — tells us the victim should obtain some compensation.[17]

Fleming, in an influential early article on probabilistic causation, had suggested that tort law's inability to cope with the inadequacy of the "but for" test was in part a result of the different problems arising within the field as a consequence of modern civilization:

> Courts have now been confronted repeatedly with tort plaintiffs whose fate depends on acceptance of probabilistic evidence based on epidemiological or other statistical evidence. Modern technology has contributed to this situation in two ways, by both creating the agents of pollution and by increasing scientific knowledge enabling more confident assessments of causation and attribution of responsibility. A principal question is whether legal routines can adapt themselves to changing scientific epistemology based on probabilistic evidence.[18]

---

17 McLachlin J., *supra* note 11 at 16.
18 Fleming, *supra* note 6 at 681.

In our view, McLachlin J. and Fleming are, taken together, correct. It is the evolving scientific (and, correspondingly, public) understanding of the uncertainty of proof identified by Fleming that gives rise to the injustice perceived by McLachlin.

The way the law regards the causal sequence of events has tended to mirror the way that science understands them, and indeed, the way in which ordinary people view the world. That is to say, scholars promoting a view of corrective justice rooted in Aristotelian thought stress the necessity of connection between wrongdoing and injury,[19] in the same way that the ancient Greeks understood the moral role of fate and the determinism of circumstances. Similarly, modern tort law developed in an era where the accepted scientific view was essentially Newtonian, dominated by ideas of cause and effect. Likewise, the problems that the law could deal with involved observable forms of injury (usually traumatic), caused by easily identified agents (usually acting by commission rather than omission, since the latter raises speculative causal issues).

Over the last one hundred years, science has come to understand that causation exists on a continuum of probabilities, and while scientists most often continue to use the shorthand of Newtonian certainty, they are really expressing ideas with varying levels of confidence.[20] As a result, legal and scientific thought on questions of cause and effect have diverged.[21]

The modern understanding of disease, injury, and illness is no longer confined to the mechanical and particularistic model. As our understanding of disease patterns progresses, science and medicine are increasingly able to attribute the source of illness in a population with a high degree of confidence. However, disease often, if not usually, has numerous potential causes (and indeed may occur naturally), and it is often difficult or impossible for a plaintiff to prove, on the balance of probabilities, that his or her specific injury

---

19   The Aristotelian view of "corrective justice" as it is applied by modern tort scholars is explained in Weinrib, *supra* note 13 at 449–50.

20   Brennan, *supra* note 1 at 483: "scientists recognize that the causal concepts they use often express probabilistic reasoning as deductive reasoning."

21   It remains a common tool of legal argumentation to suggest that one's interlocutor is "confusing correlation with causation," yet, to a scientist, there is only theoretical difference between the two: science expresses confidence about the causation of events largely based on correlation; causal hypotheses based on observed phenomena may be formed and tested through predicted "outcomes" and confounding factors reduced in experimental conditions, but in the end such experiments still produce only more correlations, though, after a sufficient consistency, the two events can be said with increasing confidence — but never absolute certainty — to be causally connected. Causality, in other words, is innately hypothetical; the purpose of much of science is to test and probe the causal hypothesis.

resulted from the defendants' negligence, or, to put it another way, that his or her injury would *not* have arisen "but for" the negligence of the defendant.

The resulting irony is that we may know with certainty (or at least with as much certainty as scientific inference can provide) that in one hundred cases of a particular injury, at least forty of those injuries were caused by exposure to a toxic substance. Yet in any individual case, because there is only a 40 percent chance that the injury was caused by the exposure, the defendant cannot be said legally to have caused the individual harm complained of. The divergence of legal and scientific conclusions in this fashion seriously undermines the law's deterrence and compensation functions, and it is our aim to show how the divergence can be significantly reduced or eliminated.

Causation of harm *in the aggregate* becomes clearer even as the individual identity of the victims, and their individual connection with each wrongdoer, is lost. "Likelihood" in an individual sense is based on the predicted causation in the aggregate population. Each concept, in other words, is conceptually reliant on the other. But is there a ground for preferring one view? In our opinion, viewing inherently probabilistic causation in the aggregate — as a definite harm in a percentage of the population rather than a probabilistic harm in an individual — provides several advantages in the resolution of mass tort claims.

This problem of "specific causation" or "individual injury attribution" is compounded when we are faced with multiple defendants. We may know that the plaintiff's injury is clearly attributable to exposure to a particular substance, but there are many potential defendants whose wrongdoing might have exposed the plaintiff to that substance and therefore it is similarly impossible to determine who is to blame (what Fleming famously called the problem of the "indeterminate defendant"[22]). Again, traditional tort law, which relies not just on blameworthiness but on causation in fact, is of little assistance.

In a system, such as ours, that relies in part upon tort victims and their lawyers to regulate the behaviour of wrongdoers, if the victims cannot recover then those whose negligence causes such widespread insidious harm might escape having to pay for, or internalize, the cost of the harm. The result — in either a negligence or strict liability regime[23] — is systemic

---

23   Fleming, *supra* note 6.
24   Although law and economics scholars disagree over the best rule to apply in particular circumstances, optimal deterrence in either analysis depends on the full internalization of at least that harm that is foreseeable. See S. Shavell, *Economic Analysis of Accident Law* (London: Harvard University Press, 1987).

undercompensation of victims and underdeterrence of wrongdoing, two profound problems for the law of torts from a functionalist perspective. Even if first-party insurance covers the costs to the victims, underdeterrence means that the overall cost of accidents is not reduced. Moreover, the business activities of the wrongdoers in such a paradigm are being externalized — heavily subsidized by either the victims (who bear their own harm or, in the case of contractual consumers, pay a "tort insurance premium" to the defendants), the public at large (in the case of social insurance), or other particular classes (through private insurance policies).[24]

Because most disease processes, particularly latent diseases, have many correlatives that might be said to increase risk, it is often difficult to ascertain who in the population of sufferers actually got their disease from exposure to any single substance, let alone whether it was the defendant before the court who made it. Mesothelioma (the disease at issue in the *Fairchild* case, discussed at length later in this chapter) involves in comparison a straightforward issue — it is, for practical purposes, always caused by inhalation of asbestos fibres. Other diseases, including most other cancers, have numerous factors associated with their occurrence; the most that can be said in most cases is that exposure to particular substances increased the risk of disease; tortious causation — even by the relaxed standard of "substantial i.e. non-*de minimus* contribution" — can in most cases never be directly proven. Parallelling the problem of the indeterminate defendant, then, is what Fleming called that of the indeterminate *plaintiff*.[25] Yet the problems of the indeterminate plaintiff and defendant, while they may be procedurally distinct, are analytically the same: the problem is the ambiguity of the causal nexus between an injured person and a person who has negligently exposed that person to risk of the sort of injury that the person has.

Dealing with the problem of probabilistic or indeterminate causation challenges lawyers to think in ways that are not necessarily familiar; in par-

---

24 The analysis here is based on basic economic principles of accident law as developed by scholars of the previous three decades. See G. Calabresi, "Some Thoughts on Risk Distribution and the Law of Torts" (1961) 70 Yale L.J. 499; G. Calabresi, *The Costs of Accidents: A Legal and Economic Analysis* (New Haven: Yale University Press, 1970); A.M. Polinsky, *An Introduction to Law and Economics*, 2d ed. (Boston: Little Brown, 1989); R.A. Posner, *Economic Analysis of Law*, 5th ed. (Boston: Little, Brown, 1998); Shavell, *supra* note 24; S. Shavell, "The Level of Litigation: Private Versus Social Optimality of Suit and of Settlement" (1999) 19 Int'l Rev. L. & Econ. 99; Kaplow & Shavell, "Fairness vs. Welfare" (2001) 114 Harv. L. Rev. 961.
25 Fleming, *supra* note 6 at 679*ff*.

ticular, it forces the law to explore ways in which liability mirrors the degree to which the tortfeasor has exposed a victim to risk, rather than in the more traditional modes of causation that are vestiges of intentional torts such as trespass.[26]

This approach in a mass-production environment makes some economic sense: Decisions made by defendants regarding the level of precaution that they will take are made, where not dictated by formal regulation, on a probabilistic basis; investments in precautions will be made up to the point of diminishing returns, based on the companies' own assessment of the aggregate of their expected liability. In other words, the behaviour of potential wrongdoers (which tort law seeks to modify and regulate) is governed by the wrongdoers' own assessment of the risk of harm that they will eventually be forced to internalize if precautions are not taken, weighed against the savings that will likely accrue if they are. If we are to assign liability on a fault-based system, then, it is not unjust — indeed it is arguably perfectly just — to assign it on the basis of increased risk, at least from a deterrence point of view.

C. LIABILITY "IN THE AIR"

The difficulty presented by ideas of causation has led to the notion, often repeated but perhaps less well understood, that there cannot be negligence or liability "in the air." That is to say, the tort has not occurred until the injury occurs, and indeed an injury is "caused" in the particular plaintiff by the particular defendant.

The doctrine was perhaps most famously articulated in *Overseas Tankship (U.K.) Ltd. v. Morts Dock & Engineering Co. Ltd.*, where Viscount Simonds said:

> It is, no doubt, proper when considering tortious liability for negligence to analyse its elements to say that the plaintiff must prove a duty owed to him by the defendant, a breach of that duty by the defendant and consequent damage. But there can be no liability until the damage has been done. It is not the act but the consequences on which tortious liability is

---

26 For a history of probabilistic analysis, see P.L. Bernstein, *Against the Gods: The Remarkable Story of Risk* (New York: Wiley, 1996). Bernstein traces the theory of probability, the root of all the modern principles of insurance, investment, and risk tolerance (and by implication substantive notions of objective reasonableness) to no earlier than 1654, a remarkably short time ago. That our legal system has yet to accept it fully is perhaps some testament to the extent to which probabilistic thinking runs against the natural grain of human thought.

founded. Just as (as it has been said) there is no such thing as negligence in the air, so there is no such thing as liability in the air.[27]

This "duty not to injure" analysis works well in individual cases but poorly in mass tort situations, where a portion of the population to whom the "duty not to injure" is owed has indeed become injured by the defendant but we cannot attribute causation in any individual case.

Nevertheless, courts have rather carelessly imported the "no liability in the air" analysis to product liability litigation involving alleged breaches of "mass duties." In *Watson v. Winget, Ltd.*,[28] Lord Denning said: "So here the wisdom of the common law lies in this, that it holds the breach of duty to be, not the carelessness in manufacture, not the putting into circulation of a faulty machine, but the wrongful infliction of damage."

Part of the problem is that much of the analysis of the "duty" has occurred in cases where the "duty" itself was not in issue. Rather the question concerned the location of the wrong for jurisdictional purposes. Analysing the causation of individual harm as the "breach of duty" has permitted courts in jurisdictions where the harm occurred to take jurisdiction over defendants who had negligently manufactured their products elsewhere. This was the case in *Moran v. Pyle National (Canada) Ltd.*[29] There, a faulty lightbulb manufactured in Ontario had failed in Saskatchewan, killing the plaintiff's husband. She sued under a statutory cause of action provided in her home province; jurisdiction depended on Saskatchewan law applying under choice of law principles, which was in turn determined by the *situs* of the tort. Dickson J. held at 405:

> If the essence of a tort is the injury or wrong, a paramount factor in determining *situs* must be the place of the invasion of one's right to bodily security. In a *Donoghue v. Stevenson* case, can carelessness in manufacture be separated from resulting injury? The jurisdictional act can well be regarded, in an appropriate case, as the infliction of injury and not the fault in manufacture. Pyle is being sued because Moran suffered harm, not because some unidentified employee of Pyle's was allegedly careless.

Later, at 409, Dickson J. suggested that this approach was fair because it accommodated the reasonable expectations of manufacturers: "By tendering his products in the market place directly or through normal distribu-

---

27 *Overseas Tankship (U.K.) Ltd. v. Morts Dock & Engineering Co. Ltd. (The "Wagon Mound")*, [1961] A.C. 388 at 425.
28 [1960] S.L.T. 321 at 331–32 (H.L.).
29 [1975] 1 S.C.R. 393.

tive channels, a manufacturer ought to assume the burden of defending those products wherever they cause harm as long as the forum into which the manufacture is taken is one that he reasonably ought to have had in his contemplation when he so tendered his goods."

Dickson J.'s approach is not inconsistent with an assertion of jurisdiction based on risk: a defendant could expect to be subject to liability in all jurisdictions where its behaviour creates a *risk* of harm, or, to put it another way, harm in a portion of the population. The duty in such a case would be a duty not to subject individual persons in one's neighbourhood to unreasonable risk, not necessarily individual harm. The breach occurs when the risk of harm materializes — that is, when harm in a portion of the population becomes inevitable, even if individual attribution is impossible. Under such circumstances, each jurisdiction where the harm has occurred in the population has an interest in providing its citizens with appropriate redress.

D. SOME APPROACHES TO INDETERMINATE CAUSATION

1) Statutory Reform of Causation Rules

Perhaps not surprisingly, some of the earliest innovations to relieve the burden of proving causation in mass-exposure situations were the result of political, rather than judicial, initiatives. In early workers' compensation laws, for instance, employees of particular businesses with which certain diseases were associated could recover without proof of causation if they developed the disease.[30] That these schemes were necessitated by systemic inability to prove scientific causation in the case of prolonged exposure diseases is made clear by McElveen and Postol:

> When states first began to compensate workers for occupational diseases, they grafted coverage for such diseases onto existing accident compensation systems. Thus, a disease or illness was considered to be "occupational" if ... it arose out of or in the course of employment. Yet establishing the causation of a disease is often complicated: a disease's etiology may be

---

30 The *Workmen's Compensation Act, 1906* (U.K.), 6 Edw. VII, c. 58, established a cause of action for employees against their employer regardless of fault. There were provisions for "deemed liability," and statutory apportionment among multiple employers for the compensation. Under the Schedules to the Act, certain diseases were deemed to have been caused by exposure in particular industries. For instance, if a miner contracted Anklyostomiasis (*ibid.* at Sch. III), he was deemed to have contracted the disease from his work at the mine, "unless the employer proves to the contrary" *ibid.* at s. 8(2).

unknown and undeterminable ... Moreover, diseases tend to develop over a period of years rather than at a single moment in time. States therefore developed various methods to determine whether a disease arose out of or in the course of employment.

The first solution to [this problem] was the development of schedules, which listed diseases that medical science had demonstrated to be employment related. Listed diseases were presumed compensable and, under some statutory schemes, the listing was conclusive .... [31]

Statutory reversal of onuses in indeterminate causation cases, or even conclusively deemed causation, is a common device, used to deal with problems as diverse as railway-related injuries in British Columbia,[32] black lung disease in the United States,[33] tobacco-related harm in British Columbia[34] and Newfoundland,[35] and damage resulting from Canadian nuclear accidents.[36]

Even in cases where the statute does not explicitly alter causation rules, courts have proven themselves willing to relax the rules of causation when the breach is of a legislative duty. In the earlier case of *Nicholson v. Atlas Steel Foundry and Engineering Co. Ltd.*,[37] the victim had worked in the defendant's steel foundry, had inhaled dust containing siliceous particles, and died of pneumoconiosis. It was alleged that the defendant had failed to provide adequate ventilation to extract the dust. The House of Lords considered the statutory duty to provide proper ventilation imposed by section 4(1) of the *Factories Act, 1937*, and Viscount Simonds said (at 618):

---

31 McElveen & Postol, "Compensating Occupational Disease Victims Under the Longshoremen's and Harbour Workers' Compensation Act" (1983) 32 Am. U.L. Rev. 717 at 720.
32 British Columbia's *Employers' Liability Act of 1891*, S.B.C. 1891, c. 10 provided that injuries suffered in certain circumstances by rail-workers are "deemed and taken to have been caused by reason of [an actionable] defect."
33 In *Usery v. Turner Elkhorn Mining Co.*, 428 U.S. 1 (1975), the Supreme Court of the United States upheld the constitutionality of the U.S. Federal *Coal Mine Health and Safety Act of 1969*, 83 Stat. 792 as amended by the *Black Lung Benefits Act of 1972*, 86 Stat. 150, 30 U.S.C. 901 et seq. (1970 ed. and Supp. IV), which applied to a particular industry, namely coal mining, and enacted a series of presumptions relating to the cause of respiratory disease in miners.
34 *Tobacco Damages and Health Care Costs Recovery Act*, S.B.C. 2000, c. 30.
35 *Tobacco Health Care Costs Recovery Act*, S.N. 2001, c. T-4.2.
36 The *Nuclear Liability Act*, R.S.C. 1985, c. N-28 at s. 4 provides that an operator of a nuclear installation is, "without proof of fault or negligence, absolutely liable for a breach of duty imposed on him." If more than one operator is at fault and it is not possible to separate the damages caused by each, they are, by virtue of s. 5, jointly and severally liable. Certain consequential damages may also according to s. 6, be "deemed ... to be attributable to that breach of duty."
37 [1957] 1 W.L.R. 613 (H.L.).

> ... if the statute prescribes a proper system of ventilation by the circulation of fresh air so as to render harmless, so far as practicable, all fumes, dust and other impurities that may be injurious to health, generated in the course of work carried on in the factory, and if it is proved that there is no system or only an inadequate system of ventilation, it requires little further to establish a causal link between that default and the illness, due to noxious dust, of a person employed in the shop. Something is required as was held in *Wardlaw*'s case. I was a party to that decision and would not in any way resile from it. But it must not be pressed too far. In the present case there was, in my opinion, ample evidence to support the appellants' case.

In other words, if the defendant's breach of its statutory duty increases exposure to a material that can cause the disease eventually contracted by the victim, the traditional rules of causation will be relaxed markedly in the circumstances. But should it make any difference whether the duty was imposed by statute or at common law?

2) Probabilistic Discounting

Courts have always accepted that where the *future* manifestation of wrong-caused injury (otherwise actionable) is uncertain, the award should be discounted on a probabilistic basis.[38] Where the negligence of the defendant causes some present injury, the future extent of that injury, the possibility that the plaintiff might develop a related injury or disease, the chances of aggravation or improvement, and all the associated costs are measured probabilistically. Thus, where there is a chance that the plaintiff's injury will diminish, damages can be discounted for that probability. Where the chances are that things will get worse, damages are increased.[39]

Courts treat past incidents, whether knowable or not, as somehow distinctly different from future eventualities, which are inherently probabilistic. It is said that probabilistic reasoning can be used to measure the extent of loss or injury in the future (because the future is inherently probabilistic) but not to determine whether a current injury was in fact caused by the defendant (because the present and past are susceptible of exact proof). But if one accepts that the causal connection between an incident of negligence and an individual's disease is unknown, and quite possibly unknowable, then a court dealing with causation-in-fact is engaged in a probabilistic

---

38 S.M. Waddams, "The Valuation of Chances" (1998) 30 Can. Bus. L.J. 86 at 87.
39 See Cassels, *supra* note 2 at 120–21.

assessment exactly parallelling the one involved in the calculation of future damages. It just chooses to pretend otherwise.

A natural objection to the discounting of *most* awards probabilistically is, of course, that to do so will not provide *restitutio ad integrum*; such an award cannot "make the victim whole."[40] Setting aside the obviously questionable underlying assumption that the award of pecuniary damages does indeed make an injured person "whole," we must remember that we are, at least notionally, concerned with all outcomes in the tort system, not only the outcomes in those few cases where both factual and legal causation cross the 50-percent threshold of likelihood.[41] Against this, it could be argued that in "under 50 percent" of cases it is better to receive something than nothing at all, and in "over 50 percent" of cases it might be more just to the defendant to avoid charging the whole of the costs. While compensation may, in individual cases, be less satisfying, deterrence will be more accurate since, overall, defendants will internalize the cost of harm. Optimal deterrence would in turn reduce the number of *future* victims.[42]

Nevertheless, the incorporation of probabilistic discounting into questions of the causation of past harm has found application in Canadian jurisprudence only when it can be characterized as a "loss of chance," and only for a brief time at that. We discuss this below.

3) Alternate Liability

The theory of alternate liability applies where two or more defendants are guilty of negligent conduct in circumstances where the conduct of just one of them must have injured the innocent plaintiff. By this theory, each of the defendants in such a case would be considered to be the cause of the plain-

---

40   Fleming, *supra* note 6 at 680.
41   Indeed, we use the 50-percent figure only for convenience, assuming, of course, that courts do require a 50-percent-plus probability. There is some evidence to suggest that in fact both judges and juries view the probabilistic threshold for civil liability at around 75 percent, closer to the "proof beyond a reasonable doubt" standard of criminal law: R.J. Simon and L. Mahan, "Quantifying Burdens of Proof" (1970–71) 5 Law & Soc. Rev. 319. For simplicity's sake, though, we here refer to the 51-percent threshold when dealing with proof on a balance of probabilities.
42   It is difficult to divine just how much support the current regime derives from its self-delusion that the compensation it provides is adequate. While this may be so in individual cases, these must be weighed against the many more cases in which compensation is denied, or not even pursued. Moreover, in choosing compensation over deterrence, courts are simply expressing an irrational (though understandable) preference to ameliorate the suffering of the party it actually sees, rather than the victims who escape its attention.

tiff's loss unless they can exculpate themselves individually. Defendants unable to meet the burden of proof are held jointly and severally liable.

The famous case of *Cook v. Lewis*,[43] is one contribution of the Supreme Court of Canada to the problem of the indeterminate defendant. Two hunting companions both negligently fired at a third, who was struck by one bullet. The Supreme Court of Canada held that, where both defendants are negligent and had rendered it impossible for the plaintiff to prove which one had caused the injury, both would be equally liable if they could not prove their causal innocence.

In reaching this decision, the Supreme Court relied upon the similar American case of *Summers v. Tice*.[44] In that case, the California Supreme Court had stated at page 4:

> [The defendants] are both wrongdoers — both negligent toward the plaintiff. They brought about a situation where the negligence of one of them injured the plaintiff, hence it should rest with them each to absolve himself if he can. The injured party has been placed by defendants in the unfair position of pointing to which defendant caused the harm. If one can escape the other may also and the plaintiff is remediless. Ordinarily defendants are in a far better position to offer evidence to determine which one caused the injury.

While the outcome of *Summers* and *Cook* may seem intuitively satisfying, the reasoning employed in the above passage seems somewhat strained. The defendants did not "[bring] about a situation where the negligence of one of them injured the plaintiff"; at least, one of them did not. How, then, is it possible to justify the imposition of liability on the "innocent" defendant?[45] One rationale offered by the courts is that the negligence of the "innocent" hunter covered up the liability of the "guilty" one. That is to say, had the "innocent" gunman not negligently fired, the plaintiff would not have been deprived of the opportunity to prove causation. But this explanation is difficult to fit within traditional conceptions of negligence, because it would, in theory, require that the "innocent" gunman could foresee that a second, "guilty" gunman would fire in the same direction at the

---

43 [1951] S.C.R. 830 [hereinafter *Cook*].
44 199 P.2d 1 (Sup. Ct. Cal. 1948) [hereinafter *Summers*].
45 Here, of course, an "innocent" and "guilty" defendant exist only in the way it can be said that Schrodinger's famous cat is neither alive nor dead — they must be conceived as entirely probabilistic assignments to the extent that the true state of affairs cannot be known. We might as well describe each defendant as, causally speaking, "innocent/guilty."

same time, and thus a duty was owed by the "innocent" gunman to the victim not to shield the "guilty" gunman from liability. If such an analysis is to be inferred (for it is nowhere explicit), then it would require that we acknowledge, at the very least, a striking relaxation of the doctrine of remoteness.

But an alternative, and perhaps more straightforward, rationale is once again to take refuge in a distributive decision — to say that, as between the reckless hunters and the innocent victim, it is better that the harm is borne by the wrongdoers, causation aside.[46] Here, a semblance of corrective justice is maintained by requiring at least that both defendants have acted carelessly towards the plaintiff and there has been, therefore, some moral wrongdoing by each "directed at" the eventual victim.

But *Cook* and *Summers*, by ostensibly relying on an onus shift when it was clear the reversed burden could not possibly be met (and indeed the rule seems to apply principally in cases — conspiracies of silence aside[47] — where the onus *cannot* be met), managed to do away with causation while retaining the pretence that they were doing nothing of the sort. They are therefore unsettling decisions for those wed to the corrective justice model, while managing to be hardly satisfying for functionalists, either.

Although the theory of alternate liability has been tailored in the United States to have application in some product liability cases,[48] the justifications offered for the *Cook v. Lewis* rule do not find ready application in mass tort situations, for a variety of reasons. Consider, for instance, that the *Cook* rule appears to apply only when the conduct of the *defendant* destroys the plaintiff's power of proof. What if it is the plaintiff who does so, through his or her own lifestyle choices, selection of products, and so on? What if *no one* is responsible for the absence of information on causation, but rather it results from the limits of scientific knowledge? This last case, moreover, counters a main justification for the rule in *Cook v. Lewis* — the

---

46 Certainly this is the traditional justification for *Summers*. See Malone, "Ruminations on Cause-In-Fact" (1956) 9 Stan. L. Rev. 60 at 66–68. Yet Rosenberg points out that reliance on the distributive rationale "surely represents a radical departure from traditional notions of culpability": D. Rosenberg, "The Causal Connection in Mass Exposure Cases: A 'Public Law' Vision of the Tort System" (1984) 97 Harv. L. Rev. 849 at 882.
47 See *Ybarra v. Spangard*, 25 Cal.2d 486, 154 P.2d 687 (Sup. Ct. Cal. 1944). In that case a surgical team bore burden of explaining how an anesthetized victim was injured in the shoulder during an appendectomy. None could explain and all were held liable.
48 See *Abel v. Eli Lilly & Co.*, 418 Mich. 311, 343 N.W.2d 164 (Sup. Ct. 1984); *Ferrigno v. Eli Lilly & Co.*, 175 N.J. Super. 551, 420 A.2d 1305 (N.J. 1980); and *Minnich v. Ashland Oil Co.*, 473 N.E.2d 1199 (Sup. Ct. Ohio 1984).

idea that the defendants are in a better position to say which of them caused the plaintiff's injury. While this may hold true in a small minority of product liability or toxic tort cases, the fact remains that scientific understanding of causation of disease processes is still primitive[49] and cases of genuinely indeterminate causation will always remain. If we hold one of several manufacturers jointly liable for an exposure-related harm, it cannot be because we believe that that defendant possesses information about the actual liability of another that could be prised out through the lawsuit; some other justification must be found.

4) Liability Based on Concert in Action, Enterprise Theory, or Market Participation

Before continuing to discuss the breadth of the extension of burden-shifting causation rules and their interaction with other emerging tort doctrines such as "loss of chance," we should describe some other ways in which legal findings of joint liability can serve to relieve the plaintiff of the burden of demonstrating exactly which defendant caused the harm complained of.

It has long been recognized that a person may be liable for harm caused by the act of another if he or she acts in concert towards the commission of a tort.[50] Yet, while a tort of "concerted action" might ease the burden on plaintiffs of proving causation, it does not represent a disconnection of the causal nexus. Rather, it widens the old notions of duty and foreseeability to capture behaviour that might before have appeared too remote to attract liability.[51]

---

49 And we here mean that the particularistic understanding of many disease processes, be they chemical, biological, or mechanical, is primitive, not that (as we emphasize here throughout) causal attribution cannot be known in an aggregate sense with some precision.

50 This is so if he or she (a) does a tortious act in concert with another or pursuant to a common design with the other, or (b) knows that another's conduct constitutes a breach of duty and gives substantial assistance or encouragement, or (c) gives substantial assistant to the other in accomplishing a tortious result and that person's own conduct, separately considered, constitutes a breach of duty to the third person: American Law Institute, *Restatement (2d) of Torts* (1979), § 876. endorsed in *Granewich v. Harding*, 985 P.2d 788 (Sup. Ct. Or. 1999).

51 See *Hymowitz v. Eli Lilly Company*, 539 N.E.2d 1069 (Ct. App. N.Y. 1988), cert. denied, 493 U.S. 944 (1989). In that case the court held that a parallel activity, without more, was not sufficient to establish a concert action claim.

Related to "concerted action" is the concept of "enterprise liability"[52] first adopted in *Hall v. E.I. duPont De Nemours & Co.*[53] In *Hall*, the plaintiffs were children who had been injured by blasting caps. Since they could not identify the particular explosives manufacturers of the caps that had injured them, the plaintiffs sought damages from six manufacturers and their trade association. The court held that each member of the blasting-cap industry could be found liable on the theory that each contributed to the failure of the trade association to set adequate industry-wide safeguards and warnings: "[W]here ... individual defendant-manufacturers cannot be identified, the existence of industry-wide standards or practices could support a finding of *joint control of risk* and a shift of the burden of proving causation to the defendants."[54]

So while, following *Hall*, a plaintiff need not identify the specific defendant that manufactured the product that caused his or her particular injury, he or she must still demonstrate that the defendants were aware of the risks of their product and possessed a joint capacity to reduce significantly or eliminate totally those risks[55] in order for the burden shift to operate.[56] Again, this is not a disconnection of the causal nexus but a broadening of the traditional requirement to connect through foreseeability the behaviour (the "controlled" risk) with the harm (to customers of the industry as a whole). Such "enterprise liability," like concerted action and the *Cook* and *Summers* cases, still relies on the idea that the defendant has, in fact, *caused* the plaintiff's harm through act or omission. The risk-based liability of *Hall* continues to require that the defendant increased the risk *to the plaintiff*.

A more flexible, but arguably far slipperier, means of approaching indeterminate causation is to impose liability on the basis of *global* risk-creation, as was accomplished through the "market share liability" designed in the DES cases in the United States, and in particular *Sindell v. Abbott Laboratories*.[57] Under these approaches, where an individual or group is

---

52 Enterprise liability is a term used in a broad array of contexts. Here it is used to describe the imposition of liability on the basis of participation in a particularly cohesive industry. Later in Part Two, we examine a different kind of "enterprise liability" — the liability imposed upon entire corporate groups based on elements of share ownership and control.
53 345 F. Supp. 353 (E.D.N.Y. 1972) [hereinafter *Hall*].
54 *Ibid.* at 374 [emphasis added].
55 *Ibid.* at 378.
56 *Ibid.* at 379–80.
57 26 Cal.3d 588 (Sup. Ct. Cal. 1980) [hereinafter *Sindell*]. From 1947 to 1971, DES had been prescribed to women as a means of preventing miscarriages. Tragically, the drug caused cancer in young women whose mothers had used the drug while pregnant.

injured by a product or process, but it is unclear which of a number of defendants involved in the activity is specifically responsible, all wrongdoers are assessed damages according to their contribution to the overall risk to the exposed population (assessed by their market share or other factors).[58]

Market-share liability bridges the conceptual gap between these types of cases, on the one hand, and true probabilistic causation, on the other. While it is in its strictest form simply a form of apportioning damages, in practice it might also be said to establish liability on a probabilistic basis — because, under market-share theory, a defendant can be found liable for negligence "in the air"; that is to say, a liable defendant need not, as in *Cook* and *Hall*, have breached its duty to the particular plaintiff before the court.

While there is still a vestige of the idea in *Sindell* that liability is being imposed through a rebuttable presumption of causation, it is difficult to confine entirely the court's reasoning in this way.[59] The breakthrough in *Sindell* is the explicit recognition that liability is almost certainly being imposed upon defendants who, while they must be shown to have breached a duty "at large," cannot be shown to have owed any duty to the particular plaintiff. The causal nexus is therefore not simply enlarged but ignored. Of course, such a bold move, generally lauded by functionalists,[60] was not without its moralist critics.[61] Even Fleming argued that courts should avoid such a radical departure, which is "not corrective, but distributive justice": "Such a break from the whole tradition of our cultures

---

After the Food and Drug Administration banned DES, a number of lawsuits were filed against its manufacturers by daughters of women who took the drug during their pregnancy. Prior to *Sindell*, many of these lawsuits were dismissed because of an inability of the plaintiffs to identify the manufacturer of the DES taken by their mother; DES had been produced in a generic form by over three hundred drug companies.

58 Richard Delgado, "Beyond *Sindell*: Relaxation of Cause-in-Fact Rules for Indeterminate Plaintiffs" (1982) 70 Cal. L. Rev. 881; Glen O. Robinson, "Multiple Causation in Tort Law: Reflections on the DES Cases" (1982) 68 Va. L. Rev. 713; Glen O. Robinson, "Probabilistic Causation and Compensation for Tortious Risk" (1985) 14 J. Legal Stud. 779.
59 *Sindell*, *supra* note 57 at 936.
60 See Kaplow & Shavell, *supra* note 25 at 1207, noting that deterrence and compensation are both optimized in a market-share regime. Indeed, Kaplow & Shavell persuasively argue that, when all members of an industry are negligent in a way that results in widespread harm, any resources spent on determining who is to blame detract from the amounts that can be dedicated to compensation, without providing any more exact deterrence, because expected liability is the same throughout the industry no matter how blame is eventually apportioned.
61 See D.A. Fischer, "Product liability — An Analysis of Market Share Liability" (1981) 34 Vand. L. Rev. 1623 at 1623, 1629–30, 1638–39.

should be at best a program for legislation, not judicial reform."[62] Indeed, since Fleming wrote, market-share liability has been enacted in several jurisdictions with respect to generalized harm of a causally indeterminate nature. For instance, in many U.S. states, "Drug Dealers' Liability Acts"[63] provide for market-share liability of drug dealers for harm caused within their "markets" as the term is statutorily defined. Similarly, tobacco costs recovery legislation in British Columbia,[64] Newfoundland,[65] and Florida[66] has contained market-share liability-apportionment schemes. There is even some suggestion that market-share theory might, at common law, support a cause of action in Canada.[67]

Nevertheless, courts remain wary of the technique. Even in DES litigation, only four states other than California — South Dakota, Washington, Wisconsin, and New York[68] — have embraced market-share liability, and

---

62 Fleming, *supra* note 6 at 668.
63 See, e.g., Arkansas: *Drug Dealer Liability Act*, 1995 Ark. Acts No. 896 (codified at Ark. Code Ann. 16-124-101 to -112 (Mich. Supp. 1997)); California: *Drug Dealer Liability Act*, 1996 Cal. Legis. Serv. 3792 (West) (codified at Cal. Health & Safety Code 11700 to 11717 (West Supp. 1998)); Illinois: *Drug Dealer Liability Act*, 1995 Ill. Leg. Serv. 89-293 (West) (codified at 740 ILL. COMP. STAT. ANN. 57/1-25 (West Supp. 1997)); Michigan: *Drug Dealer Liability Act*, 1994 Mich. Legis. Serv. 27 (West) (codified at Mich. Comp. Laws Ann. " 691.1601–691.1619 (West Supp. 1998)).
64 *Tobacco Damages and Health Care Costs Recovery Act*, S.B.C. 2000, c. 30.
65 *Tobacco Health Care Costs Recovery Act*, S.N. 2001, c. T-4.2.
66 *Medicare Third Party Liability Act*, 409.910(9)(b), Fla. Stat. (1995), considered in *Agency for Health Care Administration v. Associated Industries of Florida Inc.*, 678 So.2d 1239 (Fla. 1996).
67 In *Gariepy v. Shell Oil Co.*, (2000), 51 O.R. (3d) 181 (S.C.J.) the court declined to dismiss a claim against a defendant served *ex juris*, in part on the ground that the plaintiffs' claim for market-share liability made the extension of jurisdiction to the defendants appropriate even absent any other act by the defendants establishing the requisite "real and substantial connection" with Ontario. Cumming J. said at para. 11:

> As well, where the specific manufacturer of a defective product used by a particular class member is unknown but the product by different manufacturers is the same, then liability may be able to be determined on a market share theory: *Hall v. Du Pont de Nemours & Co.*, 345 F. Supp. 353 (E.D.N.Y. 1972) at pp. 370, 371; *Sindell v. Abbott Laboratories*, 26 Cal.3d 588, 607 P.2d 924 (1980) at para. 59.

Similarly, in *Ragoonanan Estate v. Imperial Tobacco Limited* (2000), 51 O.R. (3d) 603 (S.C.J.), the court dismissed a class action against two of three defendant manufacturers of cigarettes, on the basis that only the third actually manufactured the cigarette that had actually caused the fire that injured the representative plaintiff. In the course of doing so, the court suggested that, if the manufacturer of the fateful cigarette was not known, the plaintiff could have proceeded against all three on a market-share basis.
68 *McElhaney v. Eli Lilly & Co.*, 575 F. Supp. 228 (U.S. Dist. 1983), aff'd, 739 F.2d 340 (8th Cir. 1984); *Martin v. Abbott Laboratories Ltd.*, 689 P.2d 368 (Sup. Ct. Wash. 1984) (*en banc*); *Collins v. Eli Lilly & Co.*, 342 N.W.2d 37 (Wis.), cert. denied, 469 U.S. 826

only where plaintiffs can show that a particular product manufactured by all of the defendants named in the lawsuit caused their injuries; that a design defect in the product caused the harm and that each defendant sold the product in a manner that made it unreasonably dangerous; and that the plaintiffs are unable to identify the specific manufacturer of the product that caused their injury.[69]

Other problems remain, such as the question of how broadly or narrowly one defines the "market." Is it the national market, as provided in *Hymowitz v. Eli Lilly & Co.*?[70] There, the court reasoned that calculations based on the national market share best apportioned the defendants' liabilities, because it reflected their relative culpability in exposing the public at large to DES.[71] Then, there is a difficult question of proof — what evidence is to be used to discover the defendant's market share? How will it be introduced? In the case of gradual exposures over time (as with asbestos or tobacco, for instance, as opposed to DES), how does one deal with the constantly shifting market shares involved, as manufacturers enter or leave the market?

For these reasons among others, many U.S. jurisdictions have rejected market-share liability, even in DES litigation. The most formidable objection to the adoption of market-share liability is that which goes to the heart of any system of probabilistic liability: that is, that it is incompatible with the traditional notion of tort law as a system of individual responsibility.[72]

5) Liability for Medical Monitoring

Another interesting way in which risk-based liability is being introduced into judgments is through claims for medical monitoring. That is, plain-

---

(1984); *Hymowitz v. Eli Lilly & Co.*, 539 N.E.2d 1069 (N.Y.), cert. denied, 493 U.S. 944 (1989) [hereinafter *Hymowitz*]. Still, these courts do not agree on all the relevant criteria for the application of the doctrine. Courts in Washington and Wisconsin, for instance, did not require that the plaintiff join a substantial share of potential manufacturers in order to maintain a market-share liability action: *Martin, supra* at 383. *Collins, supra* at 50. In *Martin, ibid.* the court also imposed a presumption of equal market share, forcing the defendant to prove his actual share in order to reduce his liability.

69 Kenneth R. Lepage, "Lead-Based Paint Litigation and the Problem of Causation: Toward a Unified Theory of Market Share Liability" (1995) 37 B.C. L. Rev. 155 at 159.
70 *Hymowitz, supra* note 68 at 1078.
71 *Ibid.*
72 Shirley H. Fang, "*Santiago v. Sherwin-Williams Co.*: Rejection of Market Share Liability in Lead-Based Paint Litigation" (1995) 43 Buffalo L. Rev. 725 at 744; Rodney L. Eshelman, "Lead Paint Litigation: Why Market-Share Liability Doesn't Add Up" (May 2000) 24(4) For the Defense 28.

tiffs argue that the defendant's negligence has exposed them to greater risk of harm and that, although the harm has not yet manifested itself (and indeed will not become manifest in many of the plaintiffs), the risk itself has caused loss in the form of the costs associated with medical tests and procedures necessary either to prevent or to detect onset.

Medical monitoring as a remedy is discussed in some detail in Chapter Three. In a sense, a medical-monitoring award can be seen as probabilistic because it is unrelated to the actual causation of injury (as that term is traditionally understood) and might represent a "discounted" assessment of damages, though this latter point is more difficult. The claim is perhaps most closely analogous to the economic loss asserted in *Rivtow Marine Ltd. v. Washington Iron Works*,[73] where the Court allowed compensation for "down time" incurred when (probabilistically) dangerous cranes were taken out of commission after one of them had failed on account of cracks.

6) From Burden-Shifting and "Loss of Chance" to Probabilistic Causation

The principles that we have described so far elucidate the move away from the joint liability of traditionally defined wrongdoers (i.e., those who have owed, and breached, a duty to the particular plaintiff, and that breach has demonstrably caused the harm) towards a more results-focused liability based on distributive principles. In the latter theory, it is not necessary to demonstrate a causal relationship between wrongdoer and wronged — the necessity of causation-in-fact has been relieved to serve the ends of deterrence and compensation. Concert-in-action, enterprise liability, and, more starkly, market-share liability represent a trend towards a functionalist approach to mass exposure torts and away from the moralistic viewpoint.

a) Onus-Shifting

As discussed, one of the simplest ways of dealing with causal uncertainty is onus-shifting. Once a plaintiff has established a sufficiently high degree of "probabilistic" evidence, the burden of proof might be shifted to the defendant. The leading example of this approach was the English case of *McGhee v. National Coal Board*.[74] The plaintiff, who was employed to clean out brick kilns, developed dermatitis. The condition was likely caused by exposure to coal dust and aggravated by the fact that the employer did not provide washing facilities (this was the negligence allegation). At trial, the plaintiff's action

---

73 [1974] S.C.R. 1189.
74 *McGhee v. National Coal Board*, [1972] 3 All E.R. 1008 [hereinafter *McGhee*].

was dismissed on the ground that he had not demonstrated that the provision of washing facilities would have prevented the condition. However, on appeal the House of Lords held that the absence of such facilities had materially increased the risk. Lord Reid said that a plaintiff will succeed "if he can shew [sic] that fault of the defender caused or materially contributed to his injury. There may have been two separate causes but it is enough if one of the causes arose from the fault of the defender. The pursuer does not have to prove that this cause would of itself have been enough to cause him injury."[75]

Essentially, in such circumstances, the court is asking whether the defendant negligently created an unreasonable risk of harm to the plaintiff. If so, then the court may be willing to infer that the risk was, in fact, the cause of the plaintiff's injuries (so long as those injuries come within the area of risk created). From a policy perspective, this makes good sense. Ordinarily the plaintiff will not be in a good position to demonstrate conclusively that his or her injuries were caused by a particular product or process. The defendant has better information about the technology and the risks, and is better situated to take precautions to prevent harm. By shifting the onus of proof to the defendant, the court ensures that the plaintiff receives the benefit of the doubt, and is not left helpless because of the inadequacy of medical and technical knowledge. As Lord Wilberforce stated: "[I]t is a sound principle that where a person has, by breach of a duty of care, created a risk, and injury occurs within that area of risk, the loss should be borne by him unless he shows that it has some other cause."[76]

On the other hand, onus reversals seem, to many, to deviate too far from the corrective justice model, and threaten to broaden liability too far. Indeed, in 1988, the same court that decided *McGhee* arguably emasculated it in the medical-negligence case *Wilsher v. Essex Area Health Authority*.[77] The plaintiff was unable to establish that his retinal condition was caused by the admittedly negligent treatment, and was not a preexisting condition. The House of Lords overruled the lower courts, which had relied on *McGhee* in favour of the plaintiff. Reasserting the traditional individualistic requirements of proof, Lord Bridge concluded: "whether we like it or not, the law, which only Parliament can change, requires proof of fault causing damage as the basis of liability in tort. We should do society nothing but disservice if we made the forensic process still more unpredictable and hazardous by distorting the law to accommodate the exigencies of what may seem hard cases."[78]

---

75   Ibid. at 1010.
76   Ibid. at 1012.
77   *Wilsher v. Essex Area Health Authority*, [1988] A.C. 1074 (H.L.) [hereinafter *Wilsher*].
78   Ibid. at 1092.

Other courts in Canada and the United States have shown a similar reluctance to relax too far the rules of causal proof. Yet, while such rules protect defendants against unfounded lawsuits, they also serve to bar many deserving plaintiffs from compensation.

In *Snell v. Farrell*,[79] the Supreme Court of Canada reacted to the uncertainty of the House of Lords with ambivalence of its own. In *Snell*, Sopinka J. seemed to reject the *McGhee* approach, though on the assumption that it was unnecessary to resolve the problems of causation. He stated:

> I have examined the alternatives arising out of the *McGhee* case. They were that the plaintiff simply prove that the defendant created a risk that the injury which occurred would occur. Or, what amounts to the same thing, that the defendant has the burden of disproving causation. *If I were convinced that defendants who have a substantial connection to the injury were escaping liability because plaintiffs cannot prove causation under currently applied principles, I would not hesitate to adopt one of these alternatives.* In my opinion, however, properly applied, the principles relating to causation are adequate to the task.[80]

In the end, the *Snell* Court found that the defendant's negligence was a significant contributing factor to the plaintiff's injuries, and thus liability could follow. In this sense, *Snell* went no further than earlier cases considering cumulative, rather than alternative, causation. Invoking Lord Bridge in *Wilsher*, who had described a "robust approach to the facts," Sopinka J. said: "The legal or ultimate burden remains with the plaintiff, but ... an inference of causation may be drawn, although positive or scientific proof of causation has not been adduced."[81]

The Supreme Court may be saying that inferences may be drawn when the evidence raises a likely case of causation. However, this would add nothing to the law and would still leave the plaintiff with the burden of proof on the balance of probabilities. But if a "robust" approach is meant to permit inferences to be drawn in the *absence* of such evidence, while providing no guiding principles, then this simply alters the law in the guise of finding facts.[82] Such an approach seems necessary only to avoid opening

---

79 (1990), 72 D.L.R. (4th) 289 (S.C.C.) [hereinafter *Snell*].
80 *Ibid.* at 299 [emphasis added].
81 *Ibid.* at 301.
82 A similar approach has been adopted where intervening events are at issue. In *Hollis v. Dow Corning Corp.*, [1995] 4 S.C.R. 634 [hereinafter *Hollis*], the defendant manufacturer of breast implants argued that, even if it had issued an appropriate warning, there was no evidence that the plaintiff's physician would have passed it along to her. Following

the floodgates to probabilistic-based litigation, a worthy goal, perhaps, but not one conducive to principled analyses along the lines proposed.

b) Probabilistic Discounting

The objection to simple onus-shifting is that it results in 100-percent liability for a defendant on the basis of a substantially smaller probability (50 percent) that the defendant's conduct caused the injury. As we have discussed, one way of moderating this apparent risk of injustice is to "discount" the defendant's liability. The idea that a plaintiff may recover for "lost opportunity," even if the chance of that opportunity materializing into gain was less than 50 percent, was first set out in *Chaplin v. Hicks*.[83] There, the defendant advertised a contest inviting applications from young women. According to the terms of the contest, twelve winners would be awarded contracts providing a weekly wage for three years. The plaintiff was selected as one of fifty finalists for one of the twelve prizes, but the defendant failed to notify her properly; she missed her interview and lost her chance (one might calculate it at 12/50ths, or 24 percent) at a prize. It was held that the defendant had breached his contract by failing to use reasonable efforts to notify the plaintiff and the jury awarded £100 damages.

It was argued that the plaintiff should receive only nominal damages since the harm suffered was too remote and speculative, that it was subject to so many contingencies that it could not be assessed. The Court of Appeal, however, upheld the jury verdict. The judges held that the mere fact that the prize was contingent did not mean that the chance of winning had no value, or that its value could not be assessed. They all referred to the fact that the plaintiff's chance of winning was about one in four, and that the jury could take this into account in determining the value of the chance.[84]

Chaplin, therefore, clearly established the principle that, at least in some cases, damages *could* be awarded for lost chances even when the chance was well under the traditional "but for" threshold of 50 percent. Thus, if a lawyer negligently permits a limitation period to expire, the

---

Cook, the majority held that this burden need not be discharged by the plaintiff, since the defendant had "creat[ed] the set of causal conditions leading to her injury" (para. 57) and thus could not rely on the uncertainty of the physician's actions to save it. But the central difficulty of *Cook* remains: if indeed the doctor had not passed on the warning, then the defendant had not "created" the conditions leading to her injury, except when viewed on a probabilistic basis, an analysis that, once again, the Court was at pains to avoid.

83 [1911] 2 K.B. 786 (C.A.) [hereinafter *Chaplin*].
84 Note that the amount awarded was still less than the "probabilistic value" of the prizes, which had an average value of around £600 (24 percent of £600 = £144).

award to the plaintiff might be discounted by the chance that he would have succeeded at trial.[85] Similarly, where a defendant neglected to take steps that could have realized for the plaintiff a profitable rezoning of property, calculations can be made of the profit to be realized, discounted by the probability of the success of the rezoning effort.[86]

Some have suggested that the chance itself should be regarded as a thing of value, and thus the expected loss "real" in its entirety.[87] But, of course, there is no "market" for most types of chance. While a lottery ticket might be resold, most opportunities that might be measured probabilistically — the chance of recovery, job prospects, and so on — are so individualistic as to make any requirement of alienability a virtual bar to recovery.

Theoretically, the concept of probabilistic valuation of chances could be used to resolve problems of causal indeterminacy in personal injury cases. Of course, when the plaintiff is able to prove on the balance of probabilities that the defendant caused his or her injury, courts will value the future extent and consequences of that injury on a probabilistic basis. Similarly, when it can be established only that there is a "substantial chance" that negligence caused a particular injury, liability and damages might be based on this chance. Thus, if the likelihood is 25 percent that the wrong caused the damages, then a quarter of the damages should be paid. Conversely (though this has not come up in the cases), it might be open to a defendant to argue that, notwithstanding that causation has been made out on a balance of probabilities, there is still only a, say, 75-percent likelihood that the wrong caused the damages, and thus the amount of liability should be reduced by 25 percent.

The advantage to this approach, of course, is that it does not depend on whether all possible causes of the injury have been identified, let alone whether they were necessarily tortious and the defendants known. However, despite some early judicial willingness to explore this avenue, it has been — at least temporarily — foreclosed.

One example is *Seyfert v. Burnaby Hospital Society*,[88] where the plaintiff, who was being treated for a fall, was misdiagnosed and developed compli-

---

85 *Kitchen v. Royal Air Force Association*, [1958] 1 W.L.R. 563 (C.A.); *Prior v. McNab* (1976), 78 D.L.R. (3d) 319 (Ont. H.C.J.).
86 *Multi-Malls Inc. v. Tex-Mall Properties Ltd.* (1980), 28 O.R. (2d) 6, aff'd (1981), 37 O.R. (2d) 133 (C.A.).
87 For an overview of loss of chance doctrine and the various philosophical positions advanced in its favour, see generally D.A. Fischer, "Tort Recovery for Loss of a Chance" (2001) 36 Wake Forest L. Rev. 605.
88 (1986), 36 C.C.L.T. 224 (B.C.S.C.) [hereinafter *Seyfert*].

cations. It was unclear, however, that the medical negligence caused the complications because they may have developed in any event. Relying on *McGhee*, McEachern C.J. held that the negligence had materially contributed to the risk of complications and awarded 25 percent of the damages, representing the lost chance of avoiding the complications and the longer period of convalescence.

McEachern C.J.'s approach to alleviating the burden of proof of causation was explicitly rejected in England,[89] and similar efforts have received a mixed and inconsistent reception in the United States.[90] The retreat from the possibilities suggested by *Seyfert* began in *Hotson v. East Berkshire Area Health Authority*.[91] In this case a child had fallen from a tree and received negligent treatment from the defendant doctor. The trial judge had found that there was a 75-percent chance that the child's eventual losses would have occurred even with appropriate care, and awarded 25-percent-damages on that basis. The House of Lords, however, analysed the trial judge's findings as indicia that the plaintiff had failed to prove "but for" causation on a balance of probabilities, and denied the award.

In *Laferriere v. Lawson*[92] the Supreme Court of Canada also overruled an award for loss of a chance. Here, the defendant doctor failed, following a biopsy in 1971, to inform the plaintiff that she had cancer. In 1978 the plaintiff died of generalized cancer. There was no doubt that the defendant was negligent, but substantial doubt that any additional treatment would have increased the plaintiff's chance of survival. Notwithstanding this doubt, the Quebec Court of Appeal awarded the plaintiff substantial damages based on the theory that she had been deprived of the opportunity or chance to seek additional treatment and improve her health. The Supreme Court of Canada reversed this element of the decision. The Court reaffirmed the traditional principles of causation whereby the plaintiff must establish causation on the balance of probabilities, at least within the four corners of the *Civil Code*.[93] Gonthier J concluded: "I do not feel it is appro-

---

89 In England, see *Hotson v. East Berkshire Area Health Authority*, [1987] A.C. 750 (H.L.) [hereinafter *Hotson*].
90 See the discussion in C.P. Reuscher, "*McMullen v. Ohio State University Hospitals*: This Isn't Vegas, But Don't Tell the Courts — Playing with Percentages and the Loss-of-chance Doctrine" (2001) 34 Akron L. Rev. 767; D.R. Carney, "*Smith v. State of Louisiana, Department of Health and Hospitals*: Loss of Chance of Survival: The Valuation Debate" (1997) 58 La. L. Rev. 339.
91 *Hotson*, *supra* note 89.
92 (1991), 78 D.L.R. (4th) 609 (S.C.C.) [hereinafter *Laferriere*]
93 McLachlin J. has written extrajudicially that *Laferriere* sets out no rules for common law courts: McLachlin, *supra* note 11 at 27–28.

priate to focus on the degree of probability of success and to compensate accordingly ..."[94] He explained:

> [I]t is only in exceptional loss of chance cases that a judge is presented with a situation where the damage can only be understood in probabilistic or statistical terms, and where it is impossible to evaluate sensibly whether or how the chance would have been realized in that particular case. The purest example of such a lost chance is that of the lottery ticket which is not placed in the draw due to the negligence of the seller of the ticket. The judge has no factual context in which to evaluate the likely result other than the realm of pure statistical chance. Effectively, the pool of factual evidence regarding the various eventualities in the particular case is dry in such cases, and the plaintiff has nothing other than statistics to elaborate the claim in damages. ... I am not prepared to conclude that particular medical conditions should be treated for purposes of causation as the equivalent of diffuse elements of pure chance, analogous to the non-specific factors of fate or fortune which influence the outcome of a lottery.[95]

The different results in *Chaplin* on the one hand, and *Hotson* and *Laferriere* on the other, reinforce the idea that courts are engaged in a results-based linguistic game when choosing between analyses based on "loss of chance" (where claims are in theory compensable) and "probabilistic causation" (where they are in theory not). In *Hotson*, for instance, was it that there was a one-in-four chance that inappropriate treatment caused the injury? Or rather was it that the negligence had taken away a 25 percent chance of recovery?[96] Is there any principled basis for deeming one compensable and the other not? Waddams, for one, suggests that *Hotson* and *Laferriere* were arguably "loss of chance" cases and both ought be compensable.[97] It is sometimes suggested that the difference lies in the form of the action — that in contract cases (*Chaplin*), proof of damage is not an element of the cause of action and therefore probabilistic reasoning is acceptable solely as an instrument of measuring the loss, whereas in negligence cases, proof of damage is an essential element of the claim and probabilis-

---

94 *Laferriere, supra* note 92 at 610.
95 *Ibid.* at 603 and 605.
96 Fleming puts it this way, *supra* note 6 at 674–75: "In sum, all that *Hotson* interdicted was the attempt, in a case where the cause of action depended on physical injury, to circumvent proof of such an injury by proof of a lost chance to avoid it. The distinction may not appeal to everybody."
97 Waddams, *supra* note 38 at 90 (discussing *Hotson*) and 95 (discussing *Laferriere*).

tic reasoning cannot be used to establish liability.[98] This distinction, which achieves doctrinal reconciliation at the expense of substantial coherence (and suggests a resurrection of old and interesting debates about concurrent liability in contract and tort), was implicitly rejected by Waddams[99] and explicitly disparaged by Black. "However," noted Black, "abandoning it does raise the question of what distinction we should adopt in its stead."[100]

The most recent authoritative discussion of the issue (before *Fairchild*, discussed below) is in *Athey v. Leonati*,[101] where the Supreme Court of Canada joined the sceptics in rejecting a purely probabilistic approach to damages assessment — whether cloaked as "loss of chance" or otherwise. The issue in *Athey* was whether automobile accidents caused the plaintiff's back injury; the trial judge held that the accidents were a minor contributing factor and awarded 25-percent damages. The Supreme Court of Canada disapproved of this method, stating:

> [The trial judge] awarded only 25 percent of the global damages because she held that the accidents were a "causation factor" of 25 percent. Taken out of context, this could be read as meaning that there was a 25 percent chance that the injury was caused by the accidents, and a 75 percent chance that it was caused by the pre-existing condition. In that case, causation would simply not be proven.[102]

The better approach, according to the Supreme Court, was to consider the facts as indicating that the accidents were a 25-percent cause of the harm — that is, a material cause that rose above *de minimus*. The analysis, however, assists only in cases where the harm might be seen — in however strained a fashion — as cumulative rather than alternative.[103] It offers little

---

98 In *De la Giroday v. Brough*, the B.C. Court of Appeal clung to the artificial and ancient distinction of actions "in trespass" and those "on the case," holding that, where damages were a necessary part of the action (as in negligence), causation that did not rise to the level of probability (at least with respect to some damages) could not, as a matter of law, trigger any liability because no cause of action was made out. *De la Giroday v. Brough* (1997), 33 B.C.L.R. (3d) 171 (C.A.), leave to appeal ref'd [1977] S.C.C.A. No. 381.
99 Waddams, *supra* note 38.
100 Vaughan Black, "Not a Chance: Comments on Waddams, The Valuation of Chances" (1998) 30 Can. Bus. L.J. 96 at 98.
101 [1996] 3 S.C.R. 458 [hereinafter *Athey*].
102 *Ibid.* at para. 42.
103 As in the English case of *Lambton v. Mellish*, [1894] 3 Ch. 163, where two merry-go-round operators were found liable in nuisance for the cacophony produced when their organs operated simultaneously, though neither would have been individually liable but for the activity of the other. See also *Corey v. Havener* (1920), 182 Mass. 250 (1902), involving two motorists passing a horse and wagon at high speed on either side, fright-

help in mass exposure cases, for instance, because exact disease processes are frequently unknown, and the extent to which a disease should be seen as alternatively caused (as is perhaps arguable with mesothelioma) or cumulatively caused (the dominant view of smoking-related lung cancer) will often be impossible to assess. This is especially true with diseases in which causes may be synergistic, that is, where multiple factors compound, rather than just increase, the risk of disease.

It is difficult to state precisely where the line is currently drawn on the use of probabilistic damages in individual tort cases. They are clearly available when the causal uncertainty is in relation to the extent of the plaintiff's future injuries (for example, the chance of improvement or deterioration).[104] They are also available in respect of opportunities of which the plaintiff has been deprived and which remain hypothetical (as in *Chaplin v. Hicks* or the personal injury victim who lost the opportunity to pursue a particular career). In these cases the defendant's wrongful conduct has clearly caused the plaintiff a loss but there is doubt about the extent or value of the loss. On the other hand, when the question is whether an injury or illness, which has in fact occurred, was caused by the defendant's wrong, the plaintiff must establish causation on the traditional balance of probabilities. The principle is usually explained in the following fashion: courts adopt a different approach depending upon whether they are assessing hypothetical events that might have occurred but for the accident, or that might yet occur in the future, and events that have in fact occurred. In the latter type of case, causation must be established on traditional grounds. As Lord Diplock stated in *Mallett v. McMonagle*:[105]

> The role of the court in making an assessment of damages which depends on its view as to *what will be and what would have been* is to be contrasted with its ordinary function in civil actions of determining what was. In determining what did happen in the past a court decides on the balance of probabilities. Anything more probable than not it treats as certain. But in assessing damages which depends on its view as to what will happen

---

ening the horse and injuring the plaintiff. More particularly, see *Bonnington Castings v. Wardlaw*, [1956] A.C. 613 (H.L.), where the plaintiff contracted pneumoconiosis from silica dust that could have originated from either or both of two machines, one of which was operated negligently and the other not. In such circumstances, the employer was held liable because the negligence had "materially contributed" to the risk. The decision, though, depended on the premise that pneumoconiosis resulted from cumulative, rather than alternative, exposure to the silica.

104 *Lewis v. Todd*, [1980] 2 S.C.R. 694 at 253.
105 [1970] A.C. 166 (H.L.).

in the future or would have happened in the future if something had not happened in the past, the court must make an estimate as to what are the chances that a particular thing will or would have happened and reflect those chances, whether they are more or less than even, in the amount of damages which it awards.[106]

We have tried to make the point in this section that these distinctions are not entirely satisfactory, in terms either of logic or of justice. We agree with Professor Black's assertion that "redescription" should not be determinative of the claims of injured persons, or of the liability of defendants. Ironically, the adoption of probabilistic reasoning and measurement in these cases, as *Athey* shows, is potentially fairer not only to plaintiffs (who would otherwise have difficulty establishing their case) but also to defendants (who, while being found liable, would have damages discounted). While it may be hoped that the Supreme Court will revisit the questions of loss of chance and probabilistic causation generally, we will move to a discussion of the application of such principles in the context of mass torts, where we argue that, paradoxically, the issues can actually be considerably simplified. We reach that point through another decision of the House of Lords, a case again not strictly of "mass tort" but one that we believe will have important ramifications in that field: *Fairchild v. Glenhaven Funeral Services Ltd.*

E. RISK-BASED LIABILITY: THE *FAIRCHILD* DECISION

Recently, proponents of assessing causation probabilistically and imposing liability on a "creation of risk" basis have gained a somewhat surprising ally — a unanimous House of Lords in the decision of *Fairchild v. Glenhaven Funeral Services Ltd.*[107] In *Fairchild*, the Lords decided that workers injured by exposure to asbestos dust could recover from the companies who negligently exposed them to the substance — and thus to the risk of disease — even though it could not be known *which* of the negligent defendants had caused the illness, and in fact recognizing that, in all likelihood, they were imposing liability on parties whose negligence did not in fact contribute to the injury. Significantly, in imposing liability, the majority of the Lords resisted the temptation to describe their action in the customary, if obfuscative, terms of "reversal of onus" or the "drawing of inferences," preferring to acknowledge openly that what they were in fact doing was rewriting the

---

106 *Ibid.* at 176 [emphasis added].
107 [2002] U.K.H.L. 22 [hereinafter *Fairchild*].

laws of liability and imposing it without any necessity that causation be shown, at least in a certain category of cases.[108]

1) Is Proof of Causation Really Necessary?

It is commonly accepted that even a single inhaled asbestos fibre can lead to mesothelioma, a fatal type of cancer that may take decades to proceed to a stage where it can be diagnosed, let alone treated. *Fairchild* involved workers, each of whom had contracted mesothelioma through the negligence of one of the several employers who had wrongfully exposed them to asbestos over the course of their respective employment histories. Because mesothelioma is almost always caused by asbestos exposure, it was accepted that the victims must have contracted it through their work.[109]

Upon reaching a unanimous decision that the victims' employers would be held jointly and severally liable to compensate the victims, the House of Lords took the opportunity to review rules of causation from ancient Rome to modern European countries. In his extensive speech on the question, the senior Law Lord, Bingham of Cornhill, said in the lead judgment:

> The problem of attributing legal responsibility where a victim has suffered a legal wrong but cannot show which of several possible candidates (all in breach of duty) is the culprit who has caused him harm is one that has vexed jurists in many parts of the world for many years. ... It is indeed a universal problem calling for some consideration by the House, however superficially, of the response to it in other jurisdictions.[110]

His Lordship then reviewed the literature by authorities on European law, and from jurisdictions in which liability had been imposed on a market-share basis,[111] and concluded: "Whether by treating an increase in risk as equivalent to a material contribution, or by putting a burden on the defen-

---

108 The Lords' speeches are discussed below.
109 Even such assumptions, however, reveal the inherent difficulty in knowing anything on more than a probabilistic basis. The recent death of noted author Stephen Jay Gould, for instance, is attributed to mesothelioma even though he had no known contact with asbestos in any workplace. If Gould *had* worked in a shipyard (where many of the asbestos cases originated) at any point in his life, the House of Lords would apparently say, without any hesitation, not that his disease was *probably* caused by that exposure but rather that it *certainly* was, even though it wasn't. This paradox results from the refusal by the Lords, like other courts, to recognize the extent to which all evidence of causation is probabilistic, a topic to which we will return later in this chapter.
110 *Fairchild, supra* note 107 at para. 23.
111 *Ibid.* at para. 29, citing *Sindell, supra* note 57 and *B. v. Bayer Nederland B.V.* (Hoge Raad, 9 October 1992, NJ 1994, 535).

dant, or by enlarging the ordinary approach to acting in concert, or on more general grounds influenced by policy considerations, most jurisdictions would, it seems, afford a remedy to the plaintiff."[112]

2) Inferences of Law and Fact versus Risk-Based Liability

As discussed earlier, the leading cases prior to *Fairchild* had been *McGhee v. National Coal Board*,[113] which was essentially overruled in *Wilsher v. Essex Area Health Authority*.[114] It would be tempting to see *Fairchild* as nothing more than a cautious return to — and extension of — the *ratio* of *McGhee*. Although in *Fairchild*, as in *Wilsher*, there may have been other factors responsible for the disease apart from a *particular* defendant's negligence, the case was more like *McGhee* to the extent that the Lords found no possible non-tortious cause of the injury.

But to focus on this aspect of the decision is to lose sight of *Fairchild*'s principle innovation. In *Fairchild*, the Lords chose to embrace *McGhee*'s outcome-oriented approach but abandoned the device of inferred causation in fact.[115] As Lord Nicholls of Birkenhead suggested:

> In an area of the law already afflicted with linguistic ambiguity I myself would not describe this process of legal reasoning as a "legal inference" or an "inference of causation." This phraseology tends to obscure the fact that when applying the principle described above the court is not, by a process of inference, concluding that the ordinary "but for" standard of

---

112 *Fairchild, ibid.* at para. 32. See also *Fairchild*, at para. 168 "[I]t is not necessarily the hallmark of a civilised and sophisticated legal system that it treats cases where strict proof of causation is impossible in exactly the same way as cases where such proof is possible," Rodger L.J.

113 *McGhee, supra* note 74.

114 *Wilsher, supra* note 77.

115 Four of five Lords rejected the use of a factual inference and three rejected the substitution of a legal inference. Lord Hutton was the dissenting voice in favour of clinging to the "factual inference" analysis, and based his speech on his reading of *McGhee*, holding that that case involved an inference of fact. Lord Bingham rejected resort to a factual or legal inference, although he seemed to have acknowledged that in *McGhee* a legal inference was used (*Fairchild, supra* note 107 at paras. 21, 34, Bingham L.J.). In Lord Nicholls's view, the Lords were applying a less stringent test rather than a factual or legal inference (*Fairchild*, at para. 45, Nicholls L.J.). Lord Hoffmann acknowledged that the House in *McGhee* made a legal inference but preferred not to resort to the same legal fiction (*Fairchild*, at para. 65 Hoffmann L.J.). Lord Rodger disagreed, holding that the increase in risk was sufficient to prove a material contribution and thus appears to have used a legal inference, as the other three Lords agreed was done in *McGhee* (*supra* note 74 at para. 168, Rodger L.J.).

causation is satisfied. *Instead, the court is applying a different and less stringent test. It were best if this were recognised openly.*[116]

As Lord Bingham observed at paragraph 35, "[w]hether, in certain limited and specific circumstances, a legal inference is drawn or a different legal approach is taken to proof of causation, may not make much practical difference," a trend towards clarity and transparency in judicial decision making is welcome:

> ... Lord Wilberforce, in one of the passages of his opinion in *McGhee* quoted in paragraph 20 above, wisely deprecated resort to fictions and it seems to me preferable, in the interests of transparency, that the courts' response to the special problem presented by cases such as these should be stated explicitly. I prefer to recognise that the ordinary approach to proof of causation is varied than to resort to the drawing of legal inferences inconsistent with the proven facts.[117]

So the decision in *Fairchild* must be seen as more than the simple preference of the earlier decision of *McGhee* over the later, more restrictive, view of *Wilsher*. Each of these cases attempted to introduce elements of probabilistic causation (i.e., exposure to risk) into the traditional "but for" test of causation-in-fact. In *Fairchild*, the majority of the Lords consciously departed from the "but for" requirement altogether.

3) Where Would Risk-Based Liability Apply?

While two of the Lords were content to decide when to apply the new rule on a case-by-case basis,[118] the three others set out the circumstances required before the rule may be applied.[119] We can reduce the requirements for the imposition of liability in *Fairchild* into four general requirements: (1) the defendant has committed a breach of a duty to the plaintiff, leading to the exposure of the plaintiff to an injurious substance; (2) the plaintiff has been injured; (3) it is impossible to determine the exact cause of the injury; (4) the wrongdoing was capable of causing the injury that in fact occurred, and there is an increase in the risk of that injury. If these conditions are found, the causation requirement will be satisfied.[120]

---

116 *Fairchild, supra*, note 107 at para. 45 [emphasis added].
117 *Ibid.* at para. 35, *per* Bingham L.J.
118 *Ibid.* at para. 118, *per* Hutton L.J. See also *ibid.* at para. 43, *per* Nicholls L.J.
119 *Ibid.* at para. 2, *per* Bingham L.J.; *ibid.* at para. 61, *per* Hoffmann L.J.; *ibid.* at para. 170, *per* Rodger L.J. Not that Lord Rodger considered the conditions listed to be necessary but not always sufficient.
120 Lord Bingham also set out the additional condition that the employment be at different times and for different periods, as was the case in *Fairchild, supra* note 107 at

Significantly, all of the Law Lords found that liability arises as a result of *risk contribution*.[121] While such a finding is not groundbreaking in cases of *cumulative* causation (i.e., where each defendant contributed, not just a risk, but an actual causal agent into the chain), it is certainly important when *alternative* independent causes are proposed, as in *Fairchild*.

Fairchild does not offer explicit guidance for a far more common situation: where there are other, possible alternative risk factors that have nothing to do with either the defendant's activities or other defendants' tortious activities[122] — in other words, where there is simply a "background risk" of the type of harm suffered. The majority of the Lords explicitly avoided deciding this point,[123] although, in their heavy reliance on the California decision of *Rutherford v. Owens-Illinois Inc.*,[124] they did suggest a willingness to embrace liability even in such cases.[125]

Another unresolved question following *Fairchild* is whether there remains any distinction between diseases that seem to develop from cumulative exposure to a substance (such as asbestosis) and those that can be caused by a single exposure from alternative possible sources (such as mesothelioma). In the former case, it is easier to consider the exposure a substantial contributing cause of the harm, as opposed to simply creating

---

paras. 2, 34, *per* Bingham L.J., but it is not clear why the principle should be applied differently when an employee works for two negligent employers at the same time.

121 See *ibid.* at para. 34, *per* Bingham L.J.; *ibid.* at para. 42, *per* Nicholls L.J.; *ibid.* at paras. 73–74, *per* Hoffmann L.J.; *ibid.* at para. 108 *per* Hutton L.J.; *ibid* at para. 168 *per* Rodger L.J.

122 Interestingly, Lord Rodger in *Fairchild* left this door open, but no other Lord explicitly mentioned these possibilities and indeed Lord Bingham's speech appeared to require that the plaintiff should rule out non-tortious causes. See *ibid.* at para. 170, *per* Rodger L.J.; *ibid* at para. 2, *per* Bingham L.J.

123 *Ibid.* at paras. 2, 34, *per* Bingham L.J.; *ibid.* at para. 118, *per* Hutton L.J.; *ibid.* at para. 170, *per* Rodger L.J. Lord Nicholls did not mention the question.

124 67 Cal. Rptr. 2d 16 (Sup. Ct. Cal. 1997) [hereinafter *Rutherford*].

125 In *Rutherford*, a judgment with which the chief justice and all save one member of the Supreme Court of California concurred, Baxter J. observed (at 19):

> Proof of causation in such cases will always present inherent practical difficulties, given the long latency period of asbestos-related disease, and the occupational settings that commonly exposed the worker to multiple forms and brands of asbestos products with varying degrees of toxicity. In general, however, no insuperable barriers prevent an asbestos-related cancer plaintiff from demonstrating that exposure to the defendant's asbestos products was, in reasonable medical probability, a substantial factor in causing or contributing to his risk of developing cancer. We conclude that plaintiffs are required to prove no more than this. In particular, they need not prove with medical exactitude that fibers from a particular defendant's asbestos-containing products were those, or among those, that actually began the cellular process of malignancy.

a risk. Lord Bingham recognized, again relying on *Rutherford*, that the distinction is difficult: "Were the law otherwise, an employer exposing his employee to asbestos dust could obtain complete immunity against mesothelioma (but not asbestosis) claims by employing only those who had previously been exposed to excessive quantities of asbestos dust. Such a result would reflect no credit on the law."[126]

F. PROPOSED APPLICATION IN MASS TORT CASES

It is possible that, in adopting a view of causation that is rooted in distributive justice and functionalist analysis, the case can be made, at least in the case of mass torts, that the rules must be applied so as to perform best the dominant utilitarian functions of the negligence system — optimal compensation and deterrence.[127] Should this position be accepted, then it is logically possible to apply the reasoning in *Fairchild* beyond the narrow circumstances of its facts and to impose probabilistic liability in cases where the risk was elevated over background levels by an identifiable wrongdoer. If such an extension of *Fairchild* is made, some form of discounted or probabilistic assessment of damages must also occur, and, if more than one wrongdoer is found, probabilistic apportionment will be required to avoid overdeterrence.

The most significant aspect of the *Fairchild* decision is the disconnection, indeed the abandonment, of a probable showing of damages caused by the act or omission of the defendant in a negligence case. It is possible that the case marks the end of analysing whether actions are "'actionable *per se*" or whether the cause is one "on the case" requiring causally connected damages as a prerequisite for the liability. In analytically disconnecting the negligence from the harm, the Lords seem to be acknowledging that proof of the causal nexus is not required to show negligence as such, though, of course, it will still be necessary to show causation (by whatever standards) in order to gain compensation.

In her essay on causation in 1998, Justice McLachlin (as she then was) wrote:

> We can reasonably predict that the rules that govern proof of causation in tort will change. What we cannot predict is the pace of the change. Will the common law process of change by small incremental steps suffice? Or

---

126 *Fairchild, supra* note 107 at para. 33.
127 See R. Posner, *supra* note 3 at 33.

will advancing public views about responsibility push the courts and/or the legislatures toward a more rapid and fundamental reappraisal?[128]

Even advocates of judicial restraint regarding causation admit that, while "the vast majority of causal problems in tort law can be resolved [through the application of] a small number of rudimentary principles," cases considering "multiple sufficient causes" (i.e., *Fairchild* and most toxic torts) are "noticeably more complex" and "the 'but for' test often fails to provide a satisfactory answer."[129]

While problems of application remain to be fully resolved,[130] judicious resort to the *Fairchild* risk-based analysis holds great promise for such com-

---

128 Fleming, *supra* note 6 at 35, McLachlin J.
129 M. McInnes, "Causation in Tort Law: Back to Basics in the Supreme Court of Canada" (1997) 35 Alta. L. Rev. 1013 at 1021. Nevertheless, McInnes, without reference to any mass tort decisions (which will of course amplify any errors inherent in the "all or nothing" "but for" approach, concludes that in such cases "courts (generally) arrive at appropriate conclusions." How McInnes is capable of making this determination without an understanding of causation-in-fact in the particular cases, though, is not made clear. The standard for judging "appropriateness" is never defined by McInnes and certainly does not seem to be measured by the yardstick of "appropriate" deterrence or "appropriate" compensation. Indeed, the rules that McInnes argues can be employed to dispose of many indeterminate-causation cases, such as the "thin skull" and "crumbling skull" rules, and the "take your victim as you find him" principle, are simply put forward as self-justifying.
130 One difficult remaining question of justice and fairness arises owing to the retroactive nature of common law liability. While it is not central to our thesis, the fear that a broad category of liability might be imposed on defendants for conduct that was not *at the time actionable* is a real one, and so we deal briefly with it here.

In *Fairchild*, the employers' negligence had been committed since at least the 1960s; the exposure to the fatal fibers in one case might have occurred as early as 1953 or as late as the 1970s. At the time of the negligent exposure, the law of England did not provide for recovery absent a showing of "but for" causation. The House of Lords was therefore reaching back and imposing liability upon defendants who not only may have had nothing to do with the injuries suffered but who at the time of their breach of duty would have had no idea that they could be liable for compensation on such a basis.

However, this problem can be eased if we accept that the focus is shifting from causation but remaining fixed on wrongdoing and, in the aggregate sense, real injury. The employers in *Fairchild* breached their duty to their employees and can be taken to have known at the time that they were doing it; *they just thought they were getting away with it*. In the case of a mass tort, the causation excuse rings hollow: they might not have foreseen harm to the eventual victims, but in the aggregate the harm was perfectly foreseeable. In such circumstances, it seems that there cannot be a strong objection based on moral grounds to the imposition of a new liability for an old wrong, provided the wrong was recognized (or ought to have been recognized) as such at the time — in other words, in situations where the liability may be novel, but the wrong is not.

plex actions, in a way that might serve the functional requirements for improved efficiency of action and fuller compensation and deterrence, while satisfying the moralist demands that tort law not punish those wrongdoers who are "innocent" in fact of causing harm.

Recent tort scholarship on the topic of causation-in-fact has focused on the debate between legal economists, who propose that tort rules must be explained or justified on the basis of utility,[131] and tort moralists, who suggest that there are irreducible interests of justice that must be catered to, presumably even at the expense of utility. The latter group has centred its attention in the causation debate on Aristotle's idea of "corrective justice," that is, justice "which plays a rectifying part in transactions between man and man."[132]

Corrective justice, which, in its most straightforward formulation "requires A to compensate B for loss caused by A's conduct (in fault-based theory, by A's *faulty* conduct),"[133] does not permit the abandonment of the causal nexus. Inevitably, the causation requirement is expressed in moral, rather than utilitarian or functionalist, terms; the law's authority is contingent on its ability to mirror reality.[134] That authority, then, is presumably diminished to the extent that the reality cannot, with certainty, be comprehended.

We can assign some weight to the concern that liability should not be imposed upon persons who have not caused harm — or at least (considering the impossibility of knowing causation with certainty) that our tort system should prefer to avoid such an outcome where possible. But, whatever validity the moralist position may have in the context of traditional, individualistic claims, it seems to have far less bite when mass tort claims are viewed — or adjudicated — in the aggregate.

We have seen how, by imposing notions of certainty upon inherently probabilistic judgments in individual cases of uncertain causation, plaintiffs who cannot meet the 50 percent threshold of likely causation will receive nothing for their injury. If these same rules are applied in the mass tort setting, a defendant who has caused an incremental increase of disease in the population will escape liability entirely providing that the precise attribution of a particular victim's disease is impossible. On the other hand, as Rosen-

---

131 Whether measured in terms of wealth maximization or the promotion of "welfare" more generally. See Kaplow & Shavell, "Fairness vs. Welfare," *supra* note 24.
132 Aristotle, *Nicomachean Ethics*, Bk. V para. 2.
133 S.R. Perry, "Tort Law" in D. Patterson, ed., *A Companion to Philosophy of Law and Legal Theory* (Oxford: Blackwell, 1996) at 74.
134 J.L. Coleman, "The Practice of Corrective Justice" (1995) 37 Ariz. L. Rev. 15 at 30: "legal theorists who invoke the concept of corrective justice mean to treat it as a substantive moral ideal."

berg points out, in cases where 51 percent of a given disease in the population can be attributed to the defendant (or where a lesser risk might otherwise, using the "material increase of risk" rules in individualistic tort cases, trigger liability), it could be unfair to impose the "crushing liability" of 100 percent attribution.[135]

We also suggest that the barrier to the imposition of probabilistic liability in individual cases is the lingering moralist objection that causation-in-fact is a required element to avoid the assignment of liability upon persons who have caused no harm, and (relatedly) the flow of compensation to persons whom the defendant did not injure. This is, we might add, related to the more pragmatic concern that litigation floodgates will open as proof of causation is relaxed. However, few courts have yet recognized the fundamental, principled distinction between mass torts and individual torts where probabilistic causation is concerned.

Much of the wind is taken from both moral and functional objections to probabilistic causation when mass tort claims are viewed in the aggregate, rather than individualistically. While an Aristotelian connection between individual wrongdoer and wronged is still arguably absent when a class action is resolved on a probabilistic basis, we can be fairly assured of two things: that the *actual* victims of any given defendant are among those compensated; and that that defendant indeed is not "innocent" of causation in fact, at least with respect to that portion of the population. In this sense, it is possible to argue that the use of probabilistic proof in mass tort claims comes much closer to the moralist ideal of individual justice than does the traditional system of individualistic litigation that, as we have shown, employs probabilistic reasoning in the least efficient way — deciding whether something "probably" did or did not happen. Viewed in the aggregate, one can argue whether the causation of disease in a particular population is 12 percent or 25 percent, but one will rarely be forced into the "all or nothing" propositions imposed by traditional tort rules. Fleming appears to agree that "class actions provide a procedural framework particularly suitable for implementing the [probabilistic discounting] formula."[136]

If there is anything left of the moral necessity of actually identifying which defendant harmed which plaintiff, it appears to be substantially out-

---

135 David Rosenberg, "The Casual Connection in Mass Exposure Cases: A 'Public Law' Vision of the Tort System" (1984) 97 Harvard L. Rev. 849 at 859, citing S. Shavell, "An Analysis of Causation and the Scope of Liability in the Law of Torts" (1981) 9 J. Legal Stud. 463 at 465. Rosenberg advocates full aggregation of all mass torts into mandatory class actions.

136 Fleming, *supra* note 6 at 680.

weighed by the advantages of mass resolution of claims. Indeed, the only reason to identify *actual* victims, individually, in such a claim would be to calculate their separate entitlement to compensation. However, at this stage there is no necessity to distribute the award on the basis of the degree of the defendant's fault; systems of need-based compensation, calculated on an insurance basis and possibly coordinated with existing social insurance plans, could provide systems for distribution (in other words, probabilistic damages work particularly well in subrogated or direct claims by insurers or governments in respect to mass torts for which health benefits or income replacement has already been provided to a group of victims).

Moreover, the question of undercompensation of particular victims, or the overcompensation of others, may be reduced in the mass tort/class action setting (at least with respect to future costs) by the pooling of damages and payment to class members either in the form of formal health insurance policies or distribution on a "'need as arises'" basis. The distribution problem might also be alleviated by a mass tort "superfund," possibly with the probabilistic assessment of injuries assessed by a "science panel" rather than by judges, as Brennan proposes.[137]

Fairchild's "no non-tortious cause" requirement, even in an individual case, could find some support among economic analysts, but only if joint and several liability is the only option. Suppose, for instance, that two tortfeasors expose a person to risk of disease that manifests itself and could have no other cause. One tortfeasor exposed the victim for one year, and the second for nine. Under *Fairchild*, the 10 percent contributor is jointly and severally liable for the entire amount of damages. This makes sense if, overall, the risk contribution among the contributors is continually varied. If in one case it is 90–10, and in the next 10–90, then the aggregate of liability of the two should roughly balance out, providing, of course, that the judgments are equally collectible (and roughly equally corrected) from each defendant.

If, on the other hand, the nine years' exposure was non-tortious, then it does not seem helpful to hold the 10 percent contributor liable for the 100 percent of the harm. This is because, viewed in the aggregate (assuming a 10–90 percent probability in each case), such a wrongdoer would have an overall exposure to liability ten times that which it should have.[138]

---

137 Brennan, *supra* note 1 at 532–33.
138 Another example should make this point clearer. Consider three *Fairchild* defendants, A, B, and C, who employed workers in the same industry and negligently exposed all of them to asbestos dust. Let us say that 100 workers who had worked for all three employers developed mesothelioma. Employer B should have foreseen that a certain

This is why market-share liability (or some other method based on *risk apportionment*) will provide roughly appropriate deterrence as well as compensation when claims are viewed in the aggregate.[139]

Practically speaking, though, such an argument loses much of its authority. In the real world, recovery for such torts will depend as much on the solvency of the defendants and their insurance choices; under such circumstances, joint and several liability will provide disincentives to insure adequately and will encourage asset-hiding and judgment proofing of companies involved in potentially dangerous activities.

In the case of "ordinary" accidents, what Oliver Wendell Holmes, Jr famously called "ungeneralized wrongs,"[140] the Aristotelian idea of corrective justice may be, if not economically optimal, at least socially appropriate. If a driver becomes distracted and momentarily drifts to the edge of an empty highway without any effect, no one would have the right to sue in tort, even if the driver had exposed someone, perhaps a nearby pedestrian, to an increased risk of harm. If, on the other hand, the pedestrian is struck, a suit will be launched and compensation paid. Punishment for the negligence "in the air," the simple creation of risk without a causal link to harm, has been left to the criminal law where available.

But, in such a case, the driver is not deliberately seeing how close to the pedestrian he can go. He derives no personal advantage from recklessness: there is ordinarily no incentive for a driver to play such a dangerous and bizarre game; indeed, quite the opposite is true, *inter alia* because the driv-

---

percentage of its own workers (perhaps 33) would have become sick owing to its negligence, although it also could have expected that they wouldn't be able to prove causation. While it might be optimal to upset A's "reasonable expectations" to the extent of making A liable for the harm it caused, it is far less advantageous to impose liability for the harm caused to all 100. Probabilistically, employer A is entirely innocent-in-fact of harming the 67 "extra" workers for whose illnesses it now must pay if *Fairchild* is applied in all 100 individual cases.

139 Kaplow & Shavell, *supra* note 24 (noting that investment in determining cause in such cases makes both plaintiffs and defendants worse off).

140 Holmes J., in perhaps the first articulation of the economic analysis of accident law, said:

Our law of torts comes from the old days of isolated, ungeneralized wrongs, assaults, slanders, and the like, where the damages might be taken to lie where they fell by legal judgment. But the torts with which our courts are kept busy today are mainly the incidents of certain well known businesses. They are injuries to person or property by railroads, factories, and the like. The liability for them is estimated, and sooner or later goes into the price paid by the public.

O.W. Holmes Jr, "The Path of the Law" (1897) 10 Harv. L. Rev. 457 at 467.

er him- or herself may well be injured in an accident.[141] In the contemporary industrial marketplace, however, incentives to create risk do exist on systemic levels. The profit motive and competitive pressures suggest that firms will tend to invest in precautions against harming their customers or strangers only if they are either required to do so by vigorously enforced regulatory sanctions or by being forced to internalize the full costs of the harm they cause. This latter effect can be theoretically achieved through tort liability. The lesson here is that optimal tort deterrence, the holy grail of the economic analysts of tort law, is most fully realizable not in the context of haphazard one-on-one accidents but when probabilistic assessments of causation are applied to the systemic decisions of businesses regarding investment in precautions.

Causation in law, of course, is impossible to disentangle from notions of legal rights. Every accident has numerous causes; if a negligent driver crosses the centreline and strikes another head-on, it can be said that the accident would not have occurred "but for" the presence of the innocent driver; the distinction between relevant causation and irrelevant causation can be defined only by the legal "rights" of the parties: one may legitimately be at the location of the accident, the other not. Causation in fact can demonstrate only a confidence that the defendant's actions contributed to the accident. Causation in law is concerned with the connection between "rightless" — or wrongful — activity and the harm.

It seems correct to say that in cases of mass exposure torts, where we can be scientifically certain that the defendant's wrongdoing has hurt members of the population but, because of individual attribution problems, it is not possible to determine whom, that liability can attach to the wrongdoing. Rosenberg put it this way in 1984:

> The preponderance rule may be adequate for the set of sporadic accident cases in which causal indeterminacy arises randomly and always signifies a substantial chance that the defendant in fact harmed no one. But the rule is neither rational nor a just means of resolving the systematic causal indeterminacy presented by mass exposure cases involving defendants whose tortious conduct has caused or will cause a statistically ascertainable increase in the incidence of a particular disease.[142]

Fairchild moves us part of the way down the road to fully probabilistic assessment of damages, but not all the way. Lord Hoffman had distin-

---

141 See F.A. Sloan, B.A. Reilly, & C.M. Schenzler, "Tort Liability Versus Other Approaches for Deterring Careless Driving" (1994) 14 Int'l Rev. L. & Econ. 53.
142 Rosenberg, *supra* note 135 at 858.

guished *Sindell*, where probabilistic causation was used, on the basis that the presence of additional manufacturers did not increase the risk (of exposure). In *Fairchild*, each of the defendants had exposed to risk the individual plaintiff before the court, and broken an independent duty to him. In other words, Weinrib's "irreducible" two-party relationship is preserved in the form of a duty, even if it is abandoned from the point of view of cause-in-fact.

In a mass tort claim with multiple defendants, it might be argued that it is impossible to link the creation of risk by each defendant to each exposed plaintiff. In such cases, the question that arises is whether the increase in aggregate risk is sufficient, so that all wrongdoers who have exposed members of the plaintiff population to the risk of injury can be held liable, without the necessity of proving the "nexus" between a particular plaintiff and a particular defendant. No doubt, in such circumstances, the courts will adopt a minimum threshold of risk, over and above background levels (somewhat analogous to the "more than *de minimus*" test of *Athey v. Leonati*) to trigger liability in a defendant.

The main significance of *Fairchild* for such cases lies in its forthright disconnection of wrongdoer and harm. If one can accept that the interests of justice require risk-based liability for the defendants in *Fairchild*, it is difficult to imagine that they do not similarly favour such liability in aggregated mass tort claims.[143] Indeed, as we have pointed out here, the risk of "moral unfairness" to defendants is reduced in the aggregate, because unlike the defendants in *Fairchild*, each of whom has not been found to have caused harm to *anyone*, in an aggregate claim one can be satisfied with statistical and epidemiological evidence that each defendant is, aside from simply being a wrongdoer, also a cause of actual harm in the population.[144]

Much will no doubt be made of the requirement in *Fairchild* that the only possible cause of the harm — mesothelioma in the victim — was the negligence of one of the defendants. But, while individual cases might fail because of the possibility of alternative, non-tortious possible causes, this too need not be a barrier in mass tort claims, for all of the reasons articulated here. If there had been a significant "background risk" of mesothelioma in *Fairchild*, it would have been possible, even likely, that the

---

[143] In fact, the consequences for mass tort actions from the elimination of causation requirements was described several years ago in M.A. Berger, "Eliminating General Causation: Notes Toward a New Theory of Justice and Toxic Torts" (1997) 97 Colum. L. Rev. 2117.

[144] Thus "notions of moral responsibility underlying tort law" are preserved: Berger, *ibid.* at 2117.

defendant was causally "innocent." In the aggregate setting, evidence can show that he or she is not. However, in the aggregate setting, the global damage can be discounted to that amount done by each defendant; in the individual setting (at least with joint and several liability), it cannot.

At this stage, then, difficulties of apportionment of liability remain. In such circumstances, and assuming that the risk contribution of the defendants cannot be otherwise calculated, the *Sindell* solution of market-share apportionment seems perfectly appropriate. Indeed, this door was explicitly left open by Lord Hoffmann, who described the "imaginative rule" created by the California Supreme Court in *Sindell*.[145] Similarly, more creative distribution paradigms will have to evolve as well.[146]

G. THE RECEPTION OF *FAIRCHILD* IN CANADA

Fairchild has been considered in only a few Canadian cases at the time of this writing. The two illustrate what might be expected in the circumstances: on the one hand, an acceptance that the *Fairchild* solution to liability might be, at least in some cases, fair; but, on the other, a general reluctance to embrace departures from traditional rules.

In *P.R.O. Holdings Ltd. v. Atlantic Speedy Propane Ltd.*,[147] the defendant's negligence had caused a fire in the plaintiff's warehouse. Subsequently, and partially as a result of market forces, the plaintiff company collapsed. At trial, Creaghan J. found that it was not necessary to relax the "but for" causation test, since it was perfectly workable in the case before him; while the defendant was liable for the damage to the warehouse, it was not liable

---

145 *Fairchild, supra* note 107 at para. 74 *per* Hoffmann L.J.
146 "Accurate" distribution of awards may in fact be impossible, because in a case with substantial background risk, the amount of the defendant's liability will compensate only that portion of the population whom it has actually harmed. The problem is one will not know which of the victims the defendant should pay. However, given the widespread availability of first-person health insurance (indeed, in Canada, the universal availability), it seems less unjust to distribute the award on the basis of probabilistic discounting. That is, if 20,000 of the 100,000 class members, each victims of disease X, became ill on account of the defendant, each of the 100,000 might receive 20 percent of full compensation to supplement the health coverage subsidized by their fellow citizens. Other options that have been explored elsewhere are mass tort "superfunds" that work alone or in conjunction with other government or private insurance. See Brennan, *supra* note 1; J.B. Weinstein, *Individual Justice in Mass Tort Litigation: The Effect of Class Actions, Consolidations, and other Multiparty Devices* (Evanston, Illinois: Northwestern University Press, 1995), c. 2.
147 [2003] N.B.J. No. 148 (Q.B.) [hereinafter *P.R.O. Holdings*].

for damage to the business itself. Curiously, though, Creaghan J. declined to apply the "material contribution" test, apparently holding that it applied only where the "but for" test was problematic. While discussing *Fairchild*, Creaghan J. did so only as it pertains to judicial restraint:

> [¶106] I take the law to be properly stated by Lord Nicholls of Birkenhead in *Fairchild v. Glenhaven Funeral Services Ltd.*, [2002] All E.R. 305 at paragraph 43:
>
>> "I need hardly add that considerable restraint is called for in any relaxation of the threshold 'but for' test of causal connection. The principle applied on these appeals is emphatically not intended to lead to such a relaxation when a plaintiff has difficulty, perhaps understandable difficulty, in discharging the burden of proof resting on him. Unless closely confined in its application this principle could become a source of injustice to defendants. There must be good reason for departing from the normal threshold "but for" test. The reason must be sufficiently weighty to justify depriving the defendant of the protection this test normally and rightly affords him, and it must be plain and obvious that this is so. Policy questions will loom large when a court has to decide whether the difficulties of proof confronting the plaintiff justify taking this exceptional course. It is impossible to be more specific."

Yet the case before Creaghan J. seemed perfect for the application of *Athey* "material contribution" rules, since they involved multiple contributing factors, most non-tortious. It appears to us that the decision in *P.R.O. Holdings* was, at least implicitly, premised not on causation but rather on remoteness and foreseeability — that is, there was a policy interest in restricting liability for business collapses that were not a foreseeable consequence of the negligent behaviour.

A briefer but more positive endorsement of the *Fairchild* principles arose in *British Columbia v. Imperial Tobacco Ltd.*[148] There, Holmes J. referred to arguments comparing the probabilistic causation rules in *Fairchild* with the onus-shifting provisions of the statutory recovery scheme advanced by the British Columbia government in its case against the tobacco industry. The court said at paragraph 166: "*Fairchild* illustrates the advance in common law remedies relating to problematic causation issues allowing issues

---

148   2003 BCSC 877, rev'd [2004] B.C.J. No. 1007 (C.A.), leave to appeal to S.C.C. granted {2004} S.C.C.A. No. 302.

to be resolved on a risk assessment basis as an alternative to the use of presumptions as in the present *Act*. Neither basis can be said to be unfair."

The most significant endorsement of Fairchild to date has been the case of *B.M. v. British Columbia (Attorney General)*.[149] Here the plaintiffs argued that the Royal Canadian Mounted Police ("RCMP") were liable in a case where their failure to investigate a complaint of domestic violence was followed seven weeks later by a more severe domestic violence situation, involving the fatal shooting of one person, the grievous wounding of another, and the suicide of the subject of the complaint. Although the trial judge found that the police had failed in their duty of care, liability was not assigned to the RCMP because the judge could not find a causal connection between the failure to exercise a duty of care and the later incident.[150] However, on appeal, Donald J.A. (dissenting) adopted the less stringent test for causation established in *Fairchild*, and did so explicitly in the name of fairness and justice:

> Where a breach of duty occurs and a loss is suffered by the person to whom the duty is owed in circumstances *where direct proof of causation is impossible, considerations of fairness and justice may require relaxation of the conventional requirements for causation*: Haag v. Marshall (1989), 39 B.C.L.R. (2d) 205 (C.A.); Snell v. Farrell, [1990] 2 S.C.R. 311; and Fairchild v. Glenhaven Funeral Services Ltd. and others, [2002] UKHL 22, 3 All E.R. 305. [Emphasis added.][151]

By way of contrast, other cases have restricted the application of *Fairchild*. Even where there is causal uncertainty, where there is adequate evidence for a judge to make a finding on the evidence (for or against causation), judges will make their findings without needing to resort to the policy-based principle in *Fairchild*. In *Cottrelle v. Gerrard*,[152] the Ontario Court of Appeal considered *Fairchild* in a medical negligence case. The plaintiff, a diabetic patient who, after losing a leg to gangrene, argued that her doctor was negligent in treating the sore that led to the amputation. Overturning the trial court, Sharpe J.A. distinguished this case from the *Fairchild* line, since in this case, "the evidence demonstrated that it is more likely than not that even if the appellant had lived up to the standard of care, the respondent would have lost her leg."[153]

---

149 2004 BCCA 402 [hereinafter *Mooney*].
150 2001 BCSC 419.
151 *Mooney, supra* note 149 at para. 10.
152 178 O.A.C. 142 (C. A.).
153 *Ibid.* at para. 31.

In *Condominium Corp. No. 7921945 v. Cochrane*[154] the issue was the causation of a condominium fire — was it started by the improperly extinguished cigarette of the defendant, or of that of another known party who smoked in the same external vicinity after the defendant? Although he referred to *Fairchild*, the trial judge chose to follow recent Supreme Court of Canada holdings, rather than relaxing the "but-for" test as suggested by *Fairchild*, and on the basis of evidence, he was able to conclude on the balance of probabilities that the fire was more likely caused by the second, not the first smoker.[155]

Finally, as we have mentioned, there will be debate about the applicability of Fairchild in situations where there is more than one possible cause of harm. In *P.D. v. Allen*,[156] the issue was whether childhood sexual abuse caused the plaintiff's later alcoholism. The Ontario Superior Court of Justice refers briefly to *Fairchild* but dismisses it as inapplicable, since the facts in the *Allen* suggest that there might be multiple causes to the injury suffered, whereas in *Fairchild*, there is just one possible cause of the cancer caused by asbestos. The court held that where other possible causes cannot be "effectively discounted" *Fairchild* has no application. The court reaffirmed that the plaintiff had the onus of proof of actual causation and had failed to establish the necessary link.

These cases affirm that *Fairchild* will find its way into Canadian law, but only gradually and accompanied by much judicial caution. The hesitancy to apply *Fairchild* in the circumstances illustrated by the above cases — where there is evidence tending to disprove causation, or where there are other possible causes — is understandable. Simply ignoring the need to prove causation in these circumstances might do an injustice to the plaintiff. But, as we have argued, it would be unfortunate if these restrictions became absolute, for that would simply result in the converse injustice — that deserving claims would be undone by causal uncertainty. And certainly where multiple claims can be aggregated, and the overall damage awarded discounted to deal with uncertainty, the fact there may be multiple possible causes should not be a bar to the use of the *Fairchild* principle.

---

154 [2004] A.J. No. 16 (Prov. Ct.).
155 *Ibid.* at para. 18.
156 [2004] O.J. No. 3042 (S.C.).

5. Problems of Proof

A. THE USE OF STATISTICAL EVIDENCE IN MASS TORT

As will be clear from the discussion in Chapter Four, we suggest that legally and morally, there is a strong case for the use of probabilistic analysis in mass tort claims. Legally, because statistics can indicate that the defendant's activity was a significant contributing factor (i.e., beyond *de minimus*) to the harm in the aggregate population, even if not in any individual case. Morally, because indications of causation within a population, even without proof of cause in any case, remove the possibility that a truly "innocent" defendant is being held responsible despite having caused no harm at all.

Yet there is a very real concern, captured by Professor Brennan, that courts may be unable to divorce themselves wholly from particularistic (Brennan calls it corpuscularian) thought, particularly in individual cases: "[I]t is not enough simply to say that courts should adopt probabilistic reasoning. They must be instructed. But given the importance of the moral concept of individual responsibility in tort law, we can expect courts to accommodate only so much probabilistic reasoning."[1]

Inescapably, probabilistic proof in mass tort claims means the admission of and reliance upon statistical evidence at every step of the legal

---

[1] T.A. Brennan, "Causal Chains and Statistical Links: The Role of Scientific Uncertainty in Hazardous-Substance Litigation" (1987–88) 73 Cornell L. Rev. 469 at 491.

analysis, from causation to damages.[2] Various judicial justifications for this approach have been made,[3] though the most frequently stated one seems simply to be based on efficiency: justice is a scarce resource, and economic rules favour the speedy and effective adjudication of as many simultaneous claims as our other priorities (chiefly concerns over individual victim compensation and litigative autonomy[4]) will permit. There is also a strong argument that statistical evidence of almost every factor in a single, aggregate trial will be more accurate "proof" than any number of individual claims, pursued on a balance of probabilities, and in fact the awards even in individual trials could similarly benefit.[5] Indeed, this seems self-evident on every issue with the exception of the eventual distribution of the award, which is of necessity an individualistic exercise.[6]

In Canadian discrimination law, as in the United States,[7] statistical evidence is increasingly employed both with respect to probabilistic characteristics of employees for the purposes of designing reasonable standards[8]

---

2   See generally L. Walker & J. Monahan, "Sampling Damages" (1998) 83 Iowa L. Rev. 545 at 546: "A complete solution of the number problem in mass torts can only be achieved by ... randomly sampling damages without apology."
3   It has been held, for instance, that statistical proof of damages is particularly appropriate "where the conduct of wrongdoers has rendered it difficult to ascertain the damages suffered with the precision otherwise possible.": *Blue Cross and Blue Shield of New Jersey, Inc. v. Phillip Morris, Inc.*, 133 F. Supp. 2d 162 (E.D.N.Y. 2001) at 169 [hereinafter *Blue Cross*], citing *New York Pattern Jury Instructions*, 2:277 Damages: General — Commentary (3d 2000).
4   Though there is reason to believe that the individual interest may actually be enhanced in aggregate claims; see, for instance, D. Hensler, "Resolving Mass Toxic Torts: Myths and Realities" (1989) U. Ill. L. Rev. 89 at 104: "The use of formal aggregative procedures may provide more litigant control over the litigation process, more opportunity for litigant participation in the process, and a better match between victims" losses and compensation for those losses"; to similar effect see Kaplow & Shavell, "Fairness vs. Welfare" (2001) 114 Harv. L. Rev. 961 at 1207.
5   See, for instance, J. Koeler & D. Shaviro, "Veridical Verdicts: Increasing Verdict Accuracy Through the Use of Overtly Probabilistic Evidence and Methods" (1990) 75 Cornell L. Rev. 247.
6   See the discussion below at notes 21 through 26 and accompanying text.
7   See *International Brotherhood of Teamsters v. United States*, 431 U.S. 324 (1977) at 329: "[O]ur cases make it unmistakably clear that 'statistical analyses have served and will continue to serve an important role in cases in which the existence of discrimination is a disputed issue."
8   *Ontario Human Rights Commission v. Etobicoke*, [1982] 1 S.C.R. 202 at 212: "It seems to me, however, that in cases such as this, statistical and medical evidence based upon observation and research on the question of aging, if not in all cases absolutely necessary, will certainly be more persuasive than the testimony of persons, albeit with great experience in fire-fighting, to the effect that fire-fighting is "a young man's game."

and to determine the characteristics of the available workforce to show disparity in hiring or promotion.[9] To make an analogy from anti-discrimination law to tort, statistics are used to establish elements of causation, not simply of damages.

Recent cases, moreover, have suggested ways in which statistical methods can be used directly to prove causation in an aggregate population. In 1986 a proceeding was commenced against Ferdinand E. Marcos on behalf of a class of 9,541 Philippine citizens (or their heirs) who had been tortured, summarily executed, or who disappeared during Marcos's rule between September 1972 and February 1986. Marcos's Estate was substituted as defendant upon his death in 1989. The court entered final judgment on 3 February 1995 in favour of the class in the amount of US$1,964,000,000. In *Hilao v. Estate of Marcos*,[10] the master had used a representative sample to determine what percentage of the total claims was invalid. The majority of the Federal Court of Appeal upheld the method at 786 to 787:

> While the district court's methodology in determining valid claims is unorthodox, it can be justified by the extraordinarily unusual nature of this case. ... Hilao's interest in the use of the statistical method ... is enormous, since adversarial resolution of each class member's claim would pose insurmountable practical hurdles. The "ancillary" interest of the judiciary in the procedure is obviously also substantial, since 9,541 individual adversarial determinations of claim validity would clog the docket of the district court for years. Under the balancing test set forth in Mathews and Doehr, the procedure used by the district court did not violate due process.

The most active American judicial advocate of probabilistic proof in mass tort claims is Senior Judge Jack Weinstein of the Federal Court, Eastern District of New York, who in a series of cases[11] and voluminous extraju-

---

9 *Blake v. Minister of Correctional Services* (1984), 5 C.H.R.R. D/2417 (Ont. Bd. of Inquiry) (statistics showed a *prima facie* case of discrimination but defendant satisfied burden of demonstrating that particular complainant was not discriminated against); *Canada (Canadian Human Rights Commission) v. v. Canada (Department of National Health and Welfare)* (1998), 38 C.C.E.L. (2d) 121 (F.C.T.D.), aff'd (1999), 41 C.C.E.L. (2d) 3 (F.C.A.) (statistics could provide evidence of systemic discrimination, or, in individual cases, circumstantial evidence of individual discrimination). See generally Vizkelety, *Proving Discrimination in Canada* (Toronto: Carswell, 1987) at 187.
10 103 F.3d 767 (9th Cir. 1996).
11 *Re DES Cases*, 789 F. Supp. 548 (E.D.N.Y. 1992); *Re Joint Eastern and Southern District Asbestos Litig.*, 726 F. Supp. 426 (E.D.N.Y. 1989); *Re "Agent Orange" Product Liability Litig.*, 689 F. Supp. 1250 (E.D.N.Y. 1988); *Blue Cross*, supra note 3.

dicial writings[12] has championed its use in aggregate actions. The use of statistics nevertheless remains controversial in the United States courts, where the litigative autonomy of individuals is frequently described as a near-fundamental human right and courts have difficulty accepting that some issues, like causation-reliance, can be proven statistically.[13] Nevertheless, statistical evidence has been introduced on virtually every element of mass tort claims in the United States[14] and is potentially far more helpful on very difficult questions, such as causation-reliance, than individual plaintiff evidence would be.[15] In a recent tobacco case, Judge Weinstein noted:

> A distinction must be drawn between substantive elements of a claim and procedural methods of proof. ... In an extreme case, for example, imagine that statistics demonstrate 99 out of 100 cases of specific causation in a

---

12 Most notably J.B. Weinstein, *Individual Justice in Mass Tort Litigation: The Effect of Class Actions, Consolidations, and other Multiparty Devices* (Evanston, Illinois: Northwestern University Press, 1995).

13 In *Small v. Lorillard Tobacco Co.*, 252 A.D.2d 1 (N.Y. App. Div. 1998) [herinafter *Small*], the First Department of New York's Appeals Division refused to certify a class action of over a million smokers because proof of reliance upon the misleading statements would need to be shown individually. However, the *Small* court did not consider whether reliance could accurately or fairly be shown statistically, and Weinstein J. (in a "derivative" action by health insurers) subsequently opined that it could be: *Blue Cross*, supra note 3 at 173–74. However, in the *Blue Cross* case, there was no distribution problem, since the statistical proof need only show how many of the insurer's customers were harmed; see also *Certified Question Unived States Dist. Court Order v. Philip Morris Inc.*, 621 N.W.2d 2 (Sup. Ct. Minn. 2001).

14 *Re Joint Eastern & Southern District Asbestos Litigation v. United States Mineral Products Company*, 52 F.3d 1124 (2d Cir. 1995); *Re Estate of Ferdinand Marcos Human Rights Litigation (sub nom. Hilao v. Estate of Marcos)*, 910 F. Supp. 1460 (D. Haw. 1995), aff'd 103 F.3d 767 (9th Cir. 1996); *Stewart v. General Motors Corp.*, 542 F.2d 445 (7th Cir. 1976), cert. denied, 433 U.S. 919 (1977); *Zippo Manufacturing Co. v. Rogers Imports*, 216 F. Supp. 670 (D.C.N.Y. 1963); see also decisions cited at note 11.

15 It would be a rare plaintiff who admitted on the stand that he or she did not rely on the defendant's deceit or misrepresentation. Similarly, other types of causation are typically skewed by human witnesses: imagine a plaintiff testifying about whether she would have heeded her physician's warning regarding the danger of breast implants. It is difficult to imagine individual testimony being accurate on this point (after all, how does even the victim know for sure what she would have done?), as indeed the Supreme Court of Canada acknowledged in the case of *Hollis v. Dow Corning Corp.*, [1995] 4 S.C.R. 634. On the other hand, statistical and survey evidence might offer fairly precise estimates of how many plaintiffs' class members actually relied on, or would have been dissuaded by, accurate warnings. While of little use in an individual case, again such information is crucial to the accurate resolution of mass claims of deception or failure to warn, where aggregate assessment of both liability and warnings could be made.

particular group. In addition, imagine statistics also demonstrate 99 out of 100 cases of reliance in the same groups. Even if these sets do not include the exact same 99 people, there is no reason one cannot accept as more likely than not reliance and causation in approximately 98 percent of the population (99% x 99% [approximately equal to] 98%). *A fortiori*, the case which depends on total damages to a plaintiff through aggregation of client-by-client claims — that is to say damages to a proportion of an entire subscriber population — can safely support the proposition that 98 persons were caused to be injured by, and relied upon, a fraud; it is this situation [plaintiff] brings to the court. Obviously, plaintiff's models are in the less than 98% category, but the problems posed are ones of degree and burdens of proof. They do not alter the substantive elements of New York State law or the procedural elements of federal law.[16]

Whatever turns out to be the reception afforded Judge Weinstein's views among members of the judiciary, increased reliance on statistical evidence in mass tort claims is gaining significant, and perhaps now overwhelming, support among American academics.[17]

There is some indication that the judiciary understands the inherently probabilistic nature of cause-in-fact analyses. In *Snell v. Farrell*,[18] the Supreme Court of Canada distinguished between scientific proof and proof on the balance of probabilities, noting that expert witnesses need not be satisfied of causation *scientifically* but only "more probably," "i.e. 51%."[19] This point, though, needs to be made about *all* evidence. As Saks and Kidd put it: "Much of the testimony that is commonly thought of as particularistic only seems so. It is far more probabilistic than we normally allow jurors (or judges) to realize."[20] Rosenberg would go further, arguing that there is no proof *except* probabilistic proof: "The concept of 'particularistic' evidence suggests that there exists a form of proof that can provide direct and actual knowledge of [the underlying facts]. 'Particularistic' evidence, how-

---

16 *Blue Cross*, supra note 3 at 172–73.
17 See, for instance, Kaplow & Shavell, *supra* note 4 at 1203 n. 580; M.J. Saks & P.D. Blank, "Justice Improved: The Unrecognized Benefits of Sampling and Aggregation in the Trial of Mass Torts" (1992) 44 Stan. L. Rev. 315; R.G. Bone, "Statistical Adjudication: Rights, Justice and Utility in a World of Process Scarcity" (1993) 46 Vand. L. Rev. 561; S. Gold, "Causation in Toxic Torts: Burdens of Proof, Standards of Persuasion, and Statistical Evidence" (1986) 96 Yale L. J. 376.
18 [1990] 2 S.C.R. 311.
19 *Ibid*. at para. 34, adopting Louisell, *Medical Malpractice*, vol. 3 at 25–57.
20 M.J. Saks & R.F. Kidd, "Human Information Processing and Adjudication: Trial by Heuristics" (1989–1990) 15 Law & Soc'y Rev. 123 at 151.

ever, is no less probabilistic than is the statistical evidence that courts purport to shun."[21]

The use of statistical sampling to prove all elements of causation in the Canadian mass tort context has not been explored. Yet there is reason to believe that Canadian courts will be receptive to the idea generally,[22] and Canadian class proceedings legislation, which permits findings of aggregate liability without individual proof, seems tailor-made for such an approach. Indeed, the provision within Canadian class action legislation for the aggregate assessment of damages deserves some further mention. The Ontario and B.C. Acts of 1992 and 1996 provide that, once liability has been established, the amount of an aggregate award may be calculated on the basis of statistical evidence[23] if, *inter alia*, "the aggregate or a part of the defendant's liability to some or all class members can reasonably be determined without proof by individual class members."[24] In fact, the Ontario Law Reform Commission report in 1982 had quite sensibly recommended that aggregate assessment should be the rule rather than the exception: "Individual proceedings relating to the assessment of monetary relief should be required only where an aggregate assessment is not feasible or where the amount of monetary relief to which class members are entitled cannot be established by consumer evidence."[25]

---

21 D. Rosenberg, "Mandatory-Litigation Class Action: the Only Option for Mass Tort Cases" (2001) 115 Harvard L. Rev. 831 at 870.

22 Recently, in the trade-mark case of *London Life Insurance Co. v. Manufacturers Life Insurance Co.* (1999), 87 C.P.R. (3d) 229 (F.C.T.D.), the plaintiff insurance company argued that a competitor's trade-mark ("New Freedom to Plan") was not registerable because it would be confused with London's own trade-mark, "Freedom 55." To help prove this proposition, London Life commissioned a telephone survey of approximately three hundred people to demonstrate that there was more widespread belief that the two slogans originated at the same company (29 percent) than when a "placebo" slogan was used that did not contain the word "freedom" (19 percent). The court admitted the evidence, yet London Life was ultimately unsuccessful, in part because the court was not convinced that the methodology employed by London Life's survey accurately represented the level of confusion in the marketplace caused by the competing slogans.

23 *Class Proceedings Act*, R.S.B.C. 1996, c. 50, s. 30; *Class Proceedings Act 1992*, S.O. 1992, c. 6, s. 24.

24 *Class Proceedings Act*, R.S.B.C. 1996, c. 50, s. 29(1)(c). See also *Class Proceedings Act 1992*, S.O. 1992, c. 6, s. 24(1)(c).

25 The Ontario Law Reform Commission, *Report on Class Actions*, 3 vols. (Toronto: Ministry of the Attorney General, 1982) at 597. A contemporary commentator noted that this represented a "mirror image of the United States Model": B.S. Duvall, Jr, "The Importance of Substance to the Study of Class Actions: A Review Essay on the Ontario Law Reform Commission Report on Class Actions" 3 Windsor Yearbook of Access to Justice 411 (Windsor, ON: University of Windsor, 1983).

Of course the Acts speak of establishing "liability," which might be read as going only to the distribution of damages. They do not speak to whether *causation* can be established without individual proof, but even in cases where such proof is possible it may be uneconomic. In a case of relatively minor but widespread damages resulting from a misrepresentation, it may be practically impossible to determine which of the class members relied on the misrepresentation to their detriment. However, through a process of sampling and extrapolation, a global number might be obtained that can permit a reasonably accurate assessment of legally valid claims. In such circumstances, it would make perfect sense to permit an aggregate or statistical finding with respect to liability as well as damages. It would appear that some settlements are already being calculated on such a basis.[26]

This willingness to aggregate claims from liability through damages seems to run counter to much of the jurisprudence in the United States, where some efforts by U.S. courts to perform assessments of damages on an aggregate basis[27] have been seen as violation of defendants' rights under the Fifth and Seventh Amendments of the U.S. constitution.[28] However, these provisions have no equivalent in Canadian law, where property and civil due process have no such explicit protection.[29]

---

26 See, for instance, the proposed CIBC VISA settlement, discussed later in Chapter 8 (see note 11). In that case, it would be difficult if not impossible to determine which class members were misled with respect to the foreign exchange fees they would be charged. However, if the court can be convinced that a certain percentage were, that should be enough to establish causation in the population. If courts were not willing to entertain the possibility of proof on the basis of sampling, settlements like that discussed would not be possible.

27 In *Cimino v. Raymark*, 751 F. Supp. 649 (E.D. Tex. 1990) the trial judge had designed a system whereby the tort victims were divided into groups by disease, and the claimant pool was "sampled" with the damages from these hearings extrapolated across the disease group as a whole.

28 *Cimino v. Raymark*, 151 F.3d 297 (5th Cir. 1998). Amendment VII to the U.S. constitution guarantees a trial by jury in federal civil court. The appeals court found that it guaranteed the defendants "to have a jury determine the distinct and separable issues of the actual damages of each of the extrapolation plaintiffs": *Cimino v. Raymark*, 151 F.3d 297 (5th Cir. 1998) at 320–21. The court also suggested (at 311) that the procedure employed by the court denied the defendants their Fifth Amendment rights to "due process." Neither a jury trial nor any due process rights are guaranteed in the Canadian constitution (at least with respect to civil trials), so it appears that objections similar to those made in *Cimino* could not succeed against the aggregate damages provisions of the Canadian legislation.

28 This analysis is supported by the Ontario Law Reform Commission's report, *supra* note 25 at 536, which explicitly considered the constitutionality question:

> Most of the American commentary relating to aggregate assessment is of limited usefulness for our purposes, since it has centred on ... whether this procedure vio-

B. DEEMED KNOWLEDGE

1) Deeming Knowledge at Common Law

Many tort claims require the court to make findings of fact with respect to the knowledge of the parties; this is one of the most significant problems of proof in law. Documentary evidence aside, one can never know with certainty what another person knows unless that person is willing to admit it. For this reason, courts have gradually expanded and refined the categories in which it will impute knowledge to a party.

Earlier in this book, we discussed circumstances in which manufacturers will be taken to have expert knowledge regarding their product, without regard to what knowledge they actually possessed. This is a legal imputation, irrebuttable to the extent that it is of no help for a manufacturer to say, "But I didn't have expert knowledge." The standard of care requires that it should, and either it did have the knowledge or it is liable for not having it. In this sense, deemed knowledge can be seen, not as an evidentiary device (as with a reversed onus), but as a policy-based extension of liability for ignorance.

In fact, the rule of law depends on deemed knowledge, since it is one of the fundamental tenets of the law that one is deemed to know what the law says, although, practically speaking, this cannot possibly be the case. The Supreme Court of Canada has adopted the rule expressed by Lord Ellenborough in *Bilbie v. Lumley*[30] as follows: "Every man must be taken to be cognizant of the law; otherwise there is no saying to what extent the excuse of ignorance might not be carried. It would be urged in almost every case." The Supreme Court in *Air Canada v. British Columbia* emphasized the rule: "The citizen is deemed to know the contents of legislation."[31]

Numerous common law rules have developed in other situations when knowledge will be imputed: a person is deemed to have knowledge of a trust imposed by statute;[32] a bank is deemed to know everything known to

---

lates the constitutional rights to trial by jury and due process [and] whether aggregate assessment constitutes a change in the substantive law of the United States and is therefore not permitted by the *Rules Enabling Act* ...

Fortunately, there is no need for the Commission to become enmeshed in the more technical aspects of this debate, as the *Rules Enabling Act* is obviously inapplicable and there are no similar constitutional rights to trial by jury or due process in civil cases in Ontario.

30 (1802), 2 East 469, 102 E.R. 448 at 472 and 449–50.
31 *Air Canada v. British Columbia*, [1989] 1 S.C.R. 1161 at para. 90.
32 *Air Canada v. M&L Travel Ltd.*, [1993] 3 S.C.R. 787 at 812.

its agent;[33] and an insurer has historically been deemed to know matters of a "public character or notoriety" regarding an insured risk.[34] Discussing "deemed knowledge" (of a statutory trust), Nation J. of the Alberta Court of Queen's Bench put it this way:

> The analysis of this case has to be taken in the context of the fact that the law deems the company and the directors to know of a statutory trust, even though they may not have actual knowledge. (P.608, *Re: Air Canada* case). This deemed knowledge makes this case unique from many as the aspect of the "knowing" requirement is deemed, and the directors' conduct has to be considered as if they had knowledge of the trust. Thus, it may well be that in cases of a breach of a statutory trust, the directors are more likely to be personally liable, where they consider themselves quite innocent, due to ignorance, but the court must ignore that so called "ignorance" and see their "innocence" in a different light due to the deeming of the knowledge of the trust.[35]

In *Canadian Indemnity*,[36] Gonthier J., writing for the Supreme Court, held that an insurer was deemed to know that a particular product contained asbestos because of the notoriety of that fact in the industry at the time. This reasoning was extended by Drost J. in *Privest Properties Ltd. v. Foundation Co. of Canada*[37] to suggest that a supervising contractor was also deemed to know of the presence of asbestos fibres in insulation. In that case, the corresponding "deemed knowledge" of the plaintiff (who had employed the supervising contractor) was fatal to a claim of failure to warn and misrepresentation.

2) Deeming Knowledge Via Statute

The most common form of statutorily deemed knowledge is found in the notice requirements of various statutes, which often provide, for instance, that "notice" of a proceeding or matter is deemed to have been received "one week after the delivery of the notice to the last known mailing address" of the

---

33 *Barwick v. English Joint Stock Bank* (1867), L.R. 2 Ex. 259; *British Mutual Banking Co. v. Charnwood Forest Railway Co.* (1887), 18 Q.B.D. 714 (C.A.); *Mackay v. Commercial Bank of New Brunswick* (1874), L.R. 5 P.C. 394; *Re Halifax Sugar Refining Co.* (1890–91), 7 Times L.R. 293.

34 *Canadian Indemnity Co. v. Canadian Johns-Manville Co.*, [1990] 2 S.C.R. 549 [hereinafter *Canadian Indemnity*].

35 *Bare Land Condominium Plan 8820814 v. Birchwood Village Greens Ltd.*, [1999] 6 W.W.R. 753 at para. 54 (Alta. Q.B.).

36 *Canadian Indemnity*, supra note 34.

37 (1995), 128 D.L.R. (4th) 577 (B.C.S.C.).

person notified. As indicated, deemed knowledge is widely accepted as a feature of contracts for insurance at common law. However, it has also been codified as a statutory term of contracts. The history of such provisions was discussed at length in *Canadian Indemnity Co.*,[38] where it was acknowledged that the deemed knowledge of an insurer as to matters of "public character and notoriety" (in that case mandated by Article 2486 of the *Civil Code* of Quebec) was a provision designed to streamline the process of proof. The Supreme Court there said: "In my opinion, art. 2486 C.C. was intended to alleviate the evidentiary problems which would be caused by a requirement that the insured prove that the insurer had actual knowledge of a fact that the insured failed to disclose." While this precedent is useful for its frank acknowledgment that the "deeming" is designed to relieve the burden on one prospective litigant, its inclusion as, in effect, a statutory contractual term distinguishes its immediate application in tort.

British Columbia's *Insurance (Marine) Act*[39] states:

> 20 ... where an insurance is effected for the assured by an agent, the agent must disclose to the insurer
> (a) every material circumstance that is known to the agent, and an agent to insure is deemed to know every circumstance that in the ordinary course of business ought to be known by or to have been communicated to the agent, and
> (b) every material circumstance that the assured is bound to disclose, unless it comes to the assured's knowledge too late to communicate it to the agent.

Land title statutes frequently state that a person dealing with a part or parcel of land is deemed to know all that he or she could find out from a perusal of the registry.[40] Similarly, the Manitoba *Limitation of Actions Act*,[41] stated in section 16(2) (which relates to actions under the *Fatal Accidents Act*):

> Where the applicant applying under subsection 14(1) for leave to begin or continue an action is a person who is entitled to bring an action under *The Fatal Accidents Act* in respect of the death of the deceased person ... the applicant shall be deemed to know of all facts that the deceased, at the time of his death, knew of and shall be deemed to have gained that knowledge at the time the deceased gained it ...

---

38 *Canadian Indemnity*, supra note 34.
39 R.S.B.C. 1979, c. 203, s. 20.
40 *White v. Lauder Developments Ltd.* (1976), 9 O.R. (2d) 363 (C.A.).
41 R.S.M. 1987, c. L-150.

These types of deemed knowledge, however, fall somewhat short of a type that would be particularly useful in the pursuit of mass claims, particularly tort claims. Actual knowledge is necessary only in torts that require a strong element of deliberacy, which also imputes upon the wrongdoer a degree of moral, as opposed to strictly legal, condemnation. It is therefore not surprising that legislatures have been loath to modify the law applicable to such claims.

There are exceptions, but even these tend to deem knowledge only for the purpose of imposing standards of reasonableness in the negligence setting. For example, the Alberta *Occupiers' Liability Act*[42] sets out an occupier's duty to a trespassing child:

> 13(1) When an occupier knows or has reason to know ... that a child trespasser is on his premises, ... the occupier owes a duty to that child to take such care as in all the circumstances of the case is reasonable to see that the child will be reasonably safe from that danger. ...
>
> (3) For the purposes of subsection (1), the occupier has reason to know that a child trespasser is on his premises if he has knowledge of facts from which a reasonable man would infer that a child is present or that the presence of a child is so probable that the occupier should conduct himself on the assumption that a child is present.

This has been interpreted as a statutory deeming of knowledge. The court in *Bates (Guardian of) v. Horkoff*[43] said:

> Mr. Horkoff was an occupier within the meaning of the Act. Assuming Shawna was a trespasser, then Mr. Horkoff is deemed to know of her presence by reason of subsection (3). On the facts, namely the frequent presence of children in the adjoining playground and the state of the fence separating the same from his backyard, a reasonable man would infer that the presence of a child was probable. Therefore, Mr. Horkoff was required to conduct himself based on the assumption that a child would be present.

C. DESTRUCTION OF DOCUMENTARY EVIDENCE

1) Introduction

Mass tort and product liability claims often involve evidence that is largely documentary in nature. Quite often, the critical answers sought by the

---

42 R.S.A. 1980, c. O-3.
43 [1991] A.J. No. 960 (Q.B.).

court, such as regarding the level of the defendants' knowledge of risks, adequacy of testing, compliance with regulatory procedures, and so on, are to be found within the "paper trail" that is kept in corporate offices and produced through the discovery process.

Under such circumstances, there may be a strong temptation for defendants, or potential defendants, to dispose of potentially incriminating paper. Indeed, it is frequently asserted that the deliberate destruction of evidence in such cases is on the rise,[44] and recent notorious cases of corporate cover-ups bears out this concern.[45] If it becomes apparent that relevant documents have been lost or destroyed, what is the plaintiff's recourse? The doctrine of "spoliation of evidence" was developed to deal with a situation where a party to a civil suit[46] (or, in some cases, a third party) loses or destroys evidence required by another party for the conduct of the litigation.

2) Particular Relevance in Product Liability Context

In the product liability context, a mass-consumer product liability case may require an inquiry into the manufacture, sale, and promotion of a product over many years. In these circumstances, the documents and evidence relevant to a singular product sold to one consumer have equal relevance to all like products and the hundreds or thousands of consumers who purchased the product. In this context, the evidence about the product originating from the manufacturer (or the absence of the evidence, as the case

---

44 Michael F. Pezzulli and Charles J. Fortunato, "Presenting and Defending a Spoliation of Evidence Case" located on <www.courtroom.com> (Dallas, Texas law firm website). See also Charles Nesson, "Incentives to Spoliate Evidence in Civil Litigation: The Need for Vigorous Judicial Action" (1991) 13 Cardozo L. Rev. 793.

45 In the wake of the collapse of U.S. energy giant Enron, Arthur Andersen LLP was found guilty of obstruction of justice, based on the destruction of documents related to the Enron collapse. The individual responsible for ordering the documents' destruction said that his orders had been given to ensure the Enron audit team's compliance with the company's document-retention policy. Arthur Andersen claimed the destruction was not in compliance with its policy but was the action of a single individual. However, the jury was convinced that Andersen had, at the very least, knowingly allowed the destruction to continue, and, at the very worst, had encouraged the destruction. See *U.S.A. v. Arthur Andersen LLP*, 374 F.3d 281 (5th Cir. 2004).

46 There are, of course, many cases, some quite contentious, dealing with the destruction of evidence in criminal cases. Often these matters are dealt with as discovery violations or as the grounds for stays of proceedings: See, for instance, the recent Supreme Court of Canada decision in *R. v. Carosella*, [1997] 1 S.C.R. 80. The application of the spoliation doctrine *per se*, however, bears only on civil proceedings, and that is the only context in which it is discussed here.

may be) may make or break the opportunity for hundreds or thousands of consumer-litigants to prove a breach of duty and consequential damages.

Also unique to this context is the fact that the evidence and documents discoverable in one case are equally relevant to all other litigation, both ongoing and prospective. This results in a situation where the evidence relevant to that product and the corresponding lawsuit should not be destroyed at the conclusion of one lawsuit, since it may continue to be relevant to numerous others. While it would seem reasonable, in the interests of prospective claims, to extend the duty to preserve the evidence at the conclusion of the lawsuit, a company's document-retention policy may standardize the systematic destruction of documents at the end of a trial.

Another consideration in the product liability context is that a manufacturer has a more sophisticated understanding of certain product dangers than does the public or the rest of the scientific community. A manufacturer's acts and omissions should not be judged by the general state of scientific knowledge but in light of the specific state of scientific knowledge of the manufacturer. At the time that a manufacturer uncovered data confirming the potential harm caused by flaws in the product, one would expect the manufacturer to abide by a duty to preserve evidence, even if the flaws in the product are not immediately discovered by the consumers and no claims are commenced in the short term. Unfortunately, without sufficient penalties to guide the behaviour of the manufacturer, the decision whether to preserve evidence about a product becomes a self-regulated exercise based on a cost-benefit analysis.

R. Sommers and A. Seibert, in their article "Intentional Destruction of Evidence: Why Procedural Remedies Are Insufficient," illustrate the problem as follows:[47]

> To illustrate, XYZ Co. manufactures and markets a highly profitable, but inherently defective mass consumer product. For decades, XYZ has known that its product is dangerous, inherently defective and its promotions misleading.
>
> To suppress evidence of its negligent, reckless or intentional wrongdoing it regularly destroys internal documents. XYZ knows that its product ... will typically kill a user after a period of twenty to thirty years of consumption ... XYZ knows that many potential plaintiffs would die before the company is even required to produce evidence in litigation.
>
> ... [I]f XYZ successfully eliminates all traces of evidence destruction, plaintiffs may only be able to advance negligence theories and recover

---

[47] (1999) 78 Can. Bar Rev. at 38–70.

modest compensatory damages. ... If XYZ's profits, derived from continued wrongdoing, exceed the quantum of projected modest compensatory damages awards, there is no incentive for the rogue company to change its tortious practices.

3) History of the Spoliation Doctrine

The spoliation doctrine can trace its origin to the Roman law of Justinian and his predecessors, where in loan transactions, certain business records were considered *prima facie* proof of the loan.[48] If the claimant would not or could not produce this evidence, his case would not only fail but he would be held to have committed fraud upon the defendant. The maxim that evolved, and that enjoyed a resurgence in the nineteenth century, was *omnia praesumuntur contra spoliatorem*: roughly, "all things are presumed against the spoliator."

In *St. Louis v. Canada*,[49] Girouard J. noted with some satisfaction that cases "where parties to a suit stand accused or guilty of withholding or destroying [documentary] evidence ... are not as frequent in England as in the United States, and it is not surprising that the decisions are not so numerous and do not present as many illustrations of the maxim."[50] Nonetheless, spoliation is not, contrary to popular belief, an American concept, even in its contemporary incarnation. The modern law of spoliation can properly be traced to the early eighteenth century and the leading English case of *Armory v. Delamirie*.[51] In that instance, a chimney-sweep boy had found a piece of jewellery and taken it to the defendant's goldsmith shop. The goldsmith's apprentice removed the stones and offered the boy threepence for them; the boy refused, and demanded the stones back. The goldsmith gave him only the empty socket, and the boy brought a suit in trover. Chief Justice Pratt directed the jury that it could consider evidence of what would be the most expensive stone that could have been mounted in the socket: "[U]nless the defendant did produce the jewel, and shew it not to be of the finest water, they should presume the strongest against him, and make the value of the best jewels the measure of their damages."

---

48 See Sandars, *The Institutes of Justinian* (1878 or 1888 eds.) at 358.
49 (1896), 25 S.C.R. 649 [hereinafter *St. Louis*].
50 *St. Louis*, ibid. at 682–83. This rather glib observation on the relative honesty of English (and by implication Canadian) litigants seems almost as applicable today; there remain only a handful of spoliation cases in Canada, and hundreds — if not thousands — on record in the United States.
51 (1722), 1 Strange 504 (K.B.) [hereinafter *Armory*].

The first (and for some time, only) significant Canadian decision on the spoliation doctrine is that of the Supreme Court of Canada in 1895, *St. Louis*, above.[52] In it, Mr. Justice Girouard[53] made a thorough and impressive study of the doctrine from its Roman inception, and examined it in the light of both the Quebec *Civil Code* and of the English common law.

St. Louis concerned an appellant who was suing the government of Canada for the value of stone and labour provided for the building of the railway. The government's defence rested on its assertion that the payroll records submitted to it for reimbursement were fraudulent; when the appellant was unable to produce the records for verification by the trial court, the government argued spoliation and the Exchequer Court agreed, denying St. Louis's claim.

At the Supreme Court of Canada, Mr. Justice Girouard held that the Quebec *Civil Code* did not allow for a *legal* presumption to be made against the spoliator, but rather one of fact.[54] In the case before him, the appellant had destroyed the evidence "long before ... the present action, at a time when he did not have any cause to suspect that the government would contest his claim."[55] Girouard J. also found that it was important that the "appellant is not in the position of a plaintiff who has wilfully destroyed his best evidence and asked to be allowed to give secondary evidence, a course which would be sanctioned by no court of justice ...."[56] His Lordship, who devoted pages to an analysis of English jurisprudence, also found that similar rules applied under the common law.

At the close of *St. Louis*, the law in Canada appeared clear on the issue of intentional spoliation; it creates a presumption that can be rebutted with "express and positive evidence to the contrary"[57] — that is, in the case of *St. Louis*, evidence that the destroyed books contained the figures that the appellant claims that they did. The presumption arises if the destruction occurs after notice that an action is imminent or under way. The Court appears to leave open the question of negligent spoliation; Girourd J. states that the appellant, who acted without fraudulent intent, was not a spoliator, and that even if he was, has rebutted the presumption that arises.[58] The

---

52 *St. Louis, supra* note 49, on appeal from the Exchequer Court.
53 The *St. Louis* Court was unanimous in result, but Girouard (Sedgewick and King JJ. concurring) wrote the judgment fully exploring the law of spoliation as it then existed and determining why it did not apply to the case at bar: *St. Louis, ibid.*
54 *Ibid.* at 670.
55 *Ibid.*
56 *Ibid.* at 673.
57 *Ibid.* at 690.
58 *Ibid.* at 689–90.

Court seems to be suggesting that, even without a demonstration of fraudulent intent, the presumption may still require rebuttal.

In 1911 the Saskatchewan Supreme Court (sitting *en banc*) considered a case in which a workman had been injured in a fall from a collapsing scaffold after the accident. The cleat that attached the scaffold to the wall had been destroyed by the defendant, and two justices of the court held that "[t]his made it impossible for the plaintiff to show what caused the accident, and therefore shifted the onus of proof to the defendant."[59] Unfortunately, the decision offers no clue as to whether the cleat's destruction was wilful or negligent. As a result, this case, while it supports *St. Louis* without referring to it, adds little to the rule established by the Supreme Court of Canada in 1895.

4) Remedies for Spoliation

a) As an Independent Tort

Some U.S. jurisdictions such as California, Alaska, and Florida have accepted spoliation as the basis for a separate tort, actionable in and of itself. Parties in those jurisdictions can commence actions for intentional spoliation and claim damages for losses resulting from the inability to prove facts or present evidence to establish liability because the evidence no longer exists. A few other jurisdictions in the United States have allowed actions for intentional spoliation to stand, but most other states have expressly rejected the recognition of a cause of action in tort for spoliation.[60]

Spoliation has been considered in several modern decisions of the British Columbia courts; that of the Court of Appeal in *Endean v. Canadian Red Cross Society*,[61] that of Burnyeat J. in *Dyk v. Protec Automotive Repairs*,[62] and that of Boyd J. in *Dawes v. Jajcaj*.[63] In *Endean*, the plaintiff had filed suit for spoliation because the Red Cross had allegedly destroyed documentary evidence regarding blood screening in the 1980s; the defendants claimed that the claim should be struck because it disclosed no recognized cause of action. At trial Mr. Justice Smith had held that, although there was as yet no tort of spoliation in Canada, the statement of claim should not be struck

---

59 *Lindsay v. Davidson*, [1911] 1 W.W.R. 125 at 129 (Sask. C.A. *en banc*). The case does not refer to the doctrine of spoliation or the maxim *omnia praesumuntur contra spoliatorem*, but the principles applied are similar.
60 See Craig E. Jones, "The Spoliation Doctrine and Expert Evidence in Civil Trials" (1998) 32 U.B.C. L. Rev. 293 at 299.
61 *Endean*, *infra* note 64.
62 [1997] B.C.J. No. 1895 (S.C.) [hereinafter *Dyk*].
63 (1995), 15 B.C.L.R. (3d) 240 (S.C.) [hereinafter *Dawes*].

on that basis. Smith J. noted that "the possibility that intentional destruction of relevant evidence may give rise to remedies in this jurisdiction has been recognized in *Dawes v. Jajcaj* ... and *Kaiser v. Bufton's Flowers*."[64] This case did not offer any judgment on the merits, and thus we can pass over the trial judge's reference only to intentional spoliation without further comment.

The Court of Appeal unanimously reversed the decision, finding no cause of action in spoliation because the spoliation presumption offers sufficient assistance to the innocent party:

> Thus, based on the authorities and the necessary consequences from these decided precedents, I am of the opinion that it is plain and obvious that to allow this action to proceed would indeed amount to an abuse of process.
>
> Accordingly, I am of the opinion that these appeals should be allowed and the order of the Honourable Mr. Justice Smith should be amended to decertify the action in spoliation pursuant to the *Class Proceedings Act*.[65]

The Court of Appeal in *Endean* was later directly challenged by subsequent decisions from Ontario. In *Coriale (Litigation guardian of) v. Sisters of St. Joseph of Sault Ste Marie*,[66] a plaintiff learned that medical records central to a tort claim in negligence had been destroyed by the defendant. The plaintiff sought to amend its statement of claim to assert the spoliation principle as warranting an evidentiary presumption against the defendants, and to assert spoliation as an independent tort.

A master allowed both amendments, and the decision was upheld by Molloy J. of the Ontario Court (General Division). Molloy J. specifically considered and rejected the British Columbia appellate decision in *Endean*, along with other contemporaneous Ontario decisions applying the B.C. appellate court's reasoning in the Ontario context,[67] finding that it was more appropriate to hear the spoliation issues at trial than to strike the spoliation pleadings prematurely. The court found this reasoning in keeping with the Supreme Court of Canada's decision in *Hunt v. Carey Canada Inc.*,[68] where-

---

64 *Endean v. Canadian Red Cross Society*, [1997] B.C.J. No. 1209 (S.C.) at para. 25, rev'd [1998] B.C.J. No. 724 (C.A.) [hereinafter *Endean*].
65 *Ibid*. (C.A.) at paras. 34–35.
66 [1998] O.J. No. 3735 (Gen. Div.) [hereinafter *Coriale*].
67 The *Rintoul/Robb Estate* companion cases: *Rintoul v. St. Joseph's Health Centre* (1998), 42 O.R. (3d) 379 (Div. Ct.) and *Robb Estate v. St. Joseph's Health Care Centre*, [1998] O.J. No. 1144 (Gen. Div.).
68 [1990] 2 S.C.R. 959.

in the Court held: "... where a statement of claim reveals a difficult and important point of law, it may well be critical that the action be allowed to proceed. Only in this way can we be sure that the common law in general, and the law of torts in particular, will continue to evolve to meet the legal challenges that arise in our modern industrial society."[68] Most significantly, Molloy J. in *Coriale* noted that the necessity of adopting a separate tort of spoliation should be tested against the reality of the facts of the case.[69]

More recent cases have built on this precedent. The ongoing case of *Spasic v. Imperial Tobacco* involves an Ontario plaintiff (now deceased) and her claim for damages from the manufacturers of tobacco products to which she was addicted and which she claimed caused her to develop lung cancer. In one of the many preliminary motions, the lower court held that a party guilty of spoliation could be held in contempt of court, a far greater sanction than the usual remedy of drawing an adverse inference against the spoliator. Cameron J. of the Ontario Court (General Division) held:

> The common law permits a superior court to exercise its inherent jurisdiction over its proceedings by finding a contempt not in the face of the court. The conduct must be designed to impede access to the courts or the proper administration of justice. ... The contempt proceedings should be invoked by ... a party to the proceedings.[70]
>
> ...
>
> Civil contempt is directed to the protection of the interests of individuals and the sanction is directed to remedying or compensating the private character of the harm done.[71]

Cameron J. clarified that, in order to invoke a finding of civil contempt by a court, the moving party (in this case, the victim of the spoliation) must prove *mens rea* and contempt on the part of the spoliator beyond a reasonable doubt. The burden the innocent party is required to meet to obtain a contempt order is (arguably impracticably) high.

The *Spasic* case has also provided encouragement that Canadian law is coming closer to recognizing spoliation as an independent actionable tort. In the aforementioned preliminary motion heard by Cameron J., the court also considered the validity of certain allegations in the plaintiff's statement of claim pertaining to spoliation. Cameron J. ruled that those portions should be struck out on the basis that the tort of spoliation was not part of

---

68 *Ibid.* at 990–91.
69 *Coriale, supra* note 66 at para 25.
70 (1998), 42 O.R. (3d) 391 at 397 (Gen. Div.).
71 *Ibid.* at 398.

the law of Ontario. On appeal from that decision, the Ontario Court of Appeal held in July 2000 that those claims ought not to have been struck out.[72] The appellate court allowed the plaintiff to include allegations of spoliation in the statement of claim without first having to prove them. The justices declined to spell out the elements of the novel tort of spoliation, holding that it was for the trial judge to determine the elements of the tort in the context of the facts that will emerge at trial.[73] The Ontario Court of Appeal has subsequently allowed spoliation pleadings to stand in the *Rintoul/Robb Estate* companion cases[74] on the basis of the *Spasic* appellate decision.[75]

The defendant tobacco manufacturers in *Spasic* tried again to have the spoliation references in the statement of claim struck out, on the basis that "the plaintiff has failed to plead the minimum level of fact disclosure" required by the Ontario Rules of Court. However, Brennan J. of the Ontario Superior Court allowed the spoliation pleadings to stand, stating that "the defendants have failed to provide a compelling reason for striking out the spoliation portion of the claim."[76] The court held that the plaintiff could not know particulars of the document-destruction and retention policies of the defendant tobacco manufacturers, and stated that to require further particulars, "... that persons should be named, or specific documents be identified, or particular acts of destruction ...," would be to require the plaintiff to plead evidence, which is contrary to Ontario's Rules of Court.[77]

Brennan J. held that "if [the plaintiff's claims of spoliation] are untrue, the time has come [for the companies] to deny them in a statement of defence."[78] In the process, the court chastised the defendant tobacco manufacturers for stalling the case with pointless motions; he asserted that "[t]his appeal should mark the end of proceedings over this statement of claim."[79]

Imperial Tobacco's motion for leave to appeal Brennan J.'s order was dismissed on 9 April 2003.[80] Carnway J. held that the order allowing the spoliation pleadings to stand was not the proper basis for an appeal at this stage of the proceedings:

---

72   *Spasic v. Imperial Tobacco Limited*(2000), 49 O.R. (3d) 699 (C.A.). Motion for leave to appeal to the Supreme Court of Canada dismissed [2000] S.C.C.A. 574.
73   See note 67.
74   See *Rintoul v. St. Joseph's Health Centre* and *Robb Estate v. St. Joseph's Health Centre*, [2001] O.J. No. 606 (Ont. C.A.).
75   *Spasic v. Imperial Tobacco*, reasons for judgment of Brennan J., [2003] O.J. No. 824 (S.C.J.).
76   *Ibid.* at para. 23.
77   *Ibid.* at para. 26.
78   *Ibid.* at para. 30.
79   *Ibid.* at para. 24.
80   [2003] O.J. No. 1797 (S.C.J.).

The possibly tenable tort of spoliation may arise from vastly different fact situations requiring a pragmatic and functional analysis ... In *Endean* and *Coriale*, the underlying facts were relatively easy to ascertain. In this matter the underlying facts, if any, are extremely difficult to ascertain ... I am unable to conclude there is a good reason to doubt the correctness of the order.

Moreover, the issue is not of such importance that leave should be granted. The issue is of considerable importance to the parties. However I find no matters of public importance nor matters relevant to the development of the law. It would be premature to do so at this stage of the proceedings.

b) As a Basis for Drawing Adverse Inferences and Presumptions

Most often, spoliation is asserted as a basis to permit the court to draw an adverse inference against the party who did not uphold his or her disclosure obligations, or to create a presumption that the evidence would have spoken against the spoliator. As Sir Arthur Channel for the Privy Council explained in the early case of *The Ophelia*: "If any one by a deliberate act destroys a document which, according to what its contents may have been, would have told strongly either for him or against him, the strongest possible presumption arises that if it had been produced it would have told against him ..."[81] The presumption or adverse inference is generally thought to be rebuttable, as was explained in the decision of *Cincinnati Insurance v. General Motors*:[82] "[T]he [spoliator] bears the burden of persuading ... a trial court that there is no reasonable possibility that lack of access to the unaltered or intact product deprived the [other party] of favorable evidence otherwise unobtainable, that is, that the [other party] was not prejudiced."

A fairly common application of the doctrine is as a presumption when assessing damages after liability is assigned; this is perhaps the least controversial modern application of the maxim, dating back to the original English case of *Armory v. Delamirie*[83] and the recent Ontario case of *Murano v. Bank of Montreal*:[84] "Where an initial finding of liability has been made, it is often stated that every reasonable presumption must be made in favour of a plaintiff because the defendant has produced the circumstances complained of: *omnia praesumuntur contra spoliatorem*."

---

81 *The Ophelia*, [1916] 2 A.C. 206 (P.C.) at 229–30 [hereinafter *The Ophelia*].
82 1994 Ohio App. LEXIS 4960 (6th App. Dist. 1994) at 11.
83 *Armory*, *supra* note 51.
84 [1995] O.J. No. 883 at para. 158 (Gen. Div.), var'd [1998] O.J. No. 2897 (C.A.).

But what of spoliation of evidence that goes to the elements of the cause of action, not to damages? Just how much ought to be presumed against the spoliator was, in the formative years of the doctrine, the subject of heated legal debate. Lord Mansfield, presiding over the Court of King's Bench in *Roe v. Harvey*,[85] applied quite strictly the Roman principle, holding that "in civil causes, the court will force parties to produce evidence which may prove against themselves; or leave the refusal to do it (after proper notice) as a strong presumption, to the jury." On the other extreme, other subsequent decisions held that, where documentary evidence had been destroyed by one party, the rules of evidence might be relaxed to allow the other party to prove its contents (through parol evidence, etc.).[86] The English courts backed away somewhat from the Roman law and from Lord Mansfield, as is apparent from this passage from *Barker v. Ray*,[87] where Lord Eldon held: "To say that once you prove spoliation you will take it for granted that the contents of the thing spoliated are what they have been alleged to be may be in a great many instances, going a great length."

So the position in English law by the mid-1800s appears to be an attempt to limit the equitable doctrine expressed in *Armory* from becoming determinative in cases of land title, where production of the deed was a prerequisite for success. The courts were apparently intent on staving off the Draconian consequences of the paper's loss or destruction and allowing a party to retain the ability to adduce evidence to save his or her interests. The resulting spoliation doctrine is properly characterized as a rebuttable presumption against the spoliator.

c) As an Evidentiary Tool

Spoliation can also be used as an evidentiary tool, as in the leading U.S. case of *Nally v. Volkswagen of America Inc.*[88] There, an expert's report was disallowed because much of the evidence forming the basis for his opinion had been destroyed. The court held that a party (or in that case, the party's expert) cannot benefit by putting him- or herself in the position of being the only person with first-hand knowledge of the evidence on which the claim (or in that case, the expert's opinion) can be grounded.

---

85 (1769), 4 Burr. 2484 at 2489.
86 See, for instance, *Cooper v. Gibbons* (1813), 3 Camp. 363; *Lawson v. Sherwood* (1816), 1 Starkie 314.
87 (1826), 2 Russ. 63 at 71.
88 539 N.E.2d 1017 (Mass. Sup. Judic. Ct. 1989).

d) To Restrict Available Defences

The spoliation doctrine can also be used to prohibit a party who destroyed evidence from asserting defences or raising allegations that are unsupportable in the absence of the missing evidence. In the United States, the court may sever portions of the statement of defence, or, in an extreme case, enter a summary judgment against the spoliating defendants.[89]

A notorious recent example of such extreme sanctions is the Australian decision of *McCabe v. British American Tobacco*.[90] There, it was revealed that Wills, the Australian subsidiary of BAT Industries plc, the UK-based tobacco giant, engaged in a comprehensive campaign to destroy all of its corporate documents, leaving it unable to comply with orders for discovery. When the company's document-destruction activities were revealed, Wills asserted at the application to strike its defence that the destruction was part of a legitimate document-retention policy employed in Australia yet devised and overseen by Australian, British, and American lawyers employed by the respective BAT companies in each country. The court's decision suggests that, after 1985, all BAT subsidiaries were directed to destroy most of their records older than five years, and to continue destroying any document after five years' time.

The lower court in *McCabe* ordered that, as a result of the intentional destruction of documents by the defendant, and its corresponding inability to live up to its discovery obligations, the statement of defence should be struck out. This left BAT Australia Services Ltd. without the ability to defend itself in the *McCabe* action, and conceivably in all other actions initiated thereafter. Judgment was rendered in favour of Ms. McCabe, with damages assessed at $700,000 (Australian Dollars).

On 6 December 2002, the decision of Eames J. in *McCabe* was overturned by the Court of Appeal of the State of Victoria, and a retrial was ordered.[91] Leave to appeal was denied by the High Court of Australia, which, while expressing "no view on the correctness of all of the Court of Appeal's statements as to principle," found that an evidentiary inference was sufficient to ensure a fair trial for all concerned: "The material that was relevant to the plaintiff's claim and has been destroyed related principally, if not exclusively, to the respondent's state of knowledge. It cannot be disputed that strong adverse inferences could be drawn if it were to be shown

---

[89] See *Friend v. Pep Boys*, 3 Phila. Co. Rptr. 363 at 372 (Pa. Com. Pl. 1979), aff'd 433 A.2d 539 (Pa. Super. Ct. 1981).
[90] [2002] V.S.C. 73 (S.C.) [hereinafter *McCabe*].
[91] [2002] V.S.C.A. 197.

at a trial that the respondent deliberately destroyed that material in order to make it unavailable for inspection and tender."[92]

Recently, in British Columbia, the Court of Appeal in *Homer Estate v. Eurocopter S.A.*[93] has confirmed that a court has the discretion to strike out an appearance or statement of defence of any party who "refuses or neglects to produce or permit to be inspected any document or other property," pursuant to Rule 2(5) of the Rules of Court. While not directly related to the issue of spoliation, the Rules of Court provide a remedy to those plaintiffs who are unable to access relevant evidence purportedly held by a defendant. The Court of Appeal confirmed that the litigants must adhere to the rules concerning discovery of documents "with that precision and sense of duty that one expects of a litigant," and that discovery of evidence should be made "thoroughly and timeously." However, the court characterized the act of striking out a statement of defence as a "draconian remedy" to be invoked only in the most egregious of cases.

5) Is There a Remedy if the Destruction Is Negligent?

The bulk of the early cases tended to deal with deliberate spoliation. But what happens when (as could more likely be proven) the evidence is destroyed or lost owing to the *negligence* of one of the parties? In the Roman law of old and subsequent early English cases, the intention of the parties was not particularly relevant; the prejudice to the innocent party was. Is there a sanction available against a negligent spoliator?

In 1914 a German auxiliary military hospital ship was seized by the Royal Navy and held as a prize of war; the British government asserted that the ship was fitted as a signal ship and as such did not come under the protection afforded relief vessels; the Prize Court agreed. The German Captain, one J.V.C. Pfeiffer, appealed the decision. Part of the determination turned on the effect of Captain Pfeiffer's destruction of the ship's logs prior to seizure, which could have proved the ship's true purpose. It gave Sir Arthur Channel, speaking for a unanimous Privy Council, an opportunity to offer a concise statement of the English law of spoliation, as reported in *The Ophelia:*[94]

> The substance of [the doctrine of spoliation] remains and is as forcible now as ever, and it is applicable not merely in prize cases, but to almost

---

92 *Cowell v. British American Tobacco Australia Services Ltd.*, [2003] HCATrans 384.
93 [2003] B.C.J. No. 929 (C.A.).
94 *Supra* note 81 at 229–30.

all kinds of disputes. If any one by a deliberate act destroys a document which, according to what its contents may have been, would have told strongly either for him or against him, the strongest possible presumption arises that if it had been produced it would have told against him; and *even if the document is destroyed by his own act, but under circumstances in which the intention to destroy evidence may be fairly considered rebutted, still he has to suffer.* He is in the position that he is without the corroboration which might have been expected in his case. [Emphasis added.]

So here is clear indication from the Privy Council that the doctrine of spoliation creates a presumption against not only the deliberate spoliator but also the negligent one. And yet the decision in *The Ophelia* remains virtually alone in twentieth-century English jurisprudence. It has been explicitly adopted into Australian law in *Allen v. Tobias and Another*[95] and reaffirmed as good law as recently as 1996,[96] but, despite being a decision (at least for some time) binding in Canada, it has not been applied in any of the cases considering spoliation here. In Canadian law, the question of negligent spoliation remains open.

---

95 (1958), 98 C.L.R. 367.
96 *Instant Colour Pty Ltd & Ors v. Canon Australia Pty Ltd.*, [1996] 763 F.C.A. 1 (AustLII).

6. The Problem of Corporate Groups

A. THE IMPLICATIONS OF THE CORPORATE GROUP

Public concern over the appropriate role of the corporation in society, and in particular its status as a legal "person," appears to be growing. Nowhere, though, is the independent legal personality of the corporation more important, or possibly more problematic, than when the corporation becomes a defendant in large-scale litigation. With the exception (particularly in Canada) of constitutional law, cases and textbooks generally do not distinguish in any principled way between corporate plaintiffs and defendants and individuals, and would likely reject any rule or principle distinguishing them as a threat to the legal personhood of the corporation, an essential aspect of modern economic life.

While treating a corporation identically as a person might simplify the process of legal rule making, it ignores the fact that, whether or not the plaintiff in a mass tort or product liability action is an individual or a corporation, the overwhelming majority of defendants in such actions are the latter. Moreover, the overwhelming majority of defendants are members of corporate groups — either subsidiaries of larger corporations (frequently transnationals), parent companies of other businesses, or, frequently, both.

A corporate group, like any person, has rights and responsibilities under the law. Unlike an ordinary person, however, the corporate group can establish separate entities to carry on particular aspects of the business: one part might do research, another manufacturing, a third might market and sell the product, a fourth might hold intellectual property or other assets. Additionally, the corporate entity changes over time through reorganizations, mergers, and take-overs.

As a result of this combination — the legal idea that each member of a corporate group is a separate "person" under the law — some important influences on how (or even whether) redress in tort might occur often escape the attention of legal commentary or are, at best, dealt with in a less than comprehensive way.

It is our belief that any meaningful discussion of mass tort or product liability law must necessarily entertain an examination of the impact of the corporate structure on issues from causation to recovery.

B. LIMITED LIABILITY AND TORT CREDITORS

Since at least the House of Lords 1897 decision in *Salomon v. Salomon & Co.*,[1] the insularity of the corporate personality has been lauded as fuelling an unparallelled engine of economic growth. By protecting owners and investors from personal liability for the debts of the corporation, the law is said to encourage investment and entrepreneurial activity. At the same time, artificial corporate "personhood" has been derided in some quarters as a means by which tortfeasors might evade liability for very serious wrongdoing.

One of the most notorious illustrations of the principle of separate corporate personality involved a New York taxi operator who ran a fleet of taxi cabs.[2] The owner had incorporated ten separate companies, each of which owned just two taxis. The plaintiff was severely injured by one of the cabs and sought to recover damages by suing the company which owned the cab. However, each cab carried only the minimum insurance required by

---

1 [1897] A.C. 22 (H.L.). For those unfamiliar with the facts of this seminal case, Mr. Salomon, a leather merchant and boot manufacturer, incorporated a company and sold his business to it; Salomon was the majority shareholder, having received shares as part of his payment for the business, as well as debentures constituting security. Eventually, the business became insolvent and was sued; Mr. Salomon claimed that he should be satisfied ahead of the unsecured creditors by virtue of his secured debenture. The Court of Appeal viewed the company as a "mere scheme" for limiting liability and putting Mr. Salomon ahead of the unsecured creditors. Nevertheless, the House of Lords regarded the corporation as properly formed, and a distinct entity, with no evidence of deception or fraud; as a result, Salomon's claim was upheld.
2 *Walkovszky v. Carlton*, 276 N.Y.S. 2d 585, 223 N.E. 2d 6 (1966, C.A.).

law ($10,000) and the company had no other assets. The plaintiff then brought an action for the remainder of the damages against the owner of all the companies on the basis that the entire business was in fact a single enterprise, and that the use of a series of separate companies was nothing more than an attempt to defraud members of the general public who might be injured by one of the cabs. The New York Court of Appeals refused to accept this invitation to "pierce the corporate veil." Judge Feld said that "the corporate form may not be disregarded merely because the assets of the corporation, together with the mandatory insurance coverage of the vehicle which struck the plaintiff, are insufficient to assure him the recovery sought."[3] The court felt that to pierce the corporate veil in order to obtain compensation for the victim of an accident, would have a negative impact on business planning and investment.

One judge, Keeting J. dissented in this case. He felt that it was clearly unfair to deprive the plaintiff of compensation and that the corporate form was, in this instance, being used in an unjust fashion. He explained that,

> The issue presented by this action is whether the policy of this State, which affords those desiring to engage in a business enterprise the privilege of limited liability through the use of the corporate device, is so strong that it will permit that privilege to continue no matter how much it is abused, no matter how irresponsibly the corporation is operated, no matter what the cost to the public.[4]

Judge Keeting held that the way in which the business was organized in this case revealed that the owner's sole purpose was to avoid financial responsibility for damages claims and that it would be against public policy to allow the corporate form to be used in this fashion.

This case reveals the basic policy conflict that arises in such cases.[5] On the one hand, the instruments of separate corporate personality and limited liability are widely used legal instruments of state economic policy that encourage capital accumulation and investment in economic development. By limiting the potential liability of investors the law provides an incentive for investment and avoids unfairly surprising remote owners with undue managerial responsibility or financial risk. On the other hand, the corpo-

---

3   Ibid. at 9.
4   Ibid. at 11.
5   For an excellent analysis of the history, advantages and problems of limited liability, see P. Blumberg, "Limited Liability and Corporate Groups" (1985–86) 11 Journal of Corporation Law 573.

rate form can easily be used to avoid taking financial responsibility for unconsented-to risks. As we explain below, tort victims are unlike commercial creditors and others who deal with corporations since they have no way of knowing in advance of the risk of dealing with a limited liability corporation, nor of protecting themselves against that risk.

Salomon v. Salomon developed limited liability in a very different social and legal context. Until the end of the nineteenth century there were no industrial enterprises made up of numerous corporations because generally a corporation could not own shares in another corporation unless it was specifically authorized to do so.[6] The protection offered by limited liability was extended only to individual investors. As Blumberg points out, no one foresaw the ramifications of the proliferation of corporate groups once share-ownership rules were relaxed:

> Both as an academic and a political matter, the application of limited liability to corporate groups has never undergone the scrutiny and debate that such a fundamental extension of the doctrine deserves. With the increasing predominance of large corporate groups on the world economic scene, and the increasing emergence of an interdependent world economic order, such re-examination is not only desirable, but inevitable.[7]

In October 1996, speaking at a conference of bankruptcy lawyers and judges in San Diego, Cornell University law professor Lynn M. LoPucki warned that corporations were increasingly availing themselves of "judgment proofing" strategies. LoPucki's thoughts were set out in an article in the *Yale Law Journal*[8] where he noted that several so-called "ownership strategies" are employed by corporate groups. Describing the "parent-subsidiary" strategy, he said: "Most large companies consist of numerous corporate entities. Limiting liability — that is, defeating part of it — is the principal reason for creating those entities."[9]

LoPucki demonstrates that frustration of liability is accepted in the courts and legal literature as the intent of the legislatures in establishing limited liability schemes, and a perfectly valid response to risk-management. He then discusses several approaches by which governments might

---

6   Phillip I. Blumberg, "The Increasing Recognition of Enterprise Principles in Determining Parent and Subsidiary Corporation Liabilities" (1996) 28 Conn. L.R. 295.
7   *Ibid.* at 297. See also, Aronofsky, "Piercing the Transnational Corporate Veil: Trends, Developments and the Need for Widespread Adoption of Enterprise Analysis" (1985) 10 N. Carolina J. of Int. L. and Commercial Reg. 31.
8   L. LoPucki, "The Death of Liability" (1996) 106 Yale L.J. 1.
9   *Ibid.* at 20–21.

attempt to counter the movement towards judgment-proofing. One of the methods suggested is through schemes of "enterprise liability" — that is, disregarding "entity law" in a way that "... [i]n its more conservative version ... is virtually indistinguishable from liberal piercing of the corporate veils within corporate groups."[10]

The problem is that limited liability was established largely to excuse shareholders from contractual liabilities, or liabilities to "voluntary creditors" — people who have contracted with the company in the knowledge of its limited status. Tort victims, though, are "involuntary creditors" in the sense that they "are not in a position to contract around any existing rule or to monitor the risk to which the firm is exposing them," according to Columbia University professor David Leebron.[11] Leebron continues: "If the law recognizes limited liability, tort victims will have no opportunity to negotiate for unlimited liability, and thus will have no chance to force shareholders and managers to fully take their losses into account."

Blumberg and others point out that the contemporary problem is the result of a historical accident. Limited liability laws were designed in a day when shareholders were individuals and corporations were forbidden to hold shares in other corporations. When this rule was relaxed and corporate groups emerged, there was no consideration in the cases or in academia regarding what effect this might have on tort liability; limited liability for shareholders was simply extended to corporations in their capacity as "persons."[12]

This chapter addresses the various ways in which the corporate structure can impede tort recovery, particularly recovery on a large-scale that might be anticipated in cases of massive environmental disasters or a widespread pattern of wrongdoing. It then goes on to examine in depth two strategies that courts and legislatures have taken to free tort law from the inherent limitations of the corporate personality: "enterprise liability" and "successor liability."

---

10   *Ibid.* at 67.
11   D. Leebron, "Limited Liability, Tort Victims, and Creditors" (1991) 91 Columbia L.R. 1565 at 1601.
12   When the spectre arose of corporations shielding their assets through subsidiaries, equitable rules allowing "veil-piercing" were established. Unfortunately, though, such techniques proved of limited utility since "fraud" or even "actual control," two traditional criteria for veil piercing, were extraordinarily difficult to prove.

C. MODERN CORPORATIONS AND "JUDGMENT-PROOFING" STRATEGIES

The efficacy of judgment-proofing as a corporate strategy has been called into question, with some scholars pointing out that, despite the availability of abusive corporate structures, most active corporations have substantial equity, and, moreover, there may be structural imperatives within corporations that necessitate a twinning of activity with assets within the same "corporate personality."[13] Certainly, the sheer number of equity-rich large corporations that are routinely able to satisfy judgments supports the argument that the expectations of shareholders, insurers, and so on have served to restrain corporations from the worst excesses of judgment-proofing strategy. On the other hand, there are certainly cases such as the Bhopal gas disaster, where limited liability has substantially insulated a parent company from liability for the tort of a thinly-financed and under-insured subsidiary.[14] Nonetheless, as LoPucki himself has recently conceded, analysis is "complicated by an almost complete lack of probative empirical evidence. As a result, the debate has been locked in the academic equivalent of door-to-door fighting."[15]

The basic problem is as basic as the essence of the corporate "personality" itself. That is to say, the fictitiousness of the corporation is perfectly congruent with other legal fictions; it is appropriate that a corporation may "own" something, since ownership is itself a legal construction rather than a reality. Similar principles can be said to govern the ability of a corporation to enter into contracts. The commission of torts, however, cannot occur at the level of legal fiction. Real people need to suffer real injuries, and the true actors who caused the harm are themselves people. LoPucki puts it succinctly:

> Liability is in nearly every instance generated by employees, but it can only be collected from assets ... The doctrine of *respondeat superior* transmits the liability to the employing (operating) entity. Once liability has been fixed against that entity, it can be collected from the assets owned by

---

13 See, e.g., James J. White, "Corporate Judgment Proofing: A Response to Lynn LoPucki's The Death of Liability" (1998) 107 Yale L.J. 1363, 1394–1412 and LoPucki's subsequent answer to White's criticism: Lynn M. LoPucki, "Virtual Judgment Proofing" (1998) 107 Yale L.J. 1413, 1415–21.
14 Jamie Cassels, *The Uncertain Promise of Law: Lessons from Bhopal* (Toronto: University of Toronto Press, 1993).
15 L. LoPucki, "The Essential Structure of Judgment Proofing" <www.lawschool.cornell.edu/lopucki/LoPucki/essential.htm#N_9_>.

that entity. The weakness in liability as a system is the lack of any generally applicable requirement that the operating entity own assets.[16]

So, essentially, judgment-proofing in the context of corporate structures generally involves the division of the operation into two separate "personalities": the asset-owning "equity company" and the "operating company," whose job it is to carry on the corporate group's business and thus will almost certainly be the party to attract tort liability. In almost all business transactions, these two corporations may be indistinguishable from a single entity; they may be represented by the same officers and may, depending on the relative advantages, enter the contractual relationships as a unit. However, with respect to tort law, they remain separate persons.

There are several "judgment-proofing" strategies routinely employed by corporate groups to reduce exposure of assets owned by the equity company for torts committed by the operating company. For instance, factories, machinery, vehicles, land, and all manner of other assets may be leased by the owning company to the operating company. If the lease is short term, the tort victim as judgment creditor, limited to recovering only the lessee's interest, would be deprived of meaningful recovery.

Increasingly in a brand-conscious world driven by high technology, a company's most valuable assets are its intellectual property, particularly in the form of patents, trademarks, software, and so on. These, too, can be owned by a separate corporation at arm's length from the operating company and either licensed or franchised to it. Recovery may be permitted only to the extent of the tortfeasor's interest in the licence or franchise. Corporations whose principal assets are their trademarks are not secretive about their isolation.[17]

Should the status of an operating company be sufficiently precarious that a successful tort action might send it into bankruptcy, corporations can take advantage of the rules with respect to secured transactions. If the operating company owns assets, it may have pledged them as security for loans from the equity company. In the case of dissolution, secured creditors outrank judgment creditors, who would again be left out of the division of assets, assuming that the amount of the loan approximates the value of the assets.

---

16   Ibid.
17   For instance, a tobacco company like JTI-Macdonald Corp., a Canadian subsidiary of international giant Japan Tobacco, sells cigarettes under the valuable trademark "Export A," which is actually owned (like most of its other brands) by a separate corporate entity, JTI-Macdonald TM Corp. See the Canadian Trade Mark Database, online at <http://strategis.ic.gc.ca/cgi-bin/sc_consu/trade-marks/search_e.pl>.

Perhaps the two most common methods of insulating assets from tort liability is through parent-subsidiary relationships, which may or may not also employ some of the strategies noted above, and through sale by asset purchase. The advantage of the parent-subsidiary relationship is that, as shareholder, the parent is entitled to dividends from its subsidiary. To be sure, the parent-subsidiary relationship is also one where courts have been most willing to "pierce the corporate veil" and extend liability beyond the tortfeasing corporation, but such successes have been few,[18] and the parent-subsidiary relationship, alone or in tandem with other of the schemes presented here, has arguably remained the favourite judgment-proofing strategy of corporations, because it presents numerous other unrelated advantages, and perhaps also because its defining characteristic — liability-free share ownership — is so fundamental to the notion of the corporate form that it appears beyond reproach.

In a sale by asset purchase, a subsidiary corporation will be transferred to another company, either within the same corporate group or unrelated to its original parent. If the purchaser buys the shares in the subsidiary, then the same company (renamed or not) simply becomes a subsidiary of its new parent, with all of its liabilities from before the sale, including tort liabilities, intact. However, liability generally does not follow the sale of assets; therefore, if the purchasing company instead simply buys all the assets of the seller's subsidiary, and sets up a "new" subsidiary of its own to carry on essentially the same business, then, in theory at least, no liability will attach to the "new" subsidiary for the wrongs of the "old" one, even though the company may be in all observable respects absolutely identical to its previous incarnation and may even have the same ultimate parent.

Obviously, each of these strategies may be — and most certainly are — used in combination with one another. For instance, a corporation may buy another company through an asset purchase, then divide it into two or more operating and owning entities, arranging a complex series of loans, licences, and leases among them. A vast, almost impenetrable web can be created that is limited only by the creative imagination of corporate attorneys and the cost involved. It is to be expected, then, that those businesses whose activities are most likely to attract large-scale tort liability are also the businesses who have invested in judgment-proofing strategies.

So how best to address the problem? Some have suggested that limited liability has itself reached the end of its social utility and ought to be

---

12 See Robert B. Thompson, "Piercing the Corporate Veil: An Empirical Study" (1991) 76 Cornell L. Rev. 1036, 1058.

abandoned.[19] Washington University professor Robert B. Thompson notes a growing academic consensus that "there may be *no* persuasive reasons to prefer limited liability over a regime of unlimited *pro rata* shareholder liability for corporate torts." He goes on:

> The most far-reaching of the recent proposals to reform limited liability law would make all shareholders liable for torts of the enterprise. The most significant departure from existing law would be the increased liability imposed on passive shareholders ... Recent commentary seeks to extend the legal concern ... to passive shareholders and remove what has in effect, been a per se rule against finding passive shareholders liable.[20]

No jurisdiction has gone this far, but the following sections canvass the ways in which courts have, when appropriate, sought to "pierce the corporate veil."

D. "PIERCING THE CORPORATE VEIL"

There are various ways in which one corporation may be held liable for the tort of another. The first, of course, is to establish that the corporation committed an independent tort. For example, even where the direct tort is caused by a subsidiary (e.g., the manufacturer of a defective product), it might be the case the parent company (e.g., which controls the intellectual property and is responsible for research and development) could be held responsible for a failure properly to undertake research into the product's risks, or to disseminate adequate information about those risks. Alternatively, as discussed earlier in this book, the principles of conspiracy may be used to implicate joint corporate tortfeasors.

Absent establishing an independent tort or conspiracy, situations where one corporation can be vicariously liable for the tort of another are very limited. Nevertheless, the principles of separate corporate personality and limited liability are not absolute. Courts will pierce the corporate veil where the business organization is designed so as to perpetrate a fraud or to pursue an unlawful purpose. Typically, this involves a person using the corporate form to do something that they are legally or contractually prohibited from doing themselves (e.g., to avoid a personal non-competition

---

19 See, for instance, Henry Hansmann & Reinier Kraakman, "Toward Unlimited Shareholder Liability for Corporate Torts" 100 Yale L.J. 1879; Janet Cooper Alexander, "Unlimited Shareholder Liability Through a Procedural Lens" 106 Harv. L. Rev. 387 ("limited liability ... threatens the animating principles of tort law").

20 Robert B. Thompson, "Unpacking Limited Liability: Direct and Vicarious Liability of Corporate Participants for Torts of the Enterprise" 47 Vanderbilt L.R. 1.

clause in a contract).[21] Also, commonly, where separate corporate personality is being used solely for the purpose of evading a debt,[22] the payment of taxes or a statutory obligation, the courts will look behind the corporate form and fix liability upon the owner. None of these exceptions has any easy application to products liability and negligence cases except in the case of a corporate reorganization after a tort has been committed with the express purpose of avoiding liability.

Apart from fraud, the primary situation in which one company might be liable for the tort of another is where the relationship is so close that the one is simply the agent or "alter ego" of the other. Here the courts may infer an agency relationship and ignore their separate personalities. Given the interconnectedness of certain corporate entities as described above, it might be thought that this would be easy to establish, but that is not the case. Ordinarily, agency is inferred not only from the fact of ownership, but from the extent of authority exercised over it by the owner, measured by the degree of day-to-day control and direction. The courts frequently state that they will disregard the corporate form only when the corporation is the "creature" or the "puppet" of its owner[23] or where one company has "complete dominion" over the other.

The factors which are relevant are set out in the judgment in *Smith, Stone and Knight Ltd. v. Birmingham Corp.*[24]

- Were the profits of the subsidiary treated as the profits of the owner?
- Was the person conducting the business of the subsidiary appointed by the owner
- Was the owner the "brains" of the venture
- Did the owner govern the venture in terms of making important strategic and investment decisions?
- Did the owner make the profits by its own skill and direction?
- Was the owner in effective and constant control?

The tests are applied in a way that separate corporate entities, acting in good faith, albeit negligently, are rarely held liable for one another's torts. It is important to note that mere ownership is not sufficient to make the

---

21   *Gilford Motor Co. Ltd. v. Horne*, [1933] Ch. 935 (C.A.).
22   *Fidelity Electronics of Canada Ltd. v. Fuss* (1995), 77 O.A.C. 34 (Div. Ct.).
23   *Wallersteiner v. Moir*, [1974] 3 All E.R. 217 at 238. Per Lord Denning, the companies "were just the *puppets* of Dr. Wallersteiner. He controlled their every movement. Each danced to his bidding. He pulled the strings. No one else got within reach of them. Transformed into legal language, they were his agents to do as he commanded."
24   [1939] 4 All E.R. 116 (K.B.).

subsidiary the agent of the parent. Even 100 percent ownership of one corporation by another is common, and does not mean that the subsidiary is simply the "alter ego" of the parent. Moreover, the fact of an overlapping or appointed board of directors is not particularly weighty. In *Gregorio v. Intrans-Corp. et al.*,[25] the Ontario Court of Appeal reaffirmed the traditional approach to limited liability. The plaintiff had purchased a truck from the defendant dealer who had purchased it from the defendant distributor. The distributor was the wholly owned subsidiary of the manufacturer. The trial judge held that the distributor was the alter ego of the manufacturer and was therefore liable in negligence in manufacturing the truck. The appeal was allowed on the basis that the trial judge had erred in finding liability on the alter ego theory. The Court of Appeal held:

> Generally, a subsidiary, even a wholly owned subsidiary, will not be found to be the alter ego of its parent unless the subsidiary is under the complete control of the parent and is nothing more than a conduit used by the parent to avoid liability. The alter ego principle is applied to prevent conduct akin to fraud that would otherwise unjustly deprive claimants of their rights ....[26]

The fact that several corporations are operated as a larger integrated economic unit is not sufficient to pierce the veil.[27] Nor is it offensive to the law that a form of corporate organization has been adopted with the intent of "hiving off" risky activities of one venture so that other members of the group are not exposed to liability. In *Adams v. Cape Industries*,[28] the court indicated it did not accept:

> [A]s a matter of law that the court is entitled to lift the corporate veil as against a defendant company which is the member of a corporate group merely because the corporate structure has been used so as to ensure that the legal liability (if any) in respect of particular future activities of the group (and correspondingly the risk of enforcement of that liability) will fall on another member of the group rather than the defendant company. Whether or not this is desirable, the right to use a corporate structure in this manner is inherent in our corporate law.

American and European courts may go somewhat further than their English and Canadian counterparts. Where, for example, the corporate tort-

---

25 (1994), 18 O.R. (3d) 527 (C.A.).
26 *Ibid.* at 536.
27 *Cunningham v. Hamilton* (1995), 29 Alta. L.R. (3d) 380 (C.A.).
28 [1990] 1 Ch. 433 at 544 (C.A.).

feasor is seriously undercapitalized or underinsured, and is simply being used as a mechanism to avoid responsibility for debts, the owner may sometimes be liable. In Canada a few cases have referred to inadequate capitalization as one factor that might incline a court to disregard the corporate form.[29] Generally, however, the veil survives intact to protect owners, investors and associated companies from liability for corporate torts.

In the United States some courts have experimented with the so-called "Deep Rock doctrine" that permits the corporate veil to be lifted whenever to do otherwise is not fair.[30] This has not been accepted in Canada, though in *Kosmopoulos v. Constitution Insurance Co. of Canada*,[31] there is *obiter* that might be thought to support it:

> As a general rule a corporation is a legal entity distinct from its shareholders: *Salomon v. Salomon & Co.*, [1897] A.C. 22 (H.L.). The law on when a court may disregard this principle by lifting the corporate veil" and regarding the company as a mere "agent" or "puppet" of its controlling shareholder or parent corporation follows no consistent principle. The best that can be said is that the "separate entities" principle is not enforced when it would yield a result "too flagrantly opposed to justice, convenience or the interests of the Revenue": L.C.B. Gower, *Modern Company Law* (4th ed. 1979), at p. 112. I have no doubt that theoretically the veil could be lifted in this case to do justice, as was done in *American Indemnity Co. v. Southern Missionary College*, [290 S.W. 2d 269], cited by the Court of Appeal of Ontario. But a number of factors lead me to think it would be unwise to do so.

The concluding words from the chapter in Gower[32] that Wilson J. quoted are these (at 138):

> The most that can be said is that the courts' policy is to lift the veil if they think that justice demands it and they are not constrained by contrary binding authority. The results in individual cases may be commendable, but it smacks of palm-tree justice rather than the application of legal rules.

The suggestion in *Constitution* that courts might take a broader view of their power to pierce the corporate veil has not been followed. Indeed, in

---

29 *De Salaberry Realties Ltd. v. M.N.R.* (1974), 46 D.L.R. (3d) 100 (F.C.T.D.).
30 See *Pepper v. Litton*, 308 U.S. 295; *Taylor v Standard Gas & Electric Co.*, 306 U.S. 307, 59 S.Ct. 543 (1939).
31 [1987] 1 S.C.R. 2 at 10–11, *per* Wilson J.
32 L.C.B. Gower, *Modern Company Law*, 4th ed. (London: Stevens & Sons, 1979).

B.G. Preeco 1 (Pacific Coast) Ltd. v. Bon Street Holdings Ltd.[33] the B.C. Court of Appeal explicitly rejected it. Seaton J.A. stated at page 37:

> I do not subscribe to the "Deep Rock doctrine" that permits the corporate veil to be lifted whenever to do otherwise is not fair (see: *Pepper v. Litton*, 308 U.S. 295 ...). That doctrine and the doctrine laid down in *Salomon v. Salomon & Co.*, [1897] A.C. 22 (H.L.), cannot co-exist. If it were possible to ignore the principles of corporate entity when a judge thought it unfair not to do so, *Salomon's* case would have afforded a good example for the application of that approach.

In *Transamerica Life Insurance Co. v. Canada Life Assurance Co.*, Sharpe J. considered whether the court would pierce the corporate veil whenever it is "just and equitable" to do so, based on the excerpt from *Constitution Insurance* referred to above. Sharpe J. rejected that submission and commented as follows:

> If accepted, the argument advanced by Transamerica would represent a significant departure from the principle established in *Salomon v. Salomon & Co.*, [1897] A.C. 22 at page 51 ... :
>
>> The company is at law a different person altogether from the subscribers to the memorandum; and, though it may be that after incorporation the business is precisely the same as it was before, and the same persons are managers, and the same hands receive the profits, the company is not in law the agent of the subscribers or trustee for them. Nor are the subscribers as members liable, in any shape or form, except to the extent and in the manner provided by the Act.[34]

In the most recent edition of Gower,[35] Sharpe J. pointed out at 433 that the test for piercing the corporate veil was articulated more narrowly as follows:

> There seem to be three circumstances only in which the courts can do so. These are: (1) When the court is construing a statute, contract or other document. (2) When the court is satisfied that a company is a "mere facade" concealing the true facts. (3) When it can be established that the company is an authorized agent of its controllers or its members, corporate or human.

---

33 (1989) 60 D.L.R. (4th) 30 (B.C.C.A.).
34 (1996), 28 O.R. (3d) 423 at 431 (Gen. Div.).
35 L.C.B. Gower, *Principles of Modern Company Law*, 5th ed. (London: Stevens & Sons, 1992) at 132–33,

Sharpe J. also referred to two recent judgments which had refused to read the "just and equitable" dictum as granting carte blanche to lift the corporate veil absent fraudulent or improper conduct.[36] He concluded:

> ... the courts will disregard the separate legal personality of a corporate entity where it is completely dominated and controlled and being used as a shield for fraudulent or improper conduct. The first element, "complete control", requires more than ownership. It must be shown that there is complete domination and that the subsidiary company does not, in fact, function independently ....
>
> The second element relates to the nature of the conduct: is there "conduct akin to fraud that would otherwise unjustly deprive claimants of their rights"?[37]

Clearly, the corporate form, and the principles of limited liability are alive and well in Canada. In the following sections, however, we describe evolving principles in other jurisdictions and in legal scholarship — specifically successor liability and enterprise liability — and suggest ways in which they affect Canadian law.

E. SUCCESSOR LIABILITY

1) Introduction

It has always been assumed, apparently as a rather unconscious application of the principles in *Salomon v. Salomon*, that when a company is transferred via share purchase, the "new," or "successor," company is liable for the torts of its "predecessor." They are, in law, the same person, regardless of the share ownership. By the same somnambular reasoning, if a company transfers its assets to another, the successor, even if carrying on the same business as its predecessor, is not liable.

Although the corporate personality confirmed in *Salomon* became the law in both the United States and Canada, various notions of so-called "enterprise liability" have been introduced both by statute and through common law in both countries, as means by which corporations might be held responsible for the wrongs of other members of their corporate groups.[38] Particularly in Canada, it has generally been assumed that, if a

---

36   W.D. Latimer Co. v. Dijon Investments Ltd. (1992), 12 O.R. (3d) 415 (Gen. Div.) and 801962 Ontario Inc. v. MacKenzie Trust Co., [1994] O.J. No. 2105 (Gen. Div.).
37   *Supra* note 34 at 433–34.
38   Enterprise liability is discussed in more detail later in Part Two.

business is sold via an asset transfer, as opposed to a share transfer, this was, absent fraud, effective as a method of restricting tort liability[39] upon the sale of a business. Yet, at least with respect to a manufacturer's liability for dangerous or defective products, this may no longer be so. Through the mechanism of "successor liability," a corporation may inherit the contingent liabilities of its predecessor corporation along with its assets.

Successor company liability is a type of enterprise liability that relies on entities' relationships chronologically rather than structurally. American cases have established that, in product liability cases, it can flow from either the continued *de facto* existence of the original company or, in some cases, from the continuation of the product line itself, following the sale of a business by asset transfer.

While successor liability theory is well developed in the United States, its presence has yet to be significantly felt in Canadian decisions; the law in the area is, as at least one Canadian judge has remarked, "in a state of flux," and it has been in that state for quite a long time. Nevertheless, there is reason to believe that some form of successor tort liability has been adopted (so far only conditionally) as part of the law of Canada.

This development has obvious and important ramifications, not only for lawyers involved in product liability litigation, but also for solicitors who may still be advising their clients that non-transference of contingent tort liability is a reason to arrange the sale of a business through asset transfer rather than by sale of shares, merger, or amalgamation. If the client is a manufacturer of a product, such assurances can simply not be made until and unless the law is settled. And if confidence in the asset-transfer method is undermined, either because of uncertainty or from the adoption of successor liability rules in Canada, the value of Canadian vendor companies' assets, relative to the value of their corresponding shares, will almost certainly decline. Anyway that this is measured, the law may be faced with a multi-billion-dollar question.

Our purpose here is to explain the theory of successor liability in product liability cases and to review the reception that the theory has received in Canadian courts.

---

39 There are, of course, established successorship rules in several fields of law, including the tax, labour and employment, and environmental law fields. However, these almost entirely statutory rules need not be canvassed in this part of the book, which is concerned with remedies available to tort victims.

2) The Asset Purchase Liability Bar

There may be, as some commentators and courts have argued, some valuable public policy considerations behind this "asset purchase liability bar." It has been said, for instance, that imposing liability on the purchaser of assets might be unduly restrictive of a company's ability to alienate its belongings, restructure, and generally conduct its own affairs.[40] Yet, there are many arguments, particularly in the area of product liability, on the other side. One could point out that asset sales, as often as not, occur between two subsidiaries of the same ultimate parent corporation. To move beyond "enterprise theory" and argue instead from first principles, should a party escape responsibility simply because of the legal device employed in the transaction? In a sense, it might be said that defeating contingent liability through asset sale is offensive to the idea behind privity of contract, or rather its obverse: Why should two parties be able to agree, by contract, to defeat the rights of an unknown third party, an "involuntary creditor," a "tort victim"?

The strangest aspect of this conundrum is that it is peculiarly Anglo-Canadian. American common law, arguably far advanced in the field of product liability generally, has embraced the concept of "successor liability" for decades. The conditions under which liability for defective products may flow through an asset sale are discussed below.

3) The Emergence of Successor Liability in U.S. Product Liability Cases

The liability of a successor corporation for the wrongs or debts of its predecessors, according to U.S. and Canadian corporation law, is generally dependent on the structure of the corporate acquisition. Corporate ownership may be transferred in one of three ways:[41]

1) through the sale of stock;
2) by a merger or consolidation[42] with another corporation; or

---

40 See, for instance, Yamin, "The Achilles Heel of the Takeover: Nature and Scope of Successor Corporation Product liability in Asset Acquisitions" (1984) 7 Harv. J.L. & Pub. Pol'y 185 at 212–14; and Comment, "A Search for the Outer Limits to Successor Corporation Liability for Defective Products of Predecessors," (1982) 51 U. Cin. L. Rev. 117 at 128.
41 Note, Torts — Product Liability — "Successor Corporation Strictly Liable for Defective Products Manufactured by the Predecessor Corporation" (1980) 27 Villanova L.R. 411, 412.
42 A merger occurs when one of the combining corporations continues to exist; a consolidation exists when all of the combining corporations are dissolved and an entirely new corporation is formed: *DOT v. PSC Resources, Inc.*, 175 N.J. Super. 447 (Super. Ct. 1980) [hereinafter *N.J. Transp. Dep't*].

3) by the sale of its assets.

In the case of a stock purchase or a merger or consolidation, the liability of the purchased, merged, or consolidated company remains. Where, however, the acquisition is in the form of a sale or other transference of all of a corporation's assets to a successor corporation, the latter is not liable for the debts and liabilities of the corporation whose assets it purchased.

There are four exceptions to this general rule of non-liability in asset acquisitions. These principles are summarized in the *Restatement of the Law (3d) of Torts: Product Liability*,[43] which provides:.

> § 12. Liability of Successor for Harm Caused by Defective Products Sold Commercially by Predecessor
>
> A successor corporation or other business entity that acquires assets of a predecessor corporation or other business entity is subject to liability for harm to persons or property caused by a defective product sold or otherwise distributed commercially by the predecessor if the acquisition:
> (a) is accompanied by an agreement for the successor to assume such liability; or
> (b) results from a fraudulent conveyance to escape liability for the debts or liabilities of the predecessor; or
> (c) constitutes a consolidation or merger with the predecessor; or
> (d) results in the successor's becoming a continuation of the predecessor.

It is generally accepted that (a) and (b) will occur rarely and (c) is fairly straightforward. It is not surprising, then, that the majority of the emerging jurisprudence concentrates on what constitutes a "continuation" of the predecessor company.

When applying the continuity of enterprise theory, U.S. courts may take into consideration several factors in determining whether a corporation is a successor to another. Such relevant factors have, for instance, included the following:

- retention of the same employees;
- retention of the same supervisory personnel;
- retention of the same production facilities in the same location;
- retention of the same name;

---

43 *Restatement of the Law (3d) of Torts: Product Liability* (1998). The American Law Insitute (ALI) is, like law reform commissions in the various Canadian provinces, an advisory group of legal scholars and experts, and its "Restatements" are often relied upon by U.S. legislatures and the judiciary.

- production of the same product;
- continuity of assets;
- continuity of general business operations; and
- the successor holding itself out as the continuation of the previous enterprise.[44]

One might also add that, in order for successor liability to apply, it is generally accepted that the predecessor corporation must have ceased to exist as an entity that could be sued. In *Shaffer v. South State Mach.*[45] the plaintiff had sued for injuries resulting from use of an allegedly defective saw. The defendant did not manufacture the saw but had acquired the assets of the manufacturer that did at Bankruptcy Court. The district court allowed the defendant's motion to dismiss, ruling that, although the applicable law of Pennsylvania embraced the "product line" exception to successor non-liability (discussed below), as well as the basic provisions now in Section 12 of *Restatement (3d)*, above, that exception does not apply when a potential remedy exists against the original manufacturer.[46]

---

44 *Gould v. A&M Battery and Tire Service*, 950 F. Supp. 653 (Dist. Ct. Pa. 1997) [hereinafter *Gould*], citing *United States v. Carolina Transformer Co.*, 978 F.2d 832 at 838 (4th Cir. 1992). The court in *Gould* rejected an interpretation of the Eighth Circuit decision in *United States v. Mexico Feed & Seed Co., Inc.*, 980 F.2d 478, 487 (8th Cir. 1992) [hereinafter *Mexico Feed & Seed*] as requiring the successor's knowledge of its predecessor's off-site disposal activities as a prerequisite to CERCLA liability. Instead the *Gould* court pointed to *United States v. Pierce*, 1995 WL 356017 (N.D.N.Y. 1995); *Elf Atochem North America v. United States*, 908 F. Supp. 275, 282 (E.D. Pa. 1995); and *United States v. Atlas Minerals and Chemicals, Inc.*, 824 F. Supp. 46, 50 (E.D. Pa. 1993) for the proposition that a broad application of the "substantial continuity" doctrine is necessary to prevent successor corporations to frustrate CERCLA's goal of facilitating payment for clean-up costs. The *Gould* court read *Mexico Feed & Seed* and subsequent cases as considering "knowledge" merely to be one factor among others, and not as dispositive in determining whether a defendant is a "successor" for the purposes of the law. Nevertheless, because federal courts enforcing CERCLA do not rely on state common law rules with respect to successorship, application of those rules in such cases is not settled: See, e.g., Allen Kezsbom and Alan V. Goldman, "The Long and Winding Road of Corporate Parent and Successor Liability Under CERCLA" BNA's Environmental Due Diligence Guide, § 231:485(d) (Oct. 1996); ibid., "Corporate Successor Liability for CERCLA Cleanup Costs: Recent Developments" (3 Mar. 1993) 7 Toxic Law Reporter (BNA) 1156, n.2; Allen Kezsbom, Anthony E. Satula, Jr, & Alan V. Goldman, "'Successor' and 'Parent' Liability for Superfund Cleanup Costs: The Evolving State of the Law" (Fall 1990) 10 Virginia Environmental Law Journal 45, 47–60.

45 995 F. Supp. 584 (Pa. 1998) [hereinafter *Shaffer*].

46 It must be noted that, in *Shaffer*, the Bankruptcy Court had set aside a fund for product liability claimants, and the plaintiff had filed a timely proof of claim in that proceeding. The possibility that the plaintiff might not recover from the claimants' fund, or that his recovery might be inadequate, the court said, did not change the fact that a possible

4) "Product Line Liability"

More recently, the traditional successor liability rules have been abandoned by several U.S. jurisdictions and a new theory for establishing successor liability has evolved based upon the similarity of continued business operations. The U.S. Environmental Protection Agency describes the development as the "product line" approach[47] and cites *Ray v. Alad Corp.*[48] and *Dawejko v. Jorgensen Steel Co.*[49]

The EPA distinguished this "product line" exception to limited liability from more traditional forms of successor liability as follows:

> This theory of establishing successor liability differs from the *de facto* and "mere continuation" exemptions in that the new approach does not examine whether there is a continuity of corporate structure or ownership (e.g., whether the predecessor and successor corporation share a common director or officer). Instead, according to the new theory, liability will be imposed if the successor corporation continues essentially the same manufacturing or business operation as its predecessor corporation, even if no continuity of ownership exists between them.

The leading case on the issue for our purposes is *Ramirez v. Amsted Indus., Inc.*[50] In that case, the New Jersey Appeal Division Court held that "where ... the successor corporation acquires all or substantially all of the assets of the predecessor for cash and continues essentially the same manufacturing operation as the predecessor corporation the successor remains liable for the product liability claims of its predecessor."[51]

---

remedy against the actual manufacturer existed. *Quaere* whether this ruling would have been made if the predecessor company was still extant, but entirely without assets, an "empty shell" kept alive for no other purpose than to shield the successor from liability. But see also *Roy v. Bolens Corp.*, 629 F. Supp. 1070 (D. Mass. 1986) (the successor liability doctrine has no application where "the original manufacturer remains in existence to respond in tort for its alleged negligence and breach of warranty").

47 United States Environmental Protection Agency, "Liability of Corporate Shareholders and Successor Corporations for Abandoned Sites under [*CERCLA*]" (memorandum, 13 June 1984), online: <www.epa.gov/compliance/resources/policies/cleanup/super-fund/corpshr-aban-mem.pdf>.
48 *Ibid.* at 14.
49 290 Pa. Super. Ct. 15 (1981).
50 171 N.J. Super. 261 (App. Div. 1979), aff'd 86 N.J. 332 (Sup. Ct. 1981) [hereinafter *Ramirez*].
51 *Ibid.* at 278., cited to 171 N.J. Super. 261 (App. Div. 1979).

5) Application of Successor Liability Rules in Canada

There is no substantive difference between corporation statutes in Canada and the United States that could lead one to conclude that successor liability is explicitly barred here. Rather, as in the United States, the robustness of the corporate veil established by statute is almost completely determined by the application of the common law.

Successor liability has not been considered in a comprehensive and authoritative way in Canada, at least since the dissent of Fullerton J.A. in *Trustee Company of Winnipeg v. Manitoba Bridge and Ironworks, Ltd.*,[52] where His Lordship set out at 189 the familiar "general rule" as follows: "'In absence of a statute or contract imposing liability, one corporation which makes a *bona fide* purchase of all the property of another is not liable for the debts of the selling corporation, nor does it hold such property subject to any lien or obligation towards the creditors of the selling corporation.'" In fact, all of the Canadian decisions on the issue that we have been able to find have been in interlocutory proceedings, where the plaintiff's theory of liability needs to meet only a low standard to proceed to trial.

About the same time as the *Ramirez* decision was affirmed in the United States, a case of successor liability was heard by Bouck J. in *Cominco Ltd. v. Westinghouse Canada Ltd.*[53] Without the benefit of any of the U.S. jurisprudence on the topic, Bouck J. took a traditional view of successor liability. Discussing whether a company, which had taken over all the assets and operations of a predecessor who failed to warn about dangerous cable, should "assume the duty to warn," Bouck J. held: "In my view, it did not. ... [B]y acquiring assets and employees of [the predecessor corporation] in May, 1972, any such duty to warn was not transferred to C.W. No. 2. This duty could only be conveyed by an express transfer of the obligation at the time of the sale. It does not occur by operation of law."[54]

The most thorough consideration of the U.S. rules of successor liability to date has been in *Suncor Inc. v. Canada Wire and Cable Limited*.[55] In that case, Forsyth J. was considering whether to grant a summary judgment by corporate defendants who claimed to be separated by an asset transfer from the alleged wrongdoing corporation. The plaintiffs were arguing alter ego, agency, or, in the alternative, successor liability. While Forsyth J. found that the arguments of agency and alter ego could not apply because the defen-

---

52 [1922] 1 W.W.R. 178 (Man. C.A.).
53 (1981), 127 D.L.R. (3d) 544 (B.C.S.C.), var'd (1983), 147 D.L.R. (3d) 279 (B.C.C.A.) [hereinafter *Cominco*].
54 *Ibid.* at 567.
55 (1993), 15 C.P.C. (3d) 201 [hereinafter *Suncor*].

dant did not exist at the time liability was allegedly incurred, he accepted that successor liability was an issue that should go to trial. The court recognized that the claim was novel in Canada, but it held:

> Unable to rely on any Canadian or English jurisprudence, the respondents turn to that of the United States. They concede that in the U.S., as in Canada, there is a general rule that a corporation which purchases all the assets of another corporation is not liable for debts and liabilities for which no consideration was paid. It appears to be that general rule which accounts for the fact that the corporate veil is pierced only for co-existing entities. However, they submit that a principle has emerged in recent case law that would permit the attachment of such liabilities on a successor corporation. In *Ramirez v. Amsted [sic] Industries Inc.* (1981) N.J., 431 A.2d 811 at 815 [A.2d], four exceptions to the general rule are enumerated. Only two of those are relevant for the purposes of this case:
>
> a) where the transaction for the transfer of assets amounts to a consolidation or merger of the two corporations;
> b) where the transferee is a mere continuation or reincarnation of the transferor.

The respondents cited several other cases that form part of this developing line, but I need discuss only the *Ramirez* case.

The reasoning in that case is persuasive. The defendant argued, as does the Applicant Group in this application, that the traditional corporate analysis ought to be applied. Clifford J. disagreed and said that the traditional approach narrowly emphasized the form rather than the practical effect of a particular corporate transaction. At 817 of *Ramirez*, he adopted the reasoning of other courts that

> The successor corporation, having reaped the benefits of continuing its predecessor's product line, exploiting its accumulated good will and enjoying the patronage of its established customers, should be made to bear some of the burdens of continuity, namely, liability for injuries caused by its defective products.

In a case where such benefits were reaped, it was thought improper to allow the form of a transaction to control questions of liability in tort. Several criteria have been developed for determining exactly when a successor corporation will be held liable for the torts of its predecessors. As pointed out by counsel, several of them may apply directly to the facts of this case. It is, however, unnecessary to go into detail on that point.

The law of successor corporate liability developed as the result of criticism that the traditional approach was inconsistent with the "rapidly developing principles of strict liability in tort" (*Ramirez* at p. 815). It was necessary to re-examine the principles underlying the traditional approach. In Canada, as in the U.S., the law of negligence has changed rapidly in recent years, and the evolution in the case law on the duty to warn, another possible issue in this case, is evidence of that change. How the traditional approach to the corporate liability of successor corporations will adapt to that change remains an open question in this country, and it would be wrong to conclude, as the Applicant Group submits, that the law is settled in this area. I am obliged to acknowledge that there exists a real possibility that courts in Canada will adopt the reasoning of the successor liability cases in the U.S. and will adapt it to suit our law of negligence. I am unable to exclude that as a possibility on the facts of this case.[56]

Forsyth J. goes on to consider the defendants' argument that the successor liability provisions in the U.S. cases were inextricably related to that country's strict liability rules. In rejecting this interpretation, Forsyth J. states at 211:

> The Applicant Group argued, perhaps correctly, that successor corporations have been found liable only in strict liability and product liability cases in the U.S but failed to persuade me beyond a reasonable doubt that such a restriction is justified in principle. I can say only that it is not manifestly clear to me that such a limitation is justified. That determination will have to be made after a detailed examination of the similarities and differences in the law of torts and of corporations in the two countries. In any event, it will be for a trial court to decide.

The defendant's application was rejected since it was not "plain and obvious" that the successor liability argument could not succeed in Canada.

In supplementary reasons[57] given after Bouck J.'s decision in *Cominco* was brought to his attention, Forsyth J. said this about the earlier British Columbia ruling:

> There is no reference by Bouck J. to the submissions of counsel on [the application of U.S.-type successor liability rules] and no discussion of the legal reasons which might justify a determination that the successor corporation could not assume the obligations of the predecessor. Since *Ramirez v. Amsted [sic] Industries Inc.* (1981), N.J., 431 A.2d 811, cited in my

---

56 *Ibid.* at 210–11.
57 [1993] A.J. No. 34 at para. 2 (Q.B.).

Reasons, was decided only two months prior to Bouck J.'s decision, it does not appear to have been cited or discussed in *Cominco*. Because legal arguments and authorities are absent and because there is no discussion of the reasons for the decision, I am not satisfied that case does settle the issue discussed in my reasons for judgment, namely, whether a Canadian court would adopt and adapt a developing trend in U.S. law that recognizes the liability of successor corporations for the torts of its predecessors. That question remains open.

[¶ 3] Also in my reasons for judgment, I stated that the Respondents conceded that

> "in the U.S., as in Canada, there is a general rule that a corporation which purchases all the assets of another corporation is not liable for debts and liabilities for which no consideration was paid."

The decision of Bouck J. appears to be no more than an application of that general rule. As was discussed in my reasons, it may be that, when presented with a complete and detailed analysis of the U.S. exceptions to that rule and their justifications, a Canadian trial judge would permit an exception to the Canadian rule.

Bouck J.'s decision was applied in *Winnipeg Condominium Corp. No. 36 v. Bird Construction Co.*,[58] where a plaintiff in construction litigation sought to add as a defendant an architectural corporation that was the successor of a dissolved partnership. Associate Chief Justice Oliphant said at paragraph 51:

> I am not satisfied that the architectural corporation is a successor corporation to the partnership or that any reasonable cause of action exists against it as such. There was no agreement on the part of the architectural corporation to assume the contingent liabilities of the partnership and, as Bouck J. held, correctly in my view, in *Cominco, supra*, that obligation cannot be imposed by operation of law.

However, Oliphant A.C.J. does not reject the reasoning developed in the U.S. product liability cases; it must be remembered that he was dealing with a case of pure negligence rather than with a manufacturing defect.[59]

---

58   [1998] M.J. No. 396 (Q.B.).
59   Moreover, the plaintiff had, knowing of the architectural corporation's existence, chosen to name the partnership as a defendant at the start of the action "to the exclusion of the architectural corporation": *ibid*. at para. 49.

He said: "I have not referred to the American authorities cited to me by counsel for the condominium corporation on the question of enterprise or successor liability. I do not think the principles articulated in them are applicable in the circumstances of this case."[60]

In *Boehler v. Blaser Jagdwaffen GmbH*,[61] Chamberlist J. considered whether to dismiss a successorship pleading on the strength of Bouck J.'s decision in *Cominco*. In deciding to allow the matter to proceed to trial, Chamberlist J. decided that Bouck's decision was not determinative of the matter, and at paragraph 21 cited *Suncor*:

> On a summary application such as this, I am not prepared to say that Justice Forsyth's view of the applicable law would not be adopted by a court hearing this trial. I agree with him that there exists a real possibility that the view of successor liability as set forth in *Ramirez* could be adopted in Canada and thus the case for summary dismissal is not as strong as it could be.

Suncor has been applied in two other cases where alleged successor corporations have sought dismissals on the pleading. In Ontario, the question of whether successor companies could be held liable was left open in *Seel Enterprises Ltd. v. Seel Mortgage Investment Corp.*[62] In that case, E. Macdonald J. said at paragraph 13: "I agree that the mere acquisition of assets of SMIC by Mutual does not lead to the assumption that it acquired or assumed the liabilities of Mutual. However, I consider that, at the pleadings stage, it is inappropriate to strike the action, even in the face of the apparent imperfections in the pleading." And in *Western Canadian Place Ltd. v. Con-Force Products Ltd.*,[63] McMahon J. also agreed that the matter was still an open issue in Canadian law. McMahon J. also appeared to offer an indication of what evidence might support a finding of successor liability:

> [¶ 53] The evidence on this application raises a genuine issue to be tried on the successor issue. Companies in the PCL Group were staffed from others. Many of the same personnel were involved in more than one PCL Group company. Some of the documents trade on good will dating back to 1906. Letters written to Western were answered on Management letterhead. Management referred to the contract, contractual liability and sub-

---

60 *Ibid.* at para. 52.
61 [2000] B.C.J. No. 931 (S.C.).
62 [1994] O.J. No. 1953 (Gen. Div.).
63 [1997] A.J. No. 1299 (Q.B.) [hereinafter *Western Canadian Place*].

trades as "ours." Paul Best in particular, sent letters on both Western and Management letterhead ...

[¶ 54] Given these facts and the undeveloped state of Canadian law of successor liability, there is a genuine issue for trial as to whether Management is the successor of 18127.

Suncor, it must be noted, was indirectly criticized in *obiter* by White J. in *E.D.L.P. v. Children's Aid Society of Metropolitan Toronto*.[64] In that case, White J. stated that *Ramirez*, cited in *Suncor*, "is not followed in many American courts, indeed in most American Courts."[65] White J. granted leave for the defendant to appeal the trial judge's decision to the Divisional Court; however, the appeal apparently was never heard.

6) Does U.S.-Style "Successor Liability" Have a Place in Canadian Tort Law?

a) Successor Liability in a Fault-Based System

It is possible that successor liability in the United States is simply an aspect of that country's so-called "strict liability" analysis in defective products cases, an analysis explicitly rejected by Canadian courts. This argument holds that the Canadian position preserves a "fault" analysis from normal negligence law, and successor liability is outside this paradigm: the successor breached no duty to the victim. Strict liability, on the other hand, finds its sources in economic analysis and overall justice. It reduces the issue to a simpler question: as between an innocent tort victim and the party who profits from the defective product, who should pay for the harm?

But there is room to argue that successor liability does not spring from, and should not be dependent upon, a "strict liability" analysis. In order to harmonize North American law on this point, however, Canadian courts may need to take a small step away from a strictly "fault-based" system of product liability.

One way to do this would be to focus on what is actually happening at the point of asset sale. If we ask whether a person's "fault" should follow

---

64 [1995] O.J. No. 3814 (Gen. Div.).
65 White J.'s analysis is representative of the problems Canadian courts are having in citing *Ramirez* as representative of the mainstream of U.S. law on successor liability. It must be remembered that *Ramirez* is a "product line liability" case, not simply a successor liability case; the fact that it is still controversial on that point does not undermine the essential fact that successor liability is well entrenched in U.S. product liability law.

along with a "thing," the answer is clearly no. However, if we ask ourselves instead whether "contingent liabilities" should flow, that is less clear. If a person buys all or substantially all of the assets of a business and intends to carry on essentially the same business, a substantial portion of the assets is "goodwill." This is an ethereal thing that is nonetheless recognized as sufficiently substantial so as to have a legal existence and high monetary value.

But the "goodwill" of a company is also "contingent." It is assumed that patrons of the product will continue to buy the product or patronize the business because of how pleased they have been with it prior to the transfer of assets; the successor company will thus reap the benefit of the predecessor's beneficial activities. This "contingent benefit" has a value at the time of purchase; for instance, the value of a trademark (clearly an asset) consists almost entirely of the goodwill attached to it.

Is it any less reasonable, then, to imagine that if one patron does not continue to buy the product, and is in fact harmed by it, then the "contingent benefit" of goodwill will be discounted to the amount of the "contingent liability" or, if you will, the *bad*will that follows the asset transfer? Clearly, the goodwill is diminished if a product turns out to be less useful than it was originally thought, or if consumers' fickle tastes shift elsewhere. Why should the goodwill *not* be diminished if the product turns out to be dangerous?[66]

Contract theorists might retort that the goodwill of a company truly is its property, whereas tort liability is something different; it involves a relationship with, or potential debt to, a third party, a tort victim. And yet courts have always upheld the principle that a company *could* transfer contingent liabilities to its successor, if the successor agreed. But what kind of system is that, when viewed from the position of the tort victim? The right to recovery in this system must depend on the altruism of the purchasing corporation, in a situation where there is no possible benefit to the successor corporation in assuming the liability. There is no policy reason for a rule that a successor may contract to gain contingent benefits in the form of the goodwill of a manufacturing operation while contracting *out* of contingent liabilities.

The only system that will offer any measure of fairness to vendor, purchaser, *and* tort victim is one patterned along the American model; contingent tort liabilities must, under limited circumstances, flow with the goodwill of the business; the value of the business assets thus ought to be

---

66 The intriguing idea that companies might be prevented from "rebranding" themselves to disassociate from past misbehaviour was explored in a recent Harvard Law Review Note: see "Badwill" (2003) 116 Harv. L. Rev. 1845.

discounted, not in the final analysis by an amount equivalent to any possible liability, but rather by one equivalent to a nominal insurance rate.

Much is made of the difference between Canadian and U.S product liability law, in particular the reluctance of Canadian courts to adopt the "strict liability" model favoured in the United States. Without the necessity of fault-finding, it is perhaps easier to impose liability on successors than it would be under an "at-fault" system such as Canada's.

b) Pleading Successor Liability in Canadian Courts

So what must a Canadian plaintiff plead in order to preserve a successorship allegation against challenge at a preliminary stage? Most of the cases do not discuss the sufficiency of the pleadings, but it appears that the standards of pleading are not difficult to meet. Some U.S. cases even suggest that successorship may be pleaded impliedly,[67] though it should be pointed out that naming the predecessor as a co-defendant may be viewed as fundamentally incompatible with any implied claim of successorship.

It may serve to note that the pleadings with respect to successorship, which were declared by the court worthy of emulation in *Western Canadian Place*,[68] said simply:

> The Defendants, 18127 Alberta Limited formerly known as PCL Construction Ltd. *and its successor or assign*, PCL Construction Management Inc. ("PCL") are corporations carrying on business in Calgary and elsewhere that at all material times, were or represented that they were highly experienced in the construction of concrete high-rise buildings and structures. [Emphasis added.][69]

It is also worthwhile noting that in *Western Canadian Place*, as in *Suncor*, allegations of agency, alter ego, and so on, were found to be *not* sufficient to support an argument of successor liability proceeding to trial. In *Suncor*, as in *Western Canadian Place*, the deficient plaintiff was given leave to amend to include specific allegations of successorship.

---

67 See, for instance, *Arch v. American Tobacco Company*, 175 F.R.D. 469 (E.D. Pa. 1997), where Newcomer J. considered but dismissed the plaintiff's "implied theory of corporate successor liability."
68 *Supra* note 63 at para. 67.
69 *Ibid.* at para. 8.

F. ENTERPRISE LIABILITY

1) Introduction

Enterprise liability is another term with a variety of meanings. It is occasionally used to describe no-fault insurance programs and strict liability schemes for inherently dangerous behaviour. However, we are not concerned in this book with any sort of "behaviour-specific liability" scheme. Rather, the term "enterprise liability" here represents the legal principle underlying the imposition of liability on groups of corporations (generally within the same ownership "family") on the basis that they are in fact a single "enterprise."

An "enterprise" might be sufficiently described for our purposes as the "constituent parts ... functioning as an integral part of a united endeavour."[70] Enterprise liability, then, is an attempt to assign liability to the entire responsible organization — not so much to pierce the corporate veil as to set it aside entirely and view the reality of the interaction of the various "constituent parts."

The academic literature supports the preservation of limited liability for passive individual shareholders, but it also favours an exception to the principle in the case of related companies that own or control the wrongdoer. For example, Leebron states: "With regard to integrated subsidiaries, there is little reason to respect the separate corporate entities when non-contractual tort claimants are involved."[71]

As we have discussed, the literature is nearly unanimous that the policy arguments in favour of limited liability between corporate entities and their voluntary commercial creditors do not apply to involuntary tort creditors.[72] Contract creditors know in advance that they are dealing with a limited liability company, voluntarily accept this risk, and take steps to protect themselves (personal guarantees) or demand *ex ante* compensation (a higher rate of return). Involuntary creditors, such as tort victims, have no choice in the matter. As between a major commercial beneficiary of a hazardous industry and involuntary creditors such as tort victims and the government as health insurer, it is reasonable and just that entities that have benefited financially from wrongdoing should bear the risk of loss.

---

70 See Phillip I. Blumberg, *The Law of Corporate Groups: Bankruptcy Law* § 1.03 at 10 (1985).
71 Leebron, "Limited Liability, Tort Victims and Creditors" (November 1991) 91 Columbia L. Rev. (7) 1565 at 1617.
72 See especially Leebron, *ibid.* Welling, *Corporate Law in Canada: The Governing Principles* (Toronto: Butterworths, 1984) at 146–49. Hansmann, "The Uneasy Case for Limiting Shareholder Liability for Corporate Torts" (1990) U. of T. Law and Economics Workshop Series WS 1990/91-(7).

Indeed, it is with respect to hazardous industries that enterprise tort liability has most successfully been asserted. Easterbrook and Fischel defend such an application on economic principles:

> Courts' greater willingness to allow creditors to reach the assets of corporate as opposed to personal shareholders is again consistent with economic principles.
>
> Allowing creditors to reach the assets of parent corporations does not create unlimited liability for any people. Thus the benefits of diversification, liquidity and monitoring by the capital markets are unaffected. Moreover, the moral hazard problem is probably greater in parent-subsidiary situations because subsidiaries have less incentive to insure ... If limited liability is absolute the parent can form a subsidiary with minimal capitalization for the purpose of engaging in risky activities. If things go well the parent captures the benefits. If things go poorly the subsidiary declares bankruptcy ... This asymmetry between benefits and costs, if limited liability were absolute, would create incentives to engage in a socially excessive amount of risky activities.[73]

The theory of enterprise liability has special appeal (and substantial problems) in the case of multinational corporate groups. Here, an interlocking network of companies, often located in different parts of the world, pursue a common global commercial purpose. Individual corporate members of the group (who may be under-financed and under-insured) may create significant risks to workers and consumers, but the traditional rules of limited liability will prevent recourse against other members of the group. In response to this dilemma some commentators have suggested the need for a new legal regime of "multinational enterprise liability." The liability of the parent corporation would be based upon the proposition that the web of companies under the financial control of the multinational are part of a single economic group with common objectives. Just as the parent corporation maintains control over the group, so must it maintain financial responsibility for its various endeavours.[74]

---

73 Easterbrook and Fischel, "Limited Liability and the Corporation" (1985) 52 University of Chicago Law Review 89 at 110–11.
74 See J.L. Westbrook, "Theories of Parent Company Liability and the Prospects for an International Settlement" (1985) 20 Texas Int'l L.J. 321; D. Aronofsky, "Piercing the Transnational Corporate Veil: Trends, Developments and the Need for Widespread Adoption of Enterprise Analysis" (1985) 10 N.C.J. Int'l L. and Com. Reg. 31; Haddon, Forbes and Simmonds, Canadian Business Organizations Law (1984) 639–52.

K. Hofstetter dismisses some attempts by host countries to abolish limited liability as "fraud and opportunism."[75] Nevertheless, Hofstetter argues that an exception to limited liability can be justified in the case of multinational corporate groups. Referring to the fact that limited liability is justified primarily as between individual shareholders and voluntary creditors, he suggests that when the paradigm is changed, it may not be justified as between corporate parents and involuntary creditors:

> Because a parent company is significantly more aware of the risks stemming from its subsidiaries activities it is a better monitor of such risks; it also tends to be less risk averse than an individual shareholder ... Likewise, an individual tort creditor having no contractual relations with a corporation will tend to be a poorer monitor of the corporation than a bank creditor.[76]

The principal barrier to such a multijurisdictional application of enterprise liability is, of course, the current constitutional requirement that, in order to establish jurisdiction the plaintiff must show that the defendant has a "real and substantial connection" with either the forum or the action.[77] While this does not preclude naming an absent parent as a defendant, until and unless the courts accept simple shareholding as constituting such a connection, the parent's involvement in the wrong must rise to the level of being otherwise actionable (i.e., through agency, conspiracy, direction and control, etc.). Because the jurisprudence in this area is evolving so rapidly, such developments are impossible to predict. Yet, needless to say, if a jurisdiction embraces the theory of enterprise liability, a failure to extend it to offshore corporations may render the courts impotent to provide redress.

There is some suggestion that the extraterritorial extension of enterprise liability is not impermissible. The United States Supreme Court has addressed a similar issue in *Pinney v. Nelson*[78] and *Thomas v. Matthiessen*,[79] in the context of the American constitution. California's law, which at that time held that out-of-state corporations (and thus their foreign directors and shareholders) were subject in California to that state's *unlimited* liability laws, was held valid and judgments under it were held to be enforceable against out-of-state corporations in their home states. However, such a prin-

---

75 Karl Hofstetter, "Multinational Enterprise Parent Liability: Efficient Legal Regimes in a World Market Environment" (1990) N.C.J. Int'l L. Com. Reg. 299.
76 *Ibid.* at 307.
77 This requirement is discussed further in chapter 9, *infra*.
78 183 U.S. 144 (1901) [hereinafter *Pinney*].
79 232 U.S. 221 (1914).

ciple appears to be in conflict with the basic choice of law rule that corporate liability rules are governed by the place of incorporation alone, rendering enforcement in truly international cases considerably more difficult.[80]

Moreover, a recent decision of the B.C. Supreme Court, *JTI-Macdonald Corp. v. British Columbia (Attorney General)*,[81] considered a statutory enterprise liability scheme contained within British Columbia's *Tobacco Damages and Health Care Costs Recovery Act* and found it unconstitutionally extraterritorial because, *inter alia*, of its impact on foreign affiliates without sufficient "connection" to the province.[82]

2) Jurisprudence

When the *Amoco Cadiz* spilled oil in the English Channel, the District Court found the parent company directly liable, but, in the alternative, held that the parent should be liable on enterprise principles":[83] "As an integrated multinational corporation which is engaged through a system of subsidiaries in the exploration, production, refining, transportation and sale of petroleum products throughout the world, Standard is responsible for the tortious acts of its wholly owned subsidiaries and instrumentalities [directly involved in the oil spill]."

---

80   As it turns out, one of the "California cases" ended up in England, with the Court of Appeal asked to decide whether one Mr. Furness, a major shareholder in Copper King Ltd. (a limited-liability U.K. company), could be held to account for Copper King's debts to a California company because of California's unlimited liability rules. The case is reported as *Risdon Iron and Locomotive Works v. Furness* (1906), 1 K.B. 49 (C.A.). The Court of Appeal said no, apparently distinguishing *Pinney* on the basis that the English shareholders, unlike the Americans in *Pinney* who had established their company for the purpose of doing business in California, could not have foreseen that they would be held liable in California law. Whether such an analysis would hold in Canada in the wake of *Morguard* and its progeny is less than clear.
81   (2000), 74 B.C.L.R. (3d) 149 (S.C.).
82   After the decision in *JTI-Macdonald, ibid.*, the legislature re-enacted the *TDHCCRA* without the enterprise liability provisions (*Tobacco Damages and Health Care Costs Recovery Act*, S.B.C. 2000 c. 30). In a subsequent decision (*British Columbia v. Imperial Tobacco Canada Limited*, 2003 BCSC 877), Holmes J. again found the Act extraterritorially impermissible, but this decision was reversed by a unanimous Court of Appeal: *British Columbia v. Imperial Tobacco Canada Ltd.*, 2004 BCCA 269. The effect of the upholding of the subsequent Act on Holmes J.'s first decision is uncertain. Arguably, if inclusion of foreign defendants on an "enterprise liability" basis is the dominant purpose of legislation, it will fail, but not if their inclusion is "necessarily incidental" to legislation properly focused on harms within a province. The authors were counsel for and consultant to the Province in the above actions.
83   *Re Oil Spill by the "Amoco Cadiz" off the Coast of France on Mar. 16, 1978*, 1984 A.M.C. 2123 (N.D. Ill. 1984) (finding No. 43), aff'd 954 F.2d 1279 (7th Cir. 1992).

The courts of several other states, such as Louisiana and North Carolina, have likewise introduced enterprise principles into their jurisprudence (including tort law) where a "single business enterprise" was involved, according to Blumberg.[84] Several other examples of court-made enterprise law are cited by Claudia M. Pardinas, legal counsel to the World Bank.[85] Pardinas also points out that the *United Nations Draft Code of Conduct on Transnational Corporations* applies to

> ... enterprises, irrespective of their country of origin and their ownership ... comprising entities in two or more countries, regardless of the legal form and fields of activity of these entities, which operate under a system of decision-making centres, in which the entities are so linked, by ownership or otherwise, that one or more of them may be able to exercise a significant influence over the activities of others and, in particular, to share knowledge, resources and responsibilities with the others.[86]

The following passage from Blumberg (at 198–99) is worth quoting at length before we leave the jurisprudence and turn to statute law:

> ... [I]n an impressive number of cases, particularly in antitrust and tort matters, an increasing number of American courts are permitting American plaintiffs to sue foreign parent or affiliated corporations in American courts, although the activities of its domestic subsidiary or affiliate and their collective participation in an integrated business are the only link to the forum.
>
> Some of these decisions rest on traditional "piercing the veil jurisprudence"; many others rest essentially on enterprise principles ... [such as] ... the nature [and] extent of the parent's exercise of control; the extent of group economic integration, financial and administrative interdependence, and employee assignment, training, and benefit programs; and the use of a common group persona. Where the parent's exercise of control extends to the day-by-day decision making process of the subsidiary, that feature will generally lead to assertion of jurisdiction, even by courts otherwise wedded to entity law.
>
> The tort cases involving product liability represent the furthest advance of assertion of American jurisdiction over foreign components of multinational groups. In product liability cases, courts, under the "stream of com-

---

84 Blumberg, *supra* note 6 at 334–35.
85 Claudia M. Pardinas, "The Enigma of the Legal Liability of Transnational Corporations" (1991) 14 Suffolk Transnational L.J. 405.
86 *Ibid.* at 441.

merce" doctrine, are increasingly asserting jurisdiction over foreign manufacturers or distributors .... In some cases ..., courts also rely on enterprise concepts to provide further support for their conclusions. The activities of a local subsidiary, particularly if integrated with the foreign parent's business where it serves as a local distributor or provides warranty service, provide a further basis for supporting such assertion of jurisdiction.

In this area, where the United States is the host country, there is thus a widespread use of enterprise principles to subject foreign components of multinational groups to American law. This action, however, does not seem to have created any significant disincentive to foreign trade or investment. The advantages for foreign multinational groups of participating in the enormous market opportunities provided by the United States not surprisingly seem to outweigh this exposure to American judicial process and possible ultimate liability.[87]

3) Statutes

The judiciary has been, as might be expected, very cautious towards undermining the principles of limited liability without some specific direction from the legislature. As a result, some governments began to impose enterprise liability by what Blumberg terms "statutes of specific application." He describes them thus:

> In other regulatory statutes, Congress has responded in a more sophisticated manner to the limitations of entity law and has specifically attempted to transcend its limitations. Such statutes are expressly made applicable not only to corporations conducting the activity being regulated, but also to other corporations in the groups of which the corporations in question are components.[88]

Blumberg identifies two types of legislation. The first is termed "pervasive statutes," which are concerned with regulating the activities of the group itself. Examples given include the *Bank Holding Company Act*, the *Savings and Loan Holding Company Act*, and the *Public Utility Holding Company Act*. The second group includes statutes that rely on standard entity law for most of their provisions but use enterprise principles for selected objectives. Blumberg cites statutes regulating railroads and trucking, air transportation, shipping, communications, and securities. Blumberg notes that these statutes "... are not concerned with group affairs, except in a number of

---

87 Blumberg, *supra* note 70 at 198–99.
88 *Ibid.* at 104.

selected areas in which regulation of the activities of the regulated company are expressly made applicable to other companies within the group as well."

There have been, at this point, only limited attempts at extending tort liability through statute to "innocent" members of corporate groups. For a period, the "superfund" legislation in the United States, CERCLA, was thought to incorporate enterprise principles in its definition of "operator"; however, the U.S. Supreme Court in *United States v. Bestfoods*,[89] while apparently considering it within the power of Congress to do so, held that Congress would have to make this provision explicit. On the subject of judicial recognition that Congress retains the power to impose enterprise liability, consider also Brandeis J.'s statement in *Cannon Mfg. Co. v. Cudahy Packing Co.*,[90] finding the corporate veil protected a foreign parent:

> Congress has not provided that a corporation of one state shall be amenable to suit in the federal court for another state in which the plaintiff resides, whenever it employs a subsidiary corporation as the instrumentality for doing business therein. ... In the case at bar, the identity of interest may have been more complete and the exercise of control over the subsidiary more intimate than in the three cases cited, but that fact has, in the absence of an applicable statute, no legal significance.

Likewise, of course, the unlimited liability laws of California at the beginning of the century (and discussed above) can be seen as "enterprise liability" statutes for tort purposes as well as contract, at least with respect to their application to members of corporate groups, as opposed to companies owned by human shareholders.

---

89 524 U.S. 51 (1998).
90 267 U.S. 333 (1925) at 336–37.

Part Three:
The Law of Aggregate Claims

7. Class Proceedings

A. INTRODUCTION

A class proceeding[1] is a lawsuit brought by one or more individuals (the "class representatives") on behalf of a group of persons similarly situated ("the class") to assert a common claim against the same defendant or group of defendants.[2] At the time of this writing, three Canadian jurisdictions have fairly advanced jurisprudence under comprehensive class action statutes: Quebec,[3] Ontario,[4] and British Columbia.[5] Of these three, Quebec's law is the oldest, originating in 1978, but the class proceeding

---

1   Canadian class actions statutes (with the exception of Saskatchewan's) prefer the term "class proceeding" to "class action," so as to emphasize that claims may be aggregated whether they are commenced as lawsuits or applications. Throughout this book we use the terms "class action" and "class proceeding" interchangeably.
2   Here we deal only with plaintiffs' class actions.
3   The Quebec law is found in *Code de Procédure Civile*, 1978, c. 8, Book IX and the *Code civil du Québec*, 1991 c. 64, ss. 2848, 2897, and 2908. Unless otherwise specified, all references herein are to the *Code de Procédure Civile* [hereinafter *Quebec Act*; section references denoted by Quebec art. __; reference to the *Code civil* will be cited as *Civil Code* s. __].
4   *Class Proceedings Act 1992*, S.O. 1992, c. 6 [hereinafter *Ontario Act*; section references denoted by Ontario s. __].
5   *Class Proceedings Act*, R.S.B.C. 1996, c. 50 [hereinafter *B.C. Act*; section references denoted by B.C. s. __].

remained under-utilized[6] until Ontario followed in 1992 and British Columbia in 1995. Recently, Saskatchewan,[7] Newfoundland,[8] Alberta,[9] and Manitoba[10] have passed similar legislation, joining other Commonwealth jurisdictions with formal class action regimes.[11] The various statutes have many features to facilitate recovery by plaintiff groups. For instance, they allow for the participation of subclasses and even individuals with divergent interests or issues,[12] as well as for the introduction of statistical evidence otherwise barred.[13] A province might provide financial assistance to plaintiffs[14] or otherwise modify the law of costs to reduce risk to plaintiffs.[15] A common feature of class actions is the extension of limitation periods so that potential class members' claims are not prejudiced between filing and certification.[16]

---

6   In fact, the filings of class actions in Quebec by 1987 represented only .04 percent of civil claims, 1/25th of the anticipated number: W.A. Bogart, "Questioning Litigation's Role — Courts and Class Actions in Canada" (1987) 62 Ind. L.J. 665 at 689–90. Ward Branch reports only 233 applications for certification in Quebec between 1984 and 1998, or an average of just over one per month: Ward Branch, *Class Actions in Canada* (Toronto: Canada Law Book, looseleaf) § 4.1950.
7   *Class Actions Act*, S.S. 2001, c. C-12.01 (came into force 1 January 2002).
8   *Class Actions Act*, S.N. 2001, c. C-18.1 (came into force 1 April 2002).
9   *Class Proceedings Act*, S.A. 2003, c. C-16.6.
10 *Class Proceedings Act*, C.C.S.M., c. C.130.
11 See, for instance, Part IVA of the *Federal Court of Australia Act 1976* (the representative proceedings provisions date from 1991 amendments); in England reform has taken the shape of the Group Litigation Order (GLO) rules, enacted as *Civil Procedure Rules 1998* (U.K.) Rules 19.10–19.15, Practice Direction 19B — Group Litigation. The GLO rules came into force in 2000.
12 Ontario ss. 6, 25; B.C. ss. 6, 27, 28; Quebec arts. 1022, 1037.
13 Ontario s. 23; B.C. s. 30.
14 Ontario *Law Society Act*, S.O. s. 59.1.
15 B.C. s. 37. Although there is no statutory presumption against costs in Quebec or Ontario, courts in the latter province at least have been reluctant to award them if the proceedings have been "reasonably pursued": Michael A. Eizenga, Michael J. Peerless, & Charles M. Wright, *Class Actions Law and Practice* (Toronto, Butterworths, 1999) at § 12.4–12.5. There is some suggestion that this may be changing: *Pearson v. Inco Ltd.*, 2002 Ont. Sup. C.J. LEXIS 104 (award of costs against the plaintiff in three pre-certification motions apparently without applying rules that differed from ordinary individual actions).
16 Ontario s. 28; B.C. s. 39. There is a difference, however, in what happens should a class proceeding fail certification. In Ontario, the limitation period resumes on final denial of certification. In British Columbia, the courts have interpreted virtually identical provisions to resume *retroactively* the running of the limitation period. Thus, in B.C., plaintiffs who would, in absence of a class proceeding, wish to proceed individually must file their myriad suits while awaiting certification. See Eizenga et al., *ibid.* at §§ 6.1–6.7.

The fact that, prior to 2002, only three provinces had in force class action statutes demonstrates that this type of litigation was not universally welcomed, being seen by some as an "Americanization" of Canada's more civilized litigative environment.[17] Particularly in Canada, where defendants usually enjoy the protection of being able to recover part of their costs if they prevail, there has been a serious concern that legislation must be drafted and applied in such a way as to continue to discourage frivolous suits. To do otherwise, defence counsel fear, may lead to a climate of "artificial" or "nuisance" settlements and an increasingly litigious business environment.[18]

No aspect of class actions in the United States has led to as much controversy, vacillation, and hand-wringing as the suitability of the aggregate device for handling mass-catastrophic tort claims. It is interesting to observe, then, that Canadian class proceedings statutes appear to have been actually drafted with such actions in mind. Consider the description provided by the Ontario Court of Appeal in the recent decision of *Carom v. Bre-X*:

> Disasters spawn litigation. Trains collide or derail, planes crash, ships sink, lakes and rivers become polluted, chemical factories explode, ordinary people eat, drink, wear or use unhealthy or defective products. People — sometimes hundreds, even thousands — are injured or killed by these events. When the crisis subsides, some of the victims turn to the courts for redress and compensation.
>
> One of the modern mechanisms for dealing with the litigation fallout from major disasters is the class action ...[19]

---

17 See, for instance, Derek J. Mullan, QC and Neo J. Tuytel, "The British Columbia Class Proceedings Act: Will it Open the Floodgates?" (1996) 14 Can. J. Ins. L. 30; P. Iacano, "Class Actions and Product Liability in Ontario: What Will Happen?" (1991–92) 13 C.I.L.R. 99. The litigiousness of Americans might be considerably overstated: when adjusted for population, American court filings are in the same general range as those in Ontario, Australia, England, and Denmark. See Marc Galanter, "Reading the Landscape of Disputes: What We Know and Don't Know (and Think We Know) About Our Allegedly Contentious and Litigious Society" (1983) 31 UCLA L. Rev. 4 at 55. Marc Galanter, "Real World Torts: An Antidote to Anecdote" (1996) 55 Md. L. Rev. 1093 at 1104–6.

18 The Alberta Law Reform Commission's *Report on Class Action Legislation* (Final Report #85, 2000) [hereinafter *Alberta Report*] lists and discusses eight popularly held objections to class actions at 55–63. Most are based on issues raised in Deborah R. Hensler et al., *Class Action Dilemmas: Pursuing Public Goals for Private Gain* (Santa Monica, CA: RAND Institute for Civil Justice, 1999). Hensler's book, incidentally, provides one of the most comprehensive overviews of class action policy in the United States.

19 *Carom v. Bre-X Minerals Ltd.* (1999), 44 O.R. (3d) 173 (S.C.J.). See also the Manitoba Law Reform Commission, *Class Proceedings* (Report #100) (Winnipeg: Manitoba Publi-

The Canadian statutes were drafted to avoid some of the shortcomings of the American approach, and the courts have interpreted them generously. As a result, there is considerable latitude for Canadian class actions to achieve global resolutions of mass tort claims beyond that possible in the United States in light of present jurisprudence.

B. THE PURPOSES OF CLAIMS AGGREGATION

It is repeatedly said that class proceedings legislation is designed to be solely procedural, and not substantive.[20] Even assuming this to be the case, we have emphasized throughout this book that a student of mass tort or product liability law cannot ignore the effect of aggregation on the outcomes of litigation. Indeed, although generally phrased in procedural terms, the principal purpose of aggregate actions remains to influence who can sue whom for what, and, most important, how successfully.

When we speak of mass torts, we are speaking of a situation where diffuse harm results from a decision or series of decisions made centrally, almost always in the course of conducting business or providing government services. Most often, these decisions involve the design and manufacture of a mass-market product, but mass torts also arise from decisions as to the design of processes or systems; thus (in the United States at least), racial discrimination can be a mass tort when it arises from a large employ-

---

cations Branch, 1999) [hereinafter *Manitoba Report*], which synopsized at 17–18 types of litigation that can benefit from claim aggregation:

> Class actions are useful in tort cases for mass disaster claims (claims arising from single incident mass accidents, such as train derailments and environmental disasters) and for creeping disaster claims (claims for bodily injury arising from consumer products, such as tobacco and asbestos, or medical products, such as intra-uterine devices, breast implants, contaminated blood, jaw implants, silver mercury fillings and heart pacemakers). Other uses include "claims of group defamation, nuisance, the principle in *Rylands v. Fletcher* (1868), L.R. 3 H.L. 330, various statutory torts, damages claims for breach of *Charter* rights, claims arising from illegal strikes, negligent house construction, and negligent misstatement."

20 *Ontario New Home Warranty Program v. Chevron Chemical Co.* (1999), 46 O.R. (3d) 130 at para. 50 (S.C.J.) [hereinafter *ONHWP*]:

> ... there is no jurisdiction conferred by the *Class Proceedings Act* to supplement or derogate from the substantive rights of the parties. It is a procedural statute and as such, neither its inherent objects nor its explicit provisions can be given effect in a manner which affects the substantive rights of either plaintiffs or defendants.

See also *Chadha v. Bayer Inc.* (2001), 54 O.R. (3d) 520 at 542 (Div. Ct.).

er's central policies;[21] dangerous working conditions might similarly become the subject of mass tort claims, as could decisions with respect to medical treatment, to the extent that the wrong is centralized and the harm diffuse.[22] Some torts that are inherently individual, like sexual assault, can be mass torts when, for instance, an allegation of supervisory failure or vicarious liability is made. In each case, there is a decision by a central entity the effects of which radiate out and cause or contribute to the harm of others.

In the "traditional" or individualistic legal regime, a tort action may be viewed as connecting the tortfeasor on one hand and its victim on the other. In a mass tort, by comparison, the tortfeasor lies at the hub of the actions that might be seen to radiate from the decisions made at the centre. When we view the matter this way, it is not difficult to see how the economy of scale in a dispute-resolution process will naturally favour the defendant, who can reuse the work involved in the defence of issues common to all the claims. The situation of the numerous plaintiffs is different; they must begin anew with each new case, even on the common issues.[23]

---

21 In Canada, discrimination has not been recognized as a tort, and such cases would usually proceed under the various human rights Acts, which have their own rules regarding aggregated and representative actions. However, it is possible for discrimination claims to proceed as actions for "unjust enrichment"; thus far, Canadian courts appear unwilling to consider class actions appropriate for such claims on grounds of preferability: *Franklin v. University of Toronto* (2001), 56 O.R. (3d) 698 (S.C.J.) (denying certification in claims of alleged systemic discrimination of female employees of university, but allowing case to proceed individually).

22 A notorious example would be the central decisions made with respect to the screening of the blood supply in many countries (including Canada, for blood-borne diseases during the 1980s); less obvious examples might be standard practices negligently adopted by hospitals or, on a larger scale, by medical self-regulatory bodies.

23 This imbalance has existed from the very beginning of mass tort law. Recall that the plaintiff in *Donoghue v. Stevenson*, filing her appeal *in forma pauperis*, was up against a relatively well-off manufacturer of consumer goods, who faced the prospect of numerous similar claims for negligence in bottling his ginger beer and who fought this first "test case" all the way to the Lords: See William McBride, "The Story of the Snail in the Bottle Case" in Peter Burns ed., *Donoghue v. Stevenson and the Modern Law of Negligence: The Paisley Papers* (Vancouver: Continuing Legal Education Society of B.C., 1991) at 25. Obviously, the litigative power of Mr. Stevenson's sole proprietorship is in turn dwarfed by that of modern consumer-goods firms.

Another central feature of numerosity of tort claims can also be traced to Ms. Donoghue's experience; the first party to file the claim faces the additional indignity of knowing that there are numerous others who will "free-ride" upon it by taking advantage of the legal work product (including perhaps the decision itself) and — to the extent that it becomes part of the public record — the discovery information paid for by the trailblazer in prosecuting their own claims.

This dichotomy is at the heart of mass tort — the defendant has mass-produced the wrong; the plaintiffs suffer the harm and bear the costs individually. This "structural asymmetry"[24] — it has been called a systemic bias in favour of defendants[25] — carries through from the manufacture of the product to the final resolution of the dispute, with the result that the plaintiffs are placed at a considerable disadvantage.[26]

It is also not difficult to foresee the results of structural asymmetry in the individual litigation of mass tort claims. Mass tort defendants will tend to overspend on litigation in individual suits because their economy of scale permits them to invest in each initial claim an amount far greater than the claim is worth;[27] this strategy makes success more likely in the early suits, compounding the advantage in the aggregate.[28] Faced with such unequal litigative power, suits are discouraged or settled for too little, and confidentiality agreements exacted by defendants at the time of settlement may preclude "free riders" from taking full advantage of the work that has been done before,[29] while the defendant is free to do so.

---

24 "Developments — The Paths of Civil Litigation" (2000) 113 Harv. L. Rev. 1752 [hereinafter "Developments"] at 1834.

25 David Rosenberg, "Mass Tort Class Actions — What the Defendants Have and Plaintiffs Don't" (2000) 37 Harv. J. Legis. 393 [hereinafter Rosenberg, "What the Defendants Have"].

26 *Blue Cross & Blue Shield of N.J., Inc. v. Philip Morris, Inc.*, 133 F. Supp. 2d 162 at 177 (E.Dist. N.Y. 2001) *per* Weinstein J. ("standard case-by-case adjudication of mass tort claims not only may deny litigation efficiencies to plaintiffs, but may afford large litigation advantages to defendants.")

27 R.J. Reynolds general counsel J. Michael Jordan described such a strategy to his fellow tobacco industry lawyers in 1988: "[t]he aggressive posture we have taken regarding depositions and discovery in general continues to make these cases extremely burdensome and expensive for plaintiffs' lawyers. ... To paraphrase General Patton, the way we won these cases was not by spending all of [R.J. Reynold's] money, but by making the other son of a bitch spend all of his." Quoted in *Haines v. Liggett Group Inc.*, 814 F. Supp. 414 at 421 (D.N.J. 1993).

28 *Ibid.* For a fuller discussion of this phenomenon, see Sally Moeller, "Class Auctions: Market Models for Attorney's Fees in Class Action Litigation" (2000) 113 Harv. L. Rev. 1827 at 1833. Moeller outlines the problem of overinvestment thus:

> Commentators customarily explain heavy spending by defendants on litigation as an attempt to overwhelm and intimidate individual plaintiffs or as a consequence of risk aversion with regard to the precedential impact of the judgment in an individual suit. Such motives aside, the most compelling reason for defendants to spend more than individual plaintiffs is that the full amount of their expected risk exceeds the individual claim.

29 Such "secret settlements" prevent disclosure of the nature of the claim, the information obtained during discovery, and the terms of settlement. See *Seattle Times Co. v. Rhinehart*, 104 S. Ct. 2199 (1984); David Rosenberg, "The Dusting of America: A

Practically speaking, the plaintiffs' bar will attempt to compensate for this inequality through a variety of aggregative strategies to achieve some kind of economy of scale. Lawyers will begin to specialize in suits regarding a particular defendant, product, or event, allowing fixed costs (expert reports, legal and factual research, etc.) to be spread across the lawyer's "inventory" of similarly situated plaintiffs — thus the emergence in the United States during the 1990s of "asbestos lawyers," "tobacco lawyers," and so on.[30] Moreover, lawyers and firms will enter into (more or less formal) cooperative agreements, which may run the gamut from co-counsel arrangements to "clearing-house" systems whereby legal or factual information regarding a mass tort is pooled and accessed at a much reduced fee.[31]

These alternative methods of claims aggregation, however, suffer from serious structural setbacks that allow them only marginal advantages over unconnected individual claims. Unless the cooperation among plaintiffs can reach the level of cooperation found within the defendant firm, the fundamental structural advantage to the defendant remains. Moreover, the existence "in the wings" of non-cooperating plaintiffs may lead to "free riding" on initial claims,[32] further discouraging meaningful economies of scale by discouraging cooperation among plaintiffs. Rosenberg and Fried explain the inefficiencies of informal cooperation in a recent book:

> The tort system is increasingly characterized by large-scale, corporately structured organizations comprised of plaintiffs' lawyers, specialists in claim-finding and investigation, and allied experts in an array of disciplines that exploit scale economies by preparing multiple business-related

---

Story of Asbestos — Carnage, Cover-up, and Litigation" (Book Review) (1986) 99 Harv. L. Rev. 1693 at 1701.

30 John C. Coffee, Jr, "Class Wars: The Dilemma of the Mass Tort Class Action" (1995) 95 Colum. L. Rev. 1343 [hereinafter Coffee, "Class Wars"] at 1358–59.

31 See generally Howard M. Erichson, "Informal Aggregation: Procedural and Ethical Implications of Coordination among Counsel in Related Lawsuits" (2000) 50 Duke L.J. 381; See also Eizenga et al., supra note 15 at § 2.5 (describing the Australian experience with group litigation strategies). For a criticism of the "litigation network" approach, see John C. Coffee, "Rescuing the Private Attorney General: Why the Model of the Lawyer as Bounty Hunter Is Not Working" (1983) 42 MD. L. Rev. 215 at 239–41, nn. 56–57.

32 "Free riding" is possible because a litigation in the ordinary course generates a significant amount of publicly available information regarding the common issues. Factual information gained through discovery or trial, legal research, and arguments all represent expensive investments by plaintiff's counsel, and each may be obtained for only token cost by a "free rider" who wishes to exploit the investor's work product, provided that the case proceeds to hearing or trial.

claims en masse. Although these organizations compete for market share and financial backing, they may share information and align litigation strategy to some degree. Yet collective action problems persist to prevent cost-effective information investment in maximizing aggregate net recovery of tort damages and hence aggregate deterrence benefit from tort litigation. In particular, the combination of high costs of organizing and monitoring collaboration compounded by agency problems and strong incentives for free-riding, to preclude plaintiffs' attorneys from efficiently achieving the maximum scale economies required for deterrence purposes.[33]

For these reasons, mass tort theorists increasingly accept that a fundamental — some say the *only* fundamental — reason for aggregating litigation is to redress the imbalance between mass tort defendants and plaintiffs, to "level the playing field" so that plaintiffs can enjoy the economies of scale that defendants have always exploited, and thereby increase their recovery.[34]

Assuming for the moment that aggregation of claims into a single "global action" advances the policy objectives of tort law (and in particular the related objectives of compensation and deterrence) in a mass tort setting, decisions remain to be made regarding the most effective way to combine them. Certainly, governments can and have enacted particular legislation to deal with some widespread injuries; this generally takes the form of an insurance scheme (formal or informal) for the victims coupled with a mechanism by which to recoup the costs of the insurance from the perceived wrongdoers. Workers' compensation laws can be viewed in this context[35] but are not necessarily related to *mass* torts; perhaps more focused examples would be the black lung[36] and childhood vaccination[37] statutes in the United States or the tobacco-related health-care costs-recovery schemes

---

33 Charles Fried & David Rosenberg, *Making Tort Law: What Should Be Done and Who Should Do It* (Washington, D.C.: American Enterprise Institute, 2003) at 90.
34 See Bruce Hay & David Rosenberg, "Sweetheart" and "Blackmail" Settlements in Class Actions: Reality and Remedy" (2000) 75 Notre Dame L. Rev. 1377 at 1383 (arguing that the elimination of wasteful redundancy is a goal secondary to increasing plaintiff recovery through exploitation of economies of scale).
35 Most schemes involve a mandatory (and generally exclusive) insurance plan to benefit injured workers, while assessing premiums from employers based on the nature of their industry, its aggregate injury record, and their individual claims history.
36 See *Black Lung Benefits Act of 1972*, 30 U.S.C. §§ 901 *et seq.*, discussed in *Usery v. Turner Elkhorn Mining Co.*, 428 U.S. 1 (1976).
37 *National Childhood Vaccination Injury Act of 1986*, Pub. L. No. 99-660, tit. III, s. 301, 100 Stat. 3755, 3756 (1986) (codified at 42 U.S.C. 300aa (1986).

of British Columbia[38] and Newfoundland.[39] Extreme and fundamental changes to tort law are also not unknown; the American *Drug Dealer's Liability Act* has been adopted in numerous U.S. jurisdictions[40] and assigns civil liability to drug dealers for all drug-related harm within the area deemed to be their "market," bypassing requirements for any showing of causation.

Other devices available to plaintiffs are voluntary joinder and test cases; the former, however, is impractical for classes over an easily manageable size, and the latter are plagued by problems of application (i.e., issue estoppel and *res judicata*). Equitable aggregation, long accepted in Anglo-American jurisprudence, is another option.

Such devices, though, are generally limited to particular types of harm and lack the fluid responsiveness of the tort litigation "marketplace." Moreover, mass tort judgments — or more often settlements — are more meticulously drafted, often over a period of years, by the very stakeholders in the dispute; it can be expected that they will be substantially more nuanced than legislation arrived at through political compromise, and indeed experience has borne this out.[41]

---

38 *Tobacco Damages and Health Care Costs Recovery Act*, S.B.C. 2000, c. 30.
39 *Tobacco Health Care Costs Recovery Act*, S. Nfld. & Lab. 2001, c. T-4.2.
40 Arkansas: *Drug Dealer Liability Act*, 1995 Ark. Acts No. 896 (codified at Ark. Code Ann. "16-124-101 to -112 (Michie Supp. 1997)); California: *Drug Dealer Liability Act*, 1996 Cal. Legis. Serv. 3792 (West) (codified at Cal. Health & Safety Code "11700 to 11717 (West Supp. 1998)); Colorado: Colo. Rev. Stat. 13-21-801 to 813; Georgia: *Drug Dealer Liability Act*, 1997 Ga. Laws 387 (codified at O.C.G.A. "51-1-46 (Supp. 1998)); Hawaii: *Drug Dealer Liability Act*, 1995 Haw. Sess. Laws ch. 203 (codified at Haw. Rev. Stat. Ann. '663D (Mich. Supp. 1997)); Illinois: *Drug Dealer Liability Act*, 1995 Ill. Leg. Serv. 89-293 (West) (codified at 740 Ill. Comp. Stat. Ann. 57/1-25 (West Supp. 1997)); Indiana: *Drug Dealer Liability Act*, 1997 Ind. Acts 2924 (codified at Ind. Code Ann. '34-1-70 (Michie Supp. 1998) (repealed by 1998 Ind. Acts. 8 (effective 1 July 1998)); Louisiana: *Louisiana Drug Dealer Liability Act*, 1997 La. Sess. Law Serv. 719 (West) (codified at La. Rev. Stat. Ann. " 9:2800.61-.76 (West Supp. 1998)); Michigan: *Drug Dealer Liability Act*, 1994 Mich. Legis. Serv. 27 (West) (codified at Mich. Comp. Laws Ann. " 691.1601-.1619 (West Supp. 1998)); Oklahoma: *Drug Dealer Liability Act*, 1994 Okla. Sess. Law Serv. ch. 179 (West) (codified at Okla. Stat. Ann. tit. 63, "2-421 to -435 (West 1997)); South Carolina: S. Carolina Stat. 44-54-10 to 140; South Dakota: *South Dakota Codified Laws* Sec. 34-20 C-1 *et seq.*; Utah: *Drug Dealer's Liability Act*, 1997 Utah Laws 1991 (codified at Utah Code Ann. "58-37e-1 to -14 (Supp. 1998)); U.S. Virgin Islands: 19 V.I.C. 641 to 658.
41 See generally Peter Schuck, "Mass Torts: An Institutional Evolutionist Perspective" (1995) 80 Cornell L. Rev. 941 [hereinafter Schuck, "Institutional Evolutionist Perspective"] at 985–87. A Canadian example of a comprehensive settlement establishing a *de facto* administrative scheme can be seen in that arising from the tainted blood litigation in Quebec, Ontario, and British Columbia. The terms of the settlement and the reasons for approval are described in the decisions of Smith J. in *Endean v. Canadian*

It is not surprising, then, that the most successful aggregative tool adopted in fault-based liability jurisdictions — the class action lawsuit — was designed sufficiently vaguely to provide a broad segment of society (potential plaintiffs and their lawyers) with some measure of regulatory power, as well as to provide otherwise marginal plaintiffs (i.e., those whose cases might not economically merit individual adjudication) with appropriate compensation.

C. FOUNDATIONS OF CANADIAN CLASS ACTION POLICY

1) Origins of Aggregative Proceedings

a) Common Law, Equity, and the Rules of Court

Prior to the advent of the class action provisions of the U.S. *Federal Rules of Civil Procedure* (discussed below), representative suits were not unknown to Anglo-American courts and had in fact been recognized in various forms for several hundred years.[42] Representative actions developed as an exception to the "necessary parties rule" in equity[43] and also from the "Bill of Peace," an equitable device for combining multiple suits.[44] Though the

---

Red Cross Society (1999), [2000] 1 W.W.R. 688 (B.C.S.C.); the decision of Winkler J. in *Parsons v. Canadian Red Cross Society*, [1999] O.J. No. 3572 (S.C.J.); and the decision of Morneau J. in *Honhon c. Canada (Procureur général)*, [1999] J.Q. no 4370 (S.C.).

42 See generally S.C. Yeazell, *From Medieval Group Litigation to the Modern Class Action* (New Haven, Yale University Press, 1987) [hereinafter Yeazell, *From Medieval to Modern*]; S.C. Yeazell, "Group Litigation and Social Context: Toward a History of the Class Action" (1977) 77 Colum. L. Rev. 866 at 867 and 872; Marcin, "Searching for the Origin of the Class Action" (1973) 23 Cath. U. L. Rev. 515 at 517–524.

43 The "necessary parties" rule in equity mandated that "all persons materially interested, either as plaintiffs or defendants in the subject matter of the bill ought to be made parties to the suit, however numerous they may be.": *West v. Randall*, 29 F. Cas. 718 (CCDRI 1820) *per* Story J. By contrast, an equitable class action could assist where, in the words of an early case, "it would be impracticable to make them all parties by name, and there would be continual abatements by death and otherwise, and no coming at justice, if all were to be parties": *Chancey v. May* (1722), Prec. Ch. 592, 24 E.R. 265 at 265. See generally Hazard, Gedid, & Sowle, "An Historical Analysis of the Binding Effect of Class Suits" (1998) 146 U. Pa. L. Rev. 1849 at 1859–60.

44 A "Bill of Peace" could be maintained where the interested persons were numerous, where they possessed a common interest in the question to be adjudicated, and where the representatives could be expected fairly to advocate the interests of all members of the group: see Charles Alan Wright, Arthur R. Miller, and Mary Kay Kane, *Federal Practice and Procedure*, 2d ed. (St. Paul, Minn.: West Publishing Co., 1986) at § 1751; Zechariah Chafee, Jr, *Some Problems of Equity* (Ann Arbor: University of Michigan Law School, 1950) at 161–67, 200–3.

cases from this early period are not numerous, the Courts of Equity did demonstrate a remarkable flexibility in their utilization of aggregative actions.[45]

The use of the equitable Bill of Peace dates to at least the seventeenth century,[46] when the Courts of Equity in England decided that they could take control over a "multiplicity" of actions where there was a commonality of interest. An early case summarizes the concept:

> So where a bill was brought by some few tenants of Greystock Manor against the lord, to settle the customs of the manor as to fines upon death and alienations; and an issue was directed to be tried at law ... and it was insisted upon, that there being but some of the tenants parties to this bill, the rest would not be bound by this trial: But my Lord Keeper (Sir Nathan Wright) held they would; and he said he remembered the case of Nether Wiersdale, between Lord Gerrard and some few tenants, and Lord Nottingham's case in the Dutchy, concerning the customs of Daintree Manor, for grinding and baking at the lord's mill and bake-house, and said in these and 100 others, all were bound, tho' only a few tenants parties; else where are such numbers, no right could be done, if all must be parties, for there would be perpetual abatements.[47]

Professor Chafee, who in 1932 undertook a systematic review of Bills of Peace as consolidative devices and vehicles for class actions, summarizes the application as follows:

> Each such separate suit sought or would have sought the recovery of money and nothing else — no injunction, specific performance, or other relief outside the competence of a jury and judge sitting at law. No equitable right or title was involved. The only reason for coming into equity was that it could settle in a single suit the common question: — was the maintenance and use of the dam a legal wrong to a lower riparian owner? Was a subscriber to the new stock a shareholder? The alternative to a bill of peace was a large number of actions at law, in each of which this common question might be disputed over and over again by the adversary and

---

45 The Chancery Court in *Wallworth v. Holt* (1841), 4 My. & Cr. 619, 41 E.R. 238 at 244, noted that "it [is] the duty of this Court to adapt its practice and course of proceeding to the existing state of society, and not by too strict an adherence to forms and rules ... to decline to administer justice, and to enforce rights for which there is no other remedy."
46 *How v. Tenants of Bromsgrove* (1681), 1 Vern. 22.
47 *Brown v. Howard* (1701), 1 Eq. Cas. Abr. 163, pl. 4.

the particular member of the multitude concerned. The same witnesses would be repeatedly called, the same arguments repeatedly made, and each successive case must receive fresh consideration by court and jury. The doctrine of *res judicata* would not apply to make the first judgment binding in the later suits.[48]

Unlike the consolidation rule of Lord Mansfield, the Bill of Peace did not require the consent of the parties to be bound by the single "test case."[49] Also, the record reveals that, although Bills of Peace were generally sought by defendants in order to settle multiple actions (or potential actions) against them, they could also be employed by "the multitude" — that is, the numerous plaintiffs. Chafee explains:

> [I]t is sometimes urged that the multitude [i.e., plaintiffs] can not bring a bill of peace ... This argument is fallacious ... the expense and vexation to each member of the multitude will be greatly reduced if he can join with the others in prosecuting or defending one suit in equity, and furthermore, a bill of peace does not lie solely for the benefit of the parties, but also to prevent the waste of judicial time and public money and the delay of other litigation.[50]

There were two prerequisites for a Bill of Peace to be granted. The first required "numerosity" — that a multitude of suits against a defendant be either "pending" or "possible"[51] — and the second that a "commonality of interest" existed across the class. The main controversy over the application of Bills of Peace as they began to be used in the United States in mass tort cases at the end of the nineteenth century concerned the latter. Chafee, citing Pomeroy and numerous cases, concludes that some degree of commonality was always required but that this requirement could be satisfied through the existence of "common question," perhaps coupled with "the kind of relief":[52]

---

48 Zechariah Chafee, Jr, "Bills of Peace with Multiple Parties" (1932) 45 Harv. L. Rev. 1297 at 1299 [hereinafter Chafee].
49 Ibid. at 1300.
50 Ibid. at 1303.
51 Ibid. at 1299–1300.
52 Pomeroy, *Treatise on Equity Jurisprudence* (1881) s. 269, cited in Chafee, *ibid.* at 1313. Pomeroy decries decisions that purported a more restrictive rule:
> This objection has been repeated as though it were conclusive; but like so much of the so-called "legal reasoning" traditional in the courts, it is a mere empty formula of words without any real meaning, because it has no foundation of fact, it is simply untrue; one arbitrary rule is contrived and insisted upon as the reason for

There is no advantage to justice in a requirement that the adversary in an ordinary bill of peace must have a property right. *Multiplicity with respect to common question makes the remedy at law sufficiently inadequate to support equitable jurisdiction.* Any attempt to require a general right of the nature of property is bound to raise difficult questions as to the meaning of the phrase. [Emphasis added.][53]

Perhaps the most useful thing about the Bill of Peace was that it provided not only a remedy, but also jurisdiction, including that over absent parties who could be bound without their consent. This aspect of its use made it controversial in the United States, because it allowed a judge exercising equitable jurisdiction to circumvent the constitutional requirement for a jury trial in high-value civil litigation, in theory to the advantage of defendants.[54]

Chafee's analysis of the Bill of Peace also provides the first justification for the limited fund doctrine:

Joinder in a single suit is especially desirable when the multitude are seeking to divide a fund or a limited liability. Here the usual disadvantages of multiplicity of suits are greatly aggravated. The objection to many separate suits is not merely the vexation and expense to the adversary of trying the same question over and over. In addition there is danger that the aggregate of the separate jury verdicts might exceed the limit of liability, and also it is impossible to make a fair distribution of the fund or limited liability to all members of the multitude except in a single proceeding where the claim of each can be adjudicated with due reference to the claims of the rest. The fund or limited liability is like a mince pie, which can not be satisfactorily divided until the carver counts the number of persons at the table.[55]

---

another equally arbitrary rule ... The jurisdiction has been exercised in a great variety of cases where the individual claimants were completely separate and distinct ... and the single decree *has* without any difficulty settled the entire controversy and determined the separate rights and obligations of each individual claimant.

53 Chafee, *ibid.* at 1309.
54 *Ibid.* at 1320: "Behind all this insistence on the formula of 'community of interest' lurks the fear that large corporate defendants will readily escape jury trials after widespread disasters." In fact, as we have seen, the availability of more universal aggregation can be expected to have the opposite effect and, moreover, is irrelevant in the Canadian context where no such right exists.
55 *Ibid.* at 1311.

While it is still occasionally invoked in the United States,[56] the Bill of Peace has remained virtually unused in contemporary Canadian legal practice since the fusion of law and equity began towards the close of the nineteenth century.[57] Nevertheless, it is still available, as was confirmed in the recent decision of *Dykun v. Odishaw*, where the Alberta Court of Appeal invoked the doctrine to frustrate a frivolous litigant who "insist[ed] on the use of public forums to indulge oblique motives."[58]

With the fusion of the courts of common law and equity in 1873,[59] rules were developed to preserve the equitable aggregate action.[60] English decisions initially continued to view class actions liberally. In 1901 the House of Lords held that "[t]he principle on which the rule is based forbids its restriction to cases for which an exact precedent can be found in the reports. ... [It] ought to be applied to the exigencies of modern life as occasion requires."[61]

This changed with the 1910 decision of the English Court of Appeal in *Markt & Co. v. Knight Steamship Co.*[62] Although the majority of the court

---

56 See, for instance, *Yuba Consol. Gold Fields v. Kilkeary*, 206 F.2d 884 (9th Cir. 1953); *Leaf River Forest Prod., Inc. v. Deakle*, 661 So.2d 188 at 192 (Miss. 1995). (The defendant applied for a Bill of Peace to consolidate several toxic tort cases. The court said that it might be possible: "while the label 'bill of peace' may not have survived the adoption of the [class action rules], the chancery court's authority to grant substantive relief through equity remains viable and available.") See also Thomas D. Rowe, Jr, "A Distant Mirror: The Bill of Peace in Early American Mass Torts and Its Implications for Modern Class Actions" (1997) 39 Ariz. L. Rev. 711.
57 See generally Paul M. Perell, *The Fusion of Law and Equity* (Toronto: Butterworths, 1990).
58 *Dykun v. Odishaw*, 2001 ABCA 204 at para. 9. The court directed that the Alberta courts refuse the issuance of any new pleadings by the plaintiff "of any new action that derives from his dispute with Canada Post or with his first lawyer ..." The court reflected at para. 8 (footnote 1):

> At equity a perpetual injunction may issue to restrain all further and repetitious proceedings at law by litigating parties where the question has been satisfactorily settled. The remedy was known as a "Bill of Peace." It issued when the Court of Chancery reached the conclusion that "a matter had been litigated enough." *Earl of Bath v. Sherwin* (1709), 4 Bro Parl Cas 373, 2 E.R. 253 (H.L.). Patently, it should only issue in the rarest of cases but it is available when justified.

59 *Supreme Court of Judicature Act, 1873* (U.K.), 36 & 37 Vict., c. 66.
60 Rule 10 of the *Supreme Court of Judicature Act, 1873* (U.K.), 36 & 37 Vict., c. 66 sched. reads: "Where there are numerous parties having the same interest in one action, one or more of such parties may sue or be sued, or may be authorised by the Court to defend in such actions, on behalf or for the benefit of all parties so interested."
61 *Taff Vale Ry. v. Amalgamated Soc'y of Ry. Servants*, [1901] A.C. 426 at 443 (H.L.).
62 [1910] 2 K.B. 1021 (C.A.).

found no reason to depart from the traditional liberal approach, the lone voice of Fletcher Moulton L.J. in offering a "sweeping denouncement" of class litigation seemed to have more influence in the years that followed,[63] and this, "combined with the widespread use of limited-liability companies, resulted in fewer class actions being brought."[64]

By the time that *General Motors of Canada Ltd. v. Naken*[65] was argued before the Supreme Court of Canada in 1982, the need for a statutory regime for class litigation was widely acknowledged. In *Naken*, the Supreme Court considered whether a U.S.-style class action could be designed within the vestigial "representative action" preserved as a rule of the Alberta court. The court held that it could not, suggesting (if regretfully) that true class litigation could not exist absent a comprehensive statutory regime. Estey J. held at 408:

> If the court were now to find that these claims may not be processed under Rule 75 it may mean, in practical terms, the end of many claims which, mathematically at least, may amount to about five million dollars. Furthermore, having regard to the practices in the modern market-place, particularly in national merchandizing of products such as automobiles, it is not an unreasonable risk that the vendor undertakes if he is now found to be exposed to class actions by dissatisfied purchasers. ... These, of course, are matters of policy more fittingly the subject of scrutiny in the legislative rather than the judicial chamber.

This idea, that class proceedings were designated by, and limited to, the four corners of statute, stalled the development of Canadian jurisprudence for nearly twenty years, despite some lower court decisions that managed to distinguish *Naken*.[66] The recent departure from that posture (indeed the reversal of *Naken*) in *Dutton* is therefore of enormous significance.

---

63 W.A. Bogart, "Questioning Litigation's Role — Courts and Class Actions in Canada" (1987) 62 Ind. L.J. 665 at 672. Bogart's article is a good overview of class litigation in the "wilderness years" before statutory reform. To this end see also: Neil J. Williams, "Consumer Class Actions in Canada — Some Proposals for Reform" (1975) 13 Osgoode Hall L.J. 1; and John A. Kazanjian, "Class Actions in Canada" (1973) 11 Osgoode Hall L.J. 397.

64 *Western Canadian Shopping Centres, Inc. v. Dutton*, 2001 SCC 46 at para. 24 [hereinafter *Dutton*].

65 (1983), 144 D.L.R. (3d) 385 (S.C.C.) [hereinafter *Naken*].

66 See, for example, *Swift Cdn. Co. v. Alberta (Pork Producers Marketing Board)* (1984), 53 A.R. 284 (C.A.); *Bradley v. Saskatchewan Wheat Pool* (1984), 31 Sask. R. 254 (Q.B.).

b) U.S. Federal Rule 23

Canadian mass tort law, and in particular product liability law, owes at least as much to U.S. jurisprudence as it does to that of the English courts.[67] It is perhaps not surprising, then, that the U.S. example in establishing a class action regime was watched closely in this country and would eventually provide an example for Canadian legislatures to follow. In order to appreciate the decisions made in the design of the Canadian class action systems, it is necessary to provide some background on the U.S. legislation and its treatment by the courts of that country.

The modern class action was established in 1966 through amendments to the U.S. *Federal Rules of Civil Procedure*, Rule 23.[68] Because in the United States tort law is generally governed by the law of each state, Rule 23 initially had little application to mass tort claims. However, state laws modelled on Rule 23 and the increasing number of "diversity" cases which, under the U.S. constitution, may be heard by the federal courts,[69] led to a body of jurisprudence based upon the wording of that rule. As a result, U.S. class action law, unlike many aspects of tort litigation in that country, is somewhat homogeneous, if hardly fully so.

Federal Rule 23(a) sets out the basic requirements for a lawsuit to proceed as a class action. The first prerequisite is "numerosity" of class members: the members of the class must be "so numerous that joinder of all members is impracticable." The second requirement has been referred to as "commonality": the existence of "questions of law or fact common to the class." Third, "typicality" is a requirement that the claims or defences of the class representatives are "typical of the claims or defenses of the class." This does not mean that all claims must be identical; for example, the fact that individual class members have suffered different damages will not by itself prevent certification. However, typicality might not be present where the facts establishing a claim of liability differ between the named plaintiffs

---

67 Mr. Justice Linden, for instance, has pointed out that the origins of manufacturer's tort liability in Canada can be traced to an American case, *MacPherson v. Buick Motor Co.*, 217 N.Y. Supp. 382 (1916), 111 N.E. 1050 (N.Y.C.A.) and two subsequent Canadian decisions (*Ross v. Dunstall* (1921), 62 S.C.R. 393 and *Buckley v. Mott* (1920), 50 D.L.R. 408 (N.S.S.C.)), not to the later House of Lords decision in *Donoghue v. Stevenson*, [1932] A.C. 562, as is generally assumed (for various expressions of the latter position see Peter Burns ed., *Donoghue v. Stevenson and the Modern Law of Negligence: The Paisley Papers* (Vancouver: Continuing Legal Education Society of B.C., 1991); Allen M. Linden, *Canadian Tort Law*, 7th ed. (Toronto, Butterworths, 2001) at 568).

68 Fed. R. Civ. P. Rule 23 [hereinafter Rule 23].

69 A "diversity" case is one in which the federal courts have jurisdiction because they involve, *inter alia*, parties from different states.

and the class members, as, for instance, with claims based on detrimental reliance on misrepresentations. Finally, Rule 23(a) requires that class representatives "fairly and adequately protect the interests" of the class.

In addition to meeting all of the Rule 23(a) criteria, a class action may be prosecuted only if it meets at least one of the criteria set forth in Rule 23(b). Suits for money damages under Rule 23 are divided into so-called "(b)(1)" and "(b)(3)" actions.

Most suits are pursued under Rule 23(b)(3), which sets out the basic rules for certification. Under it, a court must consider whether "central" or significant questions of law and fact common to class members "predominate over any questions affecting only individual members,"[70] and must find that the class action device is "superior to other available methods for the fair and efficient adjudication of the controversy." These requirements of predominance and superiority are most frequently involved when class certification is denied, and, as we will see, were of considerable concern to the Ontario Law Reform Commission when it formulated its recommendations in 1982, setting the tone for all Canadian systems to follow.

Rule 23(c)(2) requires that members of a class maintained under Rule 23(b)(3) receive "the best notice practicable under the circumstances, including individual notice to all members who can be identified through reasonable effort." Rule 23(b)(1) permits the certification of a "mandatory class," when separate lawsuits by or against individual class members would create a risk of inconsistent outcomes resulting in "incompatible standards of conduct" for the party adverse to the class or which "would as a practical matter be dispositive of the interests" of non-parties or render it more difficult for them to protect their interests. In addition, Rule 23(e) requires notice to the members of the class, regardless of whether it is maintained under Rule 23(b)(1), (b)(2), or (b)(3), before the action is dismissed or compromised.

c) Development of "Mass Tort" Class Action Claims in the United States under Rule 23

It is often said that mass tort class actions in the United States have developed through several distinct phases.[71] In each phase, American courts

---

70 In some cases, the representative plaintiff will seek damages as well as declaratory or injunctive relief and will attempt to certify the class under both Rule 23(b)(2) and (b)(3).

71 See Coffee, "Class Wars" *supra* note 30 at 1344, 1355–58; Schuck, "Institutional Evolutionist Perspective" *supra* note 41 at 944. For additional views of the history of mass tort actions, see John C. Coffee, Jr, "The Regulation of Entrepreneurial Litigation: Balancing Fairness and Efficiency in the Large Class Action" (1987) 54 U. Chi. L. Rev.

have weighed a desire to employ aggregative techniques in mass tort litigation against a respect for individual litigative autonomy and self-determination for injured plaintiffs. Throughout the jurisprudence and commentary, one question of policy has been pivotal: How does one allow group actions for recovery and still preserve individual rights? If it is not possible to satisfy both ambitions, when may individual interests be legitimately suppressed for the greater good of the class as a whole?

Interpretation of Rule 23 has tended to rely heavily on the notes of the Advisory Committee, which is in effect the "legislative" body responsible for making changes to the Rules.[72] With respect to class actions, the Advisory Committee's notes on Rule 23(b)(3) state:

> A "mass accident" resulting in injuries to numerous persons is ordinarily not appropriate for a class action because of the likelihood that significant questions, not only of damages but of liability and defenses of liability, would be present, affecting the individual in different ways. In these circumstances, a class action would degenerate in practice into multiple lawsuits separately tried.[73]

The notes reflect a very incremental approach to mass litigation, and indeed enshrine the traditional position that any system must give priority to the litigative autonomy historically said to inform tort law.[74] In this analysis, tort victims, particularly those who have suffered significant injuries, ought to

---

877; Deborah R. Hensler & Mark A. Peterson, "Understanding Mass Personal Injury Litigation: A Socio-Legal Analysis" (1993) 59 Brook. L. Rev. 961; and Judith Resnik, "Aggregation, Settlement, and Dismay" (1995) 80 Cornell L. Rev. 918.

72 By an Act of Congress, the *Federal Rules of Civil Procedure*, developed by standing and advisory committees of the Judicial Council, come into force after a period of time if Congress does not explicitly reject them: 28 U.S.C. 2072. It has been suggested by some that this process does not create binding legislation (because if it did it would be doing so outside the constitutional process of passage and presentment) and does not represent a binding precedent (because the U.S. federal judicial power, unlike that of Canadian courts, is limited to "cases and controversies," excluding the possibility of advisory opinions): See Owen M. Fiss, "The Political Theory of the Class Action" (1996) 53 Wash. & Lee L. Rev. 21 at 29. Nevertheless, the U.S. Supreme Court has routinely decided class action cases as if it was bound by Rule 23: *Eisen v. Carlisle & Jacquelin*, 417 U.S. 156 at 166–67 (1974).

73 Rule 23(b)(3) advisory committee's note to 1966 amendments (citing *Pennsylvania R.R. v. United States*, 111 F. Supp. 80 (D.N.J. 1953).

74 Roger C. Cramton, "Individualized Justice, Mass Torts, and 'Settlement Class Actions': An Introduction" (1995) 80 Cornell L. Rev. 811 at 814–15; David Rosenberg "Class Actions for Mass Torts: Doing Individual Justice by Collective Means" (1986–87) 62 Ind. L.J. 561 at 566 n.25.

be able to control their own litigation through to an individual and specific conclusion.[75] As a result, cases from the 1960s and 1970s echoed the views of the Advisory Committee and generally denied certification of mass tort claims,[76] except in some cases through consolidation or bankruptcy.[77]

In the mid-1980s, however, courts more frequently took a positive view of the aggregative approach and became increasingly willing to certify classes in mass tort actions.[78] It has been suggested that this acceptance of mass tort certification was driven in part by the siege mentality generated in judges facing an overwhelming array of mass tort litigation, particularly asbestos claims.[79] On the other hand, it appears equally valid to suggest that an increasing judicial recognition of the futility (not to mention costs, both to the parties and to society[80]) of repetitive individual litigation also played a significant role in this development. Nevertheless, deference to the goal of litigative autonomy meant that the overwhelming majority of

---

75 See Susan A.T. Koniak, "Feasting While the Widow Weeps: *Georgine v. Amchem. Prods., Inc.*" (1995) 80 Cornell L. Rev. 1045 at 1138–47; Richard L. Marcus, "They Can't Do That, Can They? Tort Reform Via Rule 23" (1995) 80 Cornell L. Rev. 858 at 889–90; David Rosenberg, "Of End Games and Openings in Mass Tort Cases: Lessons From a Special Master" (1989) 69 B.U.L. Rev. 695 at 701; Roger H. Trangsrud "Mass Trials in Mass Tort Cases: A Dissent" (1989) U. Ill. L. Rev. 69 [hereinafter Trangsrud, "A Dissent"] at 74–76. This "day in court ideal" is discussed earlier.

76 See, for example, *McDonnell Douglas Corp. v. United States Dist. Court*, 523 F.2d 1083 at 1085 (9th Cir. 1975) (Rule 23 does not "permit certifications of a class whose members have independent tort claims arising out of the same occurrence and whose representatives assert only liability for damages"); *Sanders v. Tailored Chem. Corp.*, 570 F. Supp. 1543 (E.D. Pa. 1983); *Marchesi v. Eastern Airlines, Inc.*, 68 F.R.D. 500 (E.D.N.Y. 1975); *Harrigan v. United States*, 63 F.R.D. 402 (E.D. Pa. 1974); *Hobbs v. Northeast Airlines, Inc.*, 50 F.R.D. 76 (E.D. Pa. 1970); for the contrary position see *Re Gabel*, 350 F. Supp. 624 (D.C, Cal. 1972) which was rejected by the Ninth Circuit in *McDonnell Douglas*, supra.

77 See Resnik, supra note 71 at 925–30; Judith Resnik, "From 'Cases' to 'Litigation'" (1991) 54 Law & Contempt. Probs. 5; Yeazell, *From Medieval to Modern*, supra note 42 at 64–68.

78 See *Re Asbestos School Litig.*, 789 F.2d 996 (3d Cir. 1986) ("the trend has been for courts to be more receptive to use of the class action in mass tort litigation"); see also Scott O. Wright & Joseph A. Colussi, *The Successful Use of the Class Action Device in the Management of Skywalk Tort Litigation*, 52 U.M.K.C.L. Rev. 141 (1984); Note, "Class Certification in Mass Accident Cases Under Rule 23(b)(1)" (1983) 96 Harv. L. Rev. 114.

79 See Coffee, "Class Wars," supra note 30 at 1350 n. 23, 1363–64; see also *Jenkins v. Raymark Indus.*, 782 F.2d 468, 470 (5th Cir. 1986). Professor Coffee derides such decisions to grant class certification as a reaction to the "mind-numbing boredom" of presiding over these cases: Coffee, "Class Wars" supra note 30 at 1351.

80 One frequently cited figure is from a Rand Corporation study of asbestos litigation, which calculates that transaction costs accounted for $0.61 of each asbestos-litigation dollar. See Coffee, supra note 71 at 1348 n.15. The costs of the litigation system are discussed further *infra*.

mass tort class actions certified during this period were of the Rule 23(b)(3) "opt-out" variety.[81] Significantly, in 1985 the U.S. Supreme Court suggested for the first time that the right to opt out of a class action to pursue an individualized resolution may be required by the due process protections of the Fourteenth Amendment.[82]

Emphasis on opt-out rights, however, considerably weakened the efficacy of class actions since class members had strong incentives to quarrel and bargain among themselves over the terms of their participation. Persons with the strongest factual claims, for instance, could hold out for a larger share of the award than their damages would otherwise admit; in such a case, both the class (and also the defendants, who had an interest in a single resolution to all claims) gave up more than they should to these objectors. This problem was recognized at the time, and, as a result, class counsel began increasingly to rely upon mandatory classes under Rule 23(b)(1) to achieve global resolution. Because these mandatory classes also represent a much greater move away from the individual rights model, they have proved highly controversial, as we will discuss in greater detail later.

Throughout this period, the courts struggled to overcome the focus on individuality in Rule 23(b)(3) and more frequently turned to Rule 23(b)(1) mandatory classes, though their legal justification for doing so was open to question.[83] The efforts to support such a move often led to the employment

---

81   See Rule 23(c)(2). Often, class members have two opportunities to opt out: a so-called "front-end" option under Rule 23(b)(3) at the time of certification, and a "back-end" opt-out if the claimant is unsatisfied with his or her share of the settlement as administered. See Schuck, "Institutional Evolutionist Perspective," *supra* note 41 at 963–64.

82   See *Phillips Petroleum Co. v. Shutts*, 472 U.S. 797 (1985) [hereinafter *Shutts*]. The *Shutts* decision suggests that opt-out rights may be a necessary part of all class actions involving non-resident plaintiffs. See Arthur Miller & David Crump, "Jurisdiction and Choice of Law in Multistate Actions After *Phillips Petroleum v. Shutts*" (1985) 96 Yale L.J. 1 at 52 ("There is no neat and logical means of resolving the question whether mandatory actions survive *Shutts*"). The question is still unsettled in the wake of the more recent U.S. Supreme Court decision in *Ortiz v. Fibreboard Corp.*, *infra*.

83   A number of decisions discuss the issue. See, for instance, *Jenkins v. Raymark Indus.*, 109 F.R.D. 269, 274–77 (E.D. Tex. 1985), aff'd 782 F.2d 468 (5th Cir. 1986); *Re Asbestos Sch. Litig.*, 104 F.R.D. 422 (E.D. Pa. 1984), modified 107 F.R.D. 215 (E.D. Pa. 1985), aff'd in part and rev'd in part, 789 F.2d 996 (3d Cir. 1986) cert. denied 479 U.S. 852; *Re Federal Skywalk Cases*, 93 F.R.D. 415 (W.D. Mo.), rev'd 680 F.2d 1175 (8th Cir. 1982) cert. denied 459 U.S. 988 (1982); *Dalkon Shield*, 521 F. Supp. 1188 (N.D. Cal.), modified 526 F. Supp. 887 (N.D. Cal. 1981), vacated 693 F.2d 847 (9th Cir. 1982) cert. denied 459 U.S. 1171; *Coburn v. 4-R Corp.*, 77 F.R.D. 43 (E.D. Ky. 1977), *mandamus* denied *sub nom. Union Light, Heat & Power Co. v. United States Dist. Court*, 588 F.2d 543 (6th Cir. 1978); *Hernandez v. Motor Vessel Skyward*, 61 F.R.D. 558 (S.D. Fla. 1973), aff'd 507 F.2d 1278 (5th Cir.), and aff'd 507 F.2d 1279 (5th Cir. 1975).

of the equitable doctrine of the "limited fund," which permitted mandatory aggregation of claims in cases where it appeared that the compensation available would be exhausted and permitting opt-outs or a multiplicity of actions would mean drastic inequity in the availability of damages.

The modern era of class actions in the United States has seen a remarkable blossoming of innovation in the trial courts in an attempt to preserve mass tort class actions, including the "settlement class action," where the lawsuit, motion for certification, and proposed settlement are filed at the same time. Other courts have struggled with the problem, inherent in any tort class action, raised by the spectre of future claims either by plaintiffs who are unknown at the time of settlement (having not manifest injury) or by those who are identified but the extent of whose injuries is not yet known.

The federal appellate courts were critical of such innovations and indeed revived their concerns about the use of class actions to deal with mass tort claims at all. In four cases since 1995, U.S. circuit courts have decertified class actions involving HIV-infected blood products,[84] asbestos,[85] penile implants,[86] and cigarettes[87] while wondering aloud whether mass tort class actions are ever appropriate.[88] Such objections were generally based on the old idea of "litigative autonomy," but it was also occasionally suggested that class actions create undue pressure on defendants to settle meritless cases, possibly even because of the scale of the action alone.[89]

Most recently, two U.S. Supreme Court decisions have dealt serious blows to the viability of mass tort class actions, at least those involving some claims that would be worth pursuing as individual suits. In *Amchem Products Inc. v. Windsor*,[90] a case concerning claims arising from asbestos exposure, the court refused certification of a class that included both present and future claimants on the grounds that the two groups' interests were too divergent and separate representation was required. While the deci-

---

84   *Re Rhône-Poulenc Rorer Inc.*, 51 F.3d 1293 (7th Cir. 1995), rehearing denied 1995 U.S. App. LEXIS 9693.
85   *Georgine v. Amchem Prods. Inc.*, 83 F.3d 610 (3d Cir. 1995), rehearing denied 1996 U.S. App. LEXIS 15416 (see *Amchem*, infra note 90).
86   *Re American Med. Sys., Inc.*, 75 F.3d 1069 at 1080-82 (6th Cir. 1996).
87   *Castano v. American Tobacco Co.*, 84 F.3d 734 (5th Cir. 1996).
88   See *Castano*, ibid. at 741–51; *Georgine*, supra note 85 at 626–34; *American Med.*, supra note 86 at 1078–82; *Rhône-Poulenc*, supra note 84 at 1298–1304. But see *Re Agent Orange Prods. Liab. Litig.*, 996 F.2d 1425 (2d Cir. 1993) (rejecting claim that class action settlement did not bind future claimants who had lacked an opportunity to opt out from the class).
89   See *Castano*, supra note 87 at 746; *Rhône-Poulenc*, supra note 84 at 1298–1300.
90   521 U.S. 591 (1997) [hereinafter *Amchem*].

sion's immediate application was fairly narrow, its focus on procedural fairness was thought to signal a general discomfort in the court with class actions for mass exposure torts. The *Harvard Law Review* stated:

> The *Amchem* Court's standard for satisfying the adequacy of representation requirement illustrates how a decision geared toward enhancing procedural fairness may conflict with the efficiency goal of the class action. The *Amchem* decision will make the aggregation and collective litigation of claims more difficult. Courts will require more subclasses, the new subclasses will retain additional attorneys, and settlement and adjudication will have to accommodate the separate claims of each subclass. Thus, the Court's decision in *Amchem* not only has undermined the efficiency goal of the class action, but also, instead of ensuring meaningful access to the courts, has created new hurdles for injured plaintiffs.[91]

Ortiz v. Fibreboard Corp.[92] is a more recent decision, also concerned with an asbestos claim. In *Ortiz*, the U.S. Supreme Court decertified a "mandatory" class on the basis that the limited fund that formed the basis of the settlement was arrived at by stipulation of the parties and may not have reflected the real ability of the parties to pay. However, the Court also took the opportunity to reiterate its concerns in *Amchem* regarding litigative autonomy and intra-class conflicts, which had not, in the Court's view, been adequately addressed in the process leading to the settlement for which approval was sought. The Court further suggested that mandatory classes might never be permissible, except perhaps in some limited fund cases. Taken together with *Amchem*, *Ortiz* has been criticized as "likely to leave many injured Americans with no viable legal remedy."[93]

As a result of the U.S. courts' troubled ambivalence, mass tort claims represent only a tiny proportion of class actions in that country.[94] This history makes the Canadian experience, marked by a willingness to certify and

---

91 "Developments," *supra* note 24 at 1815.
92 527 U.S. 815 (1999) [hereinafter *Ortiz*].
93 "Developments," *supra* note 24 at 1816.
94 Deborah Hensler, "Revisiting the Monster: New Myths and Realities of Class Action and Other Large Scale Litigation" (2001) 11 Duke J. of Comparative & Int'l L. 179 at 183–84 (noting that from 1990 to 1997 only one of the fifty-five U.S. Supreme Court decisions on certified class actions involved a mass tort claim, as did less than 10 percent of class action lawsuits decided by U.S. circuit courts from 1997). Unfortunately, there are no comprehensive statistics available as to how many of the approximately fifteen million civil suits filed in the United States annually are class actions; Hensler's research appears to suggest a total of several thousand pending class actions at all court levels: *Ibid.* at 184.

2) Canadian Reform

Canadian courts have repeatedly referred to class action legislation as advancing the interests of efficiency, access to justice, and the modification of the behaviour of wrongdoers and potential wrongdoers. However, while these three considerations will determine whether a class proceeding is preferable (and thus to an extent whether it will be certified), they do not speak to the desirability of class proceedings *per se*. So what are the conditions that led to such sweeping and powerful legislative reform?

Quebec's class action rules, which were introduced in 1978 and which generally followed Rule 23,[95] met with a lukewarm response and were slow to be used by litigants,[96] an experience that no doubt informed subsequent reforms in other provinces while providing some refutation to critics who feared overutilization if the class proceeding became more widespread. By the 1980s, it had become widely recognized that, without class proceedings statutes, the procedural mechanisms available in common law jurisdictions were inadequate to allow plaintiffs who had the same or a similar interest in the subject matter of the litigation to proceed effectively. Wherever the topic was studied in Commonwealth jurisdictions, recommendations invariably followed for substantive legislative reform.[97] As was said of England:

---

95 Permitting certification, for instance, if provisions providing for individual or other representative actions were "difficult or impracticable": Quebec s. 1003.
96 See note 6 and accompanying text.
97 See, for instance: *Alberta Report, supra* note 18; The Law Reform Commission, *Grouped Proceedings in the Federal Court, Report No. 46* (Canberra: Commonwealth of Australia, 1988) [hereinafter *Australia LRC Report*]; Ministry of the Attorney General, *Consultation Document: Class Action Legislation for British Columbia* (Victoria: Queen's Printer, May 1994); Canadian Bar Association, *Report of the Task Force on Systems of Civil Justice* (August 1996); *Manitoba Report, supra* note 19; Marie Swain, *Class Actions in New South Wales*, NSW Parliamentary Library Briefing Paper No. 22/96; Ontario Law Reform Commission, *Report on Class Actions*, 3 vols. (Toronto: Ministry of the Attorney General, 1982) [hereinafter *Ontario Report (1982)*]; *Report of the Attorney General's Advisory Committee on Class Actions Reform* (Toronto: Attorney General of Ontario, 1990) [hereinafter *Ontario Report (1990)*]; South African Law Commission, *The Recognition of a Class Action in South African Law* (Report, 1997) / (Working Paper 57, 1995); Scottish Law Commission, *Multi-Party Actions, Report #154* (1996); Ruth Rogers, *A Uniform Class Actions Statute*, 1995 Proceedings of the Uniform Law Conference of Canada, Appendix O [hereinafter *ULCC Model Act*]; Victorian Attorney-General's Law Reform Advisory Council, *Class Actions in Victoria: Time For A New*

As we become an increasingly mass producing and mass consuming society, one product or service with a flaw has the potential to injure or cause other loss to more and more people. Yet our civil justice system has not adapted to mass legal actions. We still largely treat them as a collection of individual cases, with the findings in one case having only limited relevance in law to all of the others.[98]

Lord Woolf, conducting an inquiry into the need for legislative reform in England, agreed, concluding that "[the absence of class proceedings legislation] causes difficulties when actions involving many parties are brought," and that, "[i]n addition to the existing procedures being difficult to use, they have proved disproportionately costly" and that "[i]t is now generally recognised, by judges, practitioners and consumer representatives, that there is a need for a new approach" to multiparty procedures.[99]

The inadequacies of the existing systems were also recognized by the Canadian courts. As described earlier, the 1983 *Naken* decision identified "the need for a comprehensive legislative scheme for the institution and conduct of class actions."[100] According to the Supreme Court, the paucity of detail in the then extant "representative action" rule indicated that it was not intended to facilitate modern multiparty proceedings and was wholly inadequate to support the undertaking of a complex and uncertain action.

By far the most important catalyst for class action reform in Canada was the 1982 report of the Ontario Law Reform Commission.[101] Indeed, it is not unrealistic to consider the 1982 report as the foundational document of Canadian class proceedings.[102] Published in three volumes, the report weighed exhaustively the elements of system design and made recommendations that have formed the basis for all class action legislation in Canada

---

Approach (Melbourne: Victorian Attorney-General, 1997) [hereinafter *Victoria Report*]; Lord Woolf, *Access to Justice* (Final Report, 1996) [hereinafter *Woolf Report*].

98 *Manitoba Report*, supra note 19 at 1–2, quoting from the National Consumer Council in its submission to Lord Woolf's inquiry in England.
99 The *Woolf Report*, supra note 97, led to changes in the English procedural rules of 1999 including detailed provisions governing "Group Litigation": United Kingdom, Civil Procedure Rules 1998, SI 1998/3132, rr. 19.10–19.15.
100 *Naken*, supra note 65 at 410.
101 *Ontario Report (1982)*, supra note 97.
102 The Supreme Court of Canada in *Hollick v. Toronto (City)*, 2001 SCC 68 [hereinafter *Hollick*] at para. 15 said: "In my view, it is essential therefore that courts not take an overly restrictive approach to the legislation, but rather interpret the Act in a way that gives full effect to the benefits foreseen by the drafters [of the Ontario Law Reform Commission Reports]."

that followed.[103] Then, in 1990, a second Ontario Law Reform Commission report was issued with a proposed Act incorporating many of the features recommended in 1982. That Act became the *Class Proceedings Act* currently in place, and British Columbia's *Class Proceedings Act* followed, with minor (but as we shall see significant) modifications in 1995.

In recent years, most of those provinces that have not yet followed the lead of Quebec, Ontario, and British Columbia have been moving in that direction. The Alberta Court of Appeal displayed evident frustration with the inadequacy of the vestigial Rules of Court-based representative-proceedings rule in *Western Canadian Shopping Centres, Inc. v. Dutton*.[104] Speaking of Alberta's Rule 42 provision, the court commented that "this area of the law is clearly in want of legislative reform to provide a more uniform and efficient way to deal with class action law suits." The Alberta Law Reform Institute undertook a thorough study of the available literature, and it too recommended the establishment of a class proceedings regime.[105] Notwithstanding the hints of imminent legislative change, the Supreme Court overturned the decision in *Dutton*[106] and allowed class proceedings to be imposed absent a statutory regime.

In 1996 the Uniform Law Conference of Canada adopted its Model Class Proceedings Act[107] (*ULCC Model Act*). This Act was drafted by delegates from British Columbia[108] and follows that province's *Class Proceedings Act* closely. The *ULCC Model Act* has in turn formed the basis for subsequent legislative proposals in Alberta, Saskatchewan, Manitoba, and Newfoundland and Labrador, each of which tracks the *Model Act*'s wording almost verbatim.

---

103 Even in British Columbia, the *Ontario Report (1982)*, *supra* note 97, has taken on some aspects of a legislative history, as Ontario cases that rely upon its recommendations regarding the goals of class litigation (access to justice, judicial economy, and behaviour modification) have been applied in B.C.: See, for instance, *Endean v. Canadian Red Cross Society* (1997), 148 D.L.R. (4th) 158 at 164 (B.C.S.C.), rev'd on other grounds, 157 D.L.R. (4th) 465 (B.C.C.A.), citing the goals as set out in *Adbool v. Anaheim Management Ltd.* (1995), 21 O.R. (3rd) 453 at 461 (Gen. Div.).

104 (1998), 228 A.R. 188 (C.A.). Much more recently, the Supreme Court, too, considered the objectives set out in the report as correctly identifying the objectives not only of legislative reform but also of class actions generally: see *Dutton*, *supra* note 64 at paras. 27–29. See also *Hollick*, *supra* note 102 at para. 15.

105 *Alberta Report*, *supra* note 18.

106 *Dutton*, *supra* note 64.

107 Ruth Rogers, *A Uniform Class Actions Statute*, 1995 Proceedings of the Uniform Law Conference of Canada <www.law.ualberta.ca/alri/ulc/95pro/3950.htm>.

108 Margaret Shone, "Memo Re: National Class Actions," (unpublished, 5 March 2001, on file with Alberta Law Reform Institute and with the author).

3) Scope of Reform

While the U.S. courts vacillated over the application of Rule 23 to mass tort claims, virtually all of the proposals for legislative reform in Canada have indicated that aggregation could assist the broadest possible variety of tort claims. The Manitoba Law Reform Commission report gives a description of the broad types of litigation that might be furthered by class proceedings statutes, a description that, in stark contrast to the U.S. approach, focuses entirely on torts:

> Class actions are useful in tort cases for mass disaster claims (claims arising from single incident mass accidents, such as train derailments and environmental disasters) and for creeping disaster claims (claims for bodily injury arising from consumer products, such as tobacco and asbestos, or medical products, such as intra-uterine devices, breast implants, contaminated blood, jaw implants, silver mercury fillings and heart pacemakers). Other uses include claims of group defamation, nuisance, the principle in *Rylands v. Fletcher*, various statutory torts, damages claims for breach of *Charter* rights, claims arising from illegal strikes, negligent house construction, and negligent misstatement.[109]

Nor was this the only significant departure envisioned from the American model. Rule 23's absolute requirements of numerosity and superiority were roundly rejected, with a strong tendency among Canadian proponents to allow class action suits whenever they can provide, on balance, foreseeable advantages over individual actions.

It is thus generally accepted that Canadian class proceedings statutes are much more plaintiff-friendly than the U.S. model:

> These differences have made class actions arising out of product liability not only viable in Canada, but a more effective remedy than that in the United States. American courts have generally been reluctant to certify actions arising out of product liability claims ... In the face of ... individual issues, American courts have been reluctant to find that the common issues predominate, and, therefore, have often refused certification. The differing Canadian legislation has led to a much more liberal approach towards certifying class proceedings in product liability claims.[110]

---

109 *Manitoba Report*, supra note 19 at 17–18.
110 Dean F. Edgell, *Product Liability Law in Canada* (Toronto: Butterworths, 2000) at 189.

4) Objectives of Reform

The general objectives of legislative reform are stated in the recent Alberta Law Reform Institute's report as fairness, certainty, and efficiency.[111] Others, including Michael Cochrane, former chair of the Attorney General's Advisory Committee on Class Action Reform (the body that oversaw the design of Ontario's *Class Proceedings Act*), are briefer still, describing the "fundamental purpose" of class actions as "one word — efficiency."[112] However, it is useful to remember that any list of goals couched in strictly procedural terms necessarily implies a fourth — the advancement of legitimate legal objectives, whatever they may be. In the case of mass tort class actions, therefore, it is helpful to be mindful not only of the goals of aggregation but also of the goals of tort law.

An early (and we shall see persistent) conceptual distinction made was between claims that were individually viable and those that were not.[113] Because considerations of "efficiency" were generally focused on achieving access to justice for plaintiffs, it is not surprising to find that the most frequently cited case in support of class actions is one where the potential recovery for individual claimants is so small as to make resolution impractical or to discourage risk-averse plaintiffs from proceeding. This conceptual framework has been carried over from the 1982 Ontario report into the jurisprudence,[114] although more recent efforts have also discussed claims that would not be pursued "for social or psychological reasons."[115]

---

[111] *Alberta Report*, supra note 18 at paras. 13–16.

[112] Michael G. Cochrane, *Class Actions: A Guide to the Class Proceedings Act* (Toronto: Canada Law Book, 1993).

[113] In fact, the Ontario Law Reform Commission, borrowing from the Harvard Law Review, divided claims into three conceptual categories: individually recoverable, individually not recoverable (but "viable" in class proceedings), and "non-viable," the last being those claims where the claimant's costs of asserting his right to his share of the class recovery would be greater than that share: *Ontario Report (1982)*, supra note 97 at 116, citing Note, "Developments in the Law — Class Actions" (1976) 89 Harv. L. Rev. 1318 at 1325. In this book we discuss the distinction more frequently made by courts and commentators between "individually viable" (which the Ontario report would call "individually recoverable") and "individually non-viable," which are those claims whose individual litigation costs would be greater than the expected amount of recovery.

[114] The Ontario Law Reform Commission described "the goal of permitting the advancement of meritorious claims which have henceforth been uneconomical to pursue because the damages for each individual plaintiff would be too small for each claimant to recover through usual court procedures": *Abdool v. Anaheim Management Ltd. (1)* (1993), 15 O.R. (3d) 39 at 45–46 (Gen. Div.), citing *Ontario Report (1982)*, supra note 97. Lord Woolf repeated this as a central concern: *Woolf Report*, supra note 97 at 223, §2.

[115] *Manitoba Report*, supra note 19 at 1–2; *Alberta Report*, supra note 18 at para. 14.

It is often said by judges that the 1982 Ontario Law Reform Commission report identified "access to justice, judicial economy, and behaviour modification" as three co-equal "goals" of class-action system design. In fact, the report listed these as "benefits" but emphasized that the choice to permit class actions placed the *goal* of "behaviour modification" over the *goal* of "conflict resolution" in the civil process:

> In order to understand the nature of the controversy surrounding class actions, it is essential to recognize the presence, in many cases, of a fundamental philosophical dispute relating to the functions that may be legitimately served by civil actions, including class actions. On the one hand, it has been argued that the only proper function of civil actions is to achieve the peaceful resolution of conflicts that might otherwise lead injured parties to take the law into their own hands. One commentator has identified this philosophy as the "Conflict Resolution Model." Although most persons agree that conflict resolution is an important function of the civil process, many have suggested that civil actions, including class actions, also play an important role in encouraging adherence to social norms by imposing appropriate costs upon wrongdoers and depriving them of the fruits of their misconduct. This philosophy has been identified as the "Behaviour Modification Model."
>
> A general review of the class action literature suggests that most, but not all, critics of class actions subscribe to the Conflict Resolution Model, while many supporters of class actions embrace the Behaviour Modification Model. An awareness of this basic philosophical difference is important in understanding and evaluating various policy arguments for and against class actions, such as the contention that class actions may serve a legitimate function by deterring wrongful conduct, or the condemnation of class actions as a means of stirring up unnecessary litigation.[116]

One must assume that the drafters of the report, in recommending class proceedings legislation, recognized on some level that they were making a decision in favour of deterrence over other objectives. We emphasize these passages here because we believe that important implications flow from the recognition that "behaviour modification" is the principal goal of class actions — it is the method through which most of its other advantages are best conferred.

Viewing "behaviour modification" as the goal of class legislation, and other "benefits" such as access to justice, compensation, and so on, as just

---

116 *Ontario Report (1982)*, *supra* note 97 at 114–15.

that — "benefits" — is, as we have seen, supported upon solid — if sometimes surprising — policy grounds. In this respect, the Ontario Law Reform Commission got it precisely right in 1982;[117] since then, Canadian courts have drifted somewhat from these early, perspicacious observations and are only now beginning to drift back.

There is also a competing interest that is sometimes articulated by those engaged in class action reform: that of "fairness to defendants." As the Alberta Law Reform Institute put it:

> Attention to the principle that defendants should be protected against unreasonable claims will ensure that the procedural balance is not tipped too far on the side of the interests of plaintiffs. The principle embodies the idea that defendants should not have to spend money or face adverse publicity as a result of unfounded claims brought against them. Further, the principle encompasses the idea that, where plaintiffs are able to make out a recognizable cause of action, the civil justice system should provide defendants with an opportunity to make their defence in a proceeding in which the rules are known, and the results can be predicted with a reasonable degree of certainty, obtained within a reasonable length of time and limited in cost[.][118]

It is helpful to view this objective, too, from the point of view of "behaviour modification" or deterrence. That is, it is quite appropriate to say that there should not be such uncertainty in the litigation system that a defendant takes too many precautions or reduces its potentially dangerous business activity below the socially optimal level.

At this stage of our review we ought to have some regard for the impact of the "efficiencies" of aggregate litigation upon tort law itself. The best litigation system, presumably, is one in which the most legitimate rights may be vindicated, at the lowest cost. In that way, by improving access to justice for tort victims, it is arguable that class actions may go beyond procedure altogether and improve the substantive tort law's ability to meet the challenges presented by a rapidly evolving society, an ability that Professor Linden has described as often constrained by economic reality:

> Lawyers usually work for fees, not for principles; litigants usually sue for money, not for ideals. Investigation of accidents is expensive. Expert witnesses must be paid for their work. In short, tort trials cost money. Lots

---

117 Nevertheless, the commission appreciated the value of deterrence only when the class contained at least some individually non-viable claims: *Ibid.* at 145.
118 *Alberta Report, supra* note 18 at para. 15.

of it. Unless there is a good chance of winning, litigants are unwise to sue, for losers must pay not only their own legal costs but also those of the winning parties. The allure of a quick settlement dulls the crusading ardour of many a claimant. Because of this, law suits which test the frontiers of tort law are difficult to finance. Only the rare case, the rare litigant and the rare lawyer become involved in such litigation.[119]

D. FEATURES OF CANADIAN CLASS ACTIONS

Canadian class proceedings are patterned on the basic template of the U.S. Federal Rule 23, although the statutes are of the more linear design favoured here. They foresee mostly opt-out actions launched by a representative plaintiff, establish formal requirements and processes for certification and notice similar to those in the United States, and similarly provide an active role for the court in overseeing notice and settlement. There are, however, some important differences that make a Canadian class action potentially very different from one launched in the United States.

1) Certifying the Class

The most significant step in a Canadian class action is certification, a process that defines the class and sets the boundaries of the action. The certification hearing is common to all Canadian legislative regimes and the common law class action outlined in *Dutton*, but it is not universal.[120] Practically speaking, certification may be dispositive of the action, since the vast majority of certified class actions are settled before trial.[121] Plaintiffs may seek certification and press their case on to trial; frequently, though, plaintiffs and defendants approach the court together and seek to certify a class for the purposes of obtaining a court-approved settlement. This latter type of class is known as a "settlement class."

---

119 Allen M. Linden, *Canadian Tort Law*, 7th ed. (Toronto, Butterworths, 2001) at 22.
120 The federal Australian scheme does not have a certification requirement, based upon the recommendations of the Australian Law Reform Commission, which found that there is "no value in imposing an additional costly procedure, with a strong risk of appeals involving further delay and expense, which will not achieve the aims of protecting parties or ensuring efficiency.": *Australia LRC Report, supra* note 97 at para. 147.
121 See generally Ward K. Branch and John C. Kleefeld, "Settling a Class Action (or How to Wrestle an Octopus)" Presented to the Canadian Institute Conference on Litigating Toxic Torts and Other Mass Wrongs (Toronto: 4–5 December 2000).

There are three possible types of classes, named for the mechanism of their imposition upon class members: opt-in,[122] opt-out,[123] and the "mandatory" class. It is not uncommon for a certification to include more than one type of class, for instance, an "opt-out" class for resident plaintiffs and an "opt-in" class for non-resident plaintiffs as provided for under the British Columbia Act. There has not yet been a true "mandatory" (i.e., no opt-out) class certified in Canada.

In Ontario and Quebec, as in the United States, any person may be part of a class without regard to residency.[124] In British Columbia, only a resident may commence a class proceeding. So far, only the Ontario courts have certified "opt-out" national classes involving residents from all provinces.[125] British Columbia's statute, and the *ULCC Model Act*,[126] provide only for "opt-in" non-resident classes.

Perhaps the most controversial aspect of the U.S.'s Rule 23 has been the "mandatory classes," whose members have no right to withdraw.[127] Mandatory actions were designed to assist when allowing opt-outs would jeopardize unacceptably the interests of other class members. While opt-out rights are required in a 23(b)(3) action because it is only those actions in which the interests of the individuals in pursuing their own lawsuits may be so strong as to outweigh the necessity of collective adjudication, mandatory classes are used where it is appropriate to diminish individual control because the collective approach is necessary, even if it may not be universally desired within the class. In either case, it is the interests of the absent potential plaintiff that might be seen to justify the procedure.

---

122 In this most straightforward type of action, only those defendants who formally join the lawsuit may benefit and are bound by any decision or settlement in the action. In this sense, the class action is nothing more than a type of voluntary joinder; no non-party is bound by the decisions of the court.

123 In an "opt-out" action, any potential member of the class who did not formally decline to participate in the lawsuit is deemed to be a member of the class and may benefit from and be bound by any decision or settlement within the action.

124 Subject to rules governing jurisdiction.

125 *Nantais v. Telectronics Proprietary (Canada) Ltd.* (1995), 127 D.L.R. (4th) 552 (Gen. Div.), leave to appeal refused (1995), 129 D.L.R. (4th) 110 (Gen. Div.); *Bendall v. McGhan Medical Corp.* (1993), 106 D.L.R. (4th) 339 (Ont. Gen. Div.) at 345; *Carom v. Bre-X Minerals Ltd.* (1999), 44 O.R. (3d) 173 (S.C.J.) [hereinafter *Carom*]; *Webb v. K-Mart Canada Ltd.* (1999), 45 O.R. (3d) 389 (S.C.J.); and *Wilson v. Servier* (2000), 50 O.R. (3d) 219 (S.C.J.).

126 *Supra* note 97, s. 16(2).

127 Rule 23(c)(2) sets out requirements of notice to opt out but applies only to actions under (b)(3). Thus, the combination is read to imply the possibility that, where the conditions of a (b)(1) action are met, no right to opt out is required.

Because the efficiency of class actions depends on optimal aggregation of classable claims, mandatory classes are of considerable interest to system-design theorists, and they are discussed at some length in section 4 below.

As described earlier, the U.S. Rule 23 requires that the representative party must demonstrate that the class is not so numerous that joinder of all parties is impractical, that there are questions of law or fact common to the class, that the claims or defences of the representative party are typical of the claims or defences of the class, and that the representative party will fairly and adequately protect the interests of the class. The class must also be defined with sufficient specificity in order to be ascertainable.

The Canadian legislation is somewhat different, requiring that there be an identifiable class of two or more persons that would be represented by the representative plaintiff. The precise numbers or identities of the class members need not be known before certification will be granted. Moreover, there is no explicit "numerosity" requirement such as exists under the U.S. Rule 23.[128]

According to the British Columbia and Ontario Acts,[129] the determination of whether the plaintiffs have satisfied the requirements for certifying their action as a class proceeding raises the following questions:

- Do the pleadings disclose a cause of action?
- Is there an identifiable class of two or more persons?
- Do the claims of the class members raise issues that are common to the class?
- Would a class proceeding be the preferable procedure for the fair and efficient resolution of the common issues?
- Are the plaintiffs "representative plaintiffs" who
  - would fairly and adequately represent the interests of the class;
  - have produced a plan for the proceeding that sets out a workable method of advancing the proceeding on behalf of a class and of notifying class members of the proceeding; and
  - do not have, on the common issues for the class, an interest in conflict with the interests of other class members.

Significantly, courts following legislation based on either the Ontario or British Columbia models may *not* refuse to certify the action as a class proceeding solely because the class is deficient in any of the following respects: because damages require individual assessment; because of a

---

128 *Peppiatt v. Nicol* (1993), 16 O.R. (3d) 133 (Gen. Div.).
129 B.C. s. 4(1); Ontario s. 5(1).

diversity of contractual relationships *vis-à-vis* different class members; because differing remedies are sought by class members; because of uncertainty over the number or identity of members; and because of the existence of subclasses within the claim.[130] The Quebec statute, while phrased differently, has recently been interpreted to similar effect.[131]

Whether the pleadings disclose a cause of action is a low-threshold test, familiar to civil litigators as that to be applied in an ordinary application to strike pleadings for disclosing "no reasonable claim." The test to be applied is whether it is "plain and obvious" that the plaintiff cannot succeed.[132]

As to the second requirement, this may be broken down into two "sub-requirements" of an identifiable class: numerosity and definition. The Canadian Acts require only that a class consist of two or more members. However, it stands to reason that the smaller the class, the less likely that a class action will be found to be the preferable procedure for resolving the issues, and so the absence of an explicit numerosity requirement is perhaps somewhat misleading.

Whether or not the class is "definable" is a more subjective question. In *Bywater v. Toronto Transit Commission*, it was said that

> [t]he purpose of the class definition is threefold: (a) it identifies those persons who have a potential claim for relief against the defendant; (b) it defines the parameters of the lawsuit so as to identify those persons who are bound by its results; and lastly, (c) it describes who is entitled to notice pursuant to the Act. Thus for the mutual benefit of the plaintiff and the

---

130 *Ontario Act*, s. 6; B.C. s. 7.
131 In Quebec, an action will be certified as a class proceeding if (1) the recourses of the class members raise identical, similar, or related questions of law or fact; (2) the alleged facts appear to warrant the conclusions sought; (3) the composition of the group makes joinder impracticable; and (4) the representative is in a position to represent adequately the interests of the class members: see Quebec art. 1003. The similarity of the requirements in all three provinces was discussed by the Supreme Court in *Dutton, supra* note 64 at para. 38.
132 *Peppiatt v. Nicol*, [1998] 71 O.T.C. 321 (Gen. Div.). This test was elaborated upon in *Abdool v. Anaheim Management Ltd.* (1995), 121 D.L.R. (4th) 496 at 511 (Ont. Div. Ct.):
  (a) All allegations of fact, unless patently ridiculous or incapable of proof, must be accepted as proved;
  (b) The defendant, in order to succeed, must show that it is plain and obvious beyond doubt that the plaintiffs could not succeed;
  (c) The novelty of the cause of action will not militate against the plaintiffs; and
  (d) The statement of claim must be read as generously as possible, with a view to accommodating any inadequacies in the form of the allegations due to drafting deficiencies.

defendant, the class definition ought not to be unduly narrow or unduly broad.[133]

Classes and subclasses may be created or deleted as the litigation proceeds.[134] However, in order to obtain certification, at lease one class must be identified.

It is questions about common issues and, more particularly, preferability that most often determine the outcome of the certification process in a mass tort claim, and so it is necessary to review each of these in somewhat greater depth.

2) Common Issues

Recall that Rule 23's "opt-out" scheme, set out under 23(b)(3), requires that the "questions of law or fact common to the members of the class predominate" over individual questions. In Canada, the situation was explained thus by Mr. Justice Smith in *Endean v. Canadian Red Cross Society*:

> The question of whether individual issues predominate over common issues, which so permeates the American law on this subject, is expressly excluded as a relevant consideration by s. 4(1)(c) of the Act. Further, a common issue need not be dispositive of the litigation. A common issue is sufficient if it is an issue of fact or law common to all claims, and that its resolution in favour of the plaintiffs will advance the interests of the class, leaving individual issues to be litigated later in separate trials, if necessary: *Harrington v. Dow Corning Corporation et al* (1996), 22 B.C.L.R. (3d) 97 at 105, 110 (S.C.).[135]

In numerous proceedings that have been certified, a determination of a common issue clearly advanced the claims of the potential classes to a significant extent. For example, the common issues in both *Campbell v. Flexwatt Corporation*[136] and *Chace v. Crane Canada*[137] concerned allegedly defective overhead radiant ceiling panels and cracking toilet tanks, respectively. In *Endean*, the common issue related to allegedly contaminated

---

133 *Bywater v. Toronto Transit Commission* (1998), 27 C.P.C. (4th) 172 at para. 10 (Ont. Gen. Div.).
134 *Peppiatt v. Nicol* (1993), 16 O.R. (3d) 133 (Gen. Div.).
135 *Endean v. Canadian Red Cross Society* (1997), 148 D.L.R. (4th) 158 at 167 (B.C.S.C.) rev'd in part on another point (1998), 157 D.L.R. (4th) 465 (C.A.).
136 (1996), 25 B.C.L.R. (3d) 329 at 343 (S.C.), rev'd in part on another point (1998) 44 B.C.L.R. (3d) 343 (C.A.).
137 (1996), 26 B.C.L.R. (3d) 339 (S.C.), aff'd (1997), 44 B.C.L.R. (3d) 264 (C.A.).

blood products, and in *Harrington v. Dow Corning Corp.*[138] the common issue was whether silicon gel breast implants were a dangerous product. Moreover, class proceedings involving a mass tort from a single event have been certified: for instance, *Bywater v. Toronto Transit Commission*,[139] where all members of the class were exposed to smoke in a subway tunnel fire.

Because of the lower threshold set by Canadian courts compared to the American, it is possible for the common issues to comprise far less than would be determinative even of the liability portion of the hearing. For instance, in *Carom v. Bre-X*,[140] the Ontario Court of Appeal found that it was appropriate to focus the class proceeding on the defendant's knowledge and representations regarding the Bre-X company's viability, while leaving plaintiff-focused issues such as reliance "on the sidelines," to be decided at individual trials.[141]

In *Tiemstra v. I.C.B.C.*,[142] the plaintiff sought to challenge the provincial automobile insurance company's policy of "no crash, no cash," which denied certain benefits if there had been no physical damage to the vehicle. The allegation was that I.C.B.C. had breached its statutory, common law, and fiduciary duties. The court rejected the proposed common issue, noting that it was not "dispositive of a significant feature" of the individual claims. The court contrasted those cases where the resolution of the common issue would advance the claims to an appreciable extent with those where the matter would be likely to dissolve into individual disputes. It distinguished the *Tiemstra* class from others that the British Columbia courts had previously certified:

> [16] If the common issue pertains to an alleged defective product ... then it is easy to see that a determination that the product in question is defective or dangerous as alleged will advance the claims to an appreciable extent ...
>
> [17] I agree with the statement in the respondent's factum:
>
>> A class action which will break down into substantial individual trials in any event does not promote judicial economy or improve access to justice, and is not the preferable procedure.[143]

---

138 2000 BCCA 605 [hereinafter *Harrington*].
139 [1988] O.J. No. 4913 (Gen. Div.).
140 *Supra* note 125.
141 In securities cases there may be a statutory "deemed reliance" that might usurp even this necessity.
142 (1997), 38 B.C.L.R. (3d) 377 (C.A.) [hereinafter *Tiemstra*].
143 *Ibid.* at paras. 16–17.

Although the *Tiemstra* decision is arguably sound given the distinctiveness of each cause of action,[144] the reasoning is perhaps awkwardly expressed. The suggestion that the prospect of devolution into individual trials should, *as a rule*, form a basis for the denial of certification is unsupportable, and resort to United States cases is of little assistance considering the fact that in that country the common issues must predominate in order for an action to be certified. A court following *Tiemstra* is left trying to deduce whether or not potential individual trials (often required with respect to damages if nothing else[145]) would be "substantial"; a *reductio* not particularly helpful.

However, the British Columbia Court of Appeal in *Harrington* has demonstrated how broad the definition of a single common issue can be in a product liability context. The allegations spanned hundreds of models of silicon breast implant from several manufacturers. Citing the apparent common knowledge base of the defendants with respect to risks, the court determined that whether breast implants were ever fit for human use was a sufficient common issue. In the court's view, if the plaintiffs were content to set the threshold of liability sufficiently high and be prepared to demonstrate that no implant could meet legal standards, the courts might allow an aggregate claim to proceed where it otherwise might not:

> As we have seen, the case management judge recognized that a risk assessment would probably require the respondent "to establish unfitness against the model of silicone gel breast implant which has the strongest claim to fitness" because "only as against that standard could the issue be said to be common to all manufacturers and all models."[146]

While the *Harrington* decision represents an interesting compromise on the "common issue" question, it does raise some concerns with respect to the notice to the class.[147]

---

144 However, the authority of *Tiemstra* might be said to be in question since the Supreme Court decision in *Rumley v. British Columbia*, discussed below.
145 Section 7(a) of the *B.C. Act* expressly provides that the court must not refuse certification merely because damages require individual assessment after determination of the common issues.
146 *Harrington*, supra note 138 at para. 35.
147 In such cases, the interests of the absentee class members would be inadequately protected if they were not informed of the strategic decision that had been made by class counsel to set a high bar in order to achieve certification. The spectre of valid individual claims (which do not rely on the allegation that *all* breast implants are unfit) being barred by such a process is very real and should be of concern to the courts. Notification of this decision was apparently possible in *Harrington* because the class members were known. However, in cases where they are not, a court will almost certainly be more reluctant to certify on such a "lowest common denominator" basis.

3) Preferability

As might be imagined, the preferability of a class action is largely determined by whether there are sufficient common issues. It may be a technical error to blend the two so closely together (as the British Columbia Court of Appeal did in *Tiemstra*, above) but, in fact, the interplay between them is considerable.

The proper analysis means that the existence of a common issue is not, on its own, sufficient to render a class action the preferable procedure, though it may in many cases lead to that conclusion. Rather, even an action with a number of common issues might be denied certification if the goals of the legislation, that is, efficiency, access to the courts, and behaviour modification of wrongdoers, are not met.

Mr. Justice Winkler in *Carom v. Bre-X Minerals Limited* summarized the approach to be taken in relation to preferability. He stated:

> The proper approach ... is to have regard to all of the individual and common issues arising from the claims in the context of the factual matrix. A class proceeding is the preferable procedure where it presents a fair, efficient and manageable method of determining the common issues which arise from the claims of multiple plaintiffs and where such determination will advance the proceeding in accordance with the goals of judicial economy, access to justice and the modification of the behaviour of wrongdoers.[148]

Some courts have gone further, holding that the preferability requirement means that, in order to defeat certification once the basic criteria are met, "the party opposing certification must present a concrete alternative to a class proceeding."[149]

In 2001 the Supreme Court of Canada pronounced on three certification decisions,[150] and it then became apparent that "preferability" is now the principal analytical threshold for class actions.[151] In *Hollick v. Toronto*

---

148 *Carom*, supra note 125 at 239.
149 Eizenga *et al.*, supra note 15 at § 2.9, citing in example *Bunn v. Ribcor* (1998), 38 C.L.R. (2d) 291; supp. reasons unreported (19 June 1998), Newmarket docket # 354/98, 355/98 (Ont. Gen. Div.).
150 The third of the "trilogy" was *Dutton*, supra note 64.
151 John C. Kleefeld, "Class Actions in Canada" (2002) 44:3 For The Defense 60 at 61 (describing the emergence of preferability as the dominant determinant of certification). See also Shelley M. Feld & Paul J. Martin, "Class Actions: Recent Developments of Importance" (Toronto, Fasken Martineau DuMoulin, 2000) <www.fasken.com> (describing the preferability in the wake of the trilogy as a question of "efficiency versus fairness").

(City), the Court confirmed that class proceedings statutes "should be construed generously" with a view to their purposes.[152] That case concerned nuisance complaints surrounding a government-operated landfill. Unlike that of British Columbia, Ontario's legislation does not list the policy factors that the court should consider in the "preferability" inquiry; nevertheless, the Court found that they were the same: judicial economy, access to justice, and behaviour modification. Noting that the Ontario government had set up a claims fund to deal with such complaints and that no claims had yet been made against it, the Court concluded that either the claims were "so small as to be non-existent or so large as to provide sufficient incentive for individual action."[153] As a result, access to justice was not in issue, and the Court otherwise found that judicial economy and behaviour modification were likewise not engaged. The certification was denied.

At perhaps the other extreme, in *Rumley v. British Columbia*,[154] the Court did approve certification of a class action in the case of the Jericho Residential School, arising from allegations of sexual and physical abuse of students that spanned five decades. Despite the inherently individualistic nature of such torts, the Court found a common issue in whether there had been systemic negligence at the school and in the government over the periods in question, and that a class action was preferable to other types of procedures.

In both cases, the government had set up compensation funds (in the Jericho School case capped at $60,000, in *Hollick* a "small claims" fund capped at $5,000). Both decisions' consideration of "preferability" seemed based in some part upon a comparison between the class action and the extant claims process; if the latter was found wanting, certification was deemed preferable.

From the deterrence point of view, there is a considerable difficulty in allowing defendants to set up their own compensation scheme as an alternative to class certification. If one of the justifications for class actions is that many victims might not know that they have been harmed or indeed might not sufficiently care to pursue claims from the compensation fund, then the defendant will pay only a fraction of the damages necessary to ensure appropriate deterrence.[155] As an example of the degree to which

---

152 *Hollick, supra* note 102 at para. 15.
153 *Ibid.* at para. 33.
154 2001 SCC 69.
155 Even after a successful litigation, for instance, many class members do not claim their shares of the aggregate award. The *Ontario Report (1982), supra* note 97 at 133–34, summarizing U.S. statistics, noted that, in 15.8 percent of cases where funds were

deterrence is undervalued by Canadian courts, the issue has not yet been fully considered in this light.

So far, the Canadian courts have seen the deterrence factor as a by-product of "access to justice," in the sense that the more claims are compensated, the greater the deterrent effect. The question of preferability is obvious in a case of numerous, low-value (i.e., non-marketable) claims, where the choice is between a class action and no action at all. However, repeated references to this type of case in the literature and jurisprudence might lead one to conclude that preferability is not as clear at the other end of the claim-value spectrum: in cases of mass tort where each claim is individually viable.[156]

4) Notice Requirements and Opt-Out Rights

Canadian class proceedings legislation is remarkably flexible on the question of notice. While setting out the factors that the court must consider when determining what notice is required in the circumstances, Ontario and British Columbia also allow that the court "may dispense with notice if ... the court considers it appropriate to do so."[157]

Similarly, while the procedure for permitting "opt-outs" is described, it is not explicitly mandatory in any Canadian legislation except that of Quebec.[158] Despite this flexibility, there has never been a "mandatory" class certified in Canada, nor has any certification occurred where notification of class members was deemed unnecessary. Still, the breadth of the discretion is intriguing.

---

made available, less than half of class members filed claims. The preferability of class proceedings over a pre-emptive defendant-driven compensation scheme derives from the fact that this unspent amount ought not accrue to the defendant if deterrence is to be optimized.

156 In *Hollick*, the Court suggests (*supra* note 102 at para. 34) that, if claims are individually viable, the defendant "will be forced to internalize the costs of its conduct." This is not quite true: in fact, even if every claim is individually viable, and indeed even if every viable claim is pursued (another question entirely), a class proceeding will result in a more accurate internalization of harm than several individual actions owing to cost-spreading of litigation investment reducing per-claim litigation costs and increasing settlement amounts closer to the optimal. This phenomenon is discussed at some length in Craig Jones, *Theory of Class Actions* (Toronto: Irwin Law, 2002).

157 B.C. s. 19(2); Ontario s. 17(2). There is no equivalent in Quebec.

158 Quebec's law describes the "right ["*droit*"] of a member to request his exclusion," (Quebec art. 1007) and the *Civil Code* states that if this right is exercised the member is not bound: *Civil Code*, s. 2848. A member will be "deemed" to have opted out if he continues an individual action after certification: Quebec art. 1008.

5) Aggregate Assessment of Damages and Non-Restitutionary Distribution

Another remarkable feature of the Canadian class action legislation is its provision for the aggregate assessment of damages: once liability has been established, the amount of an aggregate award may be calculated on the basis of statistical evidence[159] if, *inter alia*, "the aggregate or a part of the defendant's liability to some or all class members can reasonably be determined without proof by individual class members."[160] We say that this is remarkable because efforts by U.S. courts to perform similar assessments of damages on an aggregate basis have been seen as a violation of defendants' rights under the Fifth and Seventh Amendments of the U.S. constitution, provisions that have no equivalent in Canadian law, where property and civil due process have no such explicit protection.[161]

The Ontario Law Reform Commission report in 1982 had recommended that aggregate assessment should be the rule rather than the exception: "Individual proceedings relating to the assessment of monetary relief should be required only where an aggregate assessment is not feasible or where the amount of monetary relief to which class members are entitled cannot be established by consumer evidence."[162]

Canadian legislation further permits *cy pres* distribution to third parties "in any manner that may reasonably be expected to benefit class or subclass members, even though the order does not provide for monetary relief to individual class or subclass members,"[163] and this applies, apparently, even if doing so requires that persons other than the class members receive "windfalls."[164] The Ontario Law Reform Commission was well aware that this, too, had been found problematic on "fairness" grounds in the United States, an objection the commission rejected.[165]

---

159 B.C. s. 30, Ontario s. 24.
160 B.C. s. 29(1)(c). See also Ontario s. 24(1)(c).
161 See above chapter 5 notes 24 and 25.
162 *Ontario Report (1982)*, *supra* note 97 at 597. A contemporary commentator noted that this represented a "mirror image of the United States Model": Benjamin S. Duvall, Jr, "The Importance of Substance to the Study of Class Actions: A Review Essay on the Ontario Law Reform Commission Report on Class Actions" 3 Windsor Yearbook of Access to Justice 411 (Windsor, ON: University of Windsor, 1983).
163 B.C. s. 34(1); Ontario 26(4); Quebec arts. 1031–1036; Saskatchewan s. 37; *ULCC Model Act* s. 34.
164 *Ontario Report (1982)*, *supra* note 97 at 577–79.
165 Although the report endorsed *cy pres* distribution only as a "last resort" to avoid returning the money to the defendant (which was realized to weaken deterrence) or forfeit to the state. *Ibid.* at 572–81. However, note that subsequent legislation in B.C.

6) The "Common Law Class Action"

The most striking of the 2001 "trilogy" of 2001 Supreme Court cases is without a doubt *Western Canada Shopping Centres Inc. v. Dutton*.[166] In that case, two debenture holders in a failed company incorporated by the defendant had attempted to file a suit on behalf of themselves and 229 others similarly situated pursuant to Alberta's Rule 42, which was the codification of the previous equitable rules permitting (but not describing in detail) a "representative proceeding."[167]

Reversing its previous decision in *Naken v. General Motors*,[168] the Court held that the benefits of class actions had been demonstrated and should be extended to jurisdictions without comprehensive statutory regimes:

> The need to strike a balance between efficiency and fairness ... belies the suggestion that class actions should be approached restrictively. The defendants argue that *General Motors of Canada Ltd. v. Naken*, [1983] 1 S.C.R. 72, precludes a generous approach to class actions. I respectfully disagree ... [W]hen *Naken* was decided, the modern class action was very much an untested procedure in Canada. In the intervening years, the importance of the class action as a procedural tool in modern litigation has become manifest. Indeed, the reform that has been effected since *Naken* has been motivated in large part by the recognition of the benefits that class actions can offer the parties, the court system, and society: see, e.g., Ontario Law Reform Commission, *supra*, at pp. 3–4.[169]

The Court thus permitted lower courts to design proceedings along the lines of those available under statutory regimes where four conditions are met: "(1) the class is capable of clear definition; (2) there are issues of fact or law common to all class members; (3) success for one class member means success for all; and (4) the proposed representative adequately rep-

---

and the *ULCC Model Act* permit both *cy pres* distribution *and* forfeiture to the government (B.C. s. 34(5)(b); *ULCC Model Act* s. 34(5)(c)) (but not return to the defendant), rather than requiring, as the Ontario Act does, return of undistributed awards. This raises the possibility of *cy pres* distribution through government welfare services.

166 *Supra* note 64.
167 *Alberta Rules of Court*, Alta. Reg. 390/68 reads in relevant part:
> 42. Where numerous persons have a common interest in the subject of an intended action, one or more of those persons may sue or be sued or may be authorized by the Court to defend on behalf of or for the benefit of all.

168 *Supra* note 65.
169 *Dutton*, *supra* note 64 at para. 46.

resents the interests of the class."[170] Upon the satisfaction of those basic conditions, the test becomes one analogous to the "preferability" requirement of statutory certification regimes: "If these conditions are met the court must also be satisfied, in the exercise of its discretion, that there are no countervailing considerations that outweigh the benefits of allowing the class action to proceed."[171]

However, one profound difference between the "common law class action" defined in *Dutton* is the notice requirements, which may be more stringent than those under the statutes and might even require actual notice with the right to opt out:

> 49 [...] A judgment is binding on a class member only if the class member is notified of the suit and is given an opportunity to exclude himself or herself from the proceeding. This case does not raise the issue of what constitutes sufficient notice. However, prudence suggests that all potential class members be informed of the existence of the suit, of the common issues that the suit seeks to resolve, and of the right of each class member to opt out, and that this be done before any decision is made that purports to prejudice or otherwise affect the interests of class members.[172]

Though the full impact of the *Dutton* decision is not yet known, the philosophy underlying the decision may have several implications for class actions generally. The principal advance of *Dutton* was its recognition that the default position in *Naken* had changed: class proceedings may exist at common law, and (by implication) that they are modified by statute but not dependent on it. The idea that class proceedings may be designed by the courts in the interest of fair adjudication of mass torts also leaves the tantalizing suggestion that existing legislation might not be exhaustive in its description of the aggregative tools available to courts.

E. REPRESENTATIVE ACTIONS AFTER *WESTERN CANADIAN SHOPPING CENTRES v. DUTTON*

Following the Supreme Court of Canada's decision in *Western Canadian Shopping Centres, Inc. v. Dutton*, there is a live question regarding to what extent, if at all, a "traditional" representative action, as distinct from a "class action" (with its attendant notice requirements, etc.), may be brought.

---

170 *Ibid.* at para. 48.
171 *Ibid.*
172 *Ibid.* at para. 49.

1) "Representative Proceedings" and "Class Actions"

It is a recurring problem that the terms "representative proceeding" and "class action" are frequently used synonymously by the courts and, at least in the case of Manitoba, in the Rules of Court themselves.[173] For this section, we distinguish between those actions brought pursuant to the descendants of the equitable representative proceedings (originating with the fusion of law and equity under the *Supreme Court of Judicature Act, 1873*,[174] and the adoption of Rule 10 of the English *Rules of Procedure*[175]) now enshrined in most provinces' rules of court, which we will call "representative proceedings." We use the term "class actions" to refer to proceedings brought pursuant to class proceedings statutes or to the common law class action outlined in *Dutton*.

The principal difference is that a "class proceeding" has elaborate procedures to preserve a measure of representation and litigative autonomy for members of the plaintiff group, which may be an aggregate of a wide variety of claims. It is often, if not usually, expected that once one or more common issues are resolved, the "class" will break down into a multiplicity of smaller groups or individual actions to deal with non-common issues. Intraclass conflict is not only possible, it is expected in a class action. A traditional "representative proceeding" does not require such elaborate procedures, because it is available only when all members of the represented group have the same claim.

The *Dutton* decision permitted courts to design class action procedures under the aegis of the provincial representative proceedings rules, in provinces where such procedures were not embodied by statute. It set out procedures closely modelled on the class proceedings Acts of Ontario and British Columbia.

The stated purpose of *Dutton* was to fill what McLachlin C.J. referred to as "the procedural vacuum."[176] If this is so, then it was concerned only with the absence of procedures for class actions proper — that is, where plaintiffs with diverse claims and interests are aggregated. There was no

---

173 Rule 12, Class Actions. This section has been repealed and replaced with the coming into force of the *Class Proceedings Act*, C.C.S.M. c. C130.
174 (U.K.), 36 & 37 Vict., c. 66.
175 Rule 10 provided:

10. Where there are numerous parties having the same interest in one action, one or more of such parties may sue or be sued, or may be authorised by the Court to defend in such action, on behalf or for the benefit of all parties so interested.

176 *Dutton, supra* note 64 at para. 35.

"procedural vacuum" with respect to the "traditional" representative actions (which had been pursued for centuries), and *Dutton* nowhere purports to make such claims impossible. In other words, nothing in *Dutton* suggests that the traditional representative proceeding — for instance, as employed to permit litigation by a union or unincorporated association — was no longer available.

a) Representative Action

Historically, court rules permitted representative proceedings only in narrow circumstances. The classic statement is that of Lord Macnaghten in *Duke of Bedford v. Ellis*: "Given a common interest and a common grievance, a representative suit was in order if the relief sought was in its nature beneficial to all whom the plaintiff proposed to represent."[177] The standard, in other words, was the unity of relief sought. This is "especially [so] where the same measure of success applies equally to all."[178]

In the *Duke of Bedford* case, significantly, the relief sought was a declaration of statutory rights. Lord Shand said at paragraph 15:

> [A]ll [plaintiffs] ask the same remedy, which it is unnecessary to specify further than to say they all claim a declaratory decree by the court which shall give effect to their statutory privileges — the same in the case of each of them — as growers of fruit, flowers and vegetables, and an injunction to restrain the appellant from doing any act contrary to such declaratory decree. There is thus one cause or matter only in which all of the plaintiffs have an interest, and other "growers" have the same interest in it, as disclosed in the record, that matter being the disregard by the defendant of their statutory privileges, for which accordingly one and the same remedy in the form of the different heads of claim is asked.

Other English decisions declined to permit representative claims based on numerous individual contracts with a conveyor of cargo (each of which must be proven)[179] or in a suit against a corporation whose shareholders would each need to prove individual damages.[180]

It was the "unity of interest" requirement that led the Supreme Court in *Naken* to consider a "representative proceeding" inappropriate in a product liability case where there were complex and highly individualistic issues of causation and damages involved. Another way of putting this is to focus on

---

177 [1901] A.C. 1 at para. 5 [hereinafter *Duke of Bedford*].
178 *Cobbold v. Time Canada Ltd.* (1976), 13 O.R. (2d) 567 at 569 *per* Stark J.
179 *Markt & Co. v. Knight Steamship Company*, [1910] 2 K.B. 1021 (C.A.).
180 *Beeching v. Lloyd* (1855), 3 Drew. 227.

variances among available defences, as noted by MacKinnon A.C.J.O. in *Seafarers International Union of Canada v. Lawrence*: "[F]or a representative action to be properly formed, there must be a 'common interest' of the named plaintiff and those he claims to represent. If he wins, all win, because all have been injured as members of the class, and there is no separate defence available against some members of the class and not others."[181]

This distinction — between claims that were primarily individualistic in nature (yet had some common element) and those that were entirely duplicative — had been central to the Canadian jurisprudence prior to *Naken*.[182] At the same time, representative actions have long been used in Canada to advance claims either by or against unincorporated groups of persons: for example, *Bowen v. Macmillan*, above.

In more recent years, the courts of several non-class action provinces attempted to fill the "procedural vacuum" and extend the representative rule to actions where the normally required absolute unity of interest within the class was not entirely clear.[183] In most of these cases, the class members were known or ascertainable, and these cases did not present obvious problems of intraclass conflict.[184] These cases might be seen to represent a "middle ground" between traditional representative actions and true class proceedings as foreseen in *Dutton*.

b) Class Proceeding Distinguished

Class proceedings cured the inadequacy of the representative proceeding by permitting actions to be launched in the aggregate even where many, and even most, issues at stake were individualistic. A class action, as the

---

181 (1979), 24 O.R. (2d) 257 at 262 (C.A.).

182 See, for instance, *Bowen v. MacMillan* (1921), 21 O.W.N. 23 at 25 (H.C.) (representative action permitted where damages were "general ... to the class"); *Farnham v. Fingold*, [1973] 2 O.R. 132 at 136 (C.A.) (representative action not permitted "where the members of the class have damages that must be individually assessed," because, *inter alia*, it would deprive defendant of discovery) and *Shields v. Mayor*, [1952] O.J. No. 299 (C.A.) (representative action not permitted as each potential "class" member had separate contract with defendant).

183 *Cobbold v. Time Canada Ltd.* (1976), 13 O.R. 567 (H.C.J.); *Ranjoy Sales and Leasing Ltd. v. Deloitte, Haskins and Sells*, [1984] 4 W.W.R. 706 (Man. Q.B.) [hereinafter *Ranjoy*]; *International Capital Corp. v. Schafer* (1995), 130 Sask. R. 23 (Q.B.); *Guarantee Co. of North America v. Caisse populaire de Shippagan Ltée* (1988), 86 N.B.R. (2d) 342 (Q.B.); *Lee v. OCCO Developments Ltd.* (1994), 148 N.B.R. (2d) 321 (Q.B.); *Audenhove v. Nova Scotia (Attorney General)* (1994), 134 N.S.R. (2d) 294 at para. 7 (S.C.); *Horne v. Canada (Attorney General)* (1995), 129 Nfld. & P.E.I.R. 109 at para. 24 (P.E.I.S.C.).

184 For instance, in the Manitoba case of *Ranjoy*, *ibid.*, while the amount owed to each plaintiff, should liability ascertained be varied, was known.

Supreme Court has recently confirmed in the *Jericho Hill* case,[185] can be certified on a single common issue (the vicarious liability of the government) even in the face of strikingly individualistic facts (sexual assaults by several perpetrators against numerous victims). Another (though related) distinction between class and representative actions is that the litigation of common issues in a class action need not be determinative of the success of the class' claims; it simply must "move the litigation forward."

Because a class action raises issues of intraclass conflict that are not present in a representative proceeding (particularly claim-value diversity, subclasses, and a range of legal arguments available with respect to claims within the class), it is essential that class action rules contain safeguards. These safeguards require that members be given notice and the right to opt out. They also foresee the inclusion within the class of subclasses (with separate counsel).

c) The Plaintiffs' Option?

None of the safeguards of class action statutes (and, by extension, of the procedural regime established in *Dutton*) are required in a true representative proceeding, where by definition no intraclass conflict can occur.[184] Theoretically, then, if a plaintiff is prepared to meet the more restrictive standards for a representative proceeding, he or she should be relieved of going through the motions required of class actions — there should be no need for a certification hearing *per se*, or notice to those represented. This should be so whether the representative action is concurrently available with class action legislation or with the *ad hoc* procedures designed in *Dutton* (which closely follow those set out in the various class proceedings Acts).

But does such an option exist? We will examine this question from two perspectives: first, whether class proceedings Acts themselves supplant the "representative proceedings" rules; and second, whether the "common law class action" designed under those rules itself supplants ordinary representative proceedings in jurisdictions without class action statutes.

---

185 *Rumley v. British Columbia*, [2001] S.C.J. No. 39.
186 It is still possible, of course, that *some* conflict of interest between the lawyer and members of the class might still occur even if there was no intraclass conflict *per se* (i.e., the lawyer might settle the claim for too little with the acquiescence, for whatever reason, of the representative plaintiff). However, this problem would be unlikely to occur outside contingency fee arrangements in damages actions, could be largely ameliorated by appropriate court supervision, and is not discussed further here.

i) Do Statutory Class Action Regimes Supplant "Representative Proceedings" Rules?

It would appear that, in no province where class proceeding legislation has been introduced has the rule permitting representative proceedings been abandoned, though in Ontario it has been considerably modified. In British Columbia, Rule 5(11) survives unaltered, seven years after the *Class Proceedings Act* came into force. Saskatchewan appears to have followed the same path.[187] This is in contrast to the introduction of the new Federal Court class action rules; upon coming into force, the previous rule regarding representative proceedings was simultaneously repealed.[188]

In Ontario, the traditional rule has been split in two since the *Class Proceedings Act* was enacted. Defendants with the same interest may be represented by one of them following the traditional pattern. However, it would appear that plaintiffs' representative proceedings that do not fall under the *Class Proceedings Act* are now limited to a single category of claim: those made by trade unions and other unincorporated associations.[189] This is interesting, because it clearly demonstrates Ontario's determination to preserve (albeit in a limited way) representative proceedings outside the class action framework.

---

187 The traditional "representative proceeding" rule remains enshrined (as of 3 April 2002) in Saskatchewan's *Queen's Bench Rules*, Rule 70:

> 70 Where there are numerous persons having the same interest in one cause or matter, including actions for the prevention of waste or otherwise for the protection of property, one or more of such persons may sue or be sued, or may be authorized by the court to defend in such cause or matter, on behalf of or for the benefit of all persons so interested.

188 Section 114 of the *Federal Court Rules, 1998* repealed per s. 12, SOR/2002-417 (21 November 2002), *Rules Amending the Federal Court Rules, 1998*. See also the repeal of Manitoba's former "class action" Rule 12: M.R.205/2002.

189 See *Courts of Justice Act*, Reg. 194 (Amended to O. Reg. 206/02) Rules 12.07 and 12.08:

> PROCEEDING AGAINST REPRESENTATIVE DEFENDANT
> 12.07 Where numerous persons have the same interest, one or more of them may defend a proceeding on behalf or for the benefit of all, or may be authorized by the court to do so. O. Reg. 465/93, s. 2(3).
>
> PROCEEDING BY UNINCORPORATED ASSOCIATION OR TRADE UNION
> 12.08 Where numerous persons are members of an unincorporated association or trade union and a proceeding under the *Class Proceedings Act, 1992* would be an unduly expensive or inconvenient means for determining their claims, one or more of them may be authorized by the court to bring a proceeding on behalf of or for the benefit of all. O. Reg. 288/99, s. 9.

In Newfoundland, the traditional rule (Rule 7.11[190]) has been augmented by new rules following the *Class Actions Act* (Rule 7A). However, Rule 7A contains explicit reference to the representative action rule, which is preserved: "7A.11. This Rule [i.e., class action procedure] does not apply to a proceeding brought in a representative capacity under rule 7.11, 7.12 or 7.13, unless the court orders that this Rule shall apply on the terms that the court may order."

There is only one case to our knowledge directly comparing the statutory class proceedings with representative actions. In *Chace v. Crane Canada Inc.*,[191] the Court of Appeal, in the course of deciding whether a statutory class action for defective plumbing components was "preferable" to the alternatives, considered whether a proposed class action brought pursuant to the statute might otherwise be litigated as a representative action under rule 5(11) of the British Columbia *Rules of Court*. Huddart J.A., for the court, said:

> [29] It is difficult to see how the claims of more than 100 plaintiffs could be litigated other than by a class proceeding, or as individual actions. Because damages must be assessed individually, and a fund or pool of assets cannot be created in compensating damages, a representative action under Rule 5(11) of the Supreme Court Rules would not be appropriate. See *Pasco, Oregon Jack Creek Indian Band et al. v. CNR Company et al.* (1989), 34 B.C.L.R. (2d) 344 (C.A.). A multi-party action under Rule 5(2) would permit full discovery against each individual plaintiff and the possibility that each plaintiff would have to appear at trial to prove his or her case. Costs would be payable by each plaintiff jointly and severally, giving rise to potentially greater costs than recovery. The *Class Proceedings Act* was designed for multiple plaintiff claims precisely because of the difficulty in prosecuting such claims under the Rules.

The Court of Appeal here confirms that, notwithstanding the enactment of the more liberal rules of the *Class Proceedings Act*, a plaintiff might still bring a representative action without availing him- or herself of the legislative regime, providing that he or she can meet the higher threshold set out by that rule: (a) no necessity for individual damages calculation and (b) the

---

190 See *Rules of the Supreme Court, 1986* under the *Judicature Act*, S.N.L. 1986, c. 42, Schedule D, amended to Nfld. Reg. 60/02.:

> 7.11. (1) Where numerous persons have the same interest in a proceeding, not being a proceeding mentioned in rule 7.12, the proceeding may be begun, and, unless the Court otherwise orders, continued, by or against any one or more of them as representing all or as representing all except one or more of them.

191 (1997), 44 B.C.L.R. (3d) 264 (C.A.).

possibility that a single fund or pool of assets could satisfy compensation of the "class" members.

This distinction makes sense: the detailed procedural elements of class proceedings statutes, like the *Dutton* decision itself, are principally designed to provide safeguards against conflicts of interest. Notice requirements and opt-out rights, for instance, are designed to balance the interests of class members in instances of claims-value diversity. Rules for subclassing and supervision over fees and settlements are designed to avoid a conflict between class counsel (almost always working on contingency) and absent class members. It is precisely to those cases, which *Naken* confirmed were not appropriate for representative actions, that the class action rules — whether statutory or "common law" via *Dutton* — should apply.

ii) Subsequent Treatment of Dutton *in Representative Proceedings Brought Pursuant to Rules of Court*

There have been two cases of the Manitoba superior courts considering the impact of *Dutton* upon the representative proceeding rule. One, *Scott v. St. Boniface Hospital*,[192] is straightforward. After *Dutton*, the plaintiff attempted to certify an action — "To allow the action to proceed as a class action under Queen's Bench Rule 12" — following the *Dutton* pattern. The court found that the *Dutton* criteria had not been satisfied in several respects, and denied the motion. There was no suggestion in *Scott* that the plaintiffs, who were claiming for stress-related conditions after having been exposed to a low risk of blood-borne disease during routine hospital exams, could possibly have fallen within the definition of a traditional representative action. Issues of causation and damages would have been entirely individual; if the action could be aggregated, it could only be under the *Dutton* class action regime, and it was on that basis that certification was sought and denied.

The second decision, *Neufeld v. Manitoba*, is more difficult, because it was filed as a "representative action" under Rule 12 *before* the *Dutton* decision was handed down. The claim arose as a result of two decisions of the Manitoba Court of Appeal that a security program at the Winnipeg Law Courts Complex was conducted in violation of section 8 of the *Charter*.[193] The plaintiff in *Neufeld* then launched a damages suit, claiming that each of the 600,000 searches conducted under the security program was an invasion of privacy. At first instance, Master Goldberg found that the action was inappropriate for the representative action rule, because, *inter alia*,

---

192 [2002] M.J. No. 278, 2002 MBQB 196 [hereinafter *Scott*].
193 *R. v. Gillespie* (1999), 142 Man. R. (2d) 96 (C.A.); *R. v. Gillespie*, [2000] M.J. No. 218 (C.A.).

there was not a single measure of damages applicable to each possible claim.[194]

After hearing the appeal from the master's decision, *Dutton* was decided and Hamilton J. of the Court of Queen's Bench heard further arguments. She decided that, even given *Dutton*'s liberal rules, the *Neufeld* action was not appropriate for aggregate litigation, and granted the government's motion to dismiss Neufeld's personal action in its entirety. The Manitoba Court of Appeal upheld Hamilton J.'s decision with little further comment.

The decision of the Manitoba courts in *Neufeld* made no attempt to distinguish between a traditional representative action brought pursuant to the Rules and a class action brought pursuant to *Dutton* or legislation. It is possible (though by no means necessary) to read the decisions of the superior and appeal courts as suggesting that *Dutton* actions had completely supplanted traditional representative actions. They do not say so explicitly, however.[195]

Another inconclusive decision originated in the Federal Court prior to its own class action rules coming into effect, but after *Dutton*. In *Smith v. Canada (Minister of Indian Affairs and Northern Development)*,[196] ninety-eight purported descendants of members of the Horse Lake First Nation launched a suit to gain benefits from a settlement negotiated between that First Nation and the federal government. The plaintiffs brought a motion to amend their claim so as, *inter alia*, to allow it to proceed with three of the ninety-eight acting in a representative capacity for the rest.

Hugesson J. found reasons to deny representative status, noting: "... I do not think that the proposed representative litigation meets the tests laid down by the Supreme Court of Canada in the case of *Western Canadian Shopping Centres Inc. v. Dutton* ..." He also found the proposed represented group "not homogenous" and "ill defined," and noted at paragraph 8 that "... there are important differences not only between the classes but within and between members of each class ... there are some who made applications for membership that were accepted, there are some who made appli-

---

194 *Neufeld v. Manitoba*, 2001 MBQB 14. The plaintiff sought a "pool" of $300,000,000 from which individuals who were searched could claim compensation.
195 Similarly, the Alberta Court of Queen's Bench decided that a class action filed post-*Dutton* pursuant to Rule 42 could proceed using, as "default" rules, those suggested by the Alberta Law Reform Commission for class action legislation, subject to arguments that such rules were inappropriate: *Pauli v. Ace Ina Insurance*, [2002] A.J. No. 926 (Q.B.). Again, though, the plaintiff was seeking to certify pursuant to *Dutton* and made no argument that the action would have met the "traditional" test for a representative action.
196 [2002] F.C.J. No. 1455 (T.D.).

cations for membership that were refused, there are some who appealed those refusals ... and so on ... They do not have the same interest, therefore, I think they should not be treated as a class."

Moreover, Hugesson J. decided that the action as it stood, with ninety-eight individual plaintiffs, would be manageable and more convenient. This was, in other words, a case that would have been inappropriate for a "traditional" representative action, regardless of *Dutton*. But, again, the failure to distinguish between "representative" and "class" actions, as well as the hint that *Dutton* sets out exhaustive parameters for representative actions, is troublesome.

Subsequently, in another post-*Dutton* decision, *Desjarlais v. Canada*,[197] the Federal Court refused to strike out a representative action brought by certain Cree Indians "... on their own behalf and either on behalf of their living descendants, or on behalf of the living descendants of a named individual. The individuals and delineated descendants, all of whom are Cree, are direct descendants of Indians whose ancestors have lived in what is now part of Western Canada since time immemorial." However, it was expected that, in the course of the litigation, the names of the some 650 persons in the represented group would be known and revealed through particulars. It is not entirely clear whether Prothonotary Hargraves foresaw a mechanical application of the *Dutton* rules (especially those regarding notice or opt-out rights) at a later stage of the proceedings, or if it was assumed that the case would be carried forward eventually under the Federal Court's new class action rules.

---

197 [2002] F.C.J. No. 1272.

8. Some Emerging Issues Regarding Class Actions

A. IS DETERRENCE THE MOST IMPORTANT BENEFIT OF CLASS LITIGATION?

At the time of the adoption of Rule 23 in the United States, little thought went into the question of the class action's role in society beyond a rather simple ambition to provide a mechanism of benefit to individuals who were otherwise without recourse to the courts.[1] Despite the experience of almost forty years of class actions, it is still not unusual to find modern scholars discussing the purposes of aggregate litigation in essentially these terms. In a comprehensive article on developments in civil litigation, for instance, the *Harvard Law Review* in 2000 discussed the "two important functions" of "the modern class action": "... first, it provides individuals with injuries insufficient to justify the cost of a lawsuit an economically feasible avenue of redress; second, it helps relieve the burden on court dockets ... arising from mass torts ..."[2] Only somewhat later does this article discuss deterrence, and it does so only as an aspect of "procedural fair-

---

[1] See generally Arthur A. Miller, "Of Frankenstein Monsters and Shining Knights: Myth, Reality, and the 'Class Action Problem'" (1979) 92 Harv. L. Rev. 664.

[2] "Developments — The Paths of Civil Litigation" (2000) 113 Harv. L. Rev. 1752 at 1806–7.

ness," focusing again on "widespread, but individually minimal harm."[3] This pervasive emphasis on the class action's deterrent effect on numerous low-value claims has taken deep root in Canada,[4] where the goal of access to justice is described as overarching.[5]

Despite the significant differences between the U.S. and Canadian statutes, Canadian courts often rely on U.S. literature to divine their purposes, as the Supreme Court of Canada did in *Western Canadian Shopping Centres Inc. v. Dutton*,[6] where it minimized the role of deterrence by listing it third behind, purely procedural ambitions, and emphasized deterrence principally with respect to such numerous low-value claims:

> 27 Class actions offer three important advantages over a multiplicity of individual suits. First, by aggregating similar individual actions, class actions serve judicial economy by avoiding unnecessary duplication in fact-finding and legal analysis. The efficiencies thus generated free judicial resources that can be directed at resolving other conflicts, and can also reduce the costs of litigation both for plaintiffs (who can share litigation costs) and for defendants (who need litigate the disputed issue only once, rather than numerous times) ....
>
> 28 Second, by allowing fixed litigation costs to be divided over a large number of plaintiffs, class actions improve access to justice by making economical the prosecution of claims that would otherwise be too costly to prosecute individually. Without class actions, the doors of justice remain closed to some plaintiffs, however strong their legal claims. Sharing costs ensures that injuries are not left unremedied ....
>
> 29 Third, class actions serve efficiency and justice by ensuring that actual and potential wrongdoers do not ignore their obligations to the public. *Without class actions, those who cause widespread but individually minimal harm might not take into account the full costs of their conduct, because for any one plaintiff the expense of bringing suit would far exceed the likely recovery. Cost-sharing decreases the expense of pursuing legal recourse and accordingly*

---

3   *Ibid.* at 1809–10.
4   See, for instance, Dean F. Edgell, *Product Liability Law in Canada* (Toronto: Butterworths, 2000) at 179 (describing the "reason" for class proceedings as related to claims that are "uneconomic to pursue" and "not [individually] viable").
5   See, for instance, Ontario Law Reform Commission, *Report on Class Actions*, 3 vols. (Toronto: Ministry of the Attorney General, 1982) [hereinafter *Ontario Report (1982)*] at 139 ("effective access to justice is a precondition to the exercise of all other legal rights.")
6   2001 SCC 46 [hereinafter *Dutton*].

> *deters potential defendants who might otherwise assume that minor wrongs would not result in litigation* .... [Emphasis added.][7]

This is not to suggest that the Supreme Court is unaware of the basic economic principles of negligence law, which hold that optimal deterrence will be achieved when the full costs of harm are "internalized" by the wrongdoer.[8] Yet, throughout Anglo-Canadian jurisprudence and commentary (and indeed through much of the American), the goal of deterrence is referred to generally with respect to individually non-viable claims.[9] In cases involving both individually viable and non-viable claims, deterrence is regarded as something of a serendipitous side-effect of class litigation, not without value but subservient to procedural ambitions. The Ontario Law Reform Commission report, for instance, discussed deterrence as an "essentially inevitable, albeit important byproduct of class actions [involving a diversity of claims values]."[10]

It remains to be seen whether Canadian courts will recognize the regulatory, or "public law," role of class actions through an increasing emphasis on deterrence. In our view, such recognition is appropriate and helpful to the development of mass tort law generally, and would permit courts to make better and more realistic decisions when weighing the preferability of class actions at the certification stage and when assessing the appropriateness of ensuing settlements.[11]

---

7 *Ibid.* at paras. 27–29. See also *Hollick v. Toronto (City)*, 2001 SCC 68 at para. 15.

8 Indeed, in *Hollick, ibid.* at para. 15, another class action certification case decided in 2001, the Court recognized that deterrence required that "actual and potential wrongdoers modify their behaviour to take full account of the harm they are causing, or might cause, to the public."

9 Lord Woolf spoke of providing "access to justice where large numbers of people have been affected by another's conduct, but individual loss is so small that it makes an individual action economically unviable": Lord Woolf, *Access to Justice* (Final Report, 1996) at para. 2. In the report that provided the foundation for Ontario's present legislation, deterrence was featured a little more forcefully, with the Act serving to provide a "sharper sense of obligation to the public by those whose actions affect large numbers of people.": *Report of the Attorney General's Advisory Committee on Class Actions Reform* (Toronto: Attorney General of Ontario, 1990).

10 *Ontario Report (1982)*, *supra* note 5 at 145–46.

11 An example of a settlement giving appropriate regard to deterrence principles was that announced in August 2004 by CIBC (subject to court approval). The plaintiffs alleged that some CIBC VISA transactions involving foreign currency resulted in an undisclosed or inadequately disclosed mark up. The Bank agreed to settle for $16.5 million. Because it was not possible to determine which cardholders had incurred the overcharge, all CIBC VISA customers at the relevant times were given pro-rated rebates credited to their accounts, expected to total over $13 million. In order to account for those customers who no longer had accounts, CIBC agreed to pay $1 million, plus any undistributed portion of the main award, to the United Way as a *cy pres* settlement.

B. DO CLASS ACTIONS REALLY CONSERVE JUDICIAL RESOURCES?

An obvious consequence of aggregation is that per-claim litigation costs are reduced. This represents a saving not only to the class members but also to the court, which can hear thousands of claims simultaneously.[12] There is also persuasive evidence that class actions settle more frequently than individual suits, an effect that is purported to increase as aggregation becomes more complete across the class.[13]

To be sure, individual class actions can themselves be very expensive, as Chief Justice Esson warned in *Tiemstra v. Insurance Corporation of British Columbia* when he declared that "class actions have the potential for becoming monsters of complexity and cost."[14] Putting this argument in opposition to the idea of aggregation, however, misses the point, at least in part. As Professor Coffee states: "Easy as it is to point out that mass tort litigation involves high transaction costs, one must move on to the inevitable next question: 'compared to what?'"[15]

Courts have historically exploited basic aggregative techniques such as joinder of actions to take advantage of judicial-scale economies and avoid wasteful duplication of effort (not to mention the embarrassing possibility of inconsistent results on identical questions). Yet to suggest that the public purse will be spared expense with the blossoming of class action regimes ignores a central point of these laws. We have advocated at some length the view that the principal goal of class action suits is to modify behaviour through optimal aggregation and recovery. Although we have argued that the advantages of class litigation accrue to all classable claims

---

   While, as is customary, CIBC denied any wrongdoing, the settlement arrangement represents a recognition of the primacy of deterrence – that is, making the defendant pay — and the secondary importance of compensation, particularly in cases where each class member would receive only a small amount.

12   Even the notoriously expensive asbestos litigation was made considerably less so through aggregative techniques, even absent class actions. A federal study calculated that each asbestos case cost only 19 percent of the average litigation, where the average product liability claim was well above average (174 percent): Thomas E. Willging, "Mass Tort Problems and Proposals: A Report to the Mass Torts Working Group" (Federal Judicial Center 1999, available at <www.fjc.gov/public/pdf.nsf/lookup/MassTApC.pdf>) at 14.

13   One economist who has developed settlement-rate models has found that mandatory aggregation leads to virtual certainty of settlement because, *inter alia*, it eliminates the "signalling" and information uncertainty produced through the opt-out process: Yeon-Koo Che, "Equilibrium Formation of Class Suits" (1996) 62 J. Pub. Econ. 339.

14   *Tiemstra v. Insurance Corporation of British Columbia* (1996), 22 B.C.L.R. (3d) 49 at 61 (S.C.).

15   John C. Coffee, Jr, "Class Wars: The Dilemma of the Mass Tort Class Action" (1995) 95 Colum. L. Rev. 1343 at 1347 [hereinafter Coffee, "Class Wars"].

(not only individually non-viable ones), discussion of the conservation of judicial resources must begin with the recognition that the bringing of aggregate suits, which include claims that are not individually viable, is one of the purposes of a class litigation system. So, while we might seek to employ class actions to reduce consumption of judicial resources *per claim*, we have no right to expect that their employment will reduce consumption *overall*. Class actions seek to move the litigation system towards the optimal level of suit, a level it is at present well below.[16]

This misconception is pervasive[17] and contrary to the Canadian view of judicial economy as a co-equal goal of class proceedings, along with access to justice and behaviour modification. The goal of access for under-represented plaintiffs is, at least in the case of aggregated low-value suits, frequently at odds with the goal of judicial economy: "[T]he [*Class Proceeding*] *Act* is clearly designed to increase access to justice even if this does entail greater use of judicial resources ... [the] concern is not so much with too little public law litigation, but with too little."[18] This observation may lead to the conclusion that the goal of judicial-resource conservation means *ipso facto* that Canadian class action legislation is aimed at higher-value suits as

---

16 The optimal level of suit in negligence law would be where every valid action is brought. Judge Willging, for instance, *supra* note 11 at 20, reflects that "[i]n assessing whether higher claim rates are a problem, one needs to identify potential benefits as well. While higher claiming rates impose burdens on courts, defendants, and other plaintiffs, they may also represent a more complete form of justice."

17 McNeil & Fanscal, for instance, complain that when A.H. Robins (manufacturers of the notorious Dalkon Shield intra-uterine device) filed for bankruptcy and a limited fund class action was certified, "almost 200,000 claimants who had not entered the tort system notwithstanding wide publicity [of earlier individual Dalkon Shield cases] became claimants": Barry F. McNeil & Beth L. Fanscal, "Mass Torts and Class Actions: Facing Increased Scrutiny" 167 F.R.D. 483 at 491 and 494–95.

The authors argue that "[t]he greater efficiency with which mass tort resolution is dispensed, the greater the number of claimants" (at 493) and later that "it appears that certification may indeed attract new — possibly numerous — claims that would otherwise not be pursued." (at 499) Assuming tort law is being correctly applied (and McNeil & Fanscal do not suggest otherwise — their argument is entirely procedural), it is remarkable that an increase in the number of those who can vindicate their legal rights is seen as problematic.

18 Kent Roach, "Fundamental Reforms to Civil Litigation" in Ontario Law Reform Commission, *Rethinking Civil Justice: Research Studies for the Civil Justice Review (Vol. 2)* (Toronto: Ontario Law Reform Commission, 1996) at 414. The *Ontario Report (1982)* had also noticed the irony of the "judicial efficiency" objection, *supra* note 5 at 130: "Criticisms that condemn class actions aggregating individually nonrecoverable claims — based on the view that they do not contribute to judicial economy, but rather 'stir up' unnecessary litigation — implicitly assume that class actions are, in fact, effective in providing access to the courts to a broader range of individuals."

well as lower-value ones (a conclusion that might be applauded). Unfortunately, it can also lead to the unrealistic expectation that class aggregation rules will lead to an easing of the burden faced by court systems, and this certainly may not be so.

This is not to say that class litigation can never serve the goal of conserving social resources generally. Indeed, a correctly functioning class litigation regime will tend to increase deterrence, reduce the incidence of compensable accidents, promote settlement, and ease the associated costs that are currently externalized through formal and informal insurance. Assuming that the secondary benefit of increased compensation for victims is also realized, then these effects will be further enhanced. The money thus saved can be redirected into the judicial system to accommodate these cases.

Furthermore, any additional cost upon the advent of class litigation should reduce over time as market forces respond to the deterrent effect and standards for typical mass tort claims such as product liability and securities litigation are more clearly defined. At a point of equilibrium, lawsuits will be at the lowest level necessary to diminish uncertainties as to the outcomes in similar suits. In other words, an optimal level of "test cases" will monitor the threshold of tort liability (so that insurance, deterrence, and *ex post* settlement thresholds will in turn be optimized) and track the motion of the standard of care.

In our view, the objection that class actions tend to place undue stress on the judiciary, or that "if you build a superhighway there will be a traffic jam,"[19] has credibility only to the point that the cases clogging the courts should not, under the law, be brought at all. The answer is that the system incentives must be (and to a large extent are) designed to avoid this. To argue otherwise is to say that it is better to have too little enforcement and that more widespread responsibility of mass tortfeasors is a social harm in itself, presumably because it is economically stifling to hold more defendants to the established standard of care. This argument would perhaps be better directed at actually modifying the standard of care and allowing a higher degree of behaviour now considered "negligent" to be considered "reasonable," or, alternately, abandoning a fault/harm based system altogether in favour of regimes designed around no-fault or risk-based principles. As long as these options remain unpalatable, we cannot complain of the number of suits being appropriately brought.

---

18 Francis E. McGovern, "An Analysis of Mass Torts for Judges" (1995) 73 Tex. L. Rev. 1821 at 1840.

C. NEED THE REPRESENTATIVE PLAINTIFF HAVE A CLAIM AGAINST EACH DEFENDANT?

Because class actions frequently involve challenges to products and services that are generic throughout an industry, it is often the case that a single plaintiff would wish to file a claim against numerous defendants, despite the fact that, in the traditional sense, he or she would have a claim only against one — the one who caused that plaintiff's loss.[20] This presents a difficult question of policy. On the one hand, the purpose of class actions is to offer as universal a resolution to a particular claim as possible; to the extent that the defendants' activities truly were generic, it makes some sense to consider them together. Moreover, in some cases it might be that it is only through combining claims against numerous defendants that the plaintiff's claim could become financially viable; in such a case, the harm would go uncompensated and the wrong undeterred if separate proceedings were forced upon victims.

On the other hand, however, difficult questions present themselves: to the extent that the wrongs are not generic, considerable injustice can be done by haling into court a defendant about which no one has cause to complain. In the particular context of class actions, there is a danger that claims against the additional defendants will not be pursued as vigorously as those in which the plaintiff actually has a stake, and the absent class members who are victims of the additional defendants might therefore be "sold out" by the representative and plaintiffs' counsel.[21]

In *Ragoonanan Estate v. Imperial Tobacco Canada Ltd.*,[22] Cumming J. applied the traditional rule of privity to mass claims, holding that a representative plaintiff claiming that the tobacco industry had negligently failed to design "fire proof" cigarettes could proceed only against the manufacturer of the cigarette that had caused the fire in the plaintiff's case. He said at 616:

---

20 This situation should not be confused with the case of the *indeterminate* defendant, that is where a plaintiff does not know which of several of defendants actually made the product that caused the harm. These cases, and the doctrine of 'market share liability' that emerged as a result, are canvassed in Chapter 4 above.
21 Consider that this last concern, though, really is likely to arise only in high-value claims, in which the representative plaintiff is truly engaged as more than a nominal participant. In the ordinary course, the plaintiff's counsel is the real prosecutor of the claim, and when viewed in that context the inclusion of additional defendants might be viewed as less objectionable.
22 (2000), 51 O.R. (3d) 603 (S.C.J.).

In my view, and I so find, it is not sufficient in a class proceeding, for the purpose of meeting the requirement of rule 21.01(1)(b), if the pleading simply discloses a "reasonable cause of action" by the representative plaintiff against only one defendant and then puts forward a similar claim by a speculative group of putative class members against the other defendants.

This case has given rise to the "*Ragoonanan* Motion" in Ontario, by which a defendant can have a class action struck for failing to disclose a cause of action if there is not a representative plaintiff for each defendant. The Ontario Court of Appeal approved of this principle in *Hughes v. Sunbeam Corp. (Canada)*.[23]

In British Columbia, however, the law has developed differently. Despite the almost identical requirements in the statutes of both provinces, in *Campbell v. Flexwatt Corp.*,[24] the court held at paragraph 42 that, in certifying a class action under the British Columbia *Class Proceedings Act*, "there is no requirement that there be a representative plaintiff with a cause of action against every defendant." Several cases have been allowed to proceed as class actions despite the lack of *Ragoonanan*-style "privity": for example, *Harrington v. Dow Corning Corp.*[25] and *Furlan v. Shell Oil*[26] (the latter case decided in the context of a foreign defendant's challenge to service *ex juris*). None of these British Columbia cases dealt with a "*Ragoonanan* Motion" to strike a claim on the basis that it disclosed no reasonable cause of action; nevertheless, they appear to mark a departure in the underlying assumptions made by the courts in that province.

A direct "*Ragoonanan*" or "privity" challenge has been brought in a class action launched by a single representative plaintiff against Money Mart (with whom the plaintiff did business) and numerous other purveyors of "payday loans" whose contracts were allegedly similar to those of Money Mart (and thus, in the plaintiff's submission, unlawful), but with whom the plaintiff himself had no contact. At first instance, the case management judge applied *Campbell v. Flexwatt* and refused to strike the claim against the "stranger" defendants; leave to appeal has been granted.[27] One interesting aspect of this appeal is whether the court will consider affidavit evidence that there exist plaintiffs *with* causes of action against each defendant who are willing to join the claim.

---

23 (2002), 61 O.R. (3d) 433 (C.A.).
24 [1998] 6 W.W.R. 275 (B.C.C.A.).
25 [2000] 11 W.W.R. 201 (B.C.C.A.).
26 (2000), 77 B.C.L.R. (3d) 35 (C.A.).
27 *MacKinnon v. National Money Mart Co.*, 2004 BCCA 137.

D. THE "PUBLIC LAW" VISION OF CLASS COUNSEL AS PRIVATE PROSECUTOR

In a class action suit pursued to advance deterrence, the plaintiffs' attorney is acting in the capacity of private prosecutor, exercising the public's right to appropriate deterrence of wrongdoing.[28] It can be expected that entrepreneurial lawyers will be more vigorous in the prosecution of the public's interest than would be regulatory agencies set up as an alternative to the tort system, though some have proposed the latter as preferable.[29] There is no necessary conflict of interest to the extent that a lawyer might also be seeking to vindicate the rights of the class members; lawyers share with the public a desire to see the wrongdoer held liable for the appropriate amount — the maximum recovery to which they are entitled at law. The important difference is with respect to the counsel's motivation. As an agent for the class, counsel's fees must be carefully monitored to ensure that they do not inappropriately affect the members' compensation. However, from a deterrent point of view, there is no immediately apparent social interest in restricting the percentage of recovery kept by class counsel; in fact, the more the lawyer is able to keep, the more likely optimal litigation investment will be made and optimal deterrence achieved.[30]

It should be apparent by now that designing "investor incentives" in the form of plaintiffs' counsel fee structure can be one of the most important policy decisions made by legislatures or courts. Too little incentive, and neither the social interest in deterrence nor the class interest in compensation will be satisfied. On the other hand, lawyers' fees that seem to take disproportionately from the class recovery appear objectionable *per se*. But should it be so?

---

28 See generally Owen M. Fiss, "The Political Theory of the Class Action" (1996) 53 Wash. & Lee L. Rev. 21.

29 See Peter Huber, "Safety and the Second Best: The Hazards of Public Risk Management in the Courts"(1985) 85 Colum. L. Rev. 277 at 330. While we do not here cover the relative benefits of class actions vis-à-vis administrative regimes to reduce systematic business risk-taking, we share Rosenberg's doubt of the efficacy of such bureaucracies: David Rosenberg, "Class Actions for Mass Torts: Doing Individual Justice by Collective Means" (1987) 62 Ind. L.J. 561 at 579. Of Huber's proposals, Rosenberg writes: "Contrary to the strong but unexplained faith some commentators have expressed in the administrative solution ... the merits of such a solution are far from unambiguous. The history of regulatory laxity, timidity, and even co-optation in regard to certain large-scale risks does not generate optimism."

30 Providing there are sufficient safeguards in place to guard against suits filed for their nuisance value alone.

Consider the case where proposed counsel fees would consume all or virtually all of the proposed recovery. Courts and commentators have expressed a visceral opposition to such a proposal, even when the claims at issue are so small as to be individually untenable.[31] In such a case, the reaction indicates that deterrence is being considerably undervalued and the role of plaintiffs' counsel in exercising the public rights ignored. As distressing as it may seem, such an arrangement might be the only way of pursuing the wrongdoer, and courts ought to be alive to this possibility.

There is no doubt that some aspects of public disapproval of high-fee recoveries are based upon the negative perceptions of lawyers as enriching themselves excessively from the misery of others. But if one considers that the lawyers' gains in such a case would otherwise remain with the wrongdoer, the moral issue becomes more ambiguous. *Someone* is going to gain financial benefit from the injuring activity. Should it be the injurer who benefits (and who will therefore benefit from continued negligence as well), or should it be the one who (albeit for purely selfish reasons) punishes the injurer and makes recurrence of the negligence less likely?[32]

E. FINANCING THE CLASS ACTION

1) Litigation as Investment

Class actions, as we have noted, provide both private functions analogous to ordinary civil cases and regulatory functions that may properly be regarded as falling within the public interest. Accordingly, questions arise over whether they should be privately or publicly funded.

In Canada, the debate has largely been settled in favour of private funding. While statutory arrangements for public funding of class actions are

---

31 See Victor E. Schwartz, Mark A. Behrens, & Leah Lorber, "Federal Courts Should Decide Interstate Class Actions: A Call for Federal Class Action Diversity Jurisdiction Reform" (2000) 37 Harv. J. Legis. 483 at 494–95 (criticizing apparently empty "in-kind" or *cy pres* settlements that nonetheless provided class counsel with large fees).

32 This is not to say that abusive arrangements are impossible. Schwartz *et al.* refer to a case where holders of escrow accounts received refunds from the Bank of Boston of up to $8.76 each, yet some had counsel fees of $144.25 deducted from their accounts as part of a settlement: *Ibid.* at 494, citing anecdotal reports surrounding the resolution of *Kamilewicz v. Bank of Boston Corp.*, 92 F.3d 506 (7th Cir. 1996). Nevertheless, to extrapolate such apparently bizarre results to a general argument that lawyers' fees should not, as a matter of principle, consume most or all of an award (as Schwartz *et al.* do) seems unwarranted if deterrence is valued as an objective of mass tort litigation.

in place in Ontario and Quebec,[33] their limited scope and apparent lack of success[34] has ensured that it is private litigants, or rather their lawyers, who can be expected to bear the costs of prosecuting class claims.[35]

As class actions are regarded more as investment vehicles, it is possible, if not likely, that disinterested venture capitalists will be prepared to assist with funding. In *Nantais v. Telectronics Proprietary (Canada) Ltd.*, plaintiffs' counsel obtained loans, repayment of which was contingent on the success of the class action.[36] Some class counsel have proposed a broad lattitude in arranging cooperative fee-sharing agreements with outside counsel or consultants.[37] While still in its infancy, this area may be expected to develop as the structural advantages of class actions becomes more apparent to the judiciary and legislatures.

2) Cost Awards and Indemnification Agreements

One of the most difficult questions in Canadian class action law involves whether to award costs against unsuccessful plaintiffs. In the United States, Rule 23 has no cost-shifting provisions, adopting the *de facto* "own costs" rule that prevails in that country's courts generally. However, the rules for individual suits in Canada are patterned on England's "loser pays" system.

Awards of costs against unsuccessful representative plaintiffs in class proceedings are necessarily problematic, because the economy of scale is grotesquely reversed. The costs of the defendant's litigation of all classable (i.e., similar) claims can be exacted from a single representative plaintiff whose own interest in the claim might be minimal. Such cost-shifting will presumably deter valid claims from proceeding, routinely permitting

---

33 *Law Society Amendment Act (Class Proceeding Funding), 1992*, S.O. 1992, c. 7; *An Act Respecting the Class Action*, R.S.Q., c. R-21, s. 31. For a general discussion of class action funding legislation see Ward K. Branch, *Class Actions in Canada* (Aurora: Canada Law Book, 2001), chapter 8 "Funding Agency Support."

34 See, for instance: Garry D. Watson, "Fee shifting in Ontario Class Actions and the Failure of Ontario's Class Proceedings Fund to Meet its Intended Purpose," and, for a more detailed review of the Quebec Fund's operations, see Claude Desmeules, "Public Funding of Class Actions in Quebec," both in First Annual Class Actions Symposium, *Class Actions: Where Are We and Where Are We Going* (Toronto: Osgoode Hall Law School of York University, 2001).

35 Without ignoring the fact that the proceeding itself is funded also by the state, which provides the forum, and the defendant, which bears the burden of contributing its share to the overall litigation costs.

36 "Private investors help finance class action lawsuit" *Law Times* (15–21 December 1997) p. 1; "Investors betting lawsuits will bring big payoffs" *Toronto Star* (22 February 1998) p. A3.

37 James H. MacMaster and Ward K. Branch, "Financing Class Actions" </www.branmac.com/Images/classactions_financing.pdf>.

defendants to escape the costs of their wrongdoing. While it is conceivable, on the other hand, that "own costs" regimes will encourage illegitimate litigation, the parallel experiences of Ontario and British Columbia (in the latter, an "own costs" presumption applies) do not seem to bear out such concerns, and we are unaware of any suggestion that the rate of frivolous litigation is higher in British Columbia than Ontario.

British Columbia's statute changes the normal rules for the award of costs by adopting the American approach in class proceedings, with each party bearing its own costs regardless of outcome.[38] In exceptional circumstances, however, the court may award costs to punish vexatious or abusive behaviour.[39] After reviewing the competing costs regimes, Newfoundland, Saskatchewan, Manitoba, and the Federal Court adopted British Columbia's model.

The role of the "own costs" rule in furthering the purposes of class proceedings legislation was discussed in *Samos Investments Inc. v. Pattison*.[40] There, the court said:

> [24] There is little doubt that one of the main objects of the Act is to improve access to the courts for litigants who could not otherwise afford to exercise such access. Costs are an integral aspect of that overall scheme. In that regard, the Ontario Law Reform Commission identified the question of costs as "the single most important issue" that the Commission considered in designing an expanded class action procedure. In the Commission's view, the matter of costs affected not simply the efficacy of class actions, but the more fundamental question of whether class actions should be utilized at all. (Report, p. 647).
>
> ...
>
> [26] While the Ontario Legislature did not adopt the "no way" costs rule recommended by the Commission, it is apparent that the B.C. Legislature did. It is apparent from the legislative debates at the time that this was a deliberate choice, as evidenced by the following extract from Hansard, in relation to s. 37, at the time of second reading of Bill 16 (the precursor to the Act):
>
> > Hon. C. Gabelmann [then Attorney General]: I have no way of knowing why the Ontario Legislature did not follow the recommendations of the Ontario Law Reform Commission. We felt that the Ontario Law Reform Commission recommendation that there be a no-way costs rule — in other words, that each party

---

38 B.C. s. 37.
39 B.C. s. 37(2).
40 2002 BCCA 442.

> pay their own expenses, except under exceptional circumstances — was the appropriate way to go. Why the Ontario House did something else, I don't know.
>
> ...
>
> Hon. C. Gabelmann: We think as the Ontario Law Reform Commission thinks: that this cost rule is the best way to ensure fairest access to the justice system. Plaintiffs banding together know that with the exception of the exceptional circumstance provision [s. 37(2)] they are not going to have to bear the costs of the defendant if they are unsuccessful. They are each going to bear their own costs. That's an access-to-justice question that I think is straightforward.... . (B.C. Debates, June 13, 1995)

As noted by Minister Gabelmann in the above quote, the Ontario *Class Proceedings Act* departed from the Law Reform Commission's 1982 recommendations and preserved the ordinary rules. These cost-shifting rules apply unless the class proceeding was a "test case, raised a novel point of law or involved a matter of public interest," in which case the court may exercise discretion to modify the costs award.[41] This is generous wording, since most attempted class actions, broadly speaking, are by necessity "test cases" (in that their outcome will determine the fate of numerous similar claims) and many if not most (at least product liability and toxic tort cases) arguably involve a matter of public interest. Quebec's regime attempts to strike a compromise by applying a tariff that would apply for claims of between $1,000 and $3,000, therefore protecting an unsuccessful plaintiff against disproportionate costs awards.[42]

Recently, the British Columbia attorney general flirted with the idea of modifying the cost rules in the *Class Proceedings Act* to discourage unwarranted litigation,[43] though its discussion paper provided no support for the idea that *any* frivolous suits were being filed under the province's current regime, let alone at a higher rate than in Ontario or Quebec where "loser pays" systems are available.

Some recent Ontario decisions have signalled a sharp move away from a liberal approach to costs rules. In *Pearson v. Inco Ltd.*[44] and *Gariepy v. Shell*

---

41 Ontario s. 31.
42 Quebec art. 1050.1. The Quebec regime is compared to Ontario's and B.C.'s in John A. Campion and Victoria A. Stewart, "Class Actions: Procedure and Strategy" (1997) 19 Advocate's Quarterly 20 at 41–43. See also the discussion in Branch, *supra* note 29, at c. 19.
43 British Columbia Ministry of Attorney General, *Civil Liability Review (#AG02079)* (Victoria: Ministry of Attorney General, 2002) at 8.
44 [2002] O.J. No. 3532 (S.C.J.).

Oil Co.,[45] substantial costs awards ($185,000 and $175,000, respectively) were made against representative plaintiffs upon their unsuccessful certification applications.

The difficulty with cost-shifting rules is that they tend not to consider that the class action is lawyer-driven, not plaintiff-driven. In most class actions, the expenditures by plaintiffs' counsel in simply getting to certification (where cost-shifting is available) will heavily outweigh the expected recovery of the representative plaintiff alone.

In one of the first decisions under Alberta's *Class Proceedings Act*, where the 'ordinary' costs rules apply, a decision assessing a high amount against an unsuccessful plaintiff in a proposed class action was overturned on appeal. In *Pauli v. ACE INA Insurance Co.*,[46] the Alberta Court of Appeal called such an award "chilling":

> ¶ 31 Class actions are relatively new in Canada, and it is arguable that such actions increase access to justice by allowing many claimants to pool their resources to pursue claims together that they could not pursue individually because of small monetary amounts at stake. But the reality is that large cost awards against unsuccessful plaintiffs will have a chilling effect and likely discourage meritorious class actions .... In exercising the court's discretion to award costs, there needs to be a balance between encouraging class actions that have potential merit and discouraging those that may be frivolous or vexatious.
>
> ...
>
> ¶ 34 Such an award curtails access to justice because it has a chilling affect on future potential litigants. Lawyers and other third parties, who might be willing to underwrite the costs of a potentially meritorious representative action, would be unwilling to do so if they knew they would face crippling costs merely because they offered this financial assistance. Individual litigants, whose stake in the litigation is relatively small, would then be unwilling to pursue the action.

The recognition that it is generally lawyers who finance class actions has, however, cut both ways.[47] While it is generally acknowledged that some

---

45 [2002] O.J. No. 3495 (S.C.J.) [hereinafter *Gariepy*].
46 [2004] A.J. No. 883 (C.A.).
47 Nordheimer J. in *Gariepy, ibid.* at para. 6 (financial barriers against "access to justice" could be overcome by plaintiffs' lawyers, who are "as well-funded ... as ... defendant's counsel").

lawyers in Ontario are indemnifying representative plaintiffs against adverse costs awards,[48] it is clear that, without the wealth that substantially higher counsel fees produces in the United States, most cannot afford to do so, and cost-shifting rules will continue to be a significant restriction on class actions in that province.

The most plaintiff-friendly jurisdiction in Canada at present appears to be Manitoba. In that Province, the new *Class Proceedings Act*[49] permits "national" class actions on the Ontario model, but overlaid with a 'no costs' rule. It remains to be seen whether these features will make that province a national centre of class action activity but it is possible, such are the advantages of these two provisions.

F. CARRIAGE MOTIONS AND COMPETING CLAIMS

When more than one class action has been started in which the proposed classes overlap, a conflict will arise as to the "carriage" of the action — that is, which representative plaintiff will be certified to represent the class, and, more to the point, which counsel will carry the action forward. This is a problem unique to class actions and arises as a result of the binding effect of class litigation upon numerous absent persons.

Possibly as a result of differences between the respective cultures of the Canadian and American plaintiffs' bars, competing class actions within a single jurisdiction are rare in this country. At the time of this writing, there have been only two reported cases in Canada in which the court has sought to choose between competing class plaintiffs; in all other cases, it would appear that, where competition was looming, accommodation was reached among counsel (between Ontario — i.e., "national class" — counsel and those for the British Columbia class in *Wilson v. Servier*[50]).

---

48   Julius Melnitzer, "The Dog-Eat-Dog World of Class Actions" (July/August 2003) *Lexpert* 50.
49   C.C.S.M. c. 130.
50   In *Wilson v. Servier* (a Phen-Fen diet drug litigation), a national class was certified in Ontario, encompassing all provinces with the exception of Quebec: (2000), 50 O.R. (3d) 219 (S.C.J.). At the Ontario certification hearing, counsel for the representative plaintiff in a related B.C. action appeared and announced that, if the national class were certified, the B.C. plaintiff would apply for inclusion as representative of a B.C. subclass. This is in fact what happened: [2001] O.J. No. 1615 (S.C.J.), and the B.C. action was not pursued. It is possible that the B.C. action was filed as a "safety" — that is, in order to "head off" a similar action by competing, non-aligned counsel, and also to have in reserve in case B.C. claims were not accepted by the Ontario court.

In the first case to consider the question of "carriage," *Vitapharm Canada Ltd. v. F. Hoffman LaRoche Ltd.*,[51] the court was confronted with ten separate actions (all in Ontario) vying for class certification regarding alleged vitamin price-fixing conspiracies across Canada. The plaintiffs were various retail and wholesale firms, as well as some individuals. After considering the various options available, a single counsel group (which had been advancing five of the claims) was appointed lead counsel for carriage of all related class actions. The remaining pending litigations that were entirely duplicative were stayed until further order of the court. Finally, the court issued a prohibition against the commencement of new class actions related to the same subject matter without leave of the court save and except any class action commenced by the favoured counsel group.

The court set out a series of considerations to apply when deciding carriage motions:

> Factors to consider in determining who should be appointed as solicitor of record in a class action include: the nature and scope of the causes of action advanced, the theories advanced by counsel as being supportive of the claims advanced; the state of each class action, including preparation; the number, size and extent of involvement of the proposed representative plaintiffs; the relative priority of commencing the class actions; and the resources and experience of counsel. See generally *Newberg on Class Actions* (West Group, 1992), 3d ed, s. 9.35, pp. 9-96 and 9-97.

The court then applied the tests to the case before it:

> ... There is nothing in the record to suggest that any putative representative plaintiff(s) for the retail purchasers might be a preferable choice in representing class members.
>
> The record indicates both competing counsel groups have given considerable thought to the action(s) on behalf of the retail purchasers. The record also establishes that the Strosberg/Siskind counsel group has done more extensive research to this point in time into the alleged complex web of conspiracies and the appropriate approach for an economic analysis as to damages.
>
> Which counsel group should be given carriage and appointed solicitors of record in the circumstances of the class action vitamin litigation in Ontario?

---

51 (2000), 4 C.P.C. (5th) 169 (S.C.J.) [hereinafter *Vitapharm*].

The approach offered by the Borden group of having one action for the retail purchasers that proceeds in tandem with the reconstituted actions pursuing the claims of all persons other than retail purchasers introduces many disadvantages. First, it multiplies the global assessments two-fold from a probable five to ten, since it is agreed there must be a global assessment. Moreover, this must be done on a product by product basis. This means there would have to be at least five global assessments (assuming only five different products) for the reconstituted actions and five more for the Horvath action as retail purchasers were involved in respect of each product.

Thus, the approach of the actions continuing to proceed in tandem multiplies the expense significantly. It would also leave open the possibility of different, and conflicting global assessments for a given product. As well, the global assessment for a given product would be in itself meaningless without discounting, and removing, the assessment by the loss attributable to the retail purchasers in the reconstituted actions. At the same time it would be necessary to discount the global assessments in the Horvath action by the amount of the loss attributable to all claimants other than the retail purchasers, to leave remaining the isolated amount of the damages suffered by the retail purchasers. This complex determination would have to be done on a product by product basis, that is, probably at least ten times.

In my view, and I so find, the least expensive method of determining the common issues requires that all actions except the Strosberg/Siskind counsel group actions be stayed. This approach avoids needless complexities and confusion through trying to deal with the retail purchaser claimants for all products in a single class proceeding, being the Horvath action. It is preferable to have the reconstituted actions which isolate in separate actions the divergent interests that may well result from different products used by the retail purchasers. Moreover, as I have said above, there are different groups of defendants from product to product.

At the same time, having the same counsel for all the reconstituted actions allows for efficiencies in determining matters and issues of commonality that run across the different products. The reconstituted actions of the Strosberg/Siskind counsel group reflect the advice of economists that there must be a global assessment of damages on a product by product basis. The reconstituted actions are the most comprehensive of all the Ontario actions. In my view, they represent the best opportunity to meet the interests of all the class member claimants.

> In my view, while the approach suggested by the Strosberg/Siskind counsel group is in the best interests of all claimants, it also is in the best interests of the defendants as it reduces unnecessary costs to them.[52]

The *Vitapharm* decision's emphasis — entirely correct in our view — on the efficiency advantages of a single resolution of all related claims (a recognition of the advantages of "optimal aggregation") has important ramifications for any potential plaintiffs' counsel. The decision means that aspiring class counsel will have to craft carefully as broad and inclusive a claim as the circumstances will permit and put forward a representative plaintiff (or group of plaintiffs) who can adequately represent the entire group. If a proposed claim represents only a portion of a potentially larger class, the filing counsel risks having the claim swept into a bigger, broader, class action, even one filed later, and losing carriage of the action. Because it appears at this point that Canadian plaintiffs' counsel are not adopting the massive "inventory" strategies of their U.S. counterparts, a stay of proceedings granted in a carriage motion will have the effect of wiping out all the work that the unsuccessful lawyer has committed to the claim, with potentially catastrophic consequences.

A second carriage motion was dealt with recently in British Columbia. In *Richard v. British Columbia*,[53] an action had been commenced by a proposed representative plaintiff against the provincial government over abuse allegedly suffered at the government-run Woodlands School. Several months later but prior to certification, a second action was filed by the province's public guardian and trustee ("PGT"), who put forward two other individuals as putative representatives of the class. Each set of counsel then filed motions to stay proceedings in the other action, and the PGT also asked the court to order that no other action based on the same claims be permitted.

The court referred to its "wide discretion in a carriage motion," which it attributed to section 10 of the *Law and Equity Act*.[54] That section states:

> 10. In the exercise of its jurisdiction in a cause or matter before it, the court must grant, either absolutely or on reasonable conditions that to it seem just, all remedies that any of the parties may appear to be entitled to in respect of any legal or equitable claim properly brought forward by

---

52 *Ibid.* at paras. 49–56.
53 2003 BCSC 976, aff'd [2004] B.C.J. No. 1202 (C.A.).
54 R.S.B.C. 1996, c. 253.

them in the cause or matter so that, as far as possible, all matters in controversy between the parties may be completely and finally determined and all multiplicity of legal proceedings concerning any of those matters may be avoided.

The court also referred to section 12 of British Columbia's *Class Proceedings Act*, which empowers a court to "make any order it considers appropriate respecting the conduct of a class proceeding to ensure its fair and expeditious determination," and section 13, which states the court may at any time stay any proceedings related to the class proceeding on any terms that the court deems or considers appropriate.

The court reviewed the qualifications of the respective counsel, and, as in *Vitapharm, supra*, found neither lacking. Faced with apparently equally qualified representatives, the court decided to award carriage of the action to the earlier-filed action, a decision it based upon the possibility of a conflict between those class members to whom the PGT owed its statutory duty and those to whom it did not. Unfortunately, the court offered little direction regarding what criteria it would have considered — assuming a rough equality of counsel's experience and resources — had no potential for conflict been found. In the course of its reasons, the court suggested several times that the two firms working together would complement each other well and be a "formidable team"; one can expect that attempts to reach a "team building" compromise solution will likely be common in future cases.

Carriage motions can be viewed as a method of "consolidating" claims and could potentially be used to bring together claims from several jurisdictions into a single national class. Similarly, courts might also make orders facilitating "virtual" consolidation through motions for access, which might be termed "court-ordered freeloading." In a subsequent decision of *Vitapharm Canada Ltd. v. F. Hoffman-Laroche Ltd.*, the Ontario plaintiffs had sought an order in a U.S. court for access to discoveries of the same defendants being conducted in a concurrent class action there. The defendants attempted to have the Ontario court issue an injunction to prevent the U.S. court from allowing the motion. In dismissing the application for the injunction, Cumming J. said:

> The plaintiffs' U.S. Motion *prima facie* has the purpose of saving considerable time and money in the Canadian proceedings. If successful in gaining access to U.S. discovery in the U.S. Litigation, the plaintiffs can determine earlier and with greater certainty the nature and extent of the precise evidence available that is relevant to the Canadian proceedings. To deny access to the present U.S. discovery could conceivably mean that the

plaintiffs over time would have to pursue separately s. 1782 orders in respect of the corporate Niacin defendants in the U.S. Litigation. At the least, success in obtaining access to the present U.S. discovery means that the plaintiffs can much more easily determine and discard what is *not relevant* for the purpose of the Canadian proceedings.

The plaintiffs' action in seeking access to the U.S. discovery is not oppressive or unfair to the defendants in the Canadian proceedings. To the contrary. Such access is consistent with the three policy objectives underlying the *CPA [Class Proceedings Act]* — facilitating access to justice, judicial efficiency and behaviour modification. In particular, there will be significant savings in litigation costs through such access.[55]

G. COLLUSION IN SETTLEMENT

1) To the Prejudice of Claimants

Since the 1982 Ontario Law Reform Commission report, Canadian commentators, and to a lesser extent the courts, have struggled to overcome the fear of agency problems between the class members and the representative plaintiff's counsel. The perceived danger is that class proceedings will "produce compromises unfair to class members, either because the representative plaintiff has settled with the defendant for a premium on his or her own claim, thereafter discontinuing the class action, or because the class lawyer has settled in a manner designed to maximize legal fees at the expense of the recovery ..."[56] available to class members.

Professor Coffee draws a distinction between "small claimant" (i.e., not independently viable) and "large claimant" classes. In the former, he suggests, "defendants tend to resist class certification (because plaintiffs have no realistic alternative)," whereas in "large claimant classes, defendants increasingly prefer class certification for a variety of reasons, including ... their hope to reach a "reasonable" global settlement with cooperative plaintiffs' attorneys."[57] This gives rise to what Coffee calls "structural collusion" where, "even in the absence of bad faith,"

> ... suspect settlements result in large measure because of the defendants' ability to shop for favorable settlement terms, either by contacting multi-

---

55 In *Vitapharm Canada Ltd. v. F. Hoffman-Laroche Ltd.*, [2001] O.J. No. 237 (S.C.J.) at paras. 48–49.
56 *Ontario Report (1982)*, *supra* note 5 at 146.
57 Coffee, "Class Wars" *supra* note 15 at 1353.

ple plaintiffs' attorneys or by inducing them to compete against each other. At its worst, this process can develop into a reverse auction, with the low bidder among the plaintiffs' attorneys winning the right to settle with the defendant. Here, it is necessary to confront the comparatively new institution of the "settlement" class action.[58]

Sometimes, settlements can be reached that are of deceptively little utility to the class members. One method that is gaining popularity is known as the "in-kind" or "scrip" settlement, involving coupons or some other "benefit" that will accrue to class members who continue to patronize the defendant. These kinds of settlements can be inherently problematic because they come at minimum cost to the defendant (which might even generate a profit from them[59]) and are therefore inadequate or illusory as deterrent. In some cases, they provide class members with only chimeric compensation as well.[60]

The "in kind" payment strategy sometimes involves *cy pres* payments[61] to charities or other third parties. Describing one such settlement, where a food company agreed to distribute its matzo products to various charities for a period of four years, Coffee observed that the "cynically disposed might see this settlement as an excellent way of simultaneously disposing of both stale matzos and a difficult litigation."[62] But note that *cy pres* distribution need not sacrifice deterrence; indeed deterrence will be wholly preserved regardless of who gains from the largesse, provided that the

---

58 *Ibid.* at 1354.
59 Consider, for instance, a movie chain that offers class members free tickets to films in settlement of a class action, knowing that the theatregoers' purchase of snacks will offset losses and possibly more than compensate.
60 To settle the litigation arising from the alleged proclivity of certain General Motors trucks with "side saddle" fuel tanks to explode when struck, the defendant offered $1000 gift certificates — non transferable — against the purchase of a new vehicle, perhaps a 5-percent discount on the price of the truck: *Re General Motors Corp. Pick-up Truck Fuel Tank Prods. Liab. Litig.*, 55 F.3d 768 at 780–81 (3d Cir. 1995). In such cases, Coffee notes that "[o]ften, the discount is no greater than what an individual plaintiff could receive for a volume purchase, or for a cash sale, or for using a particular credit card ..." Coffee, "Class Wars" *supra* note 14 at 1367.
61 This term is occasionally spelled *"cy-près," "cy-pres,"* or (mistakenly) *"cy-prés."* We adopt the spelling used in the overwhelming majority of Canadian cases, and as it is found in the *New Shorter Oxford English Dictionary*. *Cy pres* is derived from the Norman French term meaning "near this"; in the class action setting it refers to payment of damages or settlement funds to a person other than a class member.
62 Coffee, "Class Wars" *supra* note 14 at 1368.

defendant *loses* the appropriate amount in real terms and does not simply give away useless surplus stock, as in Coffee's example.[63]

In the United States and now Canada, a process has developed whereby "settlement classes" are certified and settled virtually simultaneously. The putative representative plaintiff and defendant agree to seek the court's approval of a settlement that has been pre-arranged between the parties; the court then certifies the class and approves the settlement, usually after a single hearing. The key feature of the settlement class is that the defendant's acquiescence to certification is conditional upon the approval of the settlement; if settlement is not approved, the action proceeds as if certification had not been attempted.[64]

The potential for so-called "structural collusion" between plaintiffs' and defendants' counsel is obvious, particularly if several competing actions are vying for class status. Under such circumstances, the various aspiring class representatives are driven into a "reverse auction,"[65] compelling them to settle for less than the class's claim is worth. Even absent such competitive pressure, though, objections to the settlement class might be advanced on the basis that settlement levels will be suboptimal until and unless the defendant is being confronted with a complete aggregation of the claims for which it may be liable as the result of a particular mass tort.

Settlement classes are opposed by "the overwhelming majority of the scholarly community who have expressed a view" on the question,[66] and attempts to formalize their acceptance through legislative reform to Rule 23 have met with a "firestorm of criticism by the academic community."[67] There is a significant secondary concern that courts, faced with the opportunity to clear troublesome litigation from their docket, might certify when

---

63 For an example of a successful *cy pres*-type settlement, see *supra* note 11. While the structure of this settlement seems sound, courts must bear in mind the strong incentives for structural collusion in settlement classes, and ought to be convinced that the global amount settled for is a reasonable estimation of the eventual award, discounted for probability of its eventual success.

64 The history of the settlement class and attempts to alter Rule 23 to permit it explicitly are described in Darren M. Franklin, "The Mass Tort Defendants Strike Back: Are Settlement Class Actions a Collusive Threat or Just a Phantom Menace?" (2000) 53 Stan. L. Rev. 163.

65 John C. Coffee, Jr, "The Corruption of the Class Action: The New Technology of Collusion" (1995) 80 Cornell L. Rev. 851 at 851.

66 Eric D. Green, "What Will We Do When Adjudication Ends? We'll Settle in Bunches: Bringing Rule 23 into the Twenty-First Century" (1997) 44 UCLA L. Rev. 1773 at 1787.

67 Eric D. Green, "Advancing Individual Rights Through Group Justice" (1997) 30 U.C. Davis L. Rev. 791 at 794 (describing the opposition by 120 law professors who organized a steering committee to oppose the reform).

otherwise they might not, to the detriment of absent plaintiffs (and particularly future claimants).[68] Safeguards against inappropriate "settlement classes" are discussed below.

2) To the Prejudice of Non-Settling Defendants

A concern has also been expressed occasionally that aggressive defendant's counsel may negotiate a settlement with the plaintiff class to the detriment of other defendants. In such circumstances, "bar orders" might be sought to prevent the non-settling defendants from seeking contribution or indemnity from the settling defendants. The objection is most frequently raised by non-settling defendants, concerned that the settlement adversely affects their own rights. Bar orders to protect settling defendants have been granted in both Ontario[69] and British Columbia[70] as part of the settlement-approval process in class action suits.

In jurisdictions where defendants' liability is proportional, bar orders may not present a particular difficulty. For instance, if Defendant A to an action settles its obligations to the plaintiffs for $500,000 and Defendants B and C do not, then the action may continue against B and C. If they are each found to be 20 percent liable for the plaintiffs' damages of $1 million, then it does not matter that they cannot seek contribution or indemnity from the settling defendant; in such a case, it is the plaintiff who bears the risk.

However, in a jurisdiction with joint and several liability (such as Ontario), each defendant is liable for the full amount of the claim. If A settles for $500,000 when his or her proportion of liability (carrying on the above example) is actually $600,000, then the plaintiffs might claim the remaining $500,000 from the non-settling defendants (assuming the bar order "credits" the non-settling defendants with the amount of B's settlement) each of whom may be liable in proportion for this portion (i.e., because they were each 20 percent at fault, they would split the unpaid portion of Defendant A's share at $250,000 each).[71]

---

68 Franklin, "Defendants Strike Back," *supra* note 57 at 165 (noting that certifying courts are "sometimes neglecting the superiority requirements of Rule 23(b)(3) of the Federal Rules of Civil Procedure since litigation is not contemplated").
69 *Ontario New Home Warranty Program v. Chevron Chemical Co.* (1999), 46 O.R. (3d) 130 at 143 (S.C.J.) [hereinafter *ONHWP*]; *Millard v. North George Capital Management Ltd.* (2000), 47 C.P.C. (4th) 365 (Ont. S.C.J.) [hereinafter *Millard*].
70 *Sawatzky v. Société Chirurgicale Instrumentarium Inc.* (1999), 71 B.C.L.R. (3d) 51 (S.C.).
71 The English Court of Appeal has held that the liability of a concurrent wrongdoer who is unable to satisfy its share of liability should be divided between the concurrent wrongdoers in proportion to their respective degree of fault: *Fisher v. CHT Ltd. (No. 2)*, [1966] 2 Q.B. 475 (C.A.) at 481 and 483.

If the settlement is the result of a "limited fund" and Defendant A is insolvent, having exhausted its assets paying for the settlement, there is little prejudice to B and C because the results would be the same had Defendant A not settled first. Where A remains with assets, however, the potential for unfairness is manifest, although, of course, it is not an unfairness as great as many others that are possible within a system of joint and several liability.

This may create a strong incentive for structural collusion between plaintiffs' counsel and a defendant willing to settle; indeed, class counsel may engage his or her opponents in a "prisoner's dilemma," exacting a substantial (but not full) settlement with the promise to the defendant of escaping a portion of his or her liability, and content in the knowledge that the plaintiffs are not sacrificing the aggregate total of the award.

One method of evading the problem is for the court to issue the bar order on the condition that the plaintiffs will be able to seek damages from the non-settling defendants only on a several, rather than a joint and several, basis. This method was employed in *ONHWP*, coupled with a further cap on the liability of non-settling defendants at 35 percent.[72] Another idea, to similar effect, would be the solution negotiated in *Millard*,[73] with the plaintiffs agreeing that the non-settling defendants would have, as against the plaintiffs, the benefit of any claims for contribution and indemnity that they may have had against the settling defendants. In our earlier example, B and C would be able to claim the contribution amount of $100,000 (the difference between the settlement amount and A's actual proportional liability) from the plaintiff, thus offsetting the difference. In such case, as Farley J. noted in *Millard*, "it is the plaintiffs who have to bear the burden of not getting anything extra from the settling defendants."[74]

Such arrangements may in fact be not only desirable but necessary. Winkler J. in *ONHWP* seems to recognize that the court is *prohibited* from issuing a bar order that does in fact substantively affect the non-settling defendants' rights, at least as long as the court continues to consider the Ontario *Class Proceedings Act* as strictly procedural in nature.[75] From the point of view of procedural fairness, it may also be appropriate that any bar order contain a provision guaranteeing that the settling defendants contin-

---

72 *ONHWP*, *supra* note 69 at 140.
73 *Millard*, *supra* note 69.
74 *Ibid.* at para. 26.
75 In *ONHWP*, Winkler J. escapes this substantive/procedural trap only by arguing that the rights of contribution and indemnity are actually derivative rights of the plaintiff, and that they are thus unaffected by the court's order. See *supra* note 69 at 142–45.

ue to participate in the proceedings to the extent necessary to provide the non-settling defendants with sufficient information to assess accurately their relative liability.[76]

Courts generally have relied on the broad discretion found within the class proceedings legislation for procedural customization on orders to stay proceedings to issue bar orders,[77] and no doubt these orders can be an important tool in softening recalcitrant defendants' bargaining positions. However, because bar orders (if accompanied by conditions like those described above) will usually have the effect of diminishing the overall aggregate-claim value, they should be strictly scrutinized by the courts from the point of view of the interests of the class members.

H. "STRIKE SUITS" AND "BLACKMAIL" SETTLEMENTS

The Ontario Law Reform Commission's 1982 report addressed the common objection that class actions, by "extorting unjust settlements from defendants," would constitute a form of "legalized blackmail."[78] It was in part this concern that, at the dawn of the class action era in Canada, led the system designers to emphasize rigorous judicial oversight of the entire class process.

The term "strike action" or "strike suit" describes a class proceeding launched on a claim without apparent merit but in circumstances where a sizeable settlement can be achieved. It has become a rather notorious feature of securities litigation in the United States, because the suit can have immediate effects on share prices or shareholder and regulatory approvals of corporate initiatives:

---

76 This was a condition of the agreement in *Millard, supra* note 69; it was added as a condition in *ONHWP, ibid.* at 148–49. In *Millard*, the defendants agreed to continue to participate in the proceedings for the purpose of assessing relative liability. To objections that it would be onerous for the non-settling defendants to have to obtain the court's leave to conduct discoveries, Farley J. replied that "[t]he court in any such leave motion would be able to deal with the request to ensure that [the objecting non-settling defendant] was able to obtain what it reasonably required in the circumstances (prior discussions amongst counsel would likely be very helpful for all concerned) and the court would be able to deal with any actual or likely abuse on any side.": *supra* note 69 at para. 27. It is not clear from the reasons in *Sawatzky, supra* note 63 whether the settling defendants agreed as a condition of the bar order to make discovery and evidence available in subsequent proceedings; Brenner J. did not address the problem.
77 *ONHWP, supra* note 69 at 141; *Sawatzky, supra* note 70 at para. 63.
78 *Ontario Report (1982), supra* note 5 at 146.

In the United States, the availability of class action procedures combined with a contingency fee structure for plaintiffs' lawyers has led to the creation of an entrepreneurial sector of the legal profession known as the "strike bar." U.S. strike bar lawyers are motivated by sizable contingency fees and relative freedom to direct litigation according to their own interests. Even defendants who have done nothing wrong face Hobson's choice: to pay for a very expensive battle in the courts and eventually risk a potentially exorbitant jury damage award, or settle. Most defendants eventually swallow their indignation and make the prudent economic choice and, as a result, settlement has become the typical outcome of class action securities litigation in the United States.[79]

The methods of the "strike bar" have been described as follows:

[A] relatively small number of plaintiffs' attorneys regularly were filing class actions only hours or days after the disclosure of information that precipitated a major move in the price of a corporation's stock. It seemed apparent, even to people sympathetic to claims of open market fraud, that the moving force behind most class actions was not investors aggrieved by the defendants' alleged misrepresentations but plaintiffs' attorneys seeking to earn potentially large contingent fees. The investors in whose names class action [sic] were filed were mere figureheads; their function was to provide these attorneys with "the key to the courthouse."[80]

Securities cases provided particularly fertile ground for such actions, partly because of their potential for interfering with corporate activities (mergers and the like), but also because their impact on share price could be considerable as well. One commentator concluded that most settlements resulting from securities class actions had no relation to the merits of the cases involved.[81] As a result, federal law in the United States was amended to make "strike suits" less profitable.[82]

---

79 Steven Sharpe and James Reid, "Aspects of Class Action Securities Litigation in the United States" (1997) 28 Can. Bus. L.J. 348 at 353–54. See also John Avery, "Securities Litigation Reform: The Long and Winding Road to the Private Securities Litigation Reform Act of 1995" (1996) 51 Bus. Law 335 at 337.
80 Elliott J. Weiss, "Comment: The Impact to Date of the Lead Plaintiff Provisions of the *Private Securities Litigation Reform Act*" (1997) 39 Ariz. L. Rev. 561 at 561–62.
81 Janet Cooper Alexander, "Do the Merits Matter? A Study of Settlements in Securities Class Actions" (1991) 43 Stan. L. Rev. 497.
82 *The Private Securities Litigation Reform Act of 1995*, Pub. L. No. 104-67, 109 Stat. 737 (1995) (codified as amended in sections of 15 U.S.C.) (requiring a mandatory inquiry by the court at the conclusion of each attempted class action and permitting, *inter alia*, sanctions to be imposed on plaintiffs and lawyers who have brought forward frivolous

But allegations of "blackmail" reach beyond the peculiar economics of securities litigation. Judge Posner, writing for the Seventh Circuit Court of Appeals, has suggested that extortionate pressure can be applied in such actions simply because of the potential size of awards[83] — that, in other words, a risk-averse defendant will prefer to pay more than the expected aggregate value of the claim (i.e., the potential claim amount multiplied by the probability of recovery) than "bet the business on a single flip of the coin."[84]

In truth, there is a high degree of uncertainty over the extent to which "blackmail" suits are a problem in mass tort cases, even in the United States where the concern is sometimes said to have reached "Frankenstein monster" proportions.[85] Rosenberg counters Posner's analysis by pointing out that firms are less risk-averse than individuals, and settlement pressure tends to weigh more heavily on the most risk-averse party, almost always the plaintiff:

> First, defendant firms are structured to operate risk-neutrally and have many means of hedging against risk, notably derived from laws limiting liability and affording protection in bankruptcy, opportunities for stockholders to diversity their portfolios, and widespread availability of liability insurance. Second, the "blackmail settlement" pressure from a single, class-wide trial is not systematically directed towards defendants alone, but rather is directed at both sides of the litigation. Risk-averse class members and class counsel are no less likely than a defendant to regard a single class-wide trial with apprehension. In reality, "blackmail settlement" effects in any given case induce both sides to pay a premium for settlement, which nets out to the disadvantage of the most risk-averse.[86]

Moreover, there are three other unique characteristics of U.S. litigation that might lead to suboptimal settlements by defendants (and thus overde-

---

suits) and the *Securities Litigation Uniform Standards Act of 1998*, Pub. L. No. 105-353, 112 Stat. 3227 (1998) (also to be codified in 15 U.S.C.). See generally: David M. Levine & Adam C. Pritchard, "The Securities Litigation Uniform Standards Act of 1998: The Sun Sets on California's Blue Sky Laws" (1998) 54 Bus. Law 1 at 1–2; Richard H. Walker, David M. Levine & Adam C. Pritchard, "The New Securities Class Action: Federal Obstacles, State Detours" (1997) 39 Ariz. L. Rev. 641 at 643; and Professor Jill E. Fisch, "Class Action Reform: Lessons from Securities Litigation" (1997) 39 Ariz. L. Rev. 533.

83   *Re Rhone-Poulenc Rorer, Inc.*, 51 F.3d 1293 at 1298 (7th Cir. 1995).
84   David Rosenberg, "Mass Tort Class Actions — What the Defendants Have and Plaintiffs Don't" (2000) 37 Harv. J. Legis. 393 at 429.
85   Samuel Estreicher, "Foreword: Federal Class Actions After 30 Years" (1996) 71 N.Y.U. L. Rev. 1 at 2.
86   Rosenberg, "What the Defendants Have" *supra* note 84 at 430.

terrence[87]) potentially characterized as "blackmail." First is the unique American reliance upon the jury trial in high-stakes litigation — there is persuasive evidence that juries tend to award greater damages in aggregated cases than if the claims were heard individually.[88] This problem is largely unavoidable in the United States, where a jury trial in many federal cases is constitutionally guaranteed, but it is less of a problem in Canada, where jury trials in complex cases are increasingly rare. Second, non-compensatory damages in the United States are notoriously high,[89] a situation that does not obtain in Canada, where even $1-million punitive damages are considered extreme.[90] Finally, some U.S. jurisdictions require that, in the case of a loss at trial, the defendant post an "appeal bond" that in some cases can be even greater than the damages awarded. The intention is to avoid frivolous appeals; practically speaking, though, the appeal-bond requirement can deny the opportunity to challenge an award that is significant enough to be unpayable without liquidation of the company. In Canada there is no equivalent requirement.

---

87 In fact, the problem of overdeterrence may provide a more focused objection to high damage awards than an allegation that such suits constitute "blackmail." For instance, many commentators have speculated that insubstantial claims might achieve large settlements based on questionable evidence. Invariably, those advancing this view point to the case of silicon-gel breast implants, a case in which theories of disease causation turned out to be generally unsubstantiated as research progressed: See, for example, George L. Priest, "Procedural Versus Substantive Controls of Mass Tort Class Actions" (1997) J. Leg. Stud. 521 at 522. Yet the obsession with the anecdotal case of over-compensation of victims ignores the more endemic problem of *under*-compensation in the vast majority of cases (for instance the 80 percent of product liability actions that are never pursued). The objection also does not consider the possibility that cases like that of silicon-gel implants were built upon discoveries of inadequate testing done by the manufacturers; in this sense the question arises of the degree to which manufacturer negligence should be excused or overlooked simply because of the serendipitous eventuality that no harm occurred.
88 For a discussion of the impact of aggregation on jury awards, see Barry F. McNeil & Beth L. Fanscal, "Mass Torts and Class Actions: Facing Increased Scrutiny" 167 F.R.D. 483 at 491; Kenneth S. Berdens & Irwin A. Horowitz, "Mass Tort Civil Litigation: The Impact of Procedural Changes on Jury Decisions," (1989) 73 Judicature 22.
89 The record appears to be $145 *billion* dollars in a Florida tobacco class action: *Engle v. R.J. Reynolds Tobacco Co.*, 2000 WL 33534572 (Fla. Cir. Ct. 2000). The award was overturned on appeal.
90 In fact, the recent $1-million dollar award in *Whiten v. Pilot Insurance Co.*, 2002 SCC 18 (representing less than ½ of 1 percent of the defendant's net worth) is the largest punitive claim ever approved by the Supreme Court. For an overview of the Canadian position on punitive damages see generally: Bruce Feldthusen, "Recent Developments in the Canadian Law of Punitive Damages" (1990) 16 Can. Bus. L.J. 241.

Indeed, in Canada there are strong indications that judicial oversight has been effective in minimizing, if not eliminating altogether, the abuse of the class proceeding. There have been no articles written describing any class action settlement as "blackmail," let alone any suggestion that the problem is endemic as has been suggested of the United States. In the one case where a Canadian lawyer launched what was found by the court to be a "strike suit" (which was "settled" by the defendant for the amount of the counsel's fees without prejudice to any absent class members), the court, obviously incensed at its understanding of the arrangement, approved the dismissal of the action but made an extraordinary order (on the court's own motion) to deny the payment of fees, also invoking its inherent jurisdiction to make a further order forbidding any transfer of money by any means from the defendant (or its principals) to the plaintiff's counsel.[91]

One final type of class action "blackmail" should be mentioned: no matter how perfectly any system is designed, defendants who rely especially on the goodwill of consumers could still suffer harm from the publicity surrounding a suit. Reputational harm is, of course, not a danger unique to class actions or indeed to litigation; consumer boycotts, for instance, may have similar effect. However, defendants are uniquely vulnerable to allegations made in court documents, which are not subject to the usual constraints of libel law or tort. More to the point, class counsel have a strong pecuniary incentive to threaten the defendant's reputation in a way that boycotting consumers generally do not. It is also true that because aggregation will allow, overall, more actions to be brought, and because notice requirements may publicize the alleged wrongdoing more than the filing of individual actions would, class actions may present an additional threat to firms that are particularly sensitive to public opinion. Such defendants are well advised to work closely with counsel and public-relations experts to preserve their goodwill, and some firms have developed (or claim to have developed) special expertise in managing public-relations aspects of complex litigation. If courts are ready with appropriate sanctions for cases brought frivolously against such defendants, there is no reason to believe that reputational harm will prove a significant problem for Canadian class-action law.

All allegations of "blackmail" of defendants in the class action process must be weighed against the understanding that, whenever the defendant's superior litigation power or high court costs make it uneconomical for a

---

91 *Epstein v. First Marathon Inc.*, [2000] O.J. No. 452 (S.C.J.). In fairness to the class counsel, the reasons do not offer sufficient detail for the reader to determine whether any bad faith was involved.

plaintiff to pursue a claim that is legally valid, this too represents a form of "blackmail" — against the plaintiff. The fact that the overwhelming majority of legitimate tort claims are not brought[92] points to a system of "unjust settlements" that is routine. Such "blackmail" does not carry with it the immediacy of the occasional anecdotal case of "blackmail" of defendants only because the claims not brought are unseen, falling beneath the radar of the media and popular consciousness.[93]

I. PROBLEMS OF THE "NATIONAL CLASS" AND EXTRAPROVINCIAL NOTICE

As will be apparent from much of the discussion in this Part, there is considerable concern over whether, and how, class actions can become truly "national"; that is to say, whether it is best to decide classable claims on a province-by-province basis, or combine them into a single litigation on an "opt-out" basis.[94] If it is possible to do the latter, how should it be done?

---

92 There is a great deal of literature suggesting that the tort system is — believe it or not — *under*utilized. Claiming rates vary sharply depending on the type of incident; in the U.S., it would appear that at least one-half of persons injured in motor vehicle accidents make at least an informal attempt to collect from another party, while the overall rate of pursued tort grievances is 3.8 percent: Richard E. Miller & Austin Sarat, "Grievances, Claims, and Disputes: Assessing the Adversary Culture" (1981) 15 L. & Soc'y Rev. 525 at 544–45. See also Michael J. Saks, "Do We Really Know Anything About the Behavior of the Tort Litigation System — and Why Not?" (1992) 140 Pa. L. Rev. 1147 at 1286. ("So little compensation is achieved through the tort system that only as an act of hyperbole can it be said to be part of an injury compensation system.") The possibility that Canadian rates are lower still owing to the higher degree of social insurance is supported by recent data on the pursuit rate of medical malpractice claims in U.S. states, which suggests that those with insurance are less likely to sue (as are the poor and elderly, though likely for different reasons): E.J. Thomas, D.M. Studdert, H.R. Burstin, *et al.*, "Incidence and Types of Adverse Events and Negligent Care in Utah and Colorado" (2000) 38 Medical Care 261. See also *supra* notes 16 through 18 and accompanying text.

93 This is not entirely so; the success of the book and film *A Civil Action* and widespread awareness of mass torts that have gone largely unaddressed — Bhopal, black lung disease, asbestos, and tobacco come to mind — have led to political movements to redress systemic harm, and arguably the Canadian class action regime is a result of frustration with just this kind of "systemic blackmail" of plaintiffs.

94 As described in Chapter 7, some provinces, like British Columbia, permit certification of non-residents, but only on an "opt in" basis. For reasons that should be obvious, this type of claim will generally be far less inclusive than one certified as an "opt out" class. In this section, we are discussing national "opt out" classes exclusively. Ontario and Manitoba permit national classes on an opt-out basis, and, because the class certified in *Dutton* was national (and indeed international) in scope, it is certainly arguable that national opt-out classes are available in provinces without class proceedings legislation as well.

As one of us has discussed at length elsewhere,[95] there is substantial support for the idea that the goals of class actions and tort law generally are frustrated as national classes are subdivided for provincial resolution.

The case in favour of national classes begins by observing that torts of the type that become subject to classable claims appear increasingly to be national, and increasingly international, in scale. Several conclusions can be seen to follow from this observation, but the main one is this: In any instance where a class action is preferable to a host of individual actions, it will follow that a single national class will fulfill the stated objectives of class proceedings legislation (judicial economy, access to justice, and behaviour modification) and the empirical objectives of tort law (primarily compensation and deterrence) better than will thirteen provincial and territorial classes.

The class action relies on giving plaintiffs an economy of scale to rival defendants'.[96] Any unnecessary subdividing of the single class action into smaller actions will sacrifice some of the litigative efficiency of the whole, even where plaintiffs' counsel cooperate in bringing multiple provincial actions. In province-by-province certification, per-claim litigation costs will increase for plaintiffs at a greater rate than defendants,[97] settlement incen-

---

95 See C. Jones, *Theory of Class Actions* (Toronto: Irwin Law, 2003) and "The Case for the National Class" (2004) 1 Can. Class Action R. 29.

96 The idea that mass tort defendants treat large-scale claims as a "virtual class action," spreading per-claim litigation costs over all classable claims, was developed in a series of canonical articles by Harvard's David Rosenberg. See David Rosenberg, "A 'Public Law' Vision of the Tort System" (1984) 97 Harvard L. Rev. 849; David Rosenberg "Class Actions for Mass Torts: Doing Individual Justice by Collective Means" (1987) 62 Ind. L.J. 561; David Rosenberg, "Of End Games and Openings in Mass Tort Cases: Lessons from a Special Master" (1989) 69 B.U. L. Rev. 695; David Rosenberg, "Individual Justice and Collectivizing Risk-Based Claims in Mass-Exposure Cases (1996) 71 N.Y.U. L. Rev. 210.

97 Requiring any class to subdivide and litigate separately will necessarily increase per-claim litigation costs. Subdivision of a classable claim imposes extra per-claim costs on plaintiffs to a greater extent than on defendants, who will treat common issues — e.g., whether a product was dangerously defective — as a single question. Regardless in how many jurisdictions it is defending the product. Defendants can employ the same experts, use the same legal research, and even employ the same lawyers in each jurisdiction where the issues are common — i.e. otherwise "classable." Litigation efficiencies automatically accrue to defendants in these circumstances more than plaintiffs, who can, at best, affect only an imperfect economy of scale between jurisdictions. David Rosenberg, "Mass Tort Class Actions — What the Defendants Have and Plaintiffs Don't" (2000) 37 Harv. J. Legis. 393 (exploring the "structural asymmetry" enuring to the benefit of mass tort defendants absent optimal aggregation).

tives for defendants will decrease below the optimal,[98] compensation per claim will decrease,[99] and fewer valid claims will ever be brought.[100] Free rider problems and inter-counsel blackmail will likely increase,[101] further diminishing the efficiency of aggregate resolution.

From a purely economic perspective, the most effective plaintiff's class will be drawn from all persons, regardless of their physical location, who have suffered from the same wrong. In litigation arising from the provision of products or services on a mass scale (the majority of class action cases), the class should mirror the "market" throughout which the mass-

---

[98] As the plaintiff's per-claim litigation costs increase compared to the defendants, the expected amount for which each claim will settle will decrease. The standard model of litigation settlement holds that the defendant's "maximum offer" will be the expected judgment amount plus litigation costs. The plaintiff's "minimum demand" will be the judgment *minus* litigation costs. In ordinary circumstances, the parties will settle on average at the mean point between the maximum offer and minimum demand: See generally Steven Shavell, "Suit, Settlement, and Trial: A Theoretical Analysis under Alternative Methods for the Allocation of Legal Costs" (1982) 11 J. Legal Stud. 55. The implications of this model in aggregate systems were observed in David Rosenberg, *Mass Torts and Complex Litigation Seminar (Materials)*, Harvard Law School (Unpublished, 2002, on file with the authors).

[99] This follows directly: if settlement values are decreased according to Shavell's formula, and per claim litigation costs are simultaneously increased, then the injured plaintiff not only gets a smaller piece of the pie, she gets a smaller piece of a smaller pie.

[100] This is not difficult to demonstrate. Ward Branch, one of Canada's most prolific class action litigators, has a rule of thumb whereby he will advance a class action only if its expected return is around $1 million: See Ward Branch, "The Wheat and the Chaff: Class Action Case Selection" <www.branmac.com> (accessed November 2, 2003) at 4. Branch litigates mostly in British Columbia which is home to perhaps 10 percent of the Canadian population. In cases involving a nationally-distributed product, then, Branch will take (the B.C. portion of) the case if there has been $10 million of damages across the nation. Presumably there are lawyers in the other provinces with similar thresholds.

In a case where there has been only $5 million worth of damages, and assuming all lawyers "thresholds" are the same as Branch's, then no action will be brought anywhere in the country if it must be litigated on a "province-by-province" basis, whereas the claim certainly would be brought if a national class was permitted.

[101] "Free riding" is possible because litigation in the ordinary course generates a significant amount of publicly available information regarding the common issues. Factual information gained through discovery or trial, legal research and arguments all represent expensive investments by plaintiff's counsel, and each may be obtained for only token cost by a "free rider" who wishes to exploit the investor's work product, provided that the case proceeds to hearing or trial. If the $5-million class action referred to in the previous note was certified in Ontario, a class counsel could file in British Columbia. Once certified there, the BC counsel could do no work, expecting that Ontario counsel would be willing to share all its work product in exchange for any fraction of the fee.

produced wrong could be said to be generic. In some cases, that market will be international; in most cases, it will be at least interprovincial. Based on the types of class actions so far pursued in Canada, it seems safe to say that only in a minority of cases will the impact of a mass wrong be entirely limited to residents of a single province.

There have traditionally been several arguments made in opposition to the national opt-out class, namely: provincial legislative sovereignty, concerns over the jurisdictional reach of provincial superior courts, problems of choice of law, and the problem of notice to extraprovincial class members. Each of the first three of these problems is manageable;[102] the main concern remaining should be whether notice is, under the circumstances, sufficient to provide the constitutional imperatives of "order and fairness" to the residents of other provinces, by permitting them to "opt out" of the litigation.

It is not necessarily more difficult to effect notice for class members outside the province than it is to for those within it. Indeed, given the national scale of the most popular forms of media, notice in many cases (calculated as a percentage of expected recovery per claim) will be cheaper and more efficient in a national class than in provincial ones.[103] It is difficult to imagine a case with potential plaintiffs from several provinces, yet where notice is best handled entirely locally — that is, there is no reason to think that notice will be *more* effective simply because it is generated from within a class member's own province. In an age of increasingly national (and international) media, it may even be less so.[104]

---

102 See the discussion in Jones, "The Case for the National Class," *supra* note 95.
103 Imagine a mass tort has caused damages of $1 million across Canada, and that this loss is equally spread among ten provinces ($100,000 per province). Assuming that the class members are not known, notice must be effected through advertising. The cost of using local media within the province is $10,000; the cost of taking advantage of the national media is $50,000.

　　Under the Ontario "national opt-out class" model, the representative plaintiff could spend $10,000 in each province for local media and another $50,000 in national media to be assured of the best possible notice in the circumstances. In such a case, the total cost spread across all class members would be $150,000, or 15 percent of each class member's recovery.

　　To accomplish *exactly the same* notice under the competing ULCC model of several provincial actions, the representative plaintiff in each province would have to pay $10,000 to have only provincial coverage and a further $50,000 for national coverage, the bulk of which would be "wasted" on other provinces. Each provincial class representative would therefore pay $60,000, or 60 percent of each class member's recovery.
104 Consider a class member who resides in Manitoba and reads the *Globe and Mail* and watches CBC national television exclusively. It may not be cost-effective for a Manitoba-only class to advertise in these national sources as well as the purely local ones. On

From the point of view of basic fairness when viewing the adequacy of notice, there is one aspect of jurisdiction over a national class that does raise legitimate concerns. It might be fair to bind a person within the forum province, even if that person does not have actual notice of the suit, because it can be expected that the plaintiff's lawyers will employ all legal arguments available in the forum on that person's behalf, and seek every possible legal advantage, substantive and procedural. In a national opt-out class where notice is attempted, but individual, actual notice is not possible, the concern may exist that extraprovincial plaintiffs will be bound to a process where both the courts and plaintiffs' counsel are unfamiliar with all of the advantages — substantive and procedural — that exist in the non-resident's own jurisdiction.

Much of this problem can be abated through subclassing of non-residents by jurisdiction; in a B.C. action, for instance, there could be a subclass for Albertans, Manitobans, and so on, with the subclass's counsel familiar with the applicable law of the foreign province. However, this addresses the concern only with respect to substantive law, which the forum court is bound to apply where it is applicable. If *procedural* advantages exist in the foreign province, these will be lost to a class member swept up in the B.C. action.[105]

This argument need not be fatal to an opt-out national class,[106] but it does provide some support for the notion that the quality of notice required in such an action should be higher than that in a class limited to the forum province. There is reason to believe that Canadian courts are sensitive to

---

the other hand, the model described in the previous note suggests that a national class would *always* be able to avail itself of the most efficient combination of national and local media across the country.

[105] To give a concrete example, B.C.'s *Tobacco Damages and Health Care Costs Recovery Act*, S.B.C. 2000, c. 30, provided certain procedural advantages to plaintiffs — or plaintiff classes — in tobacco litigation. They could, for instance, introduce statistical and epidemiological evidence to prove causation, as well as damages. If a national class were certified first in Ontario, this advantage would be lost to the B.C. claimants.

[106] The deprival of *plaintiffs'* procedural advantages or conveniences available in their own jurisdiction is difficult to distinguish from the situation faced by foreign-resident defendants, who may be impleaded in and bound by the forum court, providing they have the requisite "real and substantial connection" with either the forum or the subject matter of the litigation. It is arguably equally "fair" to "sweep in" plaintiffs on a similar basis. If a defendant must be taken to expect that it could have claims against it decided in any jurisdiction where the product does harm, a consumer buying a nationally-distributed product would similarly be taken to understand that, should she eventually become a victim of a wrong with relation to that product and a member of a class action, that action might be litigated in any of the provinces.

this question, and other factors should weigh more heavily when assessing notice than the residency of the prospective class members.

Nevertheless, it may also be a good idea to consider the purpose of notice in class actions. While it is often framed as preserving litigative autonomy, the "day in court" ideal, by permitting class members to opt out and pursue their own actions, this explanation is weak, at least in the case of numerous small scale claims that are either not individually viable or would be disproportionately expensive to pursue.

In such cases, the ideas of litigative autonomy or the day in court ideal are illusory — the right to pursue a claim without any potential reward is of no practical importance to anyone. The universality of subrogation clauses in insurance agreements supports the conclusion that consumers are happy to trade their right to sue in order to achieve fuller compensation in case of a loss.

It may therefore be time to consider the purpose of notice as something other than an opportunity to opt out and pursue a claim individually: in the majority of cases, it will be most useful as a form of insurance against collusion between plaintiffs' and defendants' counsel — the "sweetheart deal" made at the expense of the class. Notice, under this paradigm, is a means for the court to conduct a poll of class members, to gauge whether those harmed feel that the redress is appropriate, before the court approves the settlement offered by counsel. Such notice would not have to reach every member of the class: like a poll, its purpose would be to gather a representative sample of class members.

If the courts were, at least in cases of lower-value claims, to adopt this view of the purpose of notice, and consider that it comported with the orderly and fair resolution of mass claims, then it should be far easier to certify a national class without being unnecessarily concerned for its theoretical impact in other jurisdictions.

Assuming a court is prepared to certify nationally, there remains the question of mechanism by which it will be done. The simplest method would be for a Court to make the certification order, and expect that other jurisdictions' courts will decline to certify a competing class, following the "full faith and credit" approach of *Morguard*. A plaintiff might, in such circumstances, seek a further order of the original court prohibiting actions in other jurisdictions, a sort of national anti-suit injunction.

Part Four:
Interjurisdictional Dimensions

9. Conflict of Laws in Large-Scale Claims

A. INTRODUCTION

Conflict of laws, or private international law as it is known in the English tradition, is a complex field in itself that has generated numerous excellent and comprehensive works. In this chapter, we provide only a general overview of the field, with particular attention to issues that are likely to arise in the context of multijurisdictional litigation of the type addressed by this book: mass torts, product liability claims, and class action suits.

B. AN OVERVIEW OF CONFLICT OF LAWS ANALYSIS

Courts operate in a framework of restraint when taking control of matters that are distant from their immediate vicinity. The reasons why they do so should be immediately apparent: to avoid inconsistent decisions and waste of judicial resources as several courts address the same question; to avoid "forum-shopping" — the practice of plaintiffs seeking out the most favourable environment for litigation; and to forestall unnecessary consideration of questions of foreign law, with which the forum court is unfamiliar. There are also considerations of "comity," that is, an inclination to defer to other jurisdictions with a greater claim to legitimate interest in the subject matter of the litigation, so as to avoid trenching on the lawmaking — and law enforcing — rights of other governments, perhaps in part in the expectation that other jurisdictions' courts will similarly defer when the situation is reversed. A system based upon a restrained approach to jurisdiction also increases the likelihood that the usually deferential courts' decisions will be enforced elsewhere.

To effect these ends, Canadian courts usually address questions involving conflict of laws sequentially.[1] First, the court considers whether it has *jurisdiction simpliciter* (sometimes called personal jurisdiction) over the defendants. This is a threshold issue and either answered in the affirmative or in the negative, without room for discretion on the part of the court.[2] If "yes," then the court proceeds to consider other conflicts questions. If "no," then the action against the defendant cannot proceed.

Second, the court will ask whether, notwithstanding that it has jurisdiction over the parties (jurisdiction over the plaintiff — at least in individual claims — may be assumed as that party, by filing its claim, has attorned to the jurisdiction of the court), it should decline to exercise that jurisdiction. The court's decision in this respect is discretionary but frequently analyses whether there is a more appropriate forum for the proposed hearing of the issues.

Third, assuming that the first two questions have been answered in favour of the court asserting its jurisdiction over the matter and parties before it, the court will turn its attention to the applicable law. That is to say, notwithstanding that the matter will be heard in the forum court, should it be the law of the forum that applies or the law of another jurisdiction; if the latter, which jurisdiction? In truth, this question is not as discrete as it appears, because many courts will consider choice of law questions when considering whether to exercise its discretion to decline jurisdiction, or even (where, for instance, jurisdiction is conferred by a local statute) whether it has jurisdiction at all.

A final aspect of the conflict of laws is the enforcement of foreign judgments: Under what circumstances will the courts of one jurisdiction enforce the decisions of another? This question ordinarily arises upon enforcement, that is, when a successful plaintiff applies to the forum court to have a foreign judgment enforced by that court. However, it might also be argued with respect to the *forum conveniens* analysis: a defendant might

---

1   *Canadian International Marketing Distributing Ltd. v. Nitsuko Ltd.* (1990), 56 B.C.L.R. (2d) 130 at 131–32 (C.A.); *Jordan v. Schatz*, 2000 BCCA 409 at para. 21.
2   *Ell v. Con-Pro Industries Ltd.* (1992), 11 B.C.A.C. 174 at 184.

say to the forum court, "You should not take jurisdiction because, in any event, your judgment on these matters will not be recognized elsewhere."

These questions are relatively straightforward in the case of an "ordinary," individualized action in tort or contract. They naturally become more difficult in the case of mass torts or other complex litigation, where the parties, putative victims, and even the causes of action may be spread across a host of jurisdictions.

As the complexity of litigation, mirroring the increasingly interjurisdictional nature of commerce, has expanded across borders, courts have struggled to develop a conceptual system to deal with events that have "happened" in several jurisdictions. Does a court take jurisdiction over a case involving a product manufactured in one jurisdiction that did harm to many? If it can deal with local victims' claims, can it also address claims where the harm was suffered elsewhere? If so, under what circumstances?

C. THE "CONSTITUTIONALIZATION" OF PRIVATE INTERNATIONAL LAW

At the same time as Canadian provinces began to design class action statutes, the law of interjurisdictional conflict in tort was undergoing a significant restatement, one that has received wide notice in the common law world.[3] This revolution was effected through two landmark cases, *Morguard Investments Ltd. v. De Savoye*[4] and *Hunt v. T&N plc*.[5]

1) Morguard

In *Morguard Investments Ltd. v. De Savoye*,[6] the Supreme Court of Canada was considering the obligations of a court to recognize the judgments and orders of sister courts in other provinces. The plaintiff in *Morguard* had previously obtained a judgment in the Alberta courts against the defendant, a British Columbian resident, who had defaulted on a land mortgage in Alberta. Under Rule 30(g) of the Alberta *Rules of Court*, the Alberta court could assume jurisdiction over such a dispute even though the defendant had been served outside Alberta territory. The question before the Supreme

---

3   See, for instance, note by Janet Walker, "Choice of Law in Tort: The Supreme Court of Canada Enters the Fray" (1995) 111 L.Q.R. 397.
4   *Morguard Investments Ltd. v. De Savoye*, [1990] 3 S.C.R. 1077 [hereinafter *Morguard*].
5   *Hunt v. T&N plc*, [1993] 4 S.C.R. 289 [hereinafter *Hunt*].
6   *Morguard*, *supra* note 4.

Court of Canada was the correctness of a subsequent decision by a British Columbia judge to enforce the Alberta judgment.

Morguard is noteworthy for two reasons. First, it held that the enforcement of extrajurisdictional Canadian judgments was not analogous to the enforcement of judgments that are truly foreign, and that the same rules should not apply. Instead of relying on arcane English rules of private international law, Canadian courts must afford one another's judgments "full faith and credit," providing that the original court indeed had properly taken jurisdiction. La Forest J. held: "As I see it, the courts in one province should give full faith and credit, to use the language of the United States Constitution, to the judgments given by a court in another province or a territory, *so long as that court has properly, or appropriately, exercised jurisdiction in the action* [emphasis added]."[7]

The second question settled in *Morguard* was whether the originating court (Alberta) had properly taken jurisdiction over a matter between parties from outside the province, such that British Columbia courts ought to respect the judgment granted. The Court held that a provincial superior court's jurisdiction is limited by principles of "order and fairness," and that, with respect to a dispute involving parties from other provinces, this principle is satisfied only where there is "a real and substantial connection" between the province assuming jurisdiction and the defendant or the subject matter of the lawsuit. Significantly, the Court attributed its departure from the traditional rules to the nature of the federal system and its essentially national marketplace: "In a world where even the most familiar things we buy and sell originate or are manufactured elsewhere, and where people are constantly moving from province to province, it is simply anachronistic to uphold a 'power theory' or a single situs for torts or contracts for the proper exercise of jurisdiction."[8]

The *Morguard* decision was one of a series in which the increasingly borderless market played a prominent role in influencing the Court's reasoning. Earlier that same year, La Forest J. said in *Thomson Newspapers Ltd. v. Canada* at paragraph 168)

> ... The courts in Canada ... cannot remain oblivious to the concrete social, political and economic realities within which our system of constitutional rights and guarantees must operate. ... [A]s the Canadian economy becomes increasingly integrated with the American and, indeed, the global economy, we should be wary of giving an interpretation to the Consti-

---

7   *Ibid.* at 1102.
8   *Ibid.* at 1108–9.

tution that shackles the government's capacity to cope with problems that other countries ... are quite able to deal with[.]⁹

But *Morguard* has one other striking feature that, while not often commented upon, may bear upon our analysis here. It seems clearly to suggest that the jurisdiction of courts does not necessarily mirror that of provincial legislatures. That is, while legislatures are territiorially limited by the constitution,[10] courts — at least provincial courts of inherent jurisdiction — are not.[11] La Forest J. noted that "[t]his Court has, in other areas of the law having extraterritorial implications, recognized the need for adapting the law to the exigencies of a federation."[12] He then cited with approval from the decision of Estey J. in *Aetna Financial Services Ltd. v. Feigelman*: "... An initial question, therefore, must be answered, namely, what is meant by 'jurisdiction' in a federal context? ... In some ways, 'jurisdiction' [of the Manitoba court] extends to the national boundaries, or, in any case, beyond the provincial boundary of Manitoba."[13] This idea of the provincial superior courts as — at least in some situations — "national" courts will be more fully explored in the subsequent decision of *Hunt v. T&N plc*, which follows.

2) Hunt

While *Morguard* hinted that the "full faith and credit" and "order and fairness" requirements were constitutional in nature,[14] this was not confirmed until the Court's decision in *Hunt v. T&N plc*,[15] where it confirmed that the requirement of "a real and substantial connection" was indeed a "constitutional imperative," such that it "has become the absolute constitutional limit on the power of each province to confer judicial jurisdiction on its courts."[16]

---

9   *Thomson Newspapers Corp. v. Canada (Director of Investigation and Research)*, [1990] 1 S.C.R. 425 [hereinafter *Thomson Newspapers*].
10 It would appear, for instance, that provincial legislatures cannot make laws "aimed at" activities occurring wholly outside the province: *Reference Re Upper Churchill Water Rights Reversion Act (1980 Newfoundland)*, [1984] 1 S.C.R. 297. What remains unclear is whether there is a "real and substantial connection" test applicable to such legislation, mirroring the test for judicial jurisdiction, following *Hunt*.
11 Vaughan Black, "The Other Side of *Hunt*: New Limits on Judicial Jurisdiction" (1993) 22 Can. Bus. L.J. 4.
12 *Morguard*, supra note 4 at 1101.
13 *Ibid.* at 1101–2, citing *Aetna Financial Services Ltd. v. Feigelman*, [1985] 1 S.C.R. 2 at 34–35.
14 See *Morguard*, supra note 4 at 1094 per La Forest J.: "For a number of these writers, there are constitutional overtones to this approach .... It is fair to say that I have found the work of these writers very helpful in my own analysis of the issues."
15 *Hunt*, supra note 5.
16 Jean Gabriel Castel, *Canadian Conflict of Laws*, 4th ed. (Toronto: Butterworths, 1997) at 54.

> They are constitutional imperatives, and as such apply to the provincial legislatures as well as to the courts .... In short, to use the expressions employed in *Morguard* at p.1100, the "integrating character of our constitutional arrangements as they apply to interprovincial mobility" calls for the courts in each province to give "full faith and credit" to the judgments of the courts of sister provinces. This, as also noted in *Morguard*, is inherent in the structure of the Canadian federation, and, as such, is beyond the power of provincial legislatures to override. This does not mean, however, that a province is debarred from enacting any legislation that may have some effect on litigation in other provinces .... But it does mean that it must respect the minimum standards of order and fairness addressed in *Morguard*.
>
> ... One must emphasize that the ideas of "comity" are not an end in themselves, but are grounded in notions of order and fairness to participants in litigation with connections to multiple jurisdictions.[17]

Hunt concerned, *inter alia*, the constitutionality of a Quebec "blocking statute" that prohibited the removal of business records from Quebec to fulfil an out-of-province court's discovery requirements. Following *Morguard*, the British Columbia Supreme Court had held that comity required it to respect the barrier erected by Quebec. However, the Supreme Court of Canada turned the question of "comity" around, and held that the Quebec statute was constitutionally inapplicable to civil proceedings in another province by virtue of the same *Morguard* principles. *Hunt* also appeared to confirm that "the Constitution may itself provide a source of court jurisdiction by prohibiting the ouster of the jurisdiction of the superior courts of a province with a real and substantial connection to the matter."[18] This jurisdiction, once properly exerted, must be respected by all other Canadian courts and, by inference, legislatures.

3) The Future Direction

The Canadian jurisprudence in the field of conflicts law should be viewed as a recognition of the internationalist reality expressed by Mr. Justice La Forest in the Supreme Court of Canada's decision in *Thompson Newspapers Ltd. v. Canada*: "[A]s the Canadian economy becomes increasingly integrated with the American and, indeed, the global economy, we should be wary of giving an interpretation to the Constitution that shackles the govern-

---

17   *Hunt, supra* note 5 at paras. 56–57.
18   Janet Walker, "Interprovincial Sovereign Immunity Revisited" (1997) 35 Osgoode Hall L.J. 379 at 389.

ment's capacity to cope with problems that other countries ... are quite able to deal with in ... planning for freedom."[19] The Supreme Court has also made similar statements to justify its reconsideration of rules for jurisdiction *forum conveniens* and choice of law. Discussing the former, Sopinka J. said in *Amchem Products v. B.C. (W.C.B.)*:

> [T]he business of litigation, like commerce itself, has become increasingly international. With the increase of free trade and the rapid growth of multi-national corporations it has become more difficult to identify one clearly appropriate forum for this type of litigation. The defendant may not be identified with only one jurisdiction. Moreover, there are frequently multiple defendants carrying on business in a number of jurisdictions and distributing their products or services world wide. As well, the plaintiffs may be a large class residing in different jurisdictions. It is often difficult to pinpoint the place where the transaction giving rise to the action took place. Frequently, there is no single forum that is clearly the most convenient or appropriate for the trial of the action but rather several which are equally suitable alternatives. In some jurisdictions, novel principles requiring joinder of all who have participated in a field of commercial activity have been developed for determining how liability should be apportioned among defendants. In this climate, courts have had to become more tolerant of the systems of other countries. The parochial attitude exemplified by *Bushby v. Munday* (1821), 5 Madd. 297, 56 E.R. 908, at p. 308 and p. 913, that "the substantial ends of justice would require that this Court should pursue its own better means of determining both the law and the fact of the case" is no longer appropriate.[20]

D. THE CONSTITUTIONAL CONTEXT

Before moving on to discuss the rules of conflicts law that inform interjurisdictional litigation, we should first set out the constitutional framework in which such rules operate. We have already seen that provincial superior courts perform dual functions: first, as truly "provincial" jurisdictions, determining the law binding in that province subject only to the Supreme Court of Canada's review; and second, as "national" institutions, with jurisdiction that extends in some cases throughout Canada. While this

---

19 *Thomson Newspapers*, supra note 9 at para. 168.
20 *Amchem Products Inc. v. British Columbia (Workers' Compensation Board)* (1993), 77 B.C.L.R. (2d) 62 (S.C.C.) at para. 20, under the heading "Choosing the Forum in Modern Litigation."

"dual nature" is an elegant solution to many conflicts problems that arise at at common law, it does not overcome the problems that can arise through the compartmentalization of the Canadian federation set out in the constitution.

1) The Legislative Authority

Under section 92 of the *Constitution Act, 1867*, the power over "property and civil rights" and "the administration of justice" within the various provinces is held by the provincial legislatures.[21] The federal government, under section 91, retains both an interprovincial trade power and the residual "peace, order, and good government" authority (as well as some particular areas, such as the criminal law and bankruptcy), which permit it also to legislate in areas relevant to mass tort and complex litigation.

In general terms, Professor Hogg describes the provincial power over "property and civil rights" as follows: "[P]roperty and civil rights in the province ... covers most of the legal relationships between persons in Canada. The law relating to property, succession, the family, contracts and torts is mainly within provincial jurisdiction under s. 92(13)."[22] Hogg describes what is meant by "civil rights" in these terms: "The civil rights referred to in the *Constitution Act, 1867* comprise primarily proprietary, contractual or tortious rights; these rights exist when a legal rule stipulates that in certain circumstances one person is entitled to something from another."[23]

So it is apparent that the law regarding liability for mass tort will generally be provincial law. But, particularly in the field of large-scale wrongs, for instance, in product liability cases, how do you determine what limitations are imposed by the constitutional limitation of provincial power to property and civil rights *within the province*?

Section 92(14) provides the necessary legislative authority for the enactment of rules of evidence and civil procedure pursuant to which claims are brought.[24] In *Attorney General (Ontario) v. Scott*, Rand J., writing for four members of the Court, said: "In the administration of justice the province is supreme in determining the procedure by which rights and duties shall be enforced ..."[25] In the same case, Abbott J. writing for himself

---

21 *Constitution Act, 1867* (U.K.) 30 & 31 Victoria, c. 3, rep in R.S.C. 1985, App. II No. 5, ss. 92(13), (14).
22 P.W. Hogg, *Constitutional Law of Canada*, 4th ed. (Scarborough, ON: Carswell, 1997) at 547.
23 *Ibid.* at 548 (21-4 looseleaf).
24 *Reference Re Status of the Supreme Court of British Columbia* (1882), 1 B.C.R. 243 (S.C.C.) [appendix to the *Thrasher* case]; see also *Hunt, supra* note 5 at 320.
25 [1956] S.C.R. 137 at 141.

and two others, referred to section 92(14): "... [I]t is clearly competent to any province to determine for the purpose of a civil action brought in such province, what evidence is to be accepted and what defences may be set up to such an action."[26]

Unlike the provinces, the federal government's authority is not geographically limited.[27] Therefore, as long as a matter falls within federal competence, it does not matter in theory that it might involve issues that lack connection to Canada.[28] However, because tort law and contract are principally the domain of the provinces, considerations of constitutional territoriality will remain at the centre of conflicts analysis.

2) Comity, Order, and Fairness

But the strict division of powers analysis is not exhaustive of the factors to be considered when provincial legal regimes can be said to overlap. Repeated references are made in the cases to the ideals of "comity" and "order and fairness." Most recently, in *Spar Aerospace*,[29] the Supreme Court of Canada said:

> 21 The three principles of comity, order and fairness serve to guide the determination of the principal private international law issues: jurisdiction *simpliciter, forum non conveniens*, choice of law, and recognition of foreign judgments. Given that these three principles are at the heart of the private international legal order, it is not surprising that the various issues are interrelated.

Comity can be defined as the deference paid by the elements of one legal system (including legislative, executive, and judicial branches) to the jurisdiction of another regarding subject matter that might arise in both places. The principle is described by La Forest J. in *Morguard v. De Savoye*:

---

26 *Ibid.* at 147.
27 See, for instance, the discussion in E. Edinger, "Territorial Limitations on Provincial Powers" (1982) 14 Ottawa L. Rev. 57 at 60–61.
28 Canada's powers in this respect are analogous to England's, following the enactment of the *Statute of Westminster 1931*, (U.K.), 22 & 23 Geo. 5, c. 4, reprinted in R.S.C. 1985, App. II, No. 27. It is often said that the English Parliament could, in theory, enact a law forbidding smoking in the streets of Paris. Practically speaking, national governments are restrained from such extraterritorial ambitions by the strictures of international law and custom, the self-interest most states have in promoting comity among nations, and the practical difficulty of enforcing domestic decisions in the courts of the countries purportedly affected.
29 *Spar Aerospace Ltd. v. American Mobile Satellite Corp.*, [2002] 4 S.C.R. 205 [hereinafter *Spar Aerospace*].

> "Comity" in the legal sense is neither a matter of absolute obligation, on the one hand, nor of mere courtesy and good will, upon the other. But it is the recognition which one nation allows within its territory to the legislative, executive, or judicial acts of another nation, having due regard both to international duty and convenience, and to the rights of its own citizens or of other persons who are under the protection of its laws ....[30]

Canadian courts have adopted the following definition of the concept, from the U.S. Supreme Court decision in *Hilton v. Guyot*: "... the recognition which one nation allows within its territory to the legislative, executive or judicial acts of another nation, having due regard both to international duty and convenience, and to the rights of its own citizens or of other persons who are under the protection of its laws."[31]

"Order and fairness" is a related concept. The Supreme Court has held that "the twin objectives sought by private international law in general and the doctrine of international comity in particular [are] order and fairness."[32] Simply expressed, "order and fairness" indicates the hope that, if each jurisdiction tends to its own legal business and overlaps with its neighbours only to the extent necessary to achieve a system of effective laws, the legal landscape will provide for the efficient resolution of disputes in accordance with the policies of the various jurisdictions. When giving effect to "order and fairness," Binnie J. observed in *Holt Cargo* that "the Court gave pre-eminence to the objective of order."[33] Or, as La Forest J. put it in *Tolofson v. Jensen*: "Order is a precondition to justice."[34]

Since the pathblazing decisions of *Morguard* and *Hunt*, and arguably even since *Moran v. Pyle National Canada Ltd.*,[35] order and fairness and comity have become constitutional principles — that is, they have been rec-

---

30 *Supra* note 4 at 1096.
31 *Hilton v. Guyot*, 159 U.S. 113 (1895) at 164, citing *R. v. Spencer*, [1985] 2 S.C.R. 278 at 283 *per* Estey J. [hereinafter *Spencer*]; *Morguard*, supra note 4 at 1096 *per* La Forest J.; *Holt Cargo Systems Inc. v. ABC Containerline N.V. (Trustees of)*, [2001] 3 S.C.R. 907 at para. 69 *per* Binnie J. [hereinafter *Holt Cargo*]; *Spar Aerospace*, *supra* note 29 at para. 19 *per* LeBel J.
32 See *Holt Cargo*, *ibid.* at para. 71 *per* Binnie J.; *Morguard*, *ibid.* at 1097; and *Hunt*, *supra* note 5 at 325 *per* La Forest J.
33 *Holt Cargo*, *supra* note 30 at para. 71.
34 *Tolofson v. Jensen*, [1994] 3 S.C.R. 1022 at para. 56 [hereinafter *Tolofson*].
35 [1974] 2 W.W.R. 586 (S.C.C.) [hereinafter *Moran*]. In *Unifund*, *infra* note 66, Binnie J. mentioned *Moran* as one of the series of cases establishing the constitutional limits of provincial jurisdiction, although it was not a constitutional case. Similarly, that *Morguard* was establishing a truly constitutional principle was confirmed only in the subsequent decision of *Hunt*.

ognized by the courts as supreme over ordinary legislation, which is invalid if it contradicts them. At least as important, because these principles have been constitutionalized, the courts must ensure that their decisions in cases involving multijurisdictional aspects conform to their constraints.

E. JURISDICTION OVER THE DEFENDANT

1) Jurisdiction *Simpliciter* and the "Real and Substantial Connection" Test

Either a court has jurisdiction *simpliciter* or it does not. Each province has statutory rules for service on foreign defendants, and the circumstances under which it can be done without leave of the court vary somewhat. However, the statutory extension of jurisdiction, as in the United States, cannot exceed the extent allowed by the constitution.

The constitutional test that has evolved in Canada requires that the plaintiff show that the foreign defendant has some "real and substantial connection" with the forum before he or she need subject him- or herself to its jurisdiction. As noted earlier, the real and substantial connection test is designed to ensure that any assumption of jurisdiction is properly restrained and comports with the dictates of "order and fairness," concepts that have now become constitutionalized.[36]

Upon a challenge to the court's jurisdiction (generally made as an interlocutory motion under the forum's Rules of Court), the burden is on the plaintiff to demonstrate a "good arguable case" that such a connection exists. This is analysed by reference to the pleadings, to see whether they allege the facts necessary to establish jurisdiction. If they do, then the burden shifts to the defendant, who may introduce evidence putting jurisdictional connections alleged into issue.

Of course, what constitutes such a "connection" is open to broad interpretation; however, at least since *Moran v. Pyle*,[37] a plaintiff who is harmed by a defective product within the jurisdiction might be able to bring the manufacturer before the domestic courts, wherever the product was made or sold. In more recent years, constitutional cases indicate that jurisdiction may be asserted on the basis of a foreseeability test: jurisdiction may be established if it was reasonably foreseeable that the defendant's activities

---

36 See *Morguard, supra* note 4 at 1108.
37 *Supra* note 34.

would bring him or her under the scrutiny of the Canadian court.[38] Foreseeability is still one of the most, if not the most, important element in the establishment of jurisdiction in Canada.[39]

Foreseeability figured prominently in the analysis of the British Columbia Court of Appeal in *Harrington v. Dow Corning Corp.* In that case, the court was considering the application of the *Class Proceedings Act*.[40] The court had two aspects of territoriality to consider. First, on the issue of whether the Act could govern actions where the tort was committed outside British Columbia but the victims (women who had received allegedly faulty breast implants) later relocated there, the court reviewed the history of the "real and substantial connection" requirement and said:

> In my view, this rule is sufficient to justify the inclusion in the resident class of all women resident in British Columbia who allege they are suffering harm from the use of silicone breast implants manufactured and put into the flow of commerce negligently by an appellant. *Any manufacturer of breast implants would understand that any injury would follow the user in whom they were implanted into whatever jurisdiction the user might reside from time to time.*[41] [Emphasis added.]

The majority in *Harrington* then went on to consider the implications of section 16(2) of the Act, which allows for foreign plaintiffs (each of whom, independently, would have no "real and substantial connection" with the province) to "opt in" to the British Columbia class action as a non-resident subclass. The court held that, where the legislation itself provided for extraterritorial operation, this would be limited in its application to situations where extraterritorial reach was constitutionally permissible:

---

38 *Moses v. Shore Boat Builders Ltd.* (1993), 106 D.L.R. (4th) 654 (B.C.C.A.), leave to appeal refused (1994), 109 D.L.R. (4th) vii (S.C.C.).

39 Foreseeability would still appear to weigh heavily in the consideration of jurisdiction in Canada, as La Forest J. explained citing *Moran v. Pyle* in *Hunt, supra* note 5 at para. 41:

> ... where a corporation that had in one province manufactured goods that were defective was sued in a province where the plaintiff suffered damage as a result. As here, the manufacturer must be taken to have known that the goods would be used outside the province of manufacture in the manner they were. Given the significant connection with the province where the injury took place, it is difficult to see how it could be said to offend the principles of order and fairness for the British Columbia courts to take jurisdiction.

40 R.S.B.C. 1996, c. 50.

41 *Harrington v. Dow Corning Corp.*, 2000 BCCA 605 at para. 84 [hereinafter *Harrington*].

It might be said that all women who suffer injury from breast implants may opt into the class proceeding because they would all come within the language of s. 16(2). But, as Mr. Justice Mackenzie noted, this procedural provision does not seek to extend the jurisdiction of British Columbia courts beyond their constitutionally recognized limits. Rather, it tells a court that the Legislature accepts, even encourages, a decision to include non-residents in class proceedings as a matter of public policy. This policy makes good sense. Section 16(2) may preclude the court from certifying a national class on an opting out basis, as was done in *Nantais, supra*. However, it accords with requirements of comity, and with the policy underlying the enactment of legislation enabling class actions to determine the liability of defendants for mass injury in one forum to the extent claimants may wish and fairness to the defendants may permit.[42]

The globalizing economy is driving an expansionist view of the courts' jurisdiction. Mr. Justice La Forest commented in *Tolofson v. Jensen*:

> As *Morguard* and *Hunt* also indicate, the courts in the various states will, in certain circumstances, exercise jurisdiction over matters that may have originated in other states. And that will be so as well where a particular transaction may not be limited to a single jurisdiction. Consequently, individuals need not in enforcing a legal right be tied to the courts of the jurisdiction where the right arose, but may choose one to meet their convenience. This fosters mobility and a world economy.[43]

2) Jurisdiction *Simpliciter* and Multiple Defendants

In large-scale claims, defendants might be included in the action who, viewed outside the context of the lawsuit, are only tenuously connected with the jurisdiction, if at all. Such defendants might be included in the claim on the basis of their participation in a conspiracy with others who are more closely connected with the jurisdiction. In some product liability claims, manufacturers who made a product that is at issue in a class action suit might be included even though the victims of that particular defendants' product were foreigners, if the court wishes to resolve all the related claims at once.

Courts appear to be flexible in their inclusion of such defendants. In the case of conspiracy, for instance, courts generally appear willing to

---

42 *Ibid.* at para. 85.
43 *Tolofson, supra* note 34 at para. 39.

extend jurisdiction over all alleged co-conspirators. As Madam Justice Loo stated in *Yu-Ccan Corp. v. Master Professional Services Ltd.*: "It makes no sense to prosecute a claim of civil conspiracy without having the principal parties to the alleged conspiracy before the court as parties."[44]

The application of jurisdiction analysis with respect to claims by extraprovincial class members appears to be heading in the same general direction, with a flexible approach allowing courts to hear claims that, considered individually, would lack the real and substantial connection with the forum.[45] This "common thread" approach permits a court that properly has jurisdiction on the basis of a connection between the jurisdiction and the subject matter of an action to extend that jurisdiction to encompass any defendants potentially liable for the wrongs alleged in that action.[46]

3) Comity Internationally after *Spar Aerospace* and *Beals v. Saldanha*

Morguard, which established an obligation among Canadian jurisdictions to respect the decisions of courts in sister provinces, was essentially an importation of the U.S. constitution's "full faith and credit" requirement. It is therefore an interesting question whether the courts' varying employment of "full faith and credit" and "order and fairness" principles leads to different standards for conflicts among provinces when compared with truly "foreign" jurisdictions, particularly the United States and its constituent states.

Since *Morguard*, the principles of comity and mutual respect for the court processes of other Canadian jurisdictions have been applied to allow enforcement of the judgments of American courts in a series of British Columbia cases culminating with *Moses v. Shore Boat Builders Ltd.*[47] In that case, a Canadian manufacturer had been sued in Alaska for products it supplied there. The manufacturer did not appear, and a default judgment granted against it was enforced in British Columbia; the Supreme Court held that the *Morguard* principles could operate internationally, as well as interprovincially.

In *Spar Aerospace*,[48] the Supreme Court revisited the constitutionalization of conflict laws and appears to have found that their constitutional

---

44 2000 BCSC 676 at para. 17.
45 *Harrington, supra* note 41.
46 *Furlan v. Shell Oil Co.*, 2000 BCCA 404 at paras. 3 and 21.
47 *Supra* note 38.
48 *Supra* note 31.

aspects are, at least in some cases, limited to interprovincial matters, that is, they do not express limits on the jurisdiction of the provinces *per se* but rather limit only the extent to which one province can impinge on the authority of another. LeBel J. wrote:

> 51 I agree with the appellants that *Morguard* and *Hunt* establish that it is a constitutional imperative that Canadian courts can assume jurisdiction only where a "real and substantial connection" exists .... However, it is important to emphasize that *Morguard* and *Hunt* were decided in the context of interprovincial jurisdictional disputes. In my opinion, the specific findings of these decisions cannot easily be extended beyond this context. In particular, the two cases resulted in the enhancing or even broadening of the principles of reciprocity and speak directly to the context of interprovincial comity within the structure of the Canadian federation; see *Morguard, supra*, at p. 1109, and *Hunt, supra*, at p. 328.
>
> 52 In *Morguard*, La Forest J. ... delimited the decision to only address the modern interprovincial context (at p. 1098):
>
>> ... there is really no comparison between the interprovincial relationships of today and those obtaining between foreign countries in the 19th century. *Indeed, in my view, there never was and the courts made a serious error in transposing the rules developed for the enforcement of foreign judgments to the enforcement of judgments from sister-provinces. The considerations underlying the rules of comity apply with much greater force between the units of a federal state*, and I do not think it much matters whether one calls these rules of comity or simply relies directly on the reasons of justice, necessity and convenience to which I have already adverted. [Emphasis added.]
>
> 53 In *Hunt, supra*, at p. 321, La Forest J. stated that a central idea in *Morguard* was comity. It is apparent from his reasons in both cases, however, that federalism was the central concern underlying both decisions. At p. 1099 of *Morguard*, La Forest J. commented that adopting the traditional English rules in the Canadian context seemed to "fly in the face of the obvious intention of the Constitution to create a single country". ... At p. 323 of *Hunt*, La Forest J. drew a clear distinction between the rules pertaining to an international situation and the rules applicable to interprovincial disputes:
>
>> ... I do not think litigation engendered against a corporate citizen located in one province by its trading and commercial activ-

ities in another province should necessarily be subject to the same rules as those applicable to international commerce.

54 *Morguard* and *Hunt* have been cited by this Court in a number of cases which seem to confirm that the "real and substantial connection" was specially crafted to address the challenges posed by multiple jurisdictions within a federation. See: *Tolofson, supra*, where La Forest J. observed, at p. 1064:

> The nature of our constitutional arrangements — a single country with different provinces exercising territorial legislative jurisdiction — would seem to me to support a rule that is certain and that ensures that an act committed in one part of this country will be given the same legal effect throughout the country. ...

... In my view, there is nothing in these cases that supports the appellants' contention that the constitutional "real and substantial connection" criterion is required in addition to the jurisdiction provisions found in Book Ten of the *C.C.Q.*

The full meaning of these passages of LeBel's judgment in *Spar Aerospace* remains unclear. However, it is difficult to avoid the conclusion that the unanimous Court apparently approved of the ability of the provincial courts to take jurisdiction over foreign (non-Canadian) defendants even in instances where the "real and substantial connection" test is not satisfied, and indeed permitted the provinces to enact legislation that facilitates this process.

LeBel J. found himself in dissent in the subsequent case of *Beals v. Saldanha*.[49] There, the Court was called upon to enforce a judgment of a Florida court, despite clear concerns (at least in LeBel's mind) that notice requirements to the defendant had been inadequate and the proceedings taken were otherwise unfair to the defendants.

There was no doubt that a "real and substantial connection" with Florida existed; the dispute was over land that the Canadian defendants bought there, the deal was concluded in Florida, and it was perfectly reasonable for the defendants to assume that they would be subject to Florida's laws in any resulting dispute. But in this case, the Florida law appeared to arrive at a profoundly unjust result. Was the connection enough?

The majority of the Court found that, as a matter of principle, the "real and substantial connection" test should govern, not as a constitutional

---

49 2003 SCC 72 [hereinafter *Beals*].

principle (the Court made it clear that the rule was subject to legislation) but rather as the common law default when deciding whether a foreign court had properly taken jurisdiction over the defendants for the purposes of enforcement of the resulting judgment in Canada. LeBel J. argued strenuously for an overriding discretion to decline enforcement on the basis of simple "fairness."

The majority, too, considered fairness, but it found that while the plaintiffs in Florida had succeeded with a weak case, their success was largely due to the defendant's decision, which the Court described as based on "negligent" legal advice, not to appear to defend the action. The majority analysed an analogous argument under section 7 of the *Charter* but declared that this section, unlike the U.S. constitution, did not protect citizens against the financial consequences of a foreign court any more than those of a Canadian court.

While the result in *Beals* appears harsh — the defendants were bankrupted as a result of a damages award more than twenty times the value of the property they had purchased in Florida — the simplicity of the analysis has considerable appeal: jurisdiction is established on the "real and substantial connection" test. An enforcing jurisdiction might still refuse to acknowledge the foreign judgment if the foreign law is grossly offensive to natural justice or domestic public policy or if the judgment resulted from fraud, but, short of that threshold, legislation restricting enforcement is the only option.

4) Jurisdiction *Forum Conveniens*

Once a court has found that it has jurisdiction *simpliciter* over a defendant, it may nevertheless decline jurisdiction on the basis of *forum non conveniens*. The name of the test is in itself something of a misnomer; it is not the most convenient forum that interests the court, but rather the most appropriate one.[50]

There may be several jurisdictions that can claim sufficient connection with the action to claim jurisdiction *simpliciter*. As Sopinka J. explained in *Amchem*,[51] at paragraph 20, "[f]requently there is no single forum that is clearly the most convenient or appropriate for the trial of the action but rather several which are equally suitable alternatives." In such cases, locating a more appropriate forum allows a court to decline to exercise its jurisdiction.

---

50   *472900 B.C. Ltd. v. Thrifty Canada, Ltd.* (1998), 57 B.C.L.R. (3d) 332 at para. 31.
51   *Amchem Products Inc. v. British Columbia (Workers' Compensation Board)*, [1993] 1 S.C.R. 897 at 912 [hereinafter *Amchem*].

In considering the most appropriate forum, the court will attempt to ensure that the claim is heard in the jurisdiction that has the closest connection with the action[52] and one that does not serve to provide a juridical advantage for one of the parties in a jurisdiction that is otherwise inappropriate.[53] In the leading Ontario case of *Muscutt v. Courcelles*, Sharpe J.A. noted:

> [41] Courts have developed a list of several factors that may be considered in determining the most appropriate forum for the action, including the following:
> - the location of the majority of the parties
> - the location of key witnesses and evidence
> - contractual provisions that specify applicable law or accord jurisdiction
> - the avoidance of a multiplicity of proceedings
> - the applicable law and its weight in comparison to the factual questions to be decided
> - geographical factors suggesting the natural forum
> - whether declining jurisdiction would deprive the plaintiff of a legitimate juridical advantage available in the domestic court[.][54]

At this stage of the analysis, the burden is on the defendant challenging jurisdiction to establish the existence of a clearly more appropriate forum.[55] This is particularly so where there is no parallel proceeding in that forum already commenced. Generally speaking, the defendant alleging a preferred jurisdiction must be prepared to attorn there.[56]

5) "Fairness and Justice"

Is the *forum conveniens* analysis exhaustive of the power of the court to exercise its discretion and decline to take jurisdiction over defendants from outside the jurisdiction? The British Columbia Court of Appeal held in *Bushell v. T&N plc* that, when a foreign defendant challenges a court's jurisdiction, after jurisdiction *simpliciter* and *forum conveniens* were dealt with, the onus remained on the plaintiff "to persuade the court that a reasonable measure

---

52 *Ibid.*
53 *Westec Aerospace Inc. v. Raytheon Aircraft Company* (1999), 173 D.L.R. (4th) 498 at para. 31 (B.C.C.A.), aff'd [2001] S.C.J. No. 23.
54 *Muscutt v. Courcelles* (2002), 60 O.R. (3d) 20 (C.A.).
55 *Amchem*, *supra* note 51 at para. 33.
56 *Cook v. Parcel, Mauro, Hultin & Spaanstra, P.C.* (1997), 143 D.L.R. (4th) 213 at para. 21 (B.C.C.A.).

of fairness and justice sufficient to meet the reasonable expectations of the national and international legal communities will be preserved if the court exercises jurisdiction."[57]

It remains unclear whether this criterion, clearly founded on the principles of comity, is simply descriptive of, or subsumed within, the *forum non conveniens* analysis on the one hand, or whether it is a stand-alone basis for challenge, requiring a third analysis after jurisdiction *simpliciter* and *forum conveniens*. Subsequent decisions have been either ambivalent or inconsistent.[58]

Such a standard, which has not been commented upon outside British Columbia, raises difficult problems of proof. How does one demonstrate what are "the reasonable expectations of the national and international legal community?" It seems too much to expect that any plaintiff naming an extraprovincial defendant should be prepared to introduce expert testimony from international lawyers regarding such "expectations."

A more reasonable approach along the same lines might be to ask, "Does the extension of jurisdiction comport with the requirements of 'order and fairness'?" However, to ask this question at the third stage is to already have it answered; presumably, if there is both a "real and substantial connection," and if the forum court is an appropriate forum for the hearing of the action, then "order and fairness" should already be satisfied and so should the "national and international legal community."

Moreover, the Supreme Court's recent decision in *Beals v. Saldanha*[59] suggests that, in most circumstances, the real and substantial connection test will suffice for establishing jurisdiction, even where the defendant is domiciled in another country. In *Beals*, the Court enforced a Florida judgment in Ontario, holding that unless the judgment was obtained by fraud, or the law applied was in violation of natural justice or was offensive to

---

57　*Bushell v. T&N., plc* (1992), 67 B.C.L.R. (2d) 330 at para. 48 (C.A.) [hereinafter *Bushell*[.
58　The court in *Bushell, ibid.* appeared to consider it an independent test. See also *Quest Vitamins Supplies Ltd. v. Hassam* (1992), 79 B.C.L.R. (2d) 85 (S.C.) at 87 and as summarized in *Valmet Paper Machinery Inc. v. Hapag-Lloyd Ag.*, [1996] B.C.J. No. 2655 (S.C.) at para. 48: "Therefore the burden is on the plaintiff in these circumstances to not only satisfy the *forum conveniens* test but also persuade the court that a reasonable measure of fairness and justice sufficient to meet the reasonable expectations of national and international legal communities will be preserved if the court exercises jurisdiction." For cases considering the "expectations" analysis to be subsumed within *forum conveniens*, see *Leisure Time Distributors Ltd. v. Calzaturificio S.C.A.R.V.A.-S.P.A.* (1996), 5 C.P.C. (4th) 320 at para. 42 (S.C.); *Seine River Resources Inc. v. Pensa Inc.* (1998), 25 C.P.C. (4th) 360 at paras. 40–50 (B.C.S.C.); *Morguard Investments Ltd. v. M.E. Pritchard Associates Ltd.* (1999), 30 C.P.C. (4th) 117 at paras. 35–37 (B.C.S.C.).
59　*Supra* note 49.

public policy in that province, it would be enforced on the basis that there was a "real and substantial connection" with Florida. It would seem odd if Canadian courts would adopt higher standards for their own exercise of jurisdiction than they require of other courts whose orders they will readily enforce.

A useful "middle ground" approach was expressed in *M.E. Pritchard* by Vickers J., who suggested that, even if jurisdiction *simpliciter* and *forum conveniens* were satisfied, the court might still exercise its discretion to decline jurisdiction if to accept it would be "vexatious or oppressive," although the circumstances in which such a finding could be made tax the imagination.[60]

F. CHOICE OF LAW AND APPLICABILITY

Once a court has determined that it is appropriate that it should hear the matter before it, the next question to be asked in the conflicts analysis is: Which law should apply to the issues raised? That is, should the common law and statutes of the forum determine the rights and remedies of the parties, or is there some other place whose laws are more appropriate?

1) Choice of Law

It has long been accepted that procedural law will always be the law of the forum court. The question at the choice of law phase is therefore which substantive law should apply.

a) In Tort-Based Claims

Choice of law in tort is, following *Tolofson v. Jensen*,[61] generally thought to be governed by the *lex loci delicti*; in other words, the action will be governed by the place of the tort, or the "place of acting." But *Tolofson* advanced the *lex loci delicti* rule in a motor vehicle case, where the delict and the injury or damage occurred at the same place and at the same time. La Forest J. held at paragraph 42 that the test would *not* be appropriate in more complex cases:

> There are situations, of course, notably where an act occurs in one place but the consequences are directly felt elsewhere, when the issue of where the tort takes place itself raises thorny issues. In such a case, it may well be that the consequences would be held to constitute the wrong. *Difficulties may also arise where the wrong directly arises out of some transnational or interprovincial activity. There territorial considerations may become muted;*

---

60 *Ibid.*
61 *Supra* note 34.

they may conflict and other considerations may play a determining role. [Emphasis added.]

Recently, in *Pearson v. Boliden*, the British Columbia Court of Appeal confirmed that the *lex loci delicti* rule is not to be applied blindly to statutory causes of action such as that conferred by the provincial *Securities Act*. Newbury J.A., for the court, wrote at paragraph 64:

> [64] I also take from the foregoing cases that the *lex loci delicti* choice of law rule is not directly applicable to the question of which provincial *Act* or *Acts* may found a statutory cause of action for misrepresentation in a prospectus. As La Forest J. observed in *Tolofson*, courts are limited in exercising their powers (as to choice of law issues) to the same extent as the provincial legislatures.[62]

It is likely that courts will, as in *Pearson*, seek a functional and pragmatic approach. In that case, the plaintiff class was subdivided according to the applicable provincial law. This is no doubt the method most respectful of legislative territoriality where the claims are dependent on provincial statutory regimes. In common law claims, of course, there may be no need for such subdivision on substantive issues, which are governed by a single law as determined by the Supreme Court of Canada.[63]

b) Choice of Forum and Law in Contract-based Cases

The traditional position on choice of law in contract is that, absent explicit agreement, the proper law of a contract is determined according to which system of law has "the closest and most real connection" with the transaction, having regard to such factors as the place of contracting, the place of performance, the place of business of the parties, and the nature and subject matter of the contract.

Where parties have agreed in advance on the appropriate forum or law for the enforcement of their contract, the court will not lightly overrule that choice, particularly where the forum chosen has a substantial connection to the matters in issue: for example, *Mithras Management Ltd. v. New Visions Entertainment Corp.*[64] The Supreme Court has held that a choice of forum

---

62 *Pearson v. Boliden*, 2002 BCCA 624. See also paras. 65 and 66.
63 An exception might be with respect to the expiry of limitation periods, which the Supreme Court held in *Tolofson v. Jensen, supra* note 34, were substantive laws. A question remains regarding the effect of provincial class action legislation, which "suspends" the running of limitation periods, upon the limitation rights accruing to defendants in other provinces. This *"Tolofson* dilemma" is discussed at some length in Craig Jones, *Theory of Class Actions* (Toronto: Irwin Law, 2002) at 183–84.
64 (1992), 90 D.L.R. (4th) 726 (Ont. Gen. Div.).

clause "ought to be taken into careful consideration by a motions judge but it is not binding," and enforcement of such a clause is subject to considerations of public policy.[65]

However, the fact that parties can agree on an alternative choice of law or an alternative forum (or both) can, in the context of large-scale claims, present considerable difficulty. What if the forum selected has no class action legislation? Can a consumer engaged in the online purchase of software, for instance, really be expected to research the law of the foreign jurisdiction named in the forum selection clause to determine what his or her procedural rights will be in the case of default of the supplier?

Recall that, in *Moran v. Pyle*, both the domestic forum and law were thought to be appropriate where the manufacturer had put its wares in the stream of commerce with the expectation that they would end up where they eventually caused injury. Similar considerations, as we have seen, informed the courts' extension of jurisdiction over breast implant claims in *Harrington v. Dow*. Could these principles also inform the choice of law in contract, at least with respect to mass marketed goods? There is every reason to think so. In *Morguard*, La Forest J. wrote:

> The above rationale is not, as I see it, limited to torts. It is interesting to observe the close parallel in the reasoning in *Moran* with that adopted by this Court in dealing with jurisdiction for the purposes of the criminal law; see Libman, *supra*. In particular, barring express or implied agreement, the reasoning in *Moran* is obviously relevant to contracts; indeed, the same activity can often give rise to an action for breach of contract and one in negligence; see *Central Trust Co. v. Rafuse*, [1986] 2 S.C.R. 147. As Professor Sharpe observes in Interprovincial Product Liability Litigation, op. cit., at pp. 19–20:
>
> > It is inconsistent to permit jurisdiction in tort claims on the basis that the defendant should reasonably have foreseen that his goods would reach the plaintiff and cause damage within the jurisdiction and, on the other hand, to refuse service out of the

---

65 *Sam Lévy & Associés Inc. v. Azco Mining Inc.*, [2001] 3 S.C.R. 978 *per* Binnie J. for the Court, citing J.-G. Castel, *Canadian Conflict of Laws*, supra note 16 at 262–63; *Sarabia v. "Oceanic Mindoro" (The)* (1996), 26 B.C.L.R. (3d) 143 (C.A.) *per* Huddart J.A. at 153 (leave to appeal refused, [1997] S.C.C.A. No. 69); *Volkswagen Canada Inc. v. Auto Haus Frohlich Ltd.*, [1986] 1 W.W.R. 380 (Alta. C.A.) *per* Kerans J.A. at 381; *Ash v. Lloyd's Corp.* (1991), 6 O.R. (3d) 235 (Gen. Div.), aff'd (1992), 9 O.R. (3d) 755 (C.A.) (leave to appeal refused, [1992] 3 S.C.R. v); *Maritime Telegraph and Telephone Co. v. Pre Print Inc.* (1996), 131 D.L.R. (4th) 471 (N.S.C.A.).

jurisdiction in contractual actions where the defendant clearly knows that his goods are going to the foreign jurisdiction.[66]

This passage still contains the proviso "barring express or implied agreement." Should such agreements overcome the substantial disadvantages that could weigh against plaintiffs in mass claims? One solution is to enact legislation, such as that in Saskatchewan, where the *Consumer Protection Act*[67] sets out when the courts of that province may take jurisdiction in certain classes of product liability claims (including, broadly, contract claims for breach of statutory warranty) and also provides that the Act will be the governing substantive law in such cases. That Act states:

> 69 (1) Subject to any regulations made by the Lieutenant Governor in Council pursuant to section 71, consumers, persons mentioned in subsection 41(1) and persons mentioned in section 64 who buy or use consumer products purchased in Saskatchewan, and manufacturers, retail sellers or warrantors who carry on business in Saskatchewan, are subject to the provisions of this Part and to the jurisdiction of the courts of Saskatchewan.
>
> (2) For the purposes of this Part, a manufacturer, retail seller or warrantor is deemed to carry on business in Saskatchewan if the manufacturer, retail seller or warrantor:
> (a) holds title to land in Saskatchewan or any interest in land in Saskatchewan for the purposes of carrying on business in Saskatchewan;
> (b) maintains an office, warehouse or place of business in Saskatchewan;
> (c) is licensed or registered pursuant to any statute of Saskatchewan entitling the manufacturer, retail seller or warrantor to do business or to sell securities of the manufacturer's, retail seller's or warrantor's own issue;
> (d) has its name and telephone number listed in a current telephone directory and the telephone is located at a place in Saskatchewan for the purposes of carrying on business in Saskatchewan;
> (e) an agent, salesman, representative or other person conducts business in Saskatchewan on the manufacturer's, retail seller's or warrantor's behalf;
> (f) directly or indirectly markets consumer products in Saskatchewan; or
> (g) otherwise carries on business in Saskatchewan.

---

66 *Morguard, supra* note 4 at para. 49.
67 S.S. 1996, c. C-30.1, s. 69.

But where a legislature does purport to extend its own law through a choice of law provision, this is not the end of the story; given that the provincial Act is subject to the constitutional limitations described earlier, the question will be whether the legislation can — constitutionally — apply in any given case. It is to this question that we now turn.

2) Applicability of Provincial Statutes

Closely related to the "constitutionalized" question of the choice of law is that of consitutional applicability. That is to say, under what circumstances may a provincial statute apply to matters that are, literally speaking, not within the borders of the province?

In *British Columbia (Director of Trade Practices) v. Ideal Credit Referral Services Ltd.*,[68] the director of trade practices proceeded on a statutory cause of action against Ideal Credit alleging deceptive or unconscionable trade practices targeted at consumers, most of whom apparently were in the United States. The defendant objected, arguing that provincial legislation could not, constitutionally or from the point of view of statutory interpretation, apply when the alleged victims of the wrongful acts were all outside the province. Lambert J.A. for the unanimous Court of Appeal rejected this argument, and wrote at paragraph 15:

> ¶ 15 I conclude, on this first inquiry, that the prohibited legislative action is the action of engaging or participating in deceptive acts or practices and that the *Trade Practices Act* is not being given an improper extra-territorial effect when it prohibits or punishes engaging in those acts or practices in the Province.

Conversely, in *Robson v. Chrysler of Canada Ltd.*,[69] the same court explicitly rejected the idea that the *Trade Practices Act* could not apply to activities occurring entirely outside British Columbia. McKenzie J.A., for the Court of Appeal, held at paragraph 21:

> The chambers judge relied on two cases for the proposition that a deceptive act or practice must involve activity in British Columbia to engage the Act: *British Columbia (Director of Trade Practices) v. Ideal Credit Referral Services Ltd.* (1997), 31 B.C.L.R. (3d) 37 (C.A.) and *Stubbe et al v. P.F. Collier & Son Limited*, [1977] 3 W.W.R. 493 (B.C.S.C.).
>
> ...

---

68 (1997), 31 B.C.L.R. (3d) 37 (C.A.).
69 [2002] B.C.J. No. 1232 (C.A.), leave to appeal to S.C.C. dismissed [2002] S.C.C.A. No. 332.

I do not think that these authorities definitively answer the questions of interpretation raised by this appeal. The American defendants are alleged to be implicated in deceptive acts or practices with respect to the consumer transactions and I do not think that it is constitutionally essential that the deceptive acts or practices take place within the province, any more than it was necessary that the negligent manufacture take place in Saskatchewan in *Moran v. Pyle*.

In *Robson*, McKenzie J.A. referred to what Lambert J.A. had said in *Ideal Credit*:[70] "... the consumer need not be present in the Province; it is only the deceptive or unconscionable act or practice which must occur in the Province, though of course it need not originate in the Province, occur totally within the Province, or be confined to the Province."[71]

It is therefore settled that British Columbia's *Trade Practices Act* may be applied where breaches of that Act "perpetrated at least in part in British Columbia" are felt by victims outside the province (as in *Ideal Credit*) or where deceptive actions that do not "take place within the Province" are felt within British Columbia (as in *Robson*). In an action under the *Trade Practices Act*, it is sufficient to connect either the wrongdoing or the harm to the province.[72]

The thrust of all these cases is the same: in order to determine the territorial applicability of a statute, there is not any one single test to be applied, nor is there a requirement that any single particular element occur within a province. Rather, the approach is to construe the statute and to examine the factors that connect the enacting jurisdiction (British Columbia), the subject matter of the legislation (the government's cause of action), and the defendants to see if there is a sufficient relationship among them.

Recently in *Unifund Assurance Co. v. Insurance Corp. of British Columbia*,[73] the Supreme Court of Canada reviewed a series of its decisions considering the territorial application of provincial statutes. *Unifund* involved

---

70   *British Columbia (Director of Trade Practices) v. Ideal Credit Referral Services Ltd.* (1997), 31 B.C.L.R. (3d) 37 (C.A.) [hereinafter *Ideal Credit*].
71   *Supra*, note 69 at para. 21.
72   In *Gregory & Co. Inc. v. Quebec Securities Commission*, [1961] S.C.R. 584, the Supreme Court ruled that a Quebec broker who published a weekly bulletin sent to persons outside Quebec and who traded securities for the accounts of such customers was subject to the jurisdiction of the Quebec Securities Commission. The converse situation occurred in *R. v. W. McKenzie Securities Ltd.* (1966), 56 D.L.R. (2d) 56 (Man. C.A.). Here brokers from outside Manitoba solicited buyers within the province via the mail and telephone. They were convicted of unlawfully trading in securities under the Manitoba *Securities Act*. Freedman J.A. held that that Manitoba statute was constitutionally applicable.
66   2003 SCC 40 [hereinafter *Unifund*].

a collision in British Columbia between a vehicle insured in Ontario by Unifund and another vehicle insured by ICBC. The Ontario *Insurance Act*, on its face, permitted Unifund to pursue an action, in Ontario, to recover from ICBC certain statutory benefits Unifund had paid to its insureds. No issue was raised as to the constitutional validity of the Ontario legislation; rather, ICBC argued that section 275 of the Act, which established the cause of action, could not constitutionally be applied to it with respect to an accident that had occurred in British Columbia.

Binnie J., for the majority of the Court, agreed that on the facts of the case, section 275 was constitutionally inapplicable to ICBC. In so holding, he set out the law regarding constitutional applicability in cases considering the purportedly extraterritorial operation of a provincial statute.

Binnie J. summarized earlier decisions concerning the territorial application of provincial statutes:

> [65] It appears from the case law that different degrees of connection to the enacting province may be required according to the subject matter of the dispute. *Broken Hill* was a tax case. In divorce matters, mere residence of the parties in the jurisdiction was regarded, at common law, as an *insufficient* "relationship." Actual domicile was required, e.g., *Kalenczuk v. Kalenczuk* (1920), 52 D.L.R. 406 (Sask. C.A.). In another context, "[m]erely going through the air space over Manitoba" was an insufficient "relation" or connection with the province to support imposition of a provincial tax "within the Province": *The Queen in Right of Manitoba v. Air Canada*, [1980] 2 S.C.R. 303, at p. 316, *per* Laskin C.J. Yet in a product liability case, the presence of the defendant manufacturer in the jurisdiction is considered unnecessary. The relationship created by the knowing dispatch of goods into the enacting jurisdiction in the reasonable expectation that they will be used there is regarded as sufficient: *Moran v. Pyle National (Canada) Ltd.*, [1975] 1 S.C.R. 393, at p. 409. In yet another context, in *The Queen v. Thomas Equipment Limited*, [1979] 2 S.C.R. 529, the "relation" requirement was satisfied for regulatory purposes where the accused, a non-resident, not only sold its products (which were *not* defective) in the enacting jurisdiction, but had hired a local agent to promote their sale. *In each case, the court assessed the relationship between the enacting jurisdiction and the out-of-province individual or entity sought to be regulated by it in light of the subject matter of the legislation to determine if the relation was "sufficient" to support the validity or applicability of the legislation in question.* [Emphasis added.][74]

---

74   *Ibid.* at para. 65.

In the case of applicability, the question is whether there is sufficient connection to apply a statute to a particular defendant. While Binnie J.'s concluding sentence suggests that the "sufficient connection" test might bear on both the applicability and the validity of provincial legislation, no court has so far explicitly found provincial legislation invalid on that basis.[75]

G. "BLOCKING PROVISIONS"

Occasionally, jurisdictions attempt to enact legislation that inhibits litigation against their nationals in other jurisdictions. These provisions are generally not recognized by Canadian courts, which have taken a dim view of their legitimacy. While such provisions are generally not specific to mass torts or product liability cases, they have most frequently been at issue in such litigation, which is, by its nature, frequently pan-jurisdictional.

"Blocking provisions" have taken the form of a foreign state's claim to exclusive jurisdiction over certain matters; attempts to protect local businesses from the discovery process; and statutes enacted to prevent the enforcement of judgments awarded abroad. Anti-suit injunctions and similar devices by foreign courts seeking to interfere unjustifiably with litigation under way in the forum court are a non-legislated method of achieving the same ends, and have met similar opposition in Canadian courts.

Article 15 of the *Code Civil* of France has been interpreted by the courts of that country as meaning that a French company has a right to have any claims against it, arising anywhere in the world, tried before a French court. In the Ontario case of *Wilson v. Servier*,[76] the French parent company of its Canadian subsidiary argued that the Canadian courts were, in light of

---

75 If the "sufficient connection" test can be used at all to challenge the validity of a provincial enactment, it would almost certainly be necessary to show that the connection among the enacting jurisdiction, the subject matter of the legislation, and the individual or entity sought to be regulated by it is so attenuated that it meets the *Churchill Falls* test — that is, the only conclusion to be drawn is that the legislation is in pith and substance in relation to extraprovincial rights. This conclusion is supported by the judgment of La Forest J. in *Hunt, supra* note 5. In that case, the *Quebec Business Concerns Records Act* prohibited production of business documents by a Quebec defendant sued in any jurisdiction outside Quebec, including the other provinces. La Forest J., relying on the principle of comity, held the Act to be constitutionally inapplicable to other provinces. He then said at para. 68: "In view of the fact that I have found the impugned Act constitutionally inapplicable because it offends against the principles enunciated in *Morguard*, it becomes unnecessary for me to consider whether it is *wholly unconstitutional because, in pith and substance, it relates to a matter outside the province.*" [Emphasis added.]

76 *Wilson v. Servier Canada Inc.* (2000), 50 O.R. (3d) 219 (S.C.J.).

Article 15, not the appropriate forum for the adjudication of a class action filed in that province against it. Mr. Justice Cumming rejected this argument, preferring to apply the principle of real and substantial connection:

> [28] Article 15 of the French *Code Civil* flies in the face of the principles of comity as discussed by La Forest J. in *Morguard Investments Ltd. v. De Savoye*, [1990] 3 S.C.R. 1077, 76 D.L.R. (4th) 256 ("*Morguard*"): see also *Hunt v. T & N plc*, [1993] 4 S.C.R. 289, 109 D.L.R. (4th) 16. It is also an affront to the due process of the courts outside of France. If the subject-matter of this action has a real and substantial connection to Ontario, there is no reason why an Ontario court should stay this proceeding so that it can be heard in France. It would be unfair to deprive the representative plaintiff and the putative class members of the right to have this matter heard in Ontario simply because Article 15 of the French *Code Civil* would prevent the enforcement of an Ontario judgment against Biofarma in France. When it properly has jurisdiction, an Ontario court should not refuse to hear a case because France refuses to accede to the accepted norms of international law and, in particular, the principle of comity.
>
> ...
>
> [30] In my view, a "blocking statute" like Article 15 of the French *Code Civil* has no place in the contemporary, interconnected world of globalization and global trade, which depends upon mutual recognition and respect for settled international norms, including the principle of comity.[77]

The Supreme Court of British Columbia confirmed this analysis in a parallel class action brought against the same defendants in British Columbia:

> [32] One of the submissions of the defendants relates to Article 15 of the French *Civil Code*. It was argued that a judgment of this court cannot be enforced in France and by reason of numerous decisions of courts in France, a French citizen, whether an individual or a corporate entity, has an absolute right, subject to narrow exceptions, to have claims adjudicated by a French court.
>
> [33] I agree with the comments of Cumming, J. in *Wilson v. Servier Canada Inc.*, supra, at 229. If the subject matter of this action has a real and substantial connection to British Columbia, this court should not refuse to hear a case because of Article 15. I also agree that it is for the plaintiff

---

77   *Ibid.* at paras. 28 and 30.

to weigh the advantages and disadvantages of commencing an action in British Columbia knowing that it may not be enforced in France.[78]

In the 1990s, the colourful airline entrepreneur Freddie Laker sued his main European competitors in the United States, alleging that they conspired to drive his upstart airline out of business through anti-competitive behaviour. In the course of the *Laker Airways* litigation, the District of Columbia Circuit Court of Appeals refused to recognize an English statute directed against anti-trust suits brought in the United States and an anti-suit injunction granted by the English Court of Appeal. The Circuit Court found that the U.S. courts had properly taken jurisdiction over the English defendants, who were allegedly implicated in a conspiracy in restraint of trade, because the consequences of the alleged wrongs had been felt in the United States. In such a case, it found that it was appropriate to apply U.S. laws, which provided, *inter alia*, for treble damages, notwithstanding that such laws may be inimical to the public policy of England, where the parties were domiciled and where the actual acts that gave rise to the allegations were said to have taken place:

> No foreign court can supersede the right and obligation of the United States courts to decide whether Congress has created a remedy for those injured by trade practices adversely affecting United States interests. Our courts are not required to stand by while Britain attempts to close a courthouse door that Congress, under its territorial jurisdiction, has opened to foreign corporations.[79]

The principles of comity can apply equally well to statutes of one province that affect litigation in another. In *Hunt v. T&N plc*, the Quebec *Business Concerns Records Act* prohibited production of business documents by a Quebec defendant sued in any jurisdiction outside Quebec, including the other provinces. La Forest J., relying on the principle of comity, held the Act to be constitutionally inapplicable to other provinces. He then said:

> In view of the fact that I have found the impugned Act constitutionally inapplicable because it offends against the principles enunciated in *Morguard*, it becomes unnecessary for me to consider whether it is *wholly unconstitutional because, in pith and substance, it relates to a matter outside the province*. Nor is it necessary for me to consider whether the statute could properly be "read down" to permit its application to jurisdictions

---

78 *Armstrong v. Servier Canada Inc.*, 2002 BCSC 1248 at paras. 32–33.
79 *Laker Airways v. Sabena*, 731 F.2d 909 at 935–36 (D.C. Cir. 1984).

outside the country, nor to consider the issue of public policy raised by the appellant. [Emphasis added.][80]

An objective reader of *Hunt* would realize that the Court was making a subjective value judgment regarding who must show comity to whom. The court presumed that the Quebec "blocking statute" was valid (i.e., that it fell, on its face, within provincial competence under section 92), as were the British Columbia Rules requiring disclosure. Competent courts in each jurisdiction could, with prima facie jurisdiction over the matter, enter mutually exclusive orders necessitated by their respective laws — the Supreme Court simply had to choose, in such a case, whose laws would prevail. In *Hunt*, one jurisdiction's courts' statutory "right" to obtain documents conflicted with another's statutory "right" to block production.

Once the subjective nature of such a decision is acknowledged, then one might try to peer behind the language of the decision to see what factors the court weighed in deciding the balance of comity. On the one hand, Quebec's interest was to "impede successful litigation" in other provinces; the interest of the British Columbia courts, on the contrary, was to promote interprovincial commerce and the "efficient allocation and conduct of litigation."[81] Thus, the Supreme Court was able to elevate the "efficient resolution" of civil disputes into a constitutional principle, an interest with which another province cannot tamper, at least without a constitutionally sound reason of its own.

H. ENFORCEMENT OF JUDGMENTS

1) Enforcement of Canadian Judgments Within Canada

Until quite recently, the question of whether the courts of one province would enforce a judgment in another province were governed by rules of private international law; that is to say, a court in British Columbia would go through the same analysis whether the enforcement sought was of a judgment from Alberta or New York. Following the early English decision of *Emanuel v. Symon*,[82] this frequently meant that the judgment would have been enforced only if the defendant had actually been present in the jurisdiction at the time jurisdiction was asserted over him or her, or otherwise

---

80 *Hunt, supra* note 5 at para. 68.
81 *Ibid.* at para. 61.
82 [1908] 1 K.B. 302 (C.A.), rev'g [1907] 1 K.B. 235.

attorned to that jurisdiction. As a result, numerous Canadian interprovincial enforcement actions were unsuccessful.[83]

This changed with *Morguard Investments Ltd. v. De Savoye*,[84] where the Supreme Court of Canada held that the enforcement of extrajurisdictional *Canadian* judgments was governed by the requirement that the various provincial superior courts afford one another's judgments "full faith and credit," providing that the original court indeed had properly taken jurisdiction.[85] The Court noted that "fair process is not an issue within the Canadian federation"[86] and so there was no reason for one province to be wary of judicial decisions emanating from another. If concerns arose, they could be settled through the authority of the Supreme Court of Canada. As a result of *Morguard*, a Canadian judgment can be resisted only on the basis that the original court lacked jurisdiction, a subject governed principally by the doctrine of "real and substantial connection," as discussed earlier in this chapter.

2) Enforcement of Canadian Judgments Internationally

Any claimant in a multijurisdictional case must consider whether the eventual judgment obtained will be enforceable against the defendant in the jurisdiction where it has assets. Enforcement of Canadian judgments in most countries is mainly a matter of treaty obligation. Bilateral treaties for the recognition and enforcement of foreign judgments generally include a process by which the judgment from the treating state can be simply registered in the enforcing state, and thereby becomes a judgment of the local court.

There is currently no bilateral treaty or multilateral international convention in force between the United States and any other country on reciprocal recognition and enforcement of judgments.[87] The full faith and credit

---

83 For example, *Walsh v. Herman* (1908), 13 C.R. 314 (S.C. (Full Court)); *Marshall v. Houghton*, [1923] 2 W.W.R. 553 (Man. C.A.); *Mattar v. Alberta Public Trustee* (1952), 5 W.W.R. (N.S.) 29 (Alta. S.C., App. Div.); *Bank of Bermuda Ltd. v. Stutz*, [1965] 2 O.R. 121 (H.C.); *Batavia Times Publishing Co. v. Davis* (1977), 82 D.L.R. (3d) 247 (Ont. H.C.), aff'd (1979), 105 D.L.R. (3d) 192 (Ont. C.A.); *Eggleton v. Broadway Agencies Ltd.* (1981), 32 A.R. 61 (Q.B.); *Weiner v. Singh* (1981), 22 C.P.C. 230 (B.C. Co. Ct.); *Re Whalen and Neal* (1982), 31 C.P.C. 1 (N.B.Q.B.).

84 *Morguard*, *supra* note 4.

85 *Ibid.* at 1102.

86 *Ibid.* at 1103.

87 In 1976 the United States and United Kingdom initialled a "Convention on the Reciprocal Recognition and Enforcement of Judgments in Civil Matters," (1977) 16 I.L.M. 71, but negotiations over the final text broke off in 1981. The United States participat-

clause of the U.S. constitution does not embrace or extend to judgments of foreign tribunals and the effect of a foreign judgment is dependent on the local laws of the states,[88] within the parameters of the U.S. constitution. Under U.S. law, an individual seeking to enforce a foreign judgment, decree, or order must file suit before a competent court. The court will determine whether to give effect to the foreign judgment.[89]

The foreign judgment must first be a valid judgment of a court of general jurisdiction, final and conclusive, and capable of being enforced in the jurisdiction of that foreign court rendering it. The American court can ascertain if there was a mistake of law or fact that would make such judgment invalid in the foreign jurisdiction that rendered it. However, courts in the United States are usually generous, often recognizing and enforcing judgments, even for amounts that would not be recoverable under U.S. law, such as costs.

Absent a treaty, whether the courts of a foreign country would enforce a judgment issued by a court in Canada depends upon the internal laws of the foreign country and the principles of "international comity." In many foreign countries, the recognition and enforcement of foreign judgments is governed by local domestic law and the principles of comity, reciprocity, and *res judicata* (that is, the issues in question have been decided already).[90]

The general principle of international comity applicable in enforcement actions is that an enforcing state claims and exercises the right to examine judgments for four causes:

1) to determine if the original court had jurisdiction;
2) to determine whether the defendant was properly served;
3) to determine if the proceedings were vitiated by fraud; and
4) to establish that the judgment is not contrary to the public policy of the enforcing country.

---

ed in the negotiation of the "Inter-American Convention on the Extraterritorial Validity of Foreign Judgments and Arbitral Awards" (1979) 18 I.L.M. 1224, but to date it has not signed the treaty (nor is expected to do so in the future).

88 Under the doctrine of *Erie Railroad Co. v. Tompkins*, 304 U.S. 64 (1938), in the absence of any treaty, federal statute, admiralty jurisdiction, or other basis for federal authority, the regulation of foreign judgments has been deemed a matter governed by state law. Thus, even federal courts generally apply state law to determine the recognition and enforcement of foreign judgments in federal cases.

89 See, for instance, the *Uniform Enforcement of Foreign Judgments Act*, 13 U.L.A. 261 (1986), and the *Uniform Foreign Money-Judgments Recognition Act*, 13 U.L.A. 149 (1986).

90 *Hilton v. Guyot*, 159 U.S. 113 (1895).

These requirements are also features of the various applicable treaties. While procedures and documentary requirements vary widely from country to country, judgments that do not involve multiple damages or punitive damages generally may be enforced, in whole or in part, upon recognition as authoritative and final, subject to the particulars cited above.[91]

It is expected that within two years that an agreement may be reached by the countries of the Hague Convention (there are forty-seven countries represented in the Hague Conference on Private International Law, including Canada, the United Kingdom, and the United States[92]), in which case the rules should be more or less uniform. Because enforcement is always predicated on the legitimacy of the jurisdiction of the original court, the draft convention, like the treaty frameworks in place in Europe, hopes to establish a model that governs both jurisdiction over international disputes and the enforcement of the eventual judgments from those disputes.

The difficulty is that courts in the United States will enforce judgments only if the U.S. due process guidelines were observed by the original court of jurisdiction. A Canadian judgment, for instance, will be recognized in the United States only if sufficient minimum contacts to the particular Canadian province or territory existed to ground the court's jurisdiction.[93] It is therefore uncertain whether the United States can accept any treaty that in any way modifies or restricts the due process rights of its residents in foreign litigation.[94]

3) Enforcement of Foreign Judgments in Canada

As described earlier, since *Morguard*, some courts have applied the principles of comity and mutual respect for the court processes of foreign courts to permit enforcement of the judgments of those courts, providing the

---

[91] Waller, "Under Seige: United States Judgments in Foreign Courts" (1993) 28 Tex. Int'l L.J. 427, 434.

[92] Argentina, Australia, Austria, Belarus, Belgium, Brazil, Brunei, Canada, China, Croatia, Cyprus, Czech Republic, Denmark, Egypt, Finland, France, Germany, Greece, Hungary, Indonesia, Ireland, Israel, Italy, Japan, Korean Republic, Luxembourg, Malaysia, Mexico, Morocco, Netherlands, the Philippines, Portugal, Slovak Republic, Slovenia, South Korea, Spain, Sweden, Switzerland, Tunisia, the United Kingdom, and the United States.

[93] Michel Youssef and Peter Finkle, "Cross-Border Shopping, Consumer Remedies and Long-Arm Legislation: To Reach Out and Touch Someone" (March 1993) 15 Adv. Q'ly. 1.

[94] See letter from Jeffrey D. Kovar (the U.S. State Department's assistant legal adviser for private international law): "the U.S. delegation believes the October 1999 draft is not an effective vehicle for achieving a convention to which the United States can become a party." <www.cptech.org/ecom/jurisdiction/kovarletter.html>.

"real and substantial connection" existed and such enforcement would not violate public policy.[95] The Supreme Court confirmed this practice in the recent case of *Beals v. Saldanha*.[96] There, the Court was called upon to enforce a judgment of a Florida court, despite clear concerns that notice requirements to the defendant had been inadequate and the proceedings taken were otherwise unfair to the defendants. The Supreme Court held that, absent evidence of fraud or a clear demonstration that the law of the foreign state violated natural justice or the public policy of the enforcing province, the judgment would be enforced. The Court also confirmed that the common law defences to enforcement of natural justice, fraud, or public policy were not exhaustive:

> 41 These defences were developed by the common law courts to guard against potential unfairness unforeseen in the drafting of the test for the recognition and enforcement of judgments. The existing defences are narrow in application. They are the most recognizable situations in which an injustice may arise but are not exhaustive.
>
> 42 Unusual situations may arise that might require the creation of a new defence to the enforcement of a foreign judgment. However, the facts of this case do not justify speculating on that possibility. Should the evolution of private international law require the creation of a new defence, the courts will need to ensure that any new defences continue to be narrow in scope, address specific facts and raise issues not covered by the existing defences.

The *Beals* Court did allow that legislation blocking the enforcement of certain types of judgments, or judgments from certain jurisdictions, might be enacted, but, practically speaking, such legislation is rare. Two examples of such provisions are found in the *Foreign Extraterritorial Measures Act*.[97]

4) Enforceability as an Element of Jurisdictional Analysis

It is sometimes suggested that enforceability of any eventual judgment should be one factor weighed by the court when assessing whether it

---

95 *Moses v. Shore Boat Builders Ltd.*, supra note 37.
96 *Supra* note 49.
97 R.S.C. 1996, c. 28. The Act forbids any enforcement of judgments granted under the U.S.'s *Cuban Liberty and Democratic Solidarity (LIBERTAD) Act of 1996*, and also permits the attorney general to direct non-enforcement of awards (or reduce their amounts) made under any foreign anti-trust or trade law.

should take jurisdiction over a matter. That is to say, a court should decline jurisdiction over a question when its efforts will be moot.

The Ontario Court of Appeal apparently considers enforceability relevant to jurisdiction, listing it among several factors in the *Muscutt* series of cases and even suggesting that enforceability might be a factor in jurisdiction *simpliciter*, not simply *forum conveniens*.[98] The British Columbia Court in *Cook v. Parcel, Maura, Hultin & Spaanstra, P.C.*[99] also described enforceability as, if not a factor in itself, at least a gauge of the reasonableness of the assumption of jurisdiction: "[While] questions of comity are usually dealt with in relation to *forum non conveniens*, rather than jurisdiction simpliciter, issues of jurisdiction and enforceability are closely intertwined. The likelihood of enforceability of a judgment can be used as a measure against which to assess the reasonableness of a finding of jurisdiction."[100]

A more preferred view is that, to the extent that enforceability is to be considered at all in establishing jurisdiction (a proposition worthy of some doubt), it should be considered as part of the court's exercise of discretion under the *forum conveniens* analysis. Even there, a persuasive case can be made that enforceability in the defendant's home jurisdiction should be irrelevant, as Sigurdson J. found in *Nutreco Canada Inc. v. F. Hoffmann-La Roche*[101] and the Australian Federal Court found in *Anglo-Australian Foods v. Von Planta*. In the latter case, the court rejected arguments that it should decline jurisdiction because the litigation could result only in a judgment that was unenforceable in Switzerland, the only jurisdiction in which the defendant had assets. The court said:

> 62. The purpose of such an exercise of the discretion can be readily understood where the judgment or decree of the Court depends upon the assistance of a foreign court for its fulfillment. There is an obvious distinction between a personal judgment in a money sum and an order or decree for performance of acts or orders of restraint. The latter may be patently futile at the time of pronouncement. ... The lack of prospect of recovery on a money judgment can be no more a cause for declining to exercise jurisdiction where an applicant seeks judgment against a foreign

---

98 *Muscutt v. Courcelles* (2002), 213 D.L.R. (4th) 577 (Ont. C.A.); *Lemmex v. Sunflight Holdings Inc.* (2002), 213 D.L.R. (4th) 627 (Ont. C.A.); *Sinclair v. Cracker Barrel Old Country Store Inc.* (2002), 213 D.L.R. (4th) 643 (Ont. C.A.); *Garaj v. DeBernardo* (2002), 213 D.L.R. (4th) 661 (Ont. C.A.); *Leufkens v. Alba Tours International Inc.* (2002), 213 D.L.R. (4th) 614 (Ont. C.A.).
99 (1997), 143 D.L.R. (4th) 213 (C.A.).
100 *Ibid.* at para. 41.
101 2001 BCSC 1146.

resident than it would where both parties were domiciled within the jurisdiction of the court.[102]

That is to say that, if a plaintiff is entitled to an empty judgment from a domestic defendant (for instance, owing to inability to pay), why is he or she not similarly permitted the same from a defendant served *ex juris*, providing the court otherwise has appropriately taken jurisdiction over the latter? This approach is consistent with the hostility shown by Canadian courts to "blocking provisions" enacted by provinces or countries hindering litigation in other jurisdictions.[103] It is for the plaintiff to weigh the advantages and disadvantages of commencing an action knowing that it might not be enforced in some or all of the jurisdictions where the foreign defendant has assets.[104]

---

92 *Re Anglo-Australian Foods*, WAG 37 of 1988 (F.C. Gen. Div.) at para. 62.
93 See the discussion of "blocking provisions" in section G, *supra*.
94 *Armstrong v. Servier Canada Inc.*, 2002 BCSC 1248 at para. 33; *Wilson v. Servier* (2000), 50 O.R. (3d) 219 (S.C.J.) at para. 29; *Petersen v. Ab Bahco Ventilation* (1979), 17 B.C.L.R. 335 at 348.

10. Interjurisdictional Class Actions

A. INTRODUCTION

As discussed, in *Western Canadian Shopping Centres v. Dutton*,[1] the Supreme Court of Canada read Alberta's representative proceeding rule as permitting a class action that was all but indistinguishable from those in jurisdictions with class proceeding legislation.

But for those interested in the ongoing debate regarding the availability of a true "national class action," it is perplexing that the most significant aspect of *Dutton* has gone virtually unnoticed: *Dutton*'s class members were "foreign investors" whose claims arose in a number of different jurisdictions.[2] In *Dutton*, the Court seems to have established consciously a regime of national — indeed international — class actions, *to be certified on an opt-out basis*. As such, the *Dutton* decision reverberates well beyond provinces that lack class proceeding legislation.

---

1   2001 SCC 46 [hereinafter *Dutton*].
2   See footnote 55 and 56, *infra*, and accompanying text. Even Branch, who considers the impact of *Dutton* on the future of the national class, does not remark on the fact that the class at issue in the case was largely extra-provincial, with the causes of action arising in a number of different jurisdictions: Ward K. Branch, "Chaos or Consistency? The National Class Action Dilemma," <www.branmac.com> (accessed November 12, 2003).

In this part we recap briefly why the province-by-province adjudication of nationwide claims undermines the principal goals of aggregate litigation, and we argue that the case in favour of the "national class" is fundamentally sound. We discuss some of the objections that have been raised to the national class in the past and then turn to the Supreme Court's reasons in *Dutton* to demonstrate that, in the aftermath of that case and the Supreme Court's other recent decisions, objections to the national class must be seen as considerably diminished.

We then consider briefly the jurisprudence on national classes and review of the legislation currently in place. We describe how courts might interpret their provinces' respective legislative regimes in light of the *Dutton* decision and the role of notice requirements in certification proceeding, consideration of which is likely to become of central importance.

B. NATIONAL CLASSES vs. PROVINCE-BY-PROVINCE CERTIFICATION

1) Why the National Class is Preferable

As we have sought to emphasize throughout this book, mass torts generally arise as a result of the systemic risks of business enterprises. The impact of a single wrongful decision in the manufacturing or marketing of a mass-produced product or service will be felt throughout the market for that product, be it a surgical device, pharmaceutical, automobile, credit card, or share offering. That market is likely to be national, and increasingly international, in scale.

In any instance where a class action is preferable to a host of individual actions, it will follow that a single national class will fulfill the stated objectives of class proceedings legislation (judicial economy, access to justice,

---

3   *Dutton, supra* note 1 at paras. 27–29.
4   The foundations of the economic analysis of tort law rules are well-articulated in a series of seminal publications by Calabresi, Posner, and Kaplow & Shavell, whose work forms the basis of the analysis of class actions: Guido Calabresi, "Some Thoughts on Risk Distribution and the Law of Torts" (1961) 70 Yale L.J. 499; Guido Calabresi, *The Costs of Accidents: A Legal and Economic Analysis* (New Haven: Yale University Press, 1970); A. Mitchell Polinsky, *An Introduction to Law and Economics*, 2d. ed. (Boston: Little Brown, 1989); Richard A. Posner, *Economic Analysis of Law*, 5th ed.(Boston: Little, Brown, 1998); Steven Shavell, *Economic Analysis of Accident Law* (London: Harvard University Press, 1987); Steven Shavell, "The Level of Litigation: Private Versus Social Optimality of Suit and of Settlement" (1999) 19 Int'l Rev. L. & Econ. 99; Louis Kaplow & Steven Shavell, "Fairness vs. Welfare" (2001) 114 Harv. L. Rev. 961.

and behaviour modification[3]) and the empirical objectives of tort law (primarily compensation and deterrence[4]) better than will thirteen provincial and territorial classes. We expand briefly on these premises in this section.[5]

The class action is superior to an individual action where it permits similarly situated plaintiffs to pool litigation resources, approaching the economy of scale that defendants in multiple related actions enjoy as a matter of course.[6] Any unnecessary subdividing of the single class action into smaller actions will sacrifice some of the litigative efficiency of the whole, even where plaintiffs' counsel cooperate in bringing multiple provincial actions.[7] In province-by-province certification, per-claim litigation costs will increase for plaintiffs at a greater rate than defendants,[8] set-

---

5   For a much fuller discussion of the economic effects of claims aggregation, see Craig Jones, *Theory of Class Actions* (Toronto: Irwin Law, 2003).

6   The idea that mass tort defendants treat large-scale claims as a "virtual class action," spreading per-claim litigation costs over all classable claims, was developed in a series of canonical articles by Harvard's David Rosenberg. See David Rosenberg, "A 'Public Law' Vision of the Tort System" (1984) 97 Harvard L. Rev. 849; David Rosenberg, "Class Actions for Mass Torts: Doing Individual Justice by Collective Means" (1987) 62 Ind. L.J. 561; David Rosenberg, "Of End Games and Openings in Mass Tort Cases: Lessons from a Special Master" (1989) 69 B.U. L. Rev. 695; David Rosenberg, "Individual Justice and Collectivizing Risk-Based Claims in Mass-Exposure Cases (1996) 71 N.Y.U. L. Rev. 210.

7   For discussion of informal aggregation strategies, see Howard M. Erichson, "Informal Aggregation: Procedural and Ethical Implications of Coordination among Counsel in Related Lawsuits" (2000) 50 Duke L.J. 381; see also Michael A. Eizenga, Michael J. Peerless, & Charles M. Wright, *Class Actions Law and Practice* (Toronto: Butterworths, 1999) at §2.5 (describing the Australian experience with group litigation strategies). For a criticism of the "litigation network" approach, see John C. Coffee, "Rescuing the Private Attorney General: Why the Model of the Lawyer as Bounty Hunter is Not Working" (1983) 42 MD. L. Rev. 215 at 239–41, nn 56–57. See also Charles Fried & David Rosenberg, *Making Tort Law: What Should be Done and Who Should Do It* (Washington D.C.: AEI Press, 2003) at 90 ("the combination of high costs of organizing and monitoring collaboration compounded by agency problems and strong incentives for free-riding converge to preclude plaintiffs' attorneys from efficiently achieving the maximum scale economies required for deterrence purposes").

8   This is tautological; forcing any class to subdivide and litigate separately will necessarily increase per-claim litigation costs. Subdivision of a classable claim imposes extra per-claim costs on plaintiffs to a greater extent than on defendants, who will treat common issues — e.g., whether a product was dangerously defective — as a single question, regardless of the number of jurisdictions in which they are defending the product. Defendants can employ the same experts, use the same legal research, and even employ the same lawyers in each jurisdiction where the issues are common — i.e., otherwise "classable." Litigation efficiencies automatically accrue to defendants in these circumstances far more than plaintiffs, who can at best effect only an imperfect economy of scale between jurisdictions. David Rosenberg, "Mass Tort Class Actions: What the Defendants Have and Plaintiffs Don't" (2000) 37 Harv. J. Legis. 393 (exploring the "structural asymmetry" inuring to the benefit of mass tort defendants absent optimal aggregation).

tlement incentives for defendants will decrease below the optimal,[9] compensation per claim will decrease,[10] and fewer valid claims will ever be brought.[11] Free rider problems and inter-counsel blackmail will likely increase,[12] further diminishing the efficiency of aggregate resolution.

Province-by-province litigation of classable claims, therefore, represents a systemic advantage for mass tort defendants over mass tort victims, despite the optimistic view of some observers.[13] In weighing the advantages

---

9   As the plaintiff's per-claim litigation costs increase compared to the defendant's, the expected amount for which each claim will settle will decrease. The standard model of litigation settlement holds that the defendant's "maximum offer" will be the expected judgment amount plus litigation costs. The plaintiff's "minimum demand" will be the judgment *minus* litigation costs. In ordinary circumstances, the parties will settle on average at the mean point between the maximum offer and minimum demand: See, generally, Steven Shavell, "Suit, Settlement, and Trial: A Theoretical Analysis under Alternative Methods for the Allocation of Legal Costs" (1982) 11 J. Legal Stud. 55. The implications of this model in aggregate systems were observed in David Rosenberg, *Mass Torts and Complex Litigation Seminar (Materials)*, Harvard Law School (Unpublished, 2002, on file with the authors).

10 This follows directly: if settlement values are decreased according to Shavell's formula, and per-claim litigation costs are simultaneously increased, then the injured plaintiff not only gets a smaller piece of the pie, he or she gets a smaller piece of a smaller pie.

11 This is not difficult to demonstrate. Ward Branch, one of Canada's most prolific class action litigators, has a "rule of thumb" whereby he will advance a class action only if its expected return is around $1 million: See Ward Branch, "The Wheat and the Chaff: Class Action Case Selection," <www.branmac.com> (accessed November 2, 2003) at 4. Branch litigates mostly in British Columbia, which is home to perhaps 10 percent of the Canadian population. In cases involving a nationally distributed product, then, Branch will take (the British Columbia portion of) the case if there has been $10 million of damages across the nation. Presumably there are lawyers in the other provinces with similar thresholds.

In a case where there has been only $5 million worth of damages, and assuming all lawyers' "thresholds" are the same as Branch's, then no action will be brought anywhere in the country if it must be litigated on a province-by-province basis, whereas the claim certainly would be brought if a national class was permitted.

12 "Free riding" is possible because litigation in the ordinary course generates a significant amount of publicly available information regarding the common issues. Factual information gained through discovery or trial, legal research, and arguments all represent expensive investments by plaintiff's counsel, and each may be obtained for only token cost by a "free rider" who wishes to exploit the investor's work product, provided that the case proceeds to hearing or trial. If the $5 million class action referred to in the previous footnote was certified in Ontario, a class counsel could file in British Columbia. Once certified there, the British Columbia counsel could do no work, expecting that Ontario counsel would be willing to share all its work product in exchange for any fraction of the fee.

13 Branch has suggested that, with class actions now available in all Canadian jurisdictions, defendants planning on contesting the case on the merits are "more likely to work ... to ensure that one action covers the whole country so as to minimize legal

of larger versus smaller classes, criticisms of the national class must account for these economic factors, but they almost never do.[14]

Ideally from an economic perspective, the plaintiff's class should be drawn from all persons, regardless of their physical location, who have suffered from the same wrong. In litigation arising from the provision of products or services on a mass scale (the majority of class action cases), the class should mirror the "market" throughout which the mass-produced wrong could be said to be generic. In some cases, that market will be international; in most cases, it will be at least interprovincial. In only a minority of cases will the impact of a mass wrong be entirely limited to residents of a single province.

The settlement approved in British Columbia, Ontario, and Quebec in the Red Cross tainted blood litigation[15] is sometimes cited as a success story of the province-by-province model,[16] but it provides no counter-argument

---

costs," and that defendants looking to settle "will want to ensure that the action or actions cover as much of the country as possible": Ward K. Branch, "Chaos or Consistency?" *supra* note 2 at 8. These assertions ignore the strong structural incentives that will encourage defendants to prefer multiple actions. It is submitted that only in cases where a defendant either (a) expects certainly to lose the full amount at stake, or (in fact, probably *and*) (b) has some other motive for avoiding protracted litigation (e.g., concern for share value or overwhelming concern over public image), will it find it advantageous to negotiate a quick, nationwide solution. If either of these preconditions do not exist, the defendants' interest will almost always be to drive up the plaintiffs' expected litigation costs as much as possible, thus depressing the expected global settlement amount.

14 O'Donnell, Gross, & Garzon enunciate (without actually endorsing) objections to the national class based on traditional rules of private international law, which they weigh against the advantage of "judicial economy": J. Vincent O'Donnell, Q.C., Benjamin David Gross, & Julia Garzon, "Multijurisdictional Class Actions in Canada: Pragmatism Over Principle?" paper presented at the Canadian Institute, September 26 & 27, 2002. <www.laverydebilly.com/pdf/conferences/020901a.pdf> (accessed November 12, 2003). But judicial economy is perhaps the least significant advantage provided by claims aggregation and indeed, given that more claims may be filed in a more efficient system as "access to justice" improves, overall savings in court costs might not occur.

15 The terms of the settlement and the reasons for approval are described in the decisions of Smith J. in *Endean v. Canadian Red Cross Society*, [2000] 1 W.W.R. 688 (S.C.); the decision of Winkler J. in *Parsons v. Canadian Red Cross Society*, [1999] O.J. No. 3572 (S.C.J.); and the decision of Morneau J. in *Honhon c. Canada (Procureur général)*, [1999] J.Q. no 4370 (S.C.).

16 Docken & Walden cite the Hepatitis C litigation and conclude that "[i]n the majority of cases, the preferable approach is multiple certifications throughout Canada." They do not specify their criteria for determining what is "preferable": Clint G. Docken, Q.C. & Andrea E. Walden, "Canadian Class Action Jurisdictional Issues: Opting IN or Opting OUT?" (paper originally presented at the Canadian Institute's Calgary Seminar on Litigating Class Actions, May 30–31, 2002) <www.docken.com/CdnInstitutePaper-May2002ClassActions.pdf> (accessed November 10, 2003).

to the advantages of the national class. Even if the teams of lawyers in the three provinces were seamlessly integrated, with no duplication of effort or free riding, the resources of three courts and three sets of plaintiffs' counsel were consumed in an often duplicative process. No one to our knowledge has suggested any reason why the three-way resolution of the Red Cross litigation was preferable to doing it all in a single jurisdiction utilizing a national class. It is perhaps only the sheer scale of the recovery involved (over a billion dollars) that has allowed the case to escape characterization as an example of a grossly inefficient process; in cases of high individual recovery or particularly high numerosity of claims, increases of per-claim litigation costs as a result of inefficiency will be masked.

2) Objections to the National Class

There are four principal arguments against the advantages of the national opt-out class.

The first objection, and the one most immediately appealing, is the idea of provincial legislative sovereignty. Suppose that British Columbia decided, as a matter of public policy, that the advantages of class actions to plaintiffs are worth the disadvantages, and so enacted class action legislation. Suppose that in the same year, Alberta, in a move to attract more business investment, decided not to have class actions. If Alberta's consumers can have access to British Columbia's class action courts (with respect to products and services offered in Alberta), then it might be said that British Columbia is undermining the sovereign authority of Alberta over "property and civil rights in the Province" under section 92(13) of the *Constitution Act, 1867*.[17]

The second objection is based on concerns over the jurisdictional reach of provincial superior courts, which of course is related to the question of notice. Class actions do not simply confer rewards on absent class mem-

---

17 Traditionally, the words "in the province" meant that the provincial legislature was competent to enact legislation "directed against *acts* done within the province": *Cowen v. British Columbia (A.G)*, [1941] S.C.R 321 at 323 *per* Duff C.J. Following the analysis in *Moran v. Pyle National (Canada) Ltd.*, [1975] 1 S.C.R. 393 and *Tolofson v. Jensen*, [1994] 3 S.C.R. 1022 [hereinafter *Tolofson*], individual torts will generally be said to occur where the harm has been suffered, and governed by the law of that jurisdiction. However, in *Tolofson*, LaForest J. foresaw the relaxation of such rules in multijurisdictional actions, and said at para. 42:

> Difficulties may also arise where the wrong directly arises out of some transnational or interprovincial activity. There territorial considerations may become muted; they may conflict and other considerations may play a determining role.

bers; they also require that the member surrender the right to litigate independently. What right does a court in British Columbia have to design a system that will, if the extra-jurisdictional class member does not act, defeat his right to sue?

The third objection relates to choice of law. If the substantive law differs by province, need all the separate laws be applied by the forum court? If the class needs to be subclassed according to province (assuming the substantive law varies accordingly), then is the aggregate resolution really more efficient in a subclassed national action when compared to province-by-province adjudication?

Finally, it might be argued that, given the concerns over the territorial reach of provincial legislation and courts, there is nothing wrong in requiring that non-residents opt-in to include themselves in the action, rather than being passively included if they do not opt out. That is to say, even if it is conceded that the national class is appropriate, it is still asserted that an opt-out certification of such a class is on balance less desirable.

a) Provincial Sovereignty

Provincial sovereignty is, after *Dutton*, fairly easy to deal with on a pragmatic basis: there is no longer any Canadian province or territory in which class actions are not possible, and so concerns that one province's regime may be particularly offensive to another are deflated. Unless a province enacts legislation barring class actions, the fear of imposing class actions where they are not welcome is considerably muted. Even if a province were to forbid class actions,[18] there are strong economic reasons to permit its citizens to be included nevertheless in a national class in a different province: assuming that the costs of consumer goods are averaged nationally rather than being determined provincially (as they apparently are[19]), then citizens

---

18 Should a province attempt to bar class actions, the efficacy of such legislation in preventing residents of that province from joining a class action in another jurisdiction would be resolved through a constitutional analysis along the lines of *Hunt* and *Servier*, discussed *infra*: in other words, it would be argued that such a statute constituted an unconstitutional "blocking provision" because it frustrated the "efficient allocation and conduct of litigation" in interjurisdictional claims. See footnote 47 and accompanying text.

19 The phenomenon of national price-averaging is easily demonstrated; visit the website of any popular retailer and see if there are different prices advertised for different provinces. Generally, there are not. This means that any difference in recoverability by province is being centrally averaged and included in the prices paid by everyone — citizens in provinces where recovery is likely to be less are paying the same "tort insurance premium" as their counterparts in provinces with more liberal rules, but getting less in return.

without the protections of class action legislation, by paying a higher tort insurance premium included in their consumables as a result of class actions in other jurisdictions, are being forced to subsidize the superior recovery of their fellows in the other provinces.[20]

There are other arguments against a blind assertion of territorial sovereignty, and these are best encapsulated by a more modern view of our constitutional federation, one with provincial legal schemes that are interpreted as complementary and mutually supportive rather than defensive and self-regarding.[21] This view of confederation is increasingly that taken by the courts, as witnessed by the constitutional leeway provided to Canada's interlocking system of provincial securities regulation.[22]

b) Jurisdiction and Notice

In the world of modern communications and mass media, there is no practical difficulty in extending notice to extra-provincial classes. Indeed, given the national scale of the most popular forms of media, notice in many cases (calculated as a percentage of expected recovery per claim) will be cheaper and more efficient in a national class than in provincial ones.[23] It

---

20 The spectre of the interprovincial subsidization of tort insurance premiums built into the price of goods and services, where recovery varies by province, is discussed in more detail in Jones, *Theory of Class Actions*, supra note 5 at 87–90.

21 Overemphasis of the "jealous territoriality" model led to one of the most impenetrable and unhelpful decisions ever issued by the Supreme Court in *Interprovincial Co-operatives Ltd. v. Dryden Chemicals Ltd.*, [1976] 1 S.C.R. 477.

22 *Multiple Access Ltd. v. McCutcheon*, [1982] 2 S.C.R. 161. Dickson J. (as he then was) for the majority noted that provincial Securities Acts had been given a "wide constitutional recognition." This forbearance of extraterritorial effects where a common interprovincial purpose was inferred continues: see, for instance, *Pearson v. Boliden Ltd.* 2002 BCCA 624.

23 Imagine a mass tort has occurred that has caused $1 million in damage across the country, and that this loss is equally spread among ten provinces ($100,000 per province). Let us say that the class members are not known, so notice must be effected through advertising. The cost of using local media within the province is $10,000; the cost of taking advantage of the national media is $50,000.

   Under the Ontario "national opt-out class" model, the representative plaintiff could spend $10,000 in each province for local media and another $50,000 in national media to be assured of the best possible notice in the circumstances. In such a case, the total cost spread across all class members would be $150,000, or 15 percent of each class member's recovery.

   To accomplish *exactly the same* notice under the competing U.L.C.C. model of several provincial actions, the representative plaintiff in each province would have to pay $10,000 to have only provincial coverage, and a further $50,000 for national coverage, the bulk of which would be "wasted" on other provinces. Each provincial class representative would therefore pay $60,000, or 60 percent of each class member's recovery.

is difficult to imagine a case with potential plaintiffs from several provinces, where notice is best handled entirely locally; that is, there is no reason to think that notice will be more effective simply because it is generated from within a class member's own province. In an age of increasingly national (and international) media, it may be even less so.[24]

Just as it is difficult to argue, after *Dutton*, that the forum province is "foisting class action legislation" on other provinces,[25] it is similarly difficult to argue, in light of recent jurisprudence, that provincial superior courts are being too ambitious with their own territorial reach when they purport to make orders binding class members across the country. Such courts, at least since *Morguard Investments Ltd. v. De Savoye*,[26] have a recognized national role, as will be expanded upon below; this supports the observation of the British Columbia Court in *Harrington v. Dow Corning*: "The demands of multi-claimant manufacturers' liability litigation require recognition of concurrent jurisdiction of courts within Canada."[27]

From the point of view of basic fairness, when viewing the adequacy of notice, there is one aspect of jurisdiction over a national class that does raise legitimate concerns. It might be fair to bind a person within the forum province even if that person does not have actual notice of the suit, because it can be expected that the plaintiff's lawyers will employ all legal arguments available in the forum on that person's behalf and seek every possible legal advantage, substantive and procedural. In a national opt-out class where notice is attempted, but individual, actual notice is not possible, the concern may exist that extra-provincial plaintiffs will be bound to a process where both the courts and plaintiffs' counsel are unfamiliar with all of the advantages — substantive and procedural — that exist in the non-resident's own jurisdiction.

Most of this problem can be abated through subclassing of non-residents by jurisdiction; in a British Columbia action, for instance, there could be a subclass for Albertans, Manitobans, and so on, with the subclass's counsel familiar with the applicable law of the foreign province. However, this abates the concern only with respect to substantive law, which the

---

24 Consider a class member who resides in Manitoba and reads the *Globe & Mail* and watches CBC national television exclusively. It may not be cost-effective for a Manitoba-only class to advertise in these national sources as well as the purely local ones. On the other hand, the model described in the previous note suggests that a national class would *always* be able to avail itself of the most efficient combination of national and local media across the country.
25 Branch, "Chaos or Consistency?" *supra* note 2 at 12.
26 [1990] 3 S.C.R. 1077 [hereinafter *Morguard*].
27 *Harrington v. Dow Corning Corp.*, 29 B.C.L.R. (3d) 88 (S.C.) at para. 18.

forum court is bound to apply where it is applicable. If *procedural* advantages exist in the foreign province, these will be lost to a class member swept up in the British Columbia action.[28]

This argument need not be fatal to an opt-out national class,[29] but it does provide some support for the notion that the quality of notice required in such an action should be higher than that in a class limited to the forum province. There is reason to believe that Canadian courts are sensitive to this question, although we will later argue that the calculus for notice is not so simple and that other factors should weigh more heavily when assessing notice than the residency of the prospective class members.

c) Choice of Law

Choice of law does indeed present a challenge in complex litigation, but it is not unique to opt-out national classes. British Columbia courts have begun to deal with provincial subclassing when the cause of action is statutory, as in *Pearson v. Boliden*;[30] an Ontario court established a British Columbia subclass to accommodate differences in the substantive law in *Wilson v. Servier*.[31] Where the claim is based on the common law, for instance in cases of products liability or negligence, of course, the applicable law may be uniform across the country, and it may be that no province-by-province subclassing is even required.[32] The same would occur if the cause of action was federal, for instance as a result of *Competition Act* claims. However, now that the federal court has class proceedings rules at its disposal,[33] any national case that could be confined to federal causes of action would almost certainly proceed there.

---

28 To give a concrete example, British Columbia's *Tobacco Damages and Health Care Costs Recovery Act*, S.B.C. 2000, c. 30 provided certain procedural advantages to plaintiffs — or plaintiff classes — in tobacco litigation. They could, for instance, introduce statistical and epidemiological evidence to prove causation, as well as damages. If a national class was certified first in Ontario, this advantage would be lost to the British Columbia claimants.

29 It is difficult to distinguish plaintiffs' deprivation of procedural advantages or conveniences available in their own jurisdiction from the situation faced by foreign-resident defendants, who are frequently hauled into court, over their objections, providing they have the requisite "real and substantial connection" with either the forum or the subject matter of the litigation. It is arguably equally "fair" to "sweep in" plaintiffs on the same basis.

30 2002 BCCA 624.

31 [2001] O.J. No. 1615 (S.C.J.).

32 As the court would find in *Webb v. K-Mart Canada Ltd.* in the context of wrongful dismissal claims: (1999) 45 O.R. (3d) 389 at 403.

33 *Federal Court Rules, 1998*, Rules 299.1 *et seq.* (added by the *Rules Amending the Federal Court Rules, 1998*, SOR 2002-417, s. 17).

Even after *Tolofson*[34] there is room for flexibility in choice of law. Judge Weinstein of the U.S. District Court for the Eastern District of New York has even proposed that differences of substantive law in a multijurisdictional claim might somehow be averaged to facilitate resolution.[35]

d) Opt-In vs. Opt-Out

Common sense dictates that a class will be more fully aggregated if it is done on an opt-out, rather than opt-in, basis. Purveyors of retail rebate schemes offer coupons at purchase, rather than discounts, because they understand that comparatively fewer people will actually redeem the certificates. Class action administrators understand that, even after a claim is settled and notice goes out that funds are available, not all people actually submit the necessary forms to claim what is owed them, and in some cases substantially fewer do.

In an opt-in action, passive claimants drop through the cracks, and not just to their own disadvantage: the value of their claims, and the costs of their injuries, do not factor into the assessment against the defendant. The claims-value they represent does not contribute to the economy of scale of the litigation, and therefore per-claim litigation costs are increased; as a result, as explained earlier, both global settlements and per-claim compensation will be decreased. The decision not to opt in (or even the failure to make the decision) does not simply deprive the passive class member of compensation, it also diminishes the recovery of his or her fellow class members that *do* opt in.

While this phenomenon has led some to the extreme conclusion that even opting out should not be possible in mass tort class actions,[36] it is not necessary to go that far to get the benefits of a more fully aggregated class through an opt-out action. While those exercising their rights to opt out do indeed diminish the recovery of others in the class, this impact is lessened

---

34 See footnote 17 *supra*.
35 In the course of dealing with the 2.4 million potential Agent Orange claims over which he presided, Weinstein J. employed a "magic wand" and "vaporized the choice-of-law problem" by invoking "national consensus law" regarding products liability, available defences, and damages, and encouraging settlement on the assumption that such a principle would be applied eventually: see Peter Schuck, *Agent Orange on Trial* (Cambridge, MA: Harvard University Press, 1987) at 128. The variety of Weinstein J.'s procedural and substantive innovations in mass tort cases are recounted with admiration in Martha Minow, "A Judge for the Situation: Judge Jack Weinstein, Creator of Temporary Administrative Agencies" (1997) 97 Colum. L. Rev. 2010.
36 See, for instance, David Rosenberg, "Mandatory-Litigation Class Action: The Only Option for Mass Tort Cases" (2001) 115 Harvard L. Rev. 831.

if those persons do go on to pursue claims of their own, which is presumably the reason for opting out (lessened, too, by the fact that, as explained earlier, there will almost always be fewer "opt-outs" in an opt-out action than "never opt-ins" in an opt-in action. Opt-out schemes, therefore, are much more likely to ensure that the defendant internalizes the full extent of the harm it has caused.

Given the demonstrable advantages of opt-out claims, departure to an opt-in system for non-resident class members should only be taken if countervailing considerations outweigh them. Within the Canadian federation, though, is there really any reason to treat members of a national class differently from an intra-provincial one?

C. JURISPRUDENCE

1) *Morguard* and *Hunt* Revisited

In *Morguard Investments Ltd. v. De Savoye*[37] the Supreme Court of Canada considered the obligations of a court to recognize the judgments and orders of sister courts in other provinces. *Morguard* held that the enforcement of extra-jurisdictional *Canadian* judgments was to be governed by the principle of "full faith and credit," subject only to the requirement that the original court indeed had properly taken jurisdiction. *Morguard* also stood for the principle that, in determining whether a court had properly taken jurisdiction, principles of "order and fairness" dictated that the appropriate test was whether there was "a real and substantial connection" between the province assuming jurisdiction and the defendant or the subject matter of the lawsuit.

La Forest J. in *Morguard* attributed his disavowal of the traditional rules to the nature of the federal system and its essentially national marketplace:

> In a world where even the most familiar things we buy and sell originate or are manufactured elsewhere, and where people are constantly moving from province to province, it is simply anachronistic to uphold a "power theory" or a single situs for torts or contracts for the proper exercise of jurisdiction.[38]

The *Morguard* decision was one of a series in which the increasingly borderless market played a prominent role in influencing the Court's reason-

---

37 *Supra* note 26.
38 *Ibid.* at 1108–9.

ing. Earlier that same year, La Forest J. said in *Thomson Newspapers Ltd. v. Canada*:

> ... The courts in Canada ... cannot remain oblivious to the concrete social, political and economic realities within which our system of constitutional rights and guarantees must operate .... [A]s the Canadian economy becomes increasingly integrated with the American and, indeed, the global economy, we should be wary of giving an interpretation to the Constitution that shackles the government's capacity to cope with problems that other countries ... are quite able to deal with[.][39]

LaForest J. noted that "[t]his Court has, in other areas of the law having extraterritorial implications, recognized the need for adapting the law to the exigencies of a federation."[40] He then cited with approval from the decision of Estey J. in *Aetna Financial Services Ltd. v. Feigelman*:

> ... An initial question, therefore, must be answered, namely, what is meant by "jurisdiction" in a federal context? ... *In some ways, 'jurisdiction' [of the Manitoba court] extends to the national boundaries, or, in any case, beyond the provincial boundary of Manitoba*....[41] [Emphasis added].

The Supreme Court acknowledged that we are not, in twenty-first-century Canada, dealing with the vast disparity of legal systems against which the original English rules of "private international law" were meant to guard. As La Forest J. noted in *Morguard*, "fair process is not an issue within the Canadian federation."[42] His Lordship had earlier expanded on those aspects of Canadian federation that made Canadian court systems well-integrated and homogenous:

> The Canadian judicial structure is so arranged that any concerns about differential quality of justice among the provinces can have no real foundation. All superior court judges — who also have superintending control over other provincial courts and tribunals — are appointed and paid by the federal authorities. And all are subject to final review by the Supreme Court of Canada, which can determine when the courts of one province have appropriately exercised jurisdiction in an action and the circumstances under which the courts of another province should recognize

---

39 *Thomson Newspapers Ltd. v. Canada*, [1990] 1 S.C.R. 425 at para. 168.
40 *Morguard, supra* note 26 at para. 40.
41 *Aetna Financial Services Ltd. v. Feigelman*, [1985] 1 S.C.R. 2 at 34–35, cited in *Morguard, ibid.* at para. 40.
42 *Morguard, supra* note 26 at para. 43.

such judgments. Any danger resulting from unfair procedure is further avoided by sub-constitutional factors, such as for example the fact that Canadian lawyers adhere to the same code of ethics throughout Canada. In fact, since *Black v. Law Society of Alberta, supra* [[1989] 1 S.C.R. 591], we have seen a proliferation of interprovincial law firms.[43]

As we noted earlier, *Morguard* recognized that the provincial superior courts are — at least in some situations — "national" courts, not simply instruments of provincial sovereignty.

The decision of *Hunt v. T&N plc.*[44] confirmed that the requirement of "a real and substantial connection" was indeed a "constitutional imperative," such that it "has become the absolute constitutional limit on the power of each province to confer judicial jurisdiction on its courts."[45]

Hunt concerned the constitutionality of a Quebec "blocking statute" that prohibited the removal of business records from Quebec to fulfil an out-of-province court's discovery requirements. Following *Morguard*, the British Columbia Supreme Court had held that comity required it to respect the barrier erected by Quebec. However, the Supreme Court of Canada turned the question of "comity" around, and it held that the Quebec statute was constitutionally inapplicable to civil proceedings in another province by virtue of the same *Morguard* principles.

Hunt confirmed that "the Constitution may itself provide a source of court jurisdiction by prohibiting the ouster of the jurisdiction of the superior courts of a province with a real and substantial connection to the matter."[46] This jurisdiction, once properly exerted, must be respected by all other Canadian courts and, by inference, legislatures.

Earlier we made the point that an objective reading of *Hunt* leads to the conclusion that the Court was acting subjectively in deciding which jurisdiction's laws should yield to the other's. The Court did not question that the Quebec "blocking statute" was valid, as were the British Columbia Rules requiring disclosure; the question was *applicability*. Competent

---

43 *Ibid.* at para. 37. The *Morguard* court did not deal directly with the problem of what would happen if the legislature of one province imposes, through statute, a procedural scheme that is unfair. Would the legislature be barred from doing so in order to preserve the "fair process" within the "Canadian federation" as a whole? Or would the courts then be instead in a position to judge whether another province's legislation constitutes "fair process"? This question was not addressed until *Hunt, infra* note 44.
44 [1993] 4 S.C.R. 289 [hereinafter *Hunt*].
45 Jean Gabriel Castel, *Canadian Conflict of Laws*, 4th ed. (Toronto: Butterworths, 1997) at 54.
46 Janet Walker, "Interprovincial Sovereign Immunity Revisited" (1997) 35 Osgoode Hall L.J. 379 at 389.

courts in each jurisdiction could, with *prima facie* jurisdiction over the matter, enter mutually exclusive orders necessitated by their respective laws — the Supreme Court simply had to choose, in such a case, whose laws would prevail. As a matter of policy, one court's statutory "right" to obtain documents conflicted with another court's statutory "right" to block production. The question is then one of characterization.

The Court chose to characterize Quebec's law as intended to "impede successful litigation" in other provinces; enforcing the British Columbia court's discovery rules, on the contrary, would promote interprovincial commerce and the "efficient allocation and conduct of litigation."[47]

This aspect of *Hunt* is rarely considered, yet here it is of utmost importance. The Court has clearly signaled that, in a consideration of provincial legislation affecting litigative rights in other provinces, the resolution will depend to an extent on whether the extra-provincial extension of provincial law will promote the "efficient resolution" of civil disputes or "impede" it. As such, the economic advantages and policy imperatives of the national opt-out class may carry the day.

2) The *Dutton* Decision

In *Western Canadian Shopping Centres Inc. v. Dutton*,[48] two debenture holders in a failed company incorporated by the defendant had attempted to file a suit on behalf of themselves and 229 others similarly situated. They sued pursuant to Alberta's rule 42, which was the codification of the previous equitable rules permitting (but not describing in detail) a "representative proceeding."[49]

Reversing its previous decision in *General Motors of Canada Ltd. v. Naken*,[50] the Court held that the benefits of class actions had been demonstrated and should be extended to jurisdictions without comprehensive statutory regimes:

> The need to strike a balance between efficiency and fairness ... belies the suggestion that class actions should be approached restrictively. The

---

47   *Hunt, supra* note 44 at para. 61.
48   *Supra* note 1.
49   Alberta Rules of Court, Alta. Reg. 390/68 reads in relevant part:
> 42. Where numerous persons have a common interest in the subject of an intended action, one or more of those persons may sue or be sued or may be authorized by the Court to defend on behalf of or for the benefit of all.
50   [1983] 1 S.C.R. 72.

> defendants argue that *General Motors of Canada Ltd. v. Naken*, [1983] 1 S.C.R. 72, precludes a generous approach to class actions. I respectfully disagree .... [W]hen *Naken* was decided, the modern class action was very much an untested procedure in Canada. In the intervening years, the importance of the class action as a procedural tool in modern litigation has become manifest. Indeed, the reform that has been effected since *Naken* has been motivated in large part by the recognition of the benefits that class actions can offer the parties, the court system, and society: see, e.g., Ontario Law Reform Commission, *supra*, at pp. 3–4.[51]

The Court thus permitted lower courts to design proceedings along the lines of those available under statutory regimes where four conditions are met:

1) the class is capable of clear definition;
2) there are issues of fact or law common to all class members;
3) success for one class member means success for all; and
4) the proposed representative adequately represents the interests of the class.[52]

Upon the satisfaction of those basic conditions, the test becomes one analogous to the "preferability" requirement of statutory certification regimes:

> If these conditions are met the court must also be satisfied, in the exercise of its discretion, that there are no countervailing considerations that outweigh the benefits of allowing the class action to proceed.[53]

However, one possible difference in the "common law class action" defined in *Dutton* is the notice requirements, which may be more stringent than those under the statutes. Nevertheless, the fact that the Court foresaw the issuance of "sufficient" notice — as opposed to actual notice — suggests that the question of notice should continue to be viewed flexibly. The Court stated as follows:

> Other procedural issues may arise. One is notice. A judgment is binding on a class member only if the class member is notified of the suit and is given an opportunity to exclude himself or herself from the proceeding. *This case does not raise the issue of what constitutes sufficient notice.* However, prudence suggests that all potential class members be informed of the

---

51   *Dutton*, *supra* note 1 at para. 46.
52   *Ibid.* at para. 48
53   *Ibid.*

existence of the suit, of the common issues that the suit seeks to resolve, and of the right of each class member to opt out, and that this be done before any decision is made that purports to prejudice or otherwise affect the interests of class members. [Emphasis added.][54]

The most important aspect of *Dutton* for present purposes is that there is nothing in the decision to suggest that the opt-out "common law class" it foresees must be restricted to provincial residents. In fact, the "class" that was eventually certified as a representative action in *Dutton* consisted of "231 foreign investors."[55] Moreover, the Supreme Court brushed aside concerns over the application of foreign laws, clearly signaling that it understood that this was a class originating in diverse jurisdictions.[56]

3) Interpreting the Legislation: Opt-In vs. Opt-Out

In 1996, the Uniform Law Conference of Canada (ULCC) adopted its *Model Class Proceedings Act*.[57] This Act was drafted by delegates from British Columbia,[58] and it follows the British Columbia Act closely. The *ULCC Model Act* has in turn formed the basis for subsequent legislative proposals in Alberta, Saskatchewan, Manitoba, and Newfoundland, each of which closely tracks the Model Act's wording.

As a result, it is commonly said that there are two basic legislative models of "national classes" available in Canada: the Ontario model, which permits national opt-out classes, subject only to competing certification in other provinces, and the British Columbia model, which permits non-residents to participate on an opt-in basis only.

---

54 *Ibid.* at para. 49.
55 *Western Canadian Shopping Centres Inc. v. Dutton* (1998), 73 Alta. L.R. (3d) 227 (C.A.). The non-resident status of the class members is not apparent in the Supreme Court decision that followed, *supra* note 1.
56 The Supreme Court held in, *Dutton*, *supra* note 1 at para. 54:

> Different investors invested at different times, in different jurisdictions, on the basis of different offering memoranda, through different agents, in different series of debentures, and learned about the underlying events through different disclosure documents. Some investors may possess rescissionary rights that others do not. The fact remains, however, that the investors raise essentially the same claims requiring resolution of the same facts.

57 Ruth Rogers, *A Uniform Class Actions Statute*, 1995 Proceedings of the Uniform Law Conference of Canada <www.law.ualberta.ca/alri/ulc/95pro/3950.htm>.
58 Margaret Shone, "Memo re: National Class Actions," (5 March 2001) [unpublished, on file with Alberta Law Reform Institute and with the authors].

This is, however, an incomplete description. In fact, neither the Ontario nor British Columbia Acts explicitly permits, or explicitly prohibits, an opt-out national class. Rather, the "models" we describe as paradigmatic have resulted from the courts' interpretation of their respective provinces' legislation. These interpretations are, after *Dutton*, subject to revision.

a) National Classes in British Columbia

British Columbia's statute deals explicitly, if incompletely, with the issue of extraterritoriality. It provides that foreign class members may benefit from, and be bound by, a decision on an opt-in basis,[59] and the British Columbia Court of Appeal, at least in *obiter*, has suggested that this is the only basis on which non-residents might be included. In *Harrington v. Dow Corning Corp.*,[60] the British Columbia Court of Appeal said at paragraph 85: "Section 16(2) may preclude the court from certifying a national class on an opting out basis, as was done [by the Ontario Court] in *Nantais*."

Subsequently, Kirkpatrick J. said in *Hoy v. Medtronic*[61] at paragraph 32: "The *Act* contemplates a class which can be subdivided into resident and non-resident sub-classes (s. 6(2)). Non-residents must opt in to the class proceeding (s. 16(2))."

A review of the foundational document that led to the British Columbia Act does not shed much light on the purposes behind section 16(2). That document outlined the "problem" with the possible national opt-out class as follows:

> A class defined in a class action brought under the Ontario Act may purport to include individuals whose cause of action arose in British Columbia. If such an individual did not opt out of the Ontario class action and attempted to sue the defendants in British Columbia, he or she would likely be met by the argument that he or she was bound by the Ontario judgment and was barred from bringing an individual action. The response of the British Columbia litigant would be that the legislation in Ontario did not bind him or her. The availability of an expanded class

---

59 Section 16(2) of the *Class Proceeding Act* reads:

> (2) Subject to subsection (4), a person who is not a resident of British Columbia may, in the manner and within the time specified in the certification order made in respect of a class proceeding, opt in to that class proceeding if the person would be, but for not being a resident of British Columbia, a member of the class involved in the class proceeding.

60 2000 BCCA 605.
61 2001 BCSC 1343.

action procedure in a number of provinces could result in several class actions involving the same defendant and the same issues being commenced in each jurisdiction. In some cases, this could undermine the goals of judicial economy which underlie class actions. These issues have not been resolved by the Ontario legislation.[62]

It is unclear how either the Ontario *or* the British Columbia model could lead to "several class actions involving the same defendant and the same issues being commenced in each jurisdiction." Presumably, the problem would occur if such actions were commenced in several different jurisdictions. The passage's conclusion, that national classes would *undermine* the goal of judicial economy, is similarly perplexing. Nevertheless, it has become an article of faith that, for whatever reason, the British Columbia statute was drafted in a way to foreclose the possibility of an opt-out national class being commenced in that province.[63]

The superior courts of the various provinces retain the inherent powers to impose national classes that they had prior to class proceedings legislation. *Dutton* recognized that superior courts have the inherent jurisdiction[64] to design national opt-out classes. The question is then whether this jurisdiction is ousted by the British Columbia Act, simply because it permits non-residents on an opt-in basis. Ordinary rules of statutory interpretation would seem to suggest not;[65] in these circum-

---

62 British Columbia, *Class Action Legislation for British Columbia* (Victoria: Ministry of the Attorney General, 1994) at 22.

63 See for instance Michael A. Eizenga & Mark T. Poland, "Conflict of Laws and the National Class" <www.siskinds.com> (accessed November 13, 2003). Eizenga's and Poland's article represents a rare, thorough, and scholarly treatment of the jurisprudence surrounding national class actions in Canada. See also, generally, the overview in Garry D. Watson, "Class Actions: the Canadian Experience" (2001) 11 Duke J. of Comp. & Int'l L. 269.

64 Provincial superior courts, like U.S. state courts, are courts of inherent jurisdiction: *Canada (Canadian Human Rights Commission) v. Canadian Liberty Net*, [1998] 1 S.C.R. 626 at para. 35 [hereinafter *Liberty Net*]. This provides a "residual source of powers, which the court may draw upon as necessary whenever it is just and equitable to do so, in particular, to ensure the observance of the due process of law, to prevent improper vexation or oppression, to do justice between the parties and to secure a fair trial between them": *Halsbury's Laws of England*, vol. 37, 4th ed. (London: Butterworths, 1982) at para. 14. The Supreme Court of Canada has accorded inherent jurisdiction both a substantive and a procedural meaning: *Société des Acadiens du Nouveau-Brunswick v. Association of Parents for Fairness in Education*, [1986] 1 S.C.R. 549 at paras. 94–95 [hereinafter *Société des Acadiens*].

65 In *Société des Acadiens, ibid.*, the Court held that a court may exercise its inherent jurisdiction in respect of matters regulated by statute as long as it does so without contravening or conflicting with a statutory provision. In fact, even in the face of com-

stances, it is at least arguable that the British Columbia courts, after *Dutton*, may certify nationally on an opt-out basis, no less than may courts in jurisdictions without class proceeding legislation.

b) National Classes in Ontario

The issue of the propriety of a nationwide opt-out class was first confronted in Canada in the 1995 case *Nantais v. Telectronics*,[66] a decision of the Ontario Court (General Division). In *Nantais*, Brockenshire J. considered whether a national class made up of the recipients of allegedly faulty heart pacemaker leads was permissible. In the decision, Brockenshire J. identified the issue as fairness to absent plaintiffs (as opposed to fairness to the defendant, as the defendants urged). Considering the American position, he found the Court's expansion of class action beyond state borders in *Phillips Petroleum Co. v. Shutts*[67] to be "most persuasive." While questioning to what extent the defendant had standing to raise the rights of absent foreign plaintiffs,[68] the analysis adopted appears to coincide generally with that in *Shutts*, with Brockenshire J. noting that part of the litigation plan submitted by the plaintiffs included actual notification of all potential class members across the country. He suggested that although an opt-out class might be permissible, in the case before him "prudence would dictate" that "non-resident" class members be provided the opportunity to opt in.[69]

---

prehensive statutory provisions, courts retain a residual discretionary power to grant relief unless they have been explicitly denied this through legislation (*Liberty Net, ibid.* at paras. 10, 32) provided that (a) the subject matter is within the jurisdiction of the court and (b) that the court has taken into consideration all the relevant factors: *Société des Acadiens, ibid.* at para. 123.

66 *Nantais v. Telectronics Proprietary (Canada) Ltd.* (1995), 127 D.L.R. (4th) 552 (Gen. Div.), leave to appeal refused (1995), 129 D.L.R. (4th) 110 (Gen. Div.), leave to appeal denied (1996), 28 O.R. (3d) 523 (C.A.) [hereinafter *Nantais*]. In fact, Professor Watson foresaw the trend after the decision in *Bendall v. McGhan Medical Corp.* (1993), 106 D.L.R. (4th) 339 (Ont. Gen. Div.): Garry D. Watson, "Initial Interpretations of Ontario's *Class Proceedings Act*: The Anaheim and the Breast Implant Actions" 18 C.P.C. (3d) 344 at 358.

67 472 U.S. 797 (1985) [hereinafter *Shutts*]. The *Shutts* decision suggests that a high standard of notice and opt-out rights may be a necessary part of all class actions involving non-resident plaintiffs. See Arthur Miller & David Crump, "Jurisdiction and Choice of Law in Multistate Actions After *Phillips Petroleum v. Shutts*" (1985) 96 Yale L.J. 1.

68 This is in contrast to the U.S. Supreme Court's decision in *Shutts, ibid.* where it was found that the defendants' interest in achieving a global settlement made it appropriate that it should be concerned with whether non-resident plaintiffs would be bound by any settlement or decision.

69 *Nantais, supra* note 66 at 567 cited to 127 D.L.R. (4th).

Interjurisdictional Class Actions   **453**

So, while Brockenshire J. did not explicitly do so, he focused on the two key principles in the U.S. due process analysis — meaningful notice and the appropriateness of opt-out classes for non-resident plaintiffs.

However, in refusing leave to appeal from the *Nantais* decision, Zuber J. of the Divisional Court did not focus on the "due process" elements enunciated in the court below, emphasizing instead that the question should be more properly left for subsequent decisions of foreign courts using a *res judicata* analysis:

> Whether the result reached in Ontario court in a class proceeding will bind members of the class in other provinces who remained passive and simply did not opt out, remains to be seen. The law of *res judicata* may have to adapt itself to the class proceeding concept. In my respectful view the order of Brockenshire J. setting out a national class, finds powerful support in the judgment of La Forest J. in *Morguard Investments Ltd. v. De Savoye*, [1990] 3 S.C.R. 1077, 76 D.L.R. (4th) 256.[70]

The issue was revisited by Winkler J. in *Carom v. Bre-X*.[71] In that case, the plaintiffs argued that Brockenshire J. in *Nantais* did not adequately consider the constitutional question; Winkler J. rejected this idea. While the analysis in *Carom* might appear confusing at times,[72] Winkler J. firmly grounded his answer in the idea of "order and fairness" established by the Supreme Court's decision in *Morguard* and *Hunt*. Unfortunately, though, he approached the constitutional question from the point of view of the general "order and fairness" of the Ontario *Class Proceedings Act*, not from the circumstances of the individual case before him:

> The CPA is a procedural statute replete with provisions guaranteeing order and fairness. Section 9 permits any member to opt-out of the class proceeding within the time provided. ...
>
> In addition s. 17 requires that proper notice of the certification, in a court approved form, must be provided to all class members. The notice must include the "manner by which and time within which class members may opt out of the proceeding." Additional notices to ensure that the

---

70 The application for leave to appeal to the Divisional Court was dismissed on October 4, 1995; reasons of Zuber J. are reproduced at the end of *Nantais, ibid.*, cited to 129 D.L.R. (4th) 110 at 113.
71 (1999) 43 O.R. (3d) 441 (Gen. Div.) [hereinafter *Carom*].
72 Winkler J. apparently considered "order and fairness" and "real and substantial connection" as criteria that must be independently satisfied, rather than the latter being an aspect of the former.

interests of the class members are protected may be ordered by the court under s. 19.[73]

The notice requirements in the Ontario Act provide for everything from actual notice to no notice at all; the court has discretion to order notice in whatever form it sees fit or to dispense with it altogether. But if, for instance, stringent notice is a requirement of "due process," as in the United States after *Shutts*, then it behooves the Ontario court to adopt procedures from the more stringent end of the spectrum when foreign members are included in the class. In other words, it is not, as the *Carom* decision suggests, the language of the statute that "guarantees" order and fairness, but rather the statute is drafted in a way that allows the courts to guarantee it in any particular case.

Carom was followed by the decision of Brockenshire J. in *Webb v. K-Mart Canada Ltd.*[74] That case involved an action launched in Ontario against K-Mart for a mass termination of employees across Canada during an episode of corporate downsizing. In approving the class, Brockenshire J. said:

> Our provincial courts systems are struggling to deal with situations where there is a nationwide impact. So are the state courts in the United States. Obviously, from the points of view of both the national corporation and its employees across the nation, there should not be great disparities in treatment arising solely from an accident of geography. The lack of comparable class action legislation elsewhere in Canada, except for British Columbia and Quebec is a telling argument for extending the reach of the Ontario legislation. We must somehow as Professor Sander says, "fit the forum to the fuss" ....
>
> Here, I regard the common interests of the class members, the commercial realities of the situation, and the broad objectives of the Ontario *Act*, as outweighing any concerns expressed over extra territorial involvement of the Ontario Court.[75]

Brockenshire J. also relied heavily on the purposes of the Ontario Act, one of which was to "modify the behaviour" of potential defendants. The fact that much of the "behaviour" being "modified" was *outside* Ontario may even have encouraged Brockenshire J. to exert jurisdiction over plaintiffs in the other provinces, because he viewed the lack of a class proceed-

---

73 *Carom*, *supra* note 71 at 451–52.
74 (1999), 45 O.R. (3d) 389 (S.C.J.) [hereinafter *Webb*].
75 *Ibid.* at 404.

ings statute in those provinces as something of an "accident," rather than as a democratic choice of the respective legislatures. This was, prior to *Dutton*, a problematic analysis from the standpoint of legislative territoriality because it extended the benefits and burdens of class proceedings into provinces where such actions were not possible.

More starkly, in a subsequent decision in the same case,[76] Brockenshire J. directed that lawyers be appointed to conduct hearings in the class members' home provinces and make recommendations as to the quantum owed by K-Mart to particular individuals. Recognizing that this represented a significant extraterritorial leap of his court's authority, the learned Justice cited La Forest J. in *Morguard*[77] and Winkler J. in *Bre-X*, who had said, "*Morguard* and *Hunt* permit the extraterritorial application of legislation where the enacting Province has a real and substantial connection with the subject matter of that action and it accords with order and fairness to assume jurisdiction."[78] The same "full faith and credit" device was rather summarily invoked to overcome objections that such persons were not "officers of the Court" within the meaning of Ontario law.[79]

In denying leave to appeal in *Webb v. K-Mart Canada Ltd.*,[80] MacFarland J. said that

> Courts must adjust to the realties of modern commercialism which is not only national but international in many instances. Practical solutions to such problems can and must be crafted to respond to modern reality. This is just such a case.

More recently, Cumming J. in *Wilson v. Servier*[81] clearly confirmed that Ontario's jurisdictional analysis for national opt-out classes was based on *Hunt*'s "due process"-based *ratio*. Cumming J. said,

> In determining procedurally whether non-Ontario residents are to be included within an Ontario class action, a court must be guided by the requirements of order and fairness: see *Hunt*, at p. 326.
>
> ...

---

76 *Webb v. K-Mart Canada Ltd.*, [1999] 45 O.R. (3d) 425 (S.C.J.).
77 *Supra* note 26 at 1095 ("The business community operates in a world economy and we correctly speak of a world community even in the face of decentralized political and legal power. Accommodating the flow of wealth, skills and peoples across state lines has now become imperative.").
78 *Webb*, above note 76 at para. 21 citing *Carom*, above note 71 at 450.
79 *Ibid.* at 431–32.
80 [1999] O.J. No. 3286 at para. 10 (S.C.J.).
81 (2000), 50 O.R. (3d) 219 (S.C.J.) [hereinafter *Servier*].

This approach is efficacious in extending the policy objectives underlying the CPA for the benefit of non-residents. If there are common issues for all Canadian claimants, this approach facilitates access to justice and judicial efficiency, and tends to inhibit potentially wrongful behaviour. This is to the advantage of all Canadians and to Canada as a federal state. This procedural flexibility serves in the nature of oil in the institutional and jurisdictional machinery of Canadian federalism. Courts in Australia and the United States, both federal states, have addressed similar issues in like manner: see generally *Femcare Ltd v. Bright*, [2000] FCA 512 (April 19, 2000) (Australia); *Shutts, supra*.[82]

Perhaps unfortunately, Cumming J. did not take this principle to its logical end, because he proposed that his court's "national jurisdiction" should be truncated by class actions begun in other provinces:

> Mass torts and defective products do not respect provincial boundaries. Complex and costly litigation is not viable for individual claimants. The procedural latitude of the CPA recognizes the authority of all provinces and the rights of their individual residents. If a non-resident of Ontario wishes to commence an action in another province, that person can opt out of the Ontario action. *If a class action is commenced and certified in either British Columbia or Quebec, that certified class proceeding will take precedence for the residents of that province.*[83] [Emphasis added.]

The passage suggests that Ontario courts would, presumably through exercise of "comity," defer to a certification in British Columbia, at least with respect to British Columbia class members. Mr. Justice Cumming offers no support for this idea,[84] and indeed *Servier* seems to run counter

---

82 *Ibid.* at paras. 84, 93.
83 *Ibid.* at para. 94.
84 He does cite at para. 79 the previous decision of Zuber J. of the Ontario Divisional Court in *Nantais, supra* note 66 at 114 (cited to 129 D.L.R. (4th)):

> It is also argued that other class proceedings may be certified in other provinces relating to the matter which is the subject of this class proceeding. In my respectful view any of these practical difficulties which may develop as the matter proceeds can be met by amending the order in question to adjust the size of the class. If it is shown that the law of another province is so substantially different as to make the trial with respect to class members from that province very difficult, the class can be redefined. *Additionally, if a class is certified in another province that group can be deleted from the Ontario class.* [Emphasis added.]

Again, the suggestion in *Nantais, supra* note 66, that the forum court could "pare down" its national class if a competing class is certified ignores the question of whether an overlapping class *can* be certified given the original certification. Perhaps,

to the spirit, if not the letter, of the rules enunciated by the Supreme Court of Canada. Moreover, the reasoning does not at all confront the more central question: why should British Columbia courts not defer to the initial decision made in Ontario to certify a national class including British Columbia residents and refuse to certify a competing class? Remember, this is not a question of *forum conveniens*; under "full faith and credit," the only ground on which the British Columbia court could refuse to recognize the Ontario "national class" certification decision would be if Ontario did not have jurisdiction over the claims (and clearly Cumming J. believes it does). This is not a question of which process provides the most order, fairness, or due process, it is a simple yes or no: did the original court properly exercise its jurisdiction? If yes, if there is sufficient "order and fairness" in Ontario to justify jurisdiction over British Columbia claims, then that is the end of the analysis; following *Morguard*, a British Columbia Court would simply not have jurisdiction to certify a subsequent,[85] competing claim, and if it did, there is no basis for assuming that it would "take precedence" over the Ontario action.[86]

At the time *Servier* was decided, there were only two other provinces where comparable actions could be begun; thus the "national class" would be preserved, at least for over half of Canada's population. Since Saskatchewan and Newfoundland now have British Columbia-pattern

---

if the originally certifying court does, in fact, qualify its certification with a commitment to reduce the national class if other jurisdictions certify (as Zuber and Cumming JJ. did), then subsequent certifications may be constitutionally permissible even under a "full faith and credit" paradigm. But if no such qualification is made, there seems to be no theoretical basis upon which a subsequent certification will "take precedence" over the original national class.

85 This problem would not arise, of course, if the British Columbia case was certified first on a province-wide basis; a subsequent certification in Ontario should then acknowledge the British Columbia jurisdiction over such cases. But this scenario, if anything, speaks to the inefficiency of the British Columbia model. Why should the efficacious resolution of the action depend on which action — provincial or national — was filed first? If the original British Columbia action was permitted to certify on a national opt-out basis, and if Ontario's courts respected the certification, the problem would not arise.

86 This raises the question again: upon whose motion would certification be refused? In this case, the defendant might wish a separate British Columbia class because its economy-of-scale advantage is more pronounced if the plaintiffs are split into two camps. Counsel for the representative plaintiff would not wish to see his or her action barred through operation of comity. In such a case, and without a national consolidation mechanism in place, the only proper route would be for the court to hear an application for the original national class.

statutes, and after the advent of the "common law class action" in *Dutton*, there are now nine (or if the territories are included, twelve) other jurisdictions that might host actions that "take precedence" over the national class with respect to those places. In such a way, the national class rather boldly forged by the Ontario courts risks being chipped away — undone, somewhat ironically, precisely because the value of aggregation has become universally recognized and class litigation has spread across the country.[87]

The Ontario courts have never openly confronted the true issue underlying the national class: that is to say, they have never acknowledged that the defendants' litigation scale economy is national, and therefore so must be the plaintiffs'. As a result, Ontario decisions are inconsistent in their defence of the opt-out national class. In *Webb v. K-Mart*, for instance, the Court said that "[t]he lack of comparable class action legislation elsewhere in Canada, except for British Columbia and Quebec, is a telling argument for extending the reach of the Ontario legislation."[88] This somewhat imperialist view echoed one U.S. court's binding of Canadian class members to its own decision, excepting only those who lived in class action provinces.[89] In *Carom*, the statute was simply described as being "replete with provisions guaranteeing order and fairness."[90] These are defensive arguments, and unconvincing ones at that. An approach based on more than deontological assertions of "justice" is needed to support a robust national class action regime. Closer to the truth might be Professor Sander's remarks, cited in *Webb*, that we must "fit the forum to the fuss."[91] However, the best

---

[87] Branch puts it this way: In the post-*Dutton* era of thirteen separate class action jurisdictions, "[t]he prospects for interjurisdictional class action chaos have been substantially magnified.": Branch, *supra* note 13 at 6.

[88] *Webb v. K-Mart*, above note 74 at 404. The Court found at para. 58:

> In my view, we have here a single corporate decision by a corporation carrying on business across the country that is alleged to have adversely affected people who are working for it from coast to coast. Our provincial court systems are struggling to deal with situations where there is a nationwide impact. So are the state courts in the United States. Obviously, from the points of view of both the national corporation and its employees across the nation, there should not be great disparities in treatment arising solely from an accident of geography .... We must somehow as Professor Sander says, "fit the forum to the fuss."

[89] This decision was additionally distasteful in that the Canadian members bound by the court received a lower level of compensation than their American counterparts. In *Lindsey v. Dow Corning Corp. (In Re Silicone Gel Breast Implant Products Liability Litigation)*, U.S. Dist. LEXIS 12521 (N.D. Al. 1 Set 1994). *Contra: Bersch v. Drexel Firestone Inc.*, 519 F.2d 974 at 986 (2d Cir. 1975).

[90] See footnote 71 and accompanying text.

[91] Cited in *Webb*, *supra* note 74 at para. 58.

explanation offered in that case for *why* we must do so is to avoid a disparity of treatment across the provinces, an assertion no more helpful than those that have come before. There are many variations among provinces on matters of substantive law, particularly tort law. Why should the recovery in *Webb* be uniform when the recovery in any "ordinary" actions should not? These questions go unanswered because they have never actually been asked. We suggest here that the Ontario approach is basically correct, but we acknowledge that it has never been adequately explained.

c) National Classes in Quebec

Like that of Ontario, Quebec's statutory regime does not mention the inclusion of non-resident members in class actions. However, unlike courts in Ontario or British Columbia, Quebec's courts have been reluctant to state definitively whether they believe it appropriate to certify an opt-out national class, and, indeed, they have yet to undertake any consideration of the "order and fairness" or "real and substantial connection" tests set out by the Supreme Court of Canada.[92]

Prior to *Morguard* and *Hunt*, the Quebec courts suggested in *obiter* that any class certified should be restricted to claimants who were either residents of Quebec or who could trace their cause of action to the province.[93] Recently, the Quebec courts appear to be interpreting the legislation more liberally. In *Masson v. Thompson*,[94] the Quebec Court of Appeal refused to overturn certification on the grounds that the opt-out class included members who were resident outside the province. A subsequent decision, *Bourque v. Laboratoires Abbott Ltée*,[95] also certified a national class. In neither of these decisions did the courts take the opportunity to canvass the issues thoroughly. Moreover, in *Bourque*, it may be that the court was reasoning along the lines of the old equitable representative actions, somewhat reducing the decision's value as a precedent.[96]

---

92 Branch, "Chaos or Consistency?," *supra* note 2.
93 *Werner v. Saab-Scania AB*, [1980] C.S. 798 (Que. S.C.), aff'd (unreported, February 19, 1982) Montreal 500-09-001005-800 (C.A.). See also *Bolduc c. Cie Montreal Trust (C.A.Q.)*, [1989] A.Q. no 705 (C.A.).
94 [1994] R.J.Q. 1032 (S.C.) aff'd [1995] R.J.Q. 329 (C.A.).
95 [1998] A.Q. no 1836 (Que. S.C.).
96 The court relied in part on the fact that the relief sought — a return of certain funds to a pension plan — would benefit all class members equally. In this sense, the inclusion of the non-resident members was irrelevant unless and until the Quebec action failed and the defendant attempted to bar subsequent actions on the same issue in other jurisdictions.

4) The Unanswered Question: Sufficiency of Notice

The leading U.S. case on the multijurisdictional reach of state class actions, mentioned in the previous section, is *Phillips Petroleum Co. v. Shutts*.[97] In that case, the Supreme Court held that a Kansas state court could not bind absent plaintiff members of the class in a "common question" class action (brought under a state rule virtually identical to federal rule 23(b)(3)) unless the plaintiffs were provided with "minimal procedural due process protection," including the right to opt out. Rehnquist J., speaking for the Court, said this at 811–12:[98]

> If the forum State wishes to bind an absent plaintiff concerning a claim for money damages or similar relief at law, it must provide minimal procedural due process protection. The plaintiff must receive notice plus an opportunity to be heard and participate in the litigation, whether in person or through counsel. The notice must be the best practicable, "reasonably calculated, under all the circumstances, to apprise interested parties of the pendency of the action and afford them an opportunity to present their objections." ... Additionally, we hold that due process requires at a minimum that an absent plaintiff be provided with an opportunity to remove himself from the class by executing and returning an "opt out" or "request for exclusion" form to the court. [Citations omitted.]

The decision of the Court was specifically restricted to class actions that seek to bind *known* plaintiffs concerning claims wholly or predominantly for money judgments.[99]

In the *DES Cases*, Weinstein J. noted that the Supreme Court decision in *Shutts* "suggest[s] the need for modified jurisdictional analysis in the special context of mass litigation."[100] The Eastern District Court found that, because national class actions are necessary to provide relief where it might otherwise be unattainable, *Shutts* adopted a lower standard of "minimal procedural due process" — replacing the "minimal contacts" standard with sufficiency of notice and the opportunity to opt out.[101]

This position can be seen as essentially analogous to those of the Ontario courts since *Nantais*: provided that the imposition of a national

---

97 *Supra* note 67.
98 *Ibid.* at 811–12.
99 There is a question whether this decision has application to types of class actions such as those seeking equitable relief. *Shutts*, above note 67 at 811.
100 *Re DES Cases*, 789 F.Supp. 552 at 576 (E.D.N.Y. 1992).
101 *Ibid.*

class did not offend a minimal due process requirement, the interests of justice required the court to engage in the "time-honored jurisdiction-stretching technique of implied consent to cope with the special problem of jurisdiction in mass class actions ...."[102] Yet *Nantais* did not impose additional requirements of notice for extra-provincial plaintiffs, nor did it examine the sufficiency of notice differently for out-of-province claims.

As mentioned, though, in *Shutts*, the class members were known and it was possible to contact most individually to apprise them of the lawsuit and their right to opt out.[103] In more typical cases, where the members are not known (and may not even know they have a claim: for example, where the product in issue has not yet failed, or the disease has not manifested), the question of what notice will suffice to bind remains open.

In Australia, too, the High Court has rejected the notion that an opt-out national class is barred from certification, provided that sufficient notice is given to non-residents. The standard of notice was recently described in *Femcare Ltd. v. Bright*[104] as follows:

> In determining what is *"reasonably"* practicable and not *"unduly"* expensive for the purposes of s. 33Y(5), the Court is bound in our view, to take account of the possible adverse consequences to a group member of the representative proceeding as well as any possible benefits. A value judgment is required. Plainly the Court would be more likely to be satisfied that personal notice is reasonably practicable and not unduly expensive if an adverse determination will have significant consequences for a group member. Moreover, s. 33Y(5) must be understood in its statutory context. This includes s. 33ZF, which empowers the Court to make any order it thinks appropriate to ensure that justice is done in the proceeding.
>
> In assessing the requirements of the judicial process it is also important to bear in mind the objects underlying s. 33Y(5). As the extract from the [Law Reform Commission's] *Grouped Proceedings* report ... shows, the objective is to find the most economical means of ensuring that the group members are informed of the proceeding and their rights. The LRC con-

---

102 *Ibid.* at 577.
103 It is interesting that in *Shutts*, the final class as certified contained 28,100 members; 3,400 had "opted out" of the class by returning the request for exclusion, and notice could not be delivered to another 1,500 members, who were also excluded. The Supreme Court did not explicitly discuss, though, whether excluding those who did not receive the notice would be constitutionally required, an important question if notice was by less certain means than registered mail, if it was effected for instance through advertisements: *Shutts*, *supra* note 67.
104 [2000] FCA 512 (H.C.A.).

sidered that *"the more at stake for each person, the more effective the notice should be."* It also took the view that the procedures adopted should not shut out the very cases for which the representative procedure is most appropriate — claims involving small individual claims which are large in aggregate. [Emphases in original.][105]

However, it is somewhat inapt to cite *Femcare*, as did Cumming J. in *Servier*, as directly analogous to the U.S. Supreme Court's decision in *Shutts* and the Ontario decisions of *Nantais* and *Bre-X* simply on the basis that Australia, too, is a federal system. While the High Court in *Femcare* was indeed seeking to define a procedure that would meet due process standards, it was doing so within the confines of a valid federal Act, as opposed to the provincial legislation in the Ontario cases. In other words, the Australian Court was not considering the extra-territorial competence of the certifying court or enabling legislation. While the decision and its reasoning are helpful on the issue of appropriate notice, it is not unreasonable to argue that notice requirements for non-resident class members ought to be somewhat more stringent than those appropriate for persons within the jurisdiction.[106] A more useful Australian example might be that of the State of Victoria's group proceedings provisions. There, the legislation allows the court to decline class members where "the person does not have sufficient connection with Australia to justify inclusion as a group member."[107] This distinction — wherein even though the legislation is based in the state, the minimal contacts are considered *with respect to the entire nation* — is similar to what we propose here. The constitutionality of the *Victoria Act*'s extra-territoriality has been upheld very recently by the High Court of Australia.[108]

This is not to say that any of the "national classes" certified in Ontario would not have been certified had this analysis been applied. In fact, they very likely would have been.[109] No case in Ontario has determined whether,

---

105 *Ibid.* at paras. 73–4.
106 This is so for a number of reasons: a non-resident member, unlike a resident, is not presumed to know the forum's law, and would not ordinarily expect to be bound by an order of the forum's court. Such a distant non-resident will also be less likely to hear of the claim but for the notice.
107 *Victoria Supreme Court Act 1986*, Part IVA ("Group Proceedings") (as amended by *Courts and Tribunals Legislation (Miscellaneous Amendments) Act 2000*) [hereinafter *Victoria Act*], s. 33KA(2)(a).
108 *Mobil Oil Limited v. Victoria*, [2002] HCA 27.
109 For instance *Nantais, supra* note 66 dealt with the wiring on heart pacemakers where the class members were notifiable and the value of each claim relatively high; similarly, *Webb v. K-Mart, supra* note 74 involved mass dismissals of employees by the defen-

as in *Shutts*, there ought to be *more* stringent notice requirements for non-resident members of an opt-out class.

There is good reason, following *Morguard* and *Hunt*, to ignore *Shutts* altogether. In the United States, state courts do not have the same "national" role as the provincial superior courts. They bear none of the indicia invoked by the Supreme Court of Canada in determining that provincial superior courts are in many senses "federal" institutions[110] — American state judges are not appointed or paid by the federal government; they are not subject to unifying decisions of a single Supreme Court,[111] and so on.

So should there be a higher standard of notice for national class claims? Recall that in *Dutton* the Supreme Court of Canada held:

> This case does not raise the issue of what constitutes sufficient notice. However, prudence suggests that all potential class members be informed of the existence of the suit, of the common issues that the suit seeks to resolve, and of the right of each class member to opt out, and that this be done before any decision is made that purports to prejudice or otherwise affect the interests of class members.[112]

But the Court, while addressing a class of foreign plaintiffs, did not suggest that their notice requirements would be different for resident plaintiffs; indeed, they seemed to be enunciating a general guideline for all actions proceeding under the inherent jurisdiction of the Court. And the guideline, it should be emphasized, focuses on "sufficient notice," not "actual notice."

---

dant, who could be taken to have known at least recent personal details of the class members; and *Carom v. Bre-X, supra* note 71, a securities fraud case, had a class that was known and was, in any event, likely be a "limited fund" case.

Only the notice in *Servier, supra* note 81, could be viewed as inadequate to a high U.S.-style "due process" standard; apart from letters to "known" plaintiffs, the court required only a single publication in two newspapers, two magazines, and a medical journal [at paras. 150–1]. *Quaere* whether such notice is sufficient to defeat the rights of persons who had taken a popular diet drug and who may not know that they are ill. However, while Cumming J. in *Servier* did consider *Shutts* in certifying the "national class" before him, he did not explicitly address whether he felt himself bound to meet the higher standard of notice alluded to in that case and others since.

110 See footnote 43 and accompanying text.
111 It comes as a surprise to many Canadian lawyers that the Supreme Court of the United States is in fact bound by the decisions of state courts on questions within the latter's constitutional purview. State courts are not bound by interpretations of state law offered by the U.S. Supreme Court. Only with respect to questions within the federal court jurisdiction is the U.S. system in any sense unified.
112 *Dutton, supra* note 1 at para. 49.

Still, there may be some who favour the *Shutts* actual notice ideal as a reasonable standard when dealing with non-resident class members. In fact, it may be problematic in its overemphasis on litigative autonomy at the expense of fuller recovery for the class. Consider a case in which actual notice is, for one reason or another, impossible. *Shutts* requires the best possible notice under the circumstances, but it appears clear that the constitutionally imperative notice for non-resident plaintiffs is a higher standard than that which might otherwise prevail in state courts.[113] Yet notice which unduly consumes funds that might otherwise go into compensation is of questionable value.

Notice requirements serve two basic purposes: firstly and most obviously, they preserve litigative autonomy for those who do not wish to be part of the class.

But secondly, and at least equally importantly, notice requirements provide an avenue for class members to influence the conduct of the litigation, for instance, by appearing to object to the certification. Class members can be a crucial barometer for the court in determining whether the structural conflict of interest between class counsel and absent class members is being successfully managed, or whether the class is instead being "sold out" by a "sweetheart deal" such as a "scrip" settlement. Courts should consider in each case how much weight should be placed on each of these factors when notice is contemplated.

For instance, in a class involving numerous low value (that is, individually non-viable) claims, notice may be irrelevant from the point of view of litigative autonomy. No class member could pursue the issue in court on his or her own in any event; no rational member would opt out. In such a case, there may be no harm in allowing the action to proceed on his or her behalf with only "sample" notice. The purpose of the "sample" would be to invite participation and facilitate feedback with respect to the adequacy of any settlement. In interjurisdictional claims, these objectives are furthered by providing a mechanism whereby even only a small number of class members can register their objections meaningfully, possibly even through hearings conducted in their own jurisdictions.

In considering what constitutes adequate notice, the residence of the class members should be a factor, but it should not be the only factor. And

---

113 See John C. Coffee Jr., "Mass Torts After 'Georgine' and 'Castano'" *New York Law Journal* (30 May 1996): "The problem for defendants is, however, that *Phillips Petroleum v. Shutts* may impose higher and more costly notice requirements on such nationwide settlements in state court ...."

within the Canadian federation, it is a factor that need not be governed by provincial borders, but instead by proximity and relative ease of access to the courts. That is to say, it may be a challenge to enable a resident of a distant, rural community to participate in a class action conducted in a metropolitan centre, regardless of whether the rural community is in the same province or a neighbouring one.

In considering the notice requirements of a national opt-out class, therefore, some conclusions might be reached:

- It is not necessary, generally, to afford a higher level of notice to non-resident members, but it is not necessarily bad to do so, recognizing that an opt-out national class will make notice more effective and/or cheaper on a per-claim basis.
- One reason to consider enhanced notice for non-resident class members is if there are marked differences in the procedural law of the various provinces that might be lost to members if they are included in the national suit.[114]
- When considering adequacy of notice, a court might consider whether the per-member potential recovery justifies extraordinary steps to provide notice.
- In cases where, due to a low potential recovery amount, notice requirements may be sacrificed, it will often be better to provide excellent notice to only part of the class than poor notice to the class as a whole (to allow greater assessment of the degree and tenor of the objections from those class members notified).

D. THE FUTURE OF THE NATIONAL CLASS

The goals of tort and regulatory law, generally, and class actions, specifically, are better realized when claims are aggregated as fully as possible within the entirety of the population affected by the unlawful act. Practically speaking, this means that national classes will result in better compensation, improved access to justice, enhanced judicial economy, and superior deterrence effects than will province-by-province adjudication of large-scale claims. There will also be a meaningful reconciliation of tort insurance pre-

---

114 See footnote 28 and accompanying text. The court will need to be aware of this predicament, because it is not likely to be raised by either plaintiff's counsel (who will be pressing for national certification) or defence counsel (whose interest in depriving the foreign members of their procedural advantages might outweigh their incentive to oppose national certification).

miums and benefits as consumers paying nationally cost-averaged prices for goods or services will enjoy uniform protections.

Ironically, *Dutton*, which extended class actions uniformly across Canada, might make those actions more difficult to pursue and less effective in securing appropriate deterrence and compensation effects. Whether class actions are launched under the British Columbia/ULCC model, under the *Dutton* "common law class action," or under the Ontario process (whereby certifications in other provinces "hive off" those jurisdictions from the Ontario-based national class), Canadian class actions threaten to devolve into province-by-province adjudication, which may prove worse than chaotic; it may be catastrophic.

But if *Dutton* contains a recipe for chaos, it also presents an unrecognized opportunity to pursue genuine national — even, where appropriate, international — class actions in any jurisdiction in the country.

In British Columbia (and provinces that have adopted the British Columbia model through the *ULCC Model Act*), it is now arguable that the provisions permitting non-residents to participate on an opt-in basis is no longer exhaustive of the options for a national class. The common law, through *Dutton*, has advanced to permit national classes on an opt-out basis, binding all those persons who receive "sufficient notice" of the suit and an opportunity to opt out. If this approach proves to be incorrect, then the answer is clear — the British Columbia model must be abandoned, the opt-in requirement repealed, and national classes should be permitted in those jurisdictions no less than in Ontario and the remaining provinces, and governed only by the *Dutton* procedures.

Even though superior to province-by-province adjudication, Ontario's "national classes," which permit the "hiving off" of other provinces if overlapping actions are filed in those jurisdictions, have been a poor substitute for a true national class, because they encourage the free-rider problem and raise the spectre of blackmail among class counsel, which was described earlier. After *Dutton*, if a robust, true national opt-out class is not developed, the only true national classes that will survive under Ontario's present regime will be those that are not viable in other jurisdictions.

Ontario, it is now clear, need not have been so timid in extending its extra-territorial reach, and it need not qualify its certifications with provisions for entire provinces to "opt out" through competing certifications. Since *Morguard* and *Hunt* recognized in the Canadian constitution the doctrine of "full faith and credit," Canadian superior courts have been required to defer to valid orders made by sister courts in other provinces. This must include certification orders, where, to begin with, the certifying court had the jurisdiction to grant certification. The advantages of pursuing national classes, as we hope to have demonstrated, far outweigh competing concerns, and *Hunt* stresses the constitutional weight to be placed on the efficient resolution of inter-provincial litigation.

Of course, many details remain to be solved, not the least of which is the need for a mechanism to facilitate the consolidation of class actions on a national basis. Elsewhere, one of us has written about several ways to achieve this,[115] utilizing a central case-management system,[116] equitable powers of the courts, and statutory reform, such as the ULCC's model *Court Jurisdiction and Proceedings Transfer Act*,[117] which has, so far, been adopted in the Yukon,[118] Saskatchewan,[119] British Columbia,[120] and Nova Scotia.[121] Until courts become familiar with national classes or a centralized process is established, class counsel may have to defend their certification in other provinces when competing claims are launched or seek injunctive relief in their forum province.

But these are details conditioned upon the realization by courts and counsel alike of the advantages of proceeding through national, as opposed to provincial, opt-out classes, and the state of the law, which currently makes this an attainable, if as yet imperfectly realized, goal.

---

115 Jones, *Theory of Class Actions, supra* note 5 at 200–9.
116 Such as the Multidistrict Litigation (MDL) process in the U.S. federal court system, which permits consolidation of similar claims to a single court, at least for disposition of interlocutory and preliminary matters. The Judicial Panel on Multidistrict Litigation has the authority to transfer "civil actions involving one or more common questions of fact ... pending in different districts ... to any district for coordinated or consolidated pre-trial proceedings ... for the convenience of parties and witnesses and [to] promote the just and efficient conduct of such actions.": 28 U.S.C. 1407(a) (1993). Even though the transferee court is not empowered to conduct a trial of the transferred actions, it "ultimately disposes of most MDL cases": Rhonda Wasserman, "Duelling Class Actions" (2000) B.U.L. Rev. 461 at 510.
117 *Proceedings of the Uniform Law Conference of Canada (1994)* at 48 <www.ulcc.ca/en/us>.
118 S.Y. 2000, c. 7.
119 S.S. 1997, c. C-41.1 (effective March 1, 2004).
120 S.B.C. 2003, c. 28.
121 S.N.S. 2003, c. 2.

The Future of Large-Scale Claims in Canada

As we stressed in the introduction to this book, the high rate of settlement of large-scale claims (particularly once certified as class actions) makes any discussion of the law in the area inherently speculative. Without a constant generation of judicial precedent, lawyers and other students of the field are left with precious little certainty regarding the law that will govern any emerging claim. Crucial and far-reaching questions going to the heart of substantive grounds of liability, conflict of laws principles, and procedural matters remain unanswered.

But this is not to say that no trends can be gleaned from the recent Canadian experience with large-scale claims. We here conclude with a summary of what are, in our view, the most significant of these.

We are of the view that the law will continue to grow to respond to the increasingly complex risks and harms that are inevitable in modern society. The law will continue to adapt to the reality that many of those harms affect large classes of persons. However, the way in which Canadian law grows will be more orderly and cautious than in the United States, and we will certainly not see the adoption of ideas such as absolute product line liability. Indeed, despite repeated calls for the adoption of strict liability from U.S. jurisprudence, it is our view that the substantive law of product liability will likely remain an analysis based on negligence principles. There are a number of reasons for the different paths that will be taken by Canadian and U.S. law. On the deterrence side, Canadian citizens rely more (rightly or wrongly) on public regulation to ensure product safety and corporate responsibility. In particular, Canadian law does promote the robust use of civil juries to police and punish corporate malfeasance as in the United States. On the compensation side, the existence of universal health insurance and various programs of income protection in Canada tend to lessen (though certainly not eliminate) the reliance on civil litigation as a source of compensation for personal injury. These differences certainly do not mean that the law will remain static.

While Canadian law will remain based on a negligence analysis, Canadian courts have shown themselves to be very sensitive to issues of corporate misconduct and to the informational imbalance between manufacturers and consumers. It is our view that the duties owed by manufacturers within the context of negligence law will continue to be viewed more strictly, particularly in the case of products designed for ingestion or intimate use, or where mistakes made in design or production could cause serious injury or death.

Canadian courts may well adopt a progressive stance with respect to the proof of product liability and other large scale claims. The law in other jurisdictions to which our Courts frequently look indicate a strong, perhaps unstoppable, movement towards the acceptance of probabilistic proof of all elements of mass claims when individualistic proof is either not possible or not economically feasible. Canadian class proceedings legislation seems particularly well-suited to innovation in this area. As such, class actions in Canada will continue to be settled through such aggregate assessments of liability and damages; distribution of awards to third parties where victims are not identifiable will become more common.

Class actions, embraced only gingerly by the Canadian bar at first, have begun to come into their own in Canada as powerful regulatory, as well as compensatory, tools. Canada's class proceedings legislation, among the most flexible and powerful in the world, will be used with increasing imagination and vigour. The period of difficult growth will continue until interjurisdictional wrinkles are worked out. As the strength and experience of the plaintiffs' bar continues to grow, the value of the class proceeding as an important element of *public law* will become more fully realized.

Just *how* the "interjurisdictional wrinkles" of multi-province or even international claims will be resolved remains to be seen. The imperial march of the "real and substantial connection" test appears to have trampled all but the last vestiges of borders among the various areas of private international law — jurisdiction, choice of law, recognition and enforcement of judgments. It is possible, if not likely, that analysis in all these areas will be subsumed with a single consideration: what is fair (in the U.S. parlance, what affords "due process") to plaintiffs and defendants? Our views of "fairness" in this context will need to evolve to more closely match the increasingly borderless economic and social community in which we live our non-legal lives.

The Supreme Court has, in the recent decision of *Canfor*, invited governments to become more involved in the pursuit of large-scale wrongdoers, particularly in areas of environmental harm or failure of stewardship. It remains to be seen whether the provinces will rise to the challenge of using the newly-enhanced tool of the *parens patraie* lawsuit to pursue environmental harms, given the potential economic consequences of bringing actions against core industries, or whether they will prefer to develop legislative schemes, such as those in the areas of contaminated-site cleanup and tobacco health care costs recovery, to set off the public harms caused by particularly dangerous industries.

Because of the number of people affected, and the potentially huge economic consequences that can attach to large scale claims, such actions, although generally framed as private law, have many "public law" overtones. As a result, such litigation, more than most, is interwoven with the political and social realities of the times. In some cases, the question becomes "what will the public tolerate?" rather than "what will the law support?" Plaintiffs, lawyers and corporations are in this sense political actors, as has perhaps been most clearly seen in the recent "fast food litigation" in the U.S. There plaintiffs strenuously blamed their obesity on the failures of vendors to alert them to the ingredients in their food; the vendors equally strenuously pled the plaintiffs' own weak will, wilful blindness and sloth. This debate led in rapid succession to a series of lawsuits, intense political discussion and lobbying efforts on all sides, a couple of legal defeats for overweight plaintiffs, proposed legislation to prevent fast food litigation and — perhaps most surprisingly of all — healthier fast food (through the focus on reducing trans fats, for instance, and the introduction of "healthy choice" menus).

Of course, most large-scale claims are considerably more mundane, but certainly from the point of view of public welfare, no less important, than the debate over fast food. How well lawyers, the courts, and legislatures deal with the development of this field may be one of the most significant legal questions of our time. It has been our ambition with this book to set out the law in something approaching its full context — considering procedural and substantive rules together with a view to judging how well they function in the result — in order that students of the topic at all levels of engagement might better understand its development.

Table of Cases

2475813 Nova Scotia Ltd. v. Rodgers, [2001] N.S.J. No. 21, 2001 NSCA 12, 189 N.S.R. (2d) 363 147
472900 B.C. Ltd. v. Thrifty Canada, Ltd., [1998] B.C.J. No. 2944, 168 D.L.R. (4th) 602, [1999] 6 W.W.R. 416 (C.A.) 413
671122 Ontario Ltd. v. Sagaz Industries Canada Inc. (1998), 40 O.R. (3d) 229, [1998] O.J. No. 2194 (Gen. Div.) 135
801962 Ontario Inc v. Mackenzie Trust Co., [1994] O.J. No. 2105 (Gen. Div.) 286

Abdool v. Anaheim Management Ltd., [1993] O.J. No. 1820, 15 O.R. (3d) 39 (Gen. Div.), aff'd [1995] O.J. No. 16, 21 O.R. (3d) 453 (Div. Ct.) 333, 335, 341
Abel v. Eli Lilly & Co., 418 Mich. 311, 343 N.W.2d 164 (Sup. Ct. 1984) 217
Abernathy v. Superior Hardwoods, Inc., 704 F.2d 963 (7th Cir. 1983) 186
Adams v. Cape Industries, [1990] 1 Ch. 433 (C.A.) 283
Admiral Ins. Co. v. Columbia Casualty Ins. Co., 194 Mich. App. 300, 486 N.W.2d 351 (Mich. Ct. App. 1992) 139
Aetna Financial Services Ltd. v. Feigelman, [1985] 1 S.C.R. 2, [1985] S.C.J. No. 1 ....401, 445
Agent Orange Prod. Liability Litigation, 996 F.2d 1425, 1993 U.S. App. LEXIS 15365 (2d Cir. 1993) 329
Aiken v. Ontario (Premier), [1999] O.J. No. 2866, 45 O.R. (3d) 266 (S.C.J.) 154

Air Canada v. British Columbia, [1989] 1 S.C.R. 1161, [1989]
S.C.J. No. 44 ....158, 256
Air Canada v. M & L Travel Ltd., [1993] 3 S.C.R. 787, [1993] S.C.J. No. 118 256
Alberta (Minister of Public Works, Supply and Services) v. Nilsson (2002),
220 D.L.R. (4th) 474, [2002] A.J. No. 1474 (C.A.) 150
Alexander & Alexander, Inc. v. Fritzen, 68 N.Y.2d 968, 503 N.E.2d 102
(Ct. App. 1986) 138
Allard v. Manahan (1974), 46 D.L.R. (3d) 614, [1974] 3 W.W.R. 588 (S.C.) 57
Alleco, Inc. v. Harry & Jeanette Weinberg Found., Inc., 665 A.2d 1038
(Md. 1995) 138
Allen v. Tobias (1958), 98 CLR 367 272
Ambrogi v. Gould, Inc., 750 F. Supp. 1233, 1990 U.S. Dist. LEXIS 15473
(M.D. Pa. 1990) 179
Amchem Prods. v. Windsor, 521 U.S. 591, 117 S. Ct. 2231 (1997) 329
Amchem Products Inc. v. British Columbia (Workers' Compensation Board),
[1993] 1 S.C.R. 897, [1993] S.C.J. No. 34, 77 B.C.L.R. (2d) 62 ......403, 413–14
American Pioneer Life Ins. Co. v. Williamson, 704 So. 2d 1361, 1997
Ala. LEXIS 385 (Ala. Sup. Ct. 1997) 188
Amertek Inc. v. Canadian Commercial Corp., [2003] O.J. No. 3177,
229 D.L.R. (4th) 419 (S.C.J.) 196
Anderson v. Stevens (1981), 125 D.L.R. (3d) 736, [1981] B.C.J. No. 1849
(S.C.) 110
Anderson v. Wilson (1999), 44 O.R. (3d) 673, [1999] O.J. No. 2494
(C.A.), leave to appeal refused [1999] S.C.C.A. No. 476 ....29, 177–78, 181
Andrews v. Grand & Toy Alberta Ltd., [1978] 2 S.C.R. 229, 83 D.L.R.
(3d) 452 ....170, 174
Andrulonis v. United States, 924 F.2d 1210, 1991 U.S. App. LEXIS 1265
(2d Cir. 1991)..57
Anns v. Merton London Borough Council, [1978] A.C. 728 (H.L.) 16–17, 128
Apache Corp. v. Moore, 960 S.W.2d 746, 1997 Tex. App. LEXIS 4031
(Tex. Ct. App. 1997) 188
Applied Equipment Corp. v. Litton Saudi Arabia Ltd., 7 Cal.4th 503,
869 P.2d 454 (Sup. Ct. Calif. 1994) 138
Arch v. American Tobacco Co., 175 F.R.D. 469, 1997 U.S. Dist.
LEXIS 7890 (E.D. Pa. 1997)...299
Arendale v. Canada Bread Co. Ltd., [1941] 2 D.L.R. 41, [1941] O.W.N. 69
(C.A.) 33, 34
Armory v. Delamirie (1722), 1 Stra. 505, 93 E.R. 664 (K.B.)......................262, 268
Armstrong v. Servier Canada Inc., 2002 BCSC 1248, [2002]
B.C.J. No. 1939, 24 C.P.C. (5th) 103 ....425, 432

Arnold v. Teno, [1978] 2 S.C.R. 287, 83 D.L.R. (3d) 609.................................170, 174
Ash v. Lloyd's Corp. (1991), 6 O.R. (3d) 235, 87 D.L.R. (4th) 65 (Gen. Div.),
    aff'd (2001) 55 O.R. (3d) 688, [2001] O.J. No. 3403 (C.A.) 418
Ashby v. White (1703), 2 Ld. Raym 938 150
Assiniboine South School Division 3 v. Hoffer (1971), 21 D.L.R. (3d) 608,
    [1971] 4 W.W.R. 746 (C.A.), aff'd (1973), 40 D.L.R. (3d) 480,
    [1973] 6 W.W.R. 765 (S.C.C.) 28
Athey v. Leonati, [1996] 3 S.C.R. 458, [1996] S.C.J. No. 102 230
Attorney General (Ontario) v. Scott, [1956] S.C.R. 137, 1 D.L.R.
    (2d) 433 404–5
Attorney General v. Blake, [2000] H.L.J. No. 47, [2001] 1 A.C. 268 197
Audenhove v. Nova Scotia (AG) (1994), 134 N.S.R. (2d) 294, [1994]
    N.S.J. No. 384 (S.C.) 353
Austin v. Rescon Const (1984) Ltd., [1989] B.C.J. No. 646, 36 B.C.L.R.
    (2d) 21 (C.A.)..196
Authorson v. Canada (Attorney General), [2003] 2 S.C.R. 40, 2003 SCC 39,
    [2003] S.C.J. No. 40 ....148, 159
Auton (Guardian ad litem of) v. British Columbia (Minister of Health),
    2004 SCC 78, rev'g (2002), 220 D.L.R. (4th) 411, [2003] 1 W.W.R. 42
    (B.C.C.A.), aff'g [2000] 8 W.W.R. 227, 78 B.C.L.R. (3d) 55 (S.C.),
    supp. reasons (2001), 197 D.L.R. (4th) 165, [2001] 3 W.W.R. 447
    (S.C.) 162–63, 164
Ayers v. Jackson, 106 N.J. 557, 525 A.2d 287 (Sup. Ct. 1987) 178–79, 181

B. v. Bayer Nederland BV (Hoge Raad, 9 October 1992, NJ 1994, 535)...............233
B.M. v. British Columbia (Attorney General), 2001 BCSC 419,
    [2001] B.C.J. No. 1160, aff'd 2004 BCCA 402, [2004]
    B.C.J. No. 1506, [2004] 10 W.W.R. 286 247
Baird v. Canada (AG), [1984] 2 F.C. 160, 148 D.L.R. (3d) 1 (C.A.).......................106
Baker v. Suzuki Motor Co. (1993), 12 Alta. L.R. (3d) 193, [1993]
    A.J. No. 605 (Q.B.) 39–40, 71–72, 73, 96, 109
Ball v. Joy Mfg. Co., 755 F. Supp. 1344, 1990 U.S. Dist. LEXIS 16011
    (S.D. W.Va. 1990) 179
Bamford v. Turnley (1862), 3 B. & S. 66, 122 E.R. 27 115
Bank of Bermuda Ltd v. Stutz, [1965] 2 O.R. 121 (H.C.J.) 427
Bare Land Condominium Plan 8820814 v. Birchwood Village Greens Ltd.,
    [1999] 6 W.W.R. 753, [1998] A.J. No. 1300 (Q.B.) 257
Barker v. Lull Engineering Co., 20 Cal.3d 413, 573 P.2d 443 (Sup. Ct. 1978) 42
Barker v. Ray (1826), 2 Russ. 63 269
Barnes v. American Tobacco Co., 161 F.3d 127, 1998 U.S. App.
    LEXIS 28624 (3d Cir. C.A.) 181

Barwick v. English Joint Stock Bank (1867), L.R. 2 Exch. 259 257
Batavia Times Publishing Co v. Davis (1977), 18 O.R. (2d) 252, 82 D.L.R.
    (3d) 247 (H.C.J.) aff'd (1979), 102 D.L.R. (3d) 192 (Ont. C.A.) 427
Bates (Guardian Of) v. Horkoff, [1991] A.J. No. 960, 119 A.R. 270 (Q.B.)........259
Bazley v. Curry, [1999] 2 S.C.R. 534 ....99, 144
Beals v. Saldanha, [2003] 3 S.C.R. 416, 2003 SCC 72,
    [2003] S.C.J. No. 77 ....412, 415–16, 430
Beeching v. Lloyd (1855), 3 Drew. 227, 61 E.R. 890...352
Belsat Video Marketing Inc. v. Astral Communications Inc. (1998),
    54 O.T.C. 84, [1998] O.J. No. 654 (Gen. Div.), aff'd (1999),
    118 O.A.C. 105, [1999] O.J. No. 343 (C.A.) 136
Bendall v. McGhan Medical Corp. (1993), 106 D.L.R. (4th) 339,
    (1993), 14 O.R. (3d) 734, [1993] O.J. No. 1948 (Gen. Div.) 339, 452
Bersch v. Drexel Firestone, Inc., 519 F.2d 974, 1975 U.S. App.
    LEXIS 14917 (2d Cir. 1975)..458
BG Preeco I (Pacific Coast) Ltd v. Bon Street Holdings Ltd. (1989),
    60 D.L.R. (4th) 30, [1989] B.C.J. No. 1032 (C.A.) 285
Bilbie v. Lumley (1802), 2 East 469, 102 E.R. 448 256
Blake v. Minister of Correctional Services (1984), 5 C.H.R.R. D/2417
    (Ont. Bd. Of Inquiry) 251
Bledsoe v. Combs, 2000 U.S. Dist. LEXIS 7434 (S.D. Ind.) 166
Blue Cross and Blue Shield of New Jersey, Inc. v. Phillip Morris, Inc.,
    133 F. Supp. 2d 162 (E.D.N.Y. 2001) 250, 251, 252, 253, 314
BMW of North America v. Gore, 646 So.2d 619, 1994 Ala. LEXIS 411
    (Ala. Sup. Ct. 1994), rev'd 517 U.S. 559, 116 S. Ct. 1589 (1996)..........186, 187
Boatland of Houston, Inc. v. Bailey, 609 S.W.2d 743, 1980 Tex.
    LEXIS 398 (Sup.Ct. 1980) 38
Boehler v. Blaser Jagdwaffen GmbH, [2000] B.C.J. No. 931,
    2000 BCSC 710..296
Bolduc c. Cie Montréal Trust (C.A.Q.), [1989] A.Q. no 705 (C.A.) 459
Bonnington Castings Ltd v. Wardlaw [1956] AC 613 (H.L.) 231
Borel v. Fibreboard Paper Products Corp., 493 F.2d 1076, 1088,
    1974 U.S. App. LEXIS 8654 (5th Cir. 1974), cert. denied
    419 U.S. 869, 95 S. Ct. 127 52
Bourque c. Laboratoires Abbott Ltée, [1998] A.Q. no 1836 (S.C.) 459
Bow Valley Husky (Bermuda) Ltd. v. Saint John Shipbuilding Ltd. (1995),
    126 D.L.R., (4th) 1, [1995] N.J. No. 150 (C.A.), var'd [1997] 3 S.C.R. 1210,
    153 D.L.R. (4th) 385, [1997] S.C.J. No. 111 ....19–20, 50, 60, 111, 113
Bowen v. MacMillan (1921), 21 O.W.N. 23, [1921] O.J. No. 160 (H.C.)................353

Bradley v. Saskatchewan Wheat Pool (1984), 31 Sask.R. 254, [1984]
    S.J. No. 234 (Q.B.) 323
Brewer v. Ravan, 680 F. Supp. 1176 (M.D. Tenn. 1988) 179
Brimner v. Via Rail Canada Inc., [2000] O.J. No. 2747, 50 O.R. (3d) 114
    (S.C.J.) 193
Bristol Tramways & Carriage Co. v. Fiat Motors Ltd., [1910] 2 K.B. 831 77
British Columbia (Director of Trade Practices) v. Ideal Credit Referral Services
    Ltd. (1997), 31 B.C.L.R. (3d) 37, [1997] B.C.J. No. 693 (C.A.) 420, 421
British Columbia v. Canadian Forest Products Ltd., [2004] 2 S.C.R. 74,
    [2004] S.C.J. No. 33 119
British Columbia v. Imperial Tobacco Canada Ltd., 2003 BCSC 877,
    [2003] B.C.J. No. 1309, 227 D.L.R. (4th) 323, rev'd 2004 BCCA 269,
    [2004] B.C.J. No. 1007, leave to appeal to S.C.C. granted [2004]
    S.C.C.A. No. 302 .... 246, 303
British Mutual Banking Co., Ltd. v. Charnwood Forest Rail. Co. (1887),
    18 Q.B.D. 714, [1886–90] All E.R. Rep. 280 (C.A.) 257
Broome v. Cassell & Co Ltd., [1972] AC 1027 (H.L.) 195
Brown v. Howard (1701) 1 Eq. Cas. Abr. 163, pl. 4 319
Brushett v. Cowan (1987), 42 C.C.L.T. 64, [1987] N.J. No. 254 (S.C.T.D.),
    rev'd in part (1990), 69 D.L.R. (4th) 743, [1990] N.J. No. 145 (C.A.) 110
Buchan v. Ortho Pharmaceutical (Canada) Ltd. (1984), 8 D.L.R.
    (4th) 373 (Ont. H.C.), aff'd (1986), 25 D.L.R. (4th) 658
    (Ont. C.A.) 23–24, 28, 51–52, 54, 55, 58, 63–64, 97
Buckley v. Lever Brothers Ltd., [1953] O.R. 704, [1953] 4 D.L.R. 16 (H.C.J.) 82
Buckley v. Mott (1919), 50 D.L.R. 408 (N.S.S.C.) 14–15, 324
Bunn v. Ribcor Holdings Inc. (1998), 38 C.L.R. (2d) 291, [1998]
    O.J. No. 1790 (Gen. Div.) 345
Burnie Port Authority v. General Jones Pty. Limited (1994),
    179 C.L.R. 520, 120 A.L.R. 42 (H.C.) 124
Burns v. Jaquays Mining Corp., 156 Ariz. 375, 752 P.2d 28 (Ct. App. 1987) 179
Burnside v. Abbott Laboratories, 351 Pa. Super. 264, 505 A.2d 973 (1985) 141
Bushell v. T & N plc (1992), 67 B.C.L.R. (2d) 330, [1992] B.C.J. No. 1120
    (C.A.) 414–15
Bux v. Slough Metals Ltd., [1974] 1 All E.R. 262 (C.A.) 106
Bywater v. Toronto Transit Commission (1998), 27 C.P.C. (4th) 172,
    [1998] O.J. No. 4913 (Gen. Div.) 176, 342, 343

Camacho v. Honda Motor Co., 741 P.2d 1240, 1987 Colo. LEXIS 575 (1987) 108
Cambridge Water Co. v. Eastern Counties Leather plc, [1994] 1 All E.R. 53,
    [1993] H.L.J. No. 41 122

Campbell v. Flexwatt Corp. (1996), 25 B.C.L.R. (3d) 329, 50 C.P.C.
(3d) 290 (S.C.), rev'd in part (1997), 44 B.C.L.R. (3d) 343,
[1997] B.C.J. No. 2477 (C.A.) 342
Campbell v. Flexwatt Corp., [1998] 6 W.W.R. 275, [1997] B.C.J. No. 2477
(C.A.) 367
Campbell v. General Motors Corp. 32 Cal.3d 112, 649 P.2d 224
(Sup. Ct. 1982) 41
Campbell v. Toronto Star Newspapers Ltd., [1990] O.J. No. 1646,
73 D.L.R. (4th) 190 (Div. Ct.) 154
Canada (Canadian Human Rights Commission) v. Canada (Department of
National Health and Welfare) (1998), 38 C.C.E.L. (2d) 121,
[1998] F.C.J. No. 432 (T.D.), aff'd [1999] F.C.J. No. 40,
41 C.C.E.L. (2d) 3 (C.A.) 251
Canada (Canadian Human Rights Commission) v. Canadian Liberty Net,
[1998] 1 S.C.R. 626, [1998] S.C.J. No. 31 451
Canada Cement Lafarge Ltd v. British Columbia Lightweight Aggregate Ltd.,
[1983] 1 S.C.R. 452, 145 D.L.R. (3d) 385........................... 135, 136, 137, 140, 141
Canada Paper Co. v. Brown (1922), 63 S.C.R. 243, 66 D.L.R. 287 199
Canada v. Saskatchewan Wheat Pool, [1983] 1 S.C.R. 205, 143 D.L.R. (3d) 9 105
Canadian Indemnity Co. v. Canadian Johns-Manville Co., [1990]
2 S.C.R. 549, [1990] S.C.J. No. 82 .... 257, 258
Canadian International Marketing Distributing Ltd v. Nitsuko Ltd. (1990),
56 B.C.L.R. (2d) 130, [1990] B.C.J. No. 569 (C.A.) 398
Canadian National Railway Co. v. Norsk Pacific Steamship Co., [1992]
1 S.C.R. 1021, 91 D.L.R. (4th) 289 17
Candler v. Crane, Christmas & Co [1951] 2 K.B. 164 (C.A.) 128
Cannon Mfg. Co. v. Cudahy Packing Co., 267 U.S. 333, 45 S. Ct. 250 (1925) 306
Caparo Industries plc v. Dickman, [1990] 1 All E.R. 568 128
Caputo v. Imperial Tobacco Ltd., [2004] O.J. No. 299, 236 D.L.R.
(4th) 348 (S.C.J.) 176
Car & General Insurance Corp. Ltd v. Seymour, [1956] S.C.R. 322,
2 D.L.R. (2d) 369 111
Carlill v. Carbolic Smoke Ball Company, [1893] 1 Q.B. 256 (C.A.) 14
Carmel Holdings Ltd v. Atkins, [1977] B.C.J. No. 687, [1977]
4 W.W.R. 655 (S.C.) 121
Carom v. Bre-X Minerals Ltd. (1999), 43 O.R. (3d) 441, [1999]
O.J. No. 281 (Gen. Div.) 453–54, 458, 462
Carom v. Bre-X Minerals Ltd. (1999), 44 O.R. (3d) 173, [1999]
O.J. No. 1662 (S.C.J.) 311, 339, 343, 345

Carom v. Bre-X Minerals Ltd. (2000), 51 O.R. (3d) 236, [2000]
O.J. No. 4014 (C.A.)..131
Carter v. Brown & Williamson Tobacco Corp., 778 So.2d 932, 2000 Fla.
LEXIS 2318 (Sup. Ct. Fla.) 53–54
Castano v. American Tobacco Co., 84 F.3d 734, 1996 U.S. App.
LEXIS 11815 (5th Cir. 1996)...329
Castle v. Davenport Campbell Co., [1952] O.R. 565, [1952] 3 D.L.R. 540 (C.A.)....35
Cates Construction v. Talbot Partners, 53 Cal. App. 4th 1420,
62 Cal. Rptr. 2d 548 (Ct. App. 1997)..188
Cayzer, Irvine & Co. v. Carron Co. (1884), 9 App. Cas. 873 (H.L.) 109
CC&L Dedicated Enterprise Fund (Trustee of) v. Fisherman (2001),
18 B.L.R. (3d) 240, [2001] O.J. No. 4622 (S.C.J.) 131
Certified Question United States Dist. Court Order v. Philip Morris,
621 N.W.2d 2, 2001 Minn. LEXIS 3 (Sup. Ct. Minn. 2001) 252
Chace v. Crane Canada Inc. (1996), 26 B.C.L.R. (3d) 339, [1996]
B.C.J. No. 1606 (S.C.), aff'd (1997), 44 B.C.L.R. (3d) 264,
[1997] B.C.J. No. 2862 (C.A.) 342
Chace v. Crane Canada Inc. (1997), 44 B.C.L.R. (3d) 264, 14 C.P.C. (4th) 197,
[1997] B.C.J. No. 2862 (C.A.) 192, 193, 356
Chadha v. Bayer Inc. (2001), 54 O.R. (3d) 520, [2001] O.J. No. 1844
(Div. Ct.), aff'd (2003), 63 O.R. (3d) 22, [2003] O.J. No. 27 (C.A.) 312
Chancey v. May (1722), Prec. Ch. 592, 24 E.R. 265 318
Chaplin v. Hicks, [1911] 2 KB 786 (C.A.) 226
Cimino v. Raymark, 151 F.3d 297, 1998 U.S. App. LEXIS 20096
(5th Cir. 1998) 255
Cimino v. Raymark, 751 F. Supp. 649, 1990 U.S. Dist. LEXIS 15708
(E.D. Tex. 1990) 255, 268
Cincinnati Ins. Co. v. General Motors Corp., 1994 Ohio App. LEXIS 4960
(6th App. Dist. 1994)..268
Cipollone v. Liggett, 644 F. Supp. 283 (D.N.J. 1986) 43, 44
Cipollone v. Liggett, 683 F. Supp 1487, 1493–95 (D. N.J. 1988),
aff'd in part, rev'd in part, 893 F.2d 541 (3d. Cir 1990),
cert. granted, 111 S. Ct. 1386 (1991) 43, 44
Cobbold v. Time Canada Ltd. (1976), 13 O.R. (2d) 567, 71 D.L.R.
(3d) 629 (H.C.J.) 352, 353
Coburn v. 4-R Corp., 77 F.R.D. 43 (E.D. Ky. 1977), mandamus denied
sub nom. Union Light, Heat & Power Co. v. United States
Dist. Court, 588 F.2d 543 (6th Cir. 1978) 328
Cohen v. Bowdoin, 288 A.2d 106, 1972 Me. LEXIS 269
(Sup. Jud. Ct. 1972)...139

Collins v. Eli Lilly Co., 342 N.W.2d 37, 116 Wis.2d 166 (Sup. Ct. 1984),
    cert. denied 469 U.S. 826, 105 S.Ct. 107 ....221, 222
Cominco Ltd v. Westinghouse Can Ltd. (1981), 127 D.L.R. (3d) 544,
    [1981] B.C.J. No. 1952 (S.C.), var'd [1983] B.C.J. No. 2339,
    147 D.L.R. (3d) 279 (C.A.) 292
Condominium Corp. No. 7921945 v. Cochrane, [2004] A.J. No. 16,
    352 A.R. 71 (Prov. Ct.) 248
Conklin v. Smith, [1978] 2 S.C.R. 1107, 88 D.L.R. (3d) 317 173
Continental Trend Resources v. Oxy USA, 101 F.3d 634, 1996 U.S. App.
    LEXIS 30742 (10th Cir. 1996) 187
Cook v. Lewis, [1951] S.C.R. 830, [1952] 1 D.L.R. 1 ....62, 216
Cook v. Parcel, Mauro, Hultin & Spaanstra, P.C. (1997), 143 D.L.R.
    (4th) 213, [1997] B.C.J. No. 428 (C.A.) 414, 431
Cooper v. Gibbons (1813), 3 Camp. 363 269
Cooper v. Hobart, [2001] 3 S.C.R. 537, [2001] S.C.J. No. 76 130
Corey v. Havener, 182 Mass. 250, 65 N.E. 69 (1902) 230
Coriale (Litigation guardian of) v. Sisters of St. Joseph of Sault Ste. Marie,
    [1998] O.J. No. 3735, 41 O.R. (3d) 347 (Gen. Div.) 266
Cotic v. Gray (1981), 33 O.R. (2d) 356, 124 D.L.R. (3d) 641 (C.A.) 107
Cotter v. Levy (2000), 95 A.C.W.S. (3d) 810 (Ont. S.C.J.) 117
Cottrelle v. Gerrard (2003), 178 O.A.C. 142, [2003] O.J. No. 4194 (C.A.) 247
Coughlin v. Kuntz, [1989] B.C.J. No. 2365, 42 B.C.L.R. (2d) 108 (C.A.) 185
Cowell v. British American Tobacco Australia Services Ltd., [2003]
    HCATrans 384..271
Cowen v. British Columbia (AG), [1941] S.C.R. 321, [1941] 2 D.L.R. 687 438
Crits v. Sylvester, [1956] O.R. 132, 1 D.L.R. (2d) 502 (C.A.) 21
Crocker v. Sundance Northwest Resorts Ltd., [1988] 1 S.C.R. 1186,
    [1988] S.C.J. No. 60 112
Crofter Hand Woven Harris Tweed Co. v. Veitch, [1942] A.C. 435 (H.L.) 136
Cunningham v. Hamilton (1995), 29 Alta. L.R. (3d) 380, [1995]
    A.J. No. 476 (C.A.) 283
Cunningham v. PFL Life Ins. Co., 42 F. Supp. 2d 872, 1999 U.S. Dist.
    LEXIS 5088 (N.D. Iowa, 1999) 139
Curtis v. State of California, 128 Cal. App. 3d 668, 180 Cal. Rptr. 843
    (5th Dist. 1982)..42

D.E. (Guardian ad litem of) v. British Columbia, [2003] B.C.J. No. 1563,
    2003 BCSC 1013 103
Dalkon Shield, 521 F. Supp. 1188 (N.D. Cal.), modified 526 F. Supp. 887
    (N.D. Cal. 1981), vacated 693 F.2d 847 (9th Cir. 1982), cert. denied
    459 U.S. 1171..328

Dallaire v. Paul Émile Martel Inc., [1989] 2 S.C.R. 419, 62 D.L.R. (4th) 182 37
Daly v. General Motors Corp., 20 Cal. 3d 725, 575 P.2d 1162 (1978) 108
Dartez v. Fibreboard Corp., 765 F.2d 456, 1985 U.S. App. LEXIS 30938
    (5th Cir. 1985) 53
Dawejko v. Jorgensen Steel Co., 290 Pa. Super. Ct. 15, 434 A.2d 106 (1981) 291
Dawes v. Jajcaj (1995), 15 B.C.L.R. (3d) 240, [1995] B.C.J. No. 2366 (S.C.) 264
De la Giroday v. Brough (1997), 33 B.C.L.R. (3d) 171, [1997] B.C.J. No. 1146
    (C.A.), leave to appeal to S.C.C. refused [1997] S.C.C.A. No. 381 230
De Salaberry Realties Ltd v. M.N.R. (1974), 46 D.L.R. (3d) 100,
    [1974] C.T.C. 295 (F.C.T.D.) 284
Denny v. Ford Motor Co., 87 N.Y.2d 248, 662 N.E.2d 730 (C.A. 1995) 94
Derdiarian v. Felix Contracting Corp., 51 N.Y.2d 308, 414 N.E.2d 666
    (Ct. App. 1980) 205
Derry v. Peek, [1886–90] All E.R. Rep. 1, 14 App. Cas. 337 (H.L.) 125
Deshane v. Deere & Co (1993), 50 C.P.R. (3d) 449, 15 O.R. (3d) 225 (C.A.) 50
Desjarlais v. Canada, [2002] F.C.J. No. 1272, 224 F.T.R. 37 (T.D.) 359
Doe v. Toronto (Metropolitan) Police Commissioners, [1989] O.J. No. 471,
    58 D.L.R. (4th) 396 (H.C.J.) 161
Donoghue v. Stevenson, [1932] A.C. 562 ....14, 16, 17, 19, 20, 28, 32, 42, 68,
    313, 324
DOT v. PSC Resources, Inc., 175 N.J. Super. 447, 419 A.2d 1151
    (N.J. Super. Ct. 1980)..288
Doyle v. Olby (Ironmongers) Limited, [1969] 2 Q.B. 158, [1969]
    2 All E.R. 119 (C.A.) 127
Dubé v. Labar, [1986] 1 S.C.R. 649, [1986] S.C.J. No. 29 111
Duca Community Credit Union Ltd. v. Giovannoli, [2000] O.J. No. 1199,
    [2000] O.T.C. 229 (S.C.J.) 137
Duke of Bedford v. Ellis, [1901] A.C. 1, [1900–03] All E.R. Rep. 694 (H.L.) 352
Dyk v. Protec Automotive Repairs, [1997] B.C.J. No. 1895, 151 D.L.R.
    (4th) 374 (S.C.) 264
Dykun v. Odishaw, [2001] A.J. No. 1002, 2001 ABCA 204 322

E.D.L.P. v. Children's Aid Society of Metropolitan Toronto, [1995]
    O.J. No. 3814 (Gen. Div.) 297
Edmonton (City) v. Lovat Tunnel Equipment Inc. (2000), 88 Alta. L.R.
    (3d) 283, [2001] 4 W.W.R. 490 (Q.B.) 21
Eggleton v. Broadway Agencies Ltd. (1981), 32 A.R. 61, [1981] A.J.
    No. 792 (Q.B.) 427
Eisen v. Carlisle & Jacquelin, 417 U.S. 156, 94 S. Ct. 2140 (1974) 326
Elf Atochem North America v. United States, 908 F. Supp. 275, 1995
    U.S. Dist. LEXIS 18258 (E.D. Pa. 1995) 290

Ell v. Con-Pro Industries Ltd. (1992), 11 B.C.A.C. 174, [1992] B.C.J. No. 513 398
Elliott v. Canadian Broadcasting Corp. (1995), 25 O.R. (3d) 302,
　[1995] O.J. No. 1710 (C.A.)..154, 155
Emanuel v. Symon, [1908] 1 K.B. 302 (C.A.), rev'g [1907] 1 K.B. 235 426
Endean v. Canadian Red Cross Society (1997), 148 D.L.R. (4th) 158,
　[1997] B.C.J. No. 1209 (S.C.), rev'd in part (1998), 157 D.L.R.
　(4th) 465, [1998] B.C.J. No. 724 (C.A.) 333, 342
Endean v. Canadian Red Cross Society (1999), 68 B.C.L.R. (3d) 350,
　[2000] 1 W.W.R. 688, [1999] B.C.J. No. 2180 (S.C.) 317, 437
Endean v. Canadian Red Cross Society, [1997] B.C.J. No. 1209, 48 D.L.R.
　(4th) 158 (S.C.), rev'd [1998] B.C.J. No. 724 (C.A.) 264–65
Engle v. R.J. Reynolds Tobacco Co, 2000 WL 33534572 (Fla. Cir. Ct. 2000)......387
Epstein v. First Marathon Inc., [2000] O.J. No. 452, 2 B.L.R. (3d) 30
　(S.C.J.) 388
Erie Railroad Co. v. Tompkins, 304 U.S. 64 (1938) 428
Escola v. Coca Cola Bottling Co., 24 Cal. 2d 453, 150 P.2d 436
　(Sup. Ct. 1944) 93
Evans v. General Motors Corp., 359 F.2d 822, 1966 U.S. App. LEXIS 6477
　(7th Cir. 1966) 108

Fairchild v. Glenhaven Funeral Services Ltd., [2002] H.L.J. No. 22, [2002]
　UKHL 22, [2002] 3 All E.R. 305 ....27, 232–33, 234, 235–36, 237, 245
Farmer v. Interbake Foods Ltd., [1981] N.S.J. No. 518, 49 N.S.R. (2d) 111
　(S.C.T.D.)...79
Farnham v. Fingold, [1973] 2 O.R. 132, 33 D.L.R. (3d) 156 (C.A.) 353
Farro v. Nutone Electrical Ltd. (1990), 68 D.L.R. (4th) 268 (Ont. C.A.) 24–25
FDIC v. Hamilton, 122 F.3d 854, 1997 U.S. App. LEXIS 20908
　(10th Cir. 1997) 187
Femcare Ltd v. Bright, [2000] FCA 512 (H.C.A.) 461–62
Ferrigno v. Eli Lilly & Co., 175 N.J. Super. 551, 420 A.2d 1305
　(Sup. Ct. 1980) 217
Fidelity Electronics of Canada Ltd. v. Fuss (1995), 77 O.A.C. 37, [1995]
　O.J. No. 4319 (Div. Ct.)..282
Filteau v. Aviation Roger Forgues (unreported, 30 January 1997,
　Quebec 200-06-000001-951, Que. S.C.) 116
Fisher v. CHT Ltd. and Others (No. 2), [1966] 2 Q.B. 475 (C.A.) 382
Fletcher v. Bealey (1885), 28 Ch.D. 688, 54 L.J.Ch. 424 199
Fontaine v. British Columbia (Official Administrator), [1998]
　1 S.C.R. 424, 156 D.L.R. (4th) 577 ....25, 33–34
Ford Motor Co. v. Nowak, 638 S.W.2d 582, 1982 Tex. App. LEXIS 5007
　(C.A. 1982) 39

Ford Motor Co. v. Sperau, 708 So.2d 111, 1997 Ala. LEXIS 386 (Ala. Sup. Ct. 1997) 188
Fording Coal Ltd v. Harnischfeger Corp Of Canada, [1990] B.C.J. No. 773, 1 B.L.R. (2d) 313 (S.C.), aff'd [1991] B.C.J. No. 3682, 8 B.C.A.C. 250 (C.A.) 73–74
Foss v. Harbottle (1843), 2 Hare 461, [1982] 2 W.L.R. 31 130
Frame v. Smith, [1987] 2 S.C.R. 99 146–47
Franklin v. University of Toronto (2001), 56 O.R. (3d) 698, [2001] O.J. No. 4321 (S.C.J.) 313
Friend v. Pep Boys, 3 Phila. Co. Rptr. 363 (Pa.Com.Pl. 1979), aff'd 433 A.2d 539 (Pa. Super. Ct. 1981) 270
Frulla v. Phillip Morris Inc., (W.D. Tenn. 10 January 1990) [unreported] 108
Furlan v. Shell Oil Co. (2000), 77 B.C.L.R. (3d) 35, [2000] B.C.J. No. 1334 (C.A.), 2000 BCCA 404, [2000] 7 W.W.R. 433 .... 367, 410

Gallant v. Beitz (1983), 42 O.R. (2d) 86, 148 D.L.R. (3d) 522 (H.C.J.) 108
Gaming Corp. of America v. Dorsey & Whitney, 88 F.3d 536, 1996 U.S. App. LEXIS 15326 (8th Cir. 1996) 139
Garaj v. De Bernardo (2002), 213 D.L.R. (4th) 661 (Ont. C.A.) 431
Gardiner v. Gray (1815), 171 E.R. 46; 4 Camp. 144 12
Gariepy v. Shell Oil Co. (2000), 51 O.R. (3d) 181, [2000] O.J. No. 3804 (S.C.J.) 221
Gariepy v. Shell Oil Co., [2002] O.J. No. 3495, 23 C.P.C. (5th) 393 (S.C.J.) 372–73
Garland v. Consumers' Gas Co., [2001] O.J. No. 4651, 57 O.R. (3d) 127 (C.A.), rev'd [2004] 1 S.C.R. 629, [2004] S.C.J. No. 21 .... 133, 134
Gee v. White Spot Ltd. (1986), 7 B.C.L.R. (2d) 235, [1986] B.C.J. No. 896 (S.C.) 77–78
General Motors of Canada Ltd. v. City National Leasing Ltd., [1989] 1 S.C.R. 641, [1989] S.C.J. No. 28 169
General Motors of Canada Ltd. v. Naken (1983), 144 D.L.R. (3d) 385, [1983] 1 S.C.R. 72 .... 323, 332, 349, 447
Georgine v. Amchem Prods., 83 F.3d 610, 1996 U.S. App. LEXIS 11191 (3d Cir. 1995), rehearing denied 1996 U.S. App. LEXIS 15416 329
Gianitsis v. American Brands, Inc., 685 F. Supp. 853, 1988 U.S. Dist. LEXIS 4268 (Dist. N.H. 1988) 47
Gilboy v. American Tobacco Co., 572 So.2d 289, 1990 La. App. LEXIS 2594 (1990) 47
Gilford Motor Co., Ltd. v. Horne, [1933] Ch. 935, [1933] All E.R. Rep. 109 (C.A.) 282
Goldthorpe v. Logan, [1943] 2 D.L.R. 519, [1943] O.W.N. 215 (C.A.) 85

Good-Wear Treaders Ltd v. D & B Holdings Ltd. (1979), 98 D.L.R. (3d) 59, [1979] N.S.J. No. 532 (C.A.), aff'g [1978] N.S.J. No. 202, 28 N.S.R. (2d) 316 (S.C.T.D.) 51, 108
Gould v. A & M Battery & Tire Serv., 950 F. Supp. 653, 1997 U.S. Dist. LEXIS 379 (Pa. Dist. Ct. 1997) 290
Granewich v. Harding, 329 Ore. 47, 985 P.2d 788 218
Grant v. Australian Knitting Mills Ltd., [1936] A.C. 85 (P.C.) 34, 77
Greaves & Co. Contractors v. Baynham, Mickle & Partners, [1975] 3 All E.R. 99, [1975] 1 W.L.R. 1095 (C.A.) 86
Greenman v. Yuba Power Products, Inc., 59 Cal. 2d 57, 377 P.2d 897 (Supt. Ct. 1963) 93
Gregorio v. Intrans-Corp. (1994), 18 O.R. (3d) 527, [1994] O.J. No. 1063 (C.A.) 283
Gregory & Co v. Quebec (Securities Commission), [1961] S.C.R. 584, 28 D.L.R. (2d) 721 421
Griesenbeck v. American Tobacco Co., 897 F. Supp. 815 (D.N.J. 1995) 108
Griffiths v. Peter Conway Ltd. [1939] 1 All E.R. 685 (C.A.)................................94
Grimshaw v. Ford Motor Co., 119 Cal. App. 3d 757, 174 Cal. Rptr. 348 (C.A. 1981) 197
Guarantee Co. of North America v. Caisse Populaire De Shippagan Ltée (1988), 86 N.B.R. (2d) 342, [1988] N.B.J. No. 42 (Q.B.) 353
Guerin v. Canada, [1984] 2 S.C.R. 335, 13 D.L.R. (4th) 321 147
Guimond v. Quebec (Attorney General), [1996] 3 S.C.R. 347, [1996] S.C.J. No. 91 159

Haig v. Bamford, [1977] 1 S.C.R. 466, 72 D.L.R. (3d) 68 128
Haines v. Liggett Group Inc., 824 F. Supp. 414 (D.N.J. 1993) 314
Halberstam v. Welch, 705 F.2d 472, 227 U.S. App. D.C. 167 (1983) 139
Hall v. E.I. duPont De Nemours & Co., 345 F.Supp. 353, 17 Fed. R. Serv.2d 835 (E.D.N.Y. 1972)...27, 219
Halphen v. Johns-Manville Sales Corp:, 484 So.2d 110 (La. 1986) 48
Hamstra v. British Columbia Rugby Union, [1989] B.C.J. No. 1521, 1 C.C.L.T. (2d) 78 (S.C.) 106
Hansen v. Mountain Fuel Supply Co., 858 P.2d 970, 218 Utah Adv. Rep. 54 (Sup. Ct. 1993) 182–83
Hansen v. Twin City Construction Co. (1982), 19 Alta. L.R. (2d) 335, 136 D.L.R. (3d) 111 (Q.B.) 19
Hanten v. School District of Riverview Gardens, 183 F.3d 799, 136 Ed. Law. Rep. 761 (8th Cir. 1999) 138, 139
Harrigan v. United States, 63 F.R.D. 402 (E.D.Pa. 1974) 327

Harrington v. Dow Corning Corp., [1997] B.C.J. No. 400, 29 B.C.L.R.
(3d) 88 (S.C.) 441
Harrington v. Dow Corning Corp., 2000 BCCA 605, [2000] B.C.J. No. 2237,
193 D.L.R. (4th) 67 (C.A.) 343, 344, 367, 408–9, 410, 450
Hedley-Byrne v. Heller, [1964] AC 465 ....127, 128
Heimler v. Calvert Caterers Ltd. (1975), 8 O.R. (2d) 1, 56 D.L.R. (3d) 643
(C.A.) 23
Henningsen v. Bloomfield Motors, Inc., 32 N.J. 358, 161 A.2d 69
(Sup. Ct. 1960) 92
Herber v. Johns-Manville Corp., 785 F.2d 79, 1986 U.S. App. LEXIS
22722 (3d Cir. 1986)..179
Hercules Managements Ltd. v. Ernst & Young, [1997] 2 S.C.R. 165,
[1997] S.C.J. No. 51 ....127, 129, 139
Hernandez v. Motor Vessel Skyward, 61 F.R.D. 558 (S.D.Fla.1973),
aff'd 507 F.2d 1278 (5th Cir. 1975) 328
Hilao v. Estate of Marcos, 103 F.3d 767, 1996 U.S. App. LEXIS 32974
(9th Cir. 1996) 251, 252
Hill v. Church of Scientology of Toronto, [1995] 2 S.C.R. 1130,
[1995] S.C.J. No. 64 190
Hilton v. Guyot, 159 U.S. 113 (1895) 406, 428
Hobbs v. Northeast Airlines Inc., 50 F.R.D. 76 (E.D.Pa. 1970) 327
Hodgkinson v. Simms, [1994] 3 S.C.R. 377, [1994] S.C.J. No. 84 147
Hollick v. Toronto (City), 2001 SCC 68, [2001] 3 S.C.R. 158,
[2001] S.C.J. No. 67 ....332, 346, 347, 362
Hollis v. Dow Corning Corp., [1995] 4 S.C.R. 634, 129 D.L.R.
(4th) 609, [1995] S.C.J. No. 104 ....23, 49–50, 52, 54–55, 58, 59–60, 61–63,
85, 90, 98, 225, 252
Holt Cargo Systems Inc. v. ABC Containerline N.V. (Trustee of), [2001]
3 S.C.R. 907, [2001] S.C.J. No. 89, 2001 SCC 90 406
Holt v. PPG Industries Canada Inc., [1983] A.J. No. 191, 25 C.C.L.T. 253
(Q.B.) 96, 97
Home Office v. Dorset Yacht, [1970] A.C. 1004 (H.L.)...................................151
Homer Estate v. Eurocopter S.A., [2003] B.C.J. No. 929, 12 B.C.L.R. (4th)
321 (C.A.) 271
Honhon c. Canada (Procureur général), [1999] J.Q. no 4370 (S.C.) 318, 437
Horne v. Canada (Minister of Agriculture (1995), 129 Nfld. & P.E.I.R. 109,
[1995] P.E.I.J. No. 60 (S.C.) 353
Horsley v. MacLaren, [1972] S.C.R. 441, 22 D.L.R. (3d) 545 205
Hotson v. East Berkshire Health Authority, [1987] A.C. 750, [1987]
H.L.J. No. 32 228

How v. Tenants of Bromsgrove (1681), 1 Vern. 22 319
Howard Estate v. British Columbia, [1999] B.C.J. No. 585, 66 B.C.L.R.
 (3d) 199 (S.C.) 160
Hoy v. Medtronic, Inc., 2001 BCSC 1343, [2001] B.C.J. No. 1968,
 94 B.C.L.R. (3d) 169 450
Huff v. Price (1990), 76 D.L.R. (4th) 138 (B.C.C.A.) 192
Huff v. White Motor Corp., 565 F.2d 104, 1977 U.S. App. LEXIS
 11296 (7th Cir. 1977) 108
Hughes v. Sunbeam Corp. (Canada) (2002), 61 O.R. (3d) 433, [2002]
 O.J. No. 3457 (C.A.) 367
Hunt v. Carey Canada Inc., [1990] 2 S.C.R. 959, [1990]
 S.C.J. No. 93 .... 140, 142, 143, 265–66
Hunt v. T & N plc (1989), 117 N.R. 361 (B.C.C.A.) 136, 143
Hunt v. T&N plc, [1993] 4 S.C.R. 289, [1993] S.C.J. No. 125,
 109 D.L.R. (4th) 16 .... 399, 401, 402, 423, 424–25, 446, 447
Hymowitz v. Eli Lilly Company, 539 N.E.2d 1069, 73 N.Y. 2d 487
 (Ct. App. N.Y. 1988), cert. denied Rexall Drug Co. v. Tigue,
 493 U.S. 944, 110 S.Ct. 350 (1989) 218, 222

I.J. Manufacturing Ltd. v. Wolkowski, [1996] B.C.J. No. 2449 (S.C.) 74
In Re North Dakota Personal Injury Asbestos Litigation No. 1, 737 F. Supp.
 1087, 1990 U.S. Dist. LEXIS 6048 (D.N.D. 1990) 139
In re Oil Spill by Amoco Cadiz off Coast of France, 1984 AMC 2123,
  1984 U.S. Dist. LEXIS 17480 (N.D. Ill. 1984), aff'd 954 F.2d 1279,
  1992 U.S. App. LEXIS 833 (7th Cir. 1992) 303
Instant Colour Pty Ltd & Ors v. Canon Australia Pty, [1996] 763 F.C.A. 1 272
International Brotherhood of Teamsters v. United States, 431 U.S. 324,
 97 S.Ct. 1843 (1977) 250
International Business Machines Co. v. Scherban, [1925] 1 W.W.R. 405
 (Sask. C.A.) 77
International Capital Corp. v. Schafer (1995), 130 Sask.R. 23, [1995]
 S.J. No. 24 (Q.B.) 353
Interprovincial Co-operatives Ltd v. Dryden Chemicals Ltd., [1976]
 1 S.C.R. 477, 53 D.L.R. (3d) 321 440

Jenkins v. Raymark Indus. Inc., 109 F.R.D. 269 (E.D. Tex. 1985),
 aff'd 782 F.2d 468 (5th Cir. 1986) 327, 328
Joan W. v. City of Chicago, 771 F.2d 1020 (7th Cir. 1985) 186
John Campbell Law Corp. v. Strata Plan 1350, [2001] B.C.J. No. 2037,
 2001 BCSC 1342 124

Jones v. Mobil Oil Canada Ltd. (1999), 72 Alta. L.R. (3d) 369, [2000]
1 W.W.R. 479 (Q.B.) 122
Jordan v. Schatz, 2000 BCCA 409, [2000] B.C.J. No. 1303, 189 D.L.R.
(4th) 62 398
JP Porter Co. Ltd. v. Bell (1954), 35 M.P.R. 13, [1955] 1 D.L.R. 62 (N.S.S.C.) 121
JTI-Macdonald Corp. v. British Columbia (Attorney General) (2000),
74 B.C.L.R. (3d) 149, [2000] B.C.J. No. 349 (S.C.) 303

K & S Partnership v. Continental Bank, 952 F.2d 971 (8th Cir. 1999) 138
Kamilewicz v. Bank of Boston Corp., 92 F.3d 506, 1996 U.S. App.
LEXIS 20100 (7th Cir. 1996) 369
Kamloops (City) v. Nielsen, [1984] 2 S.C.R. 2, 10 D.L.R. (4th) 641 17
Kearney v. Phillip Morris Inc., 916 F. Supp. 61 (D.Mass. 1996) 108
Kenora (Town) Police Service v. Savino, [1996] O.J. No. 2758,
3 C.P.C. (4th) 159 (Gen. Div.) 155
Kerr v. Danier Leather Inc. (2001), 7 C.P.C. (5th) 74, [2001]
O.J. No. 950 (S.C.J.)..131
Kitchen v. Royal Air Force Association, [1958] 1 W.L.R. 563 (C.A.) 227
Knippen v. Ford Motor Co., 178 U.S. App. D.C. 227, 546 F.2d 993
(D.C. Cir. 1976)..108
Knupffer v. London Express Newspapers Ltd., [1944] AC 116 (H.L.) 154
Kordyban v. Windmill Orchards Ltd., [2000] B.C.J. No. 407,
2000 BCSC 348 76
Kosmopoulos v. Constitution Insurance Co. of Canada, [1987] 1 S.C.R. 2,
[1987] S.C.J. No. 2 284
Kotler v. American Tobacco Co., 731 F. Supp. 50; 1990 U.S. Dist.
LEXIS 1743 (Dist. Mass. 1990), aff'd 926 F.2d 1217,
1990 U.S. App. LEXIS 21906 (1st Cir. 1990), cert. granted
and judgment vacated 505 U.S. 1215, 112 S. Ct. 3019 (1992) 47
Kreutner v. Waterloo Oxford Co-operative Inc., [2000] O.J. No. 3031,
50 O.R. (3d) 140 (C.A.)...36
Krznaric v. Chevrette, [1997] O.J. No. 4712, 154 D.L.R. (4th) 527 (Gen. Div.) 165

Lac Minerals Ltd. v. International Corona Resources Ltd., [1989]
2 S.C.R. 574, [1989] S.C.J. No. 83 ....147, 194–95
Laferrière v. Lawson, [1991] 1 S.C.R. 541, [1991] S.C.J. No. 18....................228, 229
Laker Airways v. Sabena, 731 F.2d 909, 787 A.L.R. Fed. 751 (D.C. Cir. 1984) 425
Lalese Enterprises Inc (C.O.B. Basic Stock Cookware) v. Arete Technologies
Inc., [1994] B.C.J. No. 1867, 59 C.P.R. (3d) 438 (S.C.) 71
Lambert v. Lastoplex Chemicals Co., [1972] S.C.R. 569, 25 D.L.R.
(3d) 121 ....18, 49, 55–56, 72

Lambton v. Mellish, [1894] 3 Ch 163 230
Lamke v. Futorian Corp., 1985 OK 47, 709 P.2d 684 (Sup. Ct. Okla. 1985)......108
Langmead v. Admiral Cruises, 696 So.2d 1189, 1997 Fla. App. LEXIS
    5111 (Fla. Ct. App. 1997) 188
Lawson v. Sherwood (1916), 1 Starkie 314 269
Laxton v. Orkin Exterminating Co., 639 S.W.2d 431, 1982 Tenn. LEXIS
    344 (S.C. 1982) 182
Leaf River Forest Prods. v. Deakle, 661 So.2d 188, 1995 Miss. LEXIS 455 322
LeBlanc v. Marson Canada Inc. (1995), 146 N.S.R. (2d) 392, [1995]
    N.S.J. No. 509 (C.A.)...33, 34
Lee v. OCCO Developments Ltd. (1994), 148 N.B.R. (2d) 321, [1994]
    N.B.J. No. 218 (Q.B.), aff'd (1996), 181 N.B.R. (2d) 241,
    [1996] N.B.J. No. 438 (C.A.) 353
Leisure Time Distributors Ltd. v. Calzaturificio S.C.A.R.P.A.-S.P.A. (1996),
    5 C.P.C. (4th) 320, [1996] B.C.J. No. 1963 (S.C.) 415
Lem v. Barotto Sports Ltd. (1976), 1 C.C.L.T. 180, [1976] A.J. No. 442 (C.A.) 51
Lemesurier v. Union Gas Co. Of Canada (1975), 8 O.R. (2d) 152,
    57 D.L.R. (3d) 344 (H.C.J.) 19
Lemmex v. Sunflight Holidays Inc. (2002), 213 D.L.R. (4th) 627, 60 O.R.
    (3d) 54, [2002] O.J. No. 2131 (C.A.) 431
Leufkens v. Alba Tours International Inc. (2002), 213 D.L.R. (4th) 614,
    [2002] O.J. No. 2129 (C.A.) 431
Lewis v. Todd, [1980] 2 S.C.R. 694, 115 D.L.R. (3d) 257 231
Liebeck v. McDonald's Restaurants. Inc., 1995 WL 360309 (D.N.M. 1994) 188
Life Ins. Co. of Ga. v. Parker, 726 So. 2d 619, 1998 Ala. LEXIS 303
    (Ala. Sup. Ct. 1998) 188
Lindal v. Lindal, [1981] 2 S.C.R. 629 175
Lindsay v. Davidson, [1911] 1 W.W.R. 125 (Sask. C.A.) 264
Lindsey v. Dow Corning Corp. (In re Silicone Gel Breast Implant Prods.
    Liab. Litig.), 1994 U.S. Dist. LEXIS 12521 458
London Drugs Ltd v. Kuehne & Nagel International Ltd., [1992] 3 S.C.R. 299,
    [1992] S.C.J. No. 84 111
London Life Insurance Co. v. Manufacturers Life Insurance Co. (1999),
    87 C.P.R. (3d) 229, [1999] F.C.J. No. 395 (T.D.) 254
Lonrho Ltd. v. Shell Petroleum Co. Ltd., [1982] A.C. 173 (H.L.) 135, 136, 137
Lyons v. Consumers Glass Co., [1981] B.C.J. No. 2180, 28 B.C.L.R. 319 (S.C.) 69

Macdonald v. Vapor Canada Ltd., [1977] 2 S.C.R. 134, 66 D.L.R. (3d) 1 169
Mackay v. Commercial Bank of New Brunswick (1874), L.R. 5 P.C. 394,
    43 L.J.P.C. 31 257

MacKinnon v. National Money Mart Co., 2004 BCCA 137, [2004]
B.C.J. No. 435, 44 C.P.C. (5th) 72 .... 134, 367
MacKinnon v. National Money Mart Co., 2004 BCSC 140, [2004]
B.C.J. No. 176, 25 B.C.L.R. (4th) 189 134
MacKinnon v. Vancouver City Savings Credit Union, 2004 BCSC 125,
[2004] B.C.J. No. 155, 46 C.P.C. (5th) 88 134
MacLachlan & Mitchell Homes Ltd v. Frank's Rentals & Sales Ltd.,
[1979] A.J. No. 508, 106 D.L.R. (3d) 245 (C.A.) 97
MacPherson v. Buick Motor Co., 217 N.Y. 382, 111 N.E. 1050 324
Malette v. Shulman (1990), 67 D.L.R. (4th) 321, [1990] O.J. No. 450 (C.A.) 103
Malhab c. Métromédia CMR Montréal Inc. (2003), 226 D.L.R. (4th) 722,
[2003] J.Q. no 2521 (C.A.) 157, 158
Mallett v. McMonagle, [1970] A.C. 166, [1969] 2 All E.R. 178 (H.L.) 231–32
Marchesi v. Eastern Airlines, Inc., 68 F.R.D. 500, 1975 U.S. Dist. LEXIS
16175 (E.D.N.Y. 1975) 327
Maritime Telegraph and Telephone Co. v. Pre Print Inc. (1996),
131 D.L.R. (4th) 471, [1996] N.S.J. No. 7 (C.A.) 418
Markt & Co. Ltd. v. Knight Steamship Co. Ltd., [1910] 2 KB 1021 (C.A.)....322, 352
Marschler v. G. Masser's Garage, [1956] O.R. 328, 2 D.L.R. (2d) 484 (H.C.J.)....19
Marshall v. Houghton, [1923] 2 W.W.R. 553 (Man. C.A.) 427
Martin v. Abbott Laboratories, 689 P.2d 368, 102 Wash.2d 581
(Sup. Ct. Wash. 1984) 221, 222
Masson c. Thompson, [1994] R.J.Q. 1032, J.E. 94-699 (S.C.), aff'd
[1995] R.J.Q. 329, 67 Q.A.C. 75 (C.A.) 459
Mathews v. Coca Cola Co. of Canada, [1944] O.R. 207, 2 D.L.R. 355 (C.A.) 34–35
Mattar v. Alberta (Public Trustee) (1952), 5 W.W.R. (N.S.) 29, [1952]
3 D.L.R. 399 (Alta. S.C. App. Div.) 427
Matusiak v. British Columbia and Yukon Territory Building and Construction
Trades Council, [1999] B.C.J. No. 2416 (S.C.) 145–46
Mavilia v. Stoeger Industries, 574 F. Supp. 107 (D. Mass 1983) 109
Maxey v. Canada Permanent Trust Co. (1984), 27 C.C.L.T. 238,
[1984] M.J. No. 85 (C.A.) 149
Mayburry v. Ontario (Liquor Control Board), [2001] O.J. No. 1494,
O.T.C. 271 (S.C.J.) 21–22
McCabe v. British American Tobacco Australia Services Limited, [2002]
VSC 73, rev'd [2002] V.S.C.A. 197 270
McCann v. Ottawa Sun, [1993] O.J. No. 3103, 16 O.R. (3d) 672 (Gen. Div.) 155
McDonnell Douglas Corp. v. United States Dist. Court, 523 F.2d 1083
(9th Cir. 1975) 327

McElhaney v. Eli Lilly & Co., 575 F. Supp. 228 (U.S. Dist. 1983), aff'd 739 F.2d 340 (8th Cir. 1984) 221
McGhee v. National Coal Board, [1972] 3 All E.R. 1008, 116 Sol. J. 967 (H.L.) 223–24, 234
McGlasson v. Barger, 163 Colo. 438, 431 P.2d 778 (Sup. Ct. 1967) 139
McMorran v. Dominion Stores Ltd. (1977), 14 O.R. (2d) 559, 74 D.L.R. (3d) 186 (H.C.J.) 80
McPherson v. Buick Motor Company, 217 N.Y. 382, 111 N.E. (1916) 14
Meisel v. Tolko Industries Ltd., [1991] B.C.J. No. 105 (S.C.) 40, 41, 96, 97
Merry v. Westinghouse Elec. Corp., 684 F. Supp. 847, 1988 U.S. Dist. LEXIS 3610 (M.D. Pa. 1988) 179
Metro-North Commuter R.R. v. Buckley, 521 U.S. 424, 117 S. Ct. 2113 (1997) 181
Middlesex Concrete Products & Excavating Corp. v. Carteret Industrial Assoc., 37 N.J. 507, 181 A.2d 774 (Sup. Ct. 1962) 139
Mihalchuk v. Ratke (1966), 55 W.W.R. 555, [1966] S.J. No. 43 (Q.B.) 121
Millard v. North George Capital Management Ltd., [2000] O.J. No. 1535, 47 C.P.C. (4th) 365 (S.C.J.) 382, 383
Minnich v. Ashland Oil Co., 473 N.E.2d 1199, 15 Ohio St. 3d 396 (Sup. Ct. 1984) 217
Mira Design Co v. Seascape Holdings Ltd. (1982), 36 B.C.L.R. 355, [1982] B.C.J. No. 51 (S.C.) 134
Mississauga (City) v. Keifer Recaro Seating, Inc., [2001] O.J. No. 1893 (C.A.) 21
Mithras Management Ltd v. New Visions Entertainment Corp. (1992), 90 D.L.R. (4th) 726, [1992] O.J. No. 842 (Gen. Div.) 417
Mobil Oil Australia Pty Ltd v. Victoria, [2002] HCA 27 462
Moran v. Pyle National (Canada) Ltd., [1974] 1 S.C.R. 393, 2 W.W.R. 586, 43 D.L.R. (3d) 239 ....211, 406, 407, 438
Morguard Investments Ltd. v. De Savoye, [1990] 3 S.C.R. 1077, [1990] S.C.J. No. 135 ....399–400, 401, 405–6, 407, 419, 427, 441, 444, 445–46, 455
Morguard Investments Ltd. v. M.E. Pritchard Associates Ltd. (1999), 30 C.P.C. (4th) 117, [1999] B.C.J. No. 680 (S.C.) 415
Moses v. Shore Boat Builders Ltd. (1993), 106 D.L.R. (4th) 654, [1993] B.C.J. No. 1910 (C.A.), leave to appeal to S.C.C. refused [1994] 1 S.C.R. xi, 109 D.L.R. (4th) vii 408, 410, 430
Moss v. Ferguson (1979), 35 N.S.R. (2d) 181, [1979] N.S.J. No. 798 (T.D.) 21
Multi Malls Inc v. Tex Mall Properties Ltd. (1980), 28 O.R. (2d) 6, 108 D.L.R. (3d) 399 (H.C.J.), aff'd (1981), 37 O.R. (2d) 133, 128 D.L.R. (3d) 192 (C.A.) 227
Multiple Access Ltd v. McCutcheon, [1982] 2 S.C.R. 161, 138 D.L.R. (3d) 1 440

Murano v. Bank of Montreal, [1995] O.J. No. 883, 20 B.L.R. (2d) 61
 (Gen. Div.), var'd [1998] O.J. No. 2897, 41 O.R. (3d) 222 (C.A.) 268
Murphy v. Atlantic Speedy Propane Ltd. (1979), 103 D.L.R. (3d) 545,
 35 N.S.R. (2d) 422 (T.D.)...21, 41
Murphy v. Brentwood District Council, [1990] 2 All E.R. 908,
 [1991] 1 A.C. 398 (H.L.) 17
Murray v. Sperry Rand Corp. (1979), 23 O.R. (2d) 456, 96 D.L.R. (3d) 113
 (H.C.J.) 113
Muscutt v. Courcelles (2002), 213 D.L.R. (4th) 577, [2002] O.J. No. 2128
 (C.A.) 414, 431

Nally v. Volkswagen of America, Inc., 539 N.E.2d 1017, 405 Mass. 191
 (Mass. Sup. Judic. Ct. 1989) 269
Nanaimo Immigrant Settlement Society v. British Columbia, [2001]
 B.C.J. No. 209, 84 B.C.L.R. (3d) 208 (C.A.)...159, 160
Nantais v. Telectronics Proprietary (Canada) Ltd. (1995), 25 O.R. (3d) 331,
 127 D.L.R. (4th) 552 (Gen. Div.), leave to appeal denied (1995),
 129 D.L.R. (4th) 110, 40 C.P.C. (3d) 263 (Gen. Div.), leave to appeal
 denied (1996), 28 O.R. (3d) 523, 134 D.L.R. (4th) 470
 (Gen. Div.) 29, 181, 339, 452, 453, 456, 462
Nernberg v. Shop Easy Stores Ltd. (1966), 57 D.L.R. (2d) 741,
 57 W.W.R. 162 (Sask. C.A.)...18
Neufeld v. Manitoba, [2001] M.J. No. 500, 161 Man.R. (2d) 18 (Q.B.), [2002]
 M.J. No. 374, var'd [2002] M.J. No. 374, [2002] 11 W.W.R. 395 (C.A.)........164
Neufeld v. Manitoba, 2001 MBQB 14, [2001] M.J. No. 37....................................358
Nicholson v. Atlas Steel Foundry and Engineering Co. Ltd., [1957]
 1 WLR 613 (H.L.) 213
Nicholson v. John Deere Ltd. (1986), 58 O.R. (2d) 53, 34 D.L.R.
 (4th) 542 (H.C.) 36, 38
Nix v. Temple University of Commonwealth System of Higher Educ.,
 408 Pa. Super. 369, 596 A.2d 1132 (Pa. Super. Ct. 1991) 139
Non-Marine Underwriters, Lloyd's of London v. Scalera, [2002] 1 S.C.R. 551......103
Noon v. Sailor, 2000 U.S. Dist. LEXIS 7419 (S.D. Ind.) 166
Norberg v. Wynrib, [1992] 2 S.C.R. 226, [1992] S.C.J. No. 60..........................103
Nutreco Canada Inc. v. F. Hoffman-La Roche Ltd., 2001 BCSC 1146,
 [2001] B.C.J. No. 1581, 10 C.P.C. (5th) 351 (S.C.) 431

O'Brien v. Muskin Corp., 94 N.J. 169, 463 A.2d 298 (Sup. Ct. 1983)..................38
O'Fallon v. Inecto Rapid (Canada) Ltd. et al., [1940] 4 D.L.R. 276
 (B.C.C.A.) 18, 56

O'Neal v. Home Town Bank, 237 Ga. App. 325, 514 S.E.2d 669
(Ga. Ct. App. 1999)..139
Ochoa v. Canadian Mountain Holidays Inc., [1996] B.C.J. No. 2026 (S.C.) 113
Odhavji Estate v. Woodhouse, [2003] 3 S.C.R. 263, [2003] S.C.J. No. 74 151
Ontario (Human Rights Commission) v. Etobicoke (Borough), [1982]
1 S.C.R. 202, 132 D.L.R. (3d) 14..250
Ontario New Home Warranty Program v. Chevron Chemical Co., [1999]
O.J. No. 2245, 46 O.R. (3d) 130 (S.C.J.) 312, 382, 383–84
Ortenberg v. Plamondon (1914), 24 Que. K.B. 69..157
Ortiz v. Fibreboard Corp., 527 U.S. 815, 119 S. Ct. 2295..............................328, 330
Ostash v. Sonnenberg (1968), 63 W.W.R. 257, 67 D.L.R. (2d) 311 (Alta. C.A.) 19
Overseas Tankship (U.K.) Ltd. v. Morts Dock & Engineering Co. Ltd.
(The "Wagon Mound"), [1961] A.C. 388 211

P.D. v. Allen, [2004] O.J. No. 3042, [2004] O.T.C. 645 (S.C.J.).........................248
P.R.O. Holdings Ltd. v. Atlantic Speedy Propane Ltd., [2003] N.B.J. No. 148,
[2003] N.B.R. (2d) (Supp.) No. 22 (Q.B.) 245
Pacific Mutual. Life Insurance Co. v. Haslip, 499 U.S. 1, 111 S. Ct. 1032
(1991) 187
Pack v. Warner (County) No. 5 (1964), 44 D.L.R. (2d) 215, 46 W.W.R. 422
(Alta. C.A.)..19
Palsgraf v. Long Island Railroad Company, 248 N.Y. 339, 162 N.E. 99
(N.Y.A.D. 1928), rearg. den. 249 N.Y. 511, 164 N.E. 564 (N.Y. 1928)..........205
Paoli R.R. Litig., 916 F.2d 829, 1990 U.S. App. LEXIS 16631 (3d Cir. 1990) 179
Parrott v. Carr Chevrolet, Inc., 56 Ore. App. 257, 965 P.2d 440
(Ct. App. 1998) 188
Parsons v. Canadian Red Cross Society, [1999] O.J. No. 3572,
40 C.P.C. (4th) 151 (S.C.J.) 318, 437
Passwaters v. General Motors Corp., 454 F.2d 1270, 1972 U.S. App.
LEXIS 11929 (8th Cir. 1972) 108
Patenaude v. Roy (1988), 46 C.C.L.T. 173, [1988] A.Q. no 326 (S.C.) 106
Pauli v. Ace Ina Insurance Co., [2004] A.J. No. 883, 2004 ABCA 253,
242 D.L.R. (4th) 420 ....358, 373
Pawar v. Canada, [1997] F.C.J. No. 1288, 137 F.T.R. 231 (T.D.)..........................160
Pearson v. Boliden Ltd., [2002] B.C.J. No. 2593, 222 D.L.R. (4th) 453,
2002 BCCA 624 ....107, 130, 131, 132, 417, 440, 442
Pearson v. Inco Ltd., [2002] O.J. No. 3532, 27 C.P.C. (5th) 171 (S.C.J.),
aff'd [2004] O.J. No. 317, 183 O.A.C. 168 (S.C.J.)...372
Pearson v. Inco Ltd., 2002 Ont. Sup. C.J. LEXIS 104 310
Peek v. Gurney, [1861–73] All E.R. Rep. 116, L.R. 6 H.L. 377 126

Peel (Regional Municipality) v. Canada, [1992] 3 S.C.R. 762, [1992]
    S.C.J. No. 101 ....133, 159, 193–94
Pelagatti v. Cohen, 536 A.2d 1337 (Pa. Super. Ct. 1987)...139
Pennsylvania R.R. v. United States, 111 F.Supp. 80 (D.N.J. 1953) 326
Pepper v. Litton, 308 U.S. 295, 60 S. Ct. 238 (1939) 284
Peppiatt v. Nicol (1993), 16 O.R. (3d) 133, [1993] O.J. No. 2722
    (Gen. Div.)...340, 342
Peppiatt v. Nicol (1998), 71 O.T.C. 321, [1998] O.J. No. 3370 (Gen. Div.) 341
Perlmutter v. Beth David Hospital, 308 N.Y. 100, 123 N.E.2d 792
    (C.A. 1954) 87–88, 89
Petersen v. Ab Bahco Ventilation (1979), 17 B.C.L.R. 335, 107 D.L.R. (3d) 49
    (S.C.) 432
Pettkus v. Becker, [1980] 2 S.C.R. 834, 117 D.L.R. (3d) 257 ....132, 133
Phillips Petroleum Co. v. Shutts, 472 U.S. 797, 105 S. Ct. 2965
    (1985) 328, 452, 460
Phillips v. Ford Motor Co. Of Canada, [1971] 2 O.R. 637, 18 D.L.R. (3d) 641
    (C.A.), rev'g [1970] 2 O.R. 714, 12 D.L.R. (3d) 28 (H.C.J.) 95, 96
Phillips v. Kimwood Machine Co., 269 Or. 485, 525 P.2d 1033 (1974) 42, 98
Pinney v. Nelson, 183 U.S. 144, 22 S. Ct. 52 (1901) 302
Porter v. Joe, [1979] N.S.J. No. 648, 106 D.L.R. (3d) 206 (S.C.T.D.) 106
Positive Seal Dampers Inc. v. M & I Heat Transfer Products Ltd. (1991),
    2 O.R. (3d) 225, [1991] O.J. No. 3383 (Gen. Div.) 136
Posner v. Essex Ins. Co., 178 F.3d 1209, 1999 U.S. App. LEXIS 14021
    (11th Cir. 1999)138 138
Potter v. Firestone Tire & Rubber Co., 863 P.2d 795, 6 Cal. 4th 965
    (Sup. Ct. 1993) 182, 183–84
Powder Mountain Resorts Ltd. v. British Columbia, [2001] B.C.J. No. 2172,
    94 B.C.L.R. (3d) 14 (C.A.) 150, 151
Prior v. McNab (1976), 16 O.R. (2d) 380, 78 D.L.R. (3d) 319 (H.C.J.) 227
Privest Properties Ltd v. Foundation Co of Canada, (1995), 11 B.C.L.R.
    (3d) 1, [1995] B.C.J. No. 2001 (S.C.), aff'd (1997), 31 B.C.L.R.
    (3d) 114, [1997] B.C.J. No. 427 (C.A.) 95–96, 257
Prud'homme v. Prud'homme, [2002] 4 S.C.R. 663, [2002] S.C.J. No. 86 156
Prudential Assurance Co. v. Newman Industries Ltd. (No. 2), [1982]
    1 All E.R. 354 (C.A.) 130
Pullen v. Headberg, 127 P. 954 (Colo. 1912) 139

Queen Charlotte Lodge Ltd. v. Hiway Refrigeration Ltd., [1998] B.C.J. No. 13
    (S.C.) 82
Quest Vitamin Supplies Ltd. v. Hassam (1992), 79 B.C.L.R. (2d) 85, [1992]
    B.C.J. No. 2769 (S.C.)..415

R. v. Carosella, [1997] 1 S.C.R. 80, [1997] S.C.J. No. 12 260
R. v. CLP Canmarket Lifestyle Products Corp., [1988] 2 W.W.R. 170,
    [1987] M.J. No. 591 (C.A.) 65
R. v. Gillespie (1999), 142 Man.R. (2d) 96, [1999] M.J. No. 562 (C.A.) 357
R. v. Gillespie (2000), 145 Man.R. (2d) 229, [2000] M.J. No. 218 (C.A.) 164, 357
R. v. Goldhart, [1996] 2 S.C.R. 463, 136 D.L.R. (4th) 502 27
R. v. Saskatchewan Wheat Pool, [1983] 1 S.C.R. 205, 143 D.L.R.
    (3d) 9 .... 22, 105, 106
R. v. Spencer, [1985] 2 S.C.R. 278, [1985] S.C.J. No. 60 406
R. v. The Sun Diamond, [1984] 1 F.C. 3, 25 C.C.L.T. 19 (F.C.T.D.) 117
R v. W. McKenzie Securities Ltd. (1966), 56 D.L.R. (2d) 56, 55 W.W.R. 157
    (C.A.) 421
R.J. Reynolds Tobacco Co. v. Engle, 672 So.2d 39, 1996 Fla. App.
    LEXIS 561 (Ct. App. 1996) 186
Rae v. T Eaton Co. (Maritimes) (1961), 28 D.L.R. (2d) 522, 45 M.P.R. 261
    (N.S.S.C.) 97
Ragoonanan Estate v. Imperial Tobacco Canada Ltd. (2000), 51 O.R.
    (3d) 603, [2000] O.J. No. 4597 (S.C.J.) 45, 109, 221, 366
Ramirez v. Amsted Industries, Inc., 171 N.J. Super. 261, 408 A.2d 818
    (Ct. App. Div. 1979), aff'd 86 N.J. 332, 431 A.2d 811 (Sup. Ct. 1981) 291
Ranjoy Sales & Leasing Ltd v. Deloitte Haskins & Sells Ltd., [1984]
    4 W.W.R. 706, [1984] M.J. No. 28 (Q.B.), aff'd [1985] 2 W.W.R. 534,
    [1984] M.J. No. 222 (C.A.) 353
Ray v. Alad Corp., 19 Cal. 3d 22, 560 P.2d 3 (1977) 291
Re "Agent Orange" Product Liability Litigation, 689 F. Supp. 1250,
    1988 U.S. Dist. LEXIS 6833 (E.D.N.Y. 1988) 251, 252
Re American Medical Systems, Inc., 75 F.3d 1069 (6th Cir. 1996) 329
Re Anglo-Australian Foods Ltd. No., WAG 37 of 1988 (F.C. Gen. Div.) 431–32
Re Asbestos School Litigation, 104 F.R.D. 422 (E.D. Pa. 1984), modified
    107 F.R.D. 215 (E.D. Pa. 1985), aff'd in part, rev'd in part,
    789 F.2d 996 (3d Cir.) 328
Re DES Cases, 789 F. Supp. 548, 1992 U.S. Dist. LEXIS 5560
    (E.D.N.Y. 1992) 251, 252, 460–61
Re Federal Skywalk Cases, 93 F.R.D. 415 (W.D. Mo. 1982), rev'd 680
    F.2d 1175 (8th Cir.) cert. denied 459 U.S. 988 (1982) 328
Re Gabel, 350 F. Supp. 624, 17 Fed. R. Serv. 2d 857 (D.C. Cal. 1972) 327
Re General Motors Corporation Pick-Up Truck Fuel Tank Products Liability
    Litigation, 55 F.3d 768, 1995 U.S. App. LEXIS 8815 (3d Cir. 1995) 380
Re Halifax Sugar Refining Co. (1890–91), 7 Times L.R. 293 257

Re Joint Eastern & Southern Dist. Asbestos Litigation, 726 F. Supp. 426,
    1989 U.S. Dist. LEXIS 14683 (E. & S.D. N.Y. 1989) 251, 252
Re Rhone-Poulenc Rorer Inc., 51 F.3d 1293, 1995 U.S. App. LEXIS 5504
    (7th Cir. 1995), rehearing denied 1995 U.S. App. LEXIS 9693 .... 329, 386
Re School Asbestos Litigation, 789 F.2d 996, 1986 U.S. App. LEXIS
    24808 (3d Cir. 1986) 327
Re Whalen and Neal (1982), 31 C.P.C. 1 (N.B.Q.B.) 427
Reference re Status of the Supreme Court of British Columbia (1882),
    1 B.C.R. 243 (S.C.C.) 404
Reference Re Upper Churchill Water Rights Reversion Act 1980
    (Newfoundland), [1984] 1 S.C.R. 297, 8 D.L.R. (4th) 1 401
Reid v. Ford Motor Co., [2003] B.C.J. No. 2489, 2003 BCSC 1632 31
Rentway Canada Ltd v. Laidlaw Transport Ltd., [1989] O.J. No. 786,
    49 C.C.L.T. 150 (H.C.J.) 38, 39
Richard v. British Columbia, [2003] B.C.J. No. 1466, 2003 BCSC 976,
    aff'd [2004] B.C.J. No. 1202, 2004 BCCA 337, 30 B.C.L.R. (4th) 336 377
Rintoul et al. v. St. Joseph's Health Centre (1998), 42 O.R. (3d) 379,
    [1998] O.J. No. 4074 (Div. Ct.) 265, 267
Risdon Iron and Locomotive Works v. Furness, [1906] 1 KB 49 303
Rivtow Marine Ltd v. Washington Iron Works, [1974] S.C.R. 1189,
    40 D.L.R. (3d) 530 .... 28–29, 59, 223
Robb v. Canadian Red Cross Society, [2000] O.J. No. 2396 (S.C.), rev'd
    [2001] O.J. No. 4605 (C.A.) 57
Robb v. St. Joseph's Health Care Centre, [1998] O.J. No. 1144, 64 O.T.C. 161
    (Gen. Div.) 265, 267
Robb v. St. Joseph's Health Care Centre; Rintoul v. St. Joseph's Health Care
    Centre, [2001] O.J. No. 606, 5 C.P.C. (5th) 252 (C.A.) 267
Robinson v. Reed-Prentice Div. of Package Machinery Co. 49 N.Y.2d 471,
    403 N.E.2d 440 (C.A. 1980) 41
Robitaille v. Constructions Desourdy Inc. (1998), 78 A.C.W.S. (3d) 877
    (Que. C.A.) 116
Robitaille v. Vancouver Hockey Club Ltd., [1981] B.C.J. No. 555,
    30 B.C.L.R. 286 (C.A.) 185
Robson v. Chrysler Canada Ltd., [2002] B.C.J. No. 1232, 2 B.C.L.R. (4th) 1
    (C.A.), leave to appeal to S.C.C. ref'd [2002] S.C.C.A. No. 332 .... 420, 421
Roe v. Harvey (1769), 4 Burr. 2484 269
Roncarelli v. Duplessis, [1959] S.C.R. 121, 16 D.L.R. (2d) 689 150
Ross v. Dunstall (1921), 62 S.C.R. 393, 63 D.L.R. 63 .... 15, 324
Ross v. Wall (1980), 114 D.L.R. (3d) 758, [1980] B.C.J. No. 780 (C.A.) 114

Roy v. Bolens Corp., 629 F. Supp. 1070, 1986 U.S. Dist. LEXIS 28549
(Mass. 1986) 291
Roysdon v. R.J. Reynolds Tobacco Co., 849 F.2d 230, 1988 U.S. App.
LEXIS 8038 (6th Cir. 1988)...45
Rudder v. Microsoft Corp. (1999), 47 C.C.L.T. (2d) 168, [1999] O.J.
No. 3778 (S.C.J.)...113
Rumley v. British Columbia, [2001] 3 S.C.R. 184, 2001 SCC 69,
[2001] S.C.J. No. 39 ....346, 354
Rumley v. H.M.T.Q., [2001] 3 S.C.R. 184 103
Rutherford v. Owens-Illinois, Inc., 67 Cal. Rptr. 2d 16, 16 Cal. 4th 953
(Sup. Ct. Cal. 1997) 236
Ryan v. Victoria (City), [1999] 1 S.C.R. 201, 168 D.L.R. (4th) 513 ....22, 120
Rylands v. Fletcher (1868), L.R. 3 (H.L.) 120–21, 312

Sacks v. Phillip Morris Inc., 1996 U.S. Dist. Lexis 15184 (D.Md.),
aff'd 139 F.3d. 892 (4th Cir. (Md.) 1998) 108
Salomon v. Salomon & Co., [1897] A.C. 22 (H.L.) 274
Sam Lévy & Associés Inc. v. Azco Mining Inc., [2001] 3 S.C.R. 978,
[2001] S.C.J. No. 90 418
Samos Investments Inc. v. Pattison, [2002] B.C.J. No. 1771,
2002 BCCA 442, 216 D.L.R. (4th) 646 371
Sanders v. Tailored Chem. Corp., 570 F. Supp. 1543 (E.D. Pa. 1983) 327
Sarabia v. Oceanic Mindoro (The) (1996), 26 B.C.L.R. (3d) 143, [1996]
B.C.J. No. 2154 (C.A.), leave to appeal to S.C.C. ref'd [1997]
S.C.C.A. No. 69 418
Sauvé v. Canada (AG), [1993] 2 S.C.R. 438, [1993] S.C.J. No. 59 165
Sawatzky v. Société Chirurgicale Instrumentarium Inc. (1999),
71 B.C.L.R. (3d) 51, [1999] B.C.J. No. 1814 (S.C.)............................382, 384
Scarola v. Shell Canada Ltée, [2003] J.Q. no 8973 (S.C.) 29
Schachter v. Canada, [1992] 2 S.C.R. 679, 93 D.L.R. (4th) 1,
[1992] S.C.J. No. 68 165
Schulz v. Leeside Developments Ltd. (1978), 90 D.L.R. (3d) 98, [1978]
5 W.W.R. 620 (B.C.C.A.) 50
Scott v. St. Boniface General Hospital, 2002 MBQB 196, [2002] M.J. No. 278,
[2002] 11 W.W.R. 463, aff'd 2003 MBCA 90, [2003] M.J. No. 219..............357
Seafarers International Union of Canada et al. v. Lawrence (1979),
24 O.R. (2d) 257, 97 D.L.R. (3d) 324 (C.A.) 155, 353
Seattle Times Co. v. Rhinehart, 104 S. Ct. 2199, 467 U.S. 20 (1984) 314
Seel Enterprises (1985) Ltd. v. Seel Mortgage Investment Corp., [1994]
O.J. No. 1953 (Gen. Div.) 296

Seine River Resources Inc. v. Pensa Inc. (1998), 25 C.P.C. (4th) 360,
[1998] B.C.J. No. 2090 (S.C.) 415
Seyfert v. Burnaby Hospital Society (1986), 27 D.L.R. (4th) 96,
36 C.C.L.T. 224 (B.C.S.C.) 227
Shaffer v. South State Mach., 995 F. Supp. 584, 1998 U.S. Dist. LEXIS
2148 (Pa. 1998) 290
Shandloff v. City Dairy, [1936] O.R. 579, 4 D.L.R. 712 (C.A.) 32–33
Shelfer v. City of London Electric Lighting Company, [1895] 1 Ch 287 116
Shewfelt v. Canada, [1997] 4 W.W.R. 292, [1997] B.C.J. No. 518 (S.C.) 164, 165
Shields v. Mayor, [1952] O.J. No. 299 (C.A.) 353
Sidhu Estate v. Bains, [1996] B.C.J. No. 1246, [1996] 10 W.W.R. 590 (C.A.) 126
Sigurdson v. Hillcrest Service Ltd., [1977] 1 W.W.R. 740, [1976] S.J. No. 389
(Q.B.) 83
Sinclair v. Cracker Barrel Old Country Store Inc. (2002), 213 D.L.R.
(4th) 643, [2002] O.J. No. 2127 (C.A.) 431
Sindell v. Abbott Laboratories, 26 Cal. 3d 588, 607 P.2d 924
(S. Ct. 1980) 5, 27, 219, 220, 233
Small v. Lorillard Tobacco Co., 252 A.D.2d 1, 679 N.Y.S.2d 593
(App. Div. 1998) 252
Smith Brothers Excavating Windsor Ltd v. Camion Equipment & Leasing Inc.
(Trustee of) (1994), 21 C.C.L.T. (2d) 113, [1994] O.J. No. 1380
(Gen. Div.) 122
Smith New Court Securities Ltd. v. Scrimgeour Vickers (Asset Management)
Ltd., [1996] H.L.J. No. 38, [1997] A.C. 254 126
Smith v. Canada (Minister of Indian Affairs and Northern Development),
[2002] F.C.J. No. 1455, 2002 FCT 1090 (T.D.) 358
Smith v. Inglis Ltd. (1978), 83 D.L.R. (3d) 215, 25 N.S.R. (2d) 38,
[1978] N.S.J. No. 495, 6 C.C.L.T. 41 (C.A.) 34, 108
Smith, Stone and Knight, Ltd. v. Birmingham Corp., [1939] 4 All E.R. 116 282
Snell v. Farrell, [1990] 2 S.C.R. 311, [1990] S.C.J. No. 73, 72 D.L.R.
(4th) 289 .... 26, 225, 253
Société des Acadiens du Nouveau-Brunswick Inc. v. Assn. of Parents for
Fairness in Education, [1986] 1 S.C.R. 549, [1986] S.C.J. No. 26 451
Société Radio-Canada v. Radio Sept-Îles Inc., [1994] R.J.Q. 1811 (C.A.) 156
Spar Aerospace Ltd. v. American Mobile Satellite Corp., [2002]
4 S.C.R. 205, [2002] S.C.J. No. 51 .... 405, 406, 410
Spasic v. Imperial Tobacco Ltd. (1998), 42 O.R. (3d) 391, [1998]
O.J. No. 4906 (Gen. Div.), var'd [2000] O.J. No. 2690, 49 O.R.
(3d) 699 (C.A.), motion for leave to appeal to S.C.C. dismissed
[2000] S.C.C.A. No. 547 266–67

Spasic Estate v. Imperial Tobacco Ltd., [2003] O.J. No. 1797 (S.C.J.) 267
Spasic Estate v. Imperial Tobacco Ltd., [2003] O.J. No. 824 (S.C.J.) 267
Spasic v. Imperial Tobacco Ltd., [1998] O.J. No. 125 (Gen. Div.) 144
Spika v. Port Alberni (City), [2002] B.C.J. No. 980, 2002 BCSC 700................124
Spinner v. City of New York, 2003 U.S. Dist. LEXIS 19298 (E.D. N.Y.)............166
St Pierre v. Ontario (Minister of Transportation & Communications),
    [1987] 1 S.C.R. 906, [1987] S.C.J. No. 27 114
St. Louis v. Canada (1896), 25 S.C.R. 649 ....262, 263
Starkman v. Canada (Attorney General), [2000] O.J. No. 3764 (S.C.J.) 137
Stern v. Imasco Ltd. (1999), 38 C.P.C. (4th) 347, [1999] O.J. No. 4235
    (S.C.J.)..131
Stewart v. General Motors Corp., 542 F.2d 445 (7th Cir. 1976), cert. denied,
    433 U.S. 919, 97 S.Ct. 2995, rehearing denied by 434 U.S. 881,
    98 S.Ct. 244 (1977)...252
Stewart v. Pettie, [1995] 1 S.C.R. 131, 121 D.L.R. (4th) 222 26
Stoldt v. Toronto, 234 Kan. 957, 678 P.2d 153 (Sup. Ct. Kan. 1984)....................138
Strand Electric and Engineering Co Ltd v. Brisford Entertainments Ltd.,
    [1952] 2 QB 246 195
Strandquist v. Coneco Equipment, [1996] A.J. No. 605, 45 Alta. L.R.
    (3d) 272 (Q.B.), aff'd [2000] A.J. No. 554, 2000 ABCA 138 79
Strata Plan 1229 v. Trivantor Investments International Ltd., [1995]
    B.C.J. No. 557, 4 B.C.L.R. (3d) 259 (S.C.) 147
Summers v. Tice, 199 P.2d 1, 33 Cal. 2d 80 (Sup. Ct. Cal. 1948)........................216
Suncor Inc v. Canada Wire & Cable Ltd. (1993), 15 C.P.C. (3d) 201, [1993]
    A.J. No. 4 (Q.B.), supplementary reasons [1993] A.J. No. 34 (Q.B.) 292, 294
Sutherland v. Canada (Attorney General), [1997] B.C.J. No. 2550,
    15 C.P.C. (4th) 329 (S.C.) 116
Swift Cdn Co. v. Alberta (Pork Producers Marketing Board) (1984),
    53 A.R. 284, [1984] A.J. No. 990 (C.A.) 323

Tabrizi v. Whallon Machine Inc., [1996] B.C.J. No. 1212, 29 C.C.L.T.
    (2d) 176 (S.C.)..40, 41
Taff Vale Rail. Co. v. Amalgamated Society of Railway Servants, [1901]
    A.C. 426 (H.L.) 322
Tanner v. Atlantic Bridge Co. (1966), 56 D.L.R. (2d) 162, 51 M.P.R. 293
    (N.S.S.C.)..56
Tardiff v. Knox County, 2003 U.S. Dist. LEXIS 19924 (D. Me.) 166
Taylor v. Standard Gas & Electric Co., 306 U.S. 307, 59 S. Ct. 543 (1939) 284
ter Neuzen v. Korn, [1995] 3 S.C.R. 674, [1995] S.C.J. No. 79 ....88, 89, 90
Terrell v. Village of University Park, 1994 WL 30960 (N.D. Ill. 1994)........186–87
The Ophelia, [1916] 2 A.C. 206 (P.C.) 268

Thomas v. Matthiessen, 232 U.S. 221, 34 S. Ct. 312 (1914) 302
Thomson Newspapers Corp v. Canada (Director of Investigation & Research),
  [1990] 1 S.C.R. 425, [1990] S.C.J. No. 23....................................401, 402–3, 445
Thornton v. Prince George School District 57, [1978] 2 S.C.R. 267,
  83 D.L.R. (3d) 480..170, 174
Tiemstra v. Insurance Corp. of British Columbia (1997), 38 B.C.L.R.
  (3d) 377, [1997] B.C.J. No. 1628 (C.A.) 343
Tiemstra v. Insurance Corp. of British Columbia, [1996] B.C.J. No. 952,
  22 B.C.L.R. (3d) 49 (S.C.), aff'd [1997] B.C.J. No. 1628, 149 D.L.R.
  (4th) 419 (C.A.)..363
Tilden Rent A Car Co v. Clendenning (1978), 18 O.R. (2d) 601, 83 D.L.R.
  (3d) 400 (C.A.)...113
TMJ Implants Prods. Liability Litigation, 113 F.3d 1484, 1997 U.S. App.
  LEXIS 11372 (8th Cir. 1997) 138
Tock v. St John's Metro Area Board, [1989] 2 S.C.R. 1181, [1989]
  S.C.J. No. 122 ....115, 124
Tolofson v. Jensen, [1994] S.C.J. No. 110, [1994]
  3 S.C.R. 1022 ....406, 409, 416, 417, 438, 443
Tompkins Hardware Ltd v. North Western Flying Services Ltd. (1982),
  139 D.L.R. (3d) 329, [1982] O.J. No. 944 (H.C.J.)..110
Torquay Hotel Co., Ltd. v. Cousins, [1969] 2 Ch. 106 (C.A.) 103
Townsview Properties Ltd v. Sun Const & Equipment Co. (1973), 2 O.R.
  (2d) 213, 42 D.L.R. (3d) 353 (H.C.J.), var'd (1974), 7 O.R. (2d) 666,
  56 D.L.R. (3d) 330 (C.A.) 196
Transamerica Life Insurance Co. of Canada v. Canada Life Insurance Co.
  (1996), 28 O.R. (3d) 423, [1996] O.J. No. 1568 (Gen. Div.), aff'd [1997]
  O.J. No. 3754 (C.A.) 285, 286
Transco v. Stockport Metropolitan Borough Council, [2003] UKHL 61 124
Trueman v. Maritime Auto & Trailer Sales Ltd., [1977] N.B.J. No. 199,
  19 N.B.R. (2d) 8 (C.A.) 83
Trustee Company of Winnipeg v. Manitoba Bridge and Ironworks Ltd.,
  [1922] 1 W.W.R. 178, 70 D.L.R. 178 (Man. C.A.) 292

Unifund Assurance Co. v. Insurance Corp. of British, [2003] 2 S.C.R. 63,
  2003 SCC 40, [2003] S.C.J. No. 39..421–22
United Australia Ltd. v. Barclays Bank Ltd., [1940] 4 All E.R. 20 (H.L.)............196
United States v. Arthur Andersen, 374 F.3d 281, 2004 U.S. App. LEXIS
  11814 (5th Cir. 2004) 260
United States v. Atlas Minerals and Chemicals, Inc., 824 F. Supp. 46,
  1993 U.S. Dist. LEXIS 6953 (E.D. Pa. 1993) 290
United States v. Bestfoods, 524 U.S. 51, 118 S. Ct. 1876 (1998) 306

United States v. Carolina Transformer Co., 978 F.2d 832, 1992 U.S. App.
LEXIS 26723 (4th Cir. 1992) 290
United States v. Mexico Feed & Seed Co., 980 F.2d 478, 1992 U.S. App.
LEXIS 29932 (8th Cir. 1992) 290
United States v. Pierce, 1995 WL 356017 (N.D. N.Y. 1995) 290
University System of New Hampshire v. United States Gypsum Co.,
756 F. Supp. 640, 1991 U.S. Dist. LEXIS 1191 (D.N.H. 1991) 139
Usery v. Turner Elkhorn Mining Co., 428 U.S. 1, 96 S. Ct. 2882 (1976) 213, 316

Valmet Paper Machinery Inc. v. Hapag-Lloyd Ag., [1996] B.C.J. No. 2655
(S.C.) 415
Van Oirschot v. Dow Chemical Canada Inc. (1995), 31 Alta. L.R. (3d) 212,
[1995] A.J. No. 611 (C.A.) 189
Vandekerhove v. Litchfield (1993), 103 D.L.R. (4th) 739, [1993] B.C.J. No. 1355
(S.C.) 132, 134
Vaughan v. Menlove (1837), 132 E.R. 490, 3 Bing.N.C. 468 (C.P.) 20
Venus Electric Ltd v. Brevel Products Ltd. (1978), 19 O.R. (2d) 417,
85 D.L.R. (3d) 282 (C.A.) 71
Verchere v. Greenpeace Canada, [2004] B.C.J. No. 864, 2004 BCCA 242........103
Vitapharm Canada Ltd. v. F. Hoffmann-La Roche Ltd., [2001] O.J. No. 237,
6 C.P.C. (5th) 245 (S.C.J.) 378–79
Vitapharm Canada Ltd. v. F. Hoffmann-Laroche Ltd. (2000), 4 C.P.C.
(5th) 169, [2000] O.J. No. 4594, [2000] O.T.C. 877 (S.C.J.) 375–77
Vlchek v. Koshel (1988), 30 B.C.L.R. (2d) 97, [1988] B.C.J. No. 1062 (S.C.) 189
Volkswagen Canada Inc. v. Auto Haus Frohlich Ltd., [1986] 1 W.W.R. 380,
[1985] A.J. No. 719 (C.A.) 418
Vorvis v. Insurance Corp. of British Columbia, [1989] 1 S.C.R. 1085,
[1989] S.C.J. No. 46 189
Voss v. Black & Decker Mfg. Co., 59 N.Y.2d 102, 450 N.E.2d 204 (C.A. 1983)....33

W.D. Latimer Co. v. Dijon Investments Ltd. (1992), 12 O.R. (3d) 415,
[1992] O.J. No. 2909 (Gen. Div.) 286
Walker v. Pioneer Construction Co. (1967) (1975), 8 O.R. (2d) 35,
56 D.L.R. (3d) 677 (H.C.J.) 114
Walkovsky v. Carlton, 276 N.Y.S.2d 585, 223 N.E.2d 6 (1996).....................274–75
Wallersteiner v. Moir, [1974] 1 WLR 991, [1974] 3 All E.R. 217 (1974) 282
Wallworth v. Holt (1841), 4 My. & Cr. 619, 41 E.R. 238 319
Walsh v. Herman (1908), 13 B.C.R. 314, [1908] B.C.J. No. 4 (Full Court) 427
Walter v. Selfe (1851), 4 De G. & Sm. 315, 64 E.R. 849 115
Ward v. Honda Motor Co., 33 Va. Cir. 400, 1994 Va. Cir. LEXIS 854 (1994) 108

Watkins v. Lundell, 169 F.3d 540, 1999 U.S. App. LEXIS 3031
(8th Cir. 1998) 187
Watson v. Buckley, [1940] 1 All E.R. 174 (K.B.) 19
Watson v. Winget, Ltd., [1960] S.L.T. 321 (H.L.) 211
Wavel Ventures Corp. v. Constantini, [1997] 4 W.W.R. 194, 193 A.R. 81
(C.A.) 28
Webb v. K-Mart Canada Ltd. (1999), 45 O.R. (3d) 389, [1999] O.J. No. 2268
(S.C.J.) 339, 442, 454, 458, 462
Webb v. K-Mart Canada Ltd. (1999), 45 O.R. (3d) 425, [1999] O.J. No. 3285
(S.C.J.) 455
Webb v. K-Mart Canada Ltd. (1999), 45 O.R. (3d) 638, [1999] O.J. No. 3286
(S.C.J) 455
Weiner v. Singh (1981), 22 C.P.C. 230, [1981] B.C.J. No. 961 (Co. Ct.) 427
Werner v. Saab-Scania AB, [1980] C.S. 798 (Que. S.C.) 459
West v. Randall, 29 F. Cas. 718 (CCDRI 1820) 318
Westec Aerospace Inc. v. Raytheon Aircraft Co. (1999), 173 D.L.R.
(4th) 498, [1999] B.C.J. No. 871, 1999 BCCA 243, aff'd [2001]
1 S.C.R. iv, [2001] S.C.J. No. 23 414
Western Canadian Place Ltd. v. Con-Force Products Ltd., [1997] A.J.
No. 1299, 208 A.R. 179 (Q.B.) 296, 299
Western Canadian Shopping Centres Inc. v. Dutton (1998), 228 A.R. 188,
[1998] A.J. No. 1364, 73 Alta. L.R. (3d) 227 (C.A.), var'd 2001 SCC 46,
[2000] S.C.J. No. 63, [2001] 2 S.C.R. 534 .... 323, 333, 341, 345, 349–50, 351,
361–62, 433–34, 447, 448–49, 463
Wharton v. Tom Harris Chevrolet Oldsmobile Cadillac Ltd., [2002]
B.C.J. No. 233, [2002] 3 W.W.R. 629 (C.A.) 78
Whistler Cable Television Ltd v. IPEC Canada Inc., [1992] B.C.J.
No. 2681, (1992) 17 C.C.L.T. (2d) 16 (S.C.) 106
White v. Lauder Dev Ltd. (1975), 9 O.R. (2d) 363, 60 D.L.R. (3d) 419 (C.A.) 258
White v. Smith & Wesson 97 F. Supp. 2d 816, 2000 U.S. Dist. LEXIS
10074 (N. Dist. Ohio 2000) 109
Whiten v. Pilot Insurance Co. [2002] 1 S.C.R. 595, [2002] S.C.J. No. 19,
209 D.L.R. (4th) 257, 2002 SCC 18 .... 190, 387
Whitwam v. Westminster Brymbo Coal Company, [1896] 2 Ch 538 195
Wild Rose Mills Ltd v. Ellison Milling Co., [1985] B.C.J. No. 489,
32 B.L.R. 125 (S.C.) 106
Wilks v. American Tobacco Co., 61 USLW 2708 (Miss. Cir. 1993) 47
Williams Elec. Co. v. Honeywell, Inc., 772 F. Supp. 1225, 1239
(N.D. Fla. 1991) 138

Williams v. Allied Automotive, Autolite Div., 704 F. Supp. 782, 1988 U.S. Dist. LEXIS 15599 (N.D. Ohio 1988) 179
Williams v. St. John (City) (1983), 53 N.B.R. (2d) 202, [1983] N.B.J. No. 72 (T.D.) 21
Willis v. FMC Machinery & Chemicals Ltd. (1976), 68 D.L.R. (3d) 127, [1976] P.E.I.J. No. 38 (S.C.) 22–23
Wilsher v. Essex Area Health Authority, [1988] A.C. 1074, [1988] H.L.J. No. 13 .... 224, 234
Wilson v. Johns-Manville Sales Corp., 684 F.2d. 111 (D.C. Cir. 1982) 184
Wilson v. Servier Canada Inc. (2000), 50 O.R. (3d) 219, [2000] O.J. No. 3392, 49 C.P.C. (4th) 233 (S.C.J.) 29, 180–81, 339, 374, 423, 424, 432, 455–56, 462
Wilson v. Servier Canada Inc., [2001] O.J. No. 1615, 11 C.P.C. (5th) 374 (S.C.J.) 374, 442
Winnipeg Condominium Corp. No. 36 v. Bird Construction Co., [1998] M.J. No. 396, [1999] 2 W.W.R. 370 (Q.B.) 295–96
Winterbottom v. Wright (1842), 152 E.R. 402, 10 M. & W. 109 .... 13, 14
Witherell v. Buchanan Estate, [1995] N.B.J. No. 475, 169 N.B.R. (2d) 14 (C.A.) 81
Woods v. Fruehauf Trailer Corp., 1988 OK 105, 765 P.2d 770 (Okla. Sup. Ct. 1988) 41
Woolwich Equitable Building Society v. Inland Revenue Comrs., [1992] H.L.J. No. 33, [1992] 3 All E.R. 737 158

Ybarra v. Spangard, 25 Cal. 2d 486, 154 P.2d 687 (Sup. Ct. Cal. 1944) 217
Yuba Consol. Gold Fields v. Kilkeary, 206 F.2d 884, 1953 U.S. App. LEXIS 3853 (9th Cir. 1953) 322
Yu-Ccan Corp. v. Master Professional Services Ltd., [2000] B.C.J. No. 839, 2000 BCSC 676 410

Zeppa v. Coca Cola Ltd., [1955] O.R. 855, [1955] 5 D.L.R. 187 (C.A.) 35
Zidaric v. Toshiba of Canada Ltd., [2000] O.J. No. 4590 (S.C.J.) 30
Zippo Manufacturing Co. v. Rogers Imports, 216 F. Supp. 670 (D.C.N.Y. 1963) 252

Index

Affirmative defences, 107–13
   contributory negligence, 108, 109–10, 111
   intervening act of another, 107–9
   voluntary assumption of risk and waiver of liability, 110–13
Aggregate assessment of damages, 348
Aggregate claims
   law of, 307–94
Aggregative proceedings
   origins of, 318–31
Alternate liability theory, 215–18
Anns test, 16n, 128
Asset purchase liability bar, 288

Beals v. Saldanha, 410–13, 430
Bill of Peace, 318, 319, 320, 321, 322
Blackmail settlements, 384–89, 391, 430
Blocking provisions, 423–26, 432
Breach of a special duty, 146–50
Breach of standards, *see* Negligence in mass tort

Burden shifting, *see* Indeterminate causation problems
"But for test", 205–10

Canadian class action policy
   foundations of, 318–37
Canadian class actions
   features of, 338–50
Care
   large-scale duties of, 16–20
   standard of, 20–25, 27, 37, 41, 75, 77, 256
Carriage motions, 374–379
Causation
   in duty-to-warn cases, 60–63
   factual, 26
   legal, 26
   problems in large-scale wrongs, 203–5
   in product liability, 26–28
Certifying the class, 338–42, 389n, 390, 433
Charter of Rights, 161–66

501

Choice of forum and law in contract-based cases, 417–20
Choice of law, 416–17, 442, 443
Claims aggregation, 312–18, 429
Class actions, 4, 5, 107, 309n, 310, 311, 312n, 318, 329, 336, 338–50, 360–94
　benefit of deterrence in, 346, 347, 360–62
　carriage motions and competing claims, 374–79
　claim of plaintiff against additional defendants, 366–67
　collusion in settlement, 379–84
　　to prejudice of claimants, 379–82
　　to prejudice of non-settling defendants, 382–84
　conservation of judicial resources, 363–65
　　financing of, 369–74
　　cost awards and indemnification agreements, 370–74
　　litigation as investment, 369–70
　investor incentives, 368–69
　issues regarding, 360–94
　"national class" and extraprovincial notice problems, 389–94
　public law-style class counsel in the private prosecutor capacity, 368–69
　"strike suits" and "blackmail" settlements, 384–89, 391
Class proceedings, 309–59
　definition of, 309
　features of Canadian class actions, 338–50
　　aggregate assessment of damages and non-restitutionary disrtibution, 348
　　certifying the class, 338–42, 389n, 390, 433
　　common issues, 342–44
　　"common law class action", 349–50
　　mandatory class, 339
　　notice requirements and opt-out rights, 347
　　opt-in class, 339
　　opt-out class, 339
　　preferability, 345–47
　foundations of Canadian class action policy, 318–37
　　Canadian reform, 331–33
　　common law, equity and rules of court, 318–23
　　objectives of reform, 335–38
　　origins of aggregative proceedings, 318–31
　　scope of reform, 334
　　U.S. Federal Rule 23, 324–31, 334, 338, 339, 340, 342, 360
　　U.S. "mass tort" class action claims under Rule 23, 325–31
　purposes of claims aggregation, 312–18
　　free riding, 313n, 314, 315, 391n, 436n
　　structural asymmetry, 314
　representative actions after *Western Canadian Shopping Centres v. Dutton*, 333, 350–59, 433
　　class proceeding distinguished, 353–54
　　class proceedings Acts vs. "representative proceedings" rules, 355–57
　　impact of *Dutton* on "representative proceedings" rule, 357–59
　　plaintiffs' option, 354–59
　　proceeding against representative defendant, 355n

proceeding by unincorporated association or trade union, 355n
representative action, 352–53
"representative proceedings" and "class actions", 351–59
Collusion in settlement, 379–84
Comity, 391–92, 402, 405–7, 410, 456
Comity internationally, 410–13, 428
"Common law class action", 349
Compensatory damages, 169–75
Complex litigation, 3, 4
Compliance with regulation, 119
Concert in action liability, 218–19
Conflict of laws in large-scale claims, 397–432
  "blocking provisions", 423–26
  choice of law and applicability, 416–23
    applicability of provincial statutes, 420–23
    choice of forum and law in contract-based claims, 417–20
    choice of law in tort-based claims, 416–17
  conflict of laws analysis, 397–99
  constitutional context and, 403–7
    comity, order and fairness ideals, 405–7
    legislative authority, 404–5
    Spar Aerospace, 405
  "constitutionalization" of private international law, 399–403
    Hunt v. T&N plc, 401–2
    Morguard Investments Ltd. v. De Savoye, 399–401, 402
  enforcement of judgments, 426–32
    Canadian judgments internationally, 427–29
    Canadian judgments within Canada, 426–27
    as an element of jurisdictional analysis, 430–32
    foreign judgments in Canada, 429–30
  future direction of, 402–3
  jurisdiction over the defendant, 407–16
    comity internationally post *Spar Aerospace* and *Beals v. Saldanha*, 410–13
    "fairness and justice", 414–16
    jurisdiction *forum conveniens*, 398 403, 413–14
    jurisdiction *simpliciter* and multiple defendants, 398, 409–10
    jurisdiction *simpliciter* and the "real and substantial connection" test, 407–9
Conspiracy, 135–44
  civil, 134–40
    "injurious purpose" test, 136–37
    "unlawful means" test, 135, 137–40
  to injure, 140, 143
  in non-commercial cases, 140–42
  requirement of agreement, 141
  requirement of intent, 141–42
  by unlawful means, 140
Constitution Act, 1867, 64, 65, 66
Constitutional claims in mass tort, 158–66
  Charter damages and bad faith/malice, 164–66
  civil *Charter* claims, 161–64
  recovery for breaches of *Charter* rights, 161–66
Consumer-expectations test, 41–42
Consumer protection legislation in Canada, 64–91
Contingent liability, 298
Contract-based product liability evolution, 11–13
Contract theory, 6
Contributory negligence, 109–10

Corporate groups
  contingent liability, 298
  enterprise liability, 218–19, 277, 286, 287, 289, 300–6
    jurisprudence, 303–5
    statutes, 305–6
  equity company vs. operating company, 279
  implications of, 273–24
  "judgment-proofing" strategies and modern corporations, 278–81
  limited liability and tort creditors, 274–77
  parent-subsidiary relationships, 280, 282–83
  "piercing the corporate veil", 280n, 281–86, 304
  the problem of, 273–306
  successor liability, 286–99
    asset purchase liability bar, 288
    consolidation, 288–89
    in a fault-based system, 297–99
    merger, 288–89
    pleading in Canadian courts, 299
    "product line liability", 291, 297
    role of U.S.-style successor liability in Canadian tort law, 297–99
    rules in Canada, 292–97
    in U.S. product liability cases, 288–90, 292, 294, 295
Cost awards, 370–374
Crown licence, 119
Cy Pres, 380, 381

Deceit, 124–27
Deemed knowledge, 256–59
Deemed reliance, 131, 343n
"Deep rock doctrine", 284–85
Defamation and hate speech, 154–58
Defective medical products in product liability, 84–91
Design defects, 15, 33, 36–48
  blended theories of liabilities, 42

  consumer-expectations test, 41–42
  design of cigarettes a danger?, 43–45
  expansion of risk-utility in tobacco litigation, 45–48
  risk-utility and tobacco case study, 43–48
  risk-utility test, 38–41, 45, 47, 109
  tests for, 37–42
Destruction of documentary evidence, 259–72
Deterence, 346, 347, 368
Detrimental reliance, 132
Duty of care, *see* Product liability causes of action; Mass tort causes of action
Duty to warn
  overview of, 48–52

Enforcement of judgments, 426–32
Enterprise liability, 218–19, 277, 286, 287, 289, 300–6

Failure to warn, 48–58
  causation analysis, 60–63
  communication style, 55–56
  compliance with standards, 58
  content of warning, 51, 52, 55–58
  duty is continual, 58–59
  duty to research risk, 52
  duty to warn, 48–52
  imputation of industry-wide danger knowledge, 53–55
  knowledge of defendant, 52–63
  knowledgeable vs. dependent user, 57–58
  learned intermediary rule, 59–60
  obviousness rule, 56–57
  in product liability claims, 48–64
  reliance on other sources, 63–64
Fairchild decision, 232–37, 238, 241, 243, 244, 245–48
Fairness and justice, 414–16
Fiduciary duties, 146–49, 194, 195
Free riding, 313n, 314, 315, 391n, 436n

Index   505

Future care losses, 170–75
  collateral benefits, 171–72
  contingency deductions, 171
  discounting to present value, 172
  duration of care, 172
  future prospects and level of care, 170–71
  lost earning capacity, 172
  taxation, 172

Hunt v. T&N plc, 136, 137, 139, 339n, 399n, 401–2, 406, 446–47

Implied condition of merchantability, 77–82
Imputation of knowledge in duty to warn, 53–55
Indemnification agreements, 370–74
Indeterminate causation problems, 203–48
  approaches to indeterminate causation, 212–32
    alternate liability, 215–18
    burden-shifting and "loss of chance" vs. probabilistic causation–onus-shifting, 223–26
    burden-shifting and "loss of chance" vs. probabilistic causation–probabilistic discounting, 226–32
    concert in action, enterprise or market share liabilities, 218–22
    liability for medical monitoring, 222–23
    probabilistic discounting, 214–15, 226–32, 240
    statutory reform of causation rules, 212–14
  causation problems in large-scale wrongs, 203–5
  inadequacy of the "but for" test, 205–10

  liability "in the air", 210–12
  proposed application in mass tort cases, 237–45
  reception of *Fairchild* in Canada, 245–48
  risk-based liability: the *Fairchild* decision, 232–37
    application of the risk-based liability rule, 235–37
    inferences of law and fact vs. risk-based liability, 234–35
    the need for proof of causation, 233–34, 236n
Industry-wide liability, 27
Injunctions, 198–99
"Injurious purpose" test, 136–37
Intentional torts, 103–4
Interjurisdictional class actions, 433–67
  jurisprudence, 444–65
    legislation for opt-in vs. opt-out national classes, 449–59
    Morguard Investments Ltd. v. De Savoye and Hunt v. T&N plc, 444–47
    national classes in British Columbia, 450–52
    national classes in Ontario, 452–59
    national classes in Quebec, 459
    sufficiency of notice, 460–65
    Western Canadian Shopping Centres Inc. v. Dutton, 447–49
  national class, 374, 389–94
  future of, 465–67
  national classes vs. province-by-province certification, 434–44
    advantages of national class, 434–38
    choice of law as disadvantage of national class, 442–43
    future of, 465–67
    jurisdictional reach and notice as a disadvantage of national class, 440–42

objections to, 438–44
opt-in vs. opt-out as a disadvantage to national class, 443–44
provincial sovereignty as a disadvantage of national class, 439–40

Interjurisdictional dimensions, 397–467

Judgment enforcement, *see* Conflict of laws in large-scale claims
Judgment-proofing strategies, 278–81
Jurisdiction and notice, 440–42
Jurisdiction *forum conveniens*, 398, 403, 413–14, 431, 457
Jurisdiction over the defendant, 407–16
Jurisdiction *simpliciter*, 398, 407–16
Jurisprudence, 4, 6, 139, 303–5, 312, 322, 353, 362, 402, 444–65
Juristic reason, 133

Large-scale claims
class actions and, 4
complex litigation and, 4
conflict of laws in, 397–432
future of in Canada, 468–70
inadequacy of reliance on precedent and, 5–6
information deficit, 4
onus of proof, 4, 24, 33–34
role and limits of law, 3–5
special problems of, 1–3
substantive vs. procedural distinction and, 3–5
Large-scale duties of care, 16–20
Law of aggregate claims, 307–94
Law of contract and tort, 2–3, 11, 13, 50, 92
Law of damages, *see* Remedies in large-scale claims
Law of implied warranties, 11
Law of negligence applicable to products, 14, 16–31

Learned intermediary rule, 59–60
Legislative standards, 22–23
Lex loci delicti, 416
Liability
contingent, 291
enterprise, 120–24, 144, 145, 218–19, 277, 286, 287, 300–6
industry-wide, 27
market-share, 5, 6, 27, 218–19
mass tort, 6–7
ordinary tort, 6
probabilistic/risk-based, 5
product, *see* Product liability causes of action
sources of, 9–200
strict, 24, 25, 44n, 46, 47, 87, 91–101, 297, 299
successor, 277, 286–99
vicarious, 24n, 100, 103n, 139n, 144–46, 281, 354
Liability from statements and silence, 124–32
Liability "in the air", 210–12
Liability sources, 9–199
Limited liability and tort creditors, 274–77
Loss of chance, *see* Indeterminate causation problems
Lost earning capacity
collateral benefits, 174
duration and discounting, 174
negative contingencies, 174
positive contingencies and lost chances, 173–74
post-accident prospects, 173
pre-accident prospects, 173

Mandatory class, 339
Manufacturing defects, 16, 32–35, 91, 107, 108
Market-share liability, 218, 222, 366
Mass tort
definition of, 1–2, 6–7
Mass tort causes of action, 102–66

breach of a special duty, 146–50
  fiduciary duties, 146–49
  voluntarily assumed duty, 149–50
breach of constitution, 106
conspiracy, 135–44
  applications of tort — *Hunt v. Carey Canada Inc.*, 142–44
  civil conspiracy, 135–40
  "injurious purpose" test, 136–37
  in non-commercial cases, 140–42
  requirement of agreement, 141
  requirement of intent, 141
  "unlawful means" test, 137–40
constitutional claims, 158–66
  Charter damages and bad faith/malice, 164–66
  civil *Charter* claims, 161–64
  claims based on the invalidity of laws, 158–60
  recovery for breaches of *Charter* rights, 161–66
defamation and hate speech, 154–58
  group defamation at common law, 154–55
  statutory actions for defamatory/ hateful statements, 155–58
intentional torts, 103–4, 106
liability from statements and silence, 124–32
  deceit, 124–27
  misrepresentation in securities cases, 130–32
  negligent misrepresentation, 127–30
misfeasance in a public office, 104, 120, 150–54
negligence and, 105–13
  affirmative defences in, 107–13
  breach of common law standards, 105
  breach of statute as evidence as mass tort, 107
  breach of statute as evidence of negligence, 105–7
nuisance-based claims, 113–24
  nuisance and negligence, 115–16
  private nuisance, 113–15
  private nuisance as a "mass tort", 116–17
  public nuisance, 117–20
  strict product liability — *Rylands v. Fletcher* actions, 120–24
statutory causes of action, 104
unjust enrichment, 132–35, 313n
vicarious liability, 139n, 144–46
Mass tort litigation
  class actions and, 5
  substantive vs. procedural distinction in, 3–5
Medical monitoring/unsafe product claims, 23, 29, 30, 31, 84–91, 178–81
Misfeasance in a public office, 104, 120, 150–54
Misrepresentation in securities cases, 130–32
Morguard investments Ltd. v. De Savoye, 399–401, 406, 407n, 410, 419n, 444–47

National class, 374, 389–94
  in British Columbia, 450–52
  certification, 434–44
  future of, 465–67
  objections to, 438–44
  in Ontario, 452–59
  in Quebec, 459
Negligence claims
  types of, 32–48
Negligence in mass tort, 105–13
Negligent misrepresentation, 127–30
Neighbour principle, 16, 50
Nuisance-based claims, 113–24

Onus of proof, 4, 34
Onus-shifting, 223–26
Opt-in class, 339, 389n
Opt-in vs. opt-out, 443–44, 449–59
Opt-out class, 339, 389n, 392, 433
Opt-out rights, 328, 347
Order and fairness, 405–7, 453, 459
Ordinary tort liability, 6–7

Parent-subsidiary relationships, 280
"Piercing the veil", 280n, 281–86, 304
Precedents
  reliance on in large-scale claims, 5
Private international law, see Conflict of laws in large-scale claims
Private nuisance, 113–17
Privity of contract, 13, 14, 79, 82–84, see Sale of Goods Act
Probabilistic analysis, 26, see Problems of proof
Probabilistic discounting, 214–15, 226–32, 240
Probabilistic/risk-based liability, 5
Problems of proof, 249–72
  deemed knowledge, 256–59
    common law deemed knowledge, 256–57
    statutorily deemed knowledge, 257–59
  destruction of documentary evidence, 259–72
  history of spoliation doctrine, 262–64
  relevance in product liability context, 260–62
  remedies for spoliation, 264–71
  spoliation, 260n, 262–72
  statistical evidence in mass tort, 249–55
Problems of proof and causation, 201–306
Product liability
  definition of, 1, 6–7

Product liability causes of action, 11–101
  consumer protection legislation in Canada, 64–84
    breach of implied warranty and privity of contract in medical context, 84–86
  division of powers, 64
  federal legislation, 64, 65–66, 68
  implied condition of merchantability, 77–82
  implied warranty of fitness for particular purpose, 70–77
  liability from warranties and implied terms, 68–69
  privity of contract, 82–84
  provincial legislation, 64, 66, 69
  rules for production and dissemination of defective medical products, 84–91
  Sale of Goods Act, 70–84
  statutory warranties and privity problems in medical context, 86–91
  strict liability in Canada, 95–101
  strict liability in U.S., 91–95
  unfair trade practices and misleading advertising, 66–68
historical foundations of, 11–16
  contract-based product liability evolution, 11–13
  law of contract, 11, 12, 13
  law of implied warranties, 11, 12, 13
  privity of contract, 13, 14
  Sale of Goods Act, 13
  tort-based product liability evolution, 13–16
principles of negligence law and, 14, 15, 16–31
  causation, 26–28
  damage and the pure economic loss bar, 28

foreseeable cause, 27–28
industry standards, 21–22, 41
large-scale duties of care, 16–20
legislative standards, 22–23
medical monitoring/unsafe product claims, 23, 29, 30, 31, 63
res ipsa loquitur, 24, 25
standard of care, 20–25, 27, 34–35
statutory standards, 22
strict liability, 24, 25, 46
in Canada, 95–101
in United States, 91–95
substantive vs. procedure in, 3–5, 312
types of negligence claims, 32–48
design defects, 15, 33, 36–48
failure to warn of risk, 48–64
manufacturing defects, 16, 32–35, 91, 107, 108
Proof of defect in negligence, 97, 98
Provincial sovereignty, 439–40
Public nuisance, 117–20
Punitive damages, 184–93
"Pure economic loss" bar, 28

"*Ragoonanan* Motion", 367
Real and substantial connection test, 407–16, 430, 453n, 459
Regulatory statutes, *see* Mass torts causes of action
Remedies in large-scale claims, 167–99
compensatory damages, 169–75
future losses, 170–75
lost earning capacity, 173–74
pain and suffering, 174–75
past losses, 170
injunctions, 198–99
restitution and disgorgement of profits, 193–98
punitive damages, 184–93
in class actions, 192–93
principles and quantum of the Canadian law, 189–92

in U.S. and Canadian product liability cases, 185–89
special issues and approaches in mass tort and product liability cases, 175–84
enhanced risk of future complications and aggravations, 183–84
fear of disease/emotional distress, 181–83
individualization vs. aggregation of damages, 175–78
medical monitoring in Canada, 180–81
medical monitoring in the United States, 178–80
statutory, 167–169
Representative actions, 352–53
Representative proceedings, 349, 351–59
Res ipsa loquitur, 24, 25, 93, 98
Restatement on product liability, 46
Restitution and disgorgement of profits, 193–98
as an alternative to civil wrongs damages, 195–96
in contractual settings and other issues, 196–97
explained and illustrated, 194–95
in mass tort cases, 197–98
Risk-based liability, 5, 232–37
Risk-utility and tobacco case study, 43–48
Risk-utility test, 38–41, 45, 47, 109
Rylands v. Fletcher, 120–24

Sale of Goods Act, 13, 68, 69, 70–84, 86, 87, 88, 90, 91
implied condition of merchantability, 77–82
implied warranty of fitness for particular purpose, 70–77
legislation of, 70
privity of contract, 82–84

Settlement class, 338, 382
Spar Aerospace, 272, 405, 410–13
Spoliation, 260n, 262–72
    as a basis for adverse inferences and presumptions, 268–69
    as a basis for independent tort, 264–68
    as a basis to restrict available defences, 270–71
    as an evidentiary tool, 269
    due to negligence, 271–72
    history of spoliation doctrine, 262–64
    remedies for, 264–71
Standard of care, *see* Product liability causes of action; Mass tort causes of action
Statutory causes of action, 104
Statutory reform of causation rules, 212–14
Statutory remedies, 167–69
Statutory standards, 22
Strict product liability, 24, 25, 44n, 46, 47, 87, 91–101, 120–24, 297, 299
Strike bar, 385
Strike suits, 384–89
Structural collusion, 379, 381, 383
Substantive law of civil obligations, 2
Successor liabilty, 277, 286–99
"Sufficient connection" test, 423

Tort-based product liability evolution, 13–16
Tort liability, 6
Tort recovery, *see* Corporate groups

Unfair trade practices and misleading advertising, 66–68
Unjust enrichment, 132–34, 313n
"Unlawful means" test, 135, 137–40
U.S. Federal Rule 23, 324–31, 334, 338, 339, 340, 342, 360

Vicarious liability, 24n, 139n, 144–46, 281
Volenti non fit injuria, 72, 110, 111, 112
Voluntarily assumed duty, 149–50
Voluntary assumption of risk and waiver of liability, 110–13

Waiver of liability, 111, 112, 113
Warranties, implied, 12–13, 70–82, 88, 168n
Warranties, statutory, 86–91
Western Canadian Shopping Centres Inc. v. Dutton, 333, 338, 341n, 350–59, 361, 433, 439, 441, 447–49, 458